ENERGY TECHNOLOGY: POWER AND TRANSPORTATION

Fourth Edition

ENERGY TECHNOLOGY: POWER AND TRANSPORTATION
Fourth Edition

Ralph C. Bohn
Dean of Continuing Education and
Professor, Division of Technology
San Jose State University
San Jose, California

Angus J. MacDonald
Professor, Division of Technology
San Jose State University
San Jose, California

CITY COLLEGE
LEARNING RESOURCE CENTRE

GLENCOE
McGraw-Hill

New York, New York
Columbus, Ohio
Mission Hills, California
Peoria, Illinois

Glencoe/McGraw-Hill

A Division of The McGraw-Hill Companies

Send all inquires to:
Glencoe/McGraw-Hill
3008 W. Willow Knolls Drive
Peoria, IL   61614-1083

ISBN 0-02-675401-0 (Text)
ISBN 0-02-676500-4 (Instructor's Resource Guide)
ISBN 0-02-675402-9 (Student Workbook)

5 6 7 8 9 10 11 12 13 14   VHJ   02 01 00 99 98 97

Table of Contents

8 Table of Contents

Preface

Energy Technology: Power and Transportation is the third title of this book which was first published in 1970. Previous titles were *Power and Energy Technology* (third edition) and *Power: Mechanics of Energy Control* (first and second editions). This book is designed to help students learn about the wide array of energy sources and how these sources are controlled to produce usable power. The third edition incorporated many changes to earlier editions. This fourth edition adds to these changes by integrating additional information throughout the book. It also adds two important chapters in the section on research and development and future trends in the area of energy technology.

A well-taught course in power and energy technology requires the integration and reinforcement of basic skills and advanced concepts of science. In particular, many principles of science and mathematics must be studied as part of the process of learning how power and energy are controlled and used in industry and society. *Correlations* of science (✳), math (✢), social studies (🌐) and language arts (✎) with power, energy and transporation technology are indicated with symbols throughout the book.

Energy Technology: Power and Transportation includes features designed to assist teachers in planning *instructional programs.* Chapter objectives, vocabulary terms, and an overview are included at the beginning of each chapter. Activities are presented at the end of the chapter. In addition, more extensive student activities are included at the end of the book.

The content contained in the first six sections of the book has been supplemented with new information. The organization of these sections remains intact since it was completely reorganized in the third edition.

The section of the book on energy sources (Section I) reflects the growing importance of solar and other alternative energy sources. Information on fossil fuels, our principle source of energy, is an important focus within these sections.

This edition continues the strong emphasis on conservation and the environment (Section II). The growing use of microprocessors and the need to store energy generated by alternative sources receive special emphasis.

The main themes and content areas of previous editions are continued. Various types of engines are studied in Sections III and IV. The emphasis on transportation is continued and strengthened. Instruction on small engines continues as an important content area. Power and energy is still presented as the study of systems and subsystems used to control, transmit, and use energy. The sections on power control and transmission (Sections V-VII) are fundamental to understanding how power is put to productive use.

Research and development and future trends in the area of power, energy, and transportation are presented throughout the book. They are explored specifically in Section VIII. This section was strengthened in this edition by adding information on the scientific method, as well as two new chapters. Transportation instruction was strengthened by the addition of a major chapter on future transportation needs. A chapter showing the effects of energy use on society was also added. The final content section, Section IX, provides information helpful to students as they prepare for careers.

Supplementary materials remain available. The *Student Workbook* includes chapter tests and a wide variety of activities, many of them of the "hands-on" type. Information on small engine repair and overhaul is presented as a series of activities in the *Student Workbook.* The *Instructor's Resource Guide* provides various types of information and materials designed to help teachers build strong, comprehensive courses in power, energy and transportation technology.

Energy Technology: Power and Transportation has been designed primarily as a school textbook. However, it will also be valuable to anyone interested in developing a basic understanding of power, energy, and transportation. The text can stand alone, independent of special teaching aids.

The most important outcome of the use of this text is *the development of an understanding of the use of power and energy in our modern society.* There will continue to be controversies over the use of nuclear energy, pollution from fossil fuels, and the potential of alternative sources of energy. These controversies will not be resolved easily. We hope that this text will help students and other readers become more aware of the problem and concerns surrounding the uses of power, energy, and technology. Only through education can we expect to meet future challenges in the dynamic field of power, energy, and transportation technology.

Sources of Energy

SECTION

Chapter 1

The Control of Energy

Energy exists in nature. It is part of every activity and every living thing.

Expanding Your Knowledge

Learning about power and energy technology will help you learn more about the world around you. As you study this chapter, you will learn to:

- Define energy and explain how it is able to produce motion, heat, and light.
- Identify the six different forms of energy and explain how energy can be changed from one form to another.
- Understand the *Law of Conservation of Energy*, which states that energy cannot be created or destroyed.
- Recognize the main elements of energy control systems.
- Explain the difference between potential energy and kinetic energy.

Building Your Word Power

Knowledge of the vocabulary used will help you develop greater understanding of power and energy. The following terms are defined and explained in this chapter. Learning these will help you learn more about the control of energy.

chemical energy
electrical energy
energy
energy control system
energy conversion
energy efficiency
friction
kinetic energy

Law of Conservation of
  Energy
light energy
mechanical energy
nuclear energy
photosynthesis
potential energy
thermal energy

The sun is the source of nearly all the energy we use and control. This chapter shows how we control energy to produce motion, heat, and light. This control involves six different forms of energy.

Energy can be changed from one form to another, but it can't be destroyed. This is a difficult concept, but understanding it is basic to understanding how energy is controlled and used. Much of the chapter is designed to help you understand this important concept.

The chapter also shows that energy always involves motion. We call motion *kinetic energy*. The one exception to "energy in motion," is "energy in storage." Stored energy, called *potential energy*, is changed to kinetic energy when we put it to work for us.

EARLY EFFORTS TO CONTROL ENERGY

Energy is the capacity to do work, or the capacity to produce motion, heat, or light. When we turn on an electric motor, drive a car, light a gas stove, or switch on a light, we are using energy.

To use energy, we must be able to *control* it. We can trace history through human efforts and successes in controlling energy. See Fig. 1-1.

The first people were hunters. They had no sources of energy except their own muscles. Muscle power, then, was the first controlled source of energy.

Eventually, people learned to make better use of their strength by using tools. For example, they discovered that wooden clubs were more effective in killing wild animals than bare hands were. The club made a person's strength more effective.

Later, people learned to grow their own food. They found that grain had a better chance of growing when the soil was turned over. To do this difficult task, they developed a special tool, the plow. At first, people pulled or pushed plows. Their physical strength limited the amount of work they could do.

Later people used animals to pull plows. Still later, animals provided the power to grind grain into flour. People could then control a form of energy greater than their own.

Centuries later, people used wind to power sailing ships. See Fig. 1-2. Wind also turned windmills to pump water and grind grain (hence, the name *windmill*). Moving water provided the energy to turn waterwheels on grain mills.

Wind and water were powerful energy sources. However, they were not dependable. People found it difficult to obtain even and steady power from these sources. They also had to use these sources at the places where they occurred in nature.

Fig. 1-1. Human progress is based on the ability to control energy.

Fig. 1-2. Harnessing wind power allowed people to explore the world. During the United States bicentennial celebration, history came to life when the "tall" ships sailed into New York Harbor.

Technology Focus

As Free As A Bird

Eons ago, in the days when stories called myths began, it is said that a master crafts-man named *Daedalus* was imprisoned on Crete, an island 69 miles off the shore of Greece. According to the myth, Daedalus escaped from the island in a very ingenious way. He made wax-and-feather wings and flew as a bird might fly across the Aegean Sea to freedom. A story? Yes. But people have long dreamed of flying under their own power. Today, with technology, it's possible.

In the late 1980s, a group* set out to recreate in a modern way the flight of Daedalus. The plane shown here, *Daedalus 88*, was designed for the job. It had a wingspan of 112 feet, but weighed only 72 pounds. In April of 1988, with a Greek cycling champion, *Kanellos Kanellopoulos*, as the power source, Daedalus 88 flew 74 miles in 3 hours and 54 minutes. The plane averaged 18.5 mph and broke three records for human-powered flight: straight-line flight, distance, and time aloft.

Although a gusty headwind caused Daedalus 88 to crash-land in the sea just 30 feet from its final destination, this "story" had a happy ending. The crash was not violent, and the unharmed pilot made it safely to shore. The old story of Daedalus included a tragedy.

According to the myth, Daedalus' son, *Icarus*, escaped with him. But in his excitement, Icarus flew higher and higher until the heat of the sun melted the wax of his wings, and he fell into the sea and drowned.

We can learn from this story today. With technology, many exciting things are possible. We can be "as free as a bird"! But when using technology, we must also use wisdom.

---

*The project was a joint venture of the Smithsonian Institution of Washington and the Dept. of Aeronautics and Astronautics of the Massachusetts Institute of Technology in Cambridge.

This situation changed with the development of the steam engine. Steam engines were first used about 300 years ago. They had many advantages over earlier sources of power. For the first time, people could fully control the *placement* of a powerful energy source. They could move the steam engine to where its power was needed. See Fig. 1-3. They could also control the *amount* of power the engine produced. Finally, they could control the *duration* of the power (how long it lasted).

Since the invention of the steam engine, people have developed many new methods of controlling energy. We control energy for transportation, heating, and cooling. By controlling energy, we can communicate instantly with people all over the world. We can even control energy to power spacecraft. Things that were impossible 100 or even 50 years ago are now common because of advancements in controlling energy. See Fig. 1-4.

Fig. 1-4. Because we have learned how to effectively control energy, we can fly coast to coast in a matter of hours.

FORMS OF ENERGY

As mentioned earlier, energy is the capacity to produce motion, heat, or light. These three products are also forms of energy:

- Mechanical energy
- Thermal energy
- Light energy

Fig. 1-3. Steam engines could be moved to where their power was needed.

Energy also has three other forms:

- Chemical energy
- Electrical energy
- Nuclear energy

The six forms of energy listed above are all related to each other. Any of these forms of energy can be converted (changed) into any of the other forms. See Fig. 1-5. For example, wood is a form of chemical energy. When wood burns, its chemical energy changes into heat energy and light energy.

Not all **energy conversions** are as simple as burning wood. For example, an automobile engine is a fairly complex tool used for energy conversion. It converts the chemical energy in gasoline or diesel fuel into mechanical energy, the energy of motion. As you will learn later, the automobile uses several different control systems to bring about this conversion and to regulate the mechanical energy.

Mechanical Energy

Mechanical energy is the most familiar form of energy because it is the energy involved in visible motion. Every moving object has mechanical energy—whether it is a hammer driving a nail, a leaf falling from a tree, or a rocket flying in space.

When we put mechanical energy to work in such devices as a hammer or an automobile, it is useful. However, mechanical energy can also be destructive. If you do not properly control the mechanical energy of a hammer, you could smash your finger.

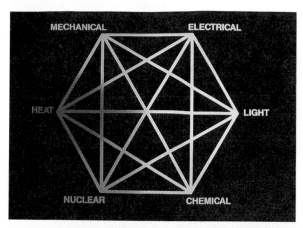

Fig. 1-5. All forms of energy are related. Each form can be converted into any other form.

To stop the car, the driver pushes the brake pedal. This pushes brake shoes against the inside of a rotating brake drum. The result is *friction*. **Friction** is heat energy produced by the resistance to movement between two surfaces touching each other. As the brake shoes rub against the brake drum, mechanical energy changes to heat energy. The air passing around the drum removes the heat. The car stops because the friction has changed motion to heat.

Friction is useful when stopping a car or helping the tires grip the road. However, friction can also be a disadvantage. In the operation of any machine, some energy is lost due to friction between moving parts. Because of this resistance to movement, more energy is required to operate the machine.

Thermal Energy (Heat)

Thermal energy is heat. It also involves motion. However, the motion in heat energy is generally not visible. (An exception might be the shimmering "heat waves" you can sometimes see above a road on a hot day.) Usually, we can only feel or see the *effects* of heat. And what we feel or see is the result of atoms or molecules in motion.

Atoms and *molecules*, the smallest particles of any substance, are always in motion. The amount of heat energy given off by a substance depends on the speed and number of atoms or molecules in motion. The faster the atoms or molecules move, the higher the heat energy (temperature). Also, the more atoms or molecules that are in motion, the greater the quantity of heat they produce.

Heat energy is an important form of energy. The sun's heat energy sustains all life on earth. Without it, our planet would be a solid chunk of ice.

We use heat energy to cook our food and heat our homes. We use it to generate electricity. It develops the mechanical energy needed to move cars, planes, boats, and even hot-air balloons. See Fig. 1-6. When we use fuels, we first burn them to produce heat. Then we put the heat energy to work for us.

Heat energy also helps us control other forms of energy. For instance, the motion developed in a car can be very dangerous if it is not controlled. We can control this mechanical energy by converting it into heat energy.

Fig. 1-6. The movement of a hot-air balloon is a visible effect of thermal energy. The "fuel" for the balloon is heated air. As the hot air rises, so does the balloon.

Light Energy

The sun produces radiant energy (heat and light). **Light energy** is the part of radiant energy that we can see. However, even though we can see it, light energy is difficult to understand. That is, it's hard to see how light does work. But just look around. Where would we be without the light from our sun?

One basic fact of life is that light is necessary for the growth of plants. Plants convert sunlight, carbon dioxide, water, and nutrients into food. This process, called **photosynthesis**, is the most important use of light energy. Without light energy, we would not have plant or animal growth. We also would not have the fossil fuels that were originally plants and animals millions of years ago. Every time we eat something or burn a fossil fuel, we are *indirectly* tapping into the light energy that came from the sun.

One *direct* way to use light energy is to use solar cells. These cells convert light directly into electricity. See Fig. 1-7. (You will learn more about these in Chapter 3.)

Chemical Energy

Chemical energy is the energy of all living things. Photosynthesis is an example of a *chemical change*. Plants and animals use the result of photosynthesis—sugar—as a source of energy. Since sugar is a chemical, it is a type of chemical energy. **Chemical energy** is energy produced by chemical changes.

Many of the most common energy sources are forms of chemical energy. Think about the fossil fuels—coal, oil, and natural gas. They are all chemicals or combinations of chemicals. All of them were produced by chemical changes.

When we need energy, we burn controlled amounts of these fuels. This burning converts the chemical energy into a certain amount of heat energy. For example, a gallon of gasoline burned in an automobile engine provides the heat energy to drive a car a certain distance.

Chemical energy can also be converted into other forms of energy. For example, a flashlight battery is a device which converts chemical energy into electrical energy. The chemicals in a battery are arranged so that an electric current will result when the ends of the battery are connected. When you turn on a flashlight, you make this connection. The battery's chemical energy changes to electrical energy and lights the bulb.

Some chemicals contain a great deal of energy that can be released all at once. These chemicals are called *explosives*. It's possible to convert the chemical energy of explosives into several forms of energy. For example, when dynamite explodes, its chemical energy changes into heat, light, and motion (wind and pressure). See Fig. 1-8. Explosive chemicals are used extensively in mining and road construction. We control the power of explosives to uncover mineral deposits and to make tunnels.

Electrical Energy

Electrical energy is the motion of tiny invisible particles of matter called *electrons*. Electrons form part of the structure of atoms. They are too small to see, even with the most powerful microscope. Therefore, we study electrical energy by watching the changes it produces.

Electrical energy has an almost limitless number of uses. We can convert it into light energy with electric lamps. Electric motors change electrical energy into mechanical energy. Electric stoves and heaters change it into thermal en-

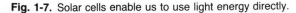
Fig. 1-7. Solar cells enable us to use light energy directly.

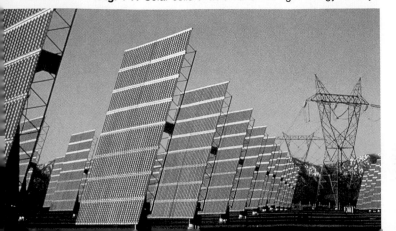

Fig. 1-8. An explosion is the rapid conversion of chemical energy into heat, light, and motion.

ergy. We also use electrical energy for radio, television, and telephone communications. See Fig. 1-9.

Electrical energy is also easy to transport from place to place. This characteristic allows us to use electrical energy almost anywhere.

Nuclear Energy

Nuclear energy is developed by changing matter into energy. Hydrogen and uranium are two kinds of matter used to produce nuclear energy. In a nuclear reaction, part of each hydrogen or uranium atom is changed into energy. This conversion decreases the amount of matter. In a nuclear reaction, a very small amount of matter is converted into a huge amount of energy.

A conversion from energy back into matter is possible but very difficult. This process involves bringing large amounts of energy together in a tiny space. It can be accomplished only under carefully controlled laboratory conditions. These conditions have been produced on only a few occasions.

The practical uses of nuclear energy are somewhat limited. The release of nuclear energy involves high operating temperatures. There is also the possibility of radiation leaks. Complex equipment and extensive safeguards are needed to safely convert nuclear energy into other energy forms.

The most common conversion takes place in nuclear power plants. These convert nuclear energy into heat energy. The heat is then used to drive steam turbines. The steam turbines operate electrical generators.

Nuclear energy also has other uses. In medicine, it is used in the form of radiation therapy to treat cancer. The United States Navy uses nuclear energy to power submarines and some large ships. See Fig. 1-10. (More detailed information about nuclear energy is presented in Chapter 5).

CONSERVATION OF ENERGY

The **Law of Conservation of Energy** states that the amount of energy in the universe is fixed. That is, energy cannot be created or destroyed. Therefore, when energy is being *used*, it is not being used up. It is being *changed* from one form to another. For example, when we exercise, we convert chemical energy (food) into mechanical energy (motion) and thermal energy (heat).

The control and use of energy consists of converting energy from one form into another. There is no energy destroyed during this process. However, some energy *is* converted into unwanted or unusable forms. In fact, it is impossible to convert one form of energy into another without wasting some energy.

To understand how energy is lost during conversion, consider a simple energy conversion system—a person riding a bicycle. When operating a bike, the rider's body converts chemical energy into mechanical energy to push the pedals. However, some of the chemical energy also changes into heat. This heat is given off through

Fig. 1-10. This submarine is powered by nuclear energy. The nuclear energy is converted to heat, which is then used to drive turbine generators.

Fig. 1-9. Electrical energy is the "lifeblood" of all kinds of communication systems.

the rider's skin. It cannot be used to move the bicycle. Heat is also generated between the moving parts of the bike and between the bike and the air. This friction further reduces the usable energy.

In many energy conversions, there is more energy lost than there is doing useful work. These types of conversions are *inefficient*. For example, automobile engines waste more than two-thirds of the total energy used to drive the cars.

Some conversions, however, are highly *efficient*. The conversion of electrical energy into mechanical energy with electric motors is one example. Only about 10% of the electrical energy is wasted. Converting energy from one form to another with little waste of energy is **energy efficiency**.

ENERGY CONTROL SYSTEMS

In the following sections of this book, you will learn about the major energy control (power) systems that have been developed over many years. Every **energy control system** has three parts:
- The original source of energy.
- All the conversions the energy goes through, including the *transmission* (moving) of energy from one place to another.
- The eventual use of the energy.

One example of an energy control system is the development, transmission, and use of electrical energy. See Fig. 1-11. The original source of energy is the fuel used at a generating plant (for example, coal). From this original source, the energy goes through the following conversions:

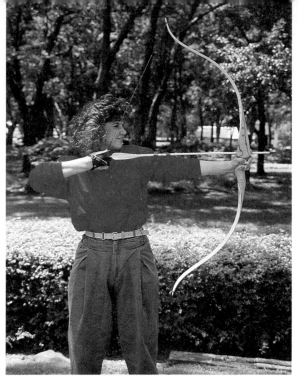

Fig. 1-12. When the stretched bowstring is released, its potential energy changes into kinetic energy and propels the arrow.

- Burning coal (chemical energy) is changed to heat energy.
- Heat energy is applied to water to produce steam (mechanical energy).
- Mechanical energy is used to drive a turbine generator, which produces electricity (electrical energy).

The electricity is then transmitted along power lines to where it is needed, such as in a home. There the electricity is used to power motors, provide light and heat, and operate radios and television sets.

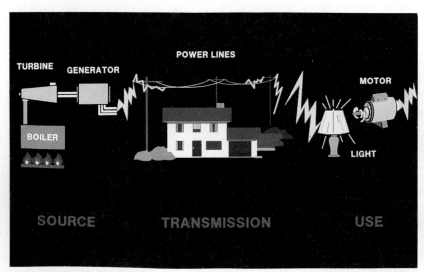

POWER LINES

TURBINE   GENERATOR

MOTOR

BOILER

LIGHT

SOURCE   TRANSMISSION   USE

Fig. 1-11. A complete energy system.

KINETIC AND POTENTIAL ENERGY

All forms of energy can be put into two categories:
- Kinetic energy
- Potential energy

See Fig. 1-12.

Kinetic Energy

Kinetic energy is energy in motion. The radiant energy that travels from the sun to the earth is a form of kinetic energy. Radiant energy produces wind and rain, which are other forms of kinetic energy. Rushing water, ocean breezes, and winter storms are all forms of kinetic energy.

Mechanical energy and electrical energy are also forms of kinetic energy. The electric current that powers a motor is an example of kinetic energy. A motor has an electrical input and a mechanical output. Whenever we use energy, it is in the form of kinetic energy.

Potential Energy

Potential energy is any form of *stored* energy. One example of potential energy is the water stored behind a dam at a hydroelectric plant. See Fig. 1-13. When energy is needed, the water is released and flows through a turbine generator. The generator produces electricity. Therefore, the overall conversion is from potential energy (stored water) into kinetic energy (electricity).

The fuel in a nuclear reactor is another form of potential energy. Uranium has a tremendous amount of stored energy. When energy is needed, engineers at the nuclear power plant start the fission process. This process produces heat, which is converted into mechanical energy, then electrical energy. The overall conversion is from potential energy (uranium) into kinetic energy (electricity).

Most of the energy under our control is in the form of potential energy. Wood, coal, oil, and natural gas are all forms of potential energy. When we need energy, we convert these sources into forms of kinetic energy. We use generating plants and various types of engines to make the energy conversions. See Fig. 1-14.

Potential energy refers to all types of available or motionless energy. A raised hammer has potential energy. When it moves downward, the hammer can drive a nail. Food is potential energy. Our bodies convert its chemical energy into kinetic energy as needed. A boulder at the top of a hill also has potential energy. This energy is released when the boulder rolls down the hill.

Another way to view potential energy is as *stored motion*. Remember that the use of energy involves motion. But potential energy can be viewed as motion waiting to occur. When the motion is needed, potential energy can be changed into one of the six forms of kinetic energy.

Fig. 1-13. Water behind a dam is potential energy. When the water is allowed to flow, it becomes kinetic energy that can be put to work generating electricity.

Fig. 1-14. An engine converts the potential energy of gasoline or diesel fuel into kinetic energy (motion).

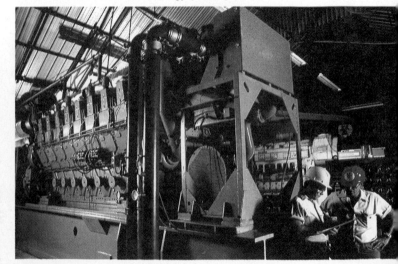

Chapter 1—Review

Testing Your Knowledge

Briefly answer each of the following questions. Write on a separate piece of paper.
1. What is energy?
2. Name one way in which early humans were able to increase their own muscle power.
3. Identify the six forms of energy. Give an example of each form.
4. Which energy conversion does a battery use to light the bulb of a flashlight?
5. Besides being forms of energy, in what way are mechanical and thermal energy similar?
6. What determines the amount of heat given off by a substance?
7. What is friction? Identify one way in which friction is useful. What is one disadvantage of friction?
8. Name three uses of nuclear energy.
9. In what form does the sun's energy travel to the earth?
10. What is photosynthesis? What energy conversion takes place during this process?
11. What energy conversion takes place when we burn a fossil fuel?
12. What is the Law of Conservation of Energy?
13. Name the three parts of an energy system.

Expressing Your Knowledge

Using complete sentences, write your answers to the following on a separate sheet of paper:
1. Why was steam power an improvement over early forms of wind and water power?
2. Electrical energy is often considered to be the most "convertible" form of energy. Describe electrical energy. Give three examples of how electrical energy is converted into other forms of energy.
3. Explain the difference between kinetic and potential energy.

Applying Your Knowledge

Follow your teacher's instructions to complete these activities:

1. Prepare a simple model or set of drawings showing the water cycle. The cycle should include (1) evaporation from the ocean, (2) clouds, (3) rain, (4) collection of water for power generation, drinking, and irrigation, and (5) distribution of water and electrical power. Present your project to the class. Then set it up as a display in the classroom.

2. Begin a *Power Notebook*. For each chapter, the notebook should have the following sections:

   a. Newspaper or magazine clippings. Attach each clipping to a page of your notebook. Use 8 ½ × 11 paper and show sources and dates. Prepare a brief review of each clipping. This could be a statement of agreement or disagreement or comments on the topic's importance or use.

   b. Vocabulary words. Define all vocabulary words shown at the beginning of each chapter. Select the five hardest words for you, and use each of these in a sentence.

   c. Answers to questions in *Testing Your Knowledge* and *Expressing Your Knowledge* found at the end of each chapter.

   d. Written assignments. Include other written assignments given by your teacher.

   Your teacher will check your notebook. Keep it neat, up-to-date, and filled with good information.

Chapter 2

The Nature and Principal Sources of Energy

To use energy, we must control it. To control energy, we must understand it—what it is and where it comes from.

Expanding Your Knowledge

As you study this chapter, you will learn to:

■ Understand three important characteristics of energy: (1) Energy is the ability to do work. (2) It always involves motion. (3) It cannot be created or destroyed.
■ Describe the origin and recovery of the fossil fuels for our use.
■ Identify the principal sources of the energy we control.
■ Recognize that all sources of energy fall within one of the following categories: exhaustible, renewable, and inexhaustible.
■ Understand how energy originates and is converted into controlled forms that are used in transportation, business, industry, and in residential and commercial areas.

Building Your Word Power

The following terms are defined and explained in this chapter. Learning these will help you learn more about the nature and principal sources of energy.

coal
exhaustible energy sources (fuels)
fossil fuels
geopressure reserves
hydroelectric energy
inexhaustible energy sources (fuels)
natural gas
oil
peat
petroleum
radiant energy
refining
renewable energy sources (fuels)
slurry
synfuels
tight sand reserves
turbine

The information presented in this chapter will help you understand both the nature of the energy we control and the sources of this energy.

There are three important characteristics of energy which must be understood. First, energy is defined as the ability or capacity to do work; second, energy always involves motion; and third, energy cannot be created or destroyed.

The main body of the chapter will give you an initial understanding of the sources of our controlled energy and how the energy is used to serve our needs. Emphasis is placed on understanding that most of the energy we control is energy from fossil fuels, hydroelectric energy, and nuclear energy.

The final section of the chapter presents, in one chart, a descriptive analysis of energy use, from source to final application in transportation, business, industry, and in commercial and residential areas. The chart also provides percentages and ratios which will expand your understanding of energy—its availability and our uses of it.

THE NATURE OF ENERGY

"Energy" is a word used by everyone. "I'm really tired. I've used up all my *energy*!", "That job took all the *energy* I had!" These and similar expressions are used every day. We use energy all the time, even when we're relaxing. The more active we become, the more energy we use.

As you look around, you'll see many examples of energy. Wind and flowing water are natural forms of energy. Wind can move sailboats and turn wind turbines (windmills) to produce electricity. Wind can also be destructive. Hurricanes and tornadoes destroy homes, turn over trucks, and knock down trees and telephone poles. A flowing stream can carry a boat or turn a turbine to produce electricity. But an uncontrolled flood can sweep away nearly everything in its path. To use energy, we must control it.

We can use fuels to produce the energy which works for us. An automobile carries people, and trucks and trains move goods across country. These are examples of controlling energy for our use. What others can you name? See Fig. 2-1.

Fig. 2-1. A crane uses energy as it lifts building materials to the upper stories of a building under construction.

Three basic energy concepts are very important in understanding the sources of energy. These will be explained later in greater detail. Remember:

■ Energy is the ability or capacity to do work.

We use energy in *all* activities, whether done by ourselves or by a machine.

■ Energy always involves motion.

Every form of energy involves motion, varying from the smallest known particles to large mechanical devices such as airplanes and ships. We can even say that energy *is* motion.

■ Energy cannot be created or destroyed.

When we use energy, we bring motion under control for our use. This often involves changing the form of the energy. The movement (motion) is not destroyed; it just continues in a different form. See Fig. 2-2.

HOW ENERGY IS USED

The history of human progress can be traced by our ability to control energy. This ability has grown over the centuries to help create the complex world in which we live. Energy powers this world and maintains the quality of life we enjoy.

Energy use can be divided into four broad areas:

■ Transportation.

Approximately one-quarter (27.1%) of the energy we control is used to move people and goods in automobiles, trucks, trains, airplanes, and ships.

■ Industrial.

This is the largest user of energy (36.6%). Energy uses in industry include heating furnaces, powering production lines, and processing raw materials.

■ Residential.

A little less than one-quarter (22.3%) is used in our homes to provide heat and light and to power the machines and equipment used there.

■ Commercial.

This area is the smallest of the four major users (14.0%). Commercial uses are similar to residential and provide the heat and light for buildings and power for office machines and computers.

Figure 2-3 graphically shows this division of use. The information is important as we study ways to conserve energy. Most progress can be made in the areas of heavy use.

Fig. 2-2. An automobile engine changes the thermal energy produced by burning gasoline into the mechanical energy of turning wheels to move the automobile. Brakes turn the mechanical energy back into thermal energy (heat from friction) to stop the car.

Fig. 2-3. The division of energy uses. Note that our largest use of energy is in industry.

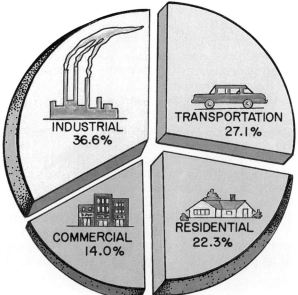

INDUSTRIAL
36.6%

TRANSPORTATION
27.1%

COMMERCIAL
14.0%

RESIDENTIAL
22.3%

GROUPING ENERGY SOURCES

The sun is our greatest and most basic source of energy. It provides the earth with vast amounts of heat and light. We call energy from the sun **radiant energy**. It warms the earth, sustains life, and produces our changing weather conditions.

The sun's energy is made available to us in many ways. For example, green plants capture and use radiant energy directly. They change sunlight, carbon dioxide, and water into food. Plants use the food for growth. The new growth is actually stored energy. Animals that eat plants take in and use this energy for survival and growth. And some energy goes into storage as fat.

Energy is also released when plants are burned. Burning plant products, such as wood, releases the energy the plants collected from the sun and stored.

Most of the energy we use is energy from the sun that nature has placed in storage. For example, coal, oil, and natural gas supply much of our energy. All three of these sources were originally plants and animals that died millions of years ago.

Flowing water is another major energy source. Again, it is the sun that provides this energy source. The sun's heat causes the water on the earth to evaporate and form clouds. The water then falls to earth as rain or snow. Some of it collects in lakes or behind dams. The water can be released from the lakes or dams and used to generate electricity.

There are many other ways in which the sun provides us with sources of energy. If we are to maintain and improve our present way of life, we must learn to make better use of our energy sources. The three basic types of energy sources are:

- Exhaustible
- Renewable
- Inexhaustible

Exhaustible Energy

Exhaustible energy sources are those which cannot be replaced once they are used. Coal, oil, natural gas, and uranium are exhaustible energy sources. These four sources supply over 95% of the energy we use.

Coal, oil, and natural gas are called **fossil fuels**. When we use these fuels, we are actually using the sun's energy that was stored as chemical energy in plants and animals millions of years ago. See Fig. 2-4.

Uranium, a metallic element, is the fuel of nuclear power plants. Like the fossil fuels, it is obtained from the ground. But our supply of uranium originated with the formation of the solar system. It is also an exhaustible energy source.

Fig. 2-4. Fossil fuels originated from ancient plants and animals that were buried in swamps and later subjected to high pressure and temperature.

A. As plants and animals died, they fell into swamps, forming a layer of organic matter. This layer was covered by sediment.

B. More plants and animals died, forming a new top layer. High pressure and temperature produced peat, the first material in the formation of fossil fuels.

C. Shifts in the earth and deposits of sand and gravel combined to raise the pressure and temperature. The end results were coal, oil, and natural gas.

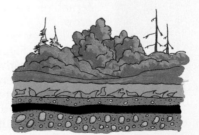
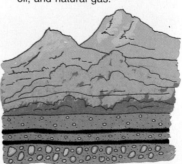

A　　　　　　　　　　B　　　　　　　　　　C

Renewable Energy

Renewable energy sources are those that can be used indefinitely if they are properly managed and maintained. Wood, plants, and waste products are renewable sources of energy.

Renewable fuels must be carefully managed or they can be lost. For example, cutting down too many trees without proper replanting could destroy wood resources. See Fig. 2-5. In the years to come, renewable sources of energy will increase in importance. This is because they can be used to replace fossil fuels.

Inexhaustible Energy

Inexhaustible energy sources are those that will always be available. They are renewed by nature and cannot be used up. Inexhaustible sources include solar energy (direct), solar salt ponds, hydroelectric energy, wind power, tides, ocean thermal energy, and geothermal energy.

The sun provides *solar energy* in the form of heat. We may use the heat directly or we may obtain it from *solar salt ponds*. Sunlight can also be changed directly into electricity with solar cells. (Refer back to Fig. 1-7.)

The sun produces the weather. The weather in turn provides rain for *hydroelectric power* and wind for *wind power*. The sun also produces temperature differences within the ocean, which provides *ocean thermal energy*.

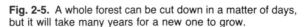
Fig. 2-5. A whole forest can be cut down in a matter of days, but it will take many years for a new one to grow.

The gravitational pull of the moon provides most of the energy for *tides*.

Geothermal energy is an inexhaustible source of heat produced by radioactive materials deep below the surface of the earth, plus heat remaining from the earth's formation.

These sources can't be exhausted. We must count on these sources as alternatives to the fossil fuels that are being depleted. Each is discussed in greater detail later in this book.

COMMON SOURCES OF ENERGY

Four of the five most used sources of energy are the four exhaustible sources of energy: coal, oil, natural gas, and uranium. The only *inexhaustible* source in common use is hydroelectric energy. Figure 2-6 shows the percentage of each of the most used sources of energy in the United States and in the world.

About 90% of all the energy used in the United States comes from fossil fuels. Oil alone provides nearly 42%, just under half of all the energy used. This dependency on oil helps explain why oil prices affect our entire economy. The only energy sources used significantly besides fossil fuels are nuclear and hydroelectric.

All alternative sources are either renewable or inexhaustible. Yet they account for less than 1% of our current usage of energy. The most widely used alternative sources are geothermal, solar, and wind.

About one-quarter of all the energy we use is in the form of electricity. Electricity provides all of our lighting and powers motors and electrical devices in homes and industries.

As with all other uses of energy, exhaustible sources supply most of the energy used to produce electrical power. Most of our electrical power comes from coal. See Fig. 2-7. Hydroelectric power, at 11.4%, is the only significant inexhaustible source. As we continue to develop alternative sources, the "other" category should grow.

Energy *reserves* are what remains of exhaustible fuels. Figure 2-8 shows a comparison of the U.S. and worldwide reserves. As you can see, oil, the most widely used fuel, is in short supply. At the present rate of usage, the world's known supplies of oil and natural gas will probably be depleted during the coming century. To avoid energy shortages, we should work *now* to develop inexhaustible or renewable supplies of energy.

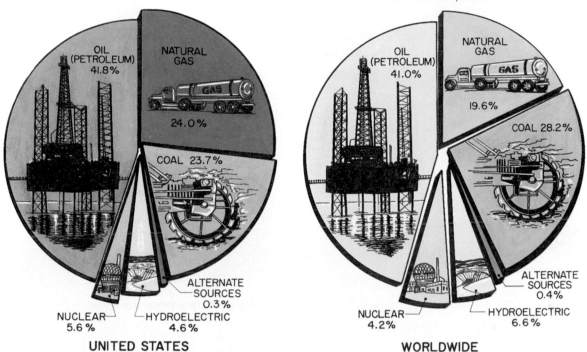

Fig. 2-6. These graphs compare the present energy usage in the U.S. with that in the entire world.

Fig. 2-7. U.S. electricity generation sources.

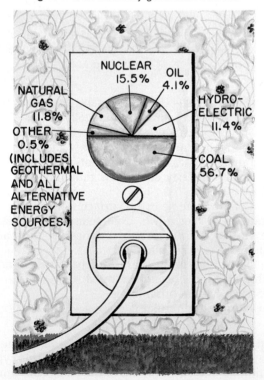

Now, let's take a closer look at four of the five major sources of energy: coal, oil, natural gas, and hydroelectric. Uranium, the source of energy for nuclear power plants, will be discussed in Chapter 5.

Coal

Coal is one of the fossil fuels. It is a solid, combustible (burnable) substance, brown to black in color. Coal is taken from the ground by both strip and underground mining.

Coal is the most abundant exhaustible fuel. As shown in Fig. 2-8, coal makes up almost 90% of all remaining exhaustible fuel resources in the United States. Worldwide, only the USSR has greater coal reserves.

At our present rate of usage, coal supplies should last 275 years or more. However, oil and natural gas have much smaller reserves. As these fuel supplies decrease, the use of coal will increase. This will reduce the length of time our coal reserves will last. Coal shortages may begin to occur in less than 200 years. This seems like a long time. But it is really a very short time compared to the millions of years it took to form the coal.

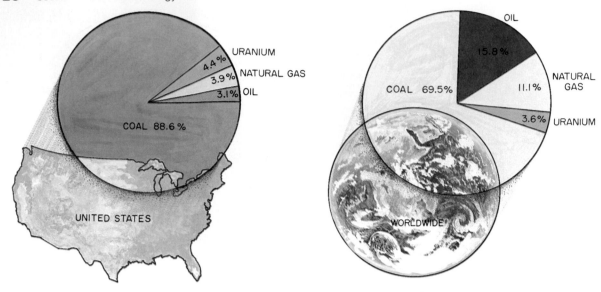

Fig. 2-8. These graphs compare U.S. and worldwide total reserves of exhaustible energy.

Location and Types of Coal. Coal reserves in the United States are abundant in the East, the Midwest, and in the Rocky Mountain states. But only a small amount of coal exists in the Far West. See Fig. 2-9.

All coal is not alike. There are several types, depending on the age and the amount of pressure placed upon the coal during formation. The first stage is called **peat**. In this stage, it is not yet coal. Peat looks like decayed wood. It will burn but produces less heat than coal. Peat may become a valuable source of energy. New processes are being developed that will permit the use of peat without transporting it. The United States has vast supplies of peat.

As time passes, pressure and heat increase and coal is formed. The following are the four classifications of coal. Each form is harder, produces more heat, and is more valuable than the last.
■ Lignite.
This type of coal is in the first stage of development. It is dark brown in color and burns well. But it does not give off enough heat to make it useful as a commercial fuel.
■ Sub-bituminous.
This type is black in color and denser than lignite. It is a common and widely used type of soft coal. It crumbles easily.

■ Bituminous.
This type is harder than sub-bituminous. It is also a common and widely-used type of soft coal.
■ Anthracite.
This type is the hardest and best coal. It is also the least common. In the U.S., Pennsylvania is the only source of anthracite coal.

Coal Mining. Coal is usually found in the earth in layers. Refer back to Fig. 2-4. These layers are often called *seams* or *veins*. Some are very thin—just a few inches thick—and have little commercial value. Seams that are mined are much larger. They are often hundreds of feet thick.

Coal may be near the surface of the earth or hundreds of feet down. Coal seams often reach the earth's surface. When this occurs, they are called *coal outcroppings*.

Since coal seams vary in depth, two mining techniques have been developed:
■ Strip, or open-pit, mining
■ Underground mining

Open-pit Mining. When coal seams are near the surface, open-pit mining is used. In this type of mining, the earth on top of the coal seam must

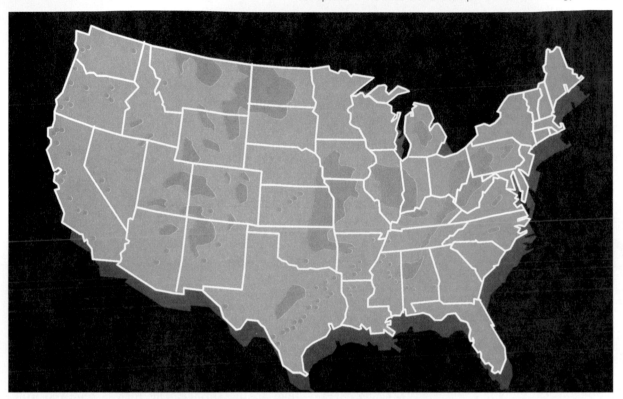

Fig. 2-9. Distribution of coal reserves in the United States.

Fig. 2-10. Coal is often moved by conveyor belts and trains.

be removed. This earth, called *overburden*, consists of topsoil and subsoil. It must be placed on land that is not over the coal seam being mined.

After the overburden has been removed, the coal is shoveled into trucks or onto a conveyor belt. It is then loaded onto trains and moved to processing plants, or, if relatively free of impurities, directly to power plants or other users. See Fig. 2-10.

The greatest problem with open-pit mining is the possibility of permanently defacing the land. After the coal is removed, the subsoil must be replaced and leveled and the topsoil placed on top of it. Even this replacement process contains one potential problem. Removing the coal lowers the final level of the land. If this condition is improperly managed, drainage and erosion problems can occur. But planning ahead can prevent problems from arising and restore the land to its natural state or for productive use.

Processes that preserve the land for future generations may be costly but they are very important. Public agencies which have the responsibility to control and regulate mining must make certain that the land is restored.

Underground Mining.
This technique is used when the coal seam is deep within the earth. Mine shafts are dug, and miners work underground mining the coal. The coal is taken to the surface by coal cars or conveyor belts.

Underground mining is often dangerous and is usually more costly than open-pit mining. However, high-grade coal such as anthracite is usually found deep within the earth. The value of this coal usually makes it economical to mine.

Coal Processing and Transportation.
When mined, coal usually contains rocks and other impurities. The mined coal must be crushed, cleaned, and sorted by size. The coal is then shipped to the consumer.

The traditional method of shipping coal is by trains. However, coal can also be shipped by pipeline. This is accomplished by crushing the coal into powder, mixing it with water, and then pumping the mixture (called **slurry**) through a pipeline. Slurry can be pumped hundreds of miles to the consumer.

Uses of Coal.
Coal used to be a major source of energy for home heating. However, it has been replaced during the last 40 to 50 years by oil and natural gas. These fuels are cleaner-burning (less polluting).

At one time, coal also fueled trains and ships. The heat from the burning coal produced steam from water. The steam powered a steam engine which drove the train or ship. Today, engines using oil have replaced almost all steam engines. But research is being done to improve the design and efficiency of steam engines. One day we may see the return of coal-fueled steam trains.

The major use of coal today is to produce electricity in power plants. See Fig. 2-11. Electrical power plants use about 85% of all coal mined.

Oil (Petroleum)[1]

Oil, or **petroleum**, is our most common source of controlled energy. As shown in Fig. 2-6, nearly 42% of our controlled energy comes from oil. Unfortunately, the worldwide supply of

---

[1]In this text, the terms "oil" and "petroleum" will be used interchangeably.

oil cannot sustain this level of consumption indefinitely. Even though new sources of oil continue to be discovered, consumption continues to exceed the rate of discovery. As a result, our known reserves of oil are decreasing.

There are three sources of oil:
- Crude oil
- Shale oil
- Tar sands

Crude Oil.
Crude oil is the main source of the oil that we use. It is a liquid trapped in pockets in the earth. Fluidity varies from very light, almost a gas, to very thick and dark.

Crude oil is obtained through a complex drilling operation. An oil derrick is placed over a carefully explored site for drilling. The derrick supports the tools and power equipment needed to drill a hole deep into the earth. Oil wells are often more than 5000 feet deep. Figure 2-12 shows a typical drilling rig.

The power source for oil drilling is usually one or more diesel engines (Chapter 14). The engine turns the rotary table which rotates the drill pipe. The bit cuts the rock as it digs deeper. Liquid mud cools the bit and brings the rock cuttings to the surface. The rock is removed from the mud and the mud is reused.

As drilling continues, lengths of drill pipe are added. Casing is used to line the hole and prevent cave-ins.

Fig. 2-11. A coal-fired electricity generating plant. The small structure at the right of the smokestack is a "scrubber" which removes sulfur dioxide before the smoke is released into the air.

Technology Focus

If You Can't Beat Them, Join Them

The United States has about 500 underground coal mine fires which have been difficult or impossible to extinguish. These fires were started by accident. The mines were abandoned when companies couldn't extinguish them. Some fires have been burning for decades. Imagine how much coal has been consumed!

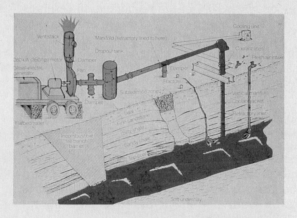

If we can't put out the fires, how can we prevent this wasteful loss of energy? The solution is to *use* the energy released by the burning coal to produce electricity. One plan is shown here. Fresh air will be provided through an intake vent. Then the hot exhaust gases will be used to produce steam to drive a turbine and an electrical generator.

Some unique design needs exist. The equipment must be compact and mobile. It must also be built on self-leveling shields in case the ground sinks due to the coal being burned below ground.

With creative thinking and the proper technology, many negative situations can be turned into positive ones. "If you can't beat them, join them."

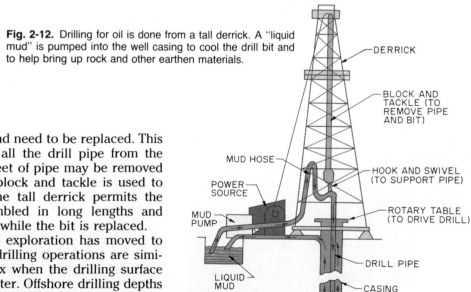

Fig. 2-12. Drilling for oil is done from a tall derrick. A "liquid mud" is pumped into the well casing to cool the drill bit and to help bring up rock and other earthen materials.

Drill bits wear and need to be replaced. This requires removal of all the drill pipe from the hole. Thousands of feet of pipe may be removed from deep holes. A block and tackle is used to remove the pipe. The tall derrick permits the pipe to be disassembled in long lengths and stored in the derrick while the bit is replaced.

Today, much oil exploration has moved to coastal waters. The drilling operations are similar but more complex when the drilling surface is many feet underwater. Offshore drilling depths are usually greater than onshore, often below 10,000 feet.

When oil is found, the casing is locked in place and oil removal begins. Most new wells have natural pressure which forces the oil to the surface. As the wells become older, pumps are used to remove the oil. See Fig. 2-13.

Shale Oil. Shale is a type of rock which contains oil. Over 80% of the remaining oil reserves in the United States are in the form of shale oil.

Extracting oil from oil shale is difficult. Workers must mine the shale like coal. The shale must then be crushed and heated until the oil is released from the rock.

When crude oil prices increased during the 1970s and early 1980s, many oil companies became interested in shale oil. But the drop in prices during the mid-1980s has discouraged the research needed to develop economical ways to remove the oil from shale. Present processes are expensive. As a result, this source of oil will have to wait until petroleum prices climb and research is resumed.

Tar Sands. Tar sands are the third source of oil. In tar sands, the oil is trapped in sand instead of shale. As with shale oil, heat is used to remove the oil.

Refining. After oil is obtained, it must be refined. Refining is the process of separating oil into several useful substances. See Fig. 2-14. This is done first by heating oil inside a tall column. As it heats up, the oil changes into vapors (gases). As the vapors rise in the column, they condense into various liquids at different levels. This part of the refining process is called *fractionating*. Each liquid formed is referred to as a *fraction*.

Fig. 2-14. Useful products are obtained from crude oil in a processing plant called a refinery.

Heavy vapors do not rise very high in the columns. They condense into fuels such as heating oil and diesel fuel. Light vapors rise higher. They condense into products (fractions) such as gasoline and kerosene.

The oil left after the fractionating process is further refined by a process called cracking. Cracking converts the less desirable fractions into gasoline.

The refining process also includes the addition of chemical compounds to the different fuels. Such compounds improve the burning and performance of the fuels in engines.

Uses of Oil. We use a great deal of oil. Many different products are produced from it, and petroleum products have a variety of uses.

Almost all transportation devices, from automobiles to jet planes, are fueled by some form of oil. The most common products are gasoline and diesel fuel. Because these fuels are easily transported and provide large amounts of energy per pound, they are presently the best energy sources for transportation.

Many homes and large buildings use oil as an energy source for heating. We also use oil to generate electricity. These uses, plus its use in transportation, have made oil the world's most important fuel.

A major user of petroleum is the petrochemical industry. Petroleum is the primary ingredient in the production of plastics. And plastics are now part of thousands of industrial and household products.

The petrochemical industry also provides photographic supplies, paints, explosives, food additives, fertilizers, and numerous other products. Many scientists believe that the remaining world supply of oil should be saved for petrochemical use. They think we should stop burning it as a fuel.

Fig. 2-13. Pumps like the one shown here are used to bring crude oil to the surface.

Oil has a major disadvantage. The pollution resulting from the use of oil and oil products, especially gasoline, seriously affects our environment. You'll learn more about this in Chapter 9.

Natural Gas

When we speak of heating or cooking with "gas," we really mean natural gas. **Natural gas** is a mixture of several types of gases. These include ethane, propane, butane, and methane. The main gas is methane.

Next to coal and petroleum, natural gas is our most widely used source of energy. It provides 24% of all the energy under our control. Most of the natural gas we use comes from Canada, Alaska, Texas, and Louisiana. Kansas, Oklahoma, and New Mexico are also important producers.

Natural gas is most commonly found in underground pools or with crude oil deposits. It is traditionally obtained by simply drilling into the deposits and collecting the gas. However, there is not enough gas in these kinds of deposits to meet the demand. Fortunately, scientists have uncovered other reserves of natural gas. The most promising reserves are:
- Geopressure reserves
- Tight sand reserves

Geopressure Reserves.
Geopressure reserves consist of natural gas dissolved under high pressure in brine (salt water). This gas-filled brine is found in pools deep within the earth. The pressure caused by the weight of the earth holds the gas suspended in the brine. Drilling into a geopressure pool relieves this pressure. It allows the natural gas to separate from the brine.

There are very large geopressure reserves. They are hard to tap because they are located so far below the surface of the earth. Scientists also need to develop better ways to separate the gas from the brine. But, geopressure reserves may be the major source of natural gas in the future.

Tight Sand Reserves.
These reserves consist of natural gas trapped in a type of hard, dense sandstone. Tight sand formations are found in the Rocky Mountain region. The gas is obtained by injecting a high-pressure fluid into the sandstone. This causes the stone to break, and that allows the gas to escape.

Processing and Using Natural Gas.
Once natural gas is collected from a reserve, it is transported through pipelines to processing plants. These plants remove impurities such as dust, water, and sulfur from the gas. They also separate special gases such as propane and butane. The remaining gas, ready to use, flows through pipelines to homes and industries.

Natural gas is our cleanest fossil fuel. It produces the least amount of pollutants when it burns. It is also cheaper than most other fuels. For these reasons, natural gas has become a major energy source for home and industry. We use it for heating, cooling, cooking, generation of electricity, and for many other purposes.

Natural gas is more difficult to transport than oil. Although it is most often transported by pipeline, it can be transported by truck or ship if it is in liquid form. See Fig. 2-15. Natural gas is liquified (changed to a liquid) by placing it under extremely high pressure and cooling it. However, the high pressure makes the transportation of liquified natural gas (LNG) potentially dangerous.

Synthetic Fuels (Synfuels)

The word "synthetic" means *artificial*, or made by human beings. *Synthetic fuels*, or **synfuels**, are liquid or gaseous fuels that are made from already existing solid fuels. Synfuels can be produced from coal, tar sands, oil shale, and from biomass (waste products).

Coal is the most likely fuel to be converted into synfuel. Scientists are now researching various processes to convert coal into liquid or gaseous fuel.

Coal Liquification.
The process of liquifying coal is not new. It was developed in Germany in 1931 by a scientist named *Friedrich Bergius*. The process is basically very simple. Coal liquifies when hydrogen is added to it under great heat and pressure. The result is synthetic oil (synoil).

Fig. 2-15. Large tankers can carry enormous amounts of liquified natural gas.

A new process being developed uses a mixture of finely ground coal and oil or water. See Fig. 2-16. The mixture does not involve costly processing, and it produces a liquid fuel usable for heating applications.

Liquified coal will be used as a replacement for oil in oil-burning power plants. And it will be used for industrial and home heating as well.

Coal Gasification. The coal gasification process consists of adding steam and hydrogen to coal under high heat and pressure. The result is a low-grade gas (syngas). This gas is then purified and upgraded. Both synoil and syngas projects are presently underway in the United States.

Future Uses. The decreased cost of oil has slowed the development of synfuels. The processing required makes them more expensive than oil. But they will become more important when oil prices go up or when the world starts running out of oil during the next century.

In the meantime, synfuels will have limited use. They are being produced mainly where there are limited supplies of oil or natural gas. South Africa, for example, has a limited supply of petroleum. Processing plants there convert coal into 55,000 barrels of synoil each day.

Fig. 2-17. The Hoover Dam, located in the Black Canyon of the Colorado River, traps behind it a body of water 115 miles long and 589 feet deep.

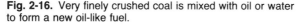

Fig. 2-16. Very finely crushed coal is mixed with oil or water to form a new oil-like fuel.

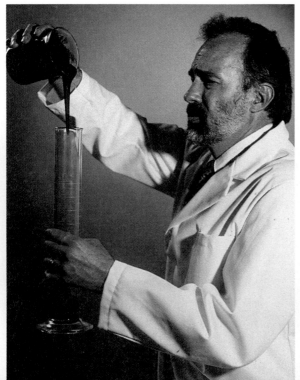

Hydroelectric Energy

Hydroelectric energy is the only significant form of inexhaustible energy presently being used. **Hydroelectric energy** is simply electrical energy produced from flowing water.

Each year the heat from the sun causes 100,000 cubic miles (416,550 km^3) of water to evaporate. This is ten times the amount of water in the Great Lakes. All of it returns to the earth as rain or snow. Rain and snow sustain our streams, rivers, lakes, and oceans. We gather runoff water into reservoirs by trapping it behind dams. See Fig. 2-17. We then use much of this water to produce electrical power.

Design and Operation. Once electricity is produced, it must be used. As a result, the rate of the flow of water through a hydroelectric plant is determined by the amount of electricity needed.

As water drains from a reservoir, it flows through a *sluice* (a special waterway or tunnel). A water **turbine** is at the end of the sluice. It is driven by the flow of water. See Fig. 2-18. The rotating (turning) turbine drives a generator that produces electricity.

Water turbines that drive electric generators operate on either the impulse or the reaction principle. The *impulse* principle is a direct push. A waterwheel operates on the impulse principle.

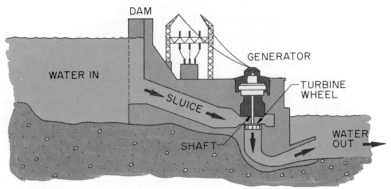

Fig. 2-18. Flowing water drives the blades of the water turbine wheel. The turbine rotates the generator shaft, producing electricity.

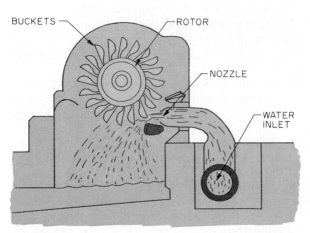

Fig. 2-19. A Pelton wheel uses the impulse force from water to rotate.

A modern version of the waterwheel is the Pelton turbine shown in Fig. 2-19. Water is directed against the turbine, causing it to rotate.

The *reaction* principle is based on the concept that as the water changes direction, it pushes against the object causing the change. Hold your hand in front of a stream of water, and deflect its motion. A reaction force will be applied to your hand.

Two turbine designs that use the reaction principle are the Francis turbine and the Kaplan turbine. In the Francis turbine, the water is directed downward; the reaction drives the turbine. The Kaplan turbine uses a propeller action to change the direction of the water flow. These two turbines are the most common designs used in hydroelectric power plants. See Fig. 2-20.

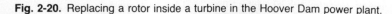

Fig. 2-20. Replacing a rotor inside a turbine in the Hoover Dam power plant.

Uses of Hydroelectric Power. Approximately 11% of all the electricity produced in the United States comes from hydroelectric power. This means that about 4% of *all* the energy we use is hydroelectric power. Most of the good hydroelectric sites are already in use. Still, the addition of new sites is expected to increase hydroelectric power by 50%-100% during the next few decades.

Hydroelectric power plants are costly and require considerable planning. Dams trap large quantities of water, forcing land to be abandoned to the growing lake. There is also the destruction of the natural environment and other side effects which must be taken into account. Wildlife may be destroyed. Even weather can be changed by placing a lake where none existed before.

Fortunately, electricity is one of the easiest forms of energy to transmit. The mountainous areas which serve as basins to store water for hydroelectric power are often miles from the cities which need the power. Transmission lines can easily carry the electricity long distances.

PRODUCING AND USING ENERGY

At the beginning of this chapter, energy use was divided into four broad categories: transportation, industrial, residential, and commercial. The sections following this division provided the primary sources for this energy. You learned that 90% of all the energy we use comes from the three fossil fuels, with oil providing nearly half of all controlled energy.

Fossil fuels release energy by burning. The heat is then used to *heat* homes and buildings or to drive engines which produce *motion*. This motion is used to power automobiles or other transportation and industrial devices. In power plants, the motion is used to drive electric generators which produce *electricity*.

As you learned in Chapter 1, we give technical names to the three forms of energy (heat, motion, and electricity) described in the previous paragraph. The heat produced by burning is called *thermal energy*. Motion is called *mechanical energy*, and electricity is called *electrical energy*. These are the three forms of energy we use the most.

We now have enough information to construct a "source to use" energy chart. See Fig. 2-21. Study this chart carefully. The following information will help you understand the chart:
■ Line width represents the amount of energy used or provided. Note that the line width representing fossil fuels is 92% of the total of all resource line widths. The line running from thermal energy to mechanical energy is two-thirds the size of the input lines to fossil fuels. This shows that two-thirds of the thermal energy is used to produce mechanical energy.
■ The box sizes are also proportional. Note that the boxes under "End Use" are proportional to the percentage shown at the right.

Now, let's work on understanding the chart. The percentages of U.S. Energy Supply show the sources of energy. Compare these with Fig. 2-6. Examine the "Resource" to "Forms of Energy" sections.
■ The energy from fossil fuels is usually thermal energy released by burning. The same is true for nuclear energy. The only useful energy from nuclear fuel is heat.
■ Hydro, the power from falling water, drives turbines. The rotation of turbines is mechanical energy.
■ Alternative sources produce all three forms of energy. Geothermal energy produces heat. Solar energy is used either for heating, or it is converted directly into electrical energy by solar cells. Wind and tides provide motion. Each of the other alternative forms provide one of these three forms of energy.

Next, look at the "Forms of Energy" to "End Use of Energy" sections.
■ The "End Use of Energy" is the same as that shown on Fig. 2-3.
■ Approximately one-third of the thermal energy produced is directly used to provide heat for homes and other buildings. Heat is also used in industrial furnaces for refining and manufacturing materials.
■ The remaining two-thirds is used to produce mechanical energy (motion). Heat drives turbines, automobile engines, boat engines, etc.
■ About half of the motion (mechanical energy) produced by engines is put to work. Nearly all of this is for transportation—automobiles, trains, airplanes, and ships. A small amount is

used in each of the other three areas. These uses include small engines around the home or around commercial buildings. Also included are farm equipment and industrial engines.

■ The remaining half of the motion drives generators to produce electricity. A very small amount of this electricity is used in transportation in the form of electric trains and subways.

■ Approximately half of the electrical energy is used in industry to power equipment and provide light and heat.

■ The remaining electricity is used in homes and buildings for light, heat for cooking and drying, and to drive electric motors for washers, air conditioners, and a host of office machines.

This chart brings together everything learned about energy up to this point. You should now know which sources are most important sources of energy, and how this energy is modified for our use.

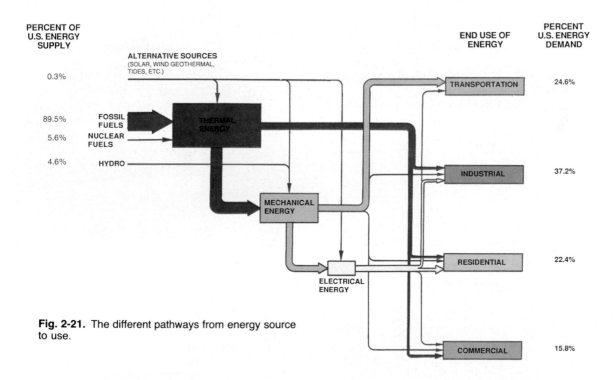

Fig. 2-21. The different pathways from energy source to use.

Chapter 2—Review

📖 Testing Your Knowledge

Briefly answer each of the following questions. Write on a separate piece of paper.

1. What is the initial or principal source of the energy we use?
2. Name the three fossil fuels.
3. Which fossil fuel is most abundant?
4. At the present time, what is the largest use of coal?
5. What is the hardest form of coal?
6. What is coal slurry?
7. What are the two main problems oil has as an energy source?
8. Natural gas contains many different kinds of gases. What is the main one?
9. What does the abbreviation "LNG" mean?
10. What are synfuels? Name two synfuels.
11. How are rain and snow used as sources of energy?
12. What is an impulse turbine? a reaction turbine?
13. Which of the four categories of energy-users consumes the most energy?
14. What are the three most common forms of energy under our control?

Expressing Your Knowledge 📖

Using complete sentences, write your answers to the following on a separate sheet of paper:

1. Explain this statement: "Energy is motion."
2. Define these terms: exhaustible energy, renewable energy, inexhaustible energy.
3. Briefly describe how fossil fuels were formed.
4. Describe open-pit mining of coal.
5. Explain the difference between crude oil, shale oil, and tar sands.
6. How is gasoline made from crude oil?
7. Describe the makeup of a geopressure reserve and tight sand reserves.
8. Define hydroelectric energy.
9. Why must we be concerned about fossil fuel supplies?

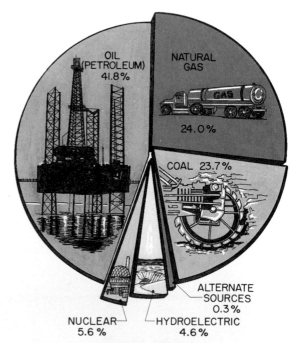

UNITED STATES

Applying Your Knowledge

Follow your teacher's instructions to complete these activities:

1. Your teacher will divide the class into 5-8 groups of students. Each group should select one of the sources of energy described in this chapter, such as shale oil or tight sand reserves of natural gas. The group should research the topic, develop posters showing production and recovery methods or other important information, and make a presentation to the class.

2. Determine the cost per cubic foot that the local utility company charges for natural gas. Many utilities print this information on the utility bill. If it isn't listed on your bill, contact your local company to obtain the current cost per cubic foot.

3. Identify the uses of natural gas in your home. In a brief report, identify each use and indicate how the use might change between seasons.

4. Read your gas meter each day for one month. The *Student Workbook* shows how meters are read. Identify the number of cubic feet used each day, each week, and for the month. Calculate the cost of gas each day, each week, and for the month. Compare your results with the utility bill. Prepare a report showing all calculations plus a table of your readings. Indicate how your results compared with the actual bill. Explain the differences.

Chapter 3

Solar Energy

Each day the sun provides the United States with 6500 times more electrical energy than is consumed. By capturing less than ¹/₁₀th of 1% (¹/₁₀₀₀) of the available solar energy, we could meet all of our energy needs, including heating and transportation.

Expanding Your Knowledge

As you study this chapter, you will learn to:

- Describe how solar energy is able to provide both heat and electricity.
- Explain how heat is moved by conduction, radiation, and convection.
- Understand the operation of a variety of passive and active solar heating systems.
- Describe how photovoltaic cells convert solar energy into electricity.
- Recognize the current level of use of solar energy to provide electrical power for home and industrial use, and provide electricity for a variety of passive and active solar heating systems.
- Recognize the current level of use of solar energy to provide electrical power for home and industrial use, and provide electricity for a variety of consumer products.
- Identify the research areas designed to make electricity from the sun a practical alternative to fossil fuels.

Building Your Word Power

The following terms are defined and explained in this chapter. Learning these will help you learn more about solar energy.

active solar heating system
conduction
convection
density
electron
greenhouse effect
kilowatt (kW)
megawatt (MW)
passive solar heating
photon
photovoltaic array
photovoltaic (PV) cells
radiation (thermal)
solar energy
solar panel (collector)
thermal mass
thermosiphoning
watt (W)

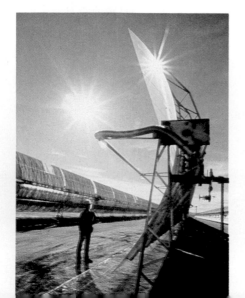

Solar energy has the potential to be a major alternative to the fossil fuels. In order to understand it, however, you must first understand how heat energy moves from one place to another.

Solar energy is becoming a practical source of heat for heating water, homes, and commercial buildings. In this chapter, emphasis is placed on the different systems which are being used to reduce the use of exhaustible fuels.

The process of converting the sun's energy directly into electricity by *photovoltaics* (solar cells) is described in detail. This level of explanation emphasizes the coming importance of this source of electricity. We already have many devices which use solar energy to produce electricity. These vary from many decades of using solar cells in light meters for photography to new uses of providing electricity for watches, calculators, and other consumer devices.

THE PROMISE OF SOLAR ENERGY

Solar energy is one of the most promising of the alternative energy sources. Most of our present energy sources are *indirect* uses of the sun's energy. The burning of fossil fuels releases solar energy stored millions of years ago. And hydroelectric energy is also an indirect use of solar energy. Heat from the sun creates the weather patterns that produce rain, the source of hydroelectric energy.

Even though most energy now in use originated from the sun, the term "**solar energy**" is commonly used to describe the *direct* control of the sun's energy. Solar energy has the potential of supplying most of the energy we need. We can use it in two ways:
■ Heating.

We can use solar energy to heat both water and buildings. Over one-quarter of our energy usage is used for these purposes. Therefore, this is an important area in which to develop solar energy.
■ Electricity.

Electricity has the most uses of any of our forms of energy. We can convert solar energy directly into electricity. We can also use it to generate steam, which can drive turbine generators. Scientists know *how* to use solar energy to generate electricity. But more research and development is needed to make solar-produced electricity more economical.

Energy in the forms of heat and electricity can satisfy most business, industry, residential, and commercial needs. Transportation devices require energy sources that can be carried by the vehicle. Some direct applications of solar energy for transportation are possible. But, at present, it is limited to experimental applications. See Fig. 3-1.

HEATING AND COOLING WITH SOLAR ENERGY

People are already using solar energy for heating. This is happening all over the world. Fossil fuels are becoming more scarce and expensive. Therefore, solar heating is becoming more popular. But using the sun for home heating is not new.

Nearly 2000 years ago, the Greeks and Romans located houses to capture the sun's heat in the winter. Roman law even made it a crime to block the sunlight from striking another person's home.

Fig. 3-1. Solar energy may someday meet most of our energy needs, even for transportation. (See feature article, p. 42.)

Technology Focus

To Race with the Sun

At first thought, the outback of Australia seems like an unlikely place to glimpse the future. But long hours of uninterrupted sunlight and long, "lonely" roads are good conditions for testing the capabilities of solar-powered vehicles.

In late 1987, Australia hosted the first Pentax World Solar Challenge, a race across the continent in solar-powered automobiles. Only 13 of the 24 entrants finished, with the last taking more than a month to finish the race. The winner, *Sunraycer* (shown here), completed the 1880-mile distance from Darwin to Adelaide in just 44 hours and 54 minutes of running time, with an average speed of 41.9 mph.

Sunraycer was engineered and built by General Motors Corporation (USA). Careful attention was given to aerodynamic efficiency in design and low rolling resistance. For power, the car used gallium-arsenide photovoltaic cells. These cells are 19-22% efficient at cool temperatures, and suffer less of a decline in hot weather than other types of cells. Sunraycer's cells powered lightweight, but costly, electric motors.

While "pure" solar cars may never replace existing automobiles, combinations may not be too far away. A combination solar and battery-powered hybrid could be a car of the near future. The Pentax World Challenge race is designed to encourage the research and development that will help perfect the concept. And experimental cars like Sunraycer allow us to test possibilities and glimpse the future.

In the United States, the 12th-century Anasazi Indians also used solar energy. Figure 3-2 shows their homes constructed under cliffs. In the winter, the sun is low in the sky. The dwellings captured the maximum amount of sunlight. In the summer, the sun is more directly overhead. The cliff shielded the homes from its intense rays.

Solar water heating dates back to the 19th century. For example, in 1896, a solar water heater installed on the roof of a California home supplied hot water for baths and other household uses.

Fig. 3-2. These cliff dwellings were heated by the low winter sun and protected from the hot summer sun by the cliffs.

During the early part of the 20th century, many people used solar water heating systems. By 1941, at least 60,000 solar water heaters had been installed. However, after World War II there was a great deal of inexpensive electricity and natural gas. This caused a decrease in the use of solar water heaters. At one point, only about 5000 solar water heaters were in use. But when gas and electricity prices increased in the 1970s, more people began using solar water heating systems.

Movement of Heat (Thermal Energy)

Before you learn about solar heating systems, you should first understand the nature of heat and temperature and how heat (thermal energy) moves from one place to another.

In Chapter 1 you learned that all forms of energy involve motion. In thermal energy, you usually cannot see the *motion*. But it is present. You can see and feel the *result*. As the air becomes warmer on a sunny day, you can feel the warmth. Sometimes you can see heat waves (turbulent hot air) rising from the surface of a hot object.

To understand heat, you must first understand the atomic structure of matter. You will recall from Chapter 1 that all matter is made of tiny units called *atoms*. An atom is the smallest unit of any basic substance (*element*). Two or more atoms combine to form a *molecule*. A molecule is the smallest particle of a substance made up of combined elements (*compound*).

Atoms and molecules are always in motion. The amount of thermal energy given off by a substance depends on the speed and number of atoms or molecules in motion. The faster they move, the higher the temperature. Also, the more atoms or molecules in motion, the greater the quantity of heat present. *Temperature* is the speed of molecular motion. *Quantity of heat* is the number and speed of molecules in motion.

In liquids and gases, molecules are free to move about. In solids, the molecules are more restricted, and motion is in the form of vibration. Thermal energy, therefore, always is identified as the motion of the atoms or molecules of a substance.

Heat moves naturally from warm to colder areas. It always seeks to balance or "even out" the temperature of objects and substances. For example, the air outside your home may be colder than the air inside. In this case, the inside heat will seek every possible route to flow to the outside. When it is hotter outside than inside, heat will attempt to flow into your home.

This movement can be understood as the movement of molecules. The warmer air has faster-moving molecules than colder air. When the fast-moving molecules meet the slower ones, they give the slower-moving molecules some of their speed. (They transfer energy.) All molecules will then move at the same speed, which is the average speed of both sets of molecules. The warm air has given some of its heat (speed of molecules) to the colder air. The result is an in-between temperature. This tendency to balance the temperature by heat flowing from warm to cold always takes place.

Heat has three ways of moving from one place to another:
- Conduction
- Radiation
- Convection

Conduction. The movement of heat through a substance is called *conduction*. Figure 3-3A shows heat moving through a solid wall by conduction. The denser the material, the more quickly the heat can move through it. **Density** refers to how closely the molecules of a substance are packed together. It is the number of molecules in a given volume. For example, concrete permits a quicker passage of heat than wood because it has greater density. Closely packed molecules collide more easily and more often than loosely packed molecules and, thus, transfer heat energy more quickly.

Radiation. Heat can also move by electromagnetic waves. These heat waves can pass through space and air without being absorbed. This form of heat transfer is called *radiation*. Through radiation, heat moves from warm objects to cooler ones. It does this with minimum warming of the air in between. Figure 3-3B shows how the sun heats a house by radiation.

Heat and light travel from the sun through space as radiant energy (electromagnetic waves). These waves do not heat the atmosphere; they just pass through it. When radiant energy hits a dark object such as the earth or an interior wall, the object absorbs the radiant energy and becomes warmer. The dark object then radiates heat, but at a much longer wavelength than the radiant energy from the sun. The dark

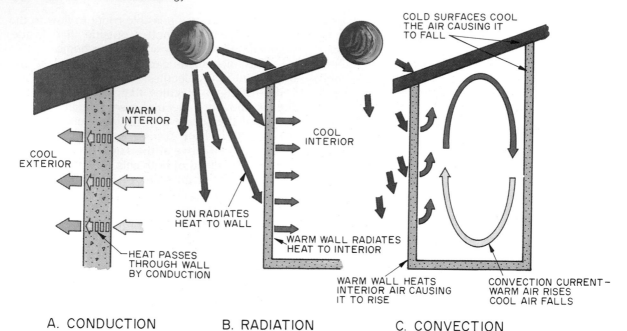

WARM INTERIOR

COOL EXTERIOR

HEAT PASSES THROUGH WALL BY CONDUCTION

A. CONDUCTION

SUN RADIATES HEAT TO WALL

COOL INTERIOR

WARM WALL RADIATES HEAT TO INTERIOR

B. RADIATION

COLD SURFACES COOL THE AIR CAUSING IT TO FALL

WARM WALL HEATS INTERIOR AIR CAUSING IT TO RISE

CONVECTION CURRENT— WARM AIR RISES COOL AIR FALLS

C. CONVECTION

Fig. 3-3. Heat moves by conduction, radiation, and convection.

object also heats the surrounding air. This is one reason why the air near the ground is warm, and gets colder the higher you go. Air is warmed by the heated surface of the earth rather than directly by the sun.

Fig. 3-4. A greenhouse is designed to receive and retain heat from the sun. The process used is called the greenhouse effect.

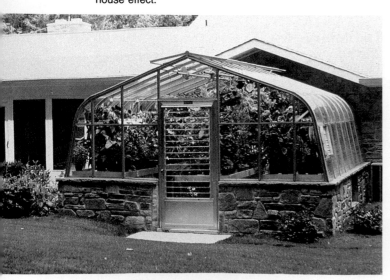

This information can be used to explain how a greenhouse is heated. The radiant energy from the sun is in the form of short wavelengths. These short waves pass through the glass walls of the greenhouse. See Fig. 3-4. The radiant energy strikes an interior wall or the ground and is absorbed. The dark surface of the wall or ground radiates heat at longer wavelengths. These wavelengths are stopped by the glass and kept inside the greenhouse. As a result, the greenhouse captures and retains the radiant energy from the sun. This process is called the **greenhouse effect.**

Convection. A third way that heat may be transferred is by *convection*. Convection is the moving of heat from warmer to colder areas by air, water, or other fluids. Heated air or water will always move to a colder area. Once there, the fluid will lose its heat. Refer back to Fig. 3-3C.

In convection, a warming and cooling process causes fluid movement. As a fluid warms up, its molecules move faster. The motion pushes the molecules apart and expands the fluid. The fluid now occupies a greater space. Therefore, it is lighter. It has less density.

Warm, light fluid rises. Colder, heavier fluid replaces it. Again, see Fig. 3-3C. When warm fluid touches a colder object, it transfers heat to that object. The fluid then cools and becomes more dense, or heavier. Gravity pulls the cooler fluid down. The fluid heats up again and the cycle repeats.

Air convects heat well only under certain conditions. The air must have enough room to set up currents (air movements). On the other hand, air trapped in a small space is a good insulator. Trapped air must transfer heat by conduction. Air molecules are much farther apart than molecules of a solid. Therefore, air conducts heat very slowly. Trapped air will help keep warm objects warm and cool objects cool.

These principles also explain how the air surrounding the earth is warmed and cooled to cause wind. As mentioned in the section on radiation, the radiant energy from the sun warms the earth. The earth in turn warms the air closest to the ground. This air becomes lighter in weight (less dense) and moves up. Colder, heavier air sinks to replace the warm air. This air movement is wind.

Preventing Heat Loss

There are two basic requirements for the successful use of solar energy. We must collect solar energy when it is available. And we must hold on to it as long as possible. Obviously, the sun's rays do not strike *any* part of the earth all the time. As one scientist put it, the sun is "a part-time performer in a full-time world." It is easy to heat a house with solar energy on sunny days. But a truly effective system captures and stores enough energy to supply heat at night and on overcast days.

Energy conservation is very important in solar heating systems. A drafty and poorly insulated house is hard to heat with solar energy. It will be warm when the sun shines. But the heat loss at night can be greater than the amount stored during the day. The first step in creating a good solar heating system is to *minimize heat loss*.

Figure 3-5 shows the many places heat can escape from a structure. Insulating roofs, walls, and floors will reduce heat loss. Caulking cracks (sealing with soft material) will also help. These conservation steps serve two purposes. They prevent heat loss during the winter. And they keep heat from entering in the summer.

Solar Heating Systems

There are two systems used for solar heating:
- Passive
- Active

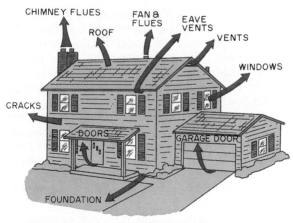

Fig. 3-5. Areas of a home most likely to allow heat loss.

Passive systems use building and landscaping design to collect, store, and transfer solar heat. *Active systems* collect solar energy and transfer the heat mechanically to where it is needed.

Passive Solar Heating

Passive solar heating is a system into which heat energy flows by natural means. These natural means include radiation, convection, and conduction.

Passive Home Heating—Direct-Gain.
The simplest kind of passive solar heating is heating living space with sunlight. See Fig. 3-6. This is called direct-gain solar heating. This type of system collects heat directly from the sun.

Fig. 3-6. Houses can be built to make good use of heat from the sun. The low winter sun will enter these large windows and help to heat the house. The large overhang will shield the window in summer.

Homes using a direct-gain system must have large windows facing south. This permits the winter sun to heat the interior using the greenhouse effect. The glass traps the sun's radiant energy inside the house. The residents use reflective curtains or insulated shades to control the amount of heat entering the home.

The house must have some type of thermal collector for heat storage. A heavy masonry (brick or stone) floor may be used to collect and store heat. When material is used in this way, it is called a **thermal mass**. Other thermal collectors include water-filled containers, concrete, and adobe.

As you know, in the northern hemisphere, the summer sun is much higher in the sky than the winter sun. To keep out the summer sun, houses with direct-gain systems use an overhang. The overhang does not keep the winter sun from shining into the house. (This is the same principle used by the Indian cliff-dwellers.)

Depending on climate, direct-gain systems can provide a part or all of the needed heat. Even on cloudy days, radiant energy will provide some heat. However, the quantity of heat will be much lower.

Most solar-heated homes have a secondary, or standby, heat source. This source is usually a gas or electric furnace or a wood stove. The standby source provides heat during extended cloudy conditions or cold spells.

Passive Home Heating—Indirect-Gain. Indirect-gain solar heating involves the use of a thermal mass. The thermal mass is located between the sun and the living area. See Fig. 3-7. It collects the sun's heat energy during the day. A large glass window keeps the heat energy from radiating outside. The wall then heats the home by both radiation and convection. The wall itself radiates heat to the living area.

In the convection process, cool air travels through vents at the bottom of the wall to the space between the glass and wall. There the air picks up heat from the wall and rises, flowing back into the room through the top vents. The vents provide temperature control. They can be closed when the house becomes warm enough. The vents are also closed at night, and the house is heated by radiation from the warm wall. See Fig. 3-7B.

An indirect-gain design can also help with summer cooling. See Fig. 3-8. Heated air between the glass and wall rises and escapes through opened vents. This action sets up a convection current that brings in cooler air from the north side of the house.

Fig. 3-7. Indirect-gain home heating.

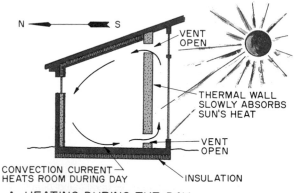

A. HEATING DURING THE DAY

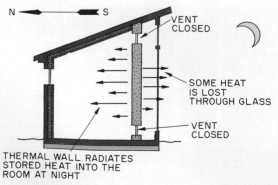

B. HEATING AT NIGHT

Fig. 3-8. Indirect-gain heating systems can also be used to help cool the home. The sun creates a convection current that draws cool air through the house.

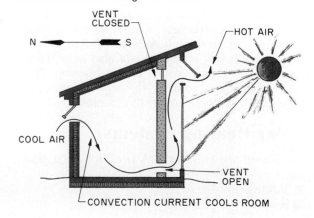

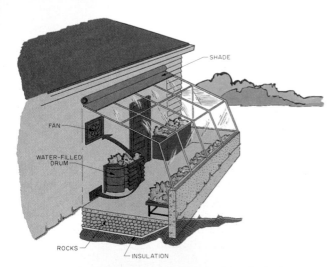

Fig. 3-9. In this indirect-gain system, the attached greenhouse provides heat to the rest of the house.

Another form of indirect-gain system is a greenhouse attached to the home. In the greenhouse shown in Fig. 3-9, "dead air" trapped between the two panes of the double-glazed glass serves as an insulator. Rocks and water-filled drums provide thermal mass to collect heat energy. Vents control the flow of the heat to the house (or to the outdoors in summer). A shade helps keep the heat in during cold nights (and keeps the sun out in the summer).

Passive Water Heating. Passive solar systems can also be used to heat water. See Fig. 3-10. These systems consist of a water storage tank, a collector, and the necessary water pipes.

Cold water is piped to the collector. Inside the collector, the water is heated directly by the sun. This causes the water to rise to the storage tank.

The principle of water circulation due to differences in temperature is called *thermosiphoning*. **Thermosiphoning** is the circulation of water by natural convection, as described earlier. The warm water expands and rises, forcing cooler water down.

Active Solar Heating

An **active solar heating system** collects solar energy and moves the energy mechanically to where it is needed. Active systems usually cost more than passive systems. But they can provide better temperature control and are more efficient. See Fig. 3-11.

Active systems normally have four parts:
- A collector to trap the sun's heat.
- A heat storage unit to retain heat until it is needed.
- A distribution system to deliver the heat where it is needed.
- Controls to regulate the system.

Most systems also have a backup system. The backup provides supplemental heat during cloudy or very cold weather.

There are two basic types of active solar heating systems. One type uses hot *water* to heat the home. The other type uses hot *air*. The two systems have much in common.

Fig. 3-11. Collectors on the roof capture solar energy to heat the interior of this home.

Fig. 3-10. A thermosiphoning water-heating system.

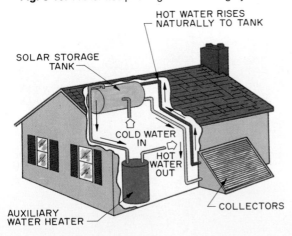

Solar Panels. One of the most important parts of any active solar heating system is the *collector*. Collectors, or solar panels, absorb heat from the sun and transfer it to water or air inside the collector. Figure 3-12 shows one type of solar collector. The frame supports the collector parts. The insulation keeps heat from radiating to the surrounding air. The *heat absorber* collects the sunlight and converts it into heat.

A heat absorber may be aluminum, copper, steel, or a combination of these materials. It is painted a flat black color or coated with an absorbent surface to increase the amount of solar energy absorbed. Painting or coating also decreases energy loss due to reflection.

The heat absorber may have tubing fastened to it. Liquid circulates through the tubing. Another type of heat absorber does not have tubes. This type consists of two sheets of metal bonded together. There are channels between the plates that allow liquid to flow between them.

Both of the heat absorbers mentioned above are for hot-water heating systems. Heat absorbers are also made to heat air rather than water. This type simply has an air space above the absorber to allow the air to circulate. A variety of absorbers can be used. See Fig. 3-13.

Both water and air collectors are sealed on top with glazing. *Glazing* is transparent or translucent glass or fiberglass. Through the greenhouse effect, the glazing traps the sun's heat in the collector. Depending on climate, the glazing may be single-, double-, or even triple-pane to reduce heat loss.

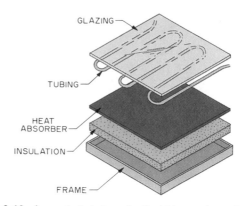

Fig. 3-12. An exploded view of a liquid-type solar collector.

Positioning Solar Panels. Solar collectors should always face south when used in the northern hemisphere. They should also face directly toward the sun. This will allow the collector to collect the most heat. The best angle for setting a collector depends on the location. In the northern part of the country, the winter sun is very low in the sky. The collector must be set at a more nearly upright angle to collect the most sunlight. The further south the house, the lower the collector angle should be.

Refer to Fig. 3-14. In Area I, the latitude is 45° north, the northern part of the United States. To face directly towards the sun in winter, the angle should be the latitude plus 15°. Hence, for heating, the panels are set at 60° (45° + 15°).

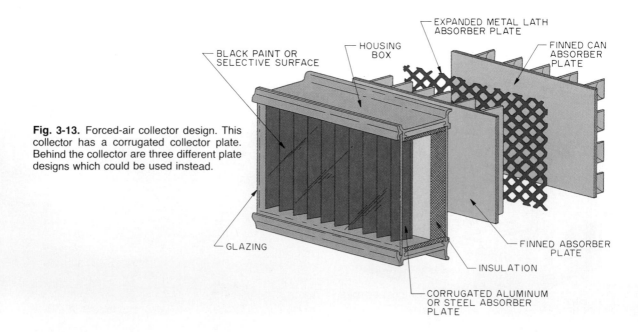

Fig. 3-13. Forced-air collector design. This collector has a corrugated collector plate. Behind the collector are three different plate designs which could be used instead.

If, however, the panels are to provide heat in the winter and cooling in the summer, a point midway between the best setting for heating and the best setting for cooling is used. This is the latitude—in this case 45°. This is also the best setting for a solar heated water system. It's the average of the best summer and winter settings, and provides heated water all year long.

If the principal need is for summer cooling or for heating a swimming pool, set the angle at latitude minus 15°. In the previous example, this provides an angle of 30°.

Area II has a latitude of 25° north, the southern part of the United States. The same procedures are used to determine solar panel angles.

Determining the number of collectors needed to heat a house is a complex procedure. The number is usually determined by a solar specialist after studying the house and location. There are three factors which are used to determine the number of panels needed:

■ The size of the house
■ How well it is insulated
■ The local climate

Active Home Heating—Hot Water. Figure 3-15 shows a typical hot-water heating system. Water circulates through a solar collector located on the roof. The sun heats the water, which is then pumped down to a heat exchanger in the storage tank. (A *heat exchanger* is a device that transfers heat from one fluid to another.)

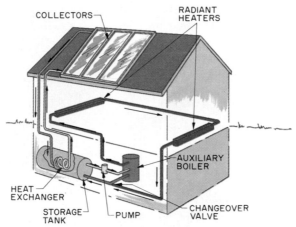
Fig. 3-15. An active solar hot-water heating system.

The hot water from the collector heats the water in the storage tank. The water is then circulated back to the collector to be reheated. This cycle keeps the water in the storage tank hot.

When heat is needed in the home, a pump sends heated water from the storage tank through the baseboard radiant heaters. These heaters radiate heat from the water to the living area. If the temperature of the storage water drops too low for efficient home heating, a changeover valve shifts the system to an auxiliary boiler. Active hot-water heating systems can also provide hot water for bathing and other uses.

Other distribution systems are possible. Pipes laid in a concrete slab under the floor can take the place of baseboard heaters. Another system uses a heat exchanger to heat air that is then circulated through the home.

Active Home Heating—Hot Air. In hot-air heating systems, the sun heats air as it circulates through solar collectors. Air from a storage area circulates through the collectors to absorb heat. The hot air then travels back to storage. This area, usually a bin of rocks, stores the heat until it is needed. See Fig. 3-16A.

At night, when the house needs heat, a fan circulates air through the storage area and around the house. See Fig. 3-16B. As long as there is enough heat in the storage area, the auxiliary heater remains off. When more heat is needed, the auxiliary heater comes on and heats the air.

Hot-air heating systems are quite flexible. If heat is needed in the house during the day, air from the collectors can be circulated through the house without going to storage. See Fig. 3-16C.

Fig. 3-14. Roof angles for best solar exposure. Area A is at 45°N latitude, the northern part of the United States. Area B is at 25°N latitude, the southern part of the United States.

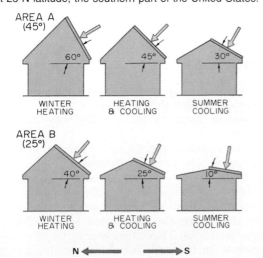

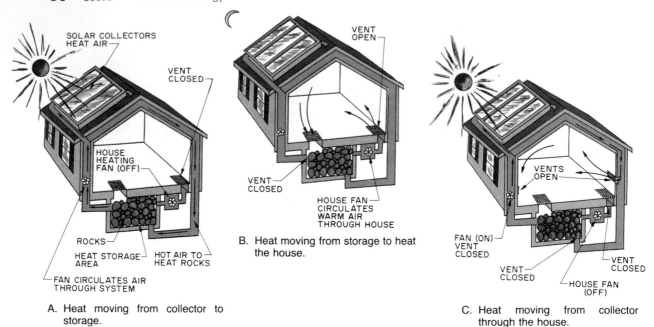

A. Heat moving from collector to storage.

B. Heat moving from storage to heat the house.

C. Heat moving from collector through the house.

Fig. 3-16. An active solar heating system that uses forced hot air.

Hot-air heating ducts must be well-insulated. The disadvantage of a hot-air system is that it is more bulky and takes much more space than a water system. Also, hot-air heating systems tend to lose more heat than water heating systems. On the positive side, hot-air systems are easy to maintain. They have no corrosion or freezing problems. They also have few summer overheating problems in the collectors.

Hot-air heating systems can also be used for summer cooling. During the night, air can be circulated through the heat storage area. This lowers the temperature of the rocks to the outside temperature. During the day, warmer air from inside the house can be cooled by circulating it over the rocks. The effectiveness of the system depends on how much cooling occurs at night.

Active Water Heating. The most popular type of solar heating system is that used to heat water for cooking, bathing, and other home uses. The system is a simplified version of the home heating system. See Fig. 3-17.

A pump is needed to circulate the water through the collector. The water is pumped from the bottom of the tank to the roof collector and into the top of the preheat tank. A mixing valve is placed at the outlet to prevent water from reaching scalding temperatures. The preheat

tank supplies the regular water heater which serves as an auxiliary heater on cloudy days or when more water is needed than the solar heater can supply.

This system can be modified. An auxiliary heating coil can be placed in the preheat tank, eliminating the need for a second tank.

In some instances, a heat exchanger is used. This system can operate with a single tank containing an auxiliary heater. See Fig. 3-18. The heat exchanger separates the collector fluid from the drinking and household water supply. The collector system often contains antifreeze to prevent freezing on cold winter nights.

Solar Cooling

Cooling of a solar heated home is usually designed around the use of cooler night air. Use of passive systems for cooling was discussed earlier.

In an active forced air system, the storage bin can also be used for summer cooling. During the night, air can be circulated through the bin, lowering the temperature of the rocks to outside temperature. During the day, warmer air from inside the house can be cooled by circulating it over the rocks. The effectiveness of the system depends on how much cooling occurs at night.

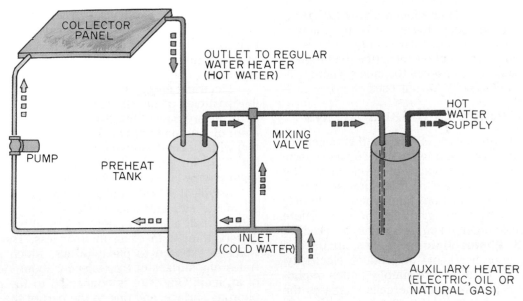

Fig. 3-17. Direct system. A pump circulates the cold water through the collector to the preheat tank. A mixing valve can be opened to add cold water if the solar water is too warm. The water passes through a regular water heater, which heats water that is too cold.

Climates which have high day and night temperatures during the summer usually require a regular air-conditioning unit to maintain indoor comfort.

 The solar heating system can provide for summer air conditioning by using an *absorption chiller.* The absorption chiller uses heat to create a cycle which removes heat from the air. The absorption principle has been used in many homes to operate refrigerators or air conditioners. They are often referred to as *gas* refrigerators or *gas* air conditioners, since natural gas has commonly been used to provide the heat for the cooling cycle.

The absorption cycle requires an input of no less than 180°F (82°C), a condition which rules out flat-plate collectors. Even though other collectors have been designed to operate at this and higher temperatures, the absorption cycle is still in the experimental stage as a solar air-conditioning system. However, we may, in the future, see air conditioners powered by solar thermal collectors.

ELECTRICITY FROM SOLAR ENERGY

The generation of electricity from solar energy has been possible since the 19th century. However, all of the early sources produced only a small amount of electricity. They were also limited to special uses such as operating electrical controls.

The search for a way to convert large amounts of solar energy into electricity has intensified during recent years. Many experimental programs are underway. We already have experimental solar power plants generating significant quantities of electricity. These plants are testing a variety of procedures which may be used in future solar power plants.

Fig. 3-18. Indirect system. A heat exchanger transfers heat from the collector to the water used in the home. The solar-heated water recirculates through the collector and heat exchanger.

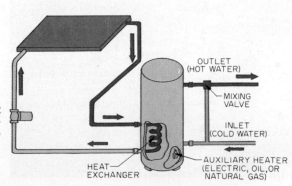

Solar power plants remain a goal for the future. Yet, even today, there are many practical uses of electricity from solar energy.

The following sections describe the progress being made to transform the sun's energy directly into electricity for our use.

Photovoltaic Cells and Arrays

The term "solar cell" is another name for photovoltaic cell and was the common term used during its early stages of development. But the term "photovoltaic" is more precise. It indicates the cell's function. Photovoltaic cells use particles of light energy called *photons*. (More about these later.) *Voltaic* means to produce electricity. **Photovoltaic cells**, then, are devices that use photons (light) to produce electricity. Photovoltaic batteries are simply groups of photovoltaic cells. Grouping the cells increases the electrical output. See Fig. 3-19.

Photovoltaic cell is often abbreviated *PV cell*. A group of PV cells is actually a *battery*. But the term "battery" is rarely used in reference to PV cells. Instead, a group of PV cells is called an **array**.

How PV Cells Operate. In order to understand PV cell operation, we need to understand both light energy and electrical energy. Remember the important energy concepts you learned in Chapter 1:

■ Energy always involves motion.
■ Energy cannot be created or destroyed.

To convert sunlight into electricity, we must change light energy into electrical energy.

Light energy is the visible portion of radiant energy. It travels to the earth in tiny energy particles called **photons**. Light consists of trillions of these tiny energy particles moving through space.

Electrical energy is the motion of tiny invisible particles of matter called **electrons**. These particles are part of the structure of atoms. Each atom of any material consists of a *nucleus* (center) with electrons moving rapidly around it. See Fig. 3-20. In a PV cell, the motion of photons (light energy) is changed to electron motion.

A typical PV cell is made from a single crystal of the element silicon. The silicon is mixed with a small amount of boron. The silicon wafer is very thin, $\frac{1}{25}$th of an inch or less. This thin wafer is exposed to phosphorous, which penetrates one surface of the wafer by about $\frac{1}{10,000}$th of an inch. One wire is connected to the phosphorous surface, and one to the part of the crystal containing only boron. See Fig. 3-21.

Phosphorous has fifteen electrons. The first band of electrons around the nucleus of any atom usually contains two electrons, and the second band eight electrons. This leaves five electrons in the outer band. Silicon has fourteen electrons with four electrons in the outer band. Since the third band normally has eight electrons (like the second band), silicon is four electrons

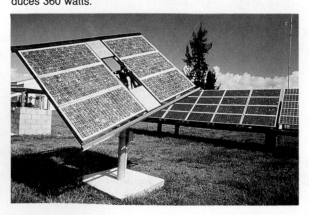

Fig. 3-19. A solar array. This passive tracking array is composed of 6 modules with 72 PV cells in each module. It produces 360 watts.

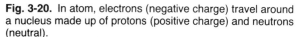

Fig. 3-20. In atom, electrons (negative charge) travel around a nucleus made up of protons (positive charge) and neutrons (neutral).

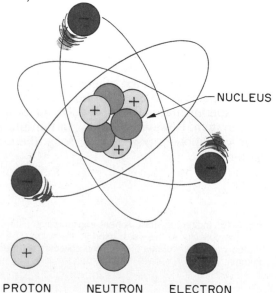

NUCLEUS

PROTON   NEUTRON   ELECTRON

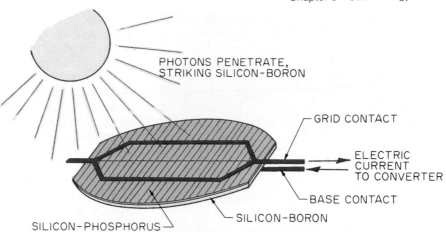

Fig. 3-21. When photons strike a solar cell, electrons are forced from the silicon-boron material to the silicon-phosphorus material. The electrons flow through the grid contact to a converter such as a light bulb which converts the electrical energy into light or a motor which converts the energy to motion. The electrons return to the silicon-boron material through the base contact.

PHOTONS PENETRATE, STRIKING SILICON-BORON

GRID CONTACT

ELECTRIC CURRENT TO CONVERTER

BASE CONTACT

SILICON-BORON

SILICON-PHOSPHORUS

short of a full third band. When a phosphorous atom bonds with a silicon atom, only four of the five electrons in the outer shell are needed to fill the third band for each atom. When materials bond, they share the outer band of electrons. As a result, the bonding of silicon and phosphorous leaves one surplus electron.

Boron is a very light material and has only five electrons—two in the first band and three in the second. When boron bonds with silicon, the four silicon outer electrons and the three boron electrons are one short of the eight needed to fill the band. The band is, therefore, unstable.

The surplus electrons from the silicon-phosphorous bond move to fill in the holes in the silicon-boron bond. See Fig. 3-22. The bonds now become stable, but the movement of electrons creates regions of negative and positive charges. The silicon-phosphorous region lost electrons and has more protons remaining than electrons. This region becomes *positively* charged. The silicon-boron region gained electrons and has more electrons than protons. This region becomes *negatively* charged.

When sunlight strikes the PV cell, the trillions of photons strike the silicon-boron bonds. Again, see Fig. 3-21. This "bombardment" knocks some of the electrons loose from the bond. Because they are negatively charged, the electrons are attracted by the positive charge of the silicon-phosphorous region. As the electrons build up in the silicon-phosphorous region, they travel over the wire connected to the silicon-phosphorous layer, to an electric light or other use of electricity, and back to the silicon-boron side of the cell. The photons continue the process, setting up a flow of electrons within the cell. These then flow through the wire to the converter and back to the cell. The flow continues in this circle as long as photons of light strike the cell. The

motion of photons of light is changed to the motion of electrons (electricity).

This is a simplified presentation of a very complex process. As you continue with future studies of PV cells and electronics, you will build upon this basic knowledge of how PV cells operate.

Fig. 3-22. This simplified graphic presentation shows how the electron moves to fill the "hole" in an incomplete band. This movement creates the negative and positive charges. (Remember, the **A** layer is directly on top of the **B** layer.)

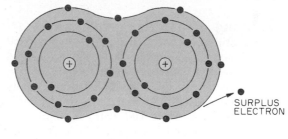

SURPLUS ELECTRON

A

A. Silicon/Phosphorus. When the electron leaves, there are more protons in the nucleus than electrons in orbit—positive charge.

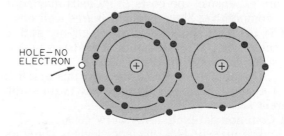

HOLE—NO ELECTRON

B

B. Silicon/Boron. When the electron arrives, there are more electrons in orbit than protons in the nucleus—negative charge.

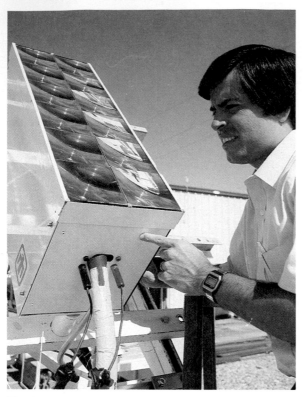

Fig. 3-23. Mirrors can be used to concentrate sunlight and increase electrical output.

PV cells from a silicon ingot. Research in both increased efficiency and reduced manufacturing costs continue.
■ Concentrating mirrors and PV cells.

Mirrors are used to concentrate the sunlight on smaller PV cells. While the cost of manufacturing is greater, efficiencies are also greater. A test cell recently converted 27.5% of the sun's energy into electricity. See Fig. 3-23.
■ Thin-film PV devices.

These devices are basically glass plates on which vapor or liquid silicon has been deposited. Thin-film devices are less efficient than other types, but they are relatively inexpensive to produce. They can also be stacked one on top of another, which increases efficiency. Present thin-film PV devices have an efficiency of 4-6%, but laboratory devices have reached 10%.

Electrical Power from Photovoltaic Cells

Solar power plants require considerable space. They must be located in places that have mostly days of sunshine. At present efficiency rates, a minimum of 20 acres of PV cells are needed to provide enough electricity for 1000 people. Desert and other arid locations are ideal for solar power.

Improving PV Cell Performance. PV cells are still too costly to compete with fossil fuels as a source of electricity. However, the gap between the two continues to narrow.

The cost of PV cells has fallen dramatically since the early 1970s. At that time, the PV cells needed to light a single 100 watt (W) light bulb cost $10,000. Today, this cost of $100 per watt has fallen to about $5 per watt. But most experts agree that the cost will need to drop to $1.50 per watt in order to compete with fossil fuels during the 1990s. In countries where fossil fuels are more expensive, the costs of PV cells may soon be competitive. Since sunlight is free, cell costs of $1 per watt should produce electricity at 6 to 7 cents per 1000 watt hours (1 kWh), a typical cost for electricity in 1987.

The ability to reduce the cost this much is not assured. Research is under way in three different areas:
■ Common flat-plate array of PV cells.

The present 11% efficiency level is being increased and 15-17% levels seem possible. Also, producing crystals in sheets or ribbons rather than bricks can eliminate the high cost of slicing

Sizing Power Plants. Electrical output is measured in **watts (W)**. In sizing power plants, engineers have learned that a continuous supply of approximately 1000 watts, or one **kilowatt (kW)**, of electrical capacity is needed per person in the United States. This includes what each of us uses plus a portion of what is used in business and industry. Therefore, 100 kilowatts of electricity is enough for a small community of 100 people.

The kilowatt is the measure used for small power plants and other types of generating units. But since many power plants are very large, a larger measure called the *megawatt* is used. A **megawatt (MW)** is one million watts. That is enough electricity for a community of 1000 people. See Fig. 3-24.

Solar power plants are also sized by kilowatts and megawatts. But since the sun's energy varies during the day, sizing is by *peak output*. That is, the maximum output which occurs at noon is used to identify the size of the plant. Since this output can't be maintained continuously, the *average* output is less. In sizing solar plants, a peak output of approximately 1600

Basic Measure = 1 watt (W) of Electricity	
1,000 watts	= 1 kilowatt (kW)—the amount of energy used by one person
1,000,000 watts	= 1 megawatt (MW)—the normal measure used to identify the size of a power plant.
1,000 kilowatts = 1 megawatt	

Fig. 3-24. Measurements used to identify electrical needs and power plant output.

Fig. 3-25. In this solar (photovoltaic) plant, trackers always point toward the sun.

watts is needed to meet the electrical needs of one person. Therefore, 100 kilowatts of solar electricity is enough for 60 people.

PV Cell Power Plants. A solar power plant using PV cells is in operation in California. See Fig. 3-25. This plant will soon provide the electricity used by a community of 10,000 people (16 megawatts). Another is currently under construction. It is even larger and will provide electricity for 60,000 people when finished. Both plants are experimental and are designed to show that PV cells can produce electricity on a large scale.

The plant shown in Fig. 3-25 has operated successfully since the installation of the first units in 1983. By mid-1984, it was operating at 6 megawatts (electricity for 4000 people), and is growing towards its planned capacity of 16 megawatts. This plant uses PV cells mounted on motor-driven trackers. Each tracker is 32 feet square and contains 256 solar modules. The initial unit for 4000 people (6 megawatts) covered 160 acres of land.

The plant is fully automatic. It starts itself at sunrise and shuts down at sunset. The trackers slowly turn through the day to "track" the sun. This means they always point directly towards the sun, making the most efficient use of solar energy.

The method used to track the sun is different from what you might expect. Rather than using light sensors, the system uses a computer. The exact location of the sun based on the date and time of the day is programmed into the computer. An accurate clock "tells" the computer the time and date, and the computer controls the tracker angles. As a result, the trackers can point directly towards the sun on all days, including cloudy and overcast ones.

Many electrical utility companies are conducting their own experiments. Although electricity from PV cells still can't compete in cost with electricity from fossil fuel plants, PV cell plants can be constructed quickly and grow as needs increase. This factor will help make PV cell plants practical as the cost per watt of cells decreases.

Small-Scale Use of PV Cells. One of the advantages of PV cells is that they can be used on a small scale. They do not require large or elaborate power equipment to work. A system that may be the home solar energy system of the future is shown in Fig. 3-26. This system combines solar electricity generation with solar hot-air heating. Using a single energy source for two useful purposes is called *cogeneration*. The panels on the roof contain PV cells. The cells convert sunlight to electricity. The electricity is either stored in storage batteries or used directly in the home. Any excess electricity could be sold to the power company for other uses.

PV cells operate more efficiently when cool. Therefore, the circulation of air through the collectors has two functions. One function is to cool the cells during operation. The other is to heat the air. The air can be stored in a heat storage area for solar heating. The heating system shown also uses an air pump. This pump provides both heat in the winter and air conditioning during the summer. The air pump is operated by electricity either from the solar cells or from the power company.

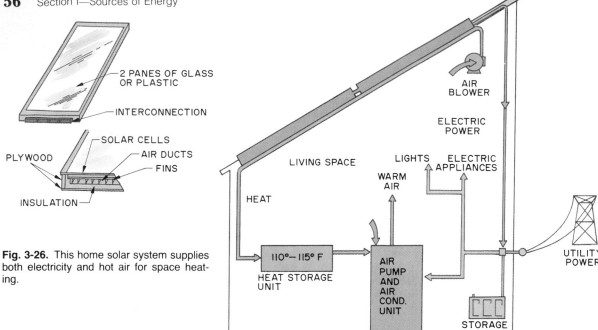

2 PANES OF GLASS
OR PLASTIC

INTERCONNECTION

SOLAR CELLS

PLYWOOD

AIR DUCTS

FINS

INSULATION

AIR BLOWER

ELECTRIC POWER

LIGHTS

ELECTRIC APPLIANCES

LIVING SPACE

WARM AIR

HEAT

110°–115° F

HEAT STORAGE UNIT

AIR PUMP AND AIR COND. UNIT

UTILITY POWER

STORAGE BATTERY

Fig. 3-26. This home solar system supplies both electricity and hot air for space heating.

The system in Fig. 3-26 is ideal since it uses both solar-generated heat and solar-generated electricity. All of the technology needed for this system is already developed. As the cost of solar cell wattage decreases, this system will become a reality.

Electrical Power from Solar Heat (Solar Thermal Conversion)

The sun's heat can also be used to produce steam to power electrical generating plants. Special collectors are used to generate the high temperatures needed to produce steam.

One generating system uses mirrors called *heliostats* to reflect sunlight and concentrate it onto a boiler at the top of a water tower. See Fig. 3-27. The heat of the concentrated sunlight converts water into high-temperature steam. The steam is then used to operate turbine generators.

Curved solar troughs are also used to concentrate solar heat. Figure 3-28 shows *parabolic troughs* focusing the sun's energy to heat a fluid used to drive a turbine generator. A power plant,

supplemented by heated steam from oil or gas, is using this principle to generate 13 megawatts of electrical power.

Practical Uses of Solar Electricity

There are many practical uses for electricity generated by PV cells and thin-film PV devices. These uses are the direct result of the research which has reduced the wattage cost to its present level. While not economical for power plants, solar electricity has found many cost-effective uses.

Fig. 3-27. This mirror plant, called Solar One, has operated in California's Mojave Desert since 1982. It can produce up to 10 MW of electrical power, enough for a community of approximately 6000 people.

Fig. 3-28. A parabolic trough solar heating system. The word "parabolic" describes the curve of the trough needed to focus heat on the line passing in front. The heated fluid can be used to drive turbines or to serve other industrial and agricultural needs.

Fig. 3-29. These devices operate from PV cells.

Devices using solar electricity are of two basic types. One type uses the electricity produced by the sun to operate the device. See Fig. 3-29. This type of design is effective whenever electricity is needed *only* when the sun shines.

The more common type of solar device uses the electricity from PV cells to charge batteries. The device is operated by the batteries. There is a growing number of these devices. Examples include calculators, cameras, and golf carts.

Large-scale uses of PV cells to produce electrical power depend on reducing the cost per watt of PV cells. However, where other sources are not available, PV cells are already used to provide electricity. This use is expected to grow in countries where fossil fuels are very expensive.

The space program has always put PV cells to practical use. See Fig. 3-30.

Fig. 3-30. Satellites are powered by panels of PV cells.

Chapter 3—Review

Testing Your Knowledge

Briefly answer each of the following questions. Write on a separate piece of paper.

1. Compare the amount of energy the sun provides the United States each day with the amount of energy we use.
2. Name two ways that the sun can provide energy for our use.
3. Identify the three ways heat moves from one place to another.
4. Under what conditions does air act as a good insulator?
5. Identify four heat-storage materials that can be used with a direct-gain passive home heating system.
6. How is an active solar heating system different from a passive solar heating system?
7. Name the four parts of an active solar heating system.
8. Why is the heat absorber of a solar collector painted black or coated with an absorbent surface?
9. What three factors determine the number of collectors needed to heat a home?
10. How is a heat exchanger used in an active water heater?
11. What is electricity?
12. Identify the three types of photovoltaic devices being developed for present and future generation of electricity.
13. In sizing electrical power plants, how many kilowatts of electricity are allowed for each individual?
14. Approximately how many acres of land would be needed for PV cells that would provide electricity for 1000 people?
15. Identify four practical uses of solar electricity.

Expressing Your Knowledge

Using complete sentences, write your answers to the following on a separate sheet of paper:

1. Define and describe atoms and molecules.
2. Explain the difference between temperature and quantity of heat.
3. Describe how an indirect-gain passive heating system heats a home.
4. Describe how a hot-air heating system can be used to provide cooling during the summer.
5. How does a photon produce a flow of electrons?

Fig. 3-31. Chart to record water temperature at different times. The experiment calls for one hour (60 minutes), but you may wish to extend the time.

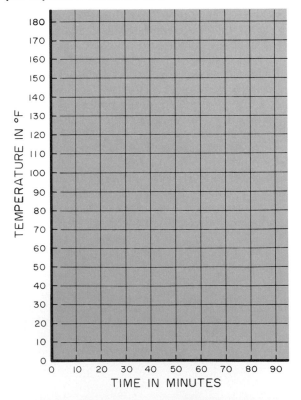

Applying Your Knowledge

Follow your teacher's instructions to complete these activities:

1. Conduct a solar energy collecting experiment. Use two small cans to see how water absorbs the sun's radiant energy. Both cans must be the same size and made of the same material. Paint one can flat black and the other one white or silver. Fill both cans to the same level, about ¾ full, with cold water. Check and record the temperature of the water in both cans. It should be the same. Place both cans on a piece of cardboard in direct sunlight for one hour. Check and record the temperature of the water in both cans every 10 minutes. A photographic darkroom thermometer is a good, rugged thermometer for this purpose. Prepare a graph like that shown in Fig. 3-31. Use it to plot the temperatures for each can of water.

   Which can absorbed and transferred more radiant energy to the water? In a brief report, explain what caused the difference.

   Repeat the experiment with ice. Fill both cans ¾ full of water and place them in a freezer (home or school) overnight. Record the frozen temperature at 32°F on your graph. Place the cans in direct sunlight and check the temperatures every 10 minutes. Record the water temperature in each as the ice starts to melt.

   In a brief report, explain differences in melting. Why did the ice take so long to melt? What was the water temperature during melting? Answer these questions in your report.

2. Conduct an experiment to determine the difference in solar energy between windows facing the sun (south) and facing away from the sun (north). Obtain two cardboard boxes. Cut off the top flaps. Paint each box white (similar to a home). The white will reflect solar energy, permitting a more accurate experiment.

   Place a thermometer in each box. Position it in such a way that you can read it from the open side. Cover the open side of each box with clear plastic. (Clear plastic food wrap is good.) Seal the boxes.

   Lay each box on its side. Place one box with the open side facing the sun (south—use a compass), and the other facing away from the sun (north). Record the temperature after 10 minutes, 20 minutes, and 30 minutes. Prepare a brief report explaining your findings.

3. Conduct an experiment to determine which materials are best for storing solar energy. Fill four small cans with different materials: sand, salt, water, and torn-up paper.

   Paint a cardboard box black. Place the four cans in the box, close it, and leave it in the sun for a half hour.

   Remove the cans and check the temperature of each can. Complete a temperature-drop table like that shown in Fig. 3-32. Stir the contents of each can occasionally to even the temperature.

   Prepare a report on your findings. Include answers to the following questions: The temperature of which material falls most slowly? Which material stores solar heat best? In what ways is this information valuable for solar energy applications?

   Try other materials like oil, dirt, gravel, foamed plastic chips, colored water, etc. Include your findings in your report.

Fig. 3-32. Temperature-drop table.

TIME

MATERIAL	2 MIN	4 MIN	6 MIN	8 MIN	10 MIN
SALT					
SAND					
WATER					
PAPER					

Chapter 4

Emerging Alternative Sources of Energy

Alternative energy sources are renewable and inexhaustible sources of energy not commonly used. Developing these resources will help reduce our dependency on the exhaustible sources of energy—the fossil fuels.

Expanding Your Knowledge

As you study this chapter, you will learn to:

■ Explain the existing and future need to develop alternatives to the fossil fuels as our primary source of energy.
■ Identify inexhaustible and exhaustible sources of energy which may emerge as important alternative energy sources.
■ Describe how the wind, the earth, oceans, salt ponds, and waste products such as garbage can be used to supply energy.
■ Understand the present stage of development of wind, geothermal, oceans, salt ponds, wood, and biomass as alternative sources of energy.
■ Describe how cogeneration and small suppliers of energy feed electricity into the existing systems.
■ Explain the need to network electrical supply lines throughout the nation.

Building Your Word Power

The following terms are defined and explained in this chapter. Learning these will help you learn more about alternative sources of energy.

alternative energy sources
biofuels
cogeneration
gasohol
geopressured energy
geothermal energy
hydrothermal energy
inverter
methanol
ocean thermal energy
petrothermal energy
solar salt ponds
tidal energy

This chapter will continue your study of alternative energy sources. In the last chapter, you learned about the potential use of solar energy. Now you will study other sources, most of which have less potential than solar energy. Yet each can make a significant contribution to our need for energy alternatives to the fossil fuels. See Fig. 4-1.

The first section describes how the wind, the earth, the oceans, and even a waste area—solar salt ponds—can be harnessed to produce energy. Each of these are either providing energy or have major research-and-development projects under way.

Renewable resources, such as wood and plants are also important sources of energy. Energy from these sources as well as that from other less desirable sources such as garbage will be explained in the second section.

At the present time, we are seeing rapid growth in the number of small energy suppliers. These suppliers are using a variety of sources of energy to produce electricity. The electricity they produce is sold to electric power companies.

THE NEED FOR NEW ENERGY SOURCES

There are two important reasons for developing new sources of energy. The first fact is already established—the world supply of fossil fuels is being depleted. Secondly, the United States has already used most of its known petroleum and natural gas reserves. Each year we become more dependent on other countries for petroleum and natural gas. Developing new energy sources can reduce the need to import fossil fuels.

INEXHAUSTIBLE SOURCES

In addition to solar energy, inexhaustible sources that are being developed as alternative sources of energy include:

Fig. 4-1. The winds and the waters hold inexhaustible energy reserves that we can tap.

 Wind
 Geothermal
 Oceans
 Solar salt ponds

Wind Energy

At one time, wind energy was an important energy source. In locations where the wind blew much of the time, people built windmills. They used the wind energy to pump water, grind grain, and perform other useful tasks.

However, wind was an unpredictable energy source. People could not control its availability. When cheap fossil fuels became available, most windmills disappeared in this country. During recent years, fossil fuels have become more and more expensive. As a result, people have again become interested in the free energy of wind. Wind energy is especially appealing because, unlike fossil fuels, it does not cause pollution.

Today's windmills are wind turbines, designed to generate electricity. The wind drives a turbine connected to a generator. As the turbine turns, the generator produces electric current.

Wind Turbine Design. An efficient wind turbine must produce electricity under many different wind conditions. It must also be strong enough to resist damage during storms. Finally, its energy production must cost less than fossil fuel energy production.

Figure 4-2 shows two basic designs for wind generators. The horizontal-axis wind turbine shown in Fig. 4-2A stands 191 feet (58 m) tall. The blades spin at 41 revolutions per minute (rpm) in winds over 40 miles (64 km) per hour.

The vertical-axis wind turbine (Fig. 4-2B) has an "egg-beater" shape. This type of wind turbine catches wind from any direction. It produces its greatest amount of electricity in winds of 35 miles (56 km) per hour.

Both of the wind turbines shown are large. Each is taller than a 20-story building. Materials and construction limit the size of turbines. Probably the largest turbine planned at present is a 7.2-megawatt (MW) turbine planned by Boeing Engineering and Construction. The tower will be 262 feet (80 m) high, with a 420-foot (128 m) blade. With the blade pointing up, the top will be over 470 feet (143 m) above the ground (about the height of a 47-story building). If operated at capacity on a continuous basis, this wind turbine would produce enough electricity for 7200 people. But, like solar energy, the capacity of a wind turbine is rated at peak (maximum) output. Since winds vary, and don't blow at all on some days, the actual average continuous output is always less than the rated capacity. A 5-megawatt wind turbine might provide an average of 1.5-2.5 mega-watts on a continuous basis. This would be enough electricity for 1500-2500 people. Hence, the 7.2-megawatt turbine will probably provide electricity for about 2500-3500 people.

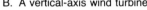

Figure 4-3 shows the operation of a typical wind turbine. As you study this diagram, note the following:

■ The wind-driven blades operate at a low speed.
■ A transmission changes this low-speed rotation into high-speed rotation for generating electricity.
■ Electricity is generated by a simple generator which operates efficiently at different wind speeds. Not shown is the *inverter* which modifies the electricity so it can be placed in the power grid to serve homes and businesses. The **inverter** changes direct current to alternating current and makes it "match" the electricity in the power grid. That is, the current from the inverter is given the same voltage and cycling rate as the current in the grid.
■ The *wind vane* measures the direction of the wind. The *anemometer* measures the speed of the wind.

Fig. 4-2. Basic wind generator designs.

B. A vertical-axis wind turbine.

A. A horizontal-axis wind turbine.

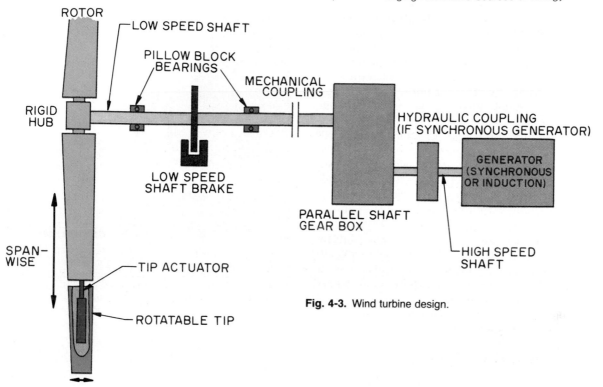

Fig. 4-3. Wind turbine design.

■ The *yaw gear* and *yaw motor* keep the wind turbine facing into the wind. They are controlled by the wind vane.

Blade design has undergone changes as turbines have developed. Early blades were flat. Modern blades are designed like an airplane wing. See Fig. 4-4. Also, the speed at which a given section of the blade travels through the air varies. The farther out its position, the faster the blade section is being moved by the air. For efficiency, the blade is twisted, and the blade gets smaller towards the blade tip. In a vertical-axis wind turbine (eggbeater), the blade is smaller at the center (fastest portion of the blade). These factors all improve efficiency.

Fig. 4-4. Airfoil design of a modern wind-turbine blade.

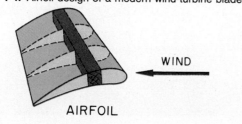

Wind-turbine efficiency is an important consideration. The greatest efficiency occurs when the wind passing over the blades is slowed by two-thirds. This provides an efficiency of just under 60%. That is, 60% of the wind passing over the blade is captured. Today, the best wind turbines are operating with 40-45% efficiency.

The cost of electrical energy produced from the wind has steadily decreased. This improvement has resulted from the development of more efficient and reliable designs. Also, production costs have decreased as designs have been improved, and the new designs have produced more electricity.

Current costs are still above that of electricity produced from fossil fuels. However, one turbine manufacturer is projecting a cost of 5.4 cents per kilowatt-hour (kWh) for a turbine that will work for 15 years. The California Energy Commission estimates that the *retail* cost of wind power will soon be between 7.5 and 11 cents per kWh. This will be about the same as consumers pay for electricity from fossil fuels and similar to the cost from other sources of electricity now available. If this projection is accurate, the use of wind turbines to generate electricity will continue to grow.

Present Status of Electricity from Wind Turbines.

There are many wind turbines in use at the present time. California, the state with the largest number of wind turbines, reports that 1% of all electricity used in the state is produced from wind turbines. For electrical production, wind turbines are grouped into farms. See Fig. 4-5.

Enough wind turbines for approximately 600 megawatts of electricity are presently in operation. Most wind turbines are on wind farms using machines in the 25- to 100-kilowatt range. Recent studies indicate that mid-range wind turbines of 200- to 800-kilowatts may be the most economical. If previous cost predictions materialize (become real), this industry will grow in the future.

Wind power is a good source of electricity for people in remote locations. It is also used to power sailboats. For the most part, wind is used for recreational sailing. See Fig. 4-6. However, experiments are underway to use large sails to help power ocean-going freighters.

Geothermal Energy

Geothermal energy is natural heat of the earth. The term "geothermal" simply means *earth heat*. It is the result of the decay of radioactive materials within the earth. The heat generated by this decay is trapped mostly inside the earth. Sometimes it escapes through geysers

Fig. 4-6. This yacht, the *Stars and Stripes,* won the America's Cup, an international race, using computer information to adjust sails and capture maximum energy from the wind. Experimental designs and practices may find practical applications in commercial vessels of the future.

and volcanos. The greater the depth, the greater the temperature of the earth. Geothermal energy has great possibilities as an energy source. See Fig. 4-7.

The greatest use of geothermal energy is to produce electricity. There are several places in the United States that are good for the production of electricity from geothermal energy.

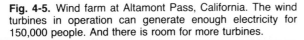

Fig. 4-5. Wind farm at Altamont Pass, California. The wind turbines in operation can generate enough electricity for 150,000 people. And there is room for more turbines.

Fig. 4-7. A source of geothermal energy for electricity. Heat radiating upwards raises the temperatures of underground rock and water. The heated water or steam rises to where it can be reached by a drilling rig. The geothermal energy is piped from the well to the electricity generating plant.

The Geysers is an area north of San Francisco, California, where magma (molten rock) is only about five miles below the surface. See Fig. 4-8. The heat from the magma produces steam that boils up out of the ground. The first geothermal power plant was built at The Geysers in 1960. There are now 20 power plants in the area. Together, they produce 1400 megawatts of electrical power, enough for a large city of 1.4 million people. Additional plants are being built. The potential capacity of the Geysers is estimated at 2000-3000 megawatts of power. This is 1% of all the electricity needed by the U.S. or 10% of the electricity used in California.

The three major types of sources of usable geothermal energy are:
- Natural steam and hot water (hydrothermal resources).
- Pressurized water and natural gas (geopressured resources).
- Magma and hot rock resources (petrothermal resources).

✳ **Natural Steam and Hot Water.** This resource is referred to as **hydrothermal energy**. It is the most easily used form of geothermal energy. Water becomes heated or vaporized into steam by contact with hot rock. The formation of steam is referred to as a *dry-steam field*. The Geysers (Fig. 4-8) uses a dry-steam field for heat. Figure 4-9 shows a drawing of the power system in operation. Dry steam from the earth passes through pipes to a turbine. The turbine drives an electrical generator. The steam then passes to a condenser. There it condenses into water and

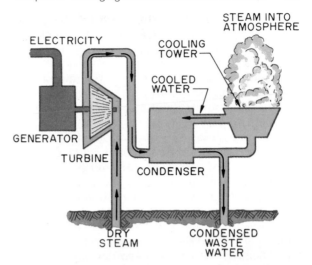

Fig. 4-9. This diagram shows how a dry-steam powered geothermal plant operates.

low-temperature steam. The water is pumped back into the ground, and the steam is exhausted into the atmosphere.

This source of geothermal energy is limited. There are just three known sites in the United States. Besides The Geysers, there are dry-steam reserves at Yellowstone and Lassen National Parks.

Hot-water fields are more common than dry-steam fields. Hot-water fields contain water ranging from 350° to 700°F (177-371°C). Water boils at 212°F (100°C) at sea level. However, underground water can reach much higher temperatures. This is because pressure on the water keeps it from changing to steam. As the hot water comes to the surface, the pressure reduces and the water "flashes." That is, some of the water changes immediately into steam. The steam is used to drive turbines.

Fields of lesser heat content also contain hot water. The temperature of the water is lower, though. The heat range is from 120° to 300°F (49-199°C). This water is not hot enough to create usable steam. However, it can be used to boil liquid that has a lower boiling point, such as ammonia. When we heat the liquid, it changes into a high-pressure gas. We can then use it to drive turbine generators.

Hot-water fields are now being developed. Experimental plants have been built in California, Utah, and Hawaii.

Fig. 4-8. The largest operating geothermal field in the U.S., The Geysers, is located in California.

Other Geothermal Reserves. Two remaining reserves comprise 99% of the available geothermal energy. However, they are more difficult to use.

Geopressured energy is a solution of natural gas in hot water trapped at high pressure underground. Approximately 14% of our reserves are of this type.

The remaining 85% of our potential geothermal energy is in the form of *magma and hot rock*. It is called **petrothermal energy**. This type is the most difficult to use.

These sources of geothermal energy are in the early steps of research and development. We know the locations of these resources. But the technology to use them in an economical and reliable fashion has not yet been developed.

We can expect research to continue. The amount of energy available is enormous—enough to supply all of our energy needs for over 10,000 years. But at the present time, only a small portion can be used economically. In the future, geothermal energy should become a significant source of energy to generate electricity.

Energy from the Oceans

There are many possibilities for using the inexhaustible energy of the oceans. We can grow plants in the oceans and then use them to manufacture fuels, such as alcohol or methanol. We can also use ocean currents and waves to drive electrical generators. But the most promising sources of energy are tides and ocean thermal energy.

 Tides. Large bodies of water raise and lower in a regular sequence twice a day. We call each raising or lowering a *tide*. Tides are caused mainly by the pull of the moon's gravity. As the earth rotates (spins) on its axis, the moon's gravity pulls on different parts of the earth. This causes water in the oceans to raise and lower. Raised water is called *high tide*. It is high for about six hours. Then the water lowers and becomes *low tide*. Low tide also lasts about six hours. This cycle occurs twice every day.

Tides vary throughout the world. To provide the flow of water to generate electricity, the variation between the high and low tides should be at least 30 feet (9.1 m). In addition, the tide must occur in a bay or estuary which can be closed by a dam. Only a limited number of places in the world meet these conditions.

Two tidal plants are now in operation, and a third is under construction. See Fig. 4-10. A small plant in northern Russia on the Bering Sea generates approximately 400 kilowatts. A large plant on the La Rance River in France generates 240 megawatts. As with other forms of alternative energy, the capacity is listed at maximum output. Since tides do not provide a constant flow of water, the plant can produce power only 25% of the time.

A tidal plant is currently under construction in North America. The plant is located on the Bay of Funday in Nova Scotia, Canada. Other possible sites for future development include Cook Inlet in Alaska, and the Gulf of California in Mexico. The Solway and Severn Estuary in England are possibilities, and there are also possible sites off the coasts of Argentina, Brazil, western Africa, Australia, and the West Indies.

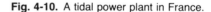

Fig. 4-10. A tidal power plant in France.

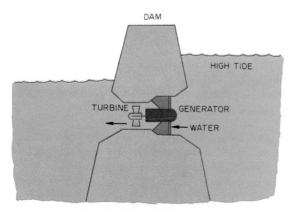

Fig. 4-11. A water turbine uses the water level difference between high tide and low tide to generate electricity.

To generate electricity using **tidal energy**, both the incoming and outgoing tides are used to turn turbines. See Fig. 4-11. A bay or estuary is closed with a dam. Water is kept in or out of the bay depending on the tide. When the tide is rising, the dam is closed. This keeps water out of the bay. When the tide is at its highest, the water is allowed to flow through the dam into the bay. The flowing water turns the turbines to produce electricity.

When the tide starts to lower, the dam is again closed. This traps the high tide water behind the dam in the bay. When the tide is at the lowest, the dam is opened. This allows the water to flow back to the ocean, again turning the electrical turbines.

While tides represent a great amount of energy on earth, the potential *usable* power is quite limited. The combination of limited sites, high costs of construction, and competition with other uses of the bay or estuary will restrict the development of tidal power.

❋ Ocean Thermal Energy.

Tropical oceans collect and store tremendous amounts of heat from the sun. It is possible to use this heat to produce electrical energy. Ocean thermal energy may have the potential for producing more than 200 times the entire world's present usage of electricity.

Producing electricity from ocean heat is called *Ocean Thermal Energy Conversion (OTEC)*. This process is based on the fact that the sun heats the oceans unevenly. Surface water

becomes hot. Deep water remains cold. The temperature difference between the hot surface water and the nearly freezing deep water can be used to produce electricity.

The OTEC system operates like a giant refrigerator. Figure 4-12 shows a diagram of the system. Basically, OTEC involves a loop between the hot surface water and the cold bottom water. A liquid, such as ammonia, circulates in the loop.

Ammonia is a liquid at a low temperature. It becomes a gas at a higher temperature. When ammonia circulates between the hot and cold water, it changes from a liquid to a gas and vice versa. When passing through the hot surface water, the ammonia changes into a gas. It expands and produces pressure. This pressure turns a turbine generator to produce electricity.

After passing through the turbine, the gas is condensed by passing through the cool bottom water. The liquified ammonia then circulates to the surface where it changes back into a gas. This process continues as the ammonia circulates between the cold and hot water. The cycle is constant as long as the temperature difference between the surface and bottom water remains the same.

Fig. 4-12. A simplified diagram of an OTEC plant in operation. Heat from the surface water vaporizes the liquid ammonia (1). The ammonia gas produces enough pressure to drive the turbine generator (2). The deep cooling water then condenses the gas into a liquid (3) to repeat the process.

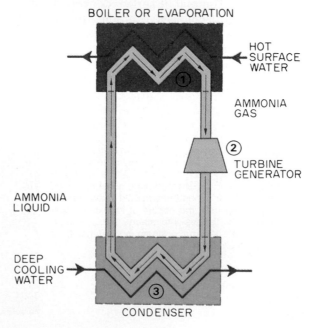

The cycle in which ammonia is used is called a *closed cycle*. The ammonia gas is sealed within the system and reused. An *open cycle* is also possible. In this cycle, the warm water is used to produce steam. See Fig. 4-13.

Producing steam with 80°F (27°C) surface water is possible, but not easy. When the pressure over a liquid is reduced, the boiling point is also lowered. If the pressure above water is reduced to ½ pound per square inch, the water will boil at 80°F, (27°C). Reducing the pressure to this level requires removing 97% of the air above the liquid.

In operation, as shown in Fig. 4-13, a vacuum pump lowers the pressure above the surface water. The warm surface water (80-84°F) (27-29°C) boils, producing steam. The steam rotates a turbine which drives a generator. The cold water (38-42°F) (3-5°C) from deep in the ocean cools the steam, condensing it back into water. As it condenses, it forms a very low pressure on the backside of the turbine. This helps rotate the turbine.

The condensed water is pure and contains no salt. The water can be used for such purposes as drinking and agriculture. It is a "bonus" of the open system.

Numerous problems remain with both the closed and open systems. The size of the plant must be enormous since it captures small amounts of energy from large amounts of water. A 100-megawatt plant would have a water flow equal to one-third the flow of the Mississippi River. A pipe 100 feet (30 m) across would be needed to carry the water.

Ocean Thermal Energy Conversion has some strong advantages. It produces no air pollution. It is also an inexhaustible source of energy. However, it has some potential environmental problems. OTEC plants will cool surface water and warm deep water. This may cause changes in the ocean environment. It may also affect the tropical climates in which the warm surface water needed for OTEC is located.

The United States could take advantage of ocean thermal energy. It is located next to areas of year-round warm surface water overlying cold deep water. Warm water from the Caribbean Sea flows northward into the Gulf of Mexico and around Florida. This current is called the Gulf Stream. Average surface temperatures are 76-80°F (20-22°C), with deep water at near freezing temperatures. These same conditions exist around Hawaii and in most tropical ocean areas.

Many countries are interested in OTEC. Experimental projects are underway. The U.S. has projects underway in Hawaii and in Florida. France, India, Japan, Sweden, and the Netherlands all have planned or operating experimental projects. While most planned projects are designed to use a closed cycle, a few will experiment with the open cycle, the newer of the two concepts.

Waves. The potential energy of ocean waves is many times greater than that of tides. However, the problems may also be greater. At this time, only one experimental system is in continuous operation. Japan has a wave-powered plant which has produced up to 150 kilowatts of electricity. Power generation occurs in a 260-foot (80-m) ship's hull, using 20 turbines.

The three types of wave machines include those that:

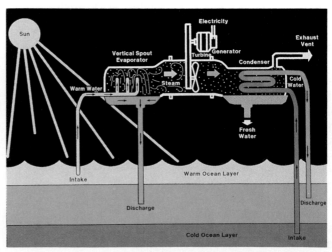

Fig. 4-13. In an open cycle, warm water from the surface of a tropical ocean is drawn into a vacuum (below atmospheric pressure) chamber. It flashes into steam and moves a turbine, generating electricity. It is then piped through cold sea water that was pumped from the bottom of the ocean. Note that when it flashes into steam, the sea water loses its salt. When the steam is condensed, the result is fresh water.

■ Use the vertical rise and fall of waves to power either water or air turbines.
■ Use to-and-fro motion to turn turbines.
■ Direct waves into a channel to maintain a flow of water to drive turbines.

The Japanese plant uses the vertical rise and fall of waves. The action compresses air which drives a turbine.

The British have studied wave power for many years. They have studied both coastal and distant ocean-wave power. Ocean waves far offshore have the greatest amount of power available. However, ocean plants would have to deal with the major problems of harsh ocean weather, plant mooring, and long electrical transmission lines.

More likely, we will see research done with small coastal devices that will be used for generating electricity. See Fig. 4-14. These will provide the knowledge needed to develop offshore plants.

Ocean Currents. Currents, such as the Gulf Stream, exist in oceans throughout the world. The energy potential, like that of waves and other alternative energy sources, is great but difficult to use.

Power from ocean currents is spread over a larger area, requiring very large extracting devices. Several designs have been planned for the Gulf Stream. Figure 4-15 shows one device. It is called a *water low-velocity energy converter*. The device operates when parachutes attached to a continuous belt are pulled by the moving current. The chutes close after completing half of the loop. The movement of the current reopens them. The movement rotates a turbine, generating electricity. When tested, this device exceeded estimated power outputs.

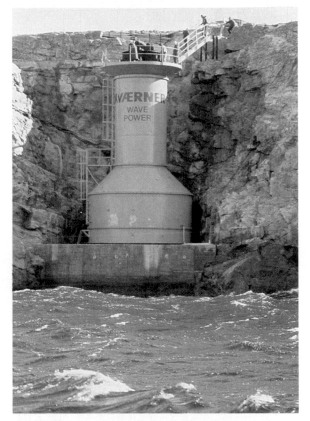

Fig. 4-14. This remote "wave generator" in Norway uses ocean waves to power a wind turbine. Wave action at the base causes a wave resonator (pump) to move up and down. This forces air up the tower, propelling a wind turbine. The generator produces 1 kilowatt of electricity, day and night.

At present, only experiments such as that just described have been undertaken. In the future, we may begin to receive some of the electricity we use from ocean currents.

Fig. 4-15. Electricity can be generated on board a ship anchored in an ocean current. The electricity would then flow through an underwater cable to shore.

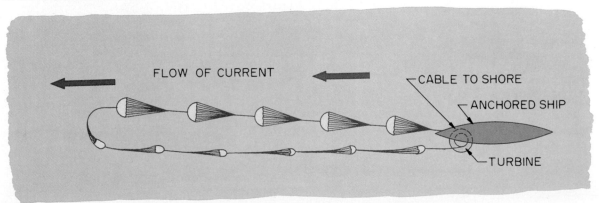

Solar Salt Ponds

Basically, **solar salt ponds** operate just the opposite of the OTEC process shown in Fig. 4-12. A solar pond is a shallow body of salt water that has a layer of fresh or less salty water near the surface. The sun's rays pass through the top layer and heat the bottom of the pond. Because the bottom water layer is heavy with salt, it holds the heat. As a result, the temperatures at the bottom of the pond can reach 250°F (121°C) while the surface layer stays fairly cool. The bottom water is prevented from boiling by the pressure of the water on top.

A loop containing a liquid such as ammonia is installed between the high- and low-temperature areas. The ammonia operates a turbine generator in the same way as in the OTEC system.

The energy possibly available from solar salt ponds is only a fraction of that from OTEC. However, solar ponds have fewer disadvantages. The electricity from solar ponds could help us meet our future energy needs.

Israel has operated test ponds for many years. A 5-megawatt plant is now in operation at the Dead Sea. And a Japanese company has successfully tested a solar pond on Hokkaido Island, a place where the temperature falls below freezing in winter.

In the United States, a test facility is being considered for the Salton Sea in Southern California. If successful, a 600-megawatt plant could be built. And it's possible to develop solar salt ponds on waste salt flats located in many other parts of the country. These could serve as energy sources in the future.

Technology Focus

The Land of Energy

Many utility companies are exploring ways of utilizing alternative sources of energy. For example, Southern California Edison (SCE), the second largest public utility in the nation, serves much of southern California. This area has a variety of resources for alternative energy. SCE generates electricity using solar, wind, hydroelectric, geothermal, and biomass—all inexhaustible or renewable sources of energy. In addition, the company has a nuclear power plant and numerous fossil fuel plants.

SCE is dedicated to developing alternative energy sources. In addition to expanding existing uses, they are investigating additional sources such as a solar salt pond at the Salton Sea. By the early 1990s, the company hopes to produce 2100 megawatts of electricity from alternative and renewable sources. This is the electricity needed by two million of the nine and one-half million people served by Southern California Edison.

SCE is just one example of companies utilizing alternative energy sources. What are companies doing in your area?

RENEWABLE SOURCES

Renewable sources are those which are constantly being replaced or renewed. These include trees and other plants that grow on the earth and those that grow in the ocean. These sources are limited. But when properly managed, they can become an important and continuous source of energy.

Using vegetation as a *planned* source of energy has many drawbacks. Most importantly, it is not an efficient source of energy. Plants capture only about 3% of the sun's energy. The remainder of the energy is lost in the process of growing the plant.

Plants convert sunlight, carbon dioxide, water, and nutrients into food. This process, photosynthesis, was described in Chapter 1. Plants and trees beautify the earth. They remove carbon dioxide from the air and return oxygen. Vegetation provides shelter for birds, animals, and humans. The use of vegetation for energy is, therefore, a bonus to the more important function of sustaining life on earth.

The renewable sources which we obtain from vegetation are:
- Wood
- Biofuels
- Gasohol
- Methanol

Wood

Wood is one of our oldest forms of energy. People have long used wood for cooking and heating. In pioneer days, wood was one of our major sources of energy. Coal and oil later replaced it.

Today, wood is often used as a fuel. Wood stoves again heat millions of American homes. Fireplaces are used both for heat and for aesthetic pleasure. In a few cases, wood also provides energy to generate electricity.

As an energy source, wood has one major disadvantage. It is not a clean-burning fuel. It creates high levels of air pollution.

Researchers are studying other uses for wood. We can convert wood to liquid and gaseous fuels easier than we can convert fossil fuels. One of these wood-based fuels is **methanol**. In the future, many car engines may be converted to burn methanol. Wood could become a major source of fuel for transportation.

The competition for the use of wood will increase in the future. Wood is a renewable resource. However, its use as a fuel will compete with its use in construction. Other competing industries include paper and furniture production. Vast forests would be necessary to sustain all these uses.

One solution might be shared usage. An industry such as a paper mill could use what it needs from the trees. The remainder could supply a utility.

Biofuels (Biomass)

Biofuels are waste products which can be used to produce energy. These include wood waste, vegetation, aquatic (water) plants, forest and farm residues, animal waste, and municipal solid wastes from plants and animals. The prefix "bio-" indicates these fuels are biological—that is, animal or vegetable. The term "biomass" is often used to describe this source of energy.

The burning of waste products is not new. The forestry industry has, for many years, provided half of its own energy needs by burning mill wastes. See Fig. 4-16. More recently, a wide variety of biomass projects have come into operation. These include:
- Farming—agricultural waste products.
- Residential and business waste products—garbage and solid waste products.
- Sewerage—by-products of waste treatment plants.

While wood can be used in its present form to produce energy, other biomass products need to be converted to a more usable form before use.

Biogas. Both animal and vegetation waste products can be used to produce *biogas*. The principal gas is methane which can be burned. The heat can be used to heat buildings or produce electricity.

Fig. 4-16. Wood wastes from this pulp and paper factory are burned to produce steam. The steam drives turbine generators to produce electricity for use in the plant. It is also used to provide heat needed within the plant.

Methane is produced from organic material, such as sewerage, garbage, and other forms of plant and animal wastes. The waste products are mixed with water, forming a *slurry* (a very heavy liquid). The slurry is placed in a tank called a *digester*, where bacteria break down the waste products into gases and sludge.

The tank must be closed and operate without the addition of air. The bacteria are *anaerobic bacteria*. They live and grow without oxygen. The bacteria are most effective at 90-100°F (32-38°C). When the slurry is broken down, sludge forms about 40% of the volume. Sludge serves as a fertilizer. The gas formed is about two-thirds methane. The remaining third is carbon dioxide mixed with small quantities of other gases. The process takes about 40 days to complete.

There are many different types of digesters, depending on the need. The simplest is a batch digester, shown in Fig. 4-17. This digester is a fiberglass tank. Slurry is added through an inlet pipe. A starter containing the bacteria is placed on top, and, after about five days, gas begins to form. The gas is removed and used. This digester needs to be emptied when filled with sludge.

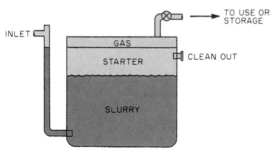

Fig. 4-17. Simple batch digester. This type is best suited to small applications. If two digesters are used, output of methane can be continuous.

Fig. 4-18. Continuous load digester. This type of digester requires the loading of approximately 1/40 the capacity of the digester each day.

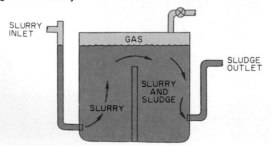

Figure 4-18 shows a continuous load digester. In this unit, approximately 1/40 of the tank capacity is added each day, with a like amount of sludge removed. The operation is then continuous.

Biogas is also available from landfill garbage dumps. These are dumps in which the garbage is covered with earth. This keeps oxygen away from the garbage. The combination of water and anaerobic bacteria produces methane gas which can be collected from the dump and used.

Figure 4-19 shows the setup of a landfill project. The gas is generated in the waste and collected by a perforated pipe. A compressor pumps the gas to an engine. The engine drives a generator, producing electricity.

Solid Biomass. Solid waste products collected by waste disposal companies can also be processed and burned to produce electricity. See Fig. 4-20. Most processes require separating combustible (burnable) substances from glass, metal, dirt, and other noncombustible materials. Combustibles which are primarily solid, such as paper and wood products, can be burned immediately. Others may require further processing.

Additional processing may involve removing water and compressing the materials into fuel pellets. The pellets can be transported and burned to produce both heat and electricity.

Methanol

Methanol, or methyl alcohol, is a clean-burning liquid fuel. It can be made from natural gas and coal. However, these sources are nonrenewable. Renewable methanol is made from wood, plants, or other biomass materials from homes, farms, and industries.

Methanol can be used as a transportation fuel. Methanol produces less energy than gasoline and burns more slowly. But with simple changes in engine design, methanol can produce as much power as gasoline. However, more fuel is consumed for each mile driven. Because it is slow-burning, methanol produces smoother engine performance.

Since fuel mileage is poorer, methanol-burning cars and buses should have larger fuel tanks. Methanol is already finding some use as a substitute for gasoline. See Fig. 4-21. Methanol could become an important source of fuel.

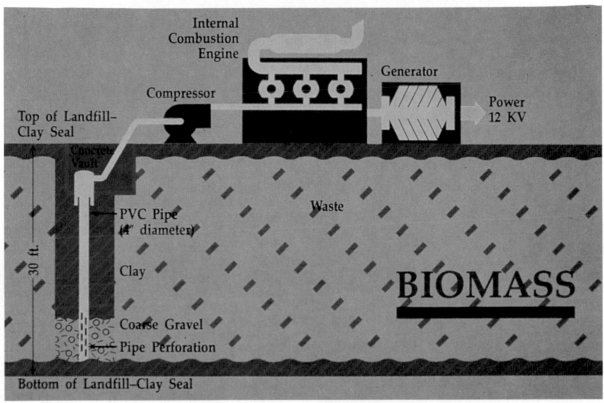

Fig. 4-19. A methane well at a landfill garbage dump.

Fig. 4-20. Each day, this resource recovery plant can convert 2000 tons of waste into clean-burning fuel.

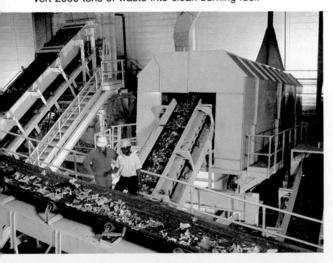

Fig. 4-21. In traffic, there will be no black smoke coming from this bus. It uses methanol, a safer fuel for public transportation.

Gasohol

Gasohol is a mixture of nine-tenths unleaded gasoline and one-tenth ethyl alcohol. It is used as a substitute for gasoline in automobiles and trucks. By using gasohol, we save 10% of the oil needed to produce gasoline.

The sources of alcohol include sweet sorghum, sugar beets, and grain. Distilleries process these crops into alcohol. The alcohol is then mixed with gasoline.

The main by-product of gasohol processing is a mash containing all the protein from the original product. This mash is not wasted. Farmers use it as a livestock food supplement.

Future of Renewable Energy Sources

Renewable energy sources are already supplying 1% or more of the electrical energy used in many parts of the country. Most of this energy is coming from biomass conversion. It is expected that the use of renewable sources will continue to increase.

COGENERATION

Cogeneration means shared use of the energy used to produce electricity. The most common cogeneration system uses fuel to power a steam turbine for the production of electricity. After the steam has passed through the turbine, the remaining heat is used to warm buildings, heat water, or provide heat for a variety of industrial processes.

Cogeneration is not a new concept. Years ago, many industries produced their own electricity and used the leftover heat for other purposes. The combination of growth of public utilities and the availability of inexpensive fossil fuels during the first half of this century eliminated most cogeneration plants. Current fuel costs have again made cogeneration economical.

Efficient use of fuel is the greatest asset of cogeneration. Electrical power plants using fossil fuels are able to use less than half the energy available in the fuel. The unused energy is usually discarded into bays, rivers, the atmosphere, or the ocean. In cogeneration, energy use is often raised to 75-80% efficiency.

Another important factor has led to the return of cogeneration. Many states have laws which require power companies to buy excess electricity produced from cogeneration. As a result, if a company produces more electricity than it needs, the power company will buy it for the same amount that it costs the power company to produce its own electricity.

Much of the current growth of cogeneration is to produce both the electricity and the heat needed by a company. Today, small generating plants are readily available to smaller companies. Small operations make use of diesel, natural gas, or gasoline engines to operate generators. The exhaust gases and engine cooling water are used to provide heat, usually to heat water or the building during winter. See Fig. 4-22.

Fig. 4-22. This company uses an engine/generator to produce by cogeneration the heat and electricity that it needs.

Smaller units for small businesses are also being manufactured. Engines/generators that produce 10-20 kilowatts are used for small business installations.

Cogeneration is also used with many biomass systems. Figure 4-16 shows wood waste products used to provide both electricity and heat.

Cogeneration is growing rapidly throughout the country. In California, the Pacific Gas and Electric Company serves nearly four million customers. In just one year, this company purchased 569 megawatts of cogenerated power. It now has contracts with potential suppliers to increase this amount to 3676 megawatts. And this is only the amount of electricity *sold* from cogeneration. It doesn't include electricity produced and used on site. This company is but one of many power companies throughout the nation purchasing electricity from cogeneration.

SMALL ENERGY SUPPLIERS

The numerous state laws requiring power companies to purchase electricity has introduced a new business into the nation. Many small suppliers are now able to produce electricity and sell it via their local power company. In the past, small suppliers were found only in remote areas where they produced electricity for their own and limited local use.

All of the alternative energy sources presented in this and previous chapters are used by small suppliers. These include hydroelectric, solar, wind, geothermal, biomass, and cogeneration. Cogeneration and biomass are used most and their use is continuing to increase throughout the nation.

The principles of operation for large or small sources are the same. Figure 4-23 shows a small 1.5-kilowatt hydroelectric project. The system includes a Pelton wheel turbine and generator. The system could be increased to five times this capacity, but would not be operable during the summer. Local conditions can greatly affect small suppliers.

If the cost of PV cells decreases to a cost-effective level, we could see rapid growth in small PV cell electricity production.

ELECTRICAL NETWORKS

As alternative sources develop, the networking of electrical transmission lines around the country will grow in importance. Inexpensive electricity produced in one portion of the nation can be sent via high-capacity electrical lines to other locations. These same lines permit the movement of "seasonal electricity" between locations. And electrical failures in one area are met with electricity purchased from another.

Networking results in a decrease in the electrical generating capacity needed by any one area. This produces lower costs for all. See Fig. 4-24.

Unfortunately, the ability to economically send electricity clear across the country doesn't exist at the present time. However, developments with *superconductors*, as described in Chapter 27, may make cross-country transmission economical. Someday, we may see electricity generated by solar energy in the Southwest distributed throughout the nation!

Fig. 4-24. The existing network of electrical power transmission lines in the western United States. Similar networks exist in other regions of the country.

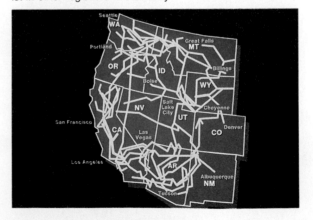

Fig. 4-23. A small hydroelectric project. Water travels 1700 feet through a 4-inch water line.

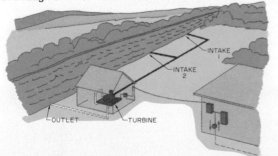

Chapter 4—Review

Testing Your Knowledge

Briefly answer each of the following questions. Write on a separate piece of paper.

1. Identify the two main reasons why we need to develop new sources of energy.
2. Name two designs for wind turbines.
3. What is the best efficiency possible for wind turbines?
4. Name the source of heat used for geothermal energy.
5. What is a geopressured energy reserve?
6. Identify the largest reserve of geothermal energy.
7. Identify the source of energy for OTEC.
8. Identify the source of biofuels.
9. How is methanol used as an energy source?
10. Identify the effects of state laws that require utility companies to buy electricity from small suppliers.
11. Name one important advantage of networking electrical utilities.

Expressing Your Knowledge

Using complete sentences, write your answers to the following on a separate sheet of paper:

1. Describe what is meant by "the output of a wind turbine is measured at peak output."
2. Explain how ocean tides are used to produce electricity.
3. Referring to the illustration below, explain what is meant by an "open cycle" in an OTEC system?
4. Describe how a solar salt pond is used as an energy source.
5. What are the advantages of cogeneration?

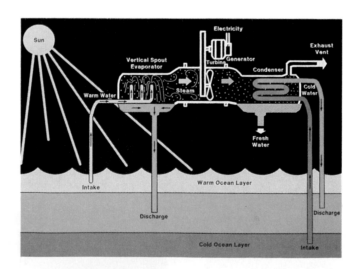

Applying Your Knowledge

Follow your teacher's instructions to complete these activities:

1. Your teacher will divide the class into eight groups. Each group should develop as many questions and answers about energy as possible and write them on 3 × 5 cards. Assign a point value such as 5, 10, or 15 points to each question, depending on the difficulty of the question. All questions should be on energy sources, as described in Chapters 2, 3, and 4. These questions can be used to play a classroom game.

   The questions written by groups 1-4 should be collected and mixed. The remaining four groups (groups 5-8) should be divided into two teams. One person on each team is asked a question. If that student answers the question correctly, his or her team gets the points. If an incorrect answer is given, the opposing team is given the opportunity to answer the question. The contest should go on for a set time, such as half a class period.

   Repeat the contest with the questions from groups 5-8 being asked of two teams composed of groups 1-4. Stop the contest after the same amount of time as was used for groups 5-8. The team with the most points wins the contest.

2. Check the population of your local community (city or county) and of your state. Using the ratio of 1 kilowatt per person, determine the kilowatts of power needed for each. Convert your answer to megawatts.

3. The population of the United States is approximately 250 million people. How many megawatts of electricity are needed to supply our nation?

Chapter 5

Nuclear Energy

Large amounts of energy can be obtained from the innermost portion of the atom—the **nucleus**. When we split the nucleus of a very heavy material such as uranium, we change matter into energy.

Expanding Your Knowledge

As you study this chapter, you will learn to:

- Explain how matter is converted to energy and used to produce heat and electricity.
- Identify nuclear fuel and how different isotopes are used.
- Describe the operation of light-water and breeder reactors.
- Identify the four major concerns people have regarding the use of nuclear energy for power.
- Explain how nuclear energy is able to supply small amounts of power over long periods of time.

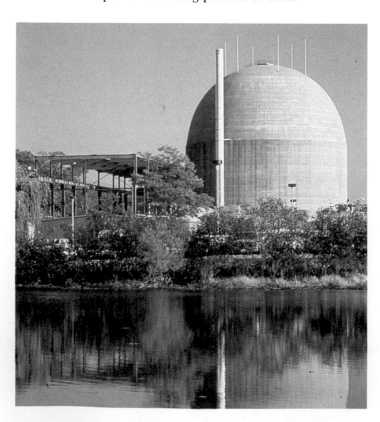

Building Your Word Power

The following terms are defined and explained in this chapter. Learning these will help you learn more about nuclear energy.

boiling-water reactor
breeder reactor
chain reaction
fission
fusion
heat exchanger
isotopes
light-water reactor
neutrons
nuclear battery
nuclear reactor
nuclear wastes
nucleus
plutonium
pressurized-water reactor
radiation (atomic)
radioactivity
thermoelectric coupling
  (thermocouple)
uranium

This chapter explains how nuclear energy is released from atoms and put to use in producing electricity.

Nuclear energy has become a large and important source of electricity in the United States and other countries. About 17% of all our electricity now comes from nuclear power plants. The two different types of nuclear plants currently producing electricity are described in detail in this chapter. A third type of plant, called a breeder reactor, is also explained since it could become a major source of nuclear power in the future.

Nuclear safety is an important concern, not only of nuclear scientists and power plant operators, but also of the general public. This chapter identifies existing concerns and provides basic knowledge that will help you make future judgments regarding the use of nuclear energy.

ENERGY FROM THE ATOM

Nuclear energy is the energy released when matter is changed into energy. The amount of energy we can obtain from nuclear reactions is almost unbelievable. *Albert Einstein* showed the relationship between matter and energy with the equation $E = mc^2$. This equation reads: *Energy equals mass times the square of the speed of light.* In simple terms, this means that tiny amounts of matter have the potential to produce giant amounts of energy.

Notice the term "*nuclear* energy." The conversion of matter into energy takes place in the *nucleus* of the atom.

There are two types of nuclear reactions:
- Fission
- Fusion

In **fission**, energy is produced when atoms are split apart. In **fusion**, energy is produced when atoms are combined. In both reactions, a small amount of matter is changed into a large amount of heat and light energy.

In this chapter, we will look at fission. Fission is an important source of power at the present time. Fusion is a possible energy source for the future. It will be studied in Chapter 25.

NUCLEAR FISSION

In Chapter 3, you learned about the tiny particles that make up an atom. (Refer back to Fig. 3-20.) You learned that electricity is the movement of electrons, the tiny particles that move around the nucleus of the atom. The nucleus contains *protons* and *neutrons*.

Nuclear fission involves only the nucleus, not the surrounding electrons. In a **nuclear reactor**, the nucleus is bombarded by **neutrons**. When a neutron enters the nucleus, the nucleus splits into two parts. See Fig. 5-1. This process produces energy. It also produces two or three free neutrons. To continue the reaction, at least

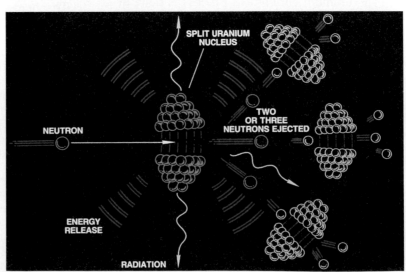

Fig. 5-1. Nuclear fission is the splitting of the nucleus of a uranium atom with a neutron. Energy is released in the form of heat. Freed neutrons then cause a chain reaction to split other nuclei.

one of the neutrons must split another uranium nucleus. When this process continues, a **chain reaction** is produced.

In a nuclear reactor, millions of uranium nuclei are split into lighter materials each second. A single fission reaction produces more than 20 million (20,000,000) times as much energy as a single chemical reaction. This energy is mainly heat. The heat is used to boil water to produce steam. The steam, in turn, operates a turbine generator.

In addition to new materials and heat energy, *radiation* is also released. You have already learned that **radiation** is the movement of energy by waves and tiny particles of light called photons.

There are many forms of radiation. Some, such as heat and light, are important for life. Other forms of radiation can be very harmful. Some of the radiation from nuclear fission is very dangerous. Since it is present in large quantities, it can cause injury and even death. During nuclear reactions, very extensive safety precautions must be taken to avoid injury from radiation.

Nuclear Fuel

Uranium is a natural radioactive substance found in the earth. *Radioactive* means that the substance releases atomic radiation.

Uranium has two major forms, called **isotopes**. One of these isotopes, uranium-235 (U-235), is rare. It makes up less than 1% of the uranium found. The other isotope is uranium-238 (U-238). This is the most common type of uranium. However, by itself U-238 is not suitable for use in present-day reactors. It must be enriched with the rare isotope U-235.

The uranium enrichment process is done in large, complex plants. This process is also the first step in creating nuclear weapons. Therefore, the plants are closely guarded. Enriched uranium is 97.5% U-238 and 2.5% U-235. This is the fuel of nuclear reactors.

Refer back to Fig. 5-1. Notice that each fission reaction releases two or three neutrons. Only one neutron is needed to sustain a chain reaction. The remaining neutrons may do one of two things:

■ They may combine with U-238 to form a substance called **plutonium**. Plutonium is *fissionable*. That is, neutrons can split its nuclei to release energy. In this way, plutonium can serve as reactor fuel.
■ The neutrons may be absorbed by control rods to regulate the reactor's energy output. This process will be described later.

Power from Nuclear Energy

At the present time, the fission of uranium is the only developed source of nuclear power. This source supplies 6% of all our power. This amounts to 17% of the electricity produced in the United States each year. Nuclear power is produced in the form of electricity at nuclear plants. See p. 78.

Once a nuclear plant is constructed, its power output is less expensive than power from other sources. One pellet of uranium costs about $7 at 1987 prices. It has the energy potential of three barrels of oil ($45) or one ton of coal ($29). All fuel costs are expected to increase in the future. However, oil and coal prices are expected to increase at greater rates than uranium. Therefore, in comparison, nuclear fuel is inexpensive. However, nuclear power plants cost much more to build than coal- or oil-burning plants. And they also cost more to operate.

Light-Water Reactors

Nuclear reactors use a liquid to transfer heat. Reactors that use ordinary water to transfer heat are called **light-water reactors**. (There are some heavy-water reactors, but they are not common. To transfer heat, heavy-water reactors use a rare type of water called *deuterium oxide*.)

There are two types of light-water reactors.
■ Boiling-water reactors
■ Pressurized-water reactors

Boiling-Water Reactors. The *core* of a nuclear reactor is the part that contains the fissionable material. In a boiling-water reactor, the core is placed inside a water-filled container called a *vessel*. See Fig. 5-2.

The heat produced by the fission reaction boils the water in the vessel. Steam collects at the top. As the steam continues to be produced, the pressure increases. This pushes the steam into the turbine. The rotating turbine drives an electrical generator.

After the steam leaves the turbine, a condenser cools it. This changes the steam back into water. A pump returns the water to the reactor vessel. The water-to-steam-to-water cycle operates continuously to produce electricity.

Pressurized-Water Reactor. Figure 5-3 shows a pressurized-water reactor. Water under very high pressure surrounds the uranium core. The high pressure permits the water to heat up to a temperature well above its normal boiling point of 212°F (100°C). The water gets very hot without changing into steam.

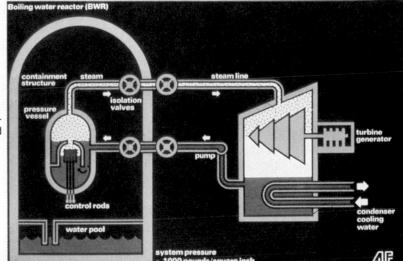

Fig. 5-2. A boiling-water reactor produces steam to operate a turbine and produce electricity.

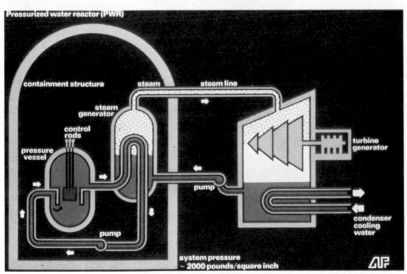

Fig. 5-3. Pressurized-water reactors use a heat exchanger and two complete water systems.

Increased pressure raises the boiling point of a liquid. As the pressure increases, molecules are held more closely together. They cannot easily move apart from each other. Changing from a liquid into a gas involves moving the molecules far apart. Therefore, the water becomes very hot but does not change into steam. This is what happens in a pressurized-water reactor. A pump moves the hot water to a heat exchanger.

A **heat exchanger** is a device that transfers heat from one fluid to another. See Fig. 5-4. The reactor produces high-temperature, high-pressure water. This water passes through the pipe

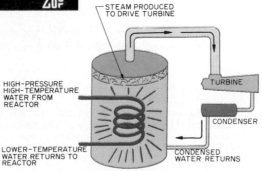

Fig. 5-4. In a pressurized-water reactor, the heat exchanger connects two separate water systems. Heat from the radioactive side produces steam in the non-radioactive side. This steam is used to drive a turbine generator.

inside the heat exchanger. The water surrounding the pipe is at a lower pressure and temperature. Heat from the reactor water passes through the walls of the pipe and heats the low-pressure water.

Since the reactor water is under high pressure, its temperature is far above the boiling point of the low-pressure water. This high temperature changes the low-temperature water to steam which drives the turbine generator. The condenser takes heat away from the steam so that it condenses back into water. The pump then sends the water back to the heat exchanger to repeat the process.

After passing through the heat exchanger, the high-pressure water returns to the reactor to be reheated. In addition to exchanging heat, the heat exchanger acts as a barrier against radiation. It prevents radiation from the reactor from traveling through the rest of the system.

In addition to their use in nuclear power plants, pressurized-water reactors are used on ships. Nuclear-powered ships include both aircraft carriers and submarines.

Controlling Reactor Output. The reaction in nuclear reactors is usually controlled with *control rods*. Control rods are made of boron, silver, and other materials. Their job is to absorb free neutrons. This limits the chain reaction.

Power plant workers can slow down or stop the reaction by inserting the control rods into the uranium core. They can speed up the reaction by pulling the rods out. (Of course, this is all done by remote control.)

Reactor Charges and By-Products. The fuel for a nuclear reactor is called the *charge*. The charge consists of packs of ½-inch diameter *fuel rods*. See Fig. 5-5. Together, many fuel rods make up a *fuel assembly*.

A typical reactor vessel contains approximately 200 fuel assemblies grouped to form the

Fig. 5-6. Lowering a fuel unit into a nuclear reactor.

core of the reactor. Movable control rods are interspersed among the fuel assemblies.

A reactor core usually has over 10,000 fuel rods placed in the 200 fuel assemblies. See Fig. 5-6. A typical charge costs more than $10 million dollars.

As described earlier, a by-product of the fission reaction is *radiation*. Radiation makes reactor water and waste products radioactive and dangerous. Special shields protect workers from the reactor's radioactivity. These shields are made of lead and concrete.

Another by-product of a fission reaction is plutonium-239. The formation of plutonium was described earlier. Plutonium is a fissionable material. Therefore, it takes part in the chain reaction. In this way, it helps provide energy for the production of electricity.

A typical reactor requires a fuel change once every three years. During the three-year period, the U-235 is slowly used up. However, the plutonium slowly builds up. At the same time, it is used as fuel. By the end of the three-year period, there is actually more plutonium taking part in the chain reaction than U-235.

After the fuel is removed, it is separated into three materials. They are uranium-238, plutonium, and waste products.

Fig. 5-5. Each nuclear fuel pellet is less than 1/2 inch in diameter. Each pellet contains the energy of 120 gallons of petroleum-based fuel. The pellets are stacked in fuel rods about 12 feet long and grouped into bundles.

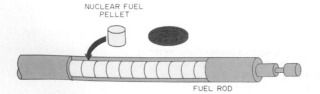

NUCLEAR FUEL
PELLET

FUEL ROD

The uranium-238 can be enriched with U-235 and reused in the reactor. At the present time, plutonium and waste products have limited use. However, an experimental reactor, the *breeder reactor*, uses both U-238 and plutonium as fuel. If breeder reactors were put into service, they would be able to use these materials.

Breeder Reactor

Ten breeder reactors have been built in the United States and abroad. However, the reactors in the U.S. are experimental, and some were shut down after testing breeder operation.

The idea of the breeder reactor is not new. Scientists first considered it as they worked on nuclear energy during the 1940s. The first electricity ever produced by a nuclear reactor was from an experimental breeder reactor in 1951.

Breeder reactors use plutonium-239 and uranium-238 as fuel. Uranium-235 is not needed. Breeder reactors convert a nonusable substance into a usable one. During fission more plutonium is created from U-238 than is used in the reactor. Therefore, the reactor "breeds," or manufactures, plutonium.

The fission reaction in breeder reactors is similar to that in light-water reactors. The major difference is in the number of neutrons released. When U-235 is split, an average of 2.5 neutrons are released. When plutonium-239 is split in a breeder reactor, an average of three neutrons are released. One of these sustains the reaction by splitting another plutonium nucleus. The other two are available to strike nearby atoms of U-238 and transform them into plutonium. If both neutrons strike, they produce an overall gain of one atom of fuel. (One atom of plutonium was used at the beginning of the reaction.)

In actual practice, for every 10 plutonium atoms split, 12 new plutonium atoms are created. At this rate, the amount of plutonium doubles in about 30 years.

Neutrons must travel very fast to produce the breeder reaction. Water slows the speed of neutrons. Therefore, water cannot be used to surround the reactor core and absorb heat energy. Instead, breeder reactors use liquid sodium. This element does not slow the neutron's speed.

Sodium is a chemically active metal. It ignites and burns when exposed to air. It also reacts chemically with water. These factors require extra precautions to be taken in designing and operating breeder reactors.

Operation of the Breeder Reactor. Figure 5-7 shows how a breeder reactor works. The reactor core produces heat. The liquid sodium surrounding the core removes the heat to a heat exchanger. The heat exchanger transfers heat from the radioactive sodium to the nonradioactive coolant. The coolant may be sodium or water. A pump sends the coolant from the heat ex-

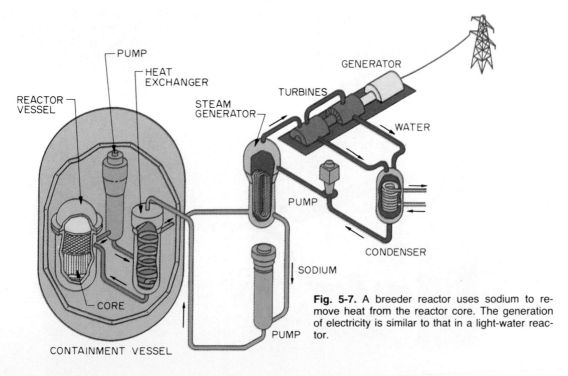

Fig. 5-7. A breeder reactor uses sodium to remove heat from the reactor core. The generation of electricity is similar to that in a light-water reactor.

changer to a device that generates steam. This steam generator produces high-pressure steam. The steam, in turn, drives a turbine to produce electricity.

Future Use. No plans currently exist for building a new breeder reactor in the United States. But France has a commercial-size breeder reactor under construction. When finished, the plant will provide all the electricity needed by a city of more than one million people.

At one time, it was thought that we would run out of U-235 by the year 2000. This was the strongest argument for the construction of breeder reactors. However, the nuclear power industry has not grown as expected. As a result, the supply of U-235 will last well into the 21st century.

Breeder reactors are also more costly to build than light-water reactors. Breeder reactors would cost an estimated 25 to 75% more than light-water reactors.

Our stockpile of U-238 continues to grow. See Fig. 5-8. Breeder reactors would put it to use. Since U-238 is by far the most abundant isotope of uranium, the use of breeder reactors would multiply our available energy from uranium by a factor of 60. Figure 5-9 shows a graphic comparison of available fuels, compared with their use. Note that the use of breeder reactors would make uranium the most abundant source of energy.

Fig. 5-8. A portion of the present U.S. stockpile of U-238. Each 12-foot-long tank contains the energy equivalent of 60 supertankers of oil.

NUCLEAR POWER SAFETY

The nuclear age began in 1945 when two atomic bombs were exploded in Japan during World War II. Nuclear power has been *controversial* since its beginning. That is, many people have strong feelings for and against nuclear power. The concerns now center on four major topics or *issues*:

- The danger of nuclear plant accidents.
- The danger of radioactivity.
- The disposal of nuclear wastes.
- The growing supply of plutonium.

Power Plant Accidents

Two major nuclear power plant accidents have occurred,—one in the United States and one in Russia. The first occurred at the Three Mile Island plant in Pennsylvania.

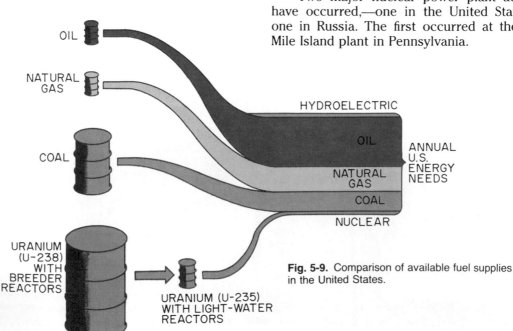

Fig. 5-9. Comparison of available fuel supplies in the United States.

Technology Focus

The China Syndrome

Some time ago, people came up with the rather funny idea that if you dug a hole deeply enough you would end up in China. The term "China syndrome" is based on this idea. But a China syndrome is not funny. It is one of the worst possible accidents that hypothetically could happen in a nuclear power plant—a *meltdown* of the fuel in the core. It would occur if the reactor core temperature were to exceed 5000°F (2782°C), the melting point of the fuel.

One of the concerns with a meltdown is that the molten fuel might melt its way through the reactor vessel and the reinforced concrete below it. The core could then continue to work its way down into the ground, "all the way to China." That is, no one knows how far it would go or what damage it would do.

A meltdown has *never* happened, but accidents at Three Mile Island and Chernobyl came dangerously close. Scientists are studying the possibility. For example, experiments are being conducted in a unique test facility at Sandia National Laboratories in New Mexico (see photo).

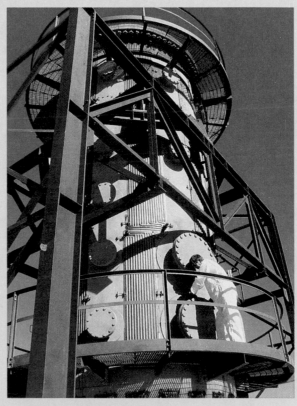

Many scientists believe that during a meltdown, the core would mix with the concrete base and solidify, or that water would cool the uranium. But no one knows for sure what would happen. And no one wants to learn from experience. Every precaution *must* be taken to prevent a China syndrome.

On March 28, 1979, a water pipe clogged at the Three Mile Island plant and a combination of mechanical failures and human errors produced a major power plant accident. The accident completely destroyed the reactor and released some radiation into the atmosphere. The apparent chain of events which occurred were:

■ When the pipe clogged, the reactor and turbine producing electricity automatically shut down.

■ This action created a back-up of heat which fused the fuel rods together, preventing them from being cooled properly.

■ Instruments were misread, other equipment failures occurred, and computers became overloaded.

■ The end result was radioactive water in the plant and a third of the reactor core reduced to rubble.

There were no injuries and the radiation leakage was not considered serious. However, the reactor was completely destroyed and thousands of people left the area for fear of radiation exposure.

The second accident occurred on April 26, 1986, in Chernobyl, Russia. This accident was far more serious than Three Mile Island. The accident led to more than 30 deaths, hundreds of injuries, and spread radiation throughout the world. It is estimated that there will be over 20,000 premature deaths in the Soviet Union due to radiation produced by the accident.

Both the Three Mile Island and the Chernobyl accidents involved human error. The accidents could have been less severe, or even eliminated, if the operators on duty had taken the correct steps in controlling the reactors. In the future, computer-controlled operation might eliminate operator errors of this type. Plant design also makes a difference. See Fig. 5-10.

Radioactivity

Great efforts have gone into nuclear reactor safety. However, there is still the danger of accidental release of radiation. In routine plant operation, there is little or no radiation released. A well-operated nuclear power plant is safe and very quiet.

Nuclear Waste Disposal

Nuclear wastes consist of new substances created during fission. In some countries, used nuclear fuel is processed to separate the waste products from the remaining uranium and plutonium. In the United States, reprocessing doesn't occur. It is less expensive to obtain new U-235 than to reclaim the unused portion.

The fuel rods are removed from the reactor after about 70% of the fuel has been used. The rods are stored in pools of water at the reactor site. After about four months, the radioactivity has decreased by about 90%. The used fuel rods are then stored at nuclear power plants for future disposal. See Fig. 5-11.

The Nuclear Waste Policy Act of 1982 established a plan to dispose of the unwanted nuclear waste. The waste, in a glass or ceramic form, will be sealed in metal canisters. The canisters will be buried in granite or salt. They will be placed in holes 2500 feet deep and covered. They can then stay there for thousands of years while the waste decays to the level of natural uranium ore.

Misuse of Plutonium

Some countries are reprocessing spent fuel and removing the unused uranium and plutonium. The plutonium is stored for future use in breeder reactors. But with added refining, it could be used in nuclear weapons. Thus, the growing supply of plutonium is a concern of many people. They are fearful that it could be stolen by terrorists or used by countries to develop nuclear arms.

Decision-Making

Our nation is faced with the need to constantly make decisions about nuclear power. We

Fig. 5-11. Storing used fuel rods in a nuclear power plant. Storage units are kept underwater. The water is circulated and particles are filtered out. Heat produced by radioactive decay is also removed from the water.

Fig. 5-10. The most important safety difference between Three Mile Island and Chernobyl was power plant design. The Three Mile Island reactor was in a containment vessel. Chernobyl, like the plant shown here, did not use containment vessels.

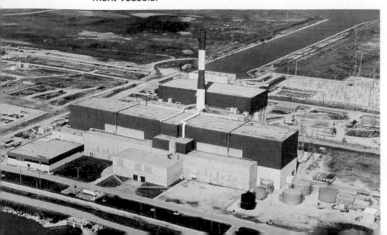

already have vast stockpiles of nuclear wastes containing plutonium. We now have over 100 nuclear plants in operation. We must all clearly understand the benefits and problems of nuclear power. Nuclear power will continue to be controversial. As citizens, we will have to make responsible decisions about its use.

At the present, there are no new nuclear power plants being planned in the U.S. Of the ones now under construction, two things are happening. Some plants are being completed and put into operation. Others are being delayed or cancelled.

Other countries are expanding their nuclear power capacity. For example, France is building 10 large new plants each year. In the United States, most nuclear power plants under construction will soon be in operation. Plant closures and the completion of new plants will have nuclear power production of electricity peak at just over 20%.

NUCLEAR AUXILIARY POWER

The nuclear wastes produced by nuclear reactors can supply small amounts of power for special situations. Only a very small amount of waste can be used in this way. There are two devices that can use nuclear wastes to develop power:
- Nuclear battery
- Thermoelectric coupling

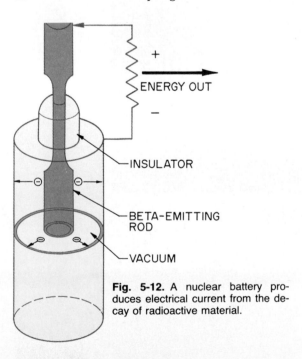

Fig. 5-12. A nuclear battery produces electrical current from the decay of radioactive material.

Nuclear Battery

The **nuclear battery** is a simple device. It uses a beta-emitting radioactive material. (A *beta particle* is a high-speed electron. To *emit* means to give off.) If the material emits enough electrons, electric current can be produced. See Fig. 5-12. The great advantage of nuclear batteries is their extra-long life.

The central part of the battery is a rod coated with the beta-emitting material. The battery container is vacuum-sealed. Electrons flow from the rod to the container wall. This produces current. Voltages from nuclear batteries can be very high. However, the actual power output of electricity is very small.

Nuclear batteries are presently used to provide power for ocean buoys and other aids to navigation. These devices require only small amounts of electricity. With nuclear batteries, the devices can be placed in remote locations.

Thermoelectric Coupling

A **thermoelectric coupling** (thermocouple) can be used to generate electricity from any heat source. "Any heat source" includes the decay of radioactive materials. A thermoelectric coupling uses two different materials joined together in a series circuit. When the coupling is heated, an electric current is generated. See Fig. 5-13.

A thermocouple system is very inefficient. Only 1 to 5% of the heat is converted into electricity. However, thermocouples have advantages that make them very useful sources of electricity. They have no moving parts, and they are silent.

Nuclear powered thermocouple units are called *radioisotopic thermoelectric generators*, or RTGs. These generators are widely used to provide power for satellites.

Fig. 5-13. A thermocouple converts heat into electricity.

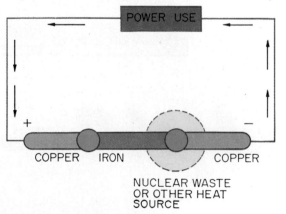

Chapter 5—Review

Testing Your Knowledge

Briefly answer each of the following questions. Write on a separate piece of paper.
1. What is the difference between fission and fusion?
2. Which isotope of uranium is relatively rare?
3. What is a light-water reactor?
4. How does a control rod control a nuclear reaction?
5. What are the four major areas of controversy surrounding nuclear power?
6. What was the initial cause of the accident at Three Mile Island?
7. What does the Nuclear Waste Policy Act of 1982 accomplish?
8. What is a current use of the nuclear battery?
9. What advantages do thermoelectric couplings have that make them useful sources of electricity?

Expressing Your Knowledge

Using complete sentences, write your answers to the following on a separate sheet of paper:
1. Describe the mathematical relationship between matter and energy.
2. Explain how plutonium is formed in a reactor fueled by uranium.
3. Briefly describe how a boiling-water reactor produces electricity from a nuclear reaction. (See illustration below.)
4. A breeder reactor produces more fuel than it uses. Explain this process.
5. How did human error contribute to the Chernobyl accident?

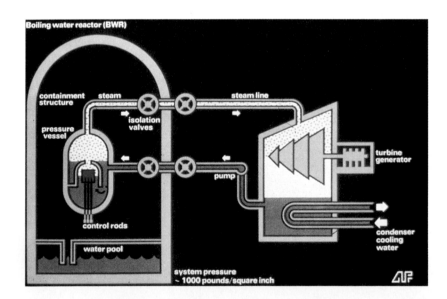

Applying Your Knowledge

Follow your teacher's instructions to complete these activities:

1. Hold either a group discussion or debate on nuclear energy. The teacher will divide the class into groups and arrange for the assignment of key issues to individual groups. Each group will do the needed research for the debate or discussion.

2. Using dominos, prepare a demonstration of a nuclear chain reaction. Set up the dominos as shown in the upper portion of Fig. 5-14A. Can you space the dominos so that the next set of hits would have the 8 front dominos hitting 16 more dominos? This reaction demonstrates an uncontrolled nuclear chain reaction. If this continued with uranium, what would be the result?

Next, set up the dominos as shown in Fig. 5-14B. This is a controlled reaction demonstration.

Describe, in a brief report, how a nuclear reactor controls the chain reaction and prevents it from running away as shown in the first demonstration.

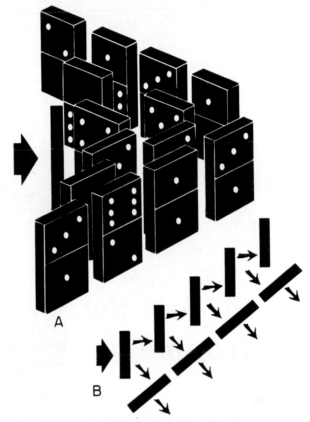

Fig. 5-14. Using dominoes to demonstrate a chain reaction.

Power and the Environment

SECTION

Chapter 6

Measuring Energy and Power

In Section I, you studied energy sources and energy control. You learned that many forms of energy—including heat, light, and motion—can be controlled. The next step is to learn how to *measure* energy.

Expanding Your Knowledge

Learning about power and energy technology will help you learn more about the world around you. As you study this chapter, you will learn to:

- Understand the difference between energy and power.
- Recognize the difference between two systems of measurement used throughout the world.
- Explain power measurements and perform a variety of mathematical problems using these measurements.
- Describe how engine power is measured, including the operation of measurement devices.
- Recognize how power is developed from energy and identify the three common forms of power.

Building Your Word Power

Knowledge of the vocabulary used will help you develop greater understanding of power and energy. The following terms are defined and explained in this chapter. Learning these will help you learn more about how energy and power are measured.

British thermal units (BTUs)
calorie (Calorie)
customary system
dynamometer
force
gravity
horsepower (hp)
International System of Units (SI)
metric system
power
pressure
speed
tachometer
torque
weight
work

In this chapter, you will learn the technical definition of terms that describe the use and measurement of energy. The most important of these are force, work, torque, power, and pressure. Emphasis is also placed on understanding the mathematical relationships between the terms. Example situations help you learn how to measure energy and power and how to calculate solutions to a variety of energy and power problems.

The metric system of measurement is introduced in this chapter. This system is used throughout the world. It's use is becoming more common in the United States as our trade with other countries increases and our industries expand.

ENERGY AND POWER

When we measure energy, we can find out how much work we can accomplish with the energy. The measurement of controlled energy is *power*. In technical terms, **power** is *energy per unit of time*. As you know, energy is the capacity to do work. Power is work accomplished in a given period of time. For example, you must use a certain amount of energy to climb a flight of stairs. Your weight and the height of the stairs determine the amount of energy needed. This energy is the same whether you walk or run up the stairs. However, the amount of *power* used is different. The faster you climb the stairs, the more power you must use.

The measurement of power is important in determining the effectiveness of any energy control system. Controlled energy, in fact, is often identified as power. Later in this book you will learn about power control and transmission devices. As you study these devices, it will be important to know how both energy and power are measured.

MEASURING SYSTEMS

The two measuring systems presently used in the United States are the customary system and the metric system. The **customary system** is the measuring system we have traditionally

used. This system is based on units such as the inch, the pound, the quart, and degrees Fahrenheit. Customary units used to measure power include horsepower, the foot-pound, pounds per square inch, and the BTU. See Fig. 6-1.

The **metric system** is the measuring system used by most of the industrialized countries of the world. This system is formally called the **International System of Units**, abbreviated **SI**.

Fig. 6-1. Basic units of measurement for the SI metric and customary systems of measurement.

Measurement	Metric Units	Customary Units
Length	millimeters centimeters meters kilometers	inches feet yards miles
Weight	grams kilograms metric tons	ounces pounds tons
Volume	milliliters liters cubic centimeters	ounces cups pints quarts gallons
Area	square centimeters square meters	square inches square feet square yards
Temperature	degrees Celsius	degrees Fahrenheit
Speed	kilometers per hour	miles per hour
Force	newtons	pounds
Torque	newton-meters	pound-feet

Pressure	pascals	pounds per
		  sq. inch
		inches of
		  mercury

Energy
  Mechanical
  Heat
 	
  Electrical
	joules
	joules
	calories
	joules
		foot-pounds
		British
		    Thermal Units
		joules

Power
  Mechanical
  Heat
  Electrical
	watts
	watts
	watts
		horsepower
		BTUs per second
		watts

The SI metric system is based on units such as the meter, the liter, the gram, and degrees Celsius. Metric units used to measure power include the newton, the watt, the joule, and the pascal. Again, see Fig. 6-1.

The metric system is easy to learn. It does not have as many units as the customary system. There are 50 units of measurement in the customary system. There are only seven in the metric system. For example, in the customary system, length can be measured according to four units: the inch, the foot, the yard, and the mile. The metric system has only one basic unit for length: the *meter*. This simplicity is possible because the metric system uses *prefixes* with its basic units. Prefixes indicate amounts smaller or larger than the basic unit. The most common prefixes are *milli-* ($\frac{1}{1000}$), *centi-* ($\frac{1}{100}$), and *kilo-* (1000). See Fig. 6-2.

The metric system is also easy to use because it is a decimal system. In a *decimal system*, all of the units and prefixes are multiples of the number 10. This means that all metric measurements can be easily multiplied and divided by 10. All you have to do is move a decimal point to the left or right. For example, 100.5 centimeters = 1.005 meters. The decimal point is moved two places to the left.

Both the customary system and the metric system are used in the United States. But most people still use the customary system in their daily measurements. The metric system is often used in industry.

MEASUREMENT CONVERSIONS

When working with energy and power, both the customary system and the metric system are used. For this reason, it is important to be able to convert a measurement from one system into a measurement in the other system.

Converting customary measurements to metric measurements is easy. You multiply the customary measurement by the metric *equivalent* of the customary unit used. Figure 6-3 shows the metric equivalents for the basic customary units. These equivalents are called *conversion factors*. To convert 10 inches into centimeters, for example, simply multiply 10 by 2.540 (the metric equivalent for 1 inch). The answer is 25.40 centimeters.

Changing a metric measurement to a customary measurement is simple, too. You multiply the metric measurement by the customary equivalent of the metric unit used. See Fig. 6-4. For example, to find out how many pounds there are in 10 kilograms, multiply 10 by 2.205 (the customary equivalent for 1 kilogram). The answer is 22.05 pounds.

Notice that equivalents are often not whole numbers. The conversion of a whole customary number usually produces a decimal metric number. For example, 20 feet is equal to 6.096 meters. This is one reason that people feel uncomfortable with the metric system. However, someday the United States may switch completely over to

Fig. 6-2. In metrics, measurements are expressed in terms relative to the basic unit of measure by using different prefixes.

Prefix + Basic Unit =		Metric term	Value
milli- (m)	+ meter (m) liter (l) gram (g)	millimeter (mm) = milliliter (ml) milligram (mg)	$\frac{1}{1000}$th of basic unit
centi- (c)	+ meter liter gram	centimeter (cm) = centiliter (cl) centigram (cg)	$\frac{1}{100}$th of basic unit
kilo- (k)	+ meter liter gram	kilometer (km) = kiloliter (kl) kilogram (kg)	1000 basic units
mega (M)	+ watt (W)	= megawatt (MW)	1,000,000 basic units
giga (G)	+ watt (W)	= gigawatt (GW)	1,000,000,000 basic units

To change a customary measurement to a metric measurement, multiply the customary measurement by the metric equivalent of the basic customary unit used.
Example: To change 127 pounds to kilograms, multiply 127 lbs. × .4536 kg = 57.61 kg

Measurement	Customary Unit	Metric Equivalent
Length	1.000 inch (in.) 1.000 foot (ft.) 1.000 yard (yd.)	2.540 centimeters (cm) .3048 meter (m) .9144 meter (m)
Distance	1.000 mile (mi.)	1.609 kilometers (km)
Area	1.000 square inch (sq. in.)	6.452 square centimeters (sq. cm)
Volume	1.000 cubic inch (cu. in.)	16.387 cubic centimeters (cu. cm)
Mass (Weight)	1.000 ounce (oz.) 1.000 pound (lb.)	28.349 grams (g) 0.4536 kilogram (kg)
Force	1.000 pound (lb.)	4.448 newtons (N)
Torque	1.000 pound-foot (lb.-ft.)	1.356 newton-meters (N-m)

Pressure	1.000 pound per square inch (psi)
	
	1.000 inch of mercury (Hg) (at 60° F)
		6895 pascals (Pa) or
		  6.895 kilopascals (kPa)
		3377 pascals (Pa) or
		  3.377 kilopascals (kPa)

Energy
  Mechanical
  Heat
 	
  Electrical
	
	1.000 foot-pound (ft.-lb.)
	1.000 British Thermal Unit (BTU)
	
	1.000 joule (J)
		
		1.356 joules (J)
		1054 joules (J),
		  252 small calories (c), or
		  0.2520 large Calorie (C)
		1.000 joule (J)

Power
  Mechanical
  Heat
 	
  Electrical
	
	1.000 horsepower (hp)
	1.000 British Thermal Unit
	  per second (BTU/s)
	1.000 watt (W)
		
		746 watts (W)
		1054 watts (W)
		
		1.000 watt (W)

Temperature	To change degrees Fahrenheit (°F) to degrees Celsius (°C), use the formula:
	°C = 0.56 (°F − 32)
	Example: Change 68° F into degrees Celsius: °C = 0.56 (68-32)
	                                 °C = 0.56 (36)
	                                 °C = 20

Fig. 6-3. Conversion table: customary to metric.

the metric system. People will begin to think in terms of metric numbers, just as they now think in terms of customary numbers. For example, we may think of a very tall person as being over two meters tall, just as we now think of a tall person as being over six feet tall. (Two meters is just over six feet, six inches.)

Metric/customary conversions do not affect our measurements of time. The traditional measurements of time—the second, minute, hour, day, and year—are universal. They are used everywhere.

MEASURING ENERGY AND POWER

As people learned to control energy, they developed ways to measure energy and power. Through measurement, it is possible to find out

To change a metric measurement to a customary measurement, multiply the metric measurement by the customary equivalent of the basic metric unit used. *Example:* Change 175 kilometers to miles. 175 km × 0.6214 mi. = 108.7 mi.

Measurement	Metric Unit	Customary Equivalent
Length	1.000 millimeter (mm) 1.000 centimeter (cm) 1.000 meter (m) 1.000 kilometer (km)	0.04 inch (in.) 0.3937 inch (in.) 3.281 feet (ft.) or 1.094 yards (yd.) 0.6214 mile (mi.)
Area	1.000 square centimeter (sq. cm)	0.1550 square inch (sq. in.)
Volume	1.000 cubic centimeter (cu. cm)	0.06102 cubic inch (cu. in.)
Mass (Weight)	1.000 gram (g) 1.000 kilogram (kg)	0.03527 ounce (oz.) 2.205 pounds (lbs.)
Force	1.000 newton (N)	0.2248 pound (lb.)
Torque	1.000 newton-meter (N-m)	0.7376 pound-foot (lb.-ft.)
Pressure	1.000 pascal (Pa) 1.000 kilopascal (kPa)	0.0001450 pound per square inch (psi) or 0.0002961 inch of mercury (in. of Hg) 0.1450 pound per square inch (psi) or 0.2961 inch of mercury (in. of Hg)

Energy
  Mechanical
  Heat
 	
  Electrical
	1.000 joule (J)
	1.000 joule (J)
	
	1.000 small calorie (c)
	
	1.000 large Calorie (C)
	
	1.000 joule (J)
		0.7376 foot-pound (ft.-lb.)
		0.0009485 British Thermal Unit (BTU)
		0.003968 British Thermal Unit (BTU)
		3.968 British Thermal Units (BTUs)
		1.000 joule (J)

Power
  Mechanical
  Heat
 	
  Electrical
	1.000 watt (W)
	1.000 watt (W)
	
	1.000 watt (W)
		0.001341 horsepower (hp)
		0.009485 British Thermal Unit per second (BTU/s)
		1.000 watt (W)

Temperature	To change degrees Celsius (°C) to degrees Fahrenheit (°F), use the formula: °F = 1.8°C + 32 Example: Change 20°C to degrees Fahrenheit: °F = 1.8 (20) + 32 °F = 36 + 32 °F = 68	

Fig. 6-4. Conversion table: metric to customary.

how much energy is needed to perform a particular task. We can also tell when we have developed enough energy to perform the task. Accurate measurement allows us to convert the correct amount of potential energy into kinetic energy. For example, we can figure out the electrical needs of a city by measuring the amount of power used by consumers. This tells us how much fuel must be converted into electrical energy at the power plant serving the city.

We commonly use a number of measurement terms to determine how much energy we have or need. In this section, you will learn how to use the following terms in calculations:

- Energy
- Work
- Power
- Force
- Torque
- Pressure
- Heat

Energy and Work

Energy has already been defined as the capacity to do work. **Work**, in turn, can be defined as useful motion, or motion that results in something useful being done. The motion produced by energy may be the movement of a rocket or the lifting of a weight. It may be the movement of electrons in a wire (electricity). It may be the movement of atoms and molecules (heat). Useful motion may also involve the *stopping* of something that is already moving. For example, the driver of a car applies the brakes to reduce the motion of the vehicle.

There is no work if nothing is accomplished. Imagine a man trying to lift a 1000-pound barrel. If he cannot move it at all, he does not perform any work. However, he *does* exert energy. Sensitive measuring instruments will show that the man gives off heat energy as he tries to lift the barrel. Arm and leg muscles are moved as the man tries to lift the barrel. Food is consumed by body cells and given off as heat during this process.

When we think in terms of measuring something, our definition of work must become more specific. Perhaps the best definition is that *work* is a measurement of mechanical energy. In the customary system, work (or mechanical energy) is measured in *foot-pounds (ft.-lbs.)*. One foot-pound of work is equal to the lifting of 1 pound a distance of 1 foot. The mathematical formula is:

Work = Weight (in pounds) × Distance (in feet)

Example problem:

How much work does a 120-pound person accomplish by climbing a 20-foot flight of stairs?

Work = 120 lbs. × 20 ft.
Work = 2400 ft.-lbs.

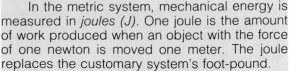

Using Metrics

In the metric system, mechanical energy is measured in *joules (J)*. One joule is the amount of work produced when an object with the force of one newton is moved one meter. The joule replaces the customary system's foot-pound.

1 J = .7376 ft.-lb.

In the metric system, electrical energy and heat energy are also measured in joules.

Power

Work is not a very complete measurement. Suppose a man were trying to move a 1000-pound barrel of nails up 20 feet to the second floor of a building. He can accomplish this task in two different ways. He could operate a crane to pick up the barrel and lift it the 20 feet in 20 seconds. Or, he could carry 100 pounds of nails up a ladder and make 10 round trips. The second method will get the nails to the second floor as well as the first method. But the second method might take 20 minutes. In each method, the amount of *work* done is the same. However, there is a big difference in the *time* it takes to do the work.

Obviously, the crane can do work much faster than the man. Since the measurement of work does not show this, we have to use another term—power. *Power* is defined as energy per second or energy per unit of time. Since energy is measured as work, power becomes work per unit of time.

Power, therefore, is a measurement of work accomplished in a given period of time. To increase power, we must do more work in a given period of time. We can also increase power by accomplishing a given amount of work in a shorter period of time.

Fig. 6-5. Force is measured in terms of weight, whether it is applied vertically or horizontally.

The crane in the previous example accomplished the same amount of work as the man. However, it accomplished the work in ¹⁄₆₀ of the time. Therefore, in the 20 seconds it took the crane to lift the nails, the crane produced 60 times the power of the man.

Horsepower (hp) is the most common measurement of power. It is based on the amount of work that a horse can do in one minute. When this standard was set, the amount of work done by the horse was multiplied by 1½. This makes 1 horsepower somewhat above the effort of a strong horse. Therefore, an engine with an output of 1 horsepower can normally do more work than a horse.

One horsepower is equal to the energy needed to lift 33,000 pounds 1 foot in 1 minute. This is the same as the energy needed to lift 550 pounds 1 foot in 1 second. In mathematical equation form:

$$1 \text{ hp} = \frac{33{,}000 \text{ foot-pounds}}{\text{minute}}$$

or

$$1 \text{ hp} = \frac{550 \text{ foot-pounds}}{\text{second}}$$

To calculate horsepower, we usually divide the foot-pounds of work by the time (in seconds) multiplied by 550. The formula is:

$$\text{hp} = \frac{\text{Weight (lbs.)} \times \text{Distance (ft.)}}{\text{Time (secs.)} \times 550}$$

Example problem:
How much horsepower does a 165-pound man develop in climbing a 20-foot flight of stairs in 12 seconds?

$$\text{hp} = \frac{165 \text{ lbs.} \times 20 \text{ ft.}}{12 \text{ sec.} \times 550}$$

$$\text{hp} = \frac{1}{2} \text{ or } 0.5$$

The *watt (W)* is a unit used to measure electrical power. It is equal to *one joule of electrical energy per second*. A toaster may use 800 watts of power. This means that 800 joules per second are needed to make the toaster's heating elements red-hot. The heating of the elements is the work that is accomplished.

In the same way, electrical energy does work in a light bulb by making a tungsten wire white-hot. A 100-watt bulb requires 100 joules per second of electrical energy to provide the correct amount of light.

Electric motors produce mechanical power. Therefore, they are usually measured by horse-

power. However, it takes a certain amount of electricity to operate a motor. For this reason, we can also measure the power of motors by watts. One horsepower is equal to 746 watts.

Using Metrics

In the metric system, power is measured in watts (W) instead of horsepower (hp). One watt of power is equal to one joule per second.
To convert horsepower to watts:
1 hp = 746 W
To convert watts to horsepower:
1 W = .001341 hp
Electrical power is measured in watts in both the customary and metric systems.

Force

Up to this point, we have used *weight* in calculating both work and horsepower. We can usually substitute *force* for weight in both calculations.

Force (F) is any push or pull on an object. The earth's **gravity** is a force that pulls down on every object on earth. When we speak of the *weight* of an object, we are really talking about how much gravity is pulling on the object. When we lift anything, we must exert a force equal to the pull of gravity on the object. Therefore, **weight** is considered to be force applied in a vertical (up and down) direction. We use pounds to measure this kind of force. See Fig. 6-5.

Force also applies to a push on an object in any direction. Again, see Fig. 6-5. Force applied in directions other than vertical is also measured in terms of weight—ounces, pounds, and tons.

The term "weight" is used instead of force only when measuring work in a vertical direction, as in simple lifting. In our calculations of work and horsepower, we will substitute force for weight. Therefore, our formula for work will be:

Work = Force × Distance

Example problem:
A man pushes a 200-pound weight a distance of 10 feet along the floor. He must exert a force of 55 pounds to slide the weight. How much work does the man accomplish?
Work = 55 lbs. × 10 ft.
Work = 550 ft.-lbs.

Technology Focus

Forces—The Known and The Unknown

Force is the mover of all nature, on earth and throughout the vast universe. Scientists have long believed that there are just four forces which produce and control all motion:

■ *Gravity*—the force of attraction between any two objects. Gravity explains why everything thrown up in the air, falls back down. It explains why the earth stays in orbit around the sun.

■ *Electromagnetism*—the force between charged particles. Electromagnetism explains how motors operate and why lightning flashes. It is the power of batteries and the attraction of electrons to protons. It's the "glue" that holds materials together.

■ *Strong force*—a binding force that occurs only within atoms. It binds the protons and neutrons together within the nucleus of an atom.

■ *Weak force*—a force that is also within atoms. It is the cause of radioactive decay.

Today, scientists are studying the possibility of a fifth or even sixth force. They have found that calculations performed according to Newton's universal law of gravitation do not always agree with actual measurements of gravitational force. And results vary.

One suspected force is related to *hypercharge*. If verified, it is a force which *counters* gravity. However, results of other tests seem to indicate a force that *helps* gravity! Either or both theories could be correct. And there could be other forces not yet suspected.

The forces beyond the major four seem to have minimum effects on earth. But they could be important forces within the universe. Or, perhaps there are earth applications that are now beyond imagination!

As we study and learn about the universe, we find that the *unknown* increases faster than the *known*. That is, the more we know, the more there is to learn.

Substituting force for weight also affects the formula for horsepower. (This is true for all situations except simple lifting. In lifting situations, force and weight are the same.) In equation form:

$$hp = \frac{Force \times Distance}{Time\ (secs.) \times 550}$$

Continuing with the last example, how much horsepower does the man produce if it takes him 20 seconds to slide the weight along the floor?

$$hp = \frac{55\ lbs. \times 10\ ft.}{20\ secs. \times 550}$$

$$hp = \frac{1}{20}\ or\ 0.05$$

Using Metrics

In the metric system, force is measured in newtons (N) instead of pounds (lbs.).

1 N = .2248 lb.

Torque

Force can also be measured in terms of *torque*. Torque is turning or twisting effort. We use torque whenever we turn a steering wheel, tighten a bolt, or twist the lid off a jar. Torque is the force applied to push the pedal of a bicycle around in a circle. It is also the force that turns the wheels on a car.

Notice that all of these examples of torque involve circular motion. **Torque** is a force applied to a radius. See Fig. 6-6. In the customary system, torque is measured in *pound-feet (lb.- ft.)*. We calculate torque by multiplying the force applied by the distance from the center of the object being turned: Torque = Force (lbs.) × Radius (ft.)

Example problem:

What is the torque when a force of 40 pounds is applied to a radius of 2 feet?

Torque = 40 lbs. × 2 ft.

Torque = 80 pound-feet

The units used to measure torque (pound-feet) and work (foot-pounds) may cause you to confuse torque with work. These terms are not the same. Torque is a certain kind of force only. It does not automatically accomplish anything. Work, on the other hand, always involves movement.

Work is force applied through a distance. The *foot* part of *foot-pounds* describes this distance. The measurement of torque also involves distance. The *feet* in *pound-feet* describes this distance. However, the distance involved in pound-feet is only the distance from the force to the center of the object being turned. Torque accomplishes work only when it moves *through* a distance. The wrench shown in Fig. 6-6 applies torque to the bolt head whether it actually moves the bolt or not.

Using Metrics

In the metric system, torque is measured in newton-meters (N-m). This is the force in newtons multiplied by the radius in meters.

The newton-meter replaces the customary system's pound-foot (lb.-ft.).

1 N-m = .7376 lb.-ft.

Pressure

Pressure is another measurement of force. Pressure is determined by the area over which a force is applied. Therefore, **pressure** is force per unit of area. For example, Fig. 6-7 shows a 100-pound weight with a base of 10 inches by 10 inches. The total area equals the length times the width.

Area = Length × Width

Area = 10 in. × 10 in.

Area = 100 sq. in.

The pressure is equal to the total force (weight) divided by the total area.

$$\text{Pressure} = \frac{\text{Force}}{\text{Area}}$$

$$\text{Pressure} = \frac{100 \text{ lbs.}}{100 \text{ sq. in.}}$$

$$\text{Pressure} = \frac{1 \text{ lb.}}{\text{sq. in.}} \text{ or } 1 \text{ lb./sq. in.}$$

Fig. 6-6. Torque is force applied to a radius. (A radius is one-half the diameter of a circle).

FORCE

RADIUS

TORQUE

Fig. 6-7. Pressure is the amount of force applied to a certain unit of area. The 100-pound block shown here applies 1 pound of force to each square inch of supporting area.

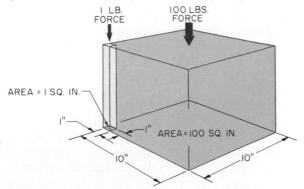

This means that the weight is "spread out" over the whole area. Each square inch of surface area supports only 1 pound. Note the units of the answer. *Pounds per square inch (psi)* is the most common unit for measuring pressure. (We use another unit—inches of mercury (in. of Hg)—to measure atmospheric pressure.)

The example in Fig. 6-7 helps to explain pressure. However, we do not commonly measure the force of solid objects in units of pressure. Units of pressure are normally used to measure the force exerted by fluids (gases or liquids).

A confined fluid under pressure exerts equal force on all enclosing surfaces. The air in an inflated balloon pushes with only a small pressure in all directions. However, it presses evenly over the entire inside surface area.

The fact that the balloon contains force can be shown by releasing the air. The escaping air can rotate a pinwheel or blow out a match.

We can calculate the total force produced by a certain amount of pressure. To do this, we simply multiply the pressure (force per unit area) by the total area. In the case of a balloon, suppose the inside surface area is 100 square inches and the pressure is ¼ pound per square inch.

Force = Pressure × Area
Force = ¼ psi × 100 sq. in.
Force = 25 lbs.

The difference between pressure and force is important. You must remember that pressure is a special measurement of force. It is force per unit of area. However, the *total* amount of force depends on the total amount of area. For example, Fig. 6-8 shows two pistons of different sizes. The small piston has an area of only 1 square inch. The large piston has an area of 10 square inches. The pressure above the piston in each cylinder is 50 pounds per square inch. However, this pressure produces different amounts of force.

Small Cylinder:
Force = Pressure × Area
Force = 50 psi × 1 sq. in.
Force = 50 lbs.

Large Cylinder:
Force = 50 psi × 10 sq. in.
Force = 500 lbs.

The large piston produces 10 times the force of the small piston. However, a given amount of air will move it only ⅟₁₀ the distance of the small piston.

Using Metrics

In the metric system, pressure is measured in *pascals (Pa)*. One pascal is the force of one newton acting on an area of one square meter.

The pascal replaces the customary unit of pounds per square inch (psi). Because the pascal is so small, measurements are often given in kilopascals (kPa).

1 kPa = .1450 psi or
.2961 in. of Hg

Heat

Heat energy is measured in **British thermal units (BTUs)**. As you recall from Chapter 1, the word "thermal" means heat. The BTU was originally used as a measurement by the British. One BTU is the heat needed to raise the temperature of 1 pound (about 1 pint) of water 1 degree Fahrenheit.

In itself, the BTU is a measurement of energy, not power. This is because power is energy per unit of time. However, we can and do measure heat energy in BTUs per hour.

We can convert heat energy into power with engines. When we do this, we lose most of the heat. It goes off into the air or is absorbed by the metal of the engine. In fact, in typical gasoline engines, only one-fifth of the available heat is changed into power. If all the available heat were

Fig. 6-8. Here the same amount of pressure (force per unit of area) is being applied to the top of each piston. However, there is 10 times as much force exerted on the large piston as there is on the small piston.

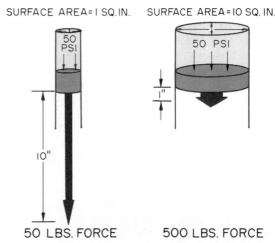

SURFACE AREA=I SQ.IN.   SURFACE AREA=IO SQ.IN.

50 PSI   50 PSI

IO"   I"

50 LBS. FORCE   500 LBS. FORCE

changed into power, a heat energy input of 2546 BTUs/hour would be needed to maintain an output of 1 horsepower. In actual practice, 10,000 to 20,000 BTUs/hour are necessary.

Another common unit of measurement for heat energy is the **calorie**. There are two kinds of calories: the small calorie (c) and the large Calorie (C). One small *calorie* is the amount of heat needed to raise the temperature of 1 cubic centimeter (about 1 tablespoon) of water 1 degree Celsius. A small calorie is much smaller than a BTU. One BTU equals 252 calories. One large *Calorie* equals 1000 times as much heat as in a small calorie. At the present time, we use the large Calorie to measure the amount of heat energy available to us in the food we eat.

The calorie is a measurement based on the metric system. However, when we fully convert to the SI metric system, we will not use the calorie. Instead, we will use the joule.

Using Metrics

In the metric system, heat energy is measured in calories (c) and joules (J). However, heat energy is expected to eventually be measured only in joules.

1 J = .238 c
1 c = 4.2 J

The joule will also replace the British thermal unit (BTU) used in the customary system to measure heat energy.

1 BTU = 1054 J or 252 c

MEASURING ENGINE POWER

We can measure the power produced by an engine with a **dynamometer**. A dynamometer determines the work that the engine can accomplish in a given period of time.

There are three basic kinds of dynamometers:
- Prony brake
- Hydraulic
- Electric

Each kind operates by putting a *load* on the engine. A load is any resistance to an engine's power. The engine is operated to its maximum power while the load is increased. A scale registers the amount of force needed to offset (balance) the engine's torque (turning force).

You can think of the dynamometer load as something that absorbs energy (converts energy

to a form it can measure and then discard). The load may be a brake lining, water, or electrical resistance. The load converts the engine's mechanical energy into heat energy. In this process, the heat energy is absorbed by air or water and discarded.

Prony Brake Dynamometer

One of the simplest and earliest developed dynamometers was the prony brake dynamometer. The prony brake is rarely used today, but its principle is the basis for all dynamometers. Basically, the prony brake consists of a braking device, a scale, and a **tachometer**. The tachometer measures the speed of the engine's rotating motion in revolutions per minute (rpm).

To understand how a prony brake works, consider the testing of a simple "engine"—a bicycle. A person pedaling a bicycle is the source of power. A stand holds the bicycle off the ground.

A braking device is attached to the top of the bicycle wheel. The braking device consists of two pieces of rough material. These pieces can be tightened against the tire. As the wheel rotates, it tries to carry the brake around with it. However, a wire attached to the scale keeps the brake from moving.

The scale shows the amount of force required to offset the torque driving the wheel. As the brake is tightened, the rider must exert more effort to turn the wheel. The scale registers this torque in pounds.

To determine horsepower, we must first calculate how much work the rider is doing. Remember, work equals force times distance. The scale tells us the force. The distance in this case is the distance around the wheel (its circumference). The formula for circumference is:

Circumference = 2πr
Where:

$$\pi = \frac{22}{7} \text{ or } 3.14$$

r = radius of a circle in feet

We also must find how far the force moves in 1 minute. To do this, we multiply the wheel circumference by the number of times the wheel revolves in 1 minute. The tachometer provides this number—the revolutions per minute (rpm). This is a measure of the wheel's *speed*. **Speed** is distance per unit of time. The formula for total distance, then, is:

Distance = Circumference (2πr) × rpm

We are now ready to calculate horsepower. First we set up the formula for horsepower. Then we "plug in" our values for force, distance, and time. (We are using the "minute" formula for horsepower because the tachometer provides a *per minute* reading.)

$$hp = \frac{Distance \times Force}{Time \ (min.) \times 33,000}$$

$$hp = \frac{2\pi r \times rpm \times F}{33,000}$$

Example problem:

A bicycle has a rear-wheel diameter of 24 inches. A person pedals the bicycle at a speed of 140 rpm (a speed of 10 miles per hour for this bike). The brake is tightened until the person is working as hard as possible to keep the wheel turning at 140 rpm. The scale reads 20 pounds. What horsepower is being produced at this speed?

$$hp = \frac{2\pi r \times rpm \times F}{33,000}$$

Where:

$$r = \frac{24 \ in.}{2} = 12 \ in. = 1 \ ft.$$

$$rpm = 140$$
$$F = 20 \ lbs.$$
$$hp = \frac{2 \times 3.14 \times 1 \times 140 \times 20}{33,000}$$

$$hp = .533$$

The prony brake dynamometer uses a different kind of braking device for automobile engines. A large brake lining and drum are used to absorb the engine's power output. The brake lining changes the engine's mechanical energy into heat energy through friction.

Hydraulic Dynamometer

The hydraulic dynamometer uses water as a brake on engine output. It is used in automobile testing. See Fig. 6-9.

In a horsepower test, the rear wheels of the car turn rollers. The rollers drive a pump that pumps water into a turbine. The turbine can be adjusted to resist the flow of water. It acts much like the brake on the prony brake dynamometer.

The turbine's resistance to the flow of water raises the water pressure. A scale registers the rate of flow and increasing pressure. The higher the pressure, the greater the power output.

As with the prony brake, the energy produced by the engine is disposed of as heat. The pumping action and the turbine's resistance to water flow raise the temperature of the water.

Electric Dynamometer

The most precise and accurate type of dynamometer is the electric dynamometer. It is used in research and development and wherever precise measurements are important.

Figure 6-10 shows how an electric dynamometer works. The engine drives a generator that produces electricity. The engine's power output is determined by the amount of electricity it produces. The electric dynamometer gives its measurements in watts. These values are then converted into horsepower.

The load on the engine is changed by changing the resistance to the flow of electricity. This is done with electrical resistors. They act much like the brake on the prony brake dynamometer. As the resistance increases, the engine must work harder to generate electricity.

As with the other dynamometers, the energy produced is disposed of as heat. As the flow of electricity increases, the heat developed at the resistors increases.

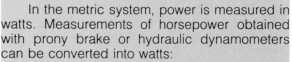

Using Metrics

In the metric system, power is measured in watts. Measurements of horsepower obtained with prony brake or hydraulic dynamometers can be converted into watts:

1 hp = 746 W

Since the electric dynamometer provides measurements directly in watts, there is no need to convert the values into metric terms. However, they may be converted into horsepower:

1 watt = .001341 hp

Fig. 6-9. Using a hydraulic dynamometer to test an automobile engine.

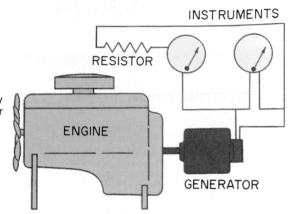

Fig. 6-10. Electric dynamometers measure engine power by the amount of electricity the power generates. The power reading is given directly in watts.

DISTINCTION: ENERGY AND POWER

At this point, you should be able to understand the difference between energy and power. The distinction is important in order to understand why we speak of *sources of energy* at one point, and why we speak of engine output in terms of *power*.

As previously defined, energy is the capacity to do work. In this definition, we are referring to potential energy. The definition can be changed to kinetic energy by defining energy as the accomplishment of work or as work performed. The measurements of energy are the same as the measurements of work: foot-pounds in mechanical energy and BTUs in heat energy. In metrics, the measurements are easier to understand. All energy is measured in joules.

Power is energy per unit of time. Horsepower, for example, is foot-pounds (energy) per unit of time. One horsepower equals 550 foot-pounds per second. Therefore, power is a measurement of energy. However, it is a specific amount of energy applied for a specific period of time. The measurement of power is in horsepower for mechanical power and in BTUs/hour for heat (thermal) power. In metrics, the measurement is easier to understand. All power is measured in watts. A watt is one joule per second.

When we study *energy sources*, we are concerned with potential energy. We know that our modern society needs kinetic energy to maintain itself. We get kinetic energy from potential energy. Therefore, the first step is to obtain potential energy.

Once we have potential energy, we put it to use by converting it into kinetic energy. We have *power* when we can apply kinetic energy over a period of time to do work.

DEVELOPING POWER FROM ENERGY

The three common forms of power in use are electrical, mechanical, and fluid. Most people easily recognize two of these forms of power. *Electrical power* provides light and operates motors. *Mechanical power* moves automobiles, trains, and airplanes.

Fluid power is equally important but not as recognizable. It is the use of fluids (gases or liquids) to produce motion. Fluid motion operates hydraulic (liquid) brakes in automobiles and air brakes in trucks. Fluid power also operates the moving parts of most heavy construction equipment, such as road graders and earth movers.

Power, like energy, can be changed from one form to another. Electrical power can operate an electric motor to produce motion per unit of time (mechanical power). The same motor can drive a hydraulic pump to produce fluid power. Mechanical power can turn a generator to produce electrical power. Each of these forms of power can easily be changed into either of the other forms.

Most of the power we develop comes from burning a fuel in an engine. This produces motion. We use this motion to power automobiles, ships, and other transportation devices. We also use it to generate electricity and operate machinery. Engineers have developed many types of engines to produce power from the energy in fuels. Sections III and IV will describe the operation of the most important of these engines.

Chapter 6—Review

Testing Your Knowledge

Briefly answer each of the following questions. Write on a separate piece of paper.

1. What is the formal name for the metric system?
2. Give the meaning of the following prefixes: milli-, centi-, and kilo-.
3. How do you convert a customary measurement into a metric measurement?
4. How much is one horsepower?
5. What is a watt?
6. How is torque measured?
7. In what units is pressure usually measured?
8. What is a British Thermal Unit (BTU)? Is it a measurement of energy or power?
9. What is a dynamometer used for? Name the three basic kinds of dynamometers and tell which is the most accurate.
10. What is the only metric measurement for energy? for power?
11. Name the three common forms of power.
12. How do we develop most of the power used to produce motion?

 Solve these problems:

13. What is the length of a 50-meter Olympic swimming pool in feet? in yards?
14. One thousand kilograms is close to a customary ton. Is it over or under one ton? By how much?
15. The distance between two cities is 60 miles. How far apart are the cities in kilometers?
16. A football field is 100 yards from goal to goal. What is the distance in meters?
17. How many watts is the equivalent of 6 horsepower?
18. Each story of a 22-story building is 10 feet. How much work does a 180-pound person do in climbing to the top of the building? If the climb takes 6 minutes, what is the average horsepower produced?

19. A 4000-pound pickup truck was pushed ½ mile by 4 people. A force of 200 pounds is required to move the truck. How much work was accomplished? How much work did each person do if each did his or her share? (Note: 5280 feet equal 1 mile).
20. A locomotive mechanic grips a wrench 3 feet from the center of a 1-inch bolt. What torque is applied to the fitting if a force of 150 pounds is needed to loosen the bolt?
21. A small engine is connected to a bicycle. The bicycle has a rear wheel with a diameter of 28 inches. At 250 rpm (approximately 21 mph), the bicycle exerts a maximum resistance of 18 pounds. What horsepower is being produced by the engine at this speed?

Expressing Your Knowledge

Using complete sentences, write your answers to the following on a separate sheet of paper:

1. Why is it important to measure energy?
2. Define work. How much is one foot-pound of work?
3. Define power in terms of energy and work.
4. How are force and torque similar?
5. Explain the difference between torque and work.
6. How are force and pressure different?
7. Explain the difference between a small calorie (c) and a large Calorie (C).
8. Explain the distinction between energy and power?

Applying Your Knowledge

Follow your teacher's instructions to complete these activities:

1. Set up an experiment to measure torque with torque wrenches. Obtain a number of torque wrenches of different lengths. Use a spring scale to pull the wrench.

   Place the wrench on a "tight bolt" or a bolt held in a vise. Using the spring scale, make a table showing force (spring scale) times the length of torque arm. Compare your calculations with the torque reading on the wrench.

   Your table should contain at least three readings with three different wrenches (different lengths).

2. Determine the horsepower you are able to develop. The procedures for conducting this activity are provided in the ***Student Workbook***.

3. Identify places in your community which use the metric system. Find out if there are plans to convert to metrics in other businesses or industries. This study can include library research, factory observations, and meeting with community leaders. Prepare a report describing your findings.

Activity Number	Wrench Length	Force	Calculated Torque	Torque Wrench Reading
1				
2				
3				
4				
5				
6				
7				
8				
9				

Chapter 7

Automated Control Systems

The automatic control of mechanical devices has grown from using simple control devices like home thermostats to the use of complex devices such as computers and microprocessors in homes, businesses, and industries. This growth has occurred in less than 20 years and is changing the ways in which we live, work, and play.

Expanding Your Knowledge

As you study this chapter, you will learn to:

- Explain what is meant by an automated control system.
- Describe the three separate functions of an automated control system and explain the purpose of each.
- Identify the difference between a microprocessor and a computer.
- Describe the operation of a microprocessor and a computer in an automated control system.
- Identify the expanding use of automated control systems.
- Describe the use of robots in modern industries.
- Discuss the social problems introduced by automated control systems and robotics.

Building Your Word Power

The following terms are defined and explained in this chapter. Learning these will help you learn more about automated control systems.

automated control
central processing unit (CPU)
computer
input
memory
microprocessor
output
programming
robot
robotics
sensing devices

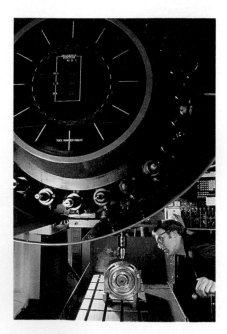

This chapter is designed to help you realize the importance of automated control in using energy and power. You will see how automated control systems work, and how sensing and control devices are used. Special emphasis is placed on understanding the use of microprocessors and computers in this process. We will also examine the growing use of robots.

The final section covers an important concern—the social effects of the increasing use of automated systems (automation), including its effects on the work force of the nation.

Fig. 7-1. A microwave oven can be set to cook at different temperatures automatically.

AUTOMATED CONTROL

All around us, things are controlled automatically. For example, a house is kept warm in winter by a furnace controlled by an instrument (sensor) that senses temperature change—a thermostat.

Another simple example is the automatic washer. After loading the machine with clothes and adding detergent, we let the machine do the rest. It fills the tub, washes, rinses, and spins. And it does all these processes automatically.

Both devices just described are relatively simple and have been in use for many years. In recent years, however, automated control has become more complex. The development of the *computer* has made complex automated control systems possible. See Fig. 7-1.

Our operating definition of **automated control** is simply *self-acting or self-adjusting*. This means that we can give an automated control system a set of directions that it will carry out automatically.

There are three separate functions of an automated control system:
■ Sensing—the "senses," usually instruments.
■ Control—the "brains," usually computers or microprocessors.
■ Operating—the "muscles," usually electric or fluid power devices.

Figure 7-2 is a graphic illustration of how these functions combine to provide automated control. Although the diagram appears simple, an automated control system is usually quite complex.

Sensing Devices

Sensing devices (sensors) are instruments that sense and measure conditions such as distance, temperature, pressure and time, and either display or pass the information on to a control device (microprocessor).

An instrument familiar to most people is the home thermostat. See Fig. 7-3. Thermostats may

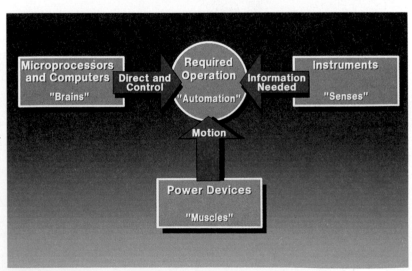

Fig. 7-2. The three basic parts of an automated control system.

be simple devices which measure and display home temperature. They also act as the *control device*, turning on the furnace when the temperature drops.

Thermostats can also be complex devices. A thermostat might contain two temperature sensing units (one to measure inside temperature and one to measure outside temperature). It may have a clock that can note the time of day or night and a microprocessor which "understands" the information and *controls* the furnace accordingly.

Your automobile also has instruments which give you operating conditions. For example, a *speedometer* measures the speed of the car, an *odometer* shows how many miles the car has been driven, and a *fuel gage* shows how much fuel is in the tank. Gages or warning lights may be used to alert the driver to problems with the engine or battery.

Following are some of the general conditions that instruments can check and report on:

■ *Temperature* control is important in homes, businesses, and industries. It is also important in many industrial processes. For example, steelmaking and welding require careful temperature control.

■ *Pressure* must be measured and controlled in all fluid power systems. Pressure gages and pressure control valves are used for this purpose.

■ *Speed* control is important in both transportation and manufacturing for efficiency and safety.

■ *Time* is important in many automated control systems. Timers are used in many home appliances. In manufacturing, each part must be delivered to the assembly line at just the right time.

■ *Dimensions* are the measurements that describe the size of objects. For example, a metal box has width, length, and height. Special instruments check the dimensions of objects as they are manufactured. See Fig. 7-4. Without this checking, automated machines could not accurately form metal, drill and tap holes, or do many other machining operations.

■ *Location* sensors are also needed in automated production. There are many types of location instruments. Some use laser beams, some use a kind of radar, and some use TV cameras. Of course, a location sensor can also be very simple, like a mechanical switch.

The things just mentioned are only a few examples of the conditions that instruments can monitor (keep track of).

Control Devices

Some automated systems can be controlled by simple devices. The automatic washer, described earlier, can be controlled by a clock which trips a series of switches.

With the development of computers and microprocessors, more detailed control is possible. The microprocessor or computer retains information and instructions and uses this data to provide more complex control.

Fig. 7-3. Practically every home has a thermostat in or near the living area. It senses temperature changes and turns the furnace on or off.

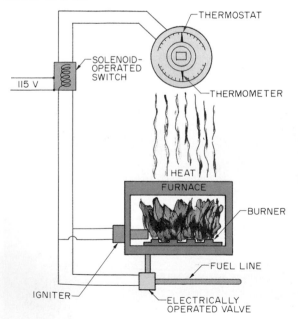

Fig. 7-4. Seventy different features of this engine block are being inspected automatically.

The terms "microprocessor" and "computer" are sometimes interchanged. But it is possible to be more precise. A **microprocessor** is a small processing unit. Microprocessors are designed to do specific tasks. The instructions to accomplish a task are built into a microprocessor during manufacturing. Sometimes a microprocessor can be given added instructions. But its basic purpose and function remain the same.

Computers are multipurpose microprocessors which can be *programmed* to perform different functions. **Programming** is the procedure used to give computers the operating instructions and data needed to perform the job. Thus the basic difference is that microprocessors have a single predetermined program while computers may have their programs changed to perform different tasks.

In an automated system, the control device (computer or microprocessor) receives information from sensing devices and provides instructions and directions to the operating devices based on this information.

Operating Devices

An automated control system is always designed to "do something." This "something" may vary from providing a smooth automobile ride to maintaining home temperatures (Fig. 7-3), to flying an airplane. See Fig. 7-5. It often involves movement or passing instructions via electronics.

In the system shown in Fig. 7-5, an automatic pilot sends instructions to all the operating devices including engines, flight controls, and landing gear. Adjustments are made by air, oil, or electric motors and other devices. These are the **output** or *operating devices* of automated systems.

MICROPROCESSOR AND COMPUTER OPERATION

We can now redesign Fig. 7-2 which showed the elements of the automated system. In that illustration, the "required operation" was shown as the center, since it was the reason the system existed. We now know the operation is the "output." Figure 7-6 shows the information flow providing the automated system. Note that the microprocessor or computer is central to the operation of the system.

The **input** may be information from instruments or sensing devices. It can also be provided by people in a variety of other ways, such as keyboarding, touching a number, or touching a specific instruction control (on mixers, microwave ovens, etc.).

Memory is stored information. Memory can include special instructions or information from a variety of sensing devices or other inputs. The memory is held until the central processing unit uses the information as it controls output.

The **central processing unit (CPU)** is the "heart" of the computer or microprocessor. It is connected to all three functions (input, memory, and output). The CPU receives information from input devices, analyzes the information using appropriate instructions from memory, and directs the output based on all the information available. The output *device* follows the instruction of the CPU, performing the needed task.

USES OF MICROPROCESSORS AND COMPUTERS

In just 20 years, the microprocessor and computer have moved from being scientific and research tools to being an integral part of nearly all businesses and industries. The following are just a few examples of the growing use of microprocessors and computers:
■ Home.

Microprocessors control refrigerators, mixers, clock radios, microwave ovens, telephones, and temperature control. Refer back to Figs. 7-1 and 7-3.
■ Automobile.

Today, nearly 10% of the cost of some modern automobiles is for computer and microprocessor electronic controls. These include the ignition and fuel systems, dash instruments, radio,

Fig. 7-5. An automatic pilot can fly and even land a plane.

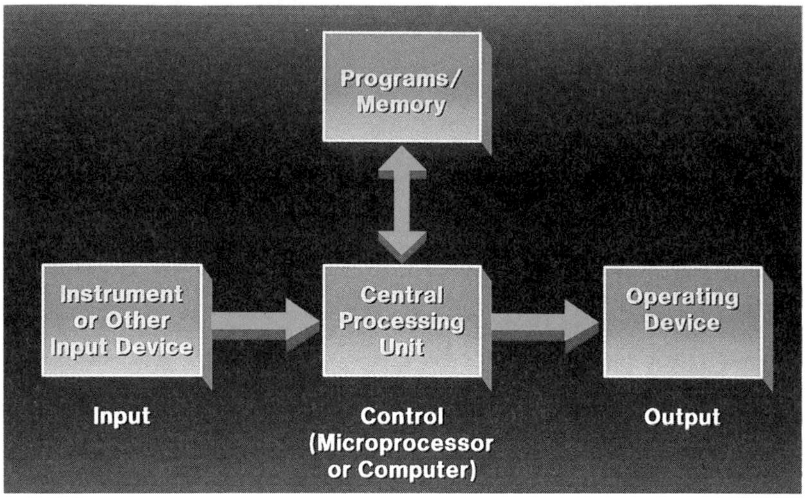

Fig. 7-6. An automated system. The microprocessor/computer is central to the operation of the system.

Programs/Memory

Instrument or Other Input Device → Central Processing Unit → Operating Device

Input

Control (Microprocessor or Computer)

Output

Technology Focus

Alcyone: Daughter of the Wind

Alcyone: Daughter of the Wind is an experimental sailing ship. It is the product of modern technology: wind tunnel testing, instrumentation measurements, and computer analysis and design.

Alcyone is 102 feet (31.1 m) long. The hull was designed with computer assistance to ensure a stable and safe vessel.

The sails, called *Turbosails*TM, are a unique design using many of the characteristics of an airplane wing. The principle of *lift*, which permits a plane to fly, is used to provide forward thrust. Each Turbosail is mounted on end and provides 3.5 to 4 times the thrust of the best conventional sail the same size. Turbosails are efficient, take up minimum deck space, and are simple to control and handle.

A *computer* is the "heart" of ship operations. The computer control system can operate the ship on sail only, diesel engine only, or a combination of both. The combination can be set to operate at a planned course and speed, with minimum fuel consumption. *Sensors* measure wind direction and intensity, speed and direction of the ship, and water characteristics. This information is continuously fed into the computer. The computer analyzes the information and determines sail, engine, and rudder settings. This information is passed on to *actuators* which automatically make the proper settings and operate the ship.

Design principles used for the Alcyone are being considered for larger ships, such as ocean-going tankers. The Alcyone has shown that electronics and computer techniques have a place in the future of navigation.

suspension, and steering. The average cost per automobile is just under $600 and is expected to rise to nearly $900 by the early 1990s.

■ Energy and power sources.

All aspects of energy and power sources are being controlled by computers and microprocessors. They have become basic to all control systems. A review of Chapters 2-5 will reveal the heavy reliance on computer and microprocessor control.

■ Transportation and manufacturing.

As with energy and power sources, all aspects of transportation and manufacturing are being controlled by computers and microprocessors. These devices operate machines, control the flow of materials for assembly, and operate production lines. They fly airplanes, control the movement and scheduling of trains, and keep track of goods being shipped.

ROBOTICS

Robotics is the study of the construction, maintenance, and use of *robots*. In the past, "robots" were thought of as machines that resemble human beings. Actually, **robots** are computer-controlled devices which perform tasks usually done by humans. The basic industrial robot in wide use today is an "arm" which moves to perform industrial operations. It is controlled by an automated control system like those previously described. Tasks are specialized and vary tremendously. They include assembly, machining, and all types of other industrial operations. See Fig. 7-7.

Some robots can identify items and locations. A "bin-picking" robot, for example, can find and pick up the proper piece from a bin of mixed pieces. This type of robot uses a vision system consisting of a TV camera and computer vision analysis which identifies the piece to be picked up by the robot. A touch-sensitive gripper tells the robot that it has picked up the correct piece.

Systems are also being developed which permit robots to move about manufacturing plants without bumping into things. Such a robot must be able to "see" people and avoid collisions by stopping operations. This is an important safety feature.

Robots can perform tasks that are dangerous for humans to do. For example, a robot in a nuclear power plant can operate in radioactive areas, locations where humans cannot safely go.

THE FUTURE OF AUTOMATED SYSTEMS

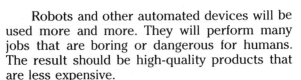

Robots and other automated devices will be used more and more. They will perform many jobs that are boring or dangerous for humans. The result should be high-quality products that are less expensive.

One of the main social concerns about automation is its displacement of human workers. Years ago, a factory might have needed hundreds of human workers. Now, with automation, the same plant can be run by only a few people. These people supervise and maintain the automated systems.

Employment is a very real concern. As automation is used more and more, there will be fewer of the traditional "blue collar" jobs available in the heavy industries. There will be a growing need for people to operate computers and maintain automated systems. However, the number of jobs created by automation is likely to be less than the number displaced. This factor could affect career decisions you will make in the future.

Automated control systems provide a good example of the advantages and disadvantages of technology. Automation will make our lives easier in many ways. But it can also force us as individuals and as a society to make some very tough decisions. Technology is changing our world rapidly. It offers both challenges and opportunities.

Fig. 7-7. Robots are used in this auto assembly line to weld parts together.

CHANGES IN MANUFACTURING PROCESS AND MATERIALS

Many improvements in both manufacturing processes and use of materials have resulted from the following factors:
- The growing world-wide competition for quality and defect-free products.
- The need for conservation of fuel and natural resources.

These needs are being met through the expansion of automated control systems and growing research efforts in the use of materials.

Process Control

The automated control systems described in this chapter are being applied to quality assurance systems. These systems assure that manufactured products are virtually defect free. Other aspects of research emphasize the use of materials that lead to products that will give trouble-free service for many years.

Figure 7-8 shows a process control system designed to monitor hundreds of manufacturing steps. In addition, quality measures check whether the manufactured product meets specifications, thus meeting quality assurance standards.

Today, manufacturing processes combine the sensing ability of sensors with the memory and analysis capabilities of computers. The result is accurate information for monitoring the quality of manufacturing. A valuable result is the ability to correct potential defects before they occur.

Use of Materials

Research in the use of materials has produced many changes in the products we use. Many new materials are stronger and provide longer life. Others are corrosion free and require less care and maintenance. Still others are less expensive and provide more economical products.

In transportation, a growing need for both quality and fuel economy has pushed the introduction of new materials. The less an automobile weighs, the less fuel it uses. As a result, many metal parts in automobiles have been replaced with plastic parts.

In the future we may see automobile frames manufactured of aluminum instead of steel. See Fig. 7-9. Also, automobile frame sections may be held together by adhesives, rather than by rivets or welds. The chassis shown in Fig. 7-9 uses a limited number of spot welds to hold the chassis together while adhesives set. Adhesives (glue) provide the bonding strength, not the spot welds.

The use of new materials for both products and fasteners will continue to grow. The result will be products with greater strength, longer life, and less weight.

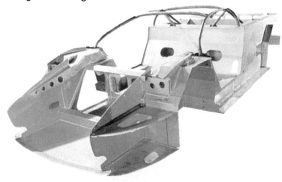

Fig. 7-9. This chassis is made of aluminum and held together by adhesives. The result is a stronger design that is also lighter in weight.

Fig. 7-8. A process control system brings together many manufacturing processes, providing information that monitors and controls the process.

Testing Your Knowledge

Briefly answer each of the following questions. Write on a separate piece of paper.
1. Identify one example of automatic control in the home.
2. What are the "brains," "senses," and "muscles" of an automated control system?
3. Name four conditions that instruments can check or monitor.
4. Identify the purpose of computer "memory."
5. Name four uses of microprocessors in the home.
6. List at least three tasks that a robotic "arm" can perform.
7. What is the main social concern for automation and automated control systems?

Expressing Your Knowledge

Using complete sentences, write your answers to the following on a separate sheet of paper.
1. Explain what is meant by an automated control system.
2. What is the major difference between a microprocessor and a computer?
3. Describe the role of a CPU in an automated control system.
4. Why is the ability to "see" important for the safe use of some robots?
5. Describe how automation and automated control systems are affecting employment. What may happen in the future?
6. Identify the two major needs of society that have resulted in improved manufacturing processes and materials.
7. Explain why weight is an important consideration in the design of transportation vehicles.

Applying Your Knowledge

Follow your teacher's instructions to complete these activities:
1. Conduct a survey of your home and describe the various automated devices in use. Include sensing devices, control devices, and operating devices.
Example: Smoke Alarm
- Sensor—senses smoke, does not react to other airborne materials, such as bug spray or perfume.
- Control—on/off (connect or disconnect alarm from power source). Power source is either battery or house current.
- Operating—buzzer, on only when smoke is present. Indicator lamp is on at all times, indicating availability of electricity to sound buzzer.

Other devices which might be in your home are a temperature sensing probe to control heat (in a roast), automatic outdoor lights, and garage door opener. Can you find others?

Develop a graphic illustration to show the results of your survey.
2. Identify how computers are used in one selected facet of energy, such as its sources, pollution control, conservation, engines, or mechanical, electrical, or fluid power systems. Your study may include library study, personal interviews, or visits to businesses and industries. Prepare a report describing how computers are used in your selected topic. You may be required to give an oral report on your topic.

Chapter 8

Conservation of Energy Resources

Energy conservation is not only using less energy. It also includes using energy in responsible ways. Good conservation practices today can help ensure adequate energy supplies in the future.

Expanding Your Knowledge

As you study this chapter, you will learn to:

- Explain why conservation of energy is important for the immediate future.
- Identify the four main areas of energy use which need to be studied in order to increase conservation.
- Explain how home energy can be saved in the high use areas of the home and in water heating.
- Describe ways that energy can be conserved in commercial, industrial, and transportation areas.
- Describe how the recycling of waste materials can aid the conservation of natural resources.

Building Your Word Power

The following terms are defined and explained in this chapter. Learning these will help you learn more about conserving our energy resources.

conservation of energy
energy efficiency rating (EER)
insulation
R-Value
recycling
waste disposal

This chapter describes the growing need for conservation and how it can be implemented. Emphasis is placed on energy conservation in the home, since this is an area in which everyone can participate. Special attention is given to the two largest uses of energy in the home—home heating and water heating. Use of insulation, window coverings, and sealing air leaks are three important methods of conserving energy.

Throughout the chapter, the role of the individual in practicing energy conservation is stressed. Without full individual support, conservation will not be successful.

THE NEED FOR CONSERVATION

Conservation of energy refers to the elimination of practices which waste energy. Conservation also includes using technology to eliminate waste and loss of energy. The easiest and quickest way to preserve our limited supply of fossil fuels is to reduce usage through conservation. Since the 1970s, when the price of oil rose rapidly due to political differences with Arab nations, we have made good progress on conserving energy. However, much more progress is possible.

Energy is one of our most important resources. Conserving our energy supplies can accomplish two things. First, we will make our present energy supplies last longer. Second, we can reduce pollution. (In the next chapter, you will learn more about how the use of energy creates pollution.)

Our nation's population continues to increase. We are developing new technologies, new labor-saving devices, and new forms of recreation. Most of these require the use of more energy. Our energy consumption could increase a great deal in the years ahead. Some power officials estimate that energy consumption could almost *triple* during the next 20 years! The increased use would force a greater use of fossil fuels at a time when we should be using less.

We could reduce our use of energy by conserving. An all-out conservation effort would result in a much smaller increase in energy use.

Conservation must occur in four areas:
- Home (residential)
- Commercial
- Industrial
- Transportation

(Refer back to Fig. 2-3.)

HOME ENERGY SAVINGS

Even though home use is below one-quarter of the total energy used, substantial energy savings can be made. Figure 8-1 shows the percentages of energy use in the home. If we apply the concept "emphasize energy savings in the areas of greatest use," we will look first at home heating and next at water heating. These two uses consume two-thirds of the energy used in the home.

Fig. 8-1. Percentages of total energy consumption for an average home. The "other" category includes home workshops, dishwashers, and the numerous powered devices in the home.

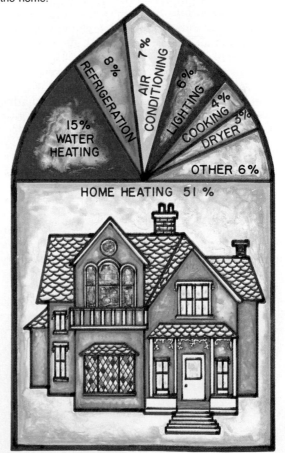

Home Heating

The heat placed in the home by the furnace is lost in three ways:

■ By conduction through walls and windows.
■ By radiation through windows.
■ By losing warm air to the outside through open doors and air leaks.

Insulation. Insulation can keep homes more comfortable in both cold and warm climates. In cold climates, insulation keeps the heat inside. In warm climates, insulation keeps the heat outside.

Insulation can be placed in ceilings, walls, and under the floor. Since hot air rises, the ceiling is the most important portion of the home to insulate. In many homes, just the walls and ceilings are insulated. But floor insulation can conserve considerable energy, especially in cold climates.

Figure 8-2 shows different forms of home insulation. Each form works in about the same manner. "Dead" air (air which doesn't move) is a good insulator. Most insulating materials trap air in thousands of tiny spaces in every cubic inch of insulation. These air spaces transmit very little heat, reducing heat transfer through the material. It's important to remember that insulation should not be "packed in." This would eliminate many of the air spaces and reduce the material's insulating properties.

Insulation effectiveness is measured by an **R-value**. R means *resistance* to heat flow. The higher the R-value, the greater the insulating power of the material. Typical home insulation values are R-11, R-19, and R-30.

Windows. Windows lose heat by radiation and conduction. They can also leak air. This is losing heat by convection. See Fig. 8-3A.

Windows can be insulated in a number of ways. The most common way is the use of some form of sealed covering. Figure 8-3B shows an unsealed window covering such as a shade or draperies. Note how convection currents carry warm air to the windowpane which loses heat by conduction.

Figure 8-3C shows a sealed covering which eliminates air leaks and the remaining heat lost by conduction. The sealed window cover could be a storm window or any of the many commercial window covers available.

Double- or triple-pane windows can reduce all three forms of energy loss shown in Fig. 8-3. Wooden frames on windows are also better insulators than metal frames.

Air Leaks. The third major loss of energy is by air leakage. Warm air may leak *out* of the home in winter and leak *into* the home in summer. Check your own home. On a cold winter day or a hot summer day, move your hand around windows and doors. Check the electrical outlets along outside walls. Do you feel an air flow? These are common places for air leaks. Plumbing and ventilation fan pipes also provide places for air to leak into or out of the home.

Air leaks are corrected by sealing the leak with either caulking compound or weather stripping. See Fig. 8-4. Caulking compound is a soft material used to fill openings and cracks. It *can't* be placed around windows or doors which open. These require weather stripping, a metal or other firm material which forms a seal around the window or door when you close it.

Water Heating

Over 3% of all the energy used in the United States is used to heat water for home use. Approximately 40% of the energy is wasted.

A gas water heater loses 55% of heat to standby loss. This is heat loss through the flue that carries away the waste heat. An electric heater loses less because it doesn't need a flue. In spite of this difference in heat loss, you may not truly be saving energy by using an electric heater. The added efficiency of the home electric water heater is more than offset by the inefficient

Fig. 8-2. Types of insulation include batt, blown-in, and insulating board.

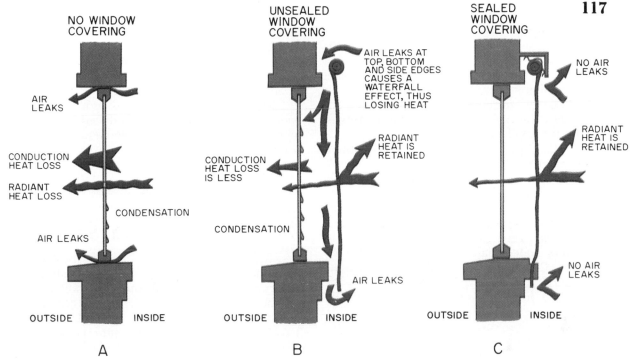

Fig. 8-3. An uninsulated window loses heat by radiation, conduction, and convection (A). An unsealed window cover reduces heat loss, but much still occurs (B). Sealing the cover improves insulation, reducing all types of heat loss (C).

use of energy in *producing* the electricity. Electrical power plants must discard over half of the heat, thereby operating at less than 50% efficiency.

Insulating a water heater is an important way to reduce a part of the standby loss. An insulation blanket can be wrapped around the tank of an electric water heater. Unless exposed, hot-water pipes can be insulated only during the construction process.

Another major way to conserve energy is to reduce the temperature and conserve on the use of hot water. Although a water heater can be kept at a temperature of 120°F (49°C), many are kept at 140°F (60°C), a temperature too high for

most home needs. Water-saving shower heads can also be used. Using such a head can reduce the water heating bills for a family of four by 25%.

Other conservation possibilities include running electric dishwashers with full loads of dishes, letting dishes dry without added heat (energy-saving cycles), and using cold water or *less* hot water for washing clothes.

Additional Home Savings

Conservation is also possible in the remaining third of home energy use. The National Bureau of Standards sponsors a program which

Fig. 8-4. Applying caulking compound and weather stripping.

identifies the efficiency of appliances used in the home. Appliances are given an **energy efficiency rating (EER)**. This rating is printed on a label that is attached to appliances. The label provides the following information:

■ The energy efficiency rating (EER) of the appliance. The higher the rating, the more efficient the appliance.

■ The efficiency range or energy consumption of similar products.

■ The estimated cost of operating the appliance for one year.

Figure 8-5 shows a typical EER label. These labels should be attached to all new refrigerators, ranges, ovens, dishwashers, freezers, washers, dryers, water heaters, furnaces, and air conditioners. Comparing these labels helps people save energy and money. And manufacturers are encouraged to construct energy-efficient appliances.

Conservation can also be practiced in the use of appliances and other electrical consumption in the home. Some of these are:

■ Use a microwave oven instead of a regular oven. The microwave is more efficient.

■ Use fluorescent lights instead of regular light bulbs.

Fig. 8-5. An EER label helps consumers pick the most energy-efficient appliance available.

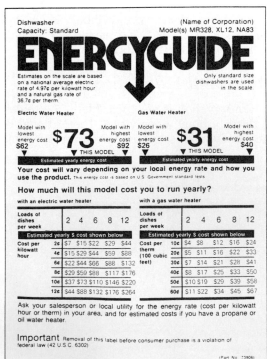

■ Adjust the air conditioner and the furnace at night. Set the air conditioner at a warmer temperature and the furnace at a lower temperature.

■ Shut off gas furnace pilot lights in summer.

If these methods are used properly, home energy consumption can be reduced by 50% or more. And what's more, people can save money without any loss of comfort!

COMMERCIAL AND INDUSTRIAL ENERGY SAVINGS

The greatest savings of energy must come from the largest users—business, industry, and government. Commercial and government uses account for over half of all the energy consumed.

Industry requires great amounts of heat. This heat is used to refine ore into metals, make glass and ceramics, and produce electrical power for millions of machines.

Conservation in business, industry, and government can be carried out in two main areas:

■ Planned conservation.

Planned practices include using cogeneration to heat buildings and water, using more efficient furnaces, controlling temperatures carefully, and shutting down furnaces when they are not needed.

■ Worker conservation practices.

Employees can make an effort to conserve energy as they work. For instance, workers can shut off truck engines while they are waiting to pick up loads. They can also keep doors to the outside shut to save on heat in the winter and air conditioning in the summer. If employees develop a "conservation attitude," energy waste can be reduced or eliminated.

TRANSPORTATION

Over one-quarter of all energy is used for transportation. This is an important area of conservation since oil provides most of the energy for transportation. Just think of the millions of cars in the United States! Most of them are powered by gasoline or diesel fuel.

There are two major ways to conserve energy in transportation. First, the weight of transportation vehicles can be reduced. For example, aluminum and plastic can be used instead of steel. Second, engines can be made more efficient.

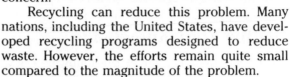

RECYCLING AND WASTE DISPOSAL

A major conservation effort is the recycling of used materials. **Recycling** is the reprocessing of used materials into a usable product or products. Recycling helps in two ways:

■ It saves energy since recycled materials require less energy than the use of new materials.
■ It reduces the need for waste disposal.

Recycling

Many states have passed recycling laws, or laws that encourage recycling. The most common laws are those requiring the payment of deposits on containers that can be recycled. These containers include aluminum cans, glass bottles, and plastic containers. Many of these state laws also establish procedures to collect and recycle the materials.

One of the oldest forms of recycling is the recycling of newspapers. Old paper can be reprocessed into newsprint at an economical cost. As a result, newspapers have been recycled for more than 50 years.

Recycling can be extended beyond the popular areas recognized above. Existing technology can recycle many waste products. Some of these are:

■ All metals, including automobiles, can be recycled. The problems are often the cost of separating metals from plastics and other materials.
■ Garbage and biological waste can be burned and converted to heat energy and electricity, or it can be processed into fertilizer. See Fig. 8-7.
■ Acids and industrial wastes can be neutralized and/or processed into useful materials.

The main problem of recycling is the combination of cost and financial incentives. In many situations, it is less expensive to discard waste and use new materials. The results may be a false economy and increased long-term costs to society in the form of landfills and hazardous wastes.

Waste Disposal

Waste disposal is a growing problem. **Waste disposal** is the discarding or destroying of sewage, garbage, and unwanted items. Many locations are used for the disposal of solid waste.

Waste also is dumped into rivers, lakes, or oceans. The hazardous nature of many waste products has made waste disposal a national concern.

Recycling can reduce this problem. Many nations, including the United States, have developed recycling programs designed to reduce waste. However, the efforts remain quite small compared to the magnitude of the problem.

The combined areas of *recycling and waste disposal* must be given a higher priority in research and development by the nations of the world.

THE FUTURE

The development of alternative energy sources requires research, capital investment, and time. Conservation practices can be put into effect quickly. Each of these approaches has the effect of reducing the need for fossil fuels. We must try to do both.

Conservation of energy is critical for both our long-term energy supplies and for the environment. Until we find a non-polluting energy source in an almost unlimited supply, we will need to carefully control the amount of energy we use.

Fig. 8-7. Waste materials can be processed into usable energy. Burning produces heat, which can be used to generate steam to operate steam turbines. The Robbins Resource Recovery Facility, a municipal waste-fired circulating fluidized bed plant to be built in a southern Chicago suburb, is designed to generate 40 MW of electric power.

Chapter 8—Review

Testing Your Knowledge

Briefly answer each of the following questions. Write on a separate piece of paper.

1. What two important things will we accomplish by practicing energy conservation?
2. Identify the four areas in which conservation must occur.
3. What percentage of our total supply of energy is consumed in homes?
4. Name the two home uses of energy which together make up two-thirds of home energy consumption.
5. Why should insulation be used in a warm climate?
6. Which insulating material would have the greater insulating power—one with an R-value of R-19 or one with an R-value of R-30?
7. Name two methods used to block air leaks.
8. Identify one way to reduce standby loss for water heaters.
9. From what areas must the largest savings in energy consumption come?
10. Name the two most important ways to conserve energy in transportation.
11. Which form of recycling has occurred for more than 50 years?

Expressing Your Knowledge

Using complete sentences, write your answers to the following on a separate sheet of paper:

1. What is meant by the "conservation of energy"?
2. Describe several ways in which heat is lost from a home.
3. Explain what an EER is and tell how it can be used to help people save energy and money.
4. Identify the two ways that recycling can help in conservation and the solving of social problems.
5. What is the main problem in the promotion of recycling?

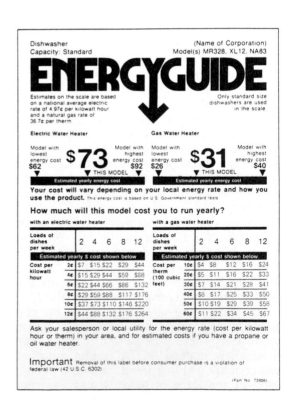

Applying Your Knowledge

Follow your teacher's instructions to complete these activities:

1. Conduct an experiment to determine which uses more energy—a bath or a shower. Use a bathtub with a shower unit. Do the following:
   - ■ Fill the tub to the normal level. Measure the depth of the water.
   - ■ How long does it take you to shower? Close the bathtub drain and allow the shower water to collect in the tub for that length of time. Measure the depth of water that has collected.
   - ■ Compare the depth of water used for a bath with that collected from the shower. Record your results.

   Can you determine the energy saved by the less wasteful method? It takes about ¼ kilowatt hour of electricity, one cubic foot of natural gas, or one ounce of oil to heat a gallon of water from 55°F (13°C) to 120°F (48°C). Determine cost savings by multiplying the energy saved by the cost of the energy.

2. Plan other experiments in your home to determine methods of conserving energy. For example, determine the cost of frequent opening and closing of the refrigerator door, or placing hot dishes in the refrigerator, or leaving the dryer running after clothes are dry, or running a partially filled dishwasher. Prepare a written report of your findings.

3. Develop an energy conservation plan for your home or school. Your plan could include the following items:
   - ■ A list of low-cost repairs that would increase energy efficiency (for example, caulking windows and weather stripping doors)
   - ■ A list of energy-conserving steps that cost nothing to perform (for example, lowering the hot water temperature and lowering the room temperature)
   - ■ A list of major steps that would conserve energy (for example, adding storm windows and adding insulation)

4. Prepare a report on energy conservation materials. Your report could include information on different types of insulation, different window coverings (for example, double- and triple-pane windows and plastic films), and weather-stripping materials.

Chapter 9

The Effects of Energy Use on the Environment

Almost every source of controlled energy produces pollution. Some sources are worse than others. Knowledge of potential pollution problems can help us to make decisions about the energy sources we use and to cope with—or even to prevent—the pollution of our environment.

Expanding Your Knowledge

As you study this chapter, you will learn to:

- Define pollution and identify the ways the use of energy causes pollution.
- Explain how smog is formed and identify its effects on people, plants, and construction materials.
- Describe the potential effects of the carbon dioxide buildup from burning fossil fuels.
- Explain how acid rain is formed and the effects it is having on the environment.
- Identify the pollution produced by burning wood and other forms of alternative energy sources.

Building Your Word Power

The following terms are defined and explained in this chapter. Learning these will help you learn more about the effects of energy use on the environment.

acid rain
carbon monoxide
earth warming
ecology
global pollution
hydrocarbons
oxident
oxidize
ozone
particulates
pollution
smog
temperature inversion
thermal pollution

Nearly every form of energy can have some negative effects on the *environment* (our natural surroundings). Some forms, like solar energy, cause minimal damage. Others, like burning wood, can produce large quantities of air pollution.

One of our major environmental concerns is the quality of the air we breathe. Use of energy is the major source of air pollution. In this chapter, you will see how energy use produces smog and places a variety of harmful gases and particles in the atmosphere. You will also find out which sources provide the greatest amounts of pollution.

The concept of "global pollution" is introduced in this chapter. The pollution produced by one country affects other nations. Two pollutants, acid rain and carbon dioxide, are of particular concern.

At the end of the chapter, we will examine how the environment can be preserved by developing alternative energy sources and controlling pollution. These two methods combined with conservation (described in the previous chapter) can help produce a more pollution-free environment in the future.

DESTROYING THE ENVIRONMENT

In the United States, we enjoy a very high standard of living. We live better than kings did in the Middle Ages. In the winter, we heat our homes with electricity, fuel oil, or natural gas. In the summer, we cool our homes with electric fans or air conditioners. We cook our food with electricity or natural gas. Electricity powers our stereos and televisions. Gasoline and diesel fuel power cars, trucks, and buses. It is easy to see that our standard of living depends on large supplies of energy.

We must pay a price for the benefits of power. Energy use has had destructive effects on our environment. Automobile engines give off harmful gases that combine to form smog. Sulfur gases from coal-fired power plants combine with water to form acid rain. Waste heat from power plants pollutes lakes and rivers. Hydroelectric power production disrupts natural biological systems. Energy use even affects the delicate temperature balance of the earth. These problems are all harmful *side effects* of energy use.

Pollution is defined as any undesirable change in the air, land, or water that harmfully affects living things. Early in this century, people thought that pollution from energy was not important. Tall smokestacks poured smoke into the city air. Factories dumped industrial wastes into the rivers. There was little pollution control of any kind. People used energy without thinking of the environment. They assumed that the atmosphere and the earth would somehow *automatically* dispose of the pollution.

This assumption was partly correct. Natural processes—photosynthesis, rain, and wind—make many side effects harmless. However, we produce pollution faster than natural processes can deal with it. As a result, pollution is damaging the environment. It reduces the quality of life for everyone.

There are many sources of pollution. Industrial wastes, trash, fertilizer runoff, sewage, and pesticides are some of them. These sources account for much of the land and water pollution. But energy use accounts for a large share of the world's air pollution.

POLLUTION FROM FOSSIL FUELS

Most of our energy comes from coal, oil, and natural gas—the fossil fuels. Natural gas is a relatively clean-burning fuel. It produces the least amount of pollution. Oil products and coal, however, produce many harmful gases when burned. These gases seriously pollute the air we breathe.

Power generation also causes water pollution. Sulfur gases from coal and oil combustion combine with water in the air. The combination falls to the earth as acid rain, polluting lakes and streams.

Power plants require lakes and streams to absorb waste heat. This heat seriously affects plant and animal life. Scientists are working to reduce all types of fossil fuel pollution.

Air Pollution

As indicated earlier, fossil fuels are the world's main source of air pollution. We cannot see many of the harmful gases produced by fossil fuel combustion. However, their effects on the environment are very real. See Fig. 9-1. In this section, we will discuss the following types of air pollution:

■ Smog
■ Carbon monoxide
■ Particulates
■ Earth warming

Smog. Automobiles are a major source of air pollution. They produce the gases that form smog. The word "smog" originally meant a mixture of smoke and fog. It is actually a brownish mass of air. Smog may be our main air pollution problem. It is present in most large industrialized cities throughout the world.

There are three conditions needed to produce smog:

■ Burning of fossil fuels, especially in gasoline and diesel engines.
■ Temperature inversion or lack of air movement. A **temperature inversion** is when warm air moves above cold air. This condition keeps the same air close to the ground all day long.
■ Sunlight which supports the chemical reaction producing smog.

We only understand part of the chemical reactions forming smog. More knowledge is necessary to gain a full understanding. Based on present knowledge, *nitrogen dioxide (NO$_2$)* is the primary cause. It is a chemical combination of nitrogen and oxygen. *NO$_2$* is the chemical symbol, or abbreviation, for nitrogen dioxide.

Our atmosphere is ⅘ nitrogen. In the high temperatures within the internal-combustion engine, nitrogen combines with oxygen to form the nitrogen dioxide. It is discharged into the atmosphere as part of the exhaust gases of the engine. Exhaust gases also include water (H$_2$O), carbon dioxide (CO$_2$), carbon monoxide (CO), and unburned fuel. Smog is formed from this exhaust in the following manner:

■ Sunlight contains *ultraviolet light*, an invisible portion of the sun's energy. The ultraviolet light is absorbed by the nitrogen dioxide (NO$_2$). This process breaks the NO$_2$ into nitrous oxide (NO) and a free atom of oxygen (O).
■ Oxygen normally has two atoms bound together, making the symbol for oxygen O$_2$. A free atom of oxygen is chemically active and unites with regular oxygen (O$_2$), forming oxygen with three atoms, O$_3$. We call this new combination **ozone**. Ozone is the most harmful part of smog.
■ This unstable condition is maintained by the ultraviolet light. As soon as the sun goes down, the reaction reverses, producing oxygen (O$_2$) and nitrogen dioxide (NO$_2$). This is why smog occurs only during the day.

The temperature inversion keeps the nitrogen dioxide in the atmosphere overnight. The next day, more nitrogen dioxide is added from burning fuel, and the smog becomes more severe. If the inversion didn't exist, the smog would disperse.

Ozone and nitrogen dioxide (the ingredients of smog) are called *oxidents*. **Oxidents** are chemical compounds which can oxidize compounds not usually oxidized by regular oxygen. When a compound is **oxidized**, it chemically unites with oxygen, forming a new compound. It is through this process that smog damages our environment.

Smog makes breathing difficult, irritates the eyes, and can injure the lungs. It is especially harmful to people who are old, weak, or ill.

Smog is also harmful to plants. It often shrivels and discolors leaves, rendering them less effective in producing food. Again, see Fig. 9-1. Smog also fades and weakens rubber, fabric, and some plastics.

Fossil fuels are also called *hydrocarbons*. **Hydrocarbons** are chemical compounds made of hydrogen and carbon. Unburned fuel from an engine consists of hydrocarbons. Free hydrocarbons also contribute to air pollution. Their effects are similar to those of smog.

Fig. 9-1. Air pollution is very harmful. Even when we can't see it, we can see its effects.

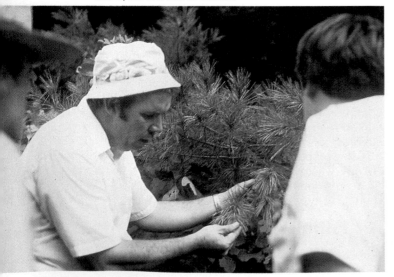

※ **Carbon Monoxide (CO).** Carbon monoxide, an exhaust emission, is the opposite of an oxident. It accepts extra oxygen during the burning process, and, when inhaled, takes it from a person's blood. In large cities, the amount of CO from automobile emissions can be 100 times greater than normal air. Carbon monoxide is colorless, odorless, and poisonous. It is the result of incomplete combustion of fossil fuels.

When carbon monoxide is inhaled, it reduces the oxygen-carrying capacity of the blood. Even small amounts are harmful to humans and animals. Large amounts of carbon monoxide can cause death.

※ **Particulates.** Fossil fuel combustion usually produces many tiny particles of matter called particulates. They include dust, smoke, ash, and other materials.

Some particulates serve a good purpose. For example, raindrops form when water vapor condenses around particles.

Most particulates, however, are harmful. Some metallic particles, such as lead, are poisonous. Some types of gasoline contain small amounts of lead added by the refinery. Lead helps gasoline burn smoothly in an engine. However, when gasoline is burned, lead particles are released into the air. Lead is very harmful to humans. Studies have shown that lead is responsible for lowering intelligence levels in children, and for causing high blood pressure in adults and deformities in the unborn.

The federal government has required the companies to reduce the amount of lead in regular gasoline. The reduction will continue and, by 1995, lead will be banned from all fuel. Also, the government has for many years required manufacturers to produce cars which use unleaded fuel.

※ **Earth Warming.** Another product of fossil fuel combustion is *carbon dioxide*. We usually think of carbon dioxide as a harmless gas. In fact, plants need carbon dioxide to grow. But fossil fuel combustion produces a *great* deal of carbon dioxide. The amount is about twice as much as plants can use. As a result, the amount of carbon dioxide builds up in the air.

Excess carbon dioxide is causing the earth to become warmer. It creates the *greenhouse effect* (Chapter 3). Like the glass of a greenhouse, carbon dioxide permits short-wave radiant energy to reach the earth where it is converted to long-wave heat energy. The carbon dioxide makes it hard for the long-wave heat energy to escape. The result is a gradual warming of the earth. See Fig. 9-2.

Recent changes could also be part of the normal cycling of earth temperature. The greenhouse effect is only one factor in long-range temperature changes. But carbon dioxide buildup does have a warming effect.

Water Pollution

Most water pollution results from the dumping of industrial wastes and improper sewage disposal. However, energy use accounts for some serious water pollution problems. Two of these problems are:
- Acid rain
- Thermal pollution

Acid Rain. Acid rain results basically from the ※ burning of coal and oil. These fuels may be burned to produce heat directly or to generate electrical power.

Coal and oil usually contain sulfur. Combustion changes sulfur into *sulfur oxides* and releases them into the air. The sulfur oxides mix with water vapor in the air. The result is sulfuric acid. When it rains, acid rain falls to the earth.

Acid rain is very harmful to all forms of life. It can collect in lakes and rivers. Fish and other animal life may die from it. As the acidity increases, fewer fish survive.

Fig. 9-2. Because of the greenhouse effect, some scientists estimate that the earth's temperature may increase by as much as 10°F (6°C) by the year 2020. This could cause glaciers and polar ice caps to melt, raising the sea level and causing flooding along the coastlines.

There has probably been acid rain since the Industrial Revolution.[1] However, it was not until the late 1950s that people began to recognize it as a problem. In 1959, Norwegians noticed fewer fish in Norwegian and Swedish lakes. They connected the decrease in fish population to acid rain. In 1969, they traced the problem to industry in Europe.

Acid rain is a growing problem. Hundreds of lakes in Norway and Sweden no longer support fish. The same is true for many lakes in the eastern United States. Lakes in the Rocky Mountains and in the South are becoming more acidic.

Acid rain harmfully affects forests. See Fig. 9-3. Many tests have been conducted which show that increased acid retards growth and even destroys trees and other plants. Acid rain may seriously decrease the use of forests for construction and as a renewable source of energy.

Acid rain is able to erode stone. It damages buildings and works of art throughout the world.

The problem of acid rain crosses national borders. Sulfur oxides from the midwestern United States produce acid rain in Canada. Sulfur oxides from China and Japan cause acid rain in our western states. All industrialized nations must cooperate to solve this problem.

Thermal Pollution. Power plants produce another form of pollution besides sulfur oxides. They release waste heat into rivers, lakes, and the oceans. This form of pollution is thermal pollution.

Thermal pollution mainly comes from power plants that use steam turbines. These plants need water to condense the steam after it is used. Less than 50% of the heat generated by fuel combustion produces power. The atmosphere and water absorb the waste heat. See Fig. 9-4.

GLOBAL POLLUTION

The growing concern for earth warming resulting from carbon dioxide and acid rain created from sulfur compounds introduces the concept of **global pollution**. Both of these sources of pollution as well as nuclear pollution are *worldwide* concerns. They affect all people on earth. Pollution created by one nation affects others.

Fig. 9-3. Art works throughout the world are being damaged by acid rain.

Fig. 9-4. Some power plants use cooling towers to release waste heat. The water cools by evaporation as it passes through the towers.

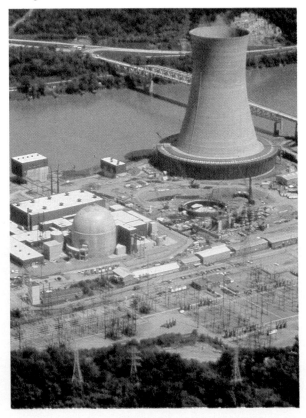

---

[1]The first Industrial Revolution was in England and lasted from 1750 to 1830. The industrial revolution in America took place in the second half of the 19th century.

In order to solve global pollution problems, people of the world must cooperate. Joint research and cooperative political efforts are needed to eliminate sources of pollution and to restore areas already damaged or destroyed.

POLLUTION FROM ALTERNATIVE SOURCES OF ENERGY

Alternative sources of energy are sources other than fossil fuels. Most alternative sources of energy are much less polluting than fossil fuels. However, each source must be thought about carefully. A few sources can cause serious pollution problems. Others may have little effect on the environment. Still others may have problems that we have not identified yet. In this section, you will learn about the problems possible with the following five sources:

■ Wood
■ Geothermal energy
■ Hydroelectric energy
■ Nuclear energy
■ Solar energy

Wood

The cost of gas and oil for heating has increased. Many people have turned to burning wood for home heating. Unfortunately, wood is not a clean-burning fuel. When it is burned, it releases two kinds of polluting materials. These are unburned chemical compounds and partially burned particles, or particulates.

Part of the wood put into a stove is not completely burned. It ends up as unburned chemical compounds released into the air. Scientists have found that some of these compounds cause cancer in animals. One compound is a cancer-causing substance that is also found in cigarette smoke.

Burning wood also produces particulates. Soot is one kind. People can inhale these particulates deep into their lungs. This makes them more likely to get respiratory (breathing-related) diseases.

Wood burning is even more polluting than burning fossil fuels. It not only causes a large share of particulate pollution, it also produces a huge amount of harmful chemical compounds. It gives off over 200 times the amount of pollution produced by burning coal. For example, several

years ago in one city in the northwestern United States, pollution from burning wood blocked out the sun for a month.

New technology might help solve the problems of burning wood. For example, one wood-burning stove design allows wood to be burned twice. The second burning removes some of the harmful unburned chemicals.

Geothermal Energy

Producing electricity from geothermal energy can also produce pollution. Most underground deposits of heat contain hydrogen sulfide gas. This gas can combine with oxygen and moisture in the air. The result is acid rain, as described earlier.

In some parts of the world, hydrogen sulfide goes into the air naturally. For example, geysers at Yellowstone National Park release hydrogen sulfide.

Geothermal plants can increase the amount of gaseous sulfur in the air. Since more of these plants may be built, it is important to find ways to prevent the release of sulfur into the air.

Hydroelectric Energy

Hydroelectric power plants create large lakes where there were only rivers. These power plants provide two major benefits. They produce pollution-free power and provide water for cities, farming, and recreation.

However, hydroelectric plants can harm the environment. The damming of a river changes the river's **ecology**. That means it affects the relationship between living things and the environment in which they live. Animals using the river may not be able to live with these changes. See Fig. 9-5.

Sometimes we can use technology to correct the problems caused by dams. For example, fish ladders built around dams permit salmon to swim upstream.

Nuclear Energy

Nuclear power plants produce almost no air pollution. However, they do produce the same thermal pollution as fossil fuel plants. Also, nuclear accidents in nuclear plants can severely pollute the air, water, and land surrounding the plant. Both of these forms of pollution were described in Chapter 5.

Fig. 9-5. Salmon swim upstream to spawn. Fish ladders are built to allow them to go around dams.

Technology Focus

To Build or Not To Build

A hydroelectric dam can profoundly affect the area in which it is located. The *Aswan High Dam* in Egypt has had both positive and negative effects. On the positive side, the dam's power station can produce up to 10 billion kilowatt-hours of electricity per year. And the giant lake created by the dam, Lake Nassar, provides water for irrigation, transportation, and recreation.

On the negative side, some scientists feel that the dam has upset the ecology of the area. For example, it ended the annual flooding of the Nile which previously deposited sediment rich in nutrients on farmlands. Nutrients also are no longer deposited in the Mediterranean Sea. A large fishing industry depended on these nutrients to feed fish. Now the fish and the industry have all but disappeared.

The benefits of the Aswan High Dam presently outweigh its harmful effects. However, when deciding whether to build a hydroelectric dam, potential harmful effects as well as expected benefits must be considered carefully. The environmental changes must not be too severe.

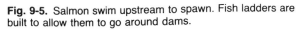

Solar Energy

As it is used today, solar energy does not cause pollution. Therefore, people are trying out solar energy for many different uses. In the future, however, solar energy may present some new pollution problems.

Someday we may collect solar energy in space. Satellites would "beam" the energy to earth with microwaves or mirrors. Some pollution problems are possible with this system.

One problem is earth warming. The satellite system would send energy to the earth that normally would have missed the earth. This could increase the temperature of the earth.

Using microwaves to "beam" down the energy could also be dangerous. Scientists know that concentrations of microwaves can be harmful to living things.

Transmitting solar energy with mirrors could also be a problem. Mirrors would provide sunlight 24 hours a day to certain places on earth. Scientists know little about the environmental effects of constant sunlight.

Other Sources

Chapter 4 presented alternative sources of energy. These sources include wind, ocean thermal energy, tides, and others. Scientists must study each source carefully to determine its environmental effects. No source is completely free of problems. But some sources are better than others. Work must be done to develop those that are more pollution-free.

PRESERVING THE ENVIRONMENT

In today's world, no country can escape the effects of pollution. But, we can control pollution from energy use in two ways. First, we can develop the more pollution-free energy sources. Second, we can reduce the amount of pollution produced at the source.

Developing Alternative Energy Sources

Much research and development has been done on alternative energy. Scientists have discovered many new energy sources. Some of these sources have added to our present energy supplies. Some have also reduced pollution. Energy is all around us at all times. The problem is to collect and control it without disturbing the environment.

Reducing Pollution

Pollution can be controlled and reduced at the source. Carmakers have made much progress in controlling automobile pollution. Control devices have reduced the amounts of hydrocarbons, nitrogen oxides, and carbon monoxide produced. See Fig. 9-6.

Sulfur oxides from coal-burning power plants can also be reduced. Sulfur can be removed from the coal before burning. This is an expensive process. However, it prevents the formation of acid rain.

Companies can also control particulate pollution. They can use filters to trap particulates in smokestacks. These filters allow only exhaust gases to pass.

We have the ability to reduce most forms of pollution. *Cost* is the major reason that pollution is not controlled better. Adding filters to smokestacks and adding pollution-control devices to cars is expensive. Removing sulfur from coal increases the cost of electrical power production. These costs are passed on to consumers. We must decide whether a clean environment is worth the cost of pollution control.

Fig. 9-6. What appears to be a small muffler on the exhaust system of this car is actually a catalytic converter. Material inside the converter helps eliminate harmful exhaust emissions.

Testing Your Knowledge

Briefly answer each of the following questions. Write on a separate piece of paper.

1. Name five ways energy use causes pollution.
2. Which energy source causes most damage to our environment?
3. Of the three fossil fuels, which pollutes the least?
4. Name the four types of air pollution caused by the use of fossil fuels.
5. What is ozone? How is it formed?
6. Identify three ways smog is harmful to people.
7. How does carbon monoxide harm people?
8. What are particulates? Name two.
9. How does lead get into the air?
10. At present, what is the most severe damage caused by acid rain?
11. What are the two forms of pollution caused by burning wood?
12. Which is more polluting, wood or coal?
13. What forms of pollution are produced by geothermal energy?
14. What form of pollution is produced by nuclear power plants?
15. Does solar energy, as used today, cause pollution?
16. What are the three ways we can control pollution caused by energy use?
17. How can acid rain be controlled?
18. What is the major reason more pollution control is not used?

Expressing Your Knowledge

Using complete sentences, write your answers to the following on a separate sheet of paper:

1. Describe how smog is formed.
2. How does carbon dioxide cause earth warming? What effect would earth warming have on sea level? (See illustration below.)
3. Describe how acid rain forms.
4. Explain how excess heat released by power plants into rivers, lakes, and the ocean is harmful.
5. How is the pollution caused by burning wood harmful?
6. Describe the benefits and problems of hydroelectric energy.
7. Explain how collecting energy in space and "beaming" it to earth could cause problems.

Applying Your Knowledge

Follow your teacher's instructions to complete these activities:

1. Conduct a "greenhouse effect" demonstration. Use two of the same kind of small cardboard boxes (such as shoe boxes) to show how energy is trapped within a greenhouse. Place a thermometer in the bottom of each box as shown in Fig. 9-7. Cover one box with a clear plastic (such as plastic food wrap). Seal the box. Make it airtight. Place both boxes on cardboard insulation in direct sunlight for one hour. Check and record the temperatures in both boxes every 10 minutes. Use a graph as shown in Fig. 3-32 to plot temperatures. Which box had the higher temperature? Why?

Conduct some added experiments with your boxes. Design and explain your own experiments, or use one or more of the following suggestions:

- Place the boxes on legs (thumbtacks will do) instead of insulation. Note effects on temperatures.
- Insulate one or both boxes and/or paint the interiors black. Note effects on temperature.
- Wrap boxes in aluminum foil. What effect does aluminum foil have? How can some of the concepts learned in this activity be used in solar heating and energy conservation?

Prepare a written report of your experiments. Include in it answers to the questions asked in this activity as well as an explanation of the greenhouse effect.

2. Identify and discuss current events that relate to pollution and environmental protection. The teacher will divide your class into groups. Each group will select or be assigned a current issue, such as oil spills, nuclear accidents, polluted water, toxic waste disposal, nuclear waste disposal, smog, acid rain, carbon dioxide in the atmosphere, or the erosion of the ozone layer. After performing research, work with your group to prepare and present a report of your group's findings to the class.

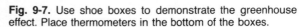

Fig. 9-7. Use shoe boxes to demonstrate the greenhouse effect. Place thermometers in the bottom of the boxes.

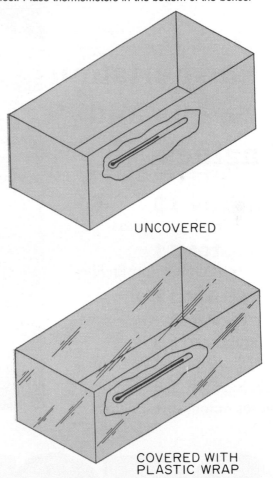

UNCOVERED

COVERED WITH PLASTIC WRAP

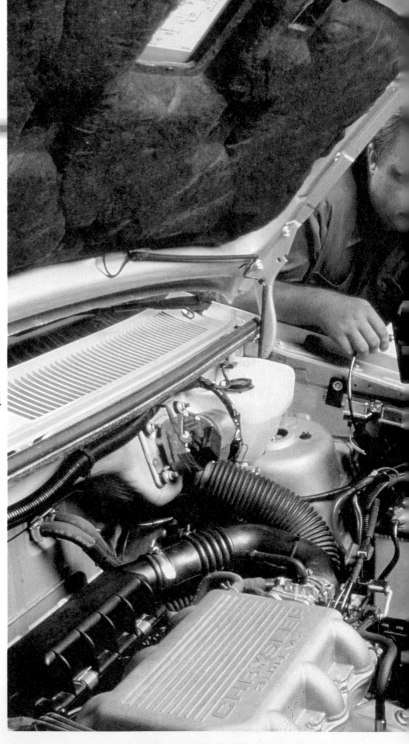

Transportation Systems and Engines

SECTION

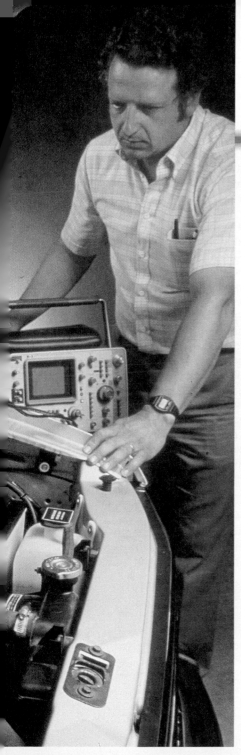

Chapter 10

Transportation Systems

Transportation is one of the largest consumers of energy. It is vital to maintaining the modern world in which we live.

Expanding Your Knowledge

Learning about power and energy technology will help you understand more about the world around you. As you study this chapter, you will learn to:

- Describe how people and goods are moved from one place to another.
- Recognize the importance of transportation in maintaining the quality of life we enjoy.
- Define many of the technical terms used in the transportation industry.
- Explain three different ways in which transportation systems are classified.
- Describe each of the five modes of transportation.
- Explain the difference between long-distance and on-site transportation.
- Explain how ships and airplanes are able to determine their position on earth by navigation.

Building Your Word Power

Knowledge of the vocabulary used will help you develop greater understanding of power and energy. The following terms are defined and explained in this chapter. Learning these will help you learn more about transportation systems.

automatic guided vehicles (AGVs)
barge
cargo
celestial navigation
chronometer
dead reckoning
electronic navigation
fix
flight plan
intermodal transportation
lift
loran
locomotives
modes, transportation

navigation
Omega
on-site transportation
passengers
piloting
radar
radio direction finder
sextant
space navigation
tractor-trailer
transportation
vehicles

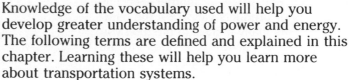

Consider the term "transportation." What thoughts come to your mind? Do you think about riding in the family car? catching a bus at the corner? semi-trailer trucks roaring along the highway? How about trains or airplanes? These things are just part of transportation—the movement of goods and people. Actually, the transportation system is very large and complex. It is an essential part of each of our lives.

In this chapter, you will learn how people and goods are moved, and how the different systems within the overall transportation system interact to provide this movement. The five primary modes of transportation (highway, air, rail, water and pipeline) will be described in detail. And you will also learn about transportation in terms of the types of items that are transported, the groups that are served, and the distance that is traveled.

THE IMPORTANCE OF TRANSPORTATION

Transportation is the movement of people and goods from one place to another. See Fig. 10-1. The goods or products vary from the natural gas which heats many homes, to the food you eat, to the electricity used in your home, to the clothes you wear, and to the machines used in factories.

The movement may involve great distances. Many of the TV sets and other electronic devices we use are manufactured in Asia, nearly halfway around the world. The distance can also be short, such as when you carry groceries from the corner store to your home.

Transportation is an industry. We rely on it every day. And transportation depends on a continuous supply of energy.

A Principal Use of Energy

All forms of transportation use some source of energy to provide the power to move people and goods. As you learned in Chapter 8, over one-quarter (27%) of all controlled energy is used for the transportation of people and goods.

The most common form of energy used comes from petroleum (oil). Most vehicles use petroleum products for fuel. Automobiles are powered by gasoline; airplanes by jet fuel; and trucks, trains, and ships by diesel oil. Petroleum is often called *the fuel of transportation*. Because it is expected to become scarce during the next century, we need to seek alternative fuels for transportation.

New fuels may be difficult to find. Most of the alternative sources of energy described in Section I are difficult to use in transportation. Solar, nuclear, wind, ocean power, and geothermal are stationary sources. Transportation requires a fuel that can be transported easily with the vehicle. Synthetic fuels such as alcohol and methanol are transportable. Unfortunately, they are made from grain and other vegetation and compete with the food market. As a result, they are a supplement but aren't manufactured in sufficient quantity to replace petroleum. Another potential fuel, hydrogen, is discussed in Chapter 26.

Some forms of transportation can use electricity or other sources of energy. Conveyors and pipelines depend on motors and pumps to provide the necessary motion. However, the major fuel source for transportation remains petroleum.

Essential for Our Way of Life

A world without any transportation is impossible. People have always transported themselves and carried goods from place to place.

Fig. 10-1. Transportation is a complex system involving the movement of people and goods.

And, rather than becoming less dependent, we are becoming more dependent. Transportation now permits us to purchase goods from all over the world. Not too many years ago, a "foreign" car was a rare sight. But today you can purchase cars from Japan, Korea, Spain, Germany, England, France, and a host of other countries from around the world. See Fig. 10-2.

The transportation of people is also important. The combination of business, tourism and pleasure, and government has made the transportation of people a giant industry.

Every day each of us uses the result of transporting goods and people from one place to another. Transportation is essential.

Elements of Transportation

The elements of transportation can be classified in a number of different ways. For our study, we will use three different classifications:
■ Things transported.

You've already learned that transportation can be classified into the movement of people or goods. Within this classification we can identify three different groups that are served: personal transportation, commercial transportation, and government transportation.
■ Carrier, or mode, of transportation.

Modes are the individual methods of transportation—highway, rail, air, water, and pipeline. This is the most common and important classification.
■ Distance items are transported.

Within this division we will examine on-site (short-distance) and off-site (long-distance) transportation.

Fig. 10-2. Transportation makes trade with other countries possible.

Fig. 10-3. Bulk cargo is handled as one unit.

MOVING PEOPLE AND GOODS

As you study transportation, a few common words gain technical meaning. People who are transported from one place to another are called **passengers**. Goods and products are referred to as **cargo**. **Freight** is another name for cargo. Devices used to move passengers and cargo are called **vehicles**.

Cargo is divided into two basic types, depending on how it is handled. *Bulk cargo* is any kind of loose cargo, such as coal, petroleum, natural gas, or milk. This kind of cargo can be handled as one complete unit. See Fig. 10-3.

The other type is called *break bulk cargo*. *Break bulk cargo* is freight that must be handled in separate units. Canned goods, TV sets, and automobile parts are examples. See Fig. 10-4.

Now let's turn our attention towards the three groups served by transportation.

Fig. 10-4. Items which must be handled separately are break bulk cargo.

Personal Transportation

Personal transportation is moving yourself from place to place. For example, when you walk to school you are engaging in personal transportation. Personal transportation also includes riding your bicycle, traveling by private automobile, using your own snowmobile or boat, or flying your own airplane.

Personal transportation is usually part of your daily routine. It can be used for business or pleasure.

Commercial Transportation

In the world of business and industry, "commercial" refers to "commerce" which means engaging in business. *Commercial transportation* is, therefore, the movement of passengers and cargo for *profit*.

Many different types of companies engage in commercial transportation. Bus companies, trucking companies, and airlines are all engaged in moving passengers and cargo for profit.

Government Transportation

Government transportation is the movement of passengers and cargo by local, state, and national governments. A major portion of our transportation system is operated by the government.

Local governments operate transportation systems. For example, sanitation systems carry away trash. Buses move people within the local community.

The national government is deeply involved in transportation. The military services move passengers and cargo throughout the world. And mail delivery is one of the nation's largest businesses.

Some forms of government transportation are referred to as *public transportation*. A system such as a subway system is operated by a government agency for the benefit of all people—the public.

TRANSPORTATION MODES

Transportation can be classified according to the methods used to transport passengers and cargo. These methods are referred to as the *modes* of transportation. The five major modes of transportation are:
- Highway transportation
- Air transportation
- Rail transportation
- Water transportation
- Pipeline transportation

Highway Transportation

Highway transportation is the movement of passengers and cargo over the nation's roads. This form of transportation serves nearly all local needs and many long-distance ones as well.

The highway system in the United States is the most advanced one in the world. The interstate highway system is supplemented by thousands of miles of connecting roads. Each city and town has a network of streets planned to serve the residents. The combination of local, state, and national highways permits the transportation of cargo and passengers to all corners of the nation.

Personal and Passenger Transportation. Because of the millions of miles of roadways, highway transportation is the primary mode used for moving people. Most adults own automobiles or other vehicles which they use to move from one place to another.

The highway system is also used for commercial passenger services. The most common commercial services are taxis and buses.

Taxis provide fast service within cities. They are often the preferred mode of transportation for businessmen and women and for people unfamiliar with the city.

The commercial passenger service that is used most is bus transportation. Regional bus companies provide transportation within a city, county, or other local division. These are *intra*state (within the state) systems. *Inter*state (between states) service is provided by larger nationwide companies. Charter companies may offer either intrastate or interstate service. These can be hired to take groups of people to specific destinations.

Commercial Cargo Service. The main commercial use of the highway system is to move cargo from one place to another. Cargo vehicles vary in size from pickup trucks to large commercial tractor-trailers carrying freight across the country. See Fig. 10-5.

There are many different types of trucks. Special-purpose vehicles usually carry bulk cargo. For example, tankers are designed to carry liquids such as gasoline, milk, or liquid chemicals. And general bulk haulers are designed to carry large quantities of sand, dirt, or gravel. The list of special-purpose vehicles is almost endless.

A. Pickup truck.

B. General bulk hauler.

Fig. 10-5. Different types and sizes of trucks are used to move cargo from place to place.

C. Tractor-trailer.

Fig. 10-6. The Concorde jet flies at 1400 miles per hour (2240 km). Passengers who travel from Europe to the United States on the Concorde arrive earlier in the day than when they left, the result of the plane flying faster than the earth rotates.

While specialized vehicles often carry bulk cargo, there are a variety of sizes of general-purpose vehicles designed to carry break bulk cargo. These vary from small local delivery vans and pickup trucks to multiple-trailer cross-country **tractor-trailers**.

The *tractor* is the basic unit of the tractor-trailer combination. Refer back to Fig. 10-5. The tractor may pull either specialized trailers or general-purpose *trailers*, thereby serving both types of cargo.

Air Transportation

In less than 90 years, air transportation has revolutionized the manner in which people travel over long distances. The first powered flight[1] in 1903 traveled just 120 feet (36.5 m). Today, giant airplanes carrying more than 500 passengers can fly nonstop across the Pacific Ocean. Planes also fly over twice the speed of sound. See Fig. 10-6.

Principles of Flight. The two main parts of an airplane are the power plant and the airframe. The power plant will be studied in later chapters of this section. Figure 10-7 shows the basic parts of the airframe.

Fig. 10-7. Parts of an airplane.

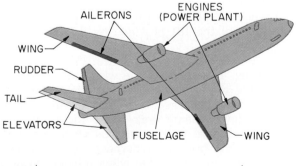

AILERONS

ENGINES (POWER PLANT)

WING

RUDDER

TAIL

ELEVATORS

FUSELAGE

WING

(AIRFRAME)

[1]By Wilbur and Orville Wright on December 17, 1903.

Technology Focus

Is Wright Wrong?

Orville and Wilbur Wright are credited with building the world's first successful powered airplane. Orville's flight on December 17, 1903, at Kitty Hawk, North Carolina is believed by most to be the first controlled flight. It lasted 12 seconds, covered 120 feet (about a third of a football field), and flew at 6.8 mph (a person can run faster). But was this really the *first* controlled flight?

According to some people in Connecticut, *Gustave Whitehead* flew a bat-winged vehicle in 1901, two years before the Wright brothers' flight. Newspaper and magazine reports describe flights by Whitehead between 1901 and 1903. But doubt remains. Some people who knew Whitehead claimed he told "tall tales" and then began believing them himself. Also, one "witness" later said he never actually saw the flight.

The controversy about the first flight may continue. But one thing is sure. Inventions very rarely result from just one person's work. There were many pioneers in aviation who contributed to the growth of powered flight.

Have you ever wondered how an airplane which may weigh more than 700,000 pounds (315,000 kg) is able to fly? An airplane can fly because of the **lift** provided by the wings. See Fig. 10-8.

As the plane moves forward, air travels over the wing. The shape of the wing causes the air traveling over the wing to move faster than the air traveling underneath. The fast-moving air creates a low-pressure area above the wing. The higher pressure underneath pushes up, producing lift. The pressure difference may be small. But the size of the wing provides a heavy upward force that is great enough to lift the heavy plane

Fig. 10-8. The shape of the wing enables an airplane to fly.

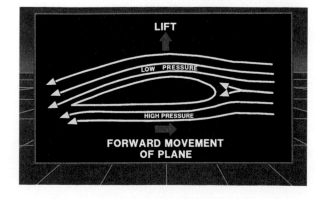

off the ground and keep it in the air. Chapter 21 will help you understand how pressure differences are able to produce a very large force.

An airplane is controlled by operating three devices:

■ Rudder.

This is an adjustable section at the rear of an airplane used to *turn* the airplane.

■ Elevators.

These are adjustable sections of the tail used to move the airplane to a higher or lower *altitude*.

■ Ailerons.

These are adjustable sections of the wing used to maintain level flight or to cause the airplane to *bank* (incline). Refer back to Fig. 10-7.

To fly the airplane, the pilot uses various combinations of these controls and the *throttle* which controls the engine power. Many planes have added controls which help the pilot control the plane during landing and takeoff, as well as during severe weather conditions.

General Aviation. General aviation refers to personal transportation provided by privately owned airplanes. Most of these planes are small. They are used for recreational flying as well as for transporting people on private business.

Commercial Aviation. Commercial aviation provides transportation of passengers and cargo for profit, often over long distances. This is one of the fastest growing parts of the transportation industry. Commercial aviation uses a variety of different types of aircraft. See Fig. 10-9.

The primary use of commercial aviation is the transport of passengers. In the past few years, larger, more efficient airplanes have been put into operation. This has permitted the cost of flying to decrease. As a result, there has been a rapid increase in the number of people flying.

People travel by air for both business and pleasure. During holiday and vacation periods, families travel long distances to be with friends and relatives. Business travel tends to dominate air travel during non-holiday/vacation periods. In many sections of the country, a person can leave home in the morning, fly to a city 300-400 miles away, spend a day working, and return home in the early evening. The San Francisco and Los Angeles areas have hundreds of *shuttle flights* in each direction each day. Shuttle service is also offered along the Atlantic coast and between other cities throughout the country.

The amount of cargo shipped by air is increasing. Many commercial companies provide overnight parcel delivery to any part of the nation. These services carry flowers, food products, and industrial products requiring quick delivery. Similar services are also provided worldwide.

Rail Transportation

In the U.S., rail transportation is one of the primary methods of moving cargo from one location to another. Some passenger services are provided, but these are less significant than cargo movement at the present time. New technology could reverse this trend.

Fig. 10-9. Commercial airplanes vary in size depending on the distance flown and the space needed for passengers.

Operation. Most trains today use steel wheels riding on heavy steel rails. These are capable of supporting heavier loads than trucks are able to carry. **Locomotives,** the train's power source, are driven by powerful diesel engines. See Fig. 10-10.

Trains carrying freight are often more than a mile long, pulling 100 or more freight cars. Each freight car is able to transport more freight than the largest truck.

There are over 200,000 miles (320,000 km) of railroad tracks in the national system of railroads in the United States. The land on which the rails are laid is called the *right-of-way* (or simply the "ways").

All railroads are connected. The tracks are all the same *gauge* (shape and width apart). This permits locomotives and railway cars to travel throughout the entire system.

Passenger Service. During much of the 19th century and the early part of the 20th century, trains provided the most rapid and safe transportation available. They carried passengers between cities and from coast to coast.

As the highway system developed, many people chose to drive their own vehicles. Today, the combination of private automobiles and safe air transportation has reduced railroad passenger service to a small percentage of the total commercial travel. Less than 10% of the people paying for travel use the train.

In 1970, Congress passed the *Rail Passenger Service Act* which established a national network of train service called *AMTRAK* (from *AM*erican *TR*avel Tr*ACK*). This act was designed to strengthen rail passenger service and help pre-

Fig. 10-11. AMTRAK trains offer long-distance passenger service.

serve the railroad as a major means of transporting passengers. Today, AMTRAK transports passengers throughout the nation. See Fig. 10-11.

A growing use of railroads for passenger service are rapid transit trains. These trains often carry passengers from suburban areas into large cities. Washington, D.C., New York, Chicago, Atlanta, San Francisco, and many other cities have developed extensive rapid transit systems.

Freight (Cargo) Service. In rail transportation, the word "cargo" is rarely used. "Freight" is the common term.

Freight trains serve more than 50,000 towns and cities. A variety of freight cars are used. Some are designed for bulk cargo, such as coal or liquids. Others carry break bulk cargo. See Fig. 10-12.

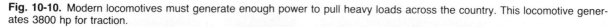

Fig. 10-10. Modern locomotives must generate enough power to pull heavy loads across the country. This locomotive generates 3800 hp for traction.

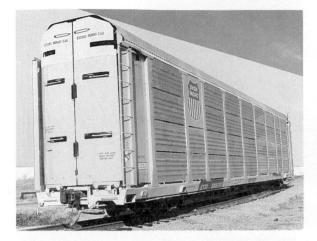

Water Transportation

With the growth of international trade, water transportation for the movement of cargo has grown at a rapid pace. Even though it is the slowest form of transportation, water transportation is inexpensive, safe, and fairly flexible. It costs less per *ton mile* to transport cargo by water than by any other means.

Passenger Service. Water transportation passenger lines are either private luxury lines or public transportation lines. Private luxury lines and riverboats are used for recreational purposes. See Fig. 10-13. This industry has grown rapidly. It provides safe and relaxing recreation.

Public water transportation lines are not common in the United States. Ferry service exists in a few places. In other parts of the world, especially Asia, ships provide transportation for thousands of people.

Cargo Service. Much cargo is transported on water. Mostly ships and barges are used.

Ships are vessels which can travel under their own power across the ocean. Many ships are designed to carry bulk cargo. Oil from oil-producing countries is shipped in supertankers to industrialized nations. See Fig. 10-14.

Fig. 10-13. In the past, riverboats were important forms of transportation for travelers. Today, they are used primarily for recreation.

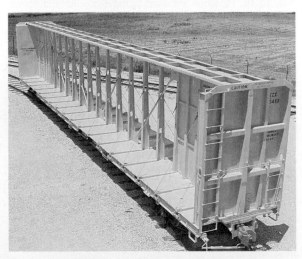

Fig. 10-12. Typical freight cars.

Fig. 10-14. A bulk cargo ship is designed for the cargo it carries.

Barges are simply "floating boxes" designed to be carried on a ship or lashed together into *tows* and pushed by a *towboat*. See Fig. 10-15. Barges are also designed for special purposes. They are used to carry many different products. Coal and grain are commonly shipped in barges.

Fig. 10-15. Special-purpose barges move large quantities of cargo.

As international trade continues to grow, the movement of cargo by water will become an increasingly important form of transportation.

Pipeline Transportation

Pipeline transportation is the movement of bulk cargo through a tube, or pipe. There are over a million miles of pipelines in the U.S. and Canada. See Fig. 10-16.

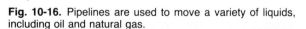

Fig. 10-16. Pipelines are used to move a variety of liquids, including oil and natural gas.

Pipelines serve many purposes. The three major systems in use today carry water, petroleum and petroleum products, and natural gas.

Pressurized pipeline systems provide water for most communities. And other pipeline systems carry away wastes and waste water.

Intermodal Transportation

The movement of passengers and cargo often requires more than one mode of transportation. When more than one mode is used, it is called **intermodal transportation**.

Passenger transportation by commercial carrier often involves more than one mode. For example, a person may travel to the airport by automobile or bus, fly to a distant city, and take a taxi or train to the hotel.

Cargo transportation is similar. For example, oil from an Alaskan oil field is transported across Alaska via pipeline. It is loaded into an oil tanker and transported to refineries in Washington, Oregon, or California.

More complex intermodal systems have developed during recent years. Truck trailers can be loaded at warehouses or manufacturing plants. They are driven to a boat dock or railroad terminal where the entire trailer is loaded and transported to a distant location. See Fig. 10-17. The trailers are then connected to another tractor and driven to their final destination.

Other Forms of Transportation

There are a few additional forms of transportation which are not included in the five modes described. Energy is moved around the nation as electricity, via a national network of electrical transmission lines. Radio and television signals are sent via electromagnetic waves.

Transportation systems for space travel and space exploration may be developed in the future. At the present time, space transportation is in the research-and-development stage. Only small amounts of cargo and a limited number of passengers are involved.

DISTANT VS. ON-SITE TRANSPORTATION

The transportation modes presented in the last section provided for passenger and cargo transportation over long distances. Long-distance transportation is not the only form of transportation. People and goods are also moved over short distances, often inside a building. When transportation occurs in the same location or over short distances, it is called **on-site transportation**.

Fig. 10-17. Truck trailers being transported on railroad flat cars. This type of intermodal transportation is referred to as "piggyback" service.

On-site transportation usually does not involve a fee or cost for transporting goods and people. As a result, the terms "passengers" and "cargo," used for long-distance transportation, are rarely used.

Devices for Moving Materials and Goods

The manufacturing process requires devices that are able to handle and move materials and goods in an efficient manner. Many special devices have been developed to make manufacturing more efficient, including:

- Conveyors.

  Conveyors are devices which move materials over a fixed path. These may be belts, rollers, or overhead carriers.
- Industrial trucks.

  The most common industrial trucks are called *forklifts* because of the fork-like device on the front of the vehicle that is used to lift and carry loads.
- Robots.

  Robotic trucks and carriers are able to move products along preplanned paths. These are called **automatic guided vehicles (AGVs)**.

People-Movers

Several on-site devices are designed to transport people. Two common devices found in many stores and office buildings are *elevators* and *escalators*. Some airports have installed *moving walkways* or *automatic train systems*.

Chairlifts and *gondolas* carry people to the top of mountains or across rivers. These devices are carried by moving cables.

NAVIGATING—KNOWING WHERE YOU ARE

Navigation is the process of planning and maintaining knowledge of your location. Both sea and air navigation use similar procedures.

Dead Reckoning

Dead reckoning is the basic planning for an air or sea trip. It is the laying down (drawing and writing) of the planned course line on a chart. This includes the distance traveled and the time needed to reach the destination. For most trips, this requires changes in course (changes in direction) at preplanned times.

For airplanes a flight plan is presented before departure. A **flight plan** describes the planned course and distance along each leg of the flight. It also includes the planned times of departure and arrival. Ships follow a similar procedure, listing departure and arrival times, ports to be visited, and major routes traveled.

During travel, the process of dead reckoning is combined with navigation. The navigator must always know the location of the ship or airplane. He or she keeps the captain informed by maintaining a plotted record of the craft's progress. Exact location is determined by obtaining a "fix." A navigation fix, the exact location of the ship or airplane, is obtained from known landmarks, from the use of electronic navigation systems, or by use of celestial measurements. The navigator is constantly obtaining a fix, which is the exact location of the ship or airplane. The navigator then revises the dead reckoning as needed. The fix usually is obtained in one of three ways: piloting, celestial navigation, or electronic navigation.

Piloting

In **piloting**, the position of the craft is determined from recognized landmarks or from aids to navigation. The navigator is responsible for navigation.

The navigator is able to determine his or her location by measuring the angle between the direction of his or her craft and the landmark. A line representing this angle is drawn on the chart. When two landmarks in different directions are measured and the lines cross, a fix is obtained. The crossing location is the position of the airplane or ship. See Fig. 10-18.

Fig. 10-18. The section of chart shown here shows navigational aids. These are indicated by the three large circles. A navigational fix is obtained by determining the angle of the navigation aid from the vessel and drawing a line on the chart as shown.

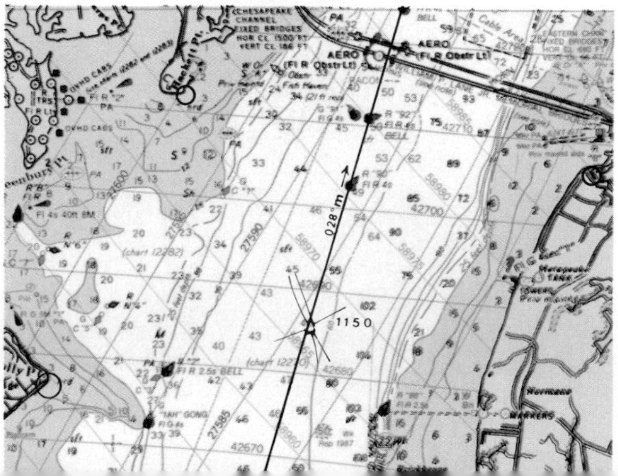

Celestial Navigation

Before the development of electronic navigation, ships and cross-ocean planes had to rely on celestial navigation, aided by piloting near land to obtain a fix. **Celestial navigation** uses the stars and the sun (celestial bodies) to determine the craft's location. It is based on the principle that at a specific time the location of the stars in the sky will be different when viewed from each location on earth. Celestial navigation, therefore, involves the following:

- Time. The navigator must know the exact time the fix is taken. A **chronometer**, an accurate clock, provides the exact time.
- Location of stars. Identified stars must be measured. The measurement is the angle of the star above the horizon. A **sextant**, an accurate device used to measure angles, measures the angle above the horizon.

Electronic Navigation

Electronic navigation permits the navigators of both ships and airplanes to know their location with a high degree of accuracy. It does this by using electronic instruments.

Radar. Radar is a system that sends a directional radio beam. When it hits a solid object, the beam bounces back. As a result, radar reveals the direction and the distance to an object, providing a fix with a single measurement. See Fig. 10-19.

Radar is especially useful in controlling airplane movements around airports. Ships use radar near land. Since radar signals travel in straight lines, and do not follow the curvature of the earth, radar is used only to watch for other ships when navigating across the ocean.

Loran. Loran is a system used by the United States to guide airplanes and ships as they approach the country. The word loran stands for "long range navigation."

Loran operates by measuring the time it takes for a radio signal sent from a known location to reach your position. Loran uses low- and medium-frequency radio signals that follow the curvature of the earth. As a result, loran has a usable range of about 1,000 miles for both airplanes and ships.

Omega. Omega is a system similar to loran. The omega system is worldwide.

Radio Direction Finder. The direction of a radio signal can be determined from the signal. Most radio station broadcast towers are plotted on charts. Also, airports broadcast signals from their towers. Airplanes and ships can use the broadcast to determine position. A *radio direction finder* identifies the origin of the signal.

With expanded use of satellites, electronic navigation will become more extensive and accurate in the future.

Space Navigation

Space navigation must be three-dimensional. In the future, if space travel becomes common, navigation will be conducted from the space vehicle. This will be far more complex and difficult than our existing earth navigation.

POWER FOR TRANSPORTATION DEVICES

As you know, transportation devices require energy to move passengers and cargo from one place to another. Airplanes, automobiles, trucks, trains, and ships are all powered by engines.

The following chapters of this section will describe these engines and explain how they provide the power necessary to move passengers and cargo to the desired location.

Fig. 10-19. Radar determines the location of a plane by sending a directional radion signal and measuring the time it takes to return.

Chapter 10—Review

Testing Your Knowledge

Briefly answer each of the following questions. Write on a separate piece of paper.

1. Name three ways in which transportation systems can be classified.
2. Give two examples of government transportation.
3. Name the five modes of transportation.
4. What is a tractor-trailer?
5. What device is used to change the altitude of an airplane?
6. What is meant by general aviation?
7. In railroading, what is a right-of-way?
8. Name three major pipeline systems in use in the United States.
9. Give two examples of on-site transportation devices that move cargo.
10. Give two examples of on-site "people-movers."
11. What fuel is the principal source of power for transportation devices?
12. What does an airplane pilot provide before departure?
13. What are the three methods for obtaining a navigation fix?
14. What does the name *loran* mean when spelled out?

Expressing Your Knowledge

Using complete sentences, write your answers to the following on a separate sheet of paper.

1. Define transportation.
2. Why may it be difficult to identify an alternate fuel to petroleum products for transportation devices?
3. How are personal and commercial transportation different?
4. What is the difference between intrastate and interstate transportation service?
5. Describe the difference between bulk cargo and break bulk cargo.
6. Briefly explain the force "lift" and tell how it enables an airplane to fly. (See illustration below.)
7. Explain what is meant by intermodal travel. Give at least one example.
8. What do we mean by *navigating*?
9. What is the principle upon which celestial navigation is based?
10. Why is space navigation more difficult than earth navigation?

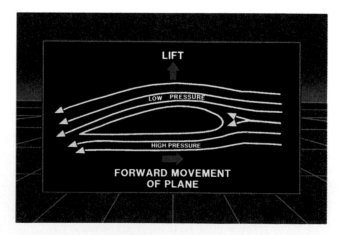

Applying Your Knowledge

Follow your teacher's instructions to complete these activities:

1. Select a trip you have recently taken or plan a trip you would like to take. Prepare a report which describes the different modes of transportation you would use. Include all modes from the time you leave your home until you return.

2. Your teacher will divide the class into five groups, one for each mode of transportation. The group will analyze the mode, identifying how it serves the local community. For example, water transportation brings foreign products, such as TV sets, across the oceans. As a group, report your findings to the class in an oral presentation.

3. Maintain a scrapbook of transportation articles and pictures from local newspapers and/or from magazines and journals. Identify categories into which the articles can be organized. For examples, you may have a section on new technology, another on social impacts of transportation, and so on.

4. Obtain a train schedule or an airplane schedule. Study the schedule and learn how to find the following information:
   ■ Departure time
   ■ Arrival time
   ■ Stops between departure and arrival locations

5. Obtain a road map of your state. List the interstate highways which travel through the state. Find a three-digit number (one that has three numbers such as 880). See if you can find out how the number was assigned. Find out the difference between odd and even-numbered interstate routes.

6. Find as many different on-site people-movers as you can. Identify their locations and explain how they are used in moving people from one place to another.

7. Obtain a navigation chart. Plan a trip between two locations on the chart. Identify the route you will travel. Plot your course, estimate your speed, establish a departure time, and determine your time of arrival. Identify landmarks that you can use for obtaining one or more navigation fixes on the trip. Note: this activity may require added information available in navigation books in the library.

148

Chapter 11

External-Combustion Engines

The idea of an external-combustion engine dates from the first century A.D. Today, these same principles are applied to create engines that are among the most powerful in the world.

Expanding Your Knowledge

As you study this chapter, you will learn to:

■ Identify the broad categories of heat engines and describe the main differences between them, including operating efficiencies.
■ Explain the three types of motion possible from heat engines.
■ Trace the historical development of the steam engine from the first engine to the development of the double-acting reciprocating steam engine.
■ Describe how a double-acting reciprocating steam engine operates.
■ Identify the two basic types of steam turbines and describe how each operates.
■ Describe how the gas within a Stirling engine produces motion.

Building Your Word Power

The following terms are defined and explained in this chapter. Learning these will help you learn more about external-combustion engines.

external-combustion engine
heat engine
internal-combustion engine
linear motion
reciprocating motion
rotary motion
steam engine
steam turbine
Stirling Cycle engine

This chapter begins your study of engines. Heat engines use heat energy to produce motion. The heat may be produced inside or outside of the engine. If produced outside, the engine is called an external-combustion engine. If produced inside the engine, it is called an internal-combustion engine. This chapter describes the different *external-combustion engines* and explains how they operate.

HEAT ENGINES

Heat engines use heat produced by the combustion (burning) of fuel. This heat is used to increase the pressure of gases. The pressurized gases are then used to produce usable motion.

As indicated earlier, there are two basic types of heat engines:
■ External-combustion
■ Internal-combustion
The difference between the two types is in *where* the gases are heated and pressurized.

In **external-combustion engines**, the heat energy is produced *outside* of the engine. This is done by burning fuels such as oil or coal, or by producing a controlled nuclear reaction. The heat is used to produce pressurized gas. Then the gas is piped into the engine, where it produces motion.

Most external-combustion engines are **steam engines**. The heat energy produced outside the engine is used to change water into steam. The steam is then used inside the engine to drive pistons or turbines.

Another type of external-combustion engine is the **Stirling Cycle engine**. Its driving force is produced by alternating expansion and contraction of a special gas.

In **internal-combustion engines**, heat and pressure are produced *inside* the engine. This is done by burning fuels such as gasoline, diesel fuel, and jet fuel. The pressure is converted into motion immediately. The next chapter will tell you about internal-combustion engines. First, however, you should know what kinds of motion we can get from heat engines.

Motion

Heat engines can produce reciprocating, rotary, and linear motion. **Reciprocating motion** is back-and-forth motion. This is the kind of motion produced in a piston engine. **Rotary motion** is spinning motion. Pressurized gases can be used to turn a rotor or turbine. **Linear motion** is motion in a straight line. Jet and rocket engines produce linear motion. See Fig. 11-1.

Engine Efficiency

When energy is changed from one form to another and put to work, some energy is lost. The amount of energy successfully converted into usable energy is expressed in terms of *efficiency*. We measure efficiency as the percentage of the available energy that is converted into usable energy. For example, about 40% of the energy produced by burning diesel oil in a diesel engine is converted into motion. The remaining 60% is lost. Most of the lost energy is in the form of unused heat.

The efficiency of the diesel engine is high compared to the locomotive steam engine. Old steam engines were less than 5% efficient. The low efficiency of steam engines is the main reason they were replaced by diesel-electric engines.

Energy conversion is usually an inefficient process. All heat engines operate with efficiencies well below 50%. As a result, less than half of the energy used is put to work. The rest is lost. This waste of energy is expensive and inefficient.

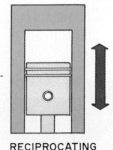

Fig. 11-1. Heat engines can produce three types of motion.

RECIPROCATING   ROTARY MOTION   LINEAR MOTION

Engine design has a great deal to do with the engine's efficiency. Designs have been changed to reduce energy losses. Designers and engineers are constantly researching new ideas to convert energy more efficiently. The better use we make of our energy, the less energy we will use.

STEAM ENGINES

The boiler is an important part of any steam engine. A *boiler* is a closed container that holds water. A heat source applied to the boiler changes the water into high-pressure steam.

The steam travels through pipes to the engine. Inside the engine, the steam pressure drives pistons or turbines. In this way, heat energy changes to mechanical energy.

The following diagram shows the main steps in steam engine operation:

Heat		Boils water changing it into steam		Steam drives engine		Mechanical energy (motion) produced
	◊		◊		◊	

Steam engines can use any energy source to produce heat. This is because the energy source never enters the engine. All of the fossil fuels (coal, oil, and natural gas) have been used to power steam engines. Other energy sources can also be used, including solar energy, geothermal energy, nuclear energy, and synfuels.

There are many different steam engine designs. Steam engines are made in hundreds of different sizes and shapes to fit special needs. However, all steam engines can be grouped into two classes:

- Reciprocating (piston) steam engines
- Steam turbines

Reciprocating (Piston) Steam Engines

Reciprocating steam engines were the first steam engines built for practical use. One of the best-known early steam engines was developed by an Englishman, *Thomas Newcomen*, in 1712. Water expands about 1700 times when it is changed into steam. Newcomen's engine made use of this expansion and the force behind it. See Fig 11-2.

Another English inventor improved on the steam engine about 50 years after Newcomen's development. *James Watt* added a special con-

denser to the Newcomen engine. This condenser was a hollow cylinder connected to the steam cylinder. The condenser cooled the steam without cooling the cylinder itself.

This new design improved the engine's efficiency. In the original Newcomen engine, the steam was cooled by cooling the cylinder. The cold cylinder reduced the temperature of the incoming steam. This in turn reduced steam pressure. Watt's design used less fuel and developed more power.

James Watt further experimented to produce the double-acting steam engine. In this engine, steam pressure pushed on both sides of the piston alternately. This was the first actual production of reciprocating motion by steam. (In the earlier engines, the steam only produced movement in one direction. The reverse movement was due to atmospheric pressure.) The double-acting design further improved the efficiency of the steam engine.

Soon, inventors made other improvements in the steam engine. They learned to increase the pressure of the steam by heating it in a boiler. In boilers, heat builds up. The higher the steam's temperature, the higher its steam pressure. The greater the pressure, the more force it could produce.

Figure 11-3 shows a reciprocating steam engine that uses high-pressure steam. Pressurized steam from the boiler flows into cylinder A. The

Fig. 11-2. The first practical steam engine was used to pump water from mine shafts. This engine was neither powerful nor efficient.

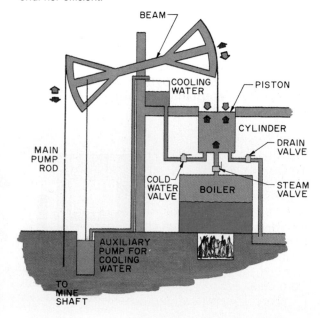

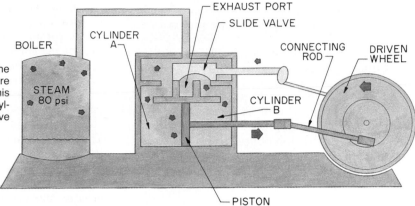

Fig. 11-3. A steam engine converts the force produced by high steam pressure into controlled, usable motion. In this drawing, steam is being supplied to cylinder A. This causes the piston to move to the right.

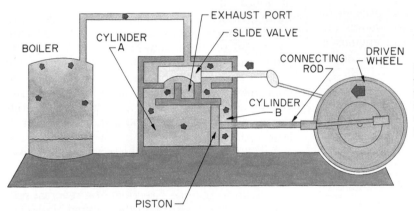

Fig. 11-4. When the side valve cuts off the steam for cylinder A, the steam enters cylinder B and pushes on the other side of the piston. The waste steam in cylinder A is pushed out the exhaust port.

steam pushes the piston to the right. This movement turns a wheel one-half turn. The rotation of the wheel pushes the slide valve to the left. The valve stops the flow of steam into cylinder A.

The steam then flows into cylinder B, as shown in Fig. 11-4. This forces the piston back to the left. As the piston moves to the left, the steam in cylinder A is pushed out through the exhaust port. The wheel makes another half-turn, completing one rotation. With this half-turn, the sliding valve moves back to the right. The cycle then begins again.

The constant back-and-forth piston movement keeps the wheel turning. The turning wheel produces mechanical energy. This energy can be used to drive generators or operate industrial machinery.

The force produced by a modern steam engine depends on the boiler pressure of the steam and the size of the piston. The force pushing the piston increases as either factor increases. We can find the amount of force with this equation from Chapter 6:

Force = Pressure × Area

The piston head is round. Therefore, we use the formula for the area of a circle to find the piston's surface area: Area of a circle $= \pi r^2$. Where:

$\pi = 3.14$

r = radius

In Fig. 11-5, for example, the radius is one-half of the 14-inch diameter. Therefore, the piston surface area is 3.14×7^2, or 154 square inches.

Fig. 11-5. Steam pressure and piston size are the two factors that determine the force produced by a steam engine.

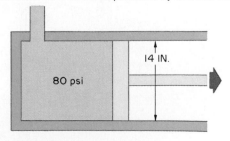

Example problem:

Find the force exerted by the piston in Fig. 11-5.

Force = Pressure × Area

Force = 80 psi × 154 sq. in.

Force = 12,320 lbs.

Steam engines brought about great changes in the way people lived. These engines introduced the age of self-propelled vehicles. Steam engines powered automobiles, trains, and ships. The steam engine mechanized agriculture. It provided power for plows, reapers, water pumps, and other farm equipment.

Steam Turbines

A **steam turbine** is a device that uses steam to produce rotary motion. Modern steam turbines are among the most powerful engines in the world. They operate on either the reaction principle or the impulse principle or both. See Fig. 11-6. These are the same principles used to drive hydraulic turbines. (See Chapter 2.)

Fig. 11-6. Steam turbines operate on either the reaction principle or the impulse principle. The two principles are shown in practice here.

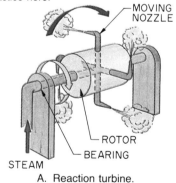

A. Reaction turbine.

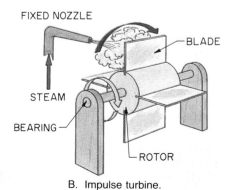

B. Impulse turbine.

In a *reaction turbine*, steam escapes from nozzles on a rotor. It applies a force that produces rotation. The force is opposite the direction of the escaping steam. The reaction turbine operates on the principle that "for every action there is an equal and opposite reaction."[1]

An *impulse turbine* has a fixed source of escaping steam. Again, see Fig. 11-6. In this engine, steam is directed against the blades of a rotor. This rotates the rotor in the same direction as the steam.

In both turbine types, the speed of the steam is important. The faster the steam moves, the greater the speed of rotation. Turbines rotate most efficiently at a speed about half that of the incoming steam. Large steam turbine rotors turn at about 10,000 revolutions per minute. Small turbine rotors turn at much higher speeds.

In impulse turbines, special nozzles increase the speed of the steam. See Fig. 11-7. Pressure forces the steam through the narrow part of the nozzle. The volume of the steam decreases, increasing its speed. (The same principle allows you to squirt water with a hose. Holding your thumb over part of the end forces the water to flow faster.)

The nozzles direct high-speed steam against blades. This causes them to *rotate*, as shown in Fig. 11-8. The blades are cup-shaped. This causes the steam to reverse direction. The reversal provides the greatest force to the moving blades.

After leaving the moving blades, the steam travels to a set of fixed blades. Again, see Fig. 11-8. These blades reverse the direction of the steam again. They direct it against another set of rotating blades. This sequence repeats until the steam loses most of its speed.

High-speed steam also travels between moving and fixed blades in reaction engines. However, the steam increases speed as it travels through the moving blades. See Fig. 11-9. The blades act like rotating nozzles. The high-speed steam applies force to the moving blades as it escapes from them.

---

[1]Newton's Third Law of Motion

Fig. 11-7. The nozzle of an impulse turbine increases the speed of the steam by decreasing its volume. The faster-moving steam then increases the speed of the turbine.

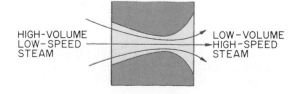

Technology Focus

A Powerful Idea

Obtaining power from steam is an ancient idea. The first steam turbine was built by *Hero* of Alexandria in the first century A.D. Hero named his device for the Greek god of the winds, *Aeolus*.

The ball of Aeolus, or *aeolipile*, consisted of a hollow metal ball mounted on pipes extending from a steam kettle. The ball was mounted in such a way that it could rotate between the supporting pipes. Two smaller L-shaped pipes came out of the ball halfway between the supports. These open-ended pipes were exactly opposite each other.

When water in the kettle was heated, steam rose through the supporting pipes into the ball. It then flowed forcefully from the L-shaped pipes, causing the ball to rotate. The energy of steam was changed into rotary motion.

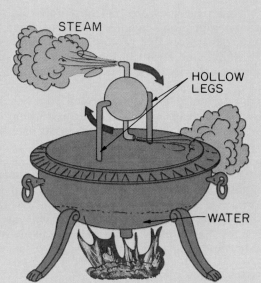

Hero's *aeolipile reaction turbine* was never put to practical use. But all important technological developments must first begin as ideas. Hero's device demonstrated principles that others applied to develop powerful engines that have influenced life through the ages.

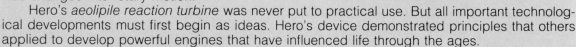

The steam then goes through fixed blades. These blades reverse the direction of the steam and direct it to another set of moving blades. This action gives some impulse power to the moving blades. Therefore, reaction turbines actually work on a combination of reaction and impulse principles.

Two things happen to steam as it moves through a turbine. It loses speed and it loses pressure. Both changes happen as the steam transfers energy to the turning blades. The pressure decrease causes an increase in steam volume. Therefore, turbine blades are *larger* in diameter and size toward the steam outlet end of

Fig. 11-8. In an impulse steam turbine, the nozzles and fixed blades direct high-speed steam to the moving blades. The moving blades are connected to an output shaft.

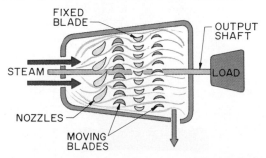

Fig. 11-9. In a reaction turbine, the steam increases in speed as it passes through the moving blades. The fixed blades direct the steam to other moving blades.

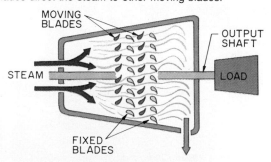

the engine. The larger diameter blades provide a mechanical advantage of force over the shorter blades. This permits the low-pressure steam to balance the force at the high-pressure end of the turbine.

Steam turbines are the most important external-combustion engines. We use them to power generators that produce large amounts of electricity. One steam turbine, for example, can supply electricity for a city of 200,000 people.

Small cogeneration systems can also use steam turbines to generate electricity. See Fig. 11-10. The steam used to drive this turbine can be used to provide heat for industrial uses and to heat buildings.

Steam turbines also power large ocean-going ships. All nuclear-fueled ships in the United States Navy are powered by steam turbines.

A variety of fuels can be used with steam turbines. Fossil fuels, nuclear fuels, geothermal energy, and almost any other heat source can be used.

STIRLING CYCLE ENGINE

Engineers in government and industry are constantly working to develop more efficient ex-

ternal-combustion engines. They are both redesigning traditional types of engines and studying new types of engines.

One promising engine under development is *Stirling Cycle engine*. It is named after its inventor, the Scottish engineer *Robert Stirling*. The Stirling engine principle is not new. It was patented in 1816. Like the Newcomen engine, the Stirling engine was first used to pump water. Today's Stirling engines have many possible uses, including electrical power generation and power for transportation.

The Stirling engine works somewhat like a reciprocating steam engine. Both engines use a gas to move a piston. And both engines use an external energy source to heat or produce the gas. In a steam engine, however, the gas (steam) is piped into a cylinder to move the piston. In a Stirling engine, the gas—usually hydrogen or helium—passes back and forth between two cylinders.

The gas used in a Stirling engine is called a *captive working gas*. It does not leave the engine after doing work. Instead, the gas is recycled to do more work.

A Stirling engine has a "hot side" and a "cold side." The hot side contains an *expansion piston* in a cylinder. The cold side contains a *compression piston* in another cylinder. Both pistons are connected to a crankshaft. This means that the movement of one piston will affect the movement of the other piston. See Fig. 11-11.

A Stirling engine is started just like an automobile engine. A starting motor turns a flywheel on the engine's crankshaft. At the same time, fuel is ignited in the combustion chamber. The heat of combustion then expands the gas contained in

Fig. 11-10. This 3.1-megawatt Centaur(R) gas turbine cogeneration system is installed at a pharmaceutical manufacturing plant. At the right is the turbine generator set with the air filter/silencer on top. In the center is the exhaust bypass valve and stack. On the left is the boiler which uses the high-temperature turbine exhaust to produce process steam.

Fig. 11-11. As the gas moves back and forth from the compression cylinder to the expansion cylinder, it produces reciprocating motion. This motion is changed to rotary motion with a crankshaft.

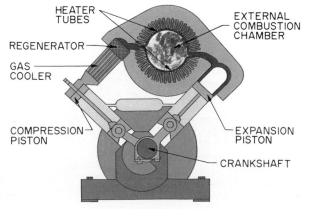

HEATER TUBES

EXTERNAL COMBUSTION CHAMBER

REGENERATOR

GAS COOLER

COMPRESSION PISTON

EXPANSION PISTON

CRANKSHAFT

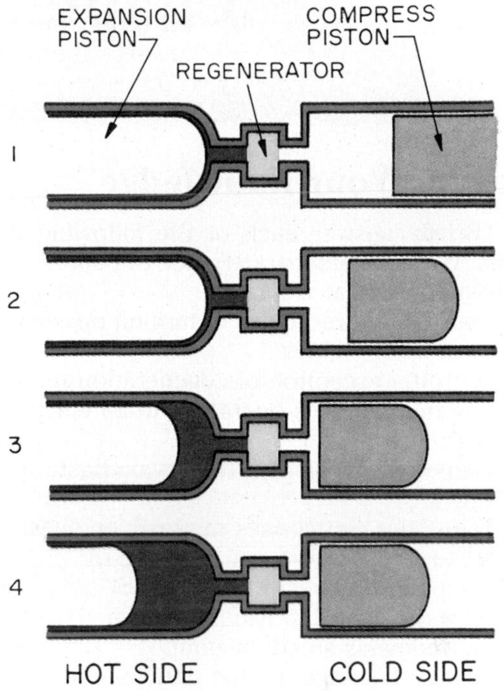

Fig. 11-12. The stages in the Stirling cycle:
Steps 1-2: Compression piston compresses gas on cold side.
Steps 2-3: Gas moves from cold side to hot side.
Steps 3-4: Heated gas expands to move expansion piston.
Steps 4-1: Gas moves from hot side to cold side.

EXPANSION PISTON

COMPRESS PISTON

REGENERATOR

1

2

3

4

HOT SIDE   COLD SIDE

heater tubes in the chamber. The pistons go through the stages shown in Fig. 11-12 to produce power.

Driven by the crankshaft, the compression piston moves up to compress the working gas on the cold side (Steps 1-2). The gas then moves through a *regenerator*. The regenerator heats the gas as it moves from the cold side to the hot side (Steps 2-3). The heated gas expands to drive the expansion piston down (Steps 3-4). The turning crankshaft then forces the expansion piston up to move the gas back to the cold side (Steps 4-1).

As the gas moves through the regenerator, the regenerator removes heat from it. Heat is also removed by a liquid cooling system. The gas then contracts, and it is ready to be compressed again.

Stirling engines have the potential to be more fuel-efficient and powerful than internal-combustion engines. They also operate much more quietly and produce far less pollution.

Stirling engines have a *multifuel* capability. This means that they can use almost any fuel, including gasoline, diesel fuel, and natural gas. Other possible fuels include methanol, coal, wood, and burnable waste products.

Stirling engines are already being used to generate electricity. Someday they may power many cars and trucks.

Testing Your Knowledge

Briefly answer each of the following questions. Write on a separate piece of paper.

1. What are heat engines?
2. Name the three types of motion possible with heat engines.
3. With the exception of cogeneration uses, do any heat engines operate with an efficiency over 50%?
4. Name two types of external-combustion engines.
5. Name the two classes of steam engines.
6. What was the first practical use of reciprocating steam engines?
7. How did James Watt improve on Newcomen's steam engine?
8. What advantage did the double-acting steam engine have over earlier steam engines?
9. The force of modern reciprocating steam engines depends on two things. What are they?
10. Why are reciprocating steam engines seldom used today?
11. Identify the two principles on which steam turbines can operate.
12. Why is the speed of the steam in a steam turbine important?
13. Name two important uses of steam turbines.

Solve this problem:

14. A steam train engine has four sets of drive wheels. Each set is driven by a single cylinder steam engine. The cylinder diameter is 14 inches and the steam pressure is 75 psi. Calculate the total force pushing the train forward from all four engines working at the same time.

Expressing Your Knowledge

Using complete sentences, write your answers to the following on a separate sheet of paper:

1. Identify the two broad categories of heat engines, and describe the main difference between the two.
2. Explain what is meant by this statement: "An engine is 30% efficient."
3. Describe the main steps in steam engine operation.
4. Why can steam engines use any energy source to produce heat?
5. Explain how confined boilers improved steam engines.
6. Describe how high-speed steam produces rotation in an impulse turbine. (See illustration below.)
7. Why is the gas in a Stirling engine called "captive working gas"?

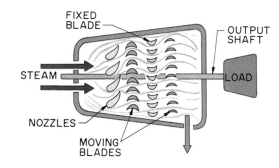

FIXED BLADE · OUTPUT SHAFT · STEAM · LOAD · NOZZLES · MOVING BLADES

Knowledge Is Power

Applying Your Knowledge

Follow your teacher's instructions to complete these activities:

1. Construct a small steam turbine. See Fig. 11-13. The materials you will need are a rectangular metal can with a metal lid (such as a spice can or any small can with a removable metal lid), small hollow tube, thread, fishing swivel, and alcohol burner or candle.

    The metal lid serves as a safety valve. If the pressure inside gets too high, it will be pushed off.

    Use only a small amount of water—1 or 2 tablespoons are enough, depending on the size of the can.

    If the tube is too large, performance will be poor. You may need to squeeze the ends to decrease size. The tubes should be glued or soldered into can. If glued, use extra glue to seal around the tube.

2. Prepare a report on old-time steam locomotives still operating in the United States. Use encyclopedia and other reference books and resource materials. Also, check with local train officials and read railroad journals, if available.

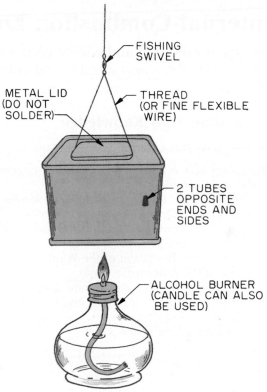

Fig. 11-13. "Hero-type" steam turbine.

Chapter 12

Internal-Combustion Engines

The most common and widely used engines throughout the world are internal-combustion engines.

Expanding Your Knowledge

As you study this chapter, you will learn to:

■ Explain how an internal-combustion engine produces motion from fuel.
■ Describe what happens during each stroke of both a two-stroke and four-stroke cycle engine.
■ Identify the primary differences between diesel and gasoline engines.
■ Describe the operation of the Wankel rotary engine in terms of the four-stroke cycle.
■ Explain how jet engines operate, including the operation of turbojet, ramjet, turbofan, and turboprop engines.
■ Describe the operation of the two types of rocket engines used for space flights.

Building Your Word Power

The following terms are defined and explained in this chapter. Learning these will help you learn more about internal-combustion engines.

compression ignition
cycle
diesel engine
engine thrust reverser
four-stroke cycle engine
gas turbine engine
gasoline piston engine
jet engine
jet propulsion
ramjet engine
rocket engine
rotary engine
stroke
Third Law of Motion
thrust
turbofan engine
turbojet engine
turboprop engine
two-stroke cycle engine

In this chapter, the operation of the most common types of internal-combustion engines is explained. We will examine the differences between two-stroke and four-stroke cycle engines. The diesel engine is presented as a simple variation of the operation of the gasoline engine.

Jet engines power most commercial airplanes and are the world's most important engine for rapid transportation over long distances. Rocket engines power space flights. These engines all operate on the same principle. This chapter contains a description of this principle and an explanation of the differences between the many engines used for air and space flights.

OUR MOST IMPORTANT ENGINE

Except for steam-powered ships, most transportation devices are powered by internal-combustion engines. These lightweight and powerful engines have made air travel possible. The rocket engine, a very powerful type of internal-combustion engine, has even propelled humans into space.

Internal-combustion engines also have important uses as stationary (fixed) engines. They run generators to produce electrical power. They also produce mechanical power for industrial machinery and equipment.

Like steam engines and Stirling Cycle engines, internal-combustion engines are *heat engines*. They burn fuel to produce pressurized gases. However, there is a big difference. In internal-combustion engines, the pressurized gases are produced *inside* the engine. The gases don't have to be piped in, as with a steam engine.

Do you remember the three kinds of motion that are possible with a heat engine? They are reciprocating motion, rotary motion, and linear motion. (Refer back to Fig. 11-1.) Different kinds of internal-combustion engines produce different kinds of motion. Gasoline and diesel piston engines produce reciprocating motion. Rotary engines produce rotary motion. Jet engines and rocket engines produce linear motion.

GASOLINE PISTON ENGINES

Wherever you happen to be at this moment, chances are that a **gasoline piston engine** isn't too far away. We are surrounded by gasoline piston engines. They are used to power automobiles. In addition, many small gasoline piston engines are used to power lawn mowers, small generators, and garden tillers. See Fig. 12-1. You will learn more about small gasoline engines in the next section of this book.

Gasoline piston engines produce reciprocating (back-and-forth) motion. A piston moves alternately from one end of a cylinder to the other. A crankshaft in the engine changes the reciprocating motion into rotary motion. See Fig. 12-2.

Fig. 12-1. Gasoline piston engines have greatly influenced our lives. For example, what would life be like without automobiles?

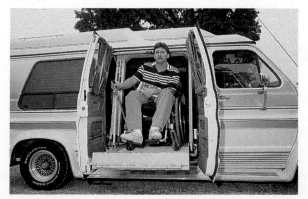

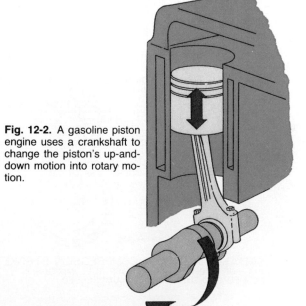

Fig. 12-2. A gasoline piston engine uses a crankshaft to change the piston's up-and-down motion into rotary motion.

There are two basic types of gasoline piston engines:

■ Four-stroke cycle engine
■ Two-stroke cycle engine

Both types of engines operate with a piston moving up and down in a cylinder. The difference is in the number of strokes that the piston makes per engine cycle. A **stroke** is the movement of the piston from one end of the cylinder to the other. A **cycle** is a complete set of piston movements. It includes all of the strokes needed to produce a power stroke.

Many times the word "stroke" or "cycle" is left out of a description of the engine. For example, *four-stroke engine* and *four-cycle engine* mean the same thing: a four-stroke cycle engine.

Four-Stroke Cycle Engines

Most modern piston engines operate on the principle of the four-stroke cycle. A German named *Karl Otto* built the first four-stroke engine in 1876. Otto's name was given to the four-stroke principle. It is still referred to as the *Otto cycle*.

In **four-stroke cycle engines** there are four separate piston strokes:

■ Intake
■ Compression
■ Power
■ Exhaust

See Fig. 12-3.

On the *intake stroke*, the piston moves down the cylinder. This creates a partial vacuum at the top of the cylinder. The intake valve is open at this time. Atmospheric pressure pushes a mixture of gasoline and air into the cylinder.

As the piston starts up on the *compression stroke*, the intake valve closes. This seals the cylinder. The piston can then compress the air-fuel mixture into a small area at the top of the cylinder. This area is called the *combustion chamber*. The piston compresses the mixture to about one-eighth its original volume. The comparison between the original and the compressed volume is called the *compression ratio*. A compression ratio of 8:1 is enough to produce high pressure in the combustion chamber.

The *power stroke* begins as a spark plug ignites (sets fire to) the compressed air-fuel mixture. The burning air-fuel mixture raises the temperature inside the cylinder. This further increases the pressure in the combustion chamber. The pressure is now about seven times the pressure before ignition. The increased pressure drives the piston down. It is the force of this downward movement that produces mechanical power.

Note that the same kind of driving force also drives the steam piston engine. You can calculate this force by multiplying the cylinder pressure by the piston area (Pressure × Area = Force).

The final stroke in the cycle is the *exhaust stroke*. Near the end of the power stroke, the exhaust valve opens. Then, as the piston moves up, it pushes the burned gases out of the cylinder.

At the end of the exhaust stroke, the piston reaches the top of the cylinder. The piston then starts down on another intake stroke. This begins a new cycle.

Fig. 12-3. The operation of a four-stroke cycle gasoline engine.

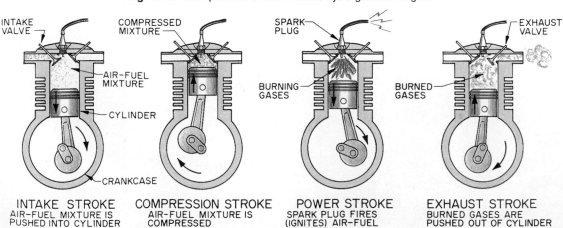

INTAKE STROKE
AIR-FUEL MIXTURE IS PUSHED INTO CYLINDER

COMPRESSION STROKE
AIR-FUEL MIXTURE IS COMPRESSED

POWER STROKE
SPARK PLUG FIRES (IGNITES) AIR-FUEL MIXTURE

EXHAUST STROKE
BURNED GASES ARE PUSHED OUT OF CYLINDER

Two-Stroke Cycle Engines

Two-stroke cycle engines contain fewer moving parts than four-stroke engines. This makes them simpler, easier to build, and much lighter in weight. However, they are much less fuel-efficient. They also give off more pollution than four-stroke engines. Therefore, two-stroke engines are generally used when light weight is more important than good fuel efficiency. The most common uses are for lawn mowers, outboard motors, and small motorcycles.

The operation of a two-stroke engine consists of a compression stroke and a power stroke. As in the four-stroke engine, there are four actions—intake, compression, power, and exhaust. However these all take place in just two strokes. See Fig. 12-4.

Most two-stroke engines do not have intake and exhaust valves. Instead, they have intake and exhaust ports (holes) in the cylinder wall. Most of these engines also have a reed valve at the bottom of the crankcase. The air-fuel mixture enters the engine through this valve. (Reed valves are explained in Chapter 15.)

As the piston moves upward on the *compression stroke*, two things happen. The piston blocks off the intake and exhaust ports. This seals in the air-fuel mixture so that the piston can compress it in the combustion chamber. At the same time, new air-fuel mixture enters the crankcase through the reed valve. This is made possible by the partial vacuum created by the upward movement of the piston.

When compression is complete, the spark plug ignites the compressed air-fuel mixture. The hot expanding gases push the piston down on the *power stroke*. As the piston passes the exhaust port, the burned gases begin to leave the engine. The piston then passes the intake port. New air-fuel mixture pushes up into the combustion chamber. The crankcase pressure built up by the downward movement of the piston causes this push.

As the new mixture enters the combustion chamber, it helps to push out the burned gases. The piston then starts back up on the next compression stroke. This begins a new cycle.

DIESEL ENGINES

The diesel engine was invented by a German mechanical engineer named *Rudolph Diesel*. He patented his design in 1892, and built a working diesel engine in 1897.

Today's diesel engines provide power for trains and buses. They also power automobiles, trucks, boats, ships, and most construction equipment. See Fig. 12-5. As stationary engines, they power generators that produce electricity.

Diesel engines operate on the same two- and four-stroke principles used in gasoline piston engines. However, diesels do not use a spark to ignite the fuel. Instead, the fuel is ignited by the intense heat of compression. This type of ignition is called **compression ignition**. See Fig. 12-6.

Fig. 12-4. The operation of a two-stroke cycle engine. The four diagrams show the position of the piston during a single cycle.

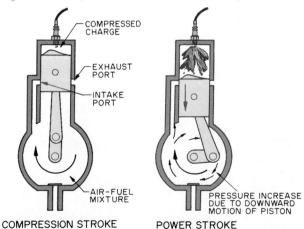

COMPRESSION STROKE
AIR-FUEL MIXTURE IS COMPRESSED. PORTS ARE SEALED.

POWER STROKE
AIR-FUEL MIXTURE IS IGNITED. PISTON IS FORCED DOWN.

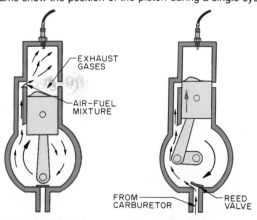

POWER STROKE
EXHAUST GASES LEAVE CYLINDER. AIR-FUEL MIXTURE ENTERS CYLINDER.

COMPRESSION STROKE
PISTON BEGINS COMPRESSION. AIR-FUEL MIXTURE ENTERS CRANKCASE.

Fig. 12-5. Diesel engines are well-suited to heavy-duty work.

Compression ignition requires an air and fuel supply system different from that of gasoline engines. In diesels, air and fuel do not enter the cylinder together. Only air is admitted on the intake stroke.

During the compression stroke, the air is compressed to $\frac{1}{16}$ to $\frac{1}{23}$ its original volume. That is, the compression ratio is from 16:1 to 23:1. This is more than twice the compression produced on the compression stroke in a gasoline engine. This high compression ratio raises the pressure and temperature inside the cylinder. The temperature inside the cylinder reaches approximately 1000°F (538°C).

At the end of the compression stroke, diesel fuel is sprayed into the cylinder. As the fuel enters the cylinder, it is ignited by the high temperature of the compressed air.

As the fuel burns, it produces very hot gases. The heated gases further raise the pressure in the cylinder. The increased pressure forces the piston down, producing the power stroke.

The diesel's higher cylinder pressures require it to be made stronger than gasoline engines. Otherwise the great amounts of pressure would damage the engine. Diesel engines are therefore larger and heavier than comparable gasoline engines. They also produce less power by weight.

The greatest advantage of the diesel engine is its fuel economy. A gasoline engine with the same horsepower as a diesel engine will weigh much less. It will also accelerate faster. However, diesel engines are about 25% more fuel-efficient than gasoline engines.

Diesel engines are used in large trucks and, to a limited extent, in American cars. As fuel prices increase in the future, diesel engines will grow in popularity. (See Chapter 14.)

ROTARY ENGINES

The **rotary engine** is often called a *Wankel engine*. See Fig. 12-7. This engine was designed by a German scientist, *Felix Wankel*, in 1958. Today Wankel engines are manufactured in a variety of sizes. They can be used as substitutes for most piston engines. Wankel engines are compact, have very little vibration, and are simple.

The Wankel engine combines features of the piston and turbine engines. Like piston engines, Wankel engines have four different actions—intake, compression, power, and exhaust. However,

Fig. 12-6. Air and fuel are supplied differently in a diesel engine than they are in a gasoline engine. The diesel's method of ignition is also different.

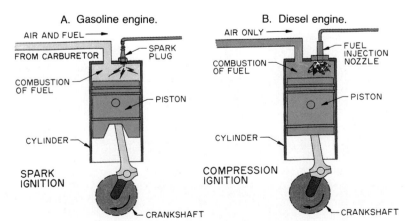

Wankel engines do not produce reciprocating motion, as piston engines do. Instead, they produce direct *rotary motion*. In this way, Wankel engines are similar to turbine engines.

Wankel engines are more fuel-efficient than turbine engines. However, Wankel engines are less fuel-efficient and more polluting than piston engines. Sealing the combustion chamber is also more difficult in Wankel engines than in piston engines.

Refer again to Fig. 12-7. The main part of the engine is a triangular *rotor*. This device plays a central part in producing the intake, compression, power, and exhaust actions. The rotor is sandwiched between the front and rear covers. It spins inside the *rotor housing*. See Fig. 12-8.

The rotor has an internal gear that meshes with a stationary gear. These gears keep the rotor properly positioned in the rotor housing at all times.

As the rotor rotates, the tips of the rotor, called the *apex seals*, press against the rotor housing. This action seals one combustion chamber from the next. The *eccentric* (off-center) *lobe* of the output shaft fits inside the rotor. As the rotor rotates, it drives the eccentric lobe of the output shaft. The output shaft spins in a fixed position. This shaft is supported by two bearings that allow easy rotation.

Because of its triangular shape, the rotor has three separate combustion chambers. See Fig. 12-9. The three chambers are in constant operation. This means that the rotor produces three power strokes for every revolution.

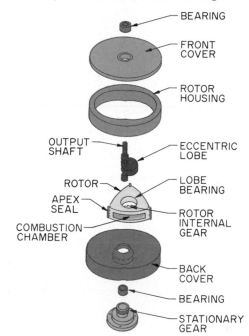

Fig. 12-8. This exploded view gives a closeup of the rotor and housing assembly on a rotary engine.

Trace the operation of the Wankel engine as shown in Fig. 12-9. Notice that one apex of the rotor has been labeled *X*.

Remember also that all three chambers are working at the same time. While one chamber is on intake and compression, the second chamber is on the power stroke. The third chamber is on the exhaust stroke.

Much research and development has been done on the Wankel engine. Engines vary in size from giant industrial engines to miniature engines. Wankel engines have been made with both single and multiple rotors. They have used fuels varying from methane gas to diesel oil. They have powered boats, automobiles, and airplanes.

Because Wankel engines are relatively lightweight and a variety of fuels may be used to operate them, the Wankel engine may become a *small* general aviation engine. See Fig. 12-10. Most small planes now use gasoline, but rotary engines are able to use the jet fuel (similar to kerosene) available at most airports. Problems remain, however. Researchers must find ways to improve fuel efficiency, prolong apex seal life, and control pollution.

Fig. 12-7. A rotary engine performs more smoothly and quietly than a piston engine.

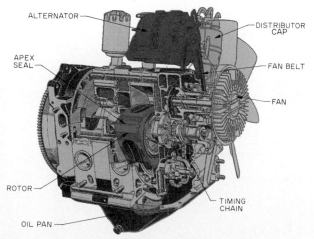

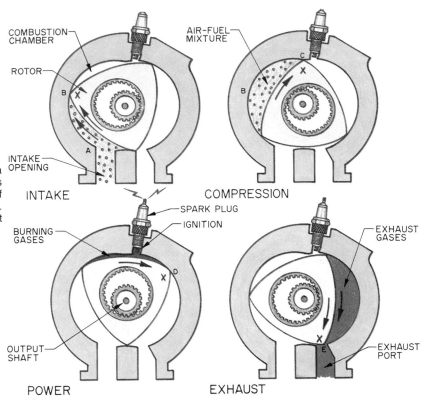

Fig. 12-9. The operation of a Wankel engine. Note that this diagram follows the action of only one combustion chamber. The other two are operating at the same time.

JET ENGINES

Jet engines can develop huge amounts of power for their size and weight. For this reason, they are used to power aircraft and missiles. They often propel aircraft at speeds over 750 miles (1200 km) per hour. See Fig. 12-11.

To understand how a jet engine works, we must review what happens to gases under pressure. Pressurized gases in a closed container exert pressure (push) equally in all directions. The forces of this pressure are in balance. For example, the air inside an expanded balloon pushes out on all surfaces with the same force. When the balloon is released, the air starts to escape.

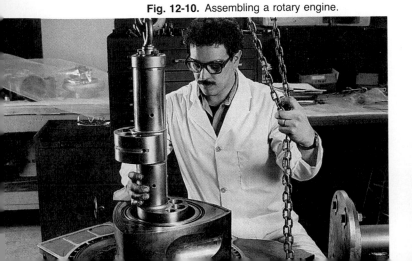

Fig. 12-10. Assembling a rotary engine.

Fig. 12-11. Jet engines are powerful!

This causes the forces inside the balloon to become imbalanced. More force is applied to the surface opposite the stem. This imbalance of force causes the balloon to be "jet-propelled" around the room.

Isaac Newton described the principle of **jet propulsion** in his **Third Law of Motion**: *To every action there is an equal and opposite reaction.* See Fig. 12-12.

Jet engines work on the principle of equal and opposite reaction. In fact, the first jet engines were called *reaction engines*. Several types of jet engines are used today. Each one uses the reaction principle in a slightly different way.

Fig. 12-12A. As the boy steps onto the dock, the "equal and opposite" reaction pushes the boat away.

Turbojet Engine

Modern jet engines are open at both ends. The **turbojet engine** is a common type of jet engine. Turbojet engines are used mainly on military aircraft. Air is brought in by an air compressor and the forward motion of the aircraft. See Fig. 12-13. The *compressor* forces the air into the combustion chamber. Here the fuel—a form of kerosene—is added and ignited. The burning fuel increases the temperature and pressure in the chamber. Pressurized gases exert a strong force in all directions.

At the same time, air is rushing in the front of the engine. This prevents gases from escaping out the front. As the pressurized gases escape out the rear, they drive a large fan called the *turbine*. The rotating turbine drives the compressor.

The escaping gases also cause an imbalance of forces inside the engine. The greater force at the front of the engine pushes it forward. This push is called **thrust**. We measure thrust in pounds or in newtons. It is the forward *force* the engine is producing at any given time. The output of a linear-motion engine (such as a jet) is always measured as thrust. Reciprocating or rotary engine output is measured as *torque*.

The action in the jet engine is continuous. Air intake, fuel addition, ignition, and thrust are all maintained on a constant basis.

Fig. 12-12B. "For every action there is an equal and opposite reaction." This principle includes all motion, whether produced by mechanical force or by pressure. The opposite reaction to the expanding gases escaping from the rear of the rocket pushes the rocket up and eventually into orbit.

Ramjet Engine

The **ramjet engine** is a very simple kind of jet engine. Basically it is little more than a hollow tube. The ramjet engine has no moving parts at the inlet, exhaust outlet, and in the combustion chamber. Ramjets are used mainly to power guided missiles.

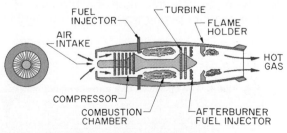

Fig. 12-13. The operation of a turbojet engine.

Technology Focus

Flying Into the 21st Century

Aviation in the 21st century promises to be exciting! Already work has begun to develop a *supersonic aerospace plane*. It will be able to take off from a runway and fly halfway around the world in less than two hours. Or, it may fly from the runway directly into orbit.

The National Aero-Space Plane program (NASP) is a joint project of the National Aeronautics and Space Administration (NASA) and the Department of Defense (DOD). By the year 2000, they plan to have operational aerospace vehicles that can travel up to 25 times the speed of sound (Mach 25). To accomplish this, new technology must be developed.

Supersonic combustion ramjet (SCRAMJET) *engines* are being developed. These will use hydrogen for fuel and fly at speeds Mach 5 to 25.

New structural *materials and designs* are needed. These must be very strong to withstand supersonic speeds. Materials must be low in weight and provide a heat shield.

Supercomputers will be used for design and flight simulations. For actual testing, an *experimental plane* called the X-30 will be built in the 1990s.

Vehicles developed by the NASP program will be able to carry passengers from an airport to a space station and back in the same day. Welcome to the 21st century!

The forward motion of the ramjet brings large amounts of air into the combustion chamber. See Fig. 12-14. The incoming air compresses the air already in the chamber. The special shape of the chamber causes this compression. Fuel addition and ignition are the same as with the turbojet. Thrust is produced the same way. Incoming air prevents the forward exhaust of burned fuel.

At high speeds, the ramjet is more efficient and more trouble-free than the turbojet. However, it cannot operate while at rest, during take-off, or at low speeds. Missiles equipped with ramjets must use a rocket engine until a very high speed is reached. At that speed, the ramjet is ignited to produce a great deal of added thrust and speed.

In the future, planes may use *turbo-ramjet* engines. They would start and operate like turbojets. When a certain speed had been reached, the engines would be shifted over to ramjet operation. The ramjet would increase both speed and efficiency.

Fig. 12-14. The operation of a ramjet engine.

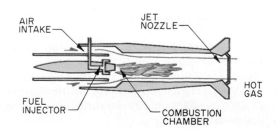

Fig. 12-15. Many jet airliners use turbofan engines. The larger fan provides additional thrust.

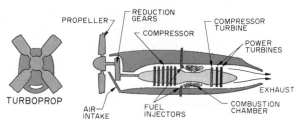

Fig. 12-16. The operation of a turboprop jet engine.

Turbofan Engine

The **turbofan engine** is similar to the turbojet engine. However, aircraft using turbofans have an additional source of propulsion. A large fan is mounted on the front of the engine. Turbines at the rear of the engine turn the fan. The fan forces huge amounts of air both into and around the engine.

 Forward motion is produced in two ways. The imbalance of forces inside the engine produces thrust. The air forced from the fan around the outside of the engine produces additional thrust.

The fan supplies the engine with a great deal of air. Combustion can take place more efficiently with more air. Therefore, the turbofan engine is more powerful and efficient at low speeds than the turbojet. For these reasons, turbofans are used to power many commercial airliners. See Fig. 12-15.

Turboprop Engine

The **turboprop engine** is very similar to the turbofan engine. The main difference is that the turboprop has a propeller instead of a fan. See Fig. 12-16.

A *compressor turbine* at the rear of the engine operates a compressor. The compressor compresses incoming air and forces it into the combustion chamber. Fuel addition and ignition are the same as in a turbojet engine. The pressurized gases resulting from combustion pass over *power turbines*. These turbines drive the propeller.

The turboprop engine has more turbines than a turbojet. They are also larger. These turbines use nearly all of the energy produced by the burning fuel to operate the compressor and propeller. Very little energy is used directly as forward thrust.

Turboprop engines are used mainly in small business airplanes. They are very effective for flights of short or medium distance.

Reverse Thrust

Jet airplanes land at high speed. Wheel brakes are unable to stop the momentum of a large, heavy airplane. The engines must be used.

An **engine thrust reverser** reverses the forward thrust of a jet engine to stop the airplane. See Fig. 12-17.

One type of engine thrust reverser is called a *target reverser* (Fig. 12-17A). After the plane lands, two doors at the back of each engine swing out. The exhaust is deflected forward by the doors, reversing the thrust. This type of reverser is used on many small and medium-sized planes.

A second type is called a *cascade reverser* (Fig. 12-17B). On large jet engines, the majority of the air taken in at the front passes through large ducts surrounding the engine core. A smaller portion of the air passes through the engine core. When the thrust is reversed, the ducts around the core are closed. At the same time a thrust reverser sleeve slides forward. This forces the exhaust air to escape forward, reversing the thrust.

Gas Turbine

The **gas turbine engine** is basically a turboprop engine without a propeller. The two engines operate on the same principles. However, they are used for different purposes. Turboprops are used only to power aircraft. Gas turbines power generators, ships, and experimental automobiles and trucks.

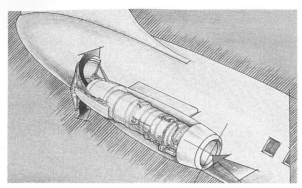

A. Target reverser.

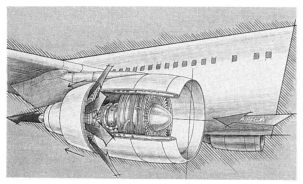

B. Cascade reverser.

Fig. 12-17. The two most common methods for reversing the thrust of jet engines. This action slows the airplane to a speed that can be managed by wheel brakes.

Fig. 12-18. Ceramic engines, such as this experimental model, can withstand very high temperatures, but ceramic parts are difficult, as well as expensive, to manufacture.

Many uses of the gas turbine are experimental. Turbines in gas turbine engines rotate at high speeds. They are also exposed to high temperatures. These conditions require the use of expensive materials and manufacturing procedures. See Fig. 12-18. Gas turbine engines are also less fuel-efficient than piston engines. These factors make the gas turbine a poor substitute for most piston engines.

ROCKET ENGINES

Rocket engines are the most powerful internal-combustion engines. A rocket engine the same size as a 100-horsepower piston engine could produce over 300,000 horsepower. Rocket engines that provide the power for space exploration are even more powerful than this. For example, the space shuttle's solid rocket boosters (SRBs) develop about 6.6 million pounds of thrust (29.4 million newtons) during takeoff. This thrust is supplemented by the three shuttle main engines which produce just under

400,000 pounds of thrust (1,750,000 newtons) each. See Fig. 12-19.

To produce their tremendous power, rocket engines use up huge amounts of fuel. A large rocket can use up over 500,000 gallons (1.9 million liters) of fuel within three minutes after takeoff.

Rocket engines, like jet engines, work on the reaction principle. The main difference is in the supply of oxygen to burn the fuel. Jet engines use

Fig. 12-19. The space shuttle is powered by rocket engines. A payload totaling 65,000 pounds (29,000 kg) can be carried in the bay.

oxygen from the air. Rocket engines carry their own oxygen supply. This makes it possible for rocket engines to operate in space, where there is no oxygen.

The operation of the rocket engine is very simple. Fuel and oxygen are mixed and ignited in the combustion chamber. The burning gases expand. They move rapidly out the exhaust port at the rear of the engine. The opposite reaction pushes the engine ahead, just as in jet engines.

Rocket engines can be divided into two types. One type uses liquid propellant (fuel). The other uses solid propellant.

Liquid-Propellant Rocket Engines

Liquid-propellant rocket engines use liquids for both the fuel and the source of oxygen. Commonly used fuels are kerosene, alcohol, and liquid hydrogen. Liquid oxygen is often used as the oxygen source. The fuel and oxygen are mixed and ignited as they enter the combustion chamber. See Fig. 12-20.

All of the United States' early space exploration efforts used liquid-fueled rockets. Power output can be regulated in liquid-propellant engines. This is one advantage they have over solid-fuel engines.

Solid-Propellant Rocket Engines

Much research and development has gone into solid-propellant rocket engines. In these engines, the fuel and oxygen are combined in a solid form. See Fig. 12-21. Solid-propellant engines are much simpler than liquid-propellant engines. The fuel does not have to be pumped to a combustion chamber. It is simply ignited and allowed to burn. This provides thrust, just as in liquid-propellant engines. Solid-fuel engines are so simple that they are used on a small scale to power model rockets.

The design of a solid-propellant engine determines its power output and duration. Once the engine is made and its fuel is ignited, its power output cannot be regulated.

Fig. 12-21. Solid-propellant rockets burn a solid chemical that contains both the fuel and the necessary oxygen.

Fig. 12-20. A liquid-propellant rocket uses both liquid fuel and liquid oxygen for combustion.

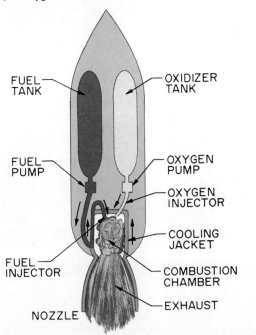

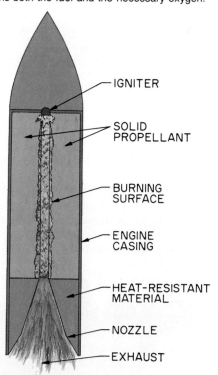

Chapter 12—Review

Testing Your Knowledge

Briefly answer each of the following questions. Write on a separate piece of paper.

1. Name the two basic types of gasoline piston engines.
2. Name (in order) the four strokes of the four-stroke engine.
3. Name three advantages two-stroke engines have over four-stroke engines.
4. Name two disadvantages of two-stroke engines as compared to four-stroke engines.
5. What is the main difference in operation between diesel and gasoline engines?
6. What is the greatest advantage of the diesel engine over the gasoline engine?
7. Wankel engines have features of what two types of engines?
8. How many combustion chambers are there in a Wankel rotor?
9. How many power strokes happen during a single rotation of the Wankel rotor?
10. What is Newton's Third Law of Motion?
11. What is the purpose of the turbine in a turbojet engine?
12. What type of jet engine is commonly used on commercial airliners?
13. What is the difference between a gas turbine engine and a turboprop engine?
14. What is the principle used to reverse the thrust of a jet engine?
15. What is the main difference between a rocket engine and a jet engine?
16. What are the two types of propellant used in rocket engines?
17. What advantage does liquid-propellant engines have over solid-propellant engines?

Solve this problem:

18. The pressure at the start of the power stroke in a small two-stroke cycle lawn mower engine is measured at 450 psi. The piston diameter is 1½ inches. What is the force pushing the piston?

Expressing Your Knowledge

Using complete sentences, write your answers to the following on a separate sheet of paper.

1. How do internal-combustion engines produce motion?
2. What is meant by the words "stroke" and "cycle" when referring to engines?
3. Describe what happens on each of the four strokes of the four-stroke cycle.
4. Describe what happens on each of the two strokes of the two-stroke cycle.
5. Explain how the fuel is ignited in a diesel engine.
6. Describe how a turbojet engine operates.
7. What is meant by "thrust"?
8. How are turbofan engines different from turbojet engines?
9. Explain how a rocket engine operates.

Applying Your Knowledge

Follow your teacher's instructions to complete these activities:

1. Conduct a "jet propulsion" contest using balloons. A balloon simply blown up and released goes in many directions. If a cork is placed in the end of the balloon, and a small hole placed in the cork, the balloon will have more flight stability. A rubber band is needed to hold the balloon tightly against the cork.

   The teacher will divide the class into teams. These teams will compete to see whose balloon will fly the farthest. Teams may use different size corks, different size holes in the corks, straws or hollow plastic tubes in the holes in corks, or other techniques. Be creative.

   All teams should use the same size balloon. Each team may have three attempts. Only the farthest flight will be counted.

   Members of the winning team must explain how they used the reaction engine operating principle or they forfeit their win.

2. The "jet propulsion" experiment can be modified by controlling the flight path. String a fishline or fine wire in the classroom. Figure 12-22 shows a fishline held by two chairs.

The insert shows a balloon taped to a soda straw or plastic tube placed on the line. Long balloons should be used to reduce friction of the balloon touching the fishline. Experiment with different design techniques in the cork to produce an effective jet "engine."

3. The teacher will divide the class into groups of 3-5 students. Each group will select a topic concerned with space exploration. These are topics such as "Colonizing the Moon," "Manned Flights to Mars," "Developing a Permanent Space Station," "Mining Meteorites," or "Manufacturing in Space." All topics should be different and the teacher must approve each topic. All members of each group should research their topic in the library. Working together, prepare a report to present to the class. Make visuals and use them in your presentation.

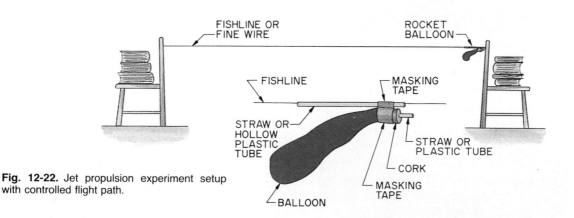

Fig. 12-22. Jet propulsion experiment setup with controlled flight path.

Chapter 13

Gasoline Automotive Engines

In the United States alone, there are about 100 million automotive gasoline engines in daily use. Nearly all use the four-stroke cycle engine.

Expanding Your Knowledge

As you study this chapter, you will learn to:

■ Name and describe the eight systems of an automotive gasoline engine (mechanical, lubrication, cooling, fuel, exhaust and emission control, ignition, starting, and charging).

■ Describe how engines are classified by number of cylinders, arrangement of cylinders, and type of valve system.

■ Explain the operating principles of the carburetor and fuel-injection systems.

■ Name five emission control devices used on automobiles and identify the type of pollution controlled by each device.

■ Describe the operation of breaker point, electronic, and computer ignition systems.

Building Your Word Power

The following words and phrases are defined and explained in the chapter. Learning these will help you learn more about gasoline automotive engines.

charging system
cooling system
emission controls
exhaust system
fuel-injection system
fuel system
ignition system
lubrication system
mechanical system
power train
starting system
system
thermostat
turbocharger

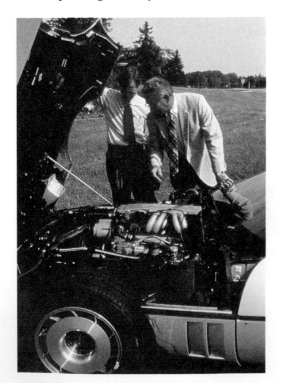

This chapter presents, in detail, the technical operation of the eight important systems used in automotive gasoline engines. Emphasis is placed on understanding the function of each system and learning how the systems work together.

In addition, the newer developments in automotive engines are presented. These include fuel injection, computerized ignition and fuel control, and turbochargers.

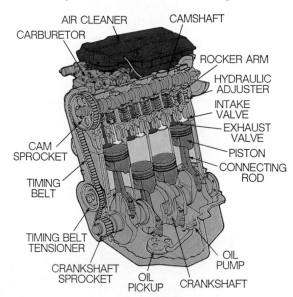

Fig. 13-1. A four-cylinder engine with an in-line arrangement.

TYPES OF AUTOMOTIVE ENGINES

Automobiles are made in a wide variety of sizes and shapes. Manufacturers use different engine designs for their automobiles. And designs are changed as improvements are made in engine fuel efficiency, power, and performance.

Engine Classifications

Automotive engines can be classified by different methods. The most basic classification is by the *number* of cylinders in the engine. Automotive engines usually have four, six, or eight cylinders.

Automotive engines can also be grouped by the *arrangement* of their cylinders. See Figs. 13-1, 13-2, and 13-3.

An engine with its cylinders arranged *in-line* is also called a straight engine. A straight or in-line-four engine has four cylinders placed one after another in a straight line (Fig. 13-1).

A *V-shaped* engine has its cylinders arranged at about a 45° angle. The most common V-shaped engines are the V-8 and V-6 engines. The V-8 engine has two banks of four cylinders each arranged in a V. The V-6 has two banks of three cylinders each (Fig. 13-2).

Opposed cylinder engines have cylinders arranged directly opposite one another. In a four-cylinder opposed engine, two cylinders are located directly across from the other two cylinders (Fig. 13-3).

Valve Classifications

A third way of grouping automotive engines is by the *type of valve system* they use. *Overhead valve* engines are also called *I-head* engines.

These engines have the valves located in the cylinder head directly above the pistons. Refer again to Fig. 13-2. The camshaft, located in the engine block, activates the valves. A system of push rods, rocker arms, and valve lifters connects the valves to the camshaft.

Overhead-camshaft engines have both the valves and the camshaft located in the cylinder head. Again, see Fig. 13-1. The camshaft operates the valves directly. This eliminates the need for push rods and rocker arms. Most modern four-cylinder engines have this design.

Other Classifications

Automotive engines are also grouped according to the type of cooling system used, the number of piston strokes per cycle, and the kind of fuel burned.

Most modern automotive engines are liquid-cooled four-stroke cycle engines. They burn either gasoline or diesel fuel. This chapter describes gasoline engines. Chapter 14 describes diesel engines.

AUTOMOTIVE ENGINE SYSTEMS

An automotive engine is actually a combination of many different systems. A **system** is a group of parts that work together. In an automotive engine, each system has its own job. Each

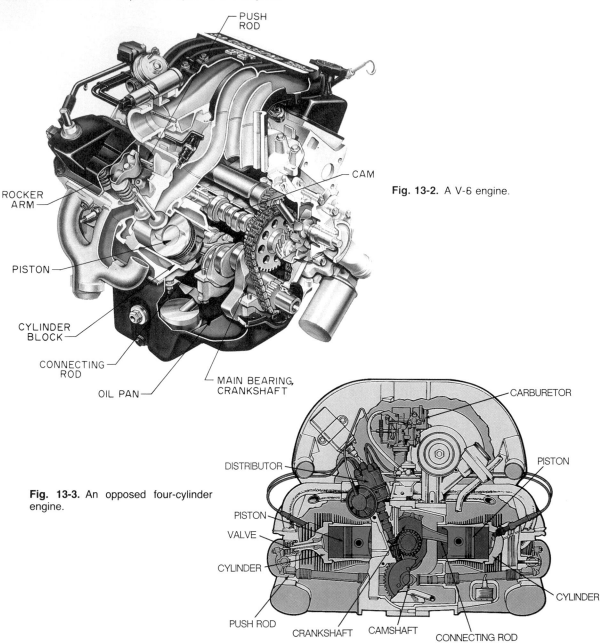

Fig. 13-2. A V-6 engine.

Fig. 13-3. An opposed four-cylinder engine.

must work properly for the engine to operate efficiently. A breakdown in one system will cause breakdowns in other systems. The result will be an inefficient or inoperable engine.

Every gasoline automotive engine consists of the following systems:

- Mechanical system
- Lubrication system
- Cooling system
- Fuel system
- Exhaust system
- Ignition system
- Starting system
- Charging system

MECHANICAL SYSTEM

The main job of the **mechanical system** is to convert heat energy into mechanical motion. It first converts heat into reciprocating motion, and then it changes this motion into rotary motion. The mechanical system consists of:

- Cylinder-block-and-head assembly
- Piston-and-crankshaft assembly
- Valve assembly

Technology Focus

Safety in Numbers

Have you ever been in a car when one drive wheel is stuck in mud or snow? The wheel just spins and the car doesn't move. This type of situation is not only frustrating, it can also be hazardous. To prevent this problem, many manufacturers are now producing cars with part-time *four-wheel-drive* systems. As the term implies, four-wheel drive provides power to all four wheels of the car. If one or two wheels are stuck, the others will pull the car free.

The new systems are different from the old four-wheel drive systems on trucks. Those were heavy and often required manually engaging the hubs on the wheels. Modern systems are engaged by a switch near the driver.

In routine driving situations, a car with a new four-wheel-drive system operates with two-wheel drive, either front-wheel or rear-wheel drive. When the driver switches to four-wheel drive, a motor connects engine power to the drive shaft going to the two wheels not usually engaged.

A four-wheel drive system is a safety feature. Cars with these systems are safer to drive in mud, snow, and ice and in rough terrain which might disable a car with only two-wheel drive.

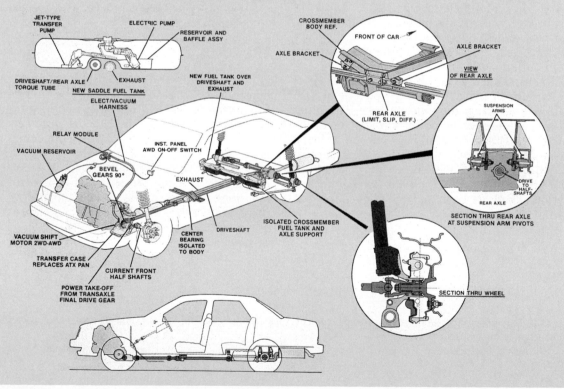

Cylinder-Block-and-Head Assembly

The backbone of the engine is the *cylinder block*. See Fig. 13-4. An *oil pan* closes the block at the bottom. A *cylinder head* seals it at the top.

All of the mechanical parts and systems needed for engine operation mount in or on the cylinder block and head. The block contains the cylinders, pistons, crankshaft, and sometimes the camshaft. The cylinder head contains most of the valve assembly.

Piston-and-Crankshaft Assembly

The piston-and-crankshaft assembly is a very important part of the engine. The *crankshaft* receives power from each of the pistons. It delivers this power to the flywheel. Figure 13-5 shows the most common crankshaft designs for in-line four, V-8, and in-line six engines. Notice the design of the crankshaft in Fig. 13-5A. Two connecting rod journals are up while two are down. Two pistons will be at the top of the cylinder— *top dead center (TDC)*— while the other two are at the bottom—*bottom dead center (BDC)*.

Each piston will be on a different stroke of the four-stroke cycle. One of the pistons at TDC will move down on the intake stroke. The other will move down on the power stroke. One of the pistons at BDC will start up on the exhaust stroke. The other will start up on the compression stroke. Figure 13-5B shows a crankshaft for a V-8 engine. This crankshaft has two connecting rods attached to each of the connecting rod bearing journals.

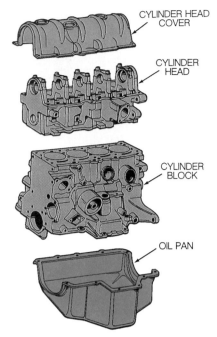

Fig. 13-4. The cylinder block and head assembly.

The piston-and-crankshaft assembly contains a smaller assembly called the *piston-and-rod assembly*. See Fig. 13-6. The upper end of the *connecting rod* is attached to the *piston* by the *piston pin*. The lower end of the connecting rod is attached to the crankshaft. The *bearing inserts* provide a low-friction surface for the rotating crankshaft. The compression and oil control *piston rings* fit around the top of the piston and press against the cylinder wall. The compression

Fig. 13-5. Different cylinder arrangements require different crankshaft designs. The numbers identify where each connecting rod attaches to the crankshaft.

A. In-line 4-cylinder. B. V-8. C. In-line 6-cylinder.

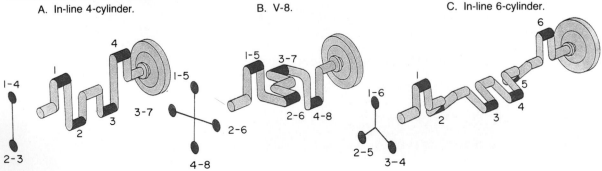

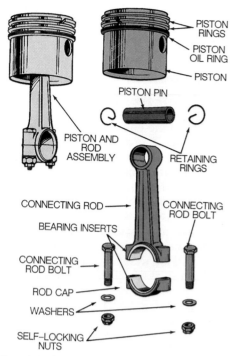

Fig. **13-6.** An automotive piston-and-rod assembly.

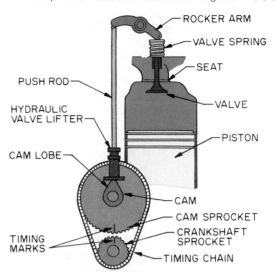

Fig. **13-7.** In an overhead-valve system, the valve assembly is driven by a camshaft in the cylinder block.

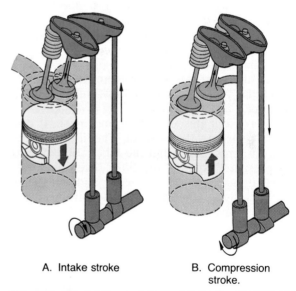

A. Intake stroke   B. Compression stroke.

Fig. **13-8.** The rotating camshaft controls the opening and closing of valves.

rings keep all the combustion pressure contained above the piston. The oil control rings keep crankcase oil from entering the combustion chamber.

Valve Assembly

Most modern automotive engines have valve assemblies mounted in the cylinder head. The valves are driven by the camshaft. The camshaft is located either in the cylinder block or above the valves in the cylinder head.

Figure 13-7 shows the basic parts of a valve assembly. A camshaft in the cylinder block drives the assembly. This type of arrangement is called an *overhead-valve system*. The basic valve assembly includes the following parts.

Camshaft. The camshaft has cams (lobes) that open the valves as it rotates. In Fig. 13-8A, the cam pushes up on other parts of the valve assembly. This opens the valve. In Fig. 13-8B, the cam has rotated to the other side. This allows the valve to close.

Hydraulic Valve Lifter, Push Rod, and Rocker Arm. These parts carry the motion of the cam lobe to the valve. The hydraulic valve lifter uses oil pressure to keep the system in adjustment. It keeps a slight pressure on the valve train in order to prevent tapping noise. It also ensures correct valve timing. The rocker arm changes the upward push of the push rod to a downward push on the valve.

Valve Spring. After the cam lobe rotates past the valve lifter, the valve spring closes the valve. The spring's pressure keeps the valve closed until the cam raises the lifter. Again, see Fig. 13-8.

Camshaft Sprocket and Timing Chain.

The crankshaft drives the camshaft through sprockets and a timing chain. Note that the camshaft sprocket is twice the size of the crankshaft sprocket. The camshaft rotates at half the speed of the crankshaft. The crankshaft must make two revolutions to open each valve in each cylinder once.

The valves must open at the correct time in relation to the piston position. Carmakers assure this by aligning *timing marks* on the camshaft and crankshaft sprockets. Again, see Fig. 13-7.

Many engines have the camshaft mounted in the cylinder head, above the valves. This type of assembly is called an *overhead-cam system*. See Fig. 13-9. This system operates the valves more directly than the overhead-valve system. The overhead-cam system allows the engine to operate at higher rpms. Four-cylinder engines commonly use overhead cams. This is because smaller engines must normally operate at higher rpms than larger engines.

In the overhead-cam system, the camshaft opens the valve by pushing down on the rocker arm. Refer again to Fig. 13-9. The *hydraulic valve adjuster* eliminates clearance and noise. It provides precision valve opening. The lifter operates from the pressure within the lubrication system. Oil pressure expands the lifter. This eliminates all clearance between the valve and the rocker arm. The hydraulic adjustment feature also permits the valve itself to expand under the heat of combustion. The adjuster compresses to permit this expansion while keeping the clearance at zero.

LUBRICATION SYSTEM

Large gasoline engines use a pressure **lubrication system**. See Fig. 13-10. The camshaft drives an oil pump located in the crankcase. The engine block, crankshaft, and camshaft all have oil passages drilled into them. The oil from the pump passes through an oil filter and into the passages. On most engines, all crankshaft and camshaft bearings, hydraulic valve lifters, and rocker arms are pressure-lubricated. Pistons, piston pins, cylinder walls, and piston rings are lubricated by a mist of oil thrown from the crankshaft.

Lubricating oil has important engine functions. Its main job is to reduce friction. It also forms a seal between the piston rings and the cylinder wall. The oil also carries heat from the piston to the oil pan. As the automobile moves, air passing over the outside of the pan cools the oil in the pan.

Gear pumps are commonly used in automotive engines. As the pump gears rotate, they force oil through the pump and into the oil filter. A blocked oil line or very high engine speeds may cause a pressure buildup. A *pressure relief valve* opens if the pressure becomes too great.

Fig. 13-10. Automobile engines use an oil pump to pick up and drive oil through the engine under pressure.

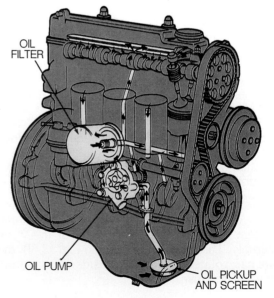

Fig. 13-9. An overhead-cam valve assembly.

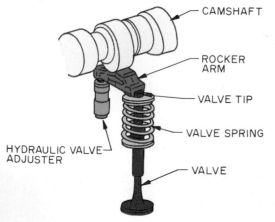

The filter removes dirt and waste materials from the oil. If the filter is clogged, the oil goes through the *filter relief valve*. Then it passes through the system. In this way lubrication of the engine continues even if the filter is completely plugged with dirt.

COOLING SYSTEM

The two types of automobile **cooling systems** are the air cooling system and the liquid cooling system.

Some auto engines use an *air cooling system*. In this type of system, air is simply passed over the engine to remove heat. However, most modern auto engines use a *liquid cooling system*. The liquid, or *coolant*, is usually water mixed with antifreeze. *Antifreeze* is a liquid that lowers both the boiling point and the freezing point of the coolant. Figure 13-11 shows the major parts of a liquid cooling system.

A *water pump* circulates the coolant from the radiator into the engine block. The coolant travels in passages around the cylinders and through the cylinder head. It removes heat as it circulates. The hot coolant then travels to the radiator. It cools as it flows through the radiator.

The *radiator* consists of many small tubes connected to thin metal fins. As hot coolant flows through the tubes, the fins absorb some of the heat. The forward motion of the automobile forces air through the radiator. The air carries away the heat. When the automobile is stopped or moving slowly, a fan forces air through the radiator. The fan is either attached to and driven by the water pump or it is driven by an electric motor.

A **thermostat** between the engine and the radiator controls the flow of coolant. If the engine is cool, the thermostat stays closed. This prevents the radiator from cooling the engine further. Once the engine reaches its correct operating temperature (usually between 150-200°F or more), the thermostat opens. In this way the thermostat maintains the most efficient engine operating temperature.

Other important parts of the cooling system are the radiator cap and the low-pressure relief valve. The *radiator cap* seals the coolant in the system. The *low-pressure relief valve* lets air or fluid into the system to keep the hoses from collapsing.

FUEL SYSTEM

An automotive **fuel system** provides a mixture of gasoline and air to the cylinders. Figure 13-12 shows the main parts of the system. The *fuel pump* pumps fuel from the fuel tank to the carburetor. The *carburetor* mixes the fuel with

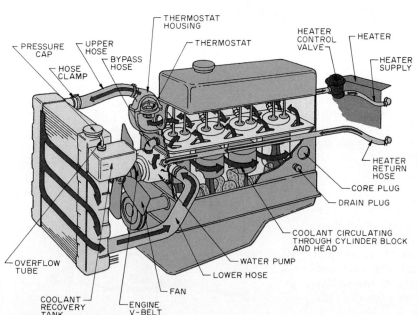

Fig. 13-11. The path of coolant through an engine.

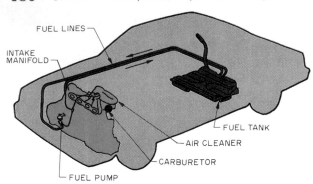

Fig. 13-12. An automotive fuel system.

clean air from the *air cleaner*. The air-fuel mixture then passes into the *intake manifold*. The intake manifold connects the carburetor to each of the engine's cylinders. When the piston moves down on the intake stroke, a vacuum is formed in the cylinder. Atmospheric pressure pushes the air-fuel mixture into the cylinder to fill the vacuum.

Fuel Pump

Some cars use an electric fuel pump to deliver fuel from the tank to the carburetor. However, most cars use a *mechanical fuel pump*. One type of fuel pump is referred to as a *diaphragm pump*. The diaphragm is operated by a cam. The cam is on the camshaft or the crankshaft. The cam pushes down on a lever on the fuel pump. The lever pulls the diaphragm up. This increases the volume of the pump chamber. The greater volume lowers the pressure in the chamber. Air pressure then pushes fuel through the inlet valve. Fuel fills the chamber.

The cam lobe then turns away from the lever. The diaphragm spring pushes the diaphragm down. This increases the chamber pressure and closes the inlet valve. The increased pressure also forces the outlet valve open. The pressure pushes fuel past the valve. It passes through the fuel line and into the carburetor.

Carburetor

As you learned earlier, pistons create a partial vacuum in the cylinders when they move down on the intake stroke. This allows atmospheric pressure to push a mixture of air and fuel into the cylinders for combustion. The *carburetor*, mounted on top of the engine, is the device that mixes the right amount of air with the right amount of fuel.

Main Fuel Circuit. Figure 13-13 shows a simple carburetor. It looks a little complicated, but begin by looking just at the right side of the drawing. A carburetor is basically a hollow tube in which fuel mixes with air. The narrow part of the tube is called the *venturi*. When air rushes through the venturi, it speeds up. (This is just like the water from a garden hose speeding up after you put your thumb over the opening.)

Besides speeding up, the air also creates a low-pressure area (partial vacuum) in the venturi. This vacuum allows atmospheric pressure to push on the fuel in the *float bowl*. The fuel flows from the bowl through the *main fuel jet* and *nozzle* into the venturi.

The fuel nozzle has a small opening. When the fuel rushes through this opening, it separates into many small droplets and mixes with the rushing air. This air-fuel mixture then flows past the *throttle plate* and into the intake manifold and cylinders.

The driver can speed up the air flow further by stepping on the accelerator pedal. Doing this opens the throttle plate further and allows more air and fuel to go to the cylinders.

Carburetors must provide different air-fuel mixtures for different operating conditions. The parts and circuits used to do this are discussed in the following sections.

Float Assembly. Fuel from the fuel pump enters the carburetor past the *float needle*. The float maintains a constant level of fuel inside the bowl. When the carburetor needs more fuel, the float tips down to pull the float needle from its seat. Fuel then flows into the bowl and brings the fuel level back up. The float then tips up to shut the needle valve.

Fig. 13-13. The carburetor mixes fuel with air.

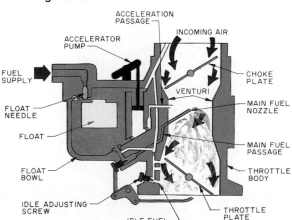

Idle Fuel Circuit. Figure 13-13 shows the fuel flow in the *main fuel circuit*. This is how the carburetor works much of the time. However, when the engine is at *idle* (not moving the car), little air flows through the venturi. This airflow cannot create a high-enough vacuum to pull fuel from the fuel nozzle. Therefore, the fuel must have another way to get into the flow of air.

To provide for fuel flow at idle, the carburetor has an *idle fuel passage*. Again, see Fig. 13-13. The vacuum below the throttle plate is enough to pull fuel out of the float bowl and through this passage. The fuel can then mix with the incoming air and travel to the cylinders.

The *idle adjusting screw* controls how much fuel flows through the idle fuel passage. By turning this screw, a mechanic can make the air-fuel mixture richer (more fuel) or leaner (less fuel).

Choke Circuit. During starting, the engine needs a rich air-fuel mixture. To supply this mixture, the *choke plate* closes partially. This restricts the entry of air. The vacuum in the cylinders then pulls in a greater amount of fuel.

Acceleration Circuit. The engine needs extra fuel to accelerate. As the driver presses the accelerator, an *accelerator pump* is depressed in the carburetor. The accelerator pump pumps extra gasoline into the *primary venturi*.

Fuel-Injection Fuel System

Many new cars have a **fuel-injection system** instead of a carburetor. The fuel-injection system does not depend on venturi action to bring fuel into the air stream. Instead, *fuel injectors* spray a measured amount of fuel into the air stream. Fuel injection controls the amount of fuel used more accurately than carburetion does. This improves fuel economy and provides pollution control. See Fig. 13-14.

In a typical fuel-injection system. Injection takes place just before the air-fuel mixture enters the combustion chamber. The system is controlled as follows:

■ Gasoline is pumped from the fuel tank to the *fuel distributor*. The distributor regulates the amount of fuel to be injected. It also sends the fuel to the proper injector just as the intake valve begins to open.

■ A *throttle plate* in the manifold controls air flow into the cylinder. The driver controls the throttle plate with the accelerator pedal.

■ When the engine is cold, a heat sensor in the engine block water jacket activates a *cold-start injector*. This injector adds extra fuel to

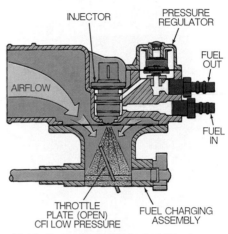

Fig. 13-14. One type of modern fuel-injection system.

the intake manifold. The cold-start injector serves the same purpose as the carburetor choke.

Fuel-injection systems cost more than carburetion systems. However, they control the fuel more precisely. This increases fuel efficiency as well as engine performance.

Turbochargers

An increasing number of modern cars use *turbochargers* to increase engine power. See Fig. 13-15. A **turbocharger** consists of an *air impellor* and an *exhaust turbine* connected to a shaft. High-pressure exhaust gases leaving the engine drive the turbine. The turbine, in turn, drives the air impellor. The air impellor forces air into the combustion chamber at a pressure higher than atmospheric pressure. This action puts more air into the cylinder. This provides higher compression for greater power output.

Turbochargers improve the performance of all engines, especially small, low-powered engines. Today, small engines are popular for reasons of fuel economy. However, they do not have the power that older and larger engines had. Adding a turbocharger to a small engine improves its overall performance, especially during passing at highway speeds.

EXHAUST SYSTEM—EMISSION CONTROL

Before the 1950s, the **exhaust system** consisted only of an exhaust manifold, muffler, and tail pipe. The *exhaust manifold* collects the ex-

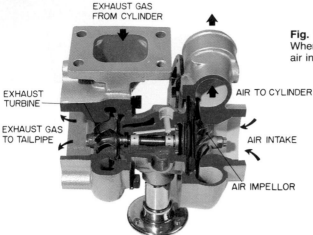

EXHAUST GAS
FROM CYLINDER

AIR TO CYLINDER

EXHAUST
TURBINE

EXHAUST GAS
TO TAILPIPE

AIR INTAKE

AIR IMPELLOR

Fig. 13-15. Turbochargers are powered by exhaust gases. When the exhaust turbine spins, the air impellor forces extra air into the cylinder.

haust gases from the combustion chambers. The *muffler* dampens exhaust noises. The *tail pipe* connects to the muffler. It carries the exhaust gases to the rear of the car.

Since the 1950s, carmakers have tried to make automotive emissions (exhaust) less harmful. They have added many controls to automotive engines. **Emission controls** reduce the amounts of harmful pollutants. See Fig. 13-16.

Positive Crankcase Ventilation(PCV) Valve

The PCV valve controls carbon monoxide and unburned fuel that "blow by" the rings into the crankcase. These gases would normally escape into the air through the crankcase breather. However, the PCV valve directs them into the intake manifold. Combustion heat reburns the gases.

Air-Injection Pump

The air-injection pump injects air into the exhaust manifold. The air provides the oxygen needed to burn any unburned fuel. Any unburned carbon monoxide is also burned and changed into carbon dioxide. This *afterburning* takes place in the exhaust manifold and catalytic converter.

Catalytic Converter

The catalytic converter continues the process of eliminating unburned fuel and carbon monoxide from the exhaust. The converter looks like a muffler. However, it has a different function. In the converter, the unburned fuel burns at a temperature low enough to prevent formation of nitrogen oxides. This helps keep nitrogen oxide emissions at a low level as well as eliminating unburned and partially burned fuel.

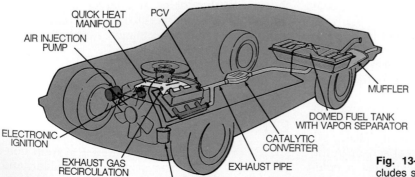

QUICK HEAT
MANIFOLD

PCV

AIR INJECTION
PUMP

MUFFLER

ELECTRONIC
IGNITION

DOMED FUEL TANK
WITH VAPOR SEPARATOR

EXHAUST GAS
RECIRCULATION

CATALYTIC
CONVERTER

EXHAUST PIPE

CARBON CANISTER

Fig. 13-16. The emission-control system includes special devices added to existing parts of the automobile engine and exhaust system.

Fuel Tank and Carbon Canister

Emission-control fuel tanks do not have vents. Therefore, unburned fuel vapors cannot escape into the air. Instead, the vapors travel through a tube to the carbon canister. During engine operation, the engine vacuum draws the vapors from the canister to the carburetor. The vapors are then drawn into the engine, where they are burned.

Exhaust Gas Recirculation (EGR) System

The EGR system reduces harmful nitrogen oxides in exhaust gases. In this system, tubing and valves connect the exhaust manifold to the intake manifold. The EGR system mixes small amounts of exhaust gas with the air-fuel mixture entering the cylinders. The exhaust gases dilute the air-fuel mixture. This makes the mixture burn at a lower temperature. The lower temperature reduces the amount of nitrogen oxides formed.

IGNITION SYSTEM

Once the air-fuel mixture is in the cylinder and is compressed by the piston, it must be ignited. High voltage must reach the spark plug and produce a spark. Delivering high voltage to the spark plug is the job of the automotive **ignition system**.

There are three basic types of automotive ignition systems:
- Breaker-point system
- Electronic ignition system
- Computerized ignition system

Breaker-Point Ignition

Figure 13-17 shows the parts of a typical breaker-point ignition system. The system has two separate electrical circuits. These are the primary circuit and the secondary circuit.

The *primary circuit* carries only low-voltage current. This circuit consists of the battery, ignition switch, ballast resistor, coil, breaker points, and condenser. The coil has two sets of windings—the primary winding and the secondary winding. When the points close, electricity flows from the battery through the primary coil winding. It continues across the points to the ground (the engine block). Then it flows back to the battery.

Electricity flowing in the primary circuit builds a magnetic field in the coil. When the points open, the current stops flowing. This causes the magnetic field to collapse. This collapse generates high voltage in the secondary coil winding. The condenser keeps current from jumping the point gap when the points open. This would cause the magnetic field to collapse accidentally.

The *secondary circuit* carries high-voltage current. This circuit consists of the coil, distributor rotor and cap, high-voltage wires, and the spark plugs. The coil produces high-voltage current. The current then travels to the *distributor cap*. A *rotor* in the cap directs the current to the

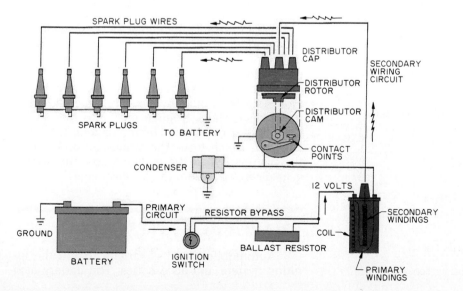

Fig. 13-17. The automotive breaker-point ignition system.

proper spark plug wire. At the spark plug, the high-voltage current sparks across the spark plug gap to ignite the fuel.

Figure 13-17 shows the ignition system of a six-cylinder engine. The *distributor cam* has six lobes. Each lobe opens and closes the points once. Therefore, the system produces a spark six times for each revolution of the cam. The distributor cam is driven by the camshaft.

The ignition system must provide a strong spark during engine starting. During starting, battery voltage may drop from 12 to 9-10 volts. Because of this drain, the ignition system is designed to operate with less voltage. When the engine is running, the charging circuit raises the voltage to over 14 volts. Since the ignition system is designed for 9-10 volts, a *ballast resistor* is placed into the circuit. It reduces ignition voltage to 9-10 volts. The ballast resistor thereby maintains ignition voltage at a constant level.

The ignition circuit operates in the following way. During starting, current bypasses the ballast resistor. This allows 9-10 volts to travel through the coil. Otherwise there would not be enough voltage to start the engine. After the engine starts, the charging voltage goes up to over 14 volts. However, the current now flows through the ballast resistor. The resistor reduces the voltage to the needed 9-10 volts.

Electronic Ignition

Many carmakers are using electronic ignition systems. These systems usually require less maintenance than breaker-point systems.

Figure 13-18 shows the parts of an electronic ignition system. The impulse generator, reluctor, and transistorized control unit replace the breaker points, condenser, and distributor cam.

The *reluctor* has iron teeth. There are as many teeth as there are cylinders in the engine.

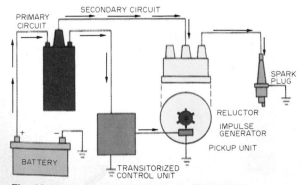

Fig. 13-18. One type of electronic ignition system.

As the reluctor turns, the teeth pass very close to the *pickup unit* of the *impulse generator*. As each tooth passes the pickup unit, it produces a small electric charge in the impulse generator. This electric charge triggers the *transistorized control unit*.

Electronic ignition eliminates the need to change breaker points. It also controls spark firing more precisely and produces a hotter spark. Electronic ignition permits easy adjustment of ignition timing. Special ignition timing can reduce amounts of nitrogen oxides and other pollutants.

Computerized Ignition and Fuel Control

Manufacturers are also adding small computers to control both ignition and fuel systems. Many sensing devices attached throughout the engine and its accessories inform the computer about engine operating conditions. The computer analyzes this information. Then it adjusts the fuel-injection system and ignition timing. Computerized ignition and fuel control reduces pollution and improves fuel economy.

STARTING SYSTEM

The **starting system** includes a starting motor, or *starter*. The starter starts the pistons moving up and down. This way, they can draw in an air-fuel mixture. The ignition system then provides the spark to ignite the mixture.

The starter is usually mounted low on the engine, toward the rear of the crankshaft. As you remember, a heavy flywheel is attached to the end of the crankshaft. The flywheel has a large *ring gear* around its outer edge.

The starter is basically an electric motor with a *drive mechanism* on it. In Fig. 13-19, the drive mechanism consists of a solenoid connected to a shift lever. (See Chapter 24.)

When the driver turns the ignition key, the motor starts turning. At the same time, the drive mechanism slides a small gear into mesh with the flywheel ring gear. The motor then turns the flywheel, which turns the crankshaft and moves the pistons. When the engine starts, the starter gear disengages from the flywheel gear.

CHARGING SYSTEM

Automobiles need electricity to run the ignition system and accessories. The battery also

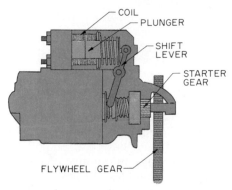

Fig. 13-19. The operation of one type of automotive starter. Normally, the starter gear is not engaged with the flywheel gear. When the driver turns the ignition key, the starter gear meshes with the flywheel gear and "cranks" the engine.

must be kept charged to operate the starting system.

Figure 13-20 shows a **charging system**. The main parts are the alternator and the voltage regulator. The illustration shows these as separate parts. However, many automotive engines have the regulator attached to the alternator.

The *alternator* is a source of electricity. It is usually driven by a belt from the engine's crankshaft. The alternator converts rotary motion into electricity. (See Chapter 24.)

The *voltage regulator* controls the output of the alternator. It maintains a constant voltage output. For the typical 12-volt system, the regulator maintains a voltage of just over 14 volts. This is the voltage needed to keep the battery fully charged and all electrical parts operating.

The regulator controls voltage by adjusting the alternator's magnetic field. When the car uses more current, the voltage drops. For example, turning on headlights causes a current drop.

Fig. 13-20. A typical automotive charging circuit.

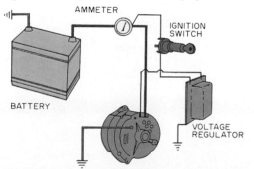

The regulator immediately supplies more current to the magnetic field. This increases alternator output. The voltage builds back up to just over 14 volts. When the lights are turned off, the regulator automatically reduces the field strength, keeping the voltage constant.

POWER TRAIN

Automobiles deliver engine power to the wheels with a *power train*. The **power train** usually includes a clutch, transmission, drive shaft, and rear end assembly.

AUTOMOBILE SERVICING

The servicing of automobiles has changed during the past two decades. Because automobiles have become more complex, service problems are more difficult to diagnose. This has resulted in two forms of specialization.

■ Emphasis on one or a small group of automobile models of a single manufacturer.

■ Emphasis on servicing one portion of an automobile.

The growing use of microprocessors and computers to control engine performance requires special engine diagnostic equipment. The shift to front-wheel drive has made front-end adjustment more important. See Fig. 13-21.

Fig. 13-21. Wheel alignment requires special equipment. Properly aligned wheels promote even tire wear and responsive steering.

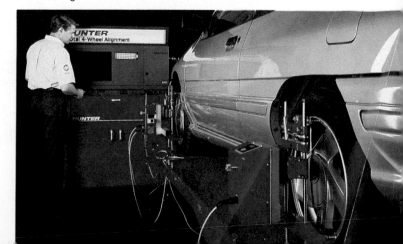

Testing Your Knowledge

Briefly answer each of the following questions. Write on a separate piece of paper.
1. Name the eight systems that every gasoline automotive engine contains.
2. Where is the camshaft located on an overhead-valve system? on an overhead-cam system?
3. How does the hydraulic valve lifter keep clearances at zero as the valve expands due to heat?
4. What is the function of a cooling system thermostat?
5. What is the function of the carburetor accelerator pump?
6. Name two advantages and one disadvantage of the fuel-injection system.
7. What are three pollutants produced by automotive engines?
8. List five emission control devices used on most new automobiles.
9. Name the three types of ignition systems used on gasoline automotive engines.
10. What is the function of the ballast resistor?
11. When a computer is used to control engine performance, which two systems does it control?
12. What is the function of the voltage regulator?
13. Name the four basic parts of the automotive power train.

Expressing Your Knowledge

Using complete sentences, write your answers to the following on a separate sheet of paper:
1. Describe three ways automotive engines are classified. Give examples of each.
2. On an in-line four-cylinder engine, the crankshaft has two connecting rod journals up while two are down. With two pistons at TDC, identify the stroke being started by each piston.
3. Describe the flow of oil in a lubrication system that has a clogged oil filter.
4. What is the main operating difference between a fuel-injection system and a carburetion system?
5. Explain how a turbocharger improves engine performance.
6. An electronic ignition system is shown below. What three advantages do electronic ignition systems have over breaker-point ignition systems?
7. Briefly describe the two forms automobile service procedures are taking.

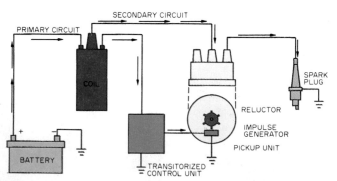

3

Applying Your Knowledge

Follow your teacher's instructions to complete these activities:

1. Conduct a survey of service stations to determine the average price of gasoline in your community. Find out the average mpg (miles per gallon) for a compact car, intermediate or sports car, and a large car. This can be obtained from stickers with EPA estimates shown on new cars. Many dealers will have a listing of EPA mileage estimates for all cars. Trucks may be substituted for cars.

Plan a trip you would like to take. Calculate the distance you will drive on the trip. From the information obtained determine the number of gallons of gasoline you would use with a compact, intermediate, and large car. Determine the cost for fuel for each size car for the trip. Prepare a report showing the information you obtained, your calculations, and your findings.

2. Check an automobile for automated control devices. They are numerous. They include power steering, power brakes, engine temperature control, heater, and fuel supply systems. Prepare a report which identifies the automated control devices that you are able to find. Select four and provide details as shown in the following example:

Example: Engine Temperature Control:
Sensor—Thermostat in engine water supply senses engine water temperature.
Control—Thermostat controls valve in engine which directs water to engine or back to radiator.
Operation—When temperature is too low, water is directed back to the engine while the engine warms up. When temperature is warm, water flows to the radiator to cool as needed.

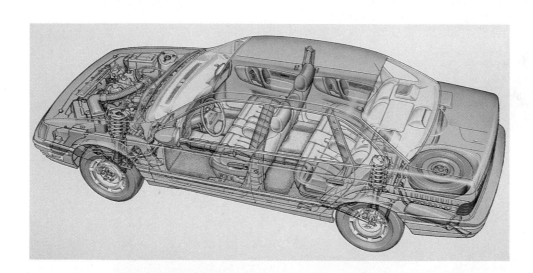

Chapter 14

Diesel Automotive Engines

Diesel engines have long been the source of power for heavy-duty trucks, trains, and ships. During the past few years, diesel engines have become more common as power sources for automobiles.

Expanding Your Knowledge

As you study this chapter, you will learn to:

- Explain why the diesel engine has grown in popularity as an automobile and truck engine.
- Identify the two major differences between gasoline and diesel engines.
- Describe the function and operation of the diesel engine fuel-injection system.
- Explain the difference between multiple-plunger and unit injector fuel-injection systems.
- Identify the type of diesel engine that requires an air blower.
- Describe the purpose and checks performed by an automotive diagnostic service center.

Building Your Word Power

The following terms are defined and explained in this chapter. Learning these will help you learn more about diesel automotive engines.

automotive diagnostic service center
four-stroke cycle diesel engine
glow plug
two-stroke cycle diesel engine

The diesel engine is similar in operation and construction to the gasoline engine. Its use is also similar. In this chapter, the important differences between the two types of engines are explained. Emphasis is placed on both the different operating characteristics and the different uses of the engines.

All diesel engines use a fuel-injection system. The different types of injections and their functions are described in detail. In the final sections, the function of glow plugs and turbochargers is presented.

DIESEL ENGINES IN AUTOMOBILES

The main advantage of diesel engines over gasoline engines is their good fuel efficiency. Diesel-powered automobiles average about 25% more miles per gallon (or kilometers per liter) than gasoline-powered automobiles.

Diesel engines, however, must be made larger, stronger, and heavier than gasoline engines. See Fig. 14-1. They must withstand combustion pressures two to three times higher than those produced in gasoline engines. The added weight needed for strength reduces the acceleration of the automobile.

Fig. 14-1. A diesel engine.

A diesel engine of the same horsepower as a gasoline engine is larger. It will not fit into the engine compartment designed for the gasoline engine. A diesel engine that *will* fit into the compartment produces lower horsepower. This further reduces the acceleration.

Diesel engine designs are being improved. Engine compartments are also being designed to accept larger engines. These factors can be expected to improve the performance of diesel-powered automobiles.

TYPES OF DIESEL ENGINES

There are two basic types of diesel engines in use today:
■ Four-stroke cycle
■ Two-stroke cycle

These engines differ in the number of piston strokes required to produce a power stroke. Their methods of intake and exhaust are also different.

Four-Stroke Cycle Diesel Engine

Four-stroke diesel engines are very similar to four-stroke gasoline engines. The piston travels from one end of the cylinder to the other four times during each cycle. The fuel is ignited at the beginning of the third stroke of each cycle. See Fig. 14-2.

Intake air flows into each cylinder through *intake valves* in the cylinder head. Exhaust gases leave through *exhaust valves*. These valves operate the same way as the valves on four-stroke gasoline engines. On the intake stroke, atmospheric pressure pushes air into the cylinder through the intake valve. The exhaust stroke forces burned gases out through the exhaust valve. During the compression and power strokes, both valves are closed.

Two-Stroke Cycle Diesel Engine

Two-stroke diesel engines are similar to two-stroke gasoline engines. They have only two strokes per cycle. The fuel is ignited on every other stroke of the piston. See Fig. 14-3.

In the two-stroke diesel engine, air is forced in and exhaust gases are forced out on a single stroke. Usually a blower forces air into the cylinder through *intake ports*. The incoming air pushes remaining exhaust gases out of the cylinder through an *exhaust valve*.

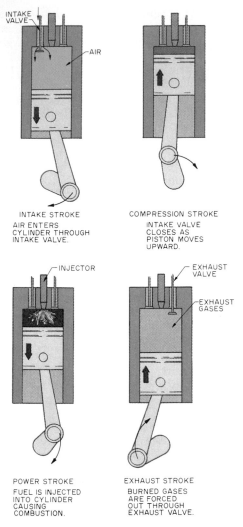

INTAKE STROKE
AIR ENTERS
CYLINDER THROUGH
INTAKE VALVE.

COMPRESSION STROKE
INTAKE VALVE
CLOSES AS
PISTON MOVES
UPWARD.

POWER STROKE
FUEL IS INJECTED
INTO CYLINDER
CAUSING
COMBUSTION.

EXHAUST STROKE
BURNED GASES
ARE FORCED
OUT THROUGH
EXHAUST VALVE.

Fig. 14-2. The diesel four-stroke cycle has the same four elements as the gasoline four-stroke cycle.

ENGINE DESIGN

The diesel engine looks much like the gasoline engine. The operations of the mechanical systems are also similar in both engines. The piston and crankshaft assembly, the valve assembly, the lubrication system, and the cooling system operate in the same way. (See Chapter 13.) However, diesel systems are built stronger to withstand higher combustion pressures.

The two major differences between gasoline and diesel engines are the way that fuel is supplied to the cylinders and the way the fuel is ignited. As explained earlier, the diesel engine does not need an ignition system. Compression heat ignites the fuel in the cylinder. A special fuel system supplies fuel to the cylinder. Diesel fuel systems are very different from gasoline fuel systems.

FUEL SYSTEM

In a gasoline engine, fuel is mixed with air in the carburetor or in the intake manifold. Diesel engines do not have carburetors. Only air flows into the combustion chamber through the intake manifold. Each intake stroke completely fills the cylinder with air. Special devices inject fuel into the air inside the cylinder. Engine power is controlled by metering the amount of fuel *injected* into the cylinders.

At idle, only a small amount of fuel is injected into each cylinder. The ratio of air to fuel may be 40 to 1. (The ratio in gasoline engines at idle is about 18 to 1.) As power needs increase,

Fig. 14-3. Four piston positions are shown in this diagram of the two-stroke diesel cycle. However, the piston moves only one complete stroke between power strokes.

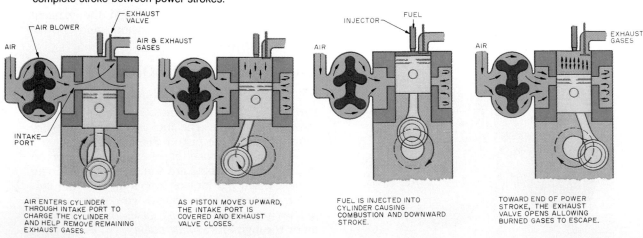

AIR ENTERS CYLINDER
THROUGH INTAKE PORT TO
CHARGE THE CYLINDER
AND HELP REMOVE REMAINING
EXHAUST GASES.

AS PISTON MOVES UPWARD,
THE INTAKE PORT IS
COVERED AND EXHAUST
VALVE CLOSES.

FUEL IS INJECTED INTO
CYLINDER CAUSING
COMBUSTION AND DOWNWARD
STROKE.

TOWARD END OF POWER
STROKE, THE EXHAUST
VALVE OPENS ALLOWING
BURNED GASES TO ESCAPE.

the amount of fuel injected increases. However, the amount of air remains the same. Therefore, the *ratio* of air to fuel decreases. The intake stroke always takes in enough air to burn all the fuel injected during full-load operation.

Fuel-Injection Systems

The main components in a diesel fuel-injection system are the fuel-injection pump and the fuel injectors. See Fig. 14-4.

The job of the *fuel injectors* is to inject a measured amount of fuel into the combustion chamber. When pressure is applied to the fuel, the injector opens and sprays fuel into the cylinder. Combustion begins immediately.

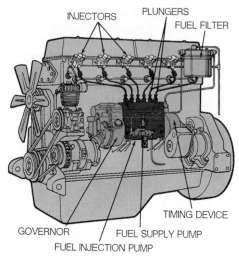

Fig. 14-4. In a multiple-plunger fuel-injection system, the injection pump supplies high-pressure fuel to each injector.

Technology Focus

A Glass Engine

An engine made of glass? Well, not quite, but in the future we may see a growing use of special types of glass called *ceramics*. For example, designers are experimenting with the use of heat-resistant ceramics to cope with the problem of engine cooling in trucks.

Truck diesel engines generate a large amount of excess heat. This heat must be transferred to the air. To accomplish this, heavy trucks have a large upright radiator at the front which allows air to enter and cool the engine. However, the radiator offers considerable

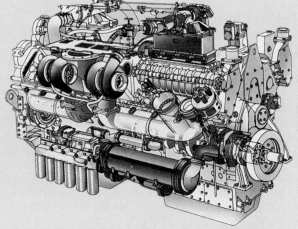

resistance to airflow, causing increased fuel consumption. Designers would like to streamline truck designs to improve fuel efficiency.

With present engines, streamlining the design to eliminate the "upright radiator" would produce engine overheating. One solution is to use ceramics. Ceramics are poor heat conductors. For example, if the inside of the cylinder wall were lined with ceramic insulation, most of the heat would stay with the burned fuel and go out the exhaust.

Ceramic parts and coatings are presently being developed. The engine shown here has ceramic coated pistons, exhaust manifold, and exhaust riser.

Problems remain. Ceramics are brittle and difficult to use. However, research and experimentation may someday come close to producing a "glass engine."

The *fuel-injection pump* produces the necessary high fuel pressure. On injection, diesel fuel must be under enough pressure to offset the pressure inside the combustion chamber (about 1000 psi during combustion). If the fuel pressure were not at least as high as the pressure in the combustion chamber during combustion, the fuel would not inject. Instead, pressure would leak from the combustion chamber into the injector nozzle.

The injection pump has two other functions. It must regulate the *amount* of fuel directed to the cylinder. It must also control the *timing* of the fuel injection.

As you recall, engine power depends on the amount of fuel supplied to the cylinders. The time at which injectors spray fuel into the cylinders is just as important. The injection pump controls this timing. It makes sure that the injectors spray fuel just before TDC (top dead center) of the compression stroke. By the time the fuel ignites, the piston will have started its downward motion.

The above discussion of the parts of an injection system is very simplified. In reality, the injection pump and injectors may not be completely separate. These two parts can be arranged in three different ways.

Multiple-Plunger System. In this system, there is a separate pumping unit (plunger) and a separate injector for each cylinder. Again, see Fig. 14-4. The plungers are all part of the fuel-injection pump. A camshaft inside the pump controls the action of the plungers. Fuel lines connect the plungers to the injectors. The amount of fuel to be injected is controlled at the fuel-injection pump.

Unit Injector System. In this system, the injection pump and injector are combined into one unit and are driven by the overhead camshaft. The plunger is a part of the injector. Pressurization, timing, and metering of the fuel all take place in the unit injector. See Fig. 14-5. An engine with this system has one unit injector for each cylinder.

Distributor System. In this system, a single injection pump supplies fuel to a distributor. The distributor directs fuel to the injectors in the right firing order. The metering of fuel is done at the pump. See Fig. 14-6.

Fuel-Injection System Operation

Diesel engines use several different injection systems. However, their operating principles are the same. Figure 14-7 shows a detailed diagram of a multiple-plunger system. By learning how this system operates, you will also learn how the other systems operate.

The multiple-plunger system contains both high- and low-pressure fuel systems. The low-pressure system consists of a fuel pump, lines, and filters, similar to the parts in a gasoline system. These parts deliver fuel from the tank to the fuel-injection pump.

The high-pressure system consists of the fuel-injection pump and the injectors. These parts supply fuel to the cylinders.

Fig. 14-5. Cutaway view of a unit injector.

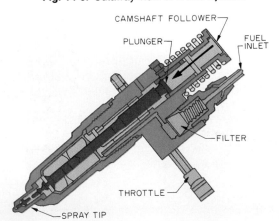

Fig. 14-6. This diagram shows the path that diesel fuel takes in a distribution injection system on a V-6 engine.

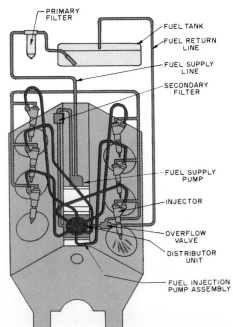

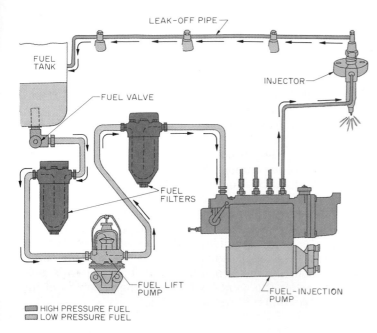

Fig. 14-7. In a multiple-plunger fuel-injection system, low-pressure fuel travels from the fuel tank to the injection pump. High-pressure fuel travels from separate plungers to the fuel injectors.

GLOW PLUGS

Because there is no spark to ignite the fuel, diesel engines can be hard to start. This is especially true in cold weather. For improved starting, diesels are often equipped with *glow plugs*. **Glow plugs** have a small wire element that gets red-hot when connected to an electrical source.

Each cylinder has a glow plug. When the diesel is to be started, current from the battery heats the glow plugs. The glow plugs then heat the fuel as it enters the cylinders. This preheating of the fuel lowers its ignition point to improve starting.

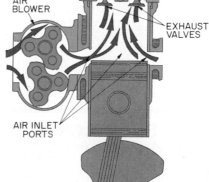

Fig. 14-8. In a two-stroke cycle engine, a blower pushes air into the cylinder.

AIR BLOWERS AND TURBOCHARGERS

Two-stroke diesel engines require an *air blower*. This device forces air into the cylinder and drives out the exhaust gases. See Fig. 14-8. When the piston reaches the bottom of the power stroke, the air inlet ports are uncovered. The blower forces air into the cylinder. The air drives the burned gases out the exhaust valve and fills the combustion chamber.

Some modern four-stroke diesel engines use a special kind of blower called a *turbocharger*. A turbocharger consists of an *air impellor* and an *exhaust turbine* connected to a shaft. High-pressure exhaust gases leaving the engine drive the turbine. The turbine, in turn, drives the air impellor. The air impellor forces air into the combustion chamber at a pressure higher than atmospheric pressure. This action puts more air into the cylinder. This provides higher compression for greater power output. See Fig. 14-9.

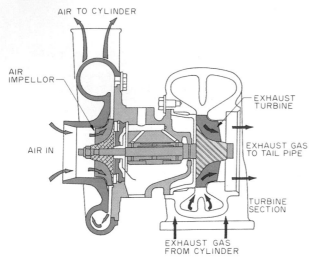

AIR TO CYLINDER

AIR
IMPELLOR

AIR IN

EXHAUST
TURBINE

EXHAUST GAS
TO TAIL PIPE

TURBINE
SECTION

EXHAUST GAS
FROM CYLINDER

Fig. 14-9. A turbocharger moves air into the compression chamber using energy provided by escaping exhaust gases.

■ Running on chassis dynamometer. This will analyze full drive-train performance and check for chassis and engine noises. The dynamometer check is often combined with the electronic diagnostic check.

■ Road testing of the automobile. This is sometimes a substitute for the dynamometer check. However, it is often conducted as a final check of the entire process.

The result of this complete analysis is a thorough understanding of the automobile performance. However, there are some things not checked in this process. Wear in transmission gears and bearings, wear in rear end bearings and gears, and air conditioning mechanical operations are difficult to diagnose in this process.

Though some components are not thoroughly checked, the automobile diagnosis provides the owner with a thorough analysis of the condition of the automobile.

AUTOMOTIVE DIAGNOSTIC SERVICE CENTERS

As automobiles, especially engines, have become more complex, the need for diagnostic service centers has grown. These centers are designed to provide a complete analysis of the condition of the automobile. See Fig. 14-10. Diagnosis service analyses are used for a variety of reasons, including:

■ Determining the cause of poor performance.

■ Determining the condition of a used automobile prior to purchase.

■ Determining the condition of the automobile as part of routine maintenance or a smog or safety check.

The diagnostic service procedure will vary among centers. Most complete diagnostic checks will involve the following:

■ Complete visual inspection of the automobile. This will include lights, fluid levels, belts and hoses, cooling system, chassis inspection, etc.

■ Electronic diagnosis and testing of engine performance. This will include testing the complete electrical system, computers and microprocessors, emission components, and engine cylinder performance.

Fig. 14-10. An automotive diagnostic service center provides a reasonably complete analysis of the condition of the automobile.

Chapter 14—Review

Testing Your Knowledge

Briefly answer each of the following questions. Write on a separate piece of paper.
1. What factor helped diesel engines grow in popularity as an automotive engine?
2. Name the two major differences between gasoline and diesel engines.
3. What is the function of the diesel engine fuel injector?
4. What is the function of the glow plug?
5. Which type of diesel engine requires an air blower?
6. Identify the purpose of an automotive diagnostic service center.
7. Name the major checking procedures used during a complete diagnostic check.

Expressing Your Knowledge

Using complete sentences, write your answers to the following on a separate sheet of paper:
1. Why must diesel engines be made heavier and stronger than gasoline engines?
2. Identify the three functions of the fuel-injection pump.
3. What is the difference between a multiple-plunger system and a unit injector system?
4. Refer to Fig. 14-9 and describe how a turbocharger functions.
5. Name the main reasons people take their automobiles to a diagnostic service center.

Applying Your Knowledge

Follow your teacher's instructions to complete these activities:
1. Find someone who owns a car with a diesel engine or visit a car dealer who sells diesel-powered cars. How do cars with diesel engines compare with cars that have gasoline engines? Make up a chart that shows the advantages and disadvantages of each and display it in the classroom.
2. There are several fuels besides gasoline and diesel fuel that can be used to run car engines. For example, LP gas, methanol, and gasohol are all being used. Find out which alternative fuels are used in your community. Gas station attendants and auto repair workers would be good sources of information. Prepare a report describing your findings.
3. With one or two classmates, visit an automotive diagnostic service center. Determine the checks performed on automobiles. Obtain examples of checks performed and problems identified. Prepare a class report on your findings.

Small Engines

SECTION

Chapter 15

Small Engine Operation

This chapter describes the operation of a single-cylinder small engine. As you learn about the operation of this engine, you'll gain an understanding of the operation of all other internal-combustion engines.

Expanding Your Knowledge

Learning about power and energy technology will help you understand more about the world around you. As you study this chapter, you will learn to:

- Identify and describe the operation of the six major systems of the small engine—mechanical, lubrication, cooling, fuel, ignition, and starting.
- Identify and describe the function of each of the main parts of the fuel system, including the air cleaner, carburetor, and fuel pump.
- Explain the operation of the float carburetor, the vacuum-feed carburetor, and the diaphragm carburetor.
- Identify and describe the function of each of the main parts of the ignition system, including the armature, flywheel magnets, breaker points, condenser, spark plug, and stop switch.
- Describe the operation of the magneto and capacitive-discharge ignition systems.

Building Your Word Power

Knowledge of the vocabulary used will help you develop greater understanding of power and energy. The following terms are defined and explained in this chapter. Learning these will help you learn more about the operation of small engines.

atomization	grounding
bearings	momentum
centrifugal force	vaporization
governor	venturi

In our nation today, a great deal of power is used in the operation of small engines. Small engines are used to power lawn mowers, weed and brush cutters, snow blowers, small boats, and a variety of other devices. Most of these devices use a simple single-cylinder small engine.

In this chapter, emphasis is placed on understanding the operation of each of the six systems which make up a small engine. Each system performs a function needed to keep the engine operating. Since small engines have a variety of uses, manufacturers have designed a number of different fuel and ignition systems for these needs. Each of these systems is also described.

SMALL ENGINE SYSTEMS

There are many different types and sizes of small engines. This chapter doesn't explain any one engine in detail. Instead, it gives you the information you need to develop a general understanding of *all* small gas engines. See Fig. 15-1.

There's a lot to learn if you really want to know how a small engine works. Basically, a small engine produces rotary motion by burning a mixture of oxygen (from air) and gasoline. To understand *how* the engine does this, you have to learn about the parts of the engine. See Fig. 15-2. You need to learn what each part looks like, what its name is, and its function. You also have to find out how the parts fit in the engine.

This chapter is divided into six sections. Each section describes one of the major small engine systems. The following are the six systems:

■ The *mechanical system* changes reciprocal motion into rotary motion.
■ The *lubrication system* lubricates (oils) engine parts to reduce friction and wear.
■ The *cooling system* removes excess heat from the engine.
■ The *fuel system* mixes air and fuel properly and delivers the mixture to the combustion chamber.
■ The *ignition system* produces the spark that ignites the fuel.
■ The *starting system* sets the engine in motion.

Study these systems separately. Once you understand each system, you can "put them together" to see how the whole engine works.

MECHANICAL SYSTEM

The mechanical system converts the reciprocating motion of the piston into useful rotary motion. Burning fuel in a sealed chamber produces high-pressure gases. As the gases expand, they push the piston. The piston is attached by a connecting rod to a crankshaft. When the piston moves down, it turns the crankshaft. The turning crankshaft provides rotating mechanical power. See Fig. 15-3. This power can then be put to work.

A small gasoline engine's mechanical system operates on either the two-stroke or four-stroke cycle. (See Chapter 12.) Two-stroke and four-stroke engines have basically the same mechanical parts. The main difference is in the control of fuel and burned gases.

Crankcase, Cylinder, and Cylinder Head

The crankcase, cylinder, and cylinder head make up the framework (body) of the engine. Together these parts form a sealed unit in which the mechanical system can work. See Fig. 15-4.

Sometimes the crankcase, cylinder, and cylinder head are made separately. Then they are bolted together. In most small engines, the cylinder head and crankcase are made as one part. This part is called the *cylinder block*.

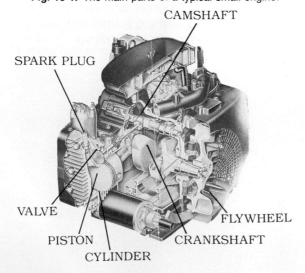
Fig. 15-1. The main parts of a typical small engine.
CAMSHAFT, SPARK PLUG, VALVE, PISTON, CYLINDER, CRANKSHAFT, FLYWHEEL

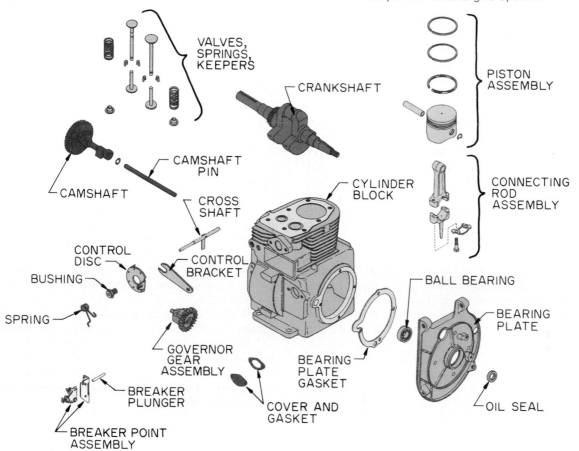

Fig. 15-2. Each of the many parts in this small engine has an important job in making the engine work.

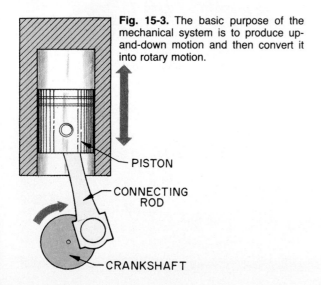

Fig. 15-3. The basic purpose of the mechanical system is to produce up-and-down motion and then convert it into rotary motion.

Fig. 15-4. In most small engines, the cylinder and crankcase are usually cast as one part, called the block. The cylinder head is bolted tightly to the block to prevent the combustion pressure from escaping.

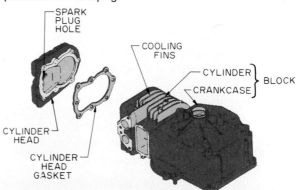

The *crankcase* is a kind of metal box. It makes up the bottom part of the engine. The crankcase has holes in two sides or ends. These holes support the crankshaft. The crankcase is usually made of aluminum. In four-stroke engines it acts as a reservoir (pool) for the engine's oil supply.

The *cylinder* is the middle part of the cylinder block. The piston moves up and down inside it. Some cylinders are made of iron. However, most small engine cylinders are aluminum. Aluminum is lightweight. It also transfers heat quickly. Some engines have an iron sleeve inside the aluminum cylinder. The outside of the cylinder has thin ribs, called *cooling fins*. Again, see Fig. 15-4. These fins help cool the engine. (Cooling fins are explained later in this chapter.)

The *cylinder head* is the top part of the engine. It is bolted tightly to the cylinder block. A *head gasket* fits between the cylinder head and cylinder block. It is made of two metal pieces that enclose a piece of soft heat-resistant material. The gasket is thin and flexible and fills the tiny irregularities and openings between the head and block. It produces a tight seal to prevent combustion pressure from escaping. Like the cylinder, the cylinder head has fins to help cool the engine. It also has a threaded hole for the spark plug.

Throughout this chapter you will see the term *combustion chamber*. The combustion chamber is not a part, but a space. This space is located in the cylinder head, just above the top of the cylinder. The bottom tip of the spark plug goes through the cylinder head into the combustion chamber. The air-fuel mixture is ignited in the combustion chamber.

Pistons

A piston is a hollow metal part that moves in the cylinder. Through the connecting rod, the movement of the piston turns the crankshaft. The piston also works as a moving seal. It seals the air-fuel mixture in the combustion chamber. It also separates the combustion chamber from the crankcase.

Most small engine pistons are made of aluminum. Figure 15-5 shows the parts of a piston.

Notice the hardened steel *piston pin* that fits into the piston. Sometimes it is called a *wrist pin*. This hollow pin attaches the piston to the connecting rod. The connecting rod is another part of the mechanical system.

Technology Focus

The Overhead Is Taking Over

For years, economy and tradition directed the manufacture of small engines. The result— L-head engines with minimum improvements during the past two decades. Today there's something new in small engines. First the Japanese and now American manufacturers are building an overhead-valve small engine and making numerous other improvements.

The overhead-valve engine shown here is aluminum with a cast-iron cylinder sleeve. It is lighter in weight and should be more durable, fuel-efficient, powerful, and easier to service than the traditional L-head engine.

You'll see the overhead-valve engine first in top-of-the-line rotary lawn mowers. However, it is expected to take over the small engine market in the future.

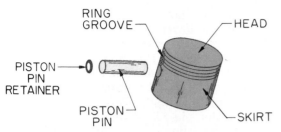

Fig. 15-5. This piston for a four-stroke engine has a flat head. Manufacturers also make piston heads with other shapes to produce greater power.

The piston is slightly smaller in diameter than the cylinder. There is a small gap between the piston and the cylinder wall. The gap is slightly larger at the top of the piston. The top of the piston is made smaller than the bottom. Pistons are made this way because of the heat produced during combustion. The heat causes the entire piston to expand. Therefore, there must be some space between the piston and the cylinder wall. The heat is most intense at the top of the piston. As a result, the piston expands more at the top than at the bottom. The piston's smaller top diameter allows for this extra expansion.

Pistons also expand unevenly across the middle. This is due to the greater amount of metal supporting the piston pin. For this reason, many pistons are not round, but slightly oval-shaped. These pistons are called *cam-ground pistons*. As a cam-ground piston expands, it becomes round like the cylinder. This keeps the piston from slapping against the cylinder wall. See Fig. 15-6.

There is a basic difference between two- and four-stroke piston heads. Four-stroke piston heads are either flat or slightly curved. Most two-stroke pistons have slanted, raised heads. The raised head directs the incoming air-fuel mixture up into the combustion chamber. The head pushes out burned gases at the same time. It also keeps the new air-fuel mixture from mixing with the burned gases. Even with this design, two-stroke engines do not exhaust burnt fuel as well as four-stroke engines.

Piston Rings

Several grooves are cut around the tops of the pistons. These grooves hold thin metal rings, called *piston rings*. The pistons in most small engines have from two to four rings. The top rings are called *compression rings*. The bottom rings are called *oil control rings*. See Fig. 15-7.

The main job of the compression rings is to seal combustion pressure inside the combustion chamber. Without this seal, some pressure would "blow by" the piston. The pressure would not push on the piston. Instead, it would escape down the cylinder wall into the crankcase. This would cause a loss of power.

The oil control rings seal the engine oil in the crankcase, away from the combustion chamber. They do this by scraping excess oil away from the cylinder wall. Oil must not get into the combustion chamber. Otherwise, the oil would burn and the engine would constantly need more oil. Too much oil in the combustion chamber would also foul the spark plug.

All pistons have either one or two compression rings. Four-stroke pistons have either one or

Fig. 15-7. Compression rings seal the combustion chamber from the crankcase.

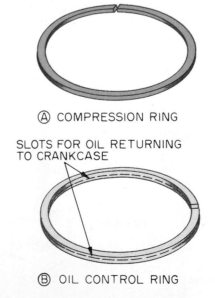

Fig. 15-6. As a cold engine warms up, a cam-ground piston expands to nearly the same size as the cylinder.

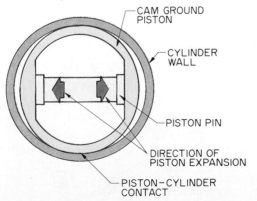

two oil rings. Two-stroke pistons do not usually have any oil rings. You will learn why when you study the *Lubrication System* section.

To provide a tight seal, the rings must press against the cylinder walls. This is done by compressing the rings into the piston grooves as the piston is put into the cylinder. The spring tension of the rings holds them tightly against the cylinder wall. This tension provides the all-important seal.

Piston rings are usually made of cast iron. Many rings are coated with chrome, which is hard and wears slowly. The chrome increases the life of the ring. It also reduces cylinder wear.

Connecting Rod

The connecting rod connects the piston to the crankshaft. It has two pieces—the rod and the rod cap. Figure 15-8 shows how the connecting rod is connected to the piston and crankshaft.

The connecting rod alternates between pushing and pulling. On the intake stroke, the connecting rod pulls the piston. On the power stroke, the piston pushes the connecting rod. The combined effect of these movements places great stress on the connecting rod.

To handle the changing stresses, the connecting rod must be very strong. Therefore, it is often made of forged steel. Some small engines do not handle heavy loads. These engines may have connecting rods made of cast steel or forged aluminum. These metals are not as strong as forged steel.

The connecting rod attaches the piston to the crankshaft. A piston pin fits through the hole at the top part of the connecting rod. This joins the connecting rod to the piston.

The bottom part of the connecting rod has a larger hole. The lower half of this hole is formed by the *rod cap*. The rod cap is attached to the rod with cap screws. This makes it possible to take off the cap and fasten the rod to the crankshaft. Both the top and bottom connecting rod holes are precisely made. This is so the crankshaft and piston pin will fit well.

Some connecting rods do not have bearings. Other connecting rods have a bearing at each end. **Bearings** are metal parts that support turning parts. They reduce friction and wear. This keeps the turning parts from being damaged or worn out quickly.

Sleeve bearings are the most common bearings used in connecting rod holes. A one-piece sleeve bearing is usually called a *bushing*. It fits into the top hole. A two-piece sleeve bearing is called an *insert bearing*. It fits the two halves of the bottom hole. See Fig. 15-9. Some small engines use *anti-friction bearings* in the bottom hole.

Crankshaft

As the connecting rod moves, it turns the crankshaft. The combined movement of the connecting rod and crankshaft changes reciprocating motion into rotary motion. The rotating crankshaft provides mechanical power to run the engine. It also provides power to do work. The crankshaft is the heart of the engine's operation. People talk about "turning over" an engine or an engine's "rpms." They are referring to the rotation of the crankshaft.

Small engine crankshafts are made of either cast iron or cast steel. Figure 15-10 shows a

Fig. 15-8. The piston has been cut away so you can see how the connecting rod attaches to the piston. The bottom part of the connecting rod consists of two parts. These parts are bolted together around the crankshaft.

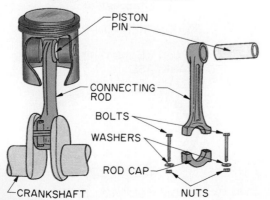

Fig. 15-9. Sleeve bearings are often inserted into the connecting rod holes. This reduces friction and wear on the connecting rod. The bearings must be lubricated to work properly.

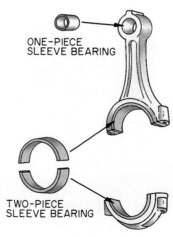

crankshaft for a one-cylinder four-stroke engine. The gear on the shaft makes it possible for the crankshaft to turn the camshaft. Crankshafts in small two-stroke engines do not have these gears. You will learn why later in this chapter.

Notice the three crankshaft *journals*. The end journals allow the crankshaft to rotate inside the cylinder block.

The connecting rod fastens to the *connecting rod journal*. Each *main journal* (end journal) fits into a hole in the end or side of the crankcase. Journals are precisely made so that the crankshaft turns smoothly.

The crank pin is offset from the main part of the shaft. A *counterweight*, opposite the crank pin, balances the crankshaft. This permits the crankshaft to maintain a balanced rotation.

The crankshaft extends through holes in the crankcase. Both ends of the crankshaft are carefully machined (shaped and sized). One end is attached to the flywheel. The other end—the *power output*—provides power to do work.

The crankshaft can fit into the crankcase either vertically (up and down) or horizontally (across). The placement depends on the engine's use. Lawn mowers, for example, have vertical crankshafts. This is so the cutting blades can be attached to the end of the crankshaft. Figure 15-11 shows how crankshaft placement affects an engine's overall design.

Crankshaft Bearings

As you know, some connecting rods use bearings to reduce friction and wear. The crankshaft main journals also need some kind of bearing surface.

Many different types of bearing surfaces can be used. In some engines designed for light loads, the bearing surfaces are simply the holes in the crankcase. On heavier-duty engines, the bearing surfaces are provided by *bearings* that fit into the crankcase holes. Figure 15-12 shows both types of bearing surfaces.

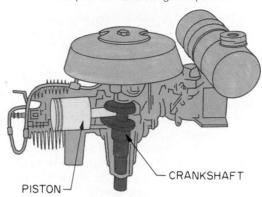

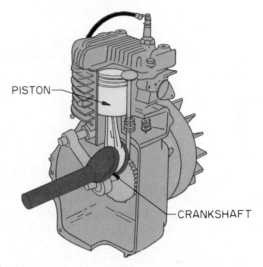

Fig. 15-11. Lawn mower engines and outboard motors usually have vertical crankshafts, such as that shown in the top drawing. In stationary engines, such as the one shown in the bottom drawing, the crankshaft is usually horizontal.

Fig. 15-12. There are two types of main bearing surfaces that can be used to support the crankshaft.

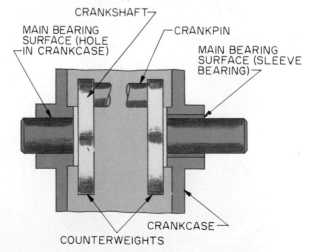

Fig. 15-10. A crankshaft has one connecting rod journal for each cylinder of the engine.

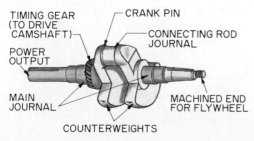

If bearings are used, they are either sleeve bearings or anti-friction bearings. *Sleeve bearings* are one-piece hollow tubes that are pressed into the crankcase holes.

Anti-friction bearings consist of steel balls or rollers inside a metal housing. This type of bearing is press-fitted onto the crankshaft journal. As the crankshaft rotates, the inner part of the bearing rotates with it. See Fig. 15-13.

Anti-friction bearings can stand heavy loads and shock. They cost more than sleeve bearings. However, they usually provide smoother performance and longer-lasting service.

Sleeve bearings and anti-friction bearings both require some kind of lubrication. Some anti-friction bearings have their own sealed-in lubrication. Sleeve bearings and other types of anti-friction bearings need another source of lubrication.

Flywheel

A heavy wheel called the *flywheel* is connected to one end of the crankshaft. A typical flywheel is shown in Fig. 15-14. Its main function is to help turn the crankshaft between power strokes. This helps maintain smooth engine operation.

To understand how the flywheel works, think about how moving objects behave. For ex-

ample, when you swing a hammer to hit a nail, the weight of the hammerhead adds force to the motion of the hammer. Basically, once you start the swing, the weight will carry the hammer to the nail. The force of the swing, along with the weight of the hammerhead, gives the hammer **momentum**.

A flywheel works in the same way. As the piston comes down on the power stroke, it turns the crankshaft and flywheel. The momentum of the heavy flywheel then keeps the crankshaft turning until the next power stroke.

Valve Train

Fuel enters the combustion chamber through a passage called the *intake port*. Burned gases leave the engine through a passage called the *exhaust port*. The intake port must be open on the intake stroke. The exhaust port must be open on the exhaust stroke. Both ports must be closed, however, during the compression and power strokes. This means that there must be a way of opening and closing the ports.

In four-stroke engines, *poppet valves* control the flow through the ports. These valves open and close to control intake and exhaust gases as they pass through the combustion chamber. Several other parts work together to open and close the valves at the right times.

As a group, the valves and their related parts are called the *valve train*. The valve train usually includes the valves, valve guides, tappets, valve springs, timing gears, and camshaft. See Fig. 15-15.

Most two-stroke engines do not have valve trains. They use a different method for intake and exhaust. This method is explained later in this chapter.

Valve Design. All four-stroke engines have two poppet valves per cylinder. One valve con-

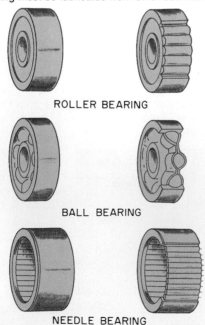

Fig. 15-13. Types of anti-friction bearings. The roller bearing is sealed with its own lubrication. The ball bearing and needle bearing must be lubricated from other sources.

ROLLER BEARING

BALL BEARING

NEEDLE BEARING

Fig. 15-14. The flywheel is attached to the crankshaft. It provides momentum, the force that keeps the flywheel rotating.

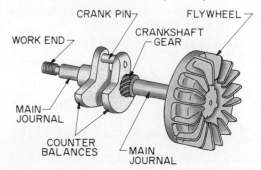

CRANK PIN

FLYWHEEL

WORK END

CRANKSHAFT GEAR

MAIN JOURNAL

COUNTER BALANCES

MAIN JOURNAL

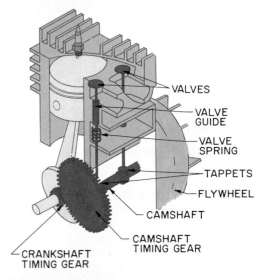

Fig. 15-15. The parts of the valve train work together to control intake and exhaust in four-stroke engines.

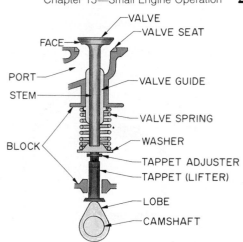

Fig. 15-16. The lobe on the camshaft causes the tappet and valve to move up. The valve spring moves the valve and tappet back down.

trols the flow of air-fuel mixture into the combustion chamber. This valve is called the *intake valve*. The other valve controls the flow of burned fuel from the engine. This valve is called the *exhaust valve*.

The valves must seal the combustion chamber during the compression and power strokes. Even the smallest leak results in a loss of power.

The valve-and-seat assembly controls the passage of gases between the port and the combustion chamber. See Fig. 15-16. The *face* is the bottom edge of the valve. It is tapered, usually at a 45° angle. The upper edge of the port is called the *seat*. It is tapered to match the valve face. Both the valve and its seat are carefully machined to match each other. This produces the most leakproof fit possible.

Valve Train Operation. The crankshaft drives the valve train and controls its speed. The crankshaft drives the valve train through two gears and a *camshaft*. The gears are called *timing gears*. Again, see Fig. 15-15. The camshaft gear is twice the size and has twice as many teeth as the crankshaft gear. As a result, the crankshaft rotates twice for each rotation of the camshaft. This allows the piston to move through the four-stroke cycle while the camshaft opens each valve once.

The camshaft has *cams*, also called *cam lobes*. These cams operate the valves. There is one cam for each valve. The lobe converts the crankshaft's rotary motion into reciprocating motion. The reciprocating motion is needed to open the valves. The design of the lobe controls how far the valve opens and how long the valve stays open.

As the camshaft turns, the cam lobes push up on the tappets. Again, see Fig. 15-16. The *tappets*, or *lifters*, push the valves open. As each tappet moves up, it compresses a *valve spring* against the engine block. As the cam lobe turns away from the tappet, the spring tension forces the valve back down. In this way the valve springs close the valves tightly. The valves stay closed until the rotating cam lobes again push up on the tappets.

Four-Stroke Cycle Operation

In Chapter 12, you learned how the four-stroke cycle works. You have just learned about the valve train, another important part of four-stroke cycle operation. Now you will learn how valve position is related to piston position. The valves and the piston must work together. The valves must open and close at just the right moment during the piston strokes. This is called *valve timing*.

Figure 15-17 shows a diagram of typical valve timing. This diagram is based on the rotation of the crankshaft. One complete turn of the crankshaft is 360°. Two piston strokes occur during each turn. Therefore, one piston stroke equals 180°. As in automotive engines, the very top of the piston's stroke is called *top dead center (TDC)* and the lowest point *bottom dead center (BDC)*.

Look again at Fig. 15-17. The intake valve opens 15° before the piston reaches TDC. It is open through the entire intake stroke (180°) and

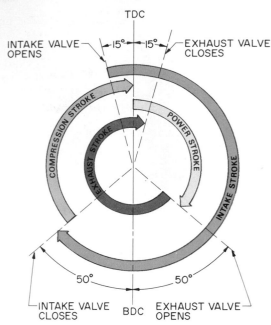

Fig. 15-17. The valves are timed to open and close according to the position of the piston. Note how the valves open slightly before or after the beginning of a new stroke.

stays open for 50° past BDC. Therefore, the intake stroke is 245° (15° + 180° + 50°), rather than 180°. This long open period permits the maximum fuel intake.

The compression stroke does not start until the intake valve closes. The intake valve was open during 50° of the upward piston movement. Therefore, the compression stroke is actually 130° (180° − 50°).

The spark plug fires just before TDC on the compression stroke. Combustion of the gases causes the power stroke. As the gases expand, the piston moves down. The exhaust valve opens at 50° before the piston reaches BDC. This makes the power stroke 130° (180° − 50°). It is the same length as the compression stroke.

The exhaust stroke lasts from 50° before BDC to 15° past TDC. This makes the exhaust stroke 245° (50° + 180° + 15°). It is the same length as the intake stroke.

Notice that between 15° before TDC and 15° after TDC, both valves are open. This happens as the exhaust stroke ends and the intake stroke begins. We call this 30° part of the timing cycle the *valve overlap.*

Valve overlap increases engine efficiency in two ways. The exhaust valve stays open long enough to allow all burnt gases to escape. The

intake valve opens early so that it will admit the most air-fuel mixture during the main part of the intake stroke.

Valves are timed to the proper piston position by aligning (lining up) *timing marks* on the timing gears. When these marks are aligned, the valves will open at the proper time.

Two-Stroke Cycle Operation

In most small two-stroke cycle engines, intake and exhaust are done without a valve train. Instead, the piston itself acts like a valve to open and close the intake and exhaust ports. Different methods are used for the intake of fuel. The most common method is the use of reed valves.

Reed Valves. A reed valve is a thin, flexible strip of steel. One end of it attaches to a small metal plate called a *reed plate.* The other end of the valve can move freely over a port in the plate. Many reed plates have several ports and several reed valves. See Fig. 15-18. Many plates have a thick metal piece called a *reed stop.* This stop keeps the reed valve from opening too far. The valve could be damaged otherwise.

The reed plate is usually attached to the inside wall of the crankcase. The reed valve controls the flow of the air-fuel mixture into the crankcase. (The following section describes how the reed valve does this.) When air pressure pushes the valve open, fuel enters the engine. Air pressure can also push the valve closed. When this happens, the valve seals the engine. Pressure builds up in the crankcase. This pressure then forces fuel into the combustion chamber.

Engine Operation. The basic operating principles of two-stroke engines were explained in Chapter 12. You are now familiar with the reed valve. Therefore, we can take a more detailed look at the actual operation of a two-stroke reed-valve engine.

Fig. 15-18. Reed valves. One has been disassembled to show the reed, reed stop, and reed plate.

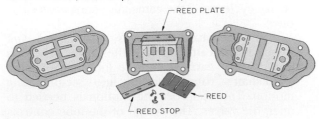

All four piston actions—intake, compression, power, and exhaust—happen in just two strokes. Intake and compression take place on the first stroke. Power and exhaust take place on the second. **A** and **B** in Fig. 15-19 show the first stroke. **C** and **D** show the second.

In **A** of Fig. 15-19, the piston is moving upward. It is passing the intake and exhaust ports. This seals the air-fuel mixture in the combustion chamber. The piston's upward movement also creates a partial vacuum in the crankcase. Atmospheric pressure then pushes air and fuel from the carburetor through the reed valve. This is how fuel enters the crankcase.

In **B** the piston has continued upward. It has compressed the fuel trapped in the combustion chamber. In the crankcase, the new air-fuel mixture has filled the vacuum. The reed valve has just closed. This seals the new air-fuel mixture in the crankcase.

Ignition takes place in **C**. The burning gases are pushing the piston down on its power stroke. This movement compresses the fuel mixture now trapped in the crankcase. In this way, pressure builds up in the crankcase.

In **D** the piston has passed the exhaust port. The burned gases are starting to escape. The piston has also passed the intake port. Crankcase pressure is pushing new air-fuel mixture into the combustion chamber. The raised head of the piston is deflecting the air-fuel mixture up. The new mixture is pushing out the burnt gases. This completes the two-stroke cycle. The cycle begins again when the piston starts back up the cylinder.

Two-stroke intake and exhaust has advantages and disadvantages. It requires fewer moving parts than a four-stroke valve train. This is an advantage in cost and maintenance. The disadvantage is in less efficient use of fuel. Some air-fuel mixture is lost as it drives out the exhaust gases. Another disadvantage is rougher, louder engine operation.

LUBRICATION SYSTEM

An engine's moving parts must be lubricated with oil. Without lubrication, an engine will soon fail. Lubrication serves the following purposes:
■ Reduces wear.

Oil produces a thin, low-friction surface. In this way, it reduces the amount of friction between parts that rub against each other. Low friction keeps parts from wearing out as quickly. This increases the life of the engine.
■ Increases efficiency.

Low friction resulting from lubrication increases the engine's efficiency. With high friction,

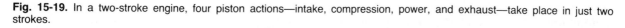

Fig. **15-19.** In a two-stroke engine, four piston actions—intake, compression, power, and exhaust—take place in just two strokes.

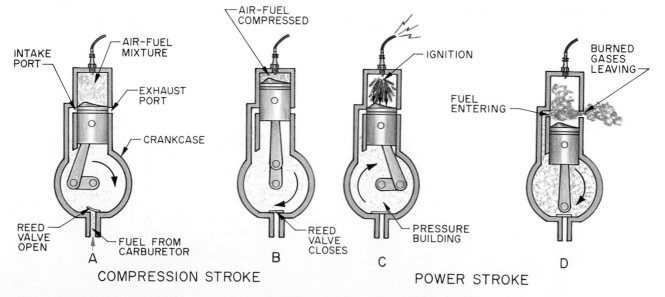

COMPRESSION STROKE   POWER STROKE

much of the power is converted into heat energy. With lubrication, more power goes to perform useful work.

■ Absorbs the shock of varying engine loads.

The piston receives a very heavy push when the fuel ignites. This places a sudden load on the piston pin, connecting rod, and crankshaft. On the return stroke, the load and force are reversed. The oil between the surfaces acts as a cushion for these continuous load changes.

■ Seals the piston rings and cylinder wall.

Oil fills the small gaps between the piston rings and the cylinder wall. This keeps the combustion gases from escaping into the crankcase.

■ Removes heat from the engine.

In a four-stroke engine, some engine heat is transferred to the oil. The oil collects in the crankcase. There, much of the heat passes through the crankcase and is cooled by the surrounding air. In this way, oil helps cool the engine.

■ Cleans the engine.

Oil circulates through the engine. As it does this, it picks up tiny particles of dirt and metal. The oil carries these particles to the oil filter or crankcase. This reduces much of the wear and damage caused by dirt between moving engine parts.

Two- and four-stroke small engines have very different lubrication systems. They are both discussed in this section. The different types and grades of oil are discussed in Chapter 17.

Two-Stroke Cycle Lubrication

The lubrication system for a two-stroke engine is very simple. You mix the oil with the fuel before filling the fuel tank. Oil and fuel then flow through the engine together. See Fig. 15-20.

The oil is much heavier and stickier than the fuel. As the oil-fuel mixture circulates, much of the oil sticks to engine parts. It coats the crankshaft, connecting rod, bearings, and cylinder walls.

Oil rings are not needed on the piston of a two-stroke engine. There is no excess oil to "scrape" back into the crankcase.

Four-Stroke Cycle Lubrication

Four-stroke engines have a separate lubrication system. Oil is not added to the fuel. The two most common types of lubrication systems used in four-stroke engines are the splash system and the pressure system.

Splash Lubrication. Most small four-stroke engines have splash lubrication systems. This type of system lubricates the engine's parts by splashing them with oil. A typical splash system is shown in Fig. 15-21.

In most splash systems, a *dipper* is attached to the bottom of the connecting rod. The dipper dips into the oil stored in the crankcase. As the connecting rod rotates, so does the dipper. As it passes through the oil, it splashes oil onto the moving engine parts.

Not all splash systems have a dipper. In some four-stroke engines, a *slinger* slings the oil against the parts. A gear on the camshaft operates the slinger. See Fig. 15-22.

Pressure Systems. Some larger one-cylinder engines use a pressure lubrication system to supply oil to an engine's moving parts. The most

Fig. 15-20. Two-stroke engines are lubricated by an oil-fuel mixture.

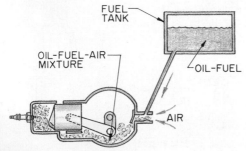

FUEL TANK

OIL-FUEL-AIR MIXTURE

OIL-FUEL

AIR

Fig. 15-21. In the simplest type of four-stroke lubrication, a dipper splashes oil on the engine parts. The dipper is either cast as part of the connecting rod or is bolted to it.

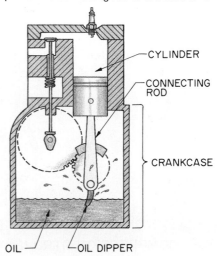

CYLINDER

CONNECTING ROD

CRANKCASE

OIL

OIL DIPPER

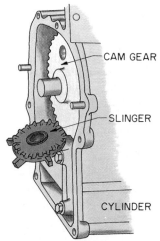

Fig. 15-22. A slinger is a gear that engages with a camshaft gear. As the camshaft turns, the slinger throws oil onto the engine parts.

important part of a pressure lubrication system is the *oil pump*. The *gear pump* in Fig. 15-23 is a commonly used type. Many other types of pumps are used in pressure systems. Either the crankshaft or the camshaft can drive the oil pump. A screen connected to the pump inlet filters the oil. This keeps dirt from entering the pump. Dirt could damage both the pump and the engine.

All pressure lubrication systems require a *pressure relief valve*. This valve keeps pressure from building up in the system. In many cases the valve is part of the pump. If the pressure rises too much, the relief valve opens. This releases oil to the inlet side of the pump and reduces the pressure in the system.

Figure 15-24 shows how oil flows through the engine. The crankcase oil is pumped to the main bearings. It enters a drilled passage in the

Fig. 15-23. In a gear pump, the teeth of the turning gears pick up the incoming oil and carry it to the outlet side.

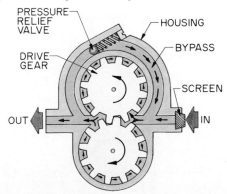

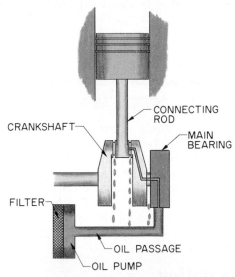

Fig. 15-24. A pressure lubrication system sends a steady stream of oil through the crankshaft to the connecting rod journal.

crankshaft and travels to the crank pin. In this way, the oil lubricates the crankshaft's bearings. The oil that reaches the crank pin also lubricates the camshaft, valve train, and piston assembly. The oil leaves the crank pin through an oil passage in the connecting rod. See Fig. 15-25. The action of the connecting rod throws the oil onto the other engine parts.

Fig. 15-25. The oil passage hole in the connecting rod provides a way for oil to reach the piston and upper cylinder wall.

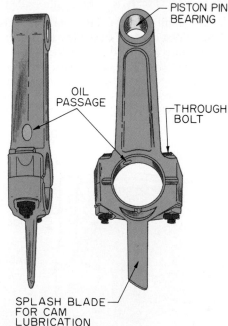

The camshaft is also lubricated by a kind of "splash system." The connecting rod splashes in the pool of oil in the crankcase. This throws oil onto the camshaft.

COOLING SYSTEM

Over two-thirds of the heat an engine produces is wasted. Less than a third of the heat is actually converted into mechanical energy. Too much heat can damage an engine's parts. Therefore, the excess heat must be removed. The exhaust gases remove much of this heat. There are two types of systems for removing the remaining heat. They are the air cooling and water cooling systems.

Air Cooling

In most small engines, waste heat is transferred to the air around the engine. The cylinder head and block are designed to transfer the heat. *Fins* cast into the cylinder head and block increase the surface area of the engine. This provides extra contact between the air and the engine. Therefore, the air around the engine can pick up more engine heat.

Engines used where there is no circulating air require a cooling fan. See Fig. 15-26. The cooling fan is part of the flywheel. Fan blades on the flywheel blow air over the cooling fins. A *shroud* directs the air over the engine.

Water Cooling

A few small engines, such as outboard motors, are water-cooled. See Fig. 15-27. In these engines, water removes the excess heat. A *water jacket* surrounds the cylinder block and head. Water circulating through the jacket absorbs heat from the engine. The water comes from the lake or river. A pump is used to move the water through the engine.

A *thermostat* prevents overcooling by controlling the water flow. As the engine temperature rises, the thermostat opens. Water then circulates through the jacket and removes heat.

As the engine temperature drops, the thermostat partially closes. This reduces water circulation. The water removes less heat. In this way, the thermostat keeps the engine at its proper temperature.

FUEL SYSTEM

The fuel system brings air and fuel together and mixes them for combustion. A fuel system includes an air cleaner, a fuel supply, a carburetor, and a governor. See Fig. 15-28.

Air Cleaner

All engines need a large amount of air for combustion. Air enters an engine through the air cleaner. See Fig. 15-29. The air cleaner removes dirt and dust particles from the air. This keeps them from entering the engine. These particles can scratch and rub the cylinder wall and the piston rings. This can cause much wear and damage.

Fig. 15-27. This cross section of a water-cooled engine shows part of the water jacket. Water circulates through the water jacket to cool the engine.

Fig. 15-26. The cooling fan is cast as part of the flywheel. The faster the crankshaft turns, the more air the fan blows across the fins.

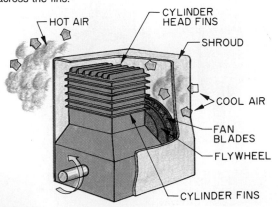

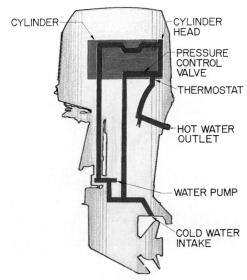

Fig. 15-28. The main parts of a small engine fuel system.

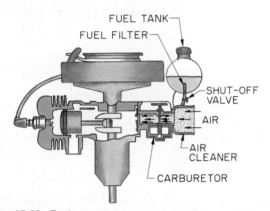

Fig. 15-29. Engines need a great deal of clean air. The air entering the engine must pass through an air cleaner before mixing with the fuel.

Fig. 15-30. Small particles of dust and dirt stick to paper filters. The cleaned air then passes through tiny holes and into the carburetor.

Air cleaners have purposes other than cleaning the air. They help quiet the rush of air into the carburetor. This makes the engine run quieter. If an engine backfires, the air cleaner also helps prevent fires.

Most air cleaners are attached to the carburetor. The air passes directly from the cleaner to the carburetor. Small engines use a dry-element or oil-foam cleaner.

Dry-Element Cleaner. The main part of a dry-element air cleaner is the dry filter. Dry filters are made of materials such as paper and felt. See Fig. 15-30. Tiny holes in the filter allow air to flow through the cleaner into the carburetor. The filter traps and holds particles of dust and dirt that cannot get through the holes.

Oil-Foam Cleaner. An oil-foam cleaner is a filter made of a plastic, sponge-like material. It is soaked in oil. See Figs. 15-31 and 15-32. Air enters the cleaner and passes through the filter. Dirt and dust particles stick to the oily filter. Only clean air enters the carburetor.

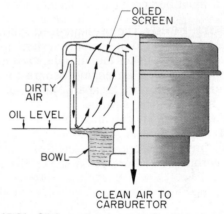

Fig. 15-31. Oil foam cleaners are a combination of a dry cleaner and an oil-bath cleaner (shown here). As air passes through an oil-bath cleaner, some dirt falls into the bowl of oil. The screen catches any dirt left in the air.

Fig. 15-32. The foam filter used in an oil-foam cleaner contains oil. As air passes through the foam, dirt sticks to the oil.

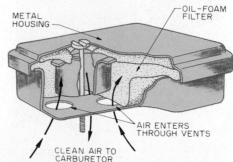

Fuel Supply

Three systems are commonly used to bring fuel into the carburetor. These are the gravity-feed, vacuum-feed, and pressure-feed systems. All three systems have a *fuel tank* and *fuel filter*.

Gravity-Feed. A simple, common method of fuel supply is the gravity-feed system. In this system the fuel tank is located above the carburetor. See Fig. 15-33. The force of gravity pushes fuel into the carburetor. No fuel pump is needed. A shutoff valve is usually located on the bottom of the tank.

Vacuum-Feed. Another common fuel-supply system is the vacuum-feed system. This system is sometimes called a *suction-feed system*. In this system, the fuel tank is located just below the carburetor. As with gravity-feed systems, no fuel pump is needed. See Fig. 15-34.

Air moving through the carburetor produces a vacuum. Atmospheric pressure pushes on the fuel in the fuel tank. Fuel passes through the fuel pipe and into the carburetor. In this system, the fuel tank must be very close to the carburetor.

Pressure-Feed. The pressure-feed system is the most complicated fuel supply system. In this system, pressure pushes fuel into the carburetor. This system is used on engines where the fuel tank and carburetor are far apart. Many outboard motors have pressure systems.

This system is similar to the fuel supply used in automotive engines. A *fuel pump* supplies the pressure to move the fuel from the tank to the carburetor. Figure 15-35 shows the loca-

tion of the fuel pump. The most common type of fuel pump is a *diaphragm pump*. This pump is similar to the automotive pump described on page 180.

Carburetor

The carburetor is the most important part of the fuel system. Its main job is to properly mix air and fuel for efficient combustion. The carburetor also controls the amount of air-fuel mixture entering the combustion chamber. See Fig. 15-36.

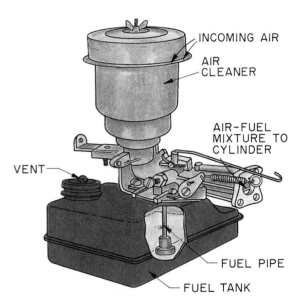

Fig. 15-34. In a vacuum-feed fuel system, the fuel tank must be very close to the carburetor. A vacuum in the carburetor causes fuel to flow from the tank.

Fig. 15-35. A pressure-feed fuel system is used when the fuel tank and carburetor are too far apart to use a gravity- or vacuum-feed system. A fuel pump pushes fuel into the carburetor.

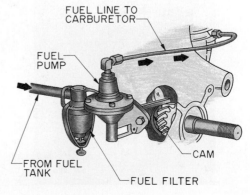

Fig. 15-33. In a gravity-feed fuel system, the fuel tank must be mounted above the carburetor. Gravity feeds the fuel from the tank to the carburetor.

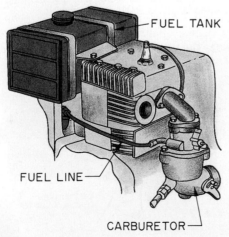

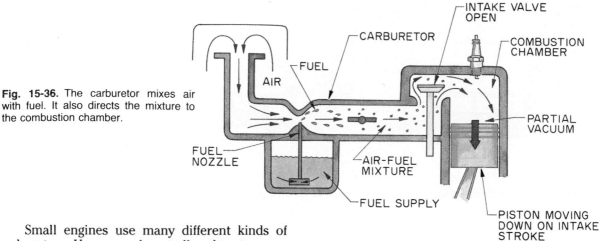

Fig. 15-36. The carburetor mixes air with fuel. It also directs the mixture to the combustion chamber.

Small engines use many different kinds of carburetors. However, almost all carburetors use the same basic parts and operating principles. This section discusses these parts and principles. Study this basic information first. Then you'll be able to understand the different carburetor types that are described later.

Venturi.
The main body of a carburetor is a tunnel-like passageway, or chamber. The chamber is wide at both ends. One end opens into the air cleaner. The other end opens into either the intake port or the intake manifold. (The *intake manifold* is the passageway to the engine.) The carburetor chamber is narrow in the middle. The narrow part is called the **venturi**. See Fig. 15-37.

To get to the combustion chamber, air must pass through the carburetor. There are two partial vacuums involved in the flow of air. One is *engine vacuum*. On the intake stroke, the pis-

Fig. 15-37. Air passing through the carburetor speeds up as it passes the venturi. This creates a partial vacuum. Atmospheric pressure can then push fuel from the fuel supply into the venturi.

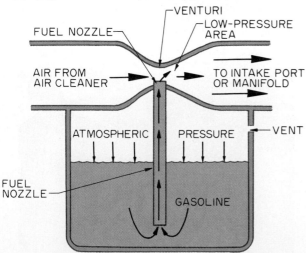

ton moves down. This creates a low-pressure area above the piston. This vacuum allows atmospheric pressure to push air through the carburetor.

The second partial vacuum is produced in the venturi. As air passes through the venturi, it speeds up. This speed increase creates a vacuum. The fuel supply is vented to the atmosphere. Therefore, the venturi vacuum allows atmospheric pressure to push fuel from the fuel supply into the venturi.

The fuel enters the venturi through a small opening. The fast-moving air atomizes the fuel. **Atomization** is the process of changing a liquid into a fine mist, or spray.

The low pressure in the venturi also lowers the fuel's boiling point. This helps vaporize the fuel. **Vaporization** changes atomized fuel into a gas. The fuel can then mix easily with the air.

Fuel Nozzle.
Fuel is pushed into the venturi through a fuel nozzle. Again, see Fig. 15-37. The fuel nozzle is simply a tube. It leads from the fuel supply to the venturi. There is low pressure at this point. Atmospheric pressure, which is higher, pushes fuel through the nozzle. The fuel then mixes with the air in the venturi.

Throttle Valve.
The throttle valve is a round, thin plate. It fits on a shaft at the cylinder end of the carburetor. See Fig. 15-38. Rotating the shaft turns the throttle to different positions. The throttle position controls the amount of air-fuel mixture entering the combustion chamber, as shown in Fig. 15-36. In this way, the throttle controls the engine's speed.

Figure 15-38 shows the throttle valve in three different positions. In the *closed* position, the valve almost completely blocks off the car-

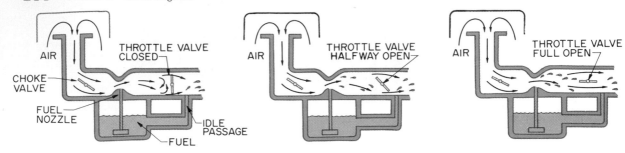

A. Engine at idle.　　　B. Engine at medium speed.　　　C. Engine at full speed.

Fig. 15-38. The throttle valve controls engine speed by controlling the amount of air and fuel entering the engine.

buretor. It lets only a small amount of air pass through. This small amount is not enough to pull fuel from the nozzle. However, a small amount of fuel can enter the carburetor through an *idle passage*. (Idling is explained later.)

In the *halfway open* position, the throttle valve is tilted at a 45° angle. See Fig. 15-38B. This time more air can pass through the carburetor. The air creates a venturi vacuum. Therefore, fuel flows out of the fuel nozzle and into the engine. The engine speeds up to a medium speed.

In the *full open* position, the valve is at a right angle to its closed position. See Fig. 15-38C. This allows the greatest amount of air-fuel mixture into the engine. The engine speeds up to its maximum speed.

There are two basic ways to control the position of the throttle:
- The engine operator can move a *throttle lever*.
- A *governor* can control the throttle position automatically. (Governors are described later in this chapter.)

Choke Valve.
The choke looks much like the throttle. It is a thin, round butterfly valve. It fits on a shaft at the air cleaner end of the carburetor. Again, see Fig. 15-38. Closing the choke reduces the amount of air entering the carburetor. The operator can usually adjust the choke with a *choke lever*.

The choke's main job is to help start cold engines. Cold engines need a richer air-fuel mixture than warm engines do. That is, they need more fuel and less air. When the choke is closed, it lets the smallest amount of air into the carburetor. This increases the engine vacuum at the fuel nozzle. The higher vacuum allows atmospheric pressure to push more fuel through the fuel nozzle. The carburetor bowl is vented to the air to maintain atmospheric pressure. Once the engine is warm, the choke is opened.

Many small engines have a *primer* instead of a choke. The operator presses the primer to pump extra fuel to the carburetor. This produces the richer mixture needed for starting. Figure 15-39 shows a typical small engine primer.

Idle Fuel Adjustment.
At times, an engine runs with the throttle closed. The rotating crankshaft does not perform any useful work. We say that the engine is *idling*. A special screw controls the proportion of air to fuel in the air-fuel mixture during idling. This screw is called the *idle fuel adjustment screw*. It is also called the *idle mixture screw*. See Fig. 15-40.

The idle fuel adjustment screw is a kind of "needle" valve. The operator turns it in or out. This reduces or increases the amount of fuel that enters the air stream.

Fig. 15-39. Primers supply extra fuel to the carburetor to help start a cold engine. The parts labeled here are (A) the governor linkage, (B) the main fuel adjustment, (C) the idle fuel adjustment, and (D) the idle speed adjustment.

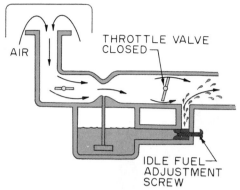

Fig. 15-40. The idle fuel adjustment screw controls the amount of fuel in the air-fuel mixture when the throttle is closed.

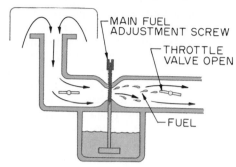

Fig. 15-41. During engine operation above idling speed, the main fuel adjustment screw controls the amount of fuel that passes through the fuel nozzle.

The usual air-fuel ratio for idling is 7-10 to 1, by weight. This means that there are between 7 and 10 pounds of air for every pound of gasoline.

Main Fuel Adjustment. When the engine runs at speeds above an idle, two things happen. First, atmospheric pressure pushes fuel up through the fuel nozzle. Second, the fuel mixes with the incoming air. The amount of fuel that passes through the nozzle can be controlled. This is done with the *main fuel adjustment screw.* See Fig. 15-41.

The main fuel adjustment screw is a needle valve. The operator turns it in or out. This controls the proportion of air to fuel at medium speeds. The usual ratio is about 15 to 1 (15 pounds of air to every pound of gasoline).

Idle Speed Adjustment. A special screw controls the amount that the throttle valve is open during idling. This screw is the *idle speed adjusting screw.*

The idle speed adjusting screw is located in an arm attached to the throttle shaft. As you turn the screw in, the end of it moves against the carburetor body. This causes the throttle valve to open. See Fig. 15-42. As the throttle opens, the idle speed (rpm) increases. If you back the screw out, the idle speed decreases.

Float Carburetor

Many small engines use float-type carburetors. These carburetors have a *float assembly.* This assembly maintains a constant supply of fuel for the carburetor. Its main parts are a float, a float bowl, and a needle valve. See Fig. 15-43.

Fig. 15-42. The engine's rpm at idle is controlled by the idle speed adjusting screw. Turning this screw in increases the idle speed. Backing it out decreases the speed.

Fig. 15-43. The parts of the float assembly work together to provide a constant supply of fuel to the carburetor.

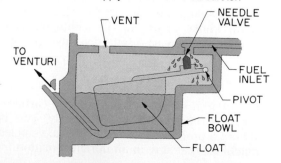

There is an air inlet at the top of the float bowl. This *vent* maintains atmospheric pressure in the bowl. The atmospheric pressure pushes the fuel from the bowl into the low pressure of the venturi.

The *float bowl* holds the fuel. Fuel travels from the bowl to the venturi. As this happens, the level of fuel in the bowl goes down. As the fuel level drops, the hollow metal *float* drops. This movement slowly pulls the *needle valve* away from the *fuel inlet seat*. More fuel then enters the bowl.

As fuel enters the bowl, the float rises. It moves the needle valve back into the fuel inlet seat. Just as much fuel enters the bowl as leaves it. The result is a constant supply of fuel to the venturi.

For proper float operation, the engine must be upright. Some engines operate in different positions. Chain saw engines and weed trimmer engines are examples. These engines can't use float carburetors. Instead, they use diaphragm or vacuum-feed carburetors.

Vacuum-Feed Carburetor

Most vacuum-feed, or *suction*, carburetors have a simpler design than float carburetors. There is no float assembly. The fuel goes directly from the fuel tank to the carburetor. Another difference is that only one needle valve is used for both the main fuel adjustment and the idle fuel adjustment. Refer back to Fig. 15-34. It shows a typical vacuum-feed carburetor.

Vacuum-feed carburetors also do not have a venturi. A specially placed throttle valve takes the place of the venturi. The throttle is in the carburetor at the end of the fuel pipe. See Fig. 15-44.

When the throttle valve is turned, it restricts the flow of air and creates a low-pressure area. This allows atmospheric pressure to push fuel up the fuel pipe and into the carburetor. Together, the throttle and the needle valve control the air-fuel ratio at all speeds.

Many vacuum-feed carburetors have a *sliding choke*. Again, see Fig. 15-44. The operator slides the choke in or out. This kind of choke works the same way as a butterfly-valve choke.

Diaphragm Carburetor

Float carburetors and vacuum-feed carburetors must be upright to work properly. This is usually not a problem. Most engines run vehicles and machines that stay in an upright position.

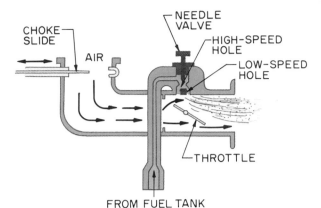

Fig. 15-44. This vacuum-feed carburetor uses only one needle valve for both high-speed and idle adjustments. This simple design works well on engines that run at fairly constant speeds.

However, some engines must operate in other positions. For example, chain saws are often turned to the side or even almost upside down. Their engines need carburetors that can work in any position. The most common carburetor used in these engines is called a *diaphragm carburetor*.

Diaphragm carburetors have a lot in common with other types of carburetors. They control engine speed with a throttle. They use a choke or a primer for starting. And they redirect fuel to an idle passage to produce a rich idling mixture.

Like float carburetors, diaphragm carburetors also maintain a constant fuel level. But this is where the big difference comes in. Instead of using a float, diaphragm carburetors use a *diaphragm* to control the fuel intake. This diaphragm is a flexible elastic disk. It fits inside the bottom of the carburetor. See Fig. 15-45.

Figure 15-45A shows how the carburetor looks before the engine is started. The fuel chamber is filled and the diaphragm supports the weight of the fuel. Notice the different parts of the carburetor. A *needle valve* fits into the *fuel inlet*. This valve controls the entry of fuel into the *fuel chamber*. The free end of the *inlet valve control lever* holds the inlet valve in place. A *spring* pushes down on the control lever and helps keep the diaphragm down. The pressure of the fuel above the diaphragm balances the pressure of the air below the diaphragm.

Now look at Fig. 15-45B. The engine has been started and there is a vacuum produced in the venturi. This vacuum reduces the pressure on the fuel in the fuel chamber. The force produced by the atmospheric pressure below the

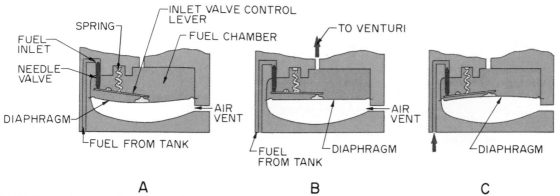

Fig. 15-45. These drawings show how a diaphragm carburetor maintains a constant fuel supply. It does this regardless of its position. (A) Diaphragm down—fuel chamber full. (B) Diaphragm rises—fuel chamber empties. (C) Diaphragm rises further—fuel enters fuel chamber.

diaphragm is now greater than the force above the diaphragm. The greater force pushes the diaphragm up as the fuel enters the venturi.

In Fig. 15-45C the force of the atmospheric pressure below the diaphragm is enough to overcome the spring tension. The control arm pivots and allows fuel to enter the fuel chamber. Fuel comes from the fuel tank located nearby. The venturi vacuum is great enough to allow the atmospheric pressure in the fuel tank to force fuel into the fuel chamber.

During operation, the diaphragm stays at a balanced position. It lets fuel enter past the inlet valve at the rate the fuel is used by the engine.

Governors

The amount of load on an engine affects its speed. When the load increases, the engine must work harder. Working harder slows the engine down. When the load lightens, the engine does not work hard. This causes the engine to speed up.

A device called a **governor** is used to even out changes in engine speed. The governor is connected to the carburetor's throttle. The governor automatically adjusts the throttle to maintain a constant speed. The governor also provides the safety feature of limiting the engine's maximum speed.

Two types of governors are commonly used on small engines. They are centrifugal and air vane governors.

Centrifugal Governors. Many governors use the principle of **centrifugal force**. This is the force that tends to push a rotating object out from its center. Governors using this force are called centrifugal, or *mechanical*, governors.

Figure 15-46 shows a common type of centrifugal governor. This type of governor fastens directly to the crankshaft. The top and bottom collars are connected by pivoting (turning) links. The top collar is connected to the throttle by linkage. (Linkage is a system of levers.)

As the crankshaft turns, it produces centrifugal force. This force pulls out on the weights held by the pivoting links. As the links move out, the upper collar drops down the shaft. See Fig. 15-47. The collar's downward movement pulls the throttle closed. This slows the engine down.

As the engine tries to speed up, the governor closes the throttle further. The faster the crankshaft tries to turn, the more the governor closes the throttle. In this way, the governor limits the engine's maximum speed.

Fig. 15-46. A centrifugal governor. The bottom collar is fastened to the crankshaft and cannot move. The top collar slides up and down according to the amount of centrifugal force produced by the turning crankshaft.

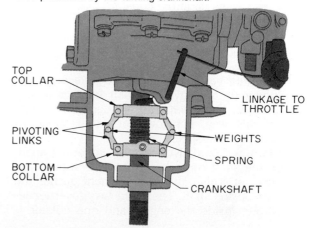

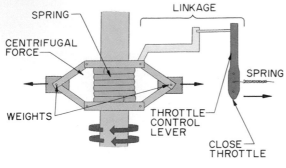

A. LIGHT LOAD

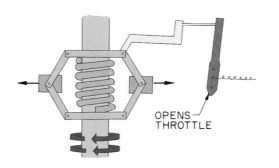

B. HEAVY LOAD

Fig. 15-47. Operation of a centrifugal governor.

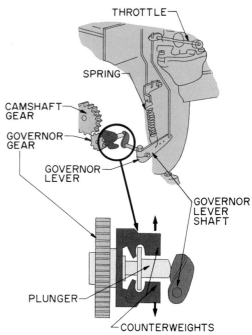

Fig. 15-48. In this type of centrifugal governor, the plunger creates centrifugal force.

Suppose that a load is put on the engine. The engine works harder and slows down. The crankshaft does not turn as fast. Therefore, the centrifugal force on the governor decreases. This causes the links to come back against the shaft. The spring pushes the collar upward. Again, see Fig. 15-47. The upward movement of the collar opens the throttle. The engine then speeds up to its original speed. This helps the engine handle the heavy load. When operating properly, the engine maintains a fairly constant speed as the load changes.

Figure 15-48 shows another type of centrifugal governor. This type of governor is operated by the camshaft. As the camshaft turns, it turns the *governor gear* attached to the *governor shaft*. A plunger on the governor shaft touches a *governor lever*. The lever in turn links to the throttle. In this way, the governor can respond to changing engine speeds.

Two weights pivot on the governor shaft. When the shaft turns, centrifugal force pulls the weights out. This outward movement pushes the plunger on the shaft. There are two governor levers—one inside the engine and one outside—

attached to the same shaft. The plunger on the inside part of the governor shaft is controlled by the centrifugal force of the weights and the plunger, which is levered by the counterweights on the inside part of the governor shaft.

A spring on the governor lever tries to hold the throttle open. But the centrifugal force overcomes the spring tension. The plunger then pushes the lever and closes the throttle. In this way, the governor limits the engine's speed as the speed increases.

Suppose a heavy load is slowing the engine down. The camshaft does not turn as fast. The governor gear slows down and the centrifugal force decreases. The weights drop back against the shaft and the plunger slides back. As the pin moves back, the lever drops. This opens the throttle. The engine speeds up to handle the load.

Air Vane Governors. Like centrifugal governors, air vane governors change engine speed to fit the load on the engine. Air vane governors operate on air flow from the flywheel. As the flywheel turns, it acts like a fan. The faster the flywheel turns, the more air flow it creates.

A small plastic or steel piece catches the flywheel air flow. This piece is called an *air vane*.

See Fig. 15-49. The air vane attaches to the throttle with a linkage. A spring holds the throttle open.

As the engine speeds up, air pushes on the vane. The vane pulls the throttle closed. In this way, the governor limits the engine's speed. The top speed can be adjusted by changing the spring tension. This makes it easier or harder for the air vane to pull the throttle closed.

A heavy load slows the engine down. The crankshaft does not turn as fast. Therefore, the flywheel slows down and throws off less air. Less air pushes against the air vane. The vane moves back to its original position. This allows the spring to pull the throttle open. The engine then speeds up to carry the load.

Exhaust

As burned gases leave an engine, they first pass through an *exhaust passageway*, or *exhaust port*. Then the gases pass through a *muffler*. The muffler is a device that reduces the noise of the escaping gases. Figure 15-50 shows the exhaust passageway and muffler for a four-stroke engine.

Here's how a muffler works. The gases leave the engine under high pressure and speed. Pushing these gases straight into the air would make them expand suddenly. This expansion would produce a very loud noise. The muffler lets the gases expand *before* they reach the outside. This reduces the pressure, so there is less noise.

IGNITION SYSTEM

A small engine ignition system must produce a spark to ignite the fuel. To do this, it must either have a source of electricity or generate its own. It must move this electricity to the combustion chamber. There the electricity must produce a high-voltage spark to ignite the air-fuel mixture. It must produce this spark at exactly the right moment. The ignition system must repeat this entire process thousands of times every minute.

Three different ignition systems are explained in this section:
■ Magneto
■ Capacitive discharge
■ Battery

Some basic knowledge of electricity and magnetism will help you understand how ignition systems work. Chapter 23 explains the principles of electricity and magnetism.

Magneto Ignition

The magneto ignition is the system most widely used in small engines. In this section you'll learn about the different parts of the system. Then you'll see how the parts all fit together in the *magneto cycle*.

The magneto system is a fairly simple kind of ignition system. It produces its own electricity and doesn't need a battery. There are five basic parts in the system. These are the armature, the magnets, the breaker points, the condenser, and the spark plug. See Fig. 15-51.

Like an automotive breaker-point ignition, the magneto system has two separate circuits—the *primary circuit* and the *secondary circuit*. As the system operates, the breaker points open and close the primary circuit. This develops, or *induces*, a current in the secondary circuit.

Armature. The armature consists of a wire coil wrapped around an iron core. The armature

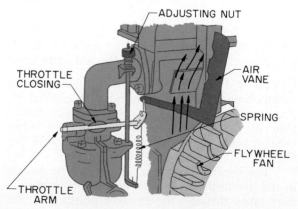

Fig. 15-49. Air vane governors are operated by air coming off the flywheel fan. The air bends the vane back and the linkage pulls the throttle closed.

Fig. 15-50. The exhaust passageway provides a way for exhaust gases to leave the engine. The muffler makes sure their exit is a fairly quiet one.

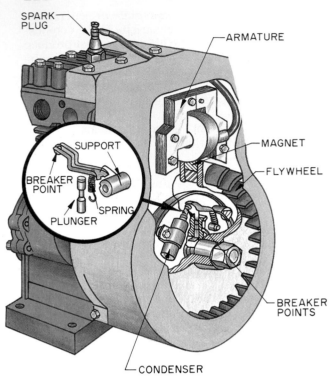

Fig. 15-51. Most small engines don't have batteries. They provide their own electric current using just the parts that make up the magneto ignition system (labeled here).

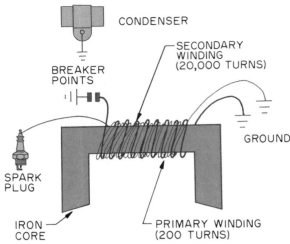

Fig. 15-52. The armature has two windings. They work together to produce high-voltage electricity for ignition.

is mounted next to the flywheel. As the flywheel turns, magnets in the flywheel rotate past the armature. This induces a low-voltage current in the coil. The armature then raises the voltage of the current by collapsing the magnetic field across the coil. This higher voltage is needed for ignition.

The armature coil has two separate windings of wire. See Fig. 15-52. The *primary winding* is a low-voltage winding. It is heavy wire. The wire is wrapped around the core between 150 and 200 times. One end of this winding attaches to the breaker points. The other end is **grounded** by connecting it to a metallic part of the engine.[1] During engine operation, current is first induced in the primary winding.

The *secondary winding* is a thinner wire than the primary winding. One end of the secondary winding connects with the spark plug. The other end is also grounded.

The secondary winding wraps around the primary winding. It is usually wrapped about 20,000 times. This is about 100 times the number of windings in the primary winding. With this ratio, the armature can act as a step-up transformer. (A *step-up transformer* is a device for increasing voltage.) Again, see Fig. 15-52. It increases the low voltage in the primary winding by 100 times. The resulting voltage gives the current a tremendous push. The current needs this push to jump a spark plug gap and ignite the air-fuel mixture.

The *armature core* is made of several plates of soft iron. The iron concentrates the magnetic field around the coil. You will see why this is important when you read about the magneto cycle.

Magnets. The magneto system needs a magnetic field to operate. Magnets are used to generate a magnetic field around the armature. The magnets are either cast into the flywheel or attached to the flywheel. See Fig. 15-53. As the flywheel turns, the magnets repeatedly induce a magnetic field in the armature. The magnets also *reverse* this magnetic field. This results in an alternating electrical current in the armature coil.

Breaker Points. The breaker points are two metal contact points located near the crankshaft. They are usually made of a heat-resistant metal. One of the points doesn't move. The other breaker point is attached to a moveable arm. See Fig. 15-54.

The breaker points act as an electric switch in the *primary circuit*. This is the path that current takes through the breaker points and the

[1]Grounding allows the flow of electricity to pass through the metal parts of the engine and back to the source. Electricity must always make a complete loop, or circuit, in order to flow.

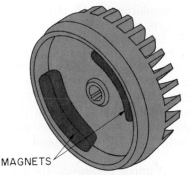

Fig. 15-53. A typical small engine flywheel. The magnets are needed to operate the magneto system.

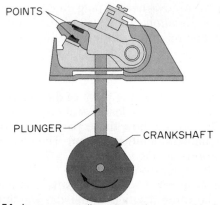

Fig. 15-54. In many small engines, the moveable breaker point is operated by a plunger. The plunger rides on the crankshaft.

primary coil winding. When the points close (touch), current flows through the primary circuit and creates a magnetic field. When the points open, the circuit is broken. The magnetic field collapses around both the primary and secondary circuits. This action reverses the magnetic field and sends high-voltage current through the *secondary circuit*. The secondary circuit consists of the secondary armature winding, the spark plug wire, and the spark plug.

The breaker points must open at just the right time to fire the spark plug. Two-stroke engines need a spark on every second piston stroke. Therefore, the points must open once for every complete rotation of the crankshaft. Some small engines do this by way of a *cam lobe* on the crankshaft. As the lobe turns, it opens and closes the points.

Other small engines have a flat spot ground on the crankshaft. The flat spot serves the same

purpose as a cam. A *plunger* rides on the crankshaft. It closes the points when it goes over the flat spot. Again, see Fig. 15-54.

Some four-stroke engines use a *camshaft* to open the points. A camshaft is a lobed shaft separate from the crankshaft. The crankshaft turns the camshaft, and the cam lobe pushes the moveable point open. The camshaft opens the point once for every two rotations of the crankshaft.

Condenser. When the breaker points open, current in the primary circuit tries to jump the gap between them. If this happens, the magneto may not generate the high ignition voltage. Current jumping between the points also burns the points. A condenser solves both of these problems.

The condenser is usually wired across the points. It acts as a temporary storage area for electric current. The condenser has a very low resistance to electrical current. As the points open, the current goes into the condenser. This keeps the current from jumping the gap. When the points are completely open, the condenser discharges its stored current back through the primary circuit to the electrical ground.

Small engines have different kinds of condensers. Most condensers consist of two or more long sheets of foil. Sheets of insulation material separate the pieces of foil. The sheets are rolled up together. Then they are placed in a small metal cylinder.

Spark Plugs

Spark plugs carry an electric charge into the combustion chamber. They then produce the spark that ignites the air-fuel mixture. There are many different sizes and kinds of spark plugs. However, the parts and operation of all plugs are much the same. Figure 15-55 shows the parts of a typical spark plug.

The top part of a spark plug is called the *terminal*. The cable that carries current from the secondary coil winding attaches to the terminal.

The *center electrode* is a heavy metal wire connected to the terminal. It carries the current to the bottom of the spark plug. A porcelain *insulator* encloses all but the bottom tip of the center electrode. The insulator protects the electrode. It also prevents the high-voltage current from escaping.

The bottom part of the insulator is inserted inside a metal *shell*. The shell is much like a bolt. It has threads and flat places for a wrench. This is so the spark plug can be screwed into the cylinder head.

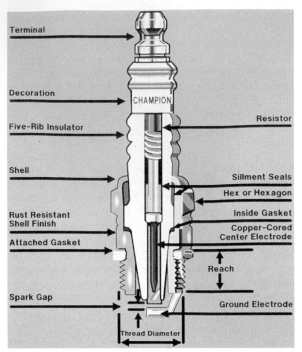

Terminal

Decoration

CHAMPION

Five-Rib Insulator

Resistor

Shell

Sillment Seals

Hex or Hexagon

Inside Gasket

Rust Resistant
Shell Finish

Copper-Cored
Center Electrode

Attached Gasket

Reach

Spark Gap

Ground Electrode

Thread Diameter

Fig. 15-55. Electric current flows down the center electrode. Then it jumps a small gap between the center and ground electrodes. The spark produced there ignites the air-fuel mixture.

The ground, or side electrode, is a wire that extends from the bottom of the shell. This electrode bends close (about 1/32 inch) to the center electrode. High-voltage current jumps the gap between the electrodes to produce the ignition spark.

Reach. Spark plugs must extend far enough into the combustion chamber to ignite the fuel. However, they must not contact the piston. This would damage both the electrodes and the piston.

How far the plug will extend depends on its reach. *Reach* refers to the length of the spark plug's threads. The cylinder head thickness determines what reach should be used.

Heat Range. Spark plugs help control their own operating temperature. All spark plugs conduct heat away from the center electrode. However, some do it faster than others.

"Heat range" is the term used to describe how fast a spark plug conducts heat away from the center electrode. The heat passes through the bottom part of the insulator. It travels to the spark plug shell. Then it goes through the shell and out to the cylinder head. The surrounding air absorbs the heat.

The insulator length determines how fast the heat gets to the cylinder head. This determines the heat range of the plug. Short, thick insulators have short heat transfer paths to the shell. They remove heat quickly. Plugs with this type of insulator are called *cold plugs*. Some spark plugs have longer, thinner insulators. Heat traveling through them does not reach the shell as quickly. The heat stays in the insulator longer. Plugs with this type of insulator are called *hot plugs*.

Several things determine the type of plug to use. These include the engine's design, how long it will be in use, and the way it is used. The plug must be hot enough to burn off excess carbon from the electrodes. Too much carbon can keep the plug from firing. However, the plug must not overheat. An overheated plug causes a condition called *preignition*. The heat of the plug ignites the air-fuel mixture before it is fully compressed.

The Magneto Cycle

You now know the parts of the magneto system. You have also learned about spark plugs. We will now see how these parts work together in the magneto ignition system. The sequence of illustrations in Fig. 15-56 will help you understand the magneto cycle.

In **A** of Fig. 15-56, the flywheel is about to carry the three magnets under the windings and U-shaped plates. The breaker points are open, and no current is flowing in either the primary or secondary circuit. Note the magnetic lines of force passing between the magnets on the flywheel.

As the flywheel moves to the position shown in **B**, the magnetic lines of force move through the U-shaped plates. These plates bring the magnetic lines of force together, providing a single path. The breaker points close when the flywheel is in the position shown in **B**. This action permits a flow of current within the primary. This flow is produced by the movement of the magnetic lines of force and locks the direction of the lines of force through the U-shaped plates. The flow of current in the primary plus the magnetic lines of force develop a strong magnetic field which surrounds the coil and U-shaped plates (**B**).

As the flywheel continues to rotate, the magnets change position, as shown in **C**. This change tries to reverse the direction of the field through the U-shaped plates, as shown by the dotted colored lines in **C**. The flow of current in the primary produces a stronger opposing field than is produced by the magnets and prevents the reversal.

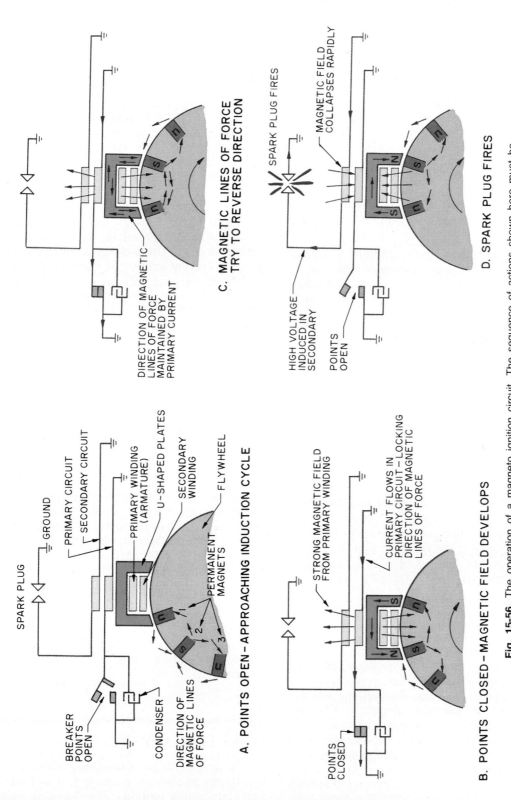

SPARK PLUG

GROUND

PRIMARY CIRCUIT

SECONDARY CIRCUIT

PRIMARY WINDING (ARMATURE)

U-SHAPED PLATES

SECONDARY WINDING

FLYWHEEL

PERMANENT MAGNETS

BREAKER POINTS OPEN

CONDENSER

DIRECTION OF MAGNETIC LINES OF FORCE

A. POINTS OPEN-APPROACHING INDUCTION CYCLE

DIRECTION OF MAGNETIC LINES OF FORCE MAINTAINED BY PRIMARY CURRENT

C. MAGNETIC LINES OF FORCE TRY TO REVERSE DIRECTION

STRONG MAGNETIC FIELD FROM PRIMARY WINDING

CURRENT FLOWS IN PRIMARY CIRCUIT-LOCKING DIRECTION OF MAGNETIC LINES OF FORCE

POINTS CLOSED

B. POINTS CLOSED-MAGNETIC FIELD DEVELOPS

SPARK PLUG FIRES

MAGNETIC FIELD COLLAPSES RAPIDLY

HIGH VOLTAGE INDUCED IN SECONDARY

POINTS OPEN

D. SPARK PLUG FIRES

Fig. 15-56. The operation of a magneto ignition circuit. The sequence of actions shown here must be repeated thousands of times per minute to keep the engine running efficiently.

As the magnets start away from the position shown in **D**, the breaker points open. This action stops the flow of current in the primary circuit, collapsing the magnetic field across the secondary. The field collapses at a very rapid rate since the path through the permanent magnets is now free to reverse direction. The combined action (reversal through the magnets and points opening) results in the field cutting the secondary windings at a rapid rate, inducing a high voltage. The voltage is high enough to jump the spark plug gap, producing a high-temperature spark. The spark ignites the air-fuel mixture.

The secondary voltage is about 10,000 volts (V) at the time the plug fires. Magneto ignition systems can produce secondary voltages of 25,000-30,000 volts when needed to fire the spark plug.

The condenser helps maintain a strong spark. As the points open, a current builds up in the condenser. When the points are completely open, the condenser discharges the current back into the primary winding. The surge of current builds up a magnetic field that cuts through the secondary winding. Because this happens at the same time that the armature field collapses, the high voltage to the spark plug is strengthened. This in turn helps the plug fire longer. The longer the plug fires, the better the ignition. In normal operation, the magneto cycle usually produces over 1000 sparks every minute.

Capacitive Discharge (CD) Ignition Systems

Many of the newer small engines have capacitive discharge (CD) ignition systems. These systems are also called *solid-state* ignitions. They have all the parts of the magneto system, except for breaker points. Instead of points, capacitive discharge systems have complex electronic parts.

Capacitive discharge systems have many advantages over magneto systems. For one thing, there is no need to service or replace points. CD systems also produce higher and more constant voltage. Therefore, there is more dependable ignition and longer spark plug life.

Like magneto systems, CD systems use flywheel magnets to produce electricity. CD systems have a capacitor (condenser), primary and secondary windings, and a spark plug. They also have three coils—the input coil, ignition coil, and trigger coil.

Figure 15-57 shows how a typical CD system works. The magnets move past the *input coil*. This develops an alternating current in the coil.

The AC current travels to the *diode rectifier*. This rectifier changes the alternating current to direct current. The direct current then charges the capacitor.

The magnets continue to rotate with the flywheel. See Fig. 15-57B. As they pass the *trigger coil*, they develop a low-voltage current in it. This current is strong enough to open the gate of the silicon-controlled rectifier (SCR). (See Chapter 24.) The SCR then opens the circuit between the capacitor and the primary winding of the *ignition coil*. This circuit is the anode-to-cathode circuit in the SCR. With this circuit open, the capacitor rapidly discharges its current.

The discharge from the capacitor causes current to surge through the primary winding. This develops a high-voltage current in the secondary winding. This voltage is high enough to jump the current across the spark plug gap.

The spark plug fires once for each rotation of the magnets. In two-stroke engines, the magnets are mounted on the flywheel or crankshaft. In four-stroke engines, the magnets are mounted on the camshaft. This is so the plug will fire on every second rotation of the crankshaft.

Battery Ignition

Since most small engines are used to power moving or portable devices, they need to be as lightweight as possible. For this reason, most small engines don't have batteries. A battery would add to the weight of the device.

However, some small stationary engines do use a battery ignition system. The advantage of a battery ignition is that it doesn't need a mechanical input to deliver electricity. When the engine is started, the battery sends current to the primary circuit. The breaker points break the circuit and induce current in the secondary circuit. This is the same thing a CD ignition or magneto ignition does. The difference is that you don't have to use the flywheel to produce a spark.

Once the engine is running, a generator or alternator supplies current. Some of this current is used for ignition. Some of it is stored by the battery.

STARTING SYSTEM

An engine in good working condition needs two things to operate. It needs fuel and momentum (continuing motion). The operator supplies the fuel by filling the gas tank. The engine, once

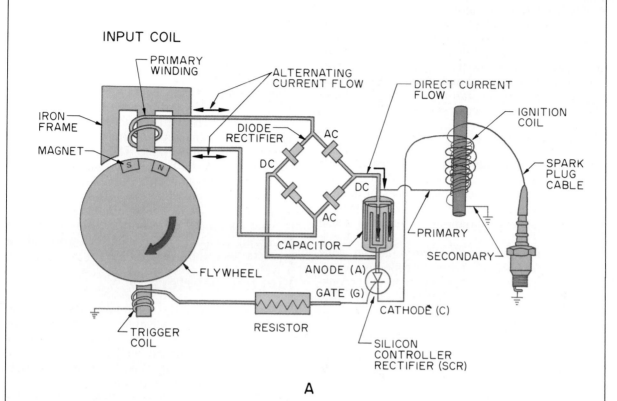

INPUT COIL

PRIMARY WINDING

IRON FRAME

MAGNET

ALTERNATING CURRENT FLOW

DIRECT CURRENT FLOW

IGNITION COIL

DIODE RECTIFIER

AC

DC

DC

AC

SPARK PLUG CABLE

PRIMARY

SECONDARY

CAPACITOR

FLYWHEEL

ANODE (A)

GATE (G)

CATHODE (C)

TRIGGER COIL

RESISTOR

SILICON CONTROLLER RECTIFIER (SCR)

A

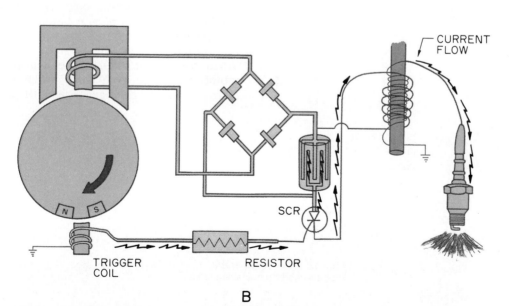

CURRENT FLOW

SCR

TRIGGER COIL

RESISTOR

B

Fig. 15-57. In CD ignition systems, electricity is generated, then stored in a capacitor. The trigger coil then opens the circuit to the ignition coil. This produces a high-voltage current in the secondary coil. (A) Charging the capacitor. (B) Discharging the capacitor and firing the spark plug.

it is running, supplies its own momentum. An engine will keep itself running for as long as its fuel supply lasts. But it cannot start itself.

An engine must get its starting momentum from an outside source. The starting system supplies the engine with this momentum. There are many different kinds of starting systems. The two basic types are manual and electric. Most small engines have manual starting systems, but some are equipped with electric starters.

Manual Starters

Some starters depend on the physical effort of the engine operator. These are called *manual*, or *hand, starters*. The two basic types of manual starters are rope starters and crank starters. There are several variations of each of these types.

The simplest of all starters is the *rope starter*. It has only two parts—a rope and a pulley. The pulley attaches directly to the crankshaft. The rope fits in a notch in the pulley. The operator must wind it around the pulley by hand and then pull it.

A more complex version of the windup rope starter is the *recoil starter*. This type has replaced most rope starters. See Fig. 15-58. A recoil starter uses a spring to rewind the rope. Pulling the rope winds a spiral *recoil spring*. Releasing the rope allows spring tension to wind the rope back on the pulley.

In a recoil starter, the rope remains on the pulley. Therefore, the pulley cannot attach directly to the crankshaft. As the operator pulls the rope, the pulley engages a one-way clutch called the *crankshaft adapter*. The crankshaft adapter is attached to the crankshaft. The momentum of the rope pulley transfers to the crankshaft. This starts the engine. The two pulleys disconnect when the rope is not being pulled.

Simple crank starters are rarely used today. *Kick starters* that are used to start motorcycles are a type of crank starter. The rider supplies the power to turn the crank. The crank turns the crankshaft. Once the engine starts, the kick starter disconnects from the crankshaft.

Another type of crank starter is used on many lawn mowers. The operator uses a crank to wind a spring tight. A button or lever releases the spring tension. The tension then works like a rope starter to turn the crankshaft.

Electric Starters

When compared to manual starters, electric starters have both advantages and disadvantages. Electric starters make it much easier for an operator to start an engine. See Fig. 15-59. However, electric starters add weight to the output device. In addition, the parts are more complex. And electric starters cost more and need a battery and generator.

All electric starters have an electric motor called the *starting motor*. A battery is needed to operate this motor. Small engine starting motors are very much like the starters used on cars. When the operator turns the ignition key, the motor turns the crankshaft. Once the engine starts, the motor disengages from the crankshaft.

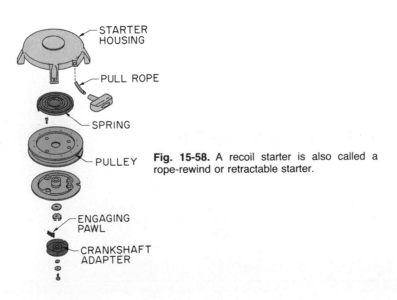

Fig. 15-58. A recoil starter is also called a rope-rewind or retractable starter.

STARTER HOUSING

PULL ROPE

SPRING

PULLEY

ENGAGING PAWL

CRANKSHAFT ADAPTER

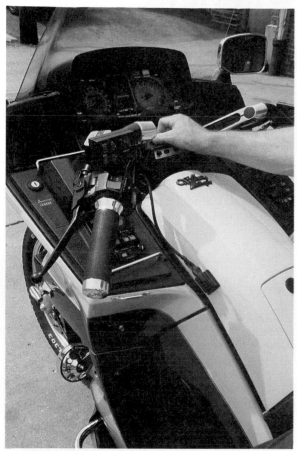

Fig. 15-59. This motorcycle is equipped with an electric starter. The battery required for starting adds weight. However, the engine is easier to start.

Stop Switch

There has to be a way to stop an engine, as well as start it. See Fig. 15-60. Most small engines are stopped by keeping the spark plug from firing. One way to do this is to ground the secondary circuit wire at the spark plug. Another way is to ground the primary circuit.

A common mechanism used to ground the secondary circuit is the stop switch (or "kill" switch). It keeps current from going to the spark plug. The spark plug can't fire, so the engine stops.

In some cases, the stop switch is connected to the breaker points. The operator uses the switch to ground the primary circuit. This keeps the magnetic field in the armature from collapsing. As a result, no spark occurs and the engine stops.

Fig. 15-60. Many engines use an off-on switch.

Chapter 15—Review

Testing Your Knowledge

Briefly answer each of the following questions. Write on a separate piece of paper.
1. Identify the six major systems of the small engine.
2. Name two functions of the crankcase.
3. What is the purpose of the ribs on the cylinder?
4. Name two functions of the piston.
5. What is the function of compression rings?
6. What is the function of the oil control rings?
7. What is the function of the connecting rod?
8. Which engine part carries the power to do work?
9. What is the function of the crankshaft counterweight?
10. What is a common name for one-piece sleeve bearings?
11. What is the function of the flywheel?
12. What is the function of the intake valve? the exhaust valve?
13. What is the function of cam lobes?
14. On a two-stroke cycle engine, which engine part acts like a valve?
15. What is the purpose of the reed valve?
16. Name the six ways the lubrication system serves the engine.
17. Name the two most common types of lubrication systems used in four-stroke engines.
18. What is the purpose of the oil pressure relief valve?
19. Name the two types of air cleaners used on small engines.
20. What is the main function of the carburetor?
21. What does the throttle valve do?
22. What carburetor part helps start a cold engine?
23. What is the ratio of gasoline to air for normal engine operation?
24. What is the advantage of using a diaphragm carburetor?
25. What device evens out changes in engine speed?
26. What is the function of the exhaust muffler?
27. Name the five basic parts of the magneto ignition system.
28. What is the function of the capacitor in the capacitive discharge system?

Expressing Your Knowledge

Using complete sentences, write your answers to the following on a separate sheet of paper:
1. Why is aluminum used for the cylinder?
2. Describe the combustion chamber.
3. What are the functions of the raised piston head in a two-stroke engine?
4. Give three reasons for using anti-friction bearings.
5. Why is the camshaft timing gear twice the size of the crankshaft timing gear?
6. What is meant by valve timing?
7. Give one advantage and two disadvantages that two-stroke engines have compared to four-stroke small engines.
8. Describe the two-stroke engine lubrication system.
9. How are most small engines cooled?
10. Give three functions of the air cleaner.
11. Describe the function of the venturi.
12. Describe how the float assembly in a float carburetor operates.
13. Describe how a vacuum-feed carburetor operates.
14. Explain how the diaphragm carburetor controls the supply of fuel to the engine.
15. Explain how an electric current is produced in the armature of the magneto ignition system.

16. Describe what happens in the magneto ignition system when the points open.
17. Describe the action in a CD system when the capacitor discharges.

Applying Your Knowledge

Follow your teacher's instructions to complete these activities:

1. Conduct an engine parts recognition contest. Assemble parts from a number of different two- and four-stroke cycle engines. The teacher will choose four students to conduct the contest. These students will identify all parts and assign points based on difficulty.

   The teacher will divide the remainder of the class into two teams. Then, each team will take turns selecting parts from the box by random selection. Random selection can be assured by attaching strings to parts and selecting strings at random. The part is given to one student on the team to identify. (The students will take turns.) If the student answers correctly, that team gets the points. If the student does not correctly identify the part, one member of the other team may answer for the points. Alternate questions between teams. The team with the highest number of points wins.

2. Compare a two-stroke cycle engine and a four-stroke cycle engine. This can be done by either assembly and disassembly or by using diagrams and pictures of engines. Identify the parts of a four-stroke engine not found in a two-stroke engine. Then, identify the parts of a two-stroke engine not found in a four-stroke engine. Prepare a report describing your findings. You may wish to prepare and include drawings.

Chapter 16

Small Engine Safety

In laboratory work, the safe way is the right way. Knowledge of dangers involved can help you avoid taking risks.

Expanding Your Knowledge

As you study this chapter, you will learn to:

- Identify a variety of accidents that might occur when operating a small engine.
- Name the general laboratory safety rules that apply during small engine activities.
- Describe safety precautions that must be taken when using gasoline, a rope starter, and when running an engine.
- Identify the precautions that must be taken whenever an engine is operated indoors.
- React to unsafe conditions in a manner that will help ensure the well-being of individuals and protect equipment from damage.
- Describe the laws protecting workers throughout the country and in your own state.

Building Your Word Power

The following terms are defined and explained in this chapter. Learning these will help you learn more about safety when working with small engines.

kickback
Occupational Safety and
    Health Act (OSHA)
solvent
ventilation
Workman's
    Compensation

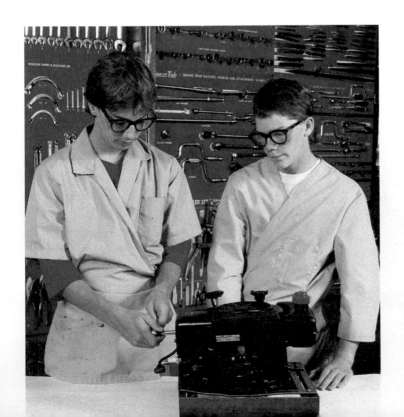

Small engines are not especially dangerous-looking objects. However, they can cause accidents and be *extremely* dangerous. Small engines can start fires. They operate at high temperatures which could result in severe burns. They can also produce harmful gases. What's more, small engines can cause electrical shocks, bad cuts, and broken bones!

Yes, small engine work *can* involve some dangerous situations. But don't let the potential dangers prevent you from participating. There is a way to avoid accidents. And this way is to develop a "safe-working" attitude.

Be serious about safety and the possibility of accidents. Sure, you can work faster if you forget about safety. But if you hurt yourself, the time you save is worthless.

This chapter will tell you about two types of safety rules. First, there are rules to follow all the time in the school lab. Second, there are special rules for working with small engines. Follow these rules and be alert to the possibility of accidents. This way you will have a good experience with small engines. See Fig. 16-1.

LABORATORY SAFETY

Most technology laboratories have a list of general safety rules posted. Following are some of the more common rules. They are very important.

■ Dress for the job.

Don't wear a tie or loose clothing. If you have long hair, tie it back or cover it. This is especially important when operating equipment with rotating parts. Loose clothing and long hair can catch in the moving parts. You can be pulled into the equipment. Jewelry, such as rings and watches, can also catch in moving parts. Remove all jewelry.

■ Protect your eyes.

Wear eye protection at all times when working in the lab. When working with power machines such as grinders, wear both safety glasses and a face shield or goggles. This will give your eyes double protection. Remember that your eyes can't be replaced. They deserve the best protection you can give them.

■ Be neat and orderly.

Don't leave parts or tools on the floor. They can cause someone to trip. Always store sharp-pointed or sharp-edged tools as soon as you finish with them. Watch for heavy objects that can fall and injure feet or legs. For example, be sure an engine is tightly mounted before you begin working on it.

■ Always use the proper tools.

Tools are designed to serve specific purposes. For example, don't use an adjustable wrench or pliers in place of a socket or box-end wrench. See Fig. 16-2. Adjustable wrenches and

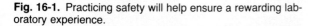
Fig. 16-1. Practicing safety will help ensure a rewarding laboratory experience.

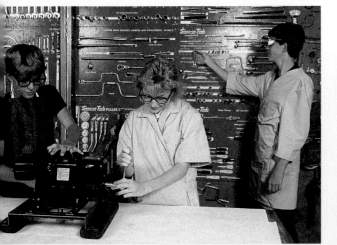

Fig. 16-2. Always use the right tool for the job. Using the wrong tool can result in damage to the tool, damage to the equipment, or injury to yourself.

pliers tend to slip more easily than box-end or socket wrenches. And slipping tools usually cause hand injuries. They can also ruin the nut or bolt. Using the right type and size of tool will prevent slipping.

■ Use tools properly.

Tool safety means more than just choosing the right tool. First, your hands shouldn't be so greasy that you can't hold the tool firmly. Second, you should always maintain a good balanced position as you use the tool. But before you use any tool, *think* about any problems that might arise. For example, when loosening a stuck bolt or nut, push the wrench with an open hand. If the bolt loosens suddenly, you won't bang your knuckles. See Fig. 16-3.

■ Work at a steady pace.

Never hurry as you work. Hurrying leads to awkward and dangerous situations. It also gives you less time to think ahead and avoid accidents.

■ Ask for help when you need it.

If you aren't sure how to do something, check the operator's manual or ask your teacher. Use only the tools and machines that you have been trained to use safely.

SMALL ENGINE SAFETY

There are safety rules for small engine work, just as there are rules for general lab work. The following pages give the most important rules. Be sure to follow these rules at all times when doing small engine work.

Preparing to Use an Engine

Before starting and running an engine, read the operator's manual carefully. The manual will explain hazards associated with running the engine. It will also point out special safety precautions that will help you.

Before you start the engine, check all safety guards and devices. Make sure they are in good condition. See that the guards are in their proper places. The operator's manual usually provides information on the proper use and maintenance of all safety devices.

Fig. 16-3. You can avoid accidents by thinking ahead. Use tools properly and make certain the engine is in a stable position. Be sure the engine is cool before you touch it.

 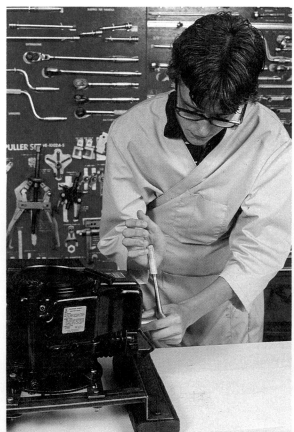

Handling Gasoline

Most small engines run on gasoline or a mixture of gasoline and oil. Gasoline is highly flammable (easily set on fire), and it is explosive. You must be *extremely careful* when working with or around gasoline.

One very important rule is to always keep gasoline in a closed container. Gasoline left in an open container will give off fumes or vapors. Under certain conditions, a spark can ignite gasoline vapors. This could cause an explosion. You can easily prevent this by storing gasoline in the proper type of container. See Fig. 16-4. Do *not* store gasoline inside your house or in a crowded area. Also, be sure to keep the cap on the engine's fuel tank.

Here are some additional rules to follow when working with gasoline:

■ Keep all flames and heat sources away from gasoline.

Know where the proper type of fire extinguisher is. And know how to *use* it. A fire may start even with the best of precautions. Be prepared!

■ Avoid breathing gasoline vapors.

Gasoline vapors are toxic (poisonous). Make sure your workplace has proper **ventilation**. That is, the area should have a good system for admitting fresh air.

■ Avoid contact with gasoline.

Many gasolines contain added chemicals. Some are poisonous when absorbed through the skin. Wash your hands thoroughly if gasoline splashes on them.

■ Never use gasoline to clean parts.

As you read ahead, instructions will call for cleaning engine parts with a *solvent*. For our uses, a **solvent** is a petroleum-based fluid that dissolves dirt, oil, and grease. Gasoline is too dangerous to use as a solvent. Kerosene is a good and fairly safe solvent.

■ Clean up gasoline spills.

Wipe up all gasoline spills *immediately*. Then place the wiping cloth in a closed, metal container. If you spill gasoline on your clothes, change clothing immediately.

Filling Fuel Tanks

Pouring fuel into a small engine fuel tank can be a dangerous situation. Remember, gasoline is highly flammable. It doesn't take a lot of heat to ignite it.

Engines get very hot when they are running. Do not pour fuel into the tank of a running engine. This would be *extremely* dangerous. Even a stopped engine that is still hot could ignite the gasoline. Wait until the engine is cool to refill the tank.

Take care as you add fuel to the tank. Touch the spout of the gasoline can to the edge of the tank. This will prevent a spark of static electricity. The spark could ignite the fuel.

Do not fill a fuel tank completely. Leave at least an inch of space at the top to allow for expansion. Try not to spill the gasoline as you pour. See Fig. 16-5. If you *do* spill or overfill, wipe up all the gasoline immediately and properly dispose of the wiping paper or cloths.

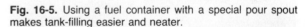
Fig. 16-5. Using a fuel container with a special pour spout makes tank-filling easier and neater.

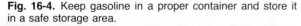
Fig. 16-4. Keep gasoline in a proper container and store it in a safe storage area.

Starting an Engine

Some small engines start with a starting rope. You should take special precautions when starting this type of engine. Never wrap the rope around your hand. Hold the rope so that you can release it easily by opening your hand. See Fig. 16-6. **Kickbacks** and engine misfires can cause a sudden pull on the rope that can pull your hand into the engine. You must be able to let go of the rope immediately.

Some small engines start with a crank. When you turn a crank, wrap your fingers around the handle. But keep your thumb next to your index finger (first finger). *Don't* wrap your thumb around the handle. You could be injured by a kickback or misfire.

Exhaust Gases

Small engines produce several different poisonous gases. The most dangerous is carbon monoxide. As you know, even a small dose of this gas can make you very ill. Large doses cause death. Each year many people die from carbon monoxide poisoning.

Fig. 16-6. This is the proper way to hold and pull a starting rope. Pull the rope out rapidly and let it rewind slowly. Be ready for kickbacks and misfires.

The key to avoiding injuries from exhaust gases is proper ventilation. Exhaust gases are harmless as long as you have plenty of fresh air. Never operate engines inside closed buildings. In fact, don't run them in *any* place where exhaust gases can build up. The only exception to this rule is a closed building that is equipped with a system for carrying the gases outside. See Fig. 16-7. In all cases, however, avoid breathing exhaust fumes as much as possible.

Running Engines

You should follow precautions when you work with a running engine. Remember the general lab rule of not wearing loose clothing. This is especially important when operating an engine. You must also keep your hair, hands, and legs away from the moving parts of the engine.

There are several other precautions to take to avoid the dangers of running engines:
■ Heat.

The cylinder and the exhaust system become very hot during operation. You can burn yourself *severely* by touching these parts. Don't get close to hot engines unless it is absolutely necessary. Allow the engine to cool first. *Never* cover a hot engine with flammable materials such as rags or plastic sheets.

Fig. 16-7. When working on a running engine indoors, use an exhaust system to conduct dangerous carbon monoxide gas to the air outside.

■ Electrical shock.

There is always the possibility of high-voltage shocks from the ignition system. These shocks are especially dangerous for persons with heart trouble. Avoid touching the parts of the ignition system while the engine is running.

■ Batteries.

Be careful when handling a small engine battery. Batteries contain acid. The acid can ruin your clothing and burn your skin. It can *blind* you if it gets into your eyes. Batteries also give off hydrogen while they are being charged. Like gasoline, hydrogen is highly flammable. It ignites easily and will explode. Keep charging batteries away from sparks, heat, and flames. Charged batteries should be kept in well-ventilated areas.

■ Noise.

Small engines can be very noisy. Never operate an engine that has a faulty exhaust system or doesn't have a muffler. Protect your ears from excessive noise by wearing ear protection. Special earmuffs and earplugs will help you avoid injury.

■ Unattended engines.

Never leave a running engine unattended. Be especially careful if children are present. Always turn off the engine before you leave the area.

■ Governor.

Never change governor settings on small engines. An engine rotating at too high a speed can damage the equipment that it operates or cause injury due to breakage or improper operation. Governor speed should be set at manufacturer's specifications.

Technology Focus

Never Out of Style

When working with small engines or devices powered by small engines, many accidents and injuries can be avoided by dressing properly. The person shown here is dressed for cutting wood with a chain saw. However, many of these safety measures apply to other uses of small engines.

■ A safety helmet should be used whenever things can fall on your head, such as when trimming or cutting trees or walking past low tree branches.

■ Ear protectors guard your hearing. Wear them when you carry or push a device with an engine or when you work close to an engine.

■ Eye protection is vital for *most* uses of small engines. The rule with eye protection is to "always use it when operating a small engine, even when you don't think you need it." School laboratories and most industrial plants require workers to wear eye protection at *all* times.

■ Appropriate protective clothing including gloves, boots, trousers with leg guards, and jackets should be worn to protect you from being cut or burnt. Clothes should fit well and have no loose ends.

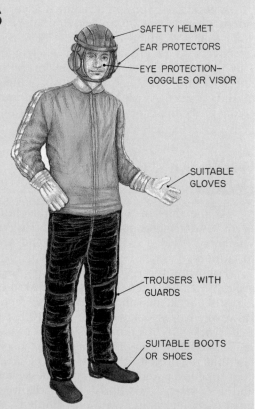

SAFETY HELMET

EAR PROTECTORS

EYE PROTECTION— GOGGLES OR VISOR

SUITABLE GLOVES

TROUSERS WITH GUARDS

SUITABLE BOOTS OR SHOES

Before using a device powered by a small engine, always consult user manuals or other instructions to find out the manufacturer's suggestions for proper dress. Follow these and use common sense. Remember, clothing is the *last* protection of your body. It won't prevent all injuries, but may prevent some and make others less severe. Safety is always in fashion!

LAWS PROTECTING WORKERS

Safety knowledge and skills learned in school laboratories will help you work safely when you take a job in business or industry. Responsibility for safety during work must be shared by employer and employees.

Occupational Safety and Health Act (OSHA)

Employers must, by law, provide employment in places free of recognized hazards that are likely to cause serious harm or death to employees. Employees, in turn, must comply with safety regulations and not expose themselves to hazards that can cause serious injury. Both of these important concepts are part of the **Occupational Safety and Health Act (OSHA)**. This federal law was passed in 1970. This is our nation's most important safety law.

A good safety program requires accurate accident records and an analysis of safety conditions that should be improved. OSHA requires employers to record and study each accident. This process includes the severity of the injury, time lost from work, and an analysis of the cause of the accident. Based upon this information, companies can act to prevent additional injuries.

Workman's Compensation (W.C.)

At the time of the American Revolution in 1776, 97% of the population lived in rural areas. Villagers provided essential goods and services to farmers.

Following the revolution, industry began to grow. Very little attention was given to safety. As a result, accidents and injuries were common. However, it was not until the late 19th century that worker protection laws were passed. In 1877, Massachusetts passed a factory inspection law that required machine guarding, guarding of floor openings and shafts, good housekeeping, and fire safety. Additional laws followed, but most early efforts met with only limited success. Most of these early safety laws did not require a sufficient number of inspectors to insure compliance.

The need for a different type of protection for workers was first recognized in Europe. This protection was designed to assist injured workers. Injured workers were often left poor and helpless. Their injuries were sometimes so severe that they could no longer work. They needed to receive some type of "compensation" when injured. This compensation was needed to provide health and medical care, and to provide funds for living until the worker was able to return to work.

By 1903 England, France, Italy, Russia, Austria, and Hungary had passed Workman's Compensation laws. In the United States, it was left to the individual states to pass laws providing Workman's Compensation (W.C.). The process was controversial, since the costs were quite high. Early laws were declared unconstitutional. In 1917, the U.S. Supreme Court ruled that Workman's Compensation laws were valid. Laws were then rapidly passed. By 1920, most states had Workman's Compensation laws. Today, all 50 states and the District of Columbia, as well as Puerto Rico, have Workman's Compensation laws in effect.

Since **Workman's Compensation laws** are state laws, many variations exist. Some laws are compulsory, and cover all employees. Others are elective for some employees and compulsory for others. Some provide options for employees. It is important for workers to know the level of protection they receive under their state Workman's Compensation laws.

Workman's Compensation laws provide protection only when injuries result from an accident occurring while working on the job. Workers are not covered for self-inflicted injuries or for injuries caused by intoxication. Benefits vary among states. The following are common benefits provided:

■ Medical payments—provided by all states.
■ Rehabilitation—special training and assistance to return to gainful employment is provided by some states.
■ Death—usually payments are made to the surviving spouse and children under 18.
■ Disability—compensation for permanent disability varies among states.

Current Laws

Today, most workers are protected by two major laws—Workman's Compensation, provided by the state, and the Occupational Safety and Health Act of the federal government. In addition, many states have passed additional laws designed to provide added worker protection. Many of these are laws that strengthen OSHA, providing additional protection for workers.

Testing Your Knowledge

Briefly answer each of the following questions. Write on a separate piece of paper.
1. What causes accidents?
2. Identify seven general laboratory safety rules.
3. Where can you find out about *special* safety precautions for running an engine?
4. List four rules to follow when working with gasoline.
5. Which parts of the engine get hot enough to cause severe burns?
6. What could happen if you touch parts of the ignition system while the engine is running?
7. In which year was OSHA passed?
8. Which benefit of Workman's Compensation is provided by all states?

Expressing Your Knowledge

Using complete sentences, write your answers to the following on a separate sheet of paper:
1. Why should gasoline be stored in a *closed* container?
2. Why should you avoid adding gasoline to a hot engine?
3. What danger is there in running an engine in an area that does not have proper ventilation? (See illustration below.)
4. Why should you not wear loose clothing when you work around a running engine?
5. Why should you be careful when handling batteries?
6. Why should you not change governor settings on small engines?
7. Identify characteristics that must be studied and recorded following an accident, as required by OSHA.
8. Under what conditions are benefits provided by Workman's Compensation laws?

Applying Your Knowledge

Follow your teacher's instructions to complete these activities:
1. The teacher will divide the class into 4-6 groups of students. Each group should select a small engine safety procedure to demonstrate. Possible demonstrations include:
    General safety procedures for working in the lab.
    Proper dress for working on small engines.
   ■ Adding fuel to small engines.
   ■ Running a small engine.
   ■ Mounting a small engine for disassembly.
   ■ Disassembly techniques.
   ■ Using tools properly.
   Each group should plan and present a demonstration using charts and other teaching aids as needed.
2. Either identify small engines around your home, or identify small-engine powered devices you would like to have to maintain a home with a lawn, trees, and shrubs. Prepare a list of safety rules and procedures to follow while using these devices.
3. Divide the class into two groups. Give each group one of the following assignments. Ask each group to report their findings to the entire class.
   1. Identify Workman's Compensation law or laws covering your state. Determine the specific benefits, exclusions, and level of protection provided to employees under your state law. Check on and identify additional laws protecting workers within your state.
   2. Identify OSHA laws that are most important to industries either close to school, in your city, or within your regions of the state. This information can be obtained from employees or from OSHA regional offices. Addresses of OSHA regional offices can be obtained by writing to OSHA, Washington, D.C. 02203.

238

Chapter 17

Maintaining and Troubleshooting Small Engines

Sooner or later, all engines develop problems from friction, heat, dust, and dirt. However, you can do a lot to slow down the wear and tear.

Expanding Your Knowledge

As you study this chapter, you will learn to:

- Identify and describe the routine maintenance procedures performed on the oil supply system, cooling system, air cleaner, fuel filter, crankcase breather, spark plug, carburetor, and battery.
- Describe what is meant by oil viscosity and oil service rating.
- Identify procedures necessary to protect an engine during short- or long-term storage.
- Explain the three conditions an engine requires for good operation (ignition, fuel, and compression) and describe how to check each condition.
- Troubleshoot an ignition, fuel, or compression problem on a small engine.

Building Your Word Power

The following terms are defined and explained in this chapter. Learning these will help you learn more about the care and maintenance of small engines.

carburetor
compression
ignition
overhaul
troubleshooting
viscosity

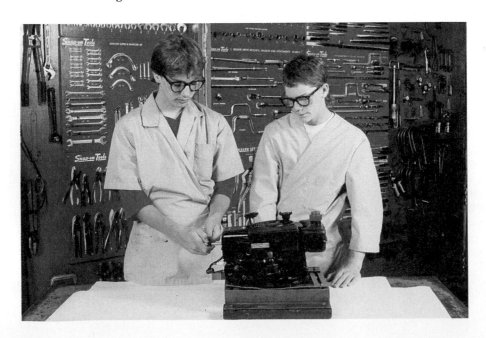

As small engines operate, many of the moving parts rub against each other. The parts gradually wear down. Dust and dirt work their way into the engine and speed up the wearing process. There is also the high temperature of combustion which puts great stress on engine materials.

All engines require care and maintenance. This chapter covers four types of engine procedures:

■ Routine maintenance.

This type of maintenance is done to prevent engine problems.

■ Engine storage.

This procedure keeps problems from developing while the engine is in storage.

■ Troubleshooting.

This is a step-by-step process for finding the source of engine problems.

■ Repair procedures.

These are general guidelines for conducting small engine repairs.

Fig. 17-1. Operating and service manuals are designed to help owners maintain and service their small engines.

ROUTINE MAINTENANCE

Most small engines provide trouble-free operation for long periods of time. However, you *do* have to care for them properly. Most small engines require routine maintenance on the following systems and parts:

■ Oil supply   ■ Crankcase breather
■ Cooling system   ■ Spark plug
■ Air cleaner   ■ Carburetor
■ Fuel filter   ■ Battery

Every engine manufacturer provides instructions for routine maintenance of its engines. When you buy a small engine or a device using one, you should receive an *owner's manual*. This manual will help you maintain the engine properly. Most manufacturers also print service and repair manuals for their engines. These manuals are usually available by request only.

Service manuals usually include more detailed information about service and repairs than owner's manuals. See Fig. 17-1. They often contain a parts list with descriptions to help you

identify and order parts. You can usually get additional information at retail stores dealing in small engines, repairs, and parts.

Many small engines have the same basic service and maintenance procedures. This chapter presents the most common ones.

Checking and Adding Oil

Two-stroke engines are usually lubricated by the oil in the oil-fuel mixture. No other engine lubrication is needed. The proper oil-fuel ratio is normally printed on the engine or in the owner's manual. Some two-stroke engines can use a premixed oil-fuel solution.

Four-stroke engines are lubricated with oil from the crankcase. Some oil can be lost while the engine is operating. Sometimes the oil slips past the piston rings into the combustion chamber, where it is burned. Another problem is worn or damaged gaskets and seals. These allow oil to leak from the engine. Both problems result in a lower oil level in the crankcase. For this reason, you should check the oil level before you start the engine. To get an accurate reading, be sure the engine is on a level surface.

The procedures for checking the oil level vary from engine to engine. Some engines have *dipsticks* which have marks on the end to show the oil level. See Fig. 17-2. To check the oil in these engines, first shut off the engine. Then pull out the dipstick. Wipe it dry. Slide the dipstick back into the crankcase, then remove it again. Examine the oil level as compared to the marks to see whether oil needs to be added.

Fig. 17–2. On engines with dipsticks, the oil level must be kept between the ADD and FULL marks.

Fig. 17-3. Many engines do not have dipsticks. Check the oil level on these engines by removing the oil filler plug. The oil level should be up to the bottom of the plug.

Many small engines don't have dipsticks. On these engines, you usually check the oil by removing the *oil filler plug*. See Fig. 17-3. The oil level should reach the bottom of this plug. If the oil level looks low, add oil until it reaches the plug level. Then replace the plug.

When you add oil to the crankcase, add it slowly. This will keep air from being trapped in the oil. Don't add too much oil. Overfilling can cause carbon to build up in the combustion chamber and on the spark plug. Overfilling can also cause oil to be thrown from the crankcase breather. (The crankcase breather is described later in this chapter.) Overfilling can interfere with engine performance, or even damage the engine.

Be careful to keep out dirt when you are adding the oil. One purpose of lubrication is to keep the engine free of "foreign" particles. Dirt can damage parts and reduce power. Keep all funnels, oil spouts, and storage containers clean. Clean away any dirt before you open the oil container.

Changing the Oil

The oil picks up carbon and dirt as it lubricates the engine. Over a period of time, the oil collects more and more impurities. The oil gradually loses its ability to lubricate properly. This is why you must regularly remove the old, dirty oil and replace it with new, clean oil. The manufacturer's instructions will tell you how often to change the oil.

Drain the oil from the engine while the oil is warm. Warm oil will flow more freely. This does two things. It allows more of the oil to be drained. It also allows the oil to carry more impurities out of the engine.

The oil drains from an *oil drain plug* on the bottom of the crankcase. See Fig. 17-4. Place a container under the drain plug to catch the oil. Then remove the plug. After all the oil has drained, replace and tighten the plug.

Place the used oil in a container and give it to a reclaiming center. Don't dump oil on the ground or into the sewer. Oil damages the environment.

Technology Focus

Stay Tuned

Cars and trucks are routinely serviced, or "tuned-up." Applied to cars and trucks, the word "tune-up" has special meanings. It refers to routine maintenance of the electrical system and fuel system. It also includes the study of engine performance and the identification of possible troubles. A tune-up usually includes changing the points, the spark plugs, and the condenser. The ignition system is also checked and adjusted. It is repaired if necessary.

Small engines are not treated the same way. Instead, the manufacturer recommends periodic (regular) maintenance. Owners may take their engines to a service center. A service center tune-up usually includes the following:

- Servicing the cooling system
- Cleaning the air cleaner, fuel filter, and crankcase breather
- Servicing (or replacing) the spark plug
- Adjusting the carburetor
- Changing the oil
- Servicing the battery

The service center mechanic will also check the engine for proper operation. From this checking, he or she can find any existing or potential problems.

Fig. 17-4. Drain oil from the engine by removing the oil drain plug. Plug location depends on the type of engine.

To add new oil, first remove the oil filler plug. Put a funnel in the hole. Pour in the new oil slowly. Fill the crankcase and replace the plug. If the engine has a dipstick, use it to check the oil level. Otherwise, fill the crankcase up to the plug. Be careful to keep dirt out of the engine.

Selecting the Right Oil

Using the *right* oil to lubricate your engine will provide the best engine performance. There are two things to consider when selecting oil for an engine:

- Viscosity
- Service rating

Viscosity. Viscosity is a measure of the thickness of an oil. It is determined by the rate at which the oil flows. For example, oils that are thick and heavy do not flow easily. These oils have a *high viscosity*. Thin, light oils flow more easily. They have a *low viscosity*.

The Society of Automotive Engineers (SAE) has set up a viscosity numbering system. The numbers used in this system are called *grades*. Thin oils have low grades, such as *SAE 10*. Heavy oils have higher grades, such as *SAE 40* or *SAE 50*. Some numbers include a W. This means that the oil can be used in freezing winter conditions. The SAE number is usually printed or stamped on the oil can. Engine manufacturers recommend certain viscosities of oil for use in their engines at different temperatures. Manufacturers generally recommend a high-viscosity oil for summer. They recommend a low-viscosity oil for winter to promote easy starting.

Multi-viscosity oils fulfill both the low- and high-viscosity requirements. For example, in cold weather, SAE 10-40 provides the same lubrication as SAE 10. In warm weather, it provides the lubrication of SAE 40. With multi-viscosity oil, you don't have to change the oil as the temperature changes.

Service Ratings. The American Petroleum Institute classifies oils according to their quality and applications. The Institute uses seven letter classifications to indicate how well an oil performs in lubrication tests. These ratings are *SA*, *SB*, *SC*, *SD*, *SE*, *SF*, and *SG*. SA is the lowest (poorest) rating. SG is the highest (best) rating.

Engines that must perform in difficult conditions need a higher class of oil. Engines exposed to less wearing conditions can use lower classes. Manufacturers usually recommend certain classes of oil for their engines. You are always safe, of course, when you use the better oils.

Cooling System

People often use small engines in dusty, dirty conditions. For example, lawn mower engines must operate with grass and dirt in the air. These materials can stick to the cooling fins. The cooling system can get clogged, and the engine can overheat. This can damage the engine seriously. Therefore, you should clean the cooling system regularly. How often a system needs cleaning depends on the operating conditions.

Practicing Safety

Do *not* clean the cooling system while the engine is hot. Let the engine cool before you clean any part of it.

Many small engines use a *blower housing* to keep out dirt and other matter. To clean the cooling system, remove the housing and brush all dirt from the flywheel vanes. See Fig. 17-5. Also clean the cooling fins on the engine cylinder and head. Wipe away all the dust. Then replace the housing.

Air Cleaner

The air that enters the engine first passes through the air cleaner. The air cleaner removes dirt from the air. This keeps the dirt from damaging the engine. You must clean the air cleaner regularly. There are two common types of air cleaners:
■ Dry element
■ Oil foam

Dry-Element Cleaners. Figure 17-6 shows how to check a dry-element air filter. You can knock the dirt free by tapping the filter sharply on a hard surface. You can also clean these filters with compressed air. Blow the air through the filter opposite the direction of normal air flow into the engine. This will remove much of the dirt collected in the filter. See Fig. 17-7.

Practicing Safety

Be careful not to point the compressed air hose toward other people when cleaning the filter.

The filter may still be dirty. Sometimes you can clean it with a non-sudsy detergent and warm water. Afterwards, rinse the filter inside

Fig. 17-5. Remove the blower housing to service the cooling system. The housing is usually bolted to the engine.

Fig. 17-6. To check a dry-element air cleaner, remove the filter cover.

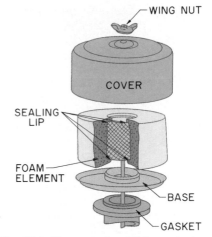

Fig. 17-8. The parts of an oil-foam air cleaner.

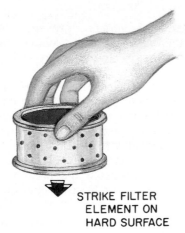

Fig. 17-7. One way to clean a dry-element air filter is to tap it on a hard surface.

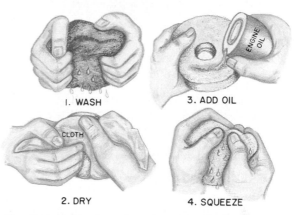

Fig. 17-9. Follow these four steps to maintain an oil-foam cleaner.

and out with clean water. Allow the filter to dry completely before using it again. (It may take a day or two to dry out completely.) If the filter is still clogged, replace it with a new filter.

Oil-Foam Cleaners. Oil-foam cleaners strain air through an oil-soaked foam filter. To service this type of cleaner, first lift off the cover. Then remove the foam filter. See Fig. 17-8. Wash the filter thoroughly in clean kerosene or liquid detergent and water. After washing the filter, dry it with a cloth. Then work some clean oil into the foam. Squeeze out any excess oil. See Fig. 17-9. Then put the filter and cap back in place.

Fuel Filter

Many small engines use a fuel filter to clean the gasoline before it reaches the carburetor.

The filter usually contains a fine wire screen. This screen traps particles of dirt that might clog small openings in the carburetor.

On many engines, the fuel filter is in the fuel tank. It is usually placed on the bottom, where the fuel line attaches. Older engines have a filter screen placed between the fuel pump and a glass bowl. A wire loop and thumbscrew hold the bowl in place. See Fig. 17-10. Some new engines have plastic filters. These are placed "in-line" between the fuel supply and the carburetor.

The in-line type of filter can't be cleaned. However, you should check it regularly to make sure it isn't blocked. First disconnect the fuel line at the carburetor. Then run fuel from the line into a small container. (If the engine has a fuel pump, you must crank the engine to make the fuel flow.) If the flow is slow, replace the filter with a new filter.

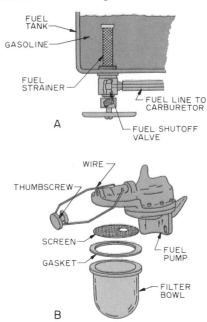

Fig. 17-10. Two common types of fuel filters are (A) filter-mounted inside fuel tank and (B) bowl type.

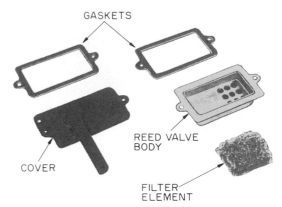

Fig. 17-11. These are the parts of a crankcase breather. To maintain the breather, simply clean the parts.

Practicing Safety

 Before testing the fuel flow, be sure to ground the spark plug high tension lead (connect it to a metal part of the engine). This will keep the engine from starting.

Fuel tank filters and glass bowl filters can be cleaned. If the fuel tank is above the filter, shut off the fuel supply with the shutoff valve. Then drain the fuel from the filter in a safe area. (With some in-tank filters, you may have to drain the tank first.) Next, take the filter apart. Clean all the parts with solvent. Make sure the parts are dry before putting the filter back together.

Crankcase Breather

In four-stroke engines, combustion pressure constantly pushes burned gases past the piston rings. The gases pass into the crankcase. Exhaust gases must not be allowed to build up in the crankcase. Otherwise, the pressure of the gases will increase. This pressure buildup can force crankcase oil out of the engine, past gaskets and seals.

Crankcase breathers prevent pressure buildup in the crankcase. They vent (release) the exhaust gases before the pressure can get too high.

There are several different types of crankcase breathers. Refer to the service manual to find out what type is used on your engine. All types need to be cleaned regularly. First, remove the breather assembly from the engine. See Fig. 17-11. Clean the parts in solvent and dry them thoroughly. Then re-install the breather. (It's a good idea to replace the breather gaskets at this time, too.)

Spark Plug

Burning fuel leaves carbon deposits on the spark plug. You should remove these deposits regularly. Use a *spark plug socket wrench* to remove the plug from the engine. See Fig. 17-12. The socket will help keep the plug from being damaged during removal. If the plug breaks, you must replace it.

Scrape the carbon deposits from the plug with a pocketknife or a wire brush. Then clean the plug with solvent. *Never use an abrasive-type cleaner on small engine spark plugs.*

Examine the plug carefully. The electrodes may be burned away. Or the porcelain insulation may be cracked. In either case, you should replace the plug. See Fig. 17-13. Adjust the gap between the electrodes to the manufacturer's specifications. To do this, first check the gap with a *wire gage*. See Fig. 17-14. Do *not* use a leaf-type feeler gage. Leaf gages can be inaccurate. Make the adjustment by bending the outer electrode. You can do this with the "gapping" part of the wire gage.

Fig. 17-12. Use a spark plug socket wrench to remove a spark plug.

There may be a gasket between the spark plug and the cylinder. Inspect the gasket before replacing the plug. If the gasket is cracked or damaged, replace it.

Also inspect the wire that leads to the spark plug. Wipe it clean and look for cracks or other damage. When you remove this wire, hold it by the connector that fits over the plug. Then pull. Never hold just the wire when pulling. This could separate the wire from the connector.

A. Spark plug in good condition.

B. Spark plug with burned electrode.

C. Spark plug with cracked porcelain.

Fig. 17-13. The spark plug on the top is in good condition. The other plugs are damaged and should be replaced.

Fig. 17-14. Use a wire gage to check for the proper spark plug gap.

Carburetor

There are three types of **carburetor** adjustments:

■ Main fuel adjustment
■ Idle fuel adjustment
■ Idle speed adjustment

Different carburetors have the adjusting screws in different places. Figure 17-15 shows one arrangement.

The carburetor fuel adjusting screws are usually needle valves. The point of a needle valve is small and fragile. It can easily be bent or distorted. Therefore, do *not* use excessive force when adjusting these valves. You can't make a proper adjustment with a damaged needle valve.

Not all small engine carburetors have the adjustments just described. In fact, some carburetors are not adjustable. With these carburetors, the settings are made at the factory. They can't be changed. When adjusting carburetors that have adjusting screws, always follow the directions provided by the manufacturer.

Main Fuel Adjustment. Adjust the main fuel screw when the engine is warm. First, open the throttle halfway. Run the engine without a load. Turn the main fuel screw in or out to get the smoothest possible operation. Usually, only partial turns of the adjusting screw are necessary.

Idle Fuel Adjustment. The idle fuel adjustment should also be made while the engine is warm. Be sure the choke is open. Close the throttle until the engine idles. Then turn the idle fuel screw in or out until the engine runs at its smoothest.

Idle Speed Adjustment. Make this final adjustment after setting the main and idle fuel screws.

Different manufacturers may give different directions for adjusting the idle speed. To be sure, *always check the manufacturer's service manual*. In general, the procedure is as follows:

Let the engine idle while you turn the idle speed screw. Use a *tachometer* for this adjustment if one is available. See Fig. 17-16. Set the engine speed to the manufacturer's specification. If you don't have a tachometer, just set the screw to the lowest speed at which the engine runs smoothly without stalling (shutting off).

Battery

An engine with an electric starter usually has a battery. The battery powers the starting motor. Battery service usually includes inspecting and cleaning, adding water, and checking and charging.

If your engine has a battery, you should check and service it regularly. Manufacturers usually provide an *equipment manual* for a device powered by a small engine. Refer to this manual for battery servicing procedures.

ENGINE STORAGE

If you won't be using an engine for some time, you should store it. How you store an engine can affect its future condition. The following tips on storage will help keep your engine in good working condition.

It is important that the engine be kept dry during storage. If you store the engine outside, protect it with a waterproof cover. Don't make the cover so tight that air can't circulate over the engine. Proper ventilation is important to prevent excessive condensation of moisture.

Fig. 17-16. A tachometer measures the speed of an engine in revolutions per minute.

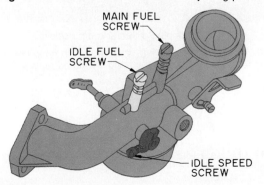

Fig. 17-15. The three main carburetor adjusting points.

MAIN FUEL SCREW

IDLE FUEL SCREW

IDLE SPEED SCREW

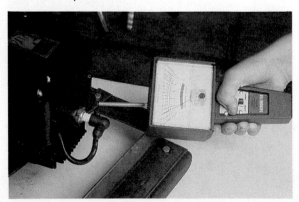

You should also drain the carburetor to prevent varnish buildup. First close the shutoff valve, then open the carburetor drain plug. Some carburetors don't have a drain plug. In this case, turn off the fuel supply from the tank, and run the engine at a fast idle until it slows down noticeably. When this happens, shut off the ignition immediately.

For short-term storage, fill the fuel tank with fresh fuel. This will keep moisture from condensing in the tank.

For storage of a month or more, you must drain the fuel tank, fuel filter bowl, and fuel lines. Let these parts dry. Then replace the tank cap and the fuel filter bowl. Draining the system prevents gum and varnish from forming within the system.

Next, remove the spark plug. Pour one or two tablespoons of engine oil into the cylinder. Crank the engine to distribute the oil. Replace the plug. Then turn the flywheel slowly by hand. As you reach the top of the compression stroke, you should feel some resistance. The flywheel may even bounce back slightly. Leave the engine in this position. The cylinder wall and piston rings are now protected from corrosion.

Engines with electric starting systems require further preparation. Disconnect the cables and be sure the battery is charged. Keep the battery in a warm place to prevent freezing.

Usually you should also prepare the piece of equipment powered by the engine. It may have belt-driven units or belts in a clutching system. Loosen all the belts. This will keep them from stretching out. If the equipment has tires, raise it off the ground. This will keep the engine weight off the tires. There will be no flat spots on the tires after storage.

TROUBLESHOOTING

Troubleshooting means checking an engine to find out what part or condition is causing poor performance. The purpose of troubleshooting is to find the trouble so that it can be corrected.

A small engine requires three conditions for good operation:
■ Ignition.
A strong spark plug must be delivered to ignite the air-fuel mixture.
■ Carburetion.
The proper air-fuel mixture must be delivered to the combustion chamber.
■ Compression.

There must be proper compression of the air-fuel mixture.

An engine may have a problem in any one of the three areas. If something is wrong, the engine will run poorly. Or, it may not run at all! Nearly all engine trouble can be traced to carburetion, compression, or ignition. As you read on, you'll see that there are many possible causes for problems in these three areas. Some of the causes are easy to correct. For example, if the engine doesn't run, it might simply be out of gas. Other causes are harder to correct.

You may decide to repair engine problems yourself, with the help of a service manual. Or, you may choose to have the more difficult work done at a small engine service center.

Ignition

Check the **ignition** by trying to generate a spark. To do this, you must first remove the spark plug wire.

Practicing Safety

Before removing the wire, make sure it is clean and dry. A dirty or damp wire can give you a shock.

Use insulated pliers to grip the wire an inch or two from the end. Hold the wire about ⅛-inch from the plug. Then crank the engine with the starting mechanism. See Fig. 17-17.

Fig. 17-17. Checking ignition by trying to generate a spark.

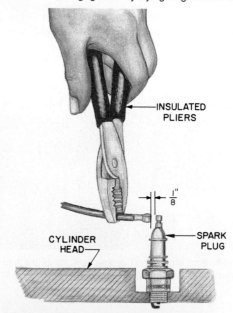

You should see a spark between the plug and the wire as you crank the engine. If there isn't a spark, something is wrong with the ignition system. Try holding the plug wire near the cylinder head while cranking the engine. If you get a spark this time, the spark plug is bad. If you don't get a spark, the problem could be any of the following:

- Incorrect breaker point gap
- Dirty or burned breaker points
- Stuck or worn breaker point plunger
- Shorted or open secondary circuit wire
- Faulty magneto system
- Condenser failure
- Sheared flywheel key
- Worn flywheel bearings

Carburetion

 When checking carburetion, first see if there is fuel in the tank. Most fuel tank caps have small vent holes. See if the vent holes are clear. A clogged vent hole keeps atmospheric pressure from pushing fuel into the carburetor. See Fig. 17-18. If the fuel tank is above the engine, make sure the shutoff valve is open. See if the choke valve operates freely.

Practicing Safety

 Remember that you are working with gasoline, which can burn or explode. Always work on a cool engine, away from open flames or heat. Work in a well-ventilated area.

Fig. 17-18. If an engine isn't getting fuel, check the fuel supply. Also clean the gas cap vent hole with a fine wire or pin.

If the engine won't start, remove the spark plug, and inspect it. The spark plug can provide important information about the engine. A good plug will look like the one in Fig. 17-13A. If the plug is *wet or black*, check the following:

- Overchoking or sticking choke plate
- Excessively rich fuel mixture
- Water in fuel
- Carburetor bowl fuel inlet valve stuck open or float level out of adjustment

If the plug is *white and dry*, check the following:

- Leaking carburetor mounting gasket
- Dirty fuel filter
- Carburetor fuel inlet valve stuck shut or float level out of adjustment
- Faulty fuel pump (if used)
- Excessively lean fuel mixture
- Fuel line kinked or smashed closed

You can do a simple check to determine whether fuel is getting to the cylinder. First, remove the spark plug. Then pour a small amount of gasoline into the cylinder. If the engine fires a few times after you replace the plug, check the possible causes of a white and dry plug.

Compression

To check **compression**, first disconnect the high-voltage wire to the spark plug. Leave the spark plug in place. Then try to turn the flywheel by hand. The flywheel should bounce back as you reach the top of the compression stroke. If it doesn't, or if it offers only small resistance to turning, the compression is low.

You can make a more accurate compression test with a *compression gage*. First remove the spark plug. Then press the rubber part of the compression gage into the spark plug hole. While holding the gage in this position, crank the engine over. Continue cranking the engine until the gage needle stops moving. The gage reading will show the amount of compression in the cylinder. Compare the reading to the manufacturer's specifications.

The following problems can cause low cylinder compression:

- Loose spark plug
- Loose cylinder head bolts
- Blown (damaged) head gasket
- Poor valve clearance adjustment
- Valve(s) sticking open
- Cracked or warped cylinder head

It's possible that the engine trouble may not be caused by any of the above problems. In this case, you will probably have to **overhaul** the engine. This means "tearing down" the engine and

checking all the parts. Major problems that can cause compression loss include the following:
■ Burned valves or valve seats
■ Badly worn or scored cylinder wall
■ Worn or broken rings
■ Broken connecting rod
■ Warped valve stems
■ Cracked cylinder block or head

REPAIR PROCEDURES

During troubleshooting, you may discover that the engine requires a major repair. Some problems, such as burned breaker points, are more easily repaired than others. However, each repair procedure requires that you disassemble and reassemble a part of the engine.

It's important to follow the engine manufacturer's procedures for any major repairs. Many procedures are the same for most small engines. However, there are some procedures that are used on only a few engines. The service manual for the engine you are repairing is the best source of information.

The following are general procedures to follow in repairing a small engine:
■ Obtain the manufacturer's service manual.
■ Find the repair you need to make in the manual.
■ Study the procedures before you do anything. This way, you'll know whether you have all the tools you need to complete the repair.
■ Assemble all the tools and cleaning supplies you'll need.
■ Repair the engine as described in the manual.
■ Clean and mark the engine parts as you make the repair. This allows you to reassemble the engine in the reverse order of disassembly.
■ After completing the repair, test the engine to make sure it runs properly.

SERVICE TOOLS AND EQUIPMENT

Servicing small engines requires a complete set of general tools and special tools for engine disassembly and repair.

General Tools

Small engine servicing requires a complete set of wrenches, pliers, screwdrivers, and general service tools. See Fig. 17-19. There are several important rules to follow when using tools:
■ Never use an open-end adjustable wrench in place of a box end, open-end, or socket wrench.
■ Use socket wrenches or box-end wrenches whenever possible. Open-end wrenches have a greater tendency to slip and cause damage to nut or bolt heads or injury to the user.
■ Use a torque wrench to tighten engine nuts and bolts to the manufacturer's specifications.
■ Avoid using pliers, vice grips, pipe wrenches, or substitutes for the proper size wrench for a nut or bolt.

Special Tools

Small engine service requires the use of many special tools, especially for engine repair. Some of these tools are shown in other illustrations in this chapter. See Figs. 17-12, 17-14, and 17-16. There are also many tools used during engine repair. See Fig. 17–20.

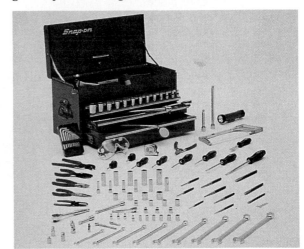

Fig. 17-19. Good tools are essential to service small engines.

Fig. 17-20. A ridge reamer is used to remove any ridge at the top of the piston. This enables removal of the piston.

Testing Your Knowledge

Briefly answer each of the following questions. Write on a separate piece of paper.
1. Name two conditions that can lower the crankcase oil level.
2. Give two reasons why you should drain oil while it is warm.
3. What is the *service rating* of an oil?
4. What liquids can you use to clean an oil-foam cleaner?
5. What types of fuel filters can be cleaned?
6. Name the three types of carburetor adjustments.
7. Why should the fuel tank be left filled during short-term storage?
8. Why should the fuel system be drained for storage of a month or more?
9. How do you protect the cylinder wall and piston rings from corrosion during storage?
10. Why should you never store a discharged battery in a cold place?
11. What three conditions does an engine require for good operation?
12. Name the two spark plug conditions that indicate carburetor trouble.

Expressing Your Knowledge

Using complete sentences, write your answers to the following on a separate sheet of paper:
1. Why does oil need to be changed in a small engine?
2. Define viscosity. Describe the viscosity characteristics of SAE 10-40 oil.
3. How do you use compressed air to clean a dry-element air filter?
4. Describe how to check an in-line type filter to make sure it is not blocked.
5. Describe how to service the crankcase breather.
6. How do you adjust the gap on a spark plug?
7. Describe how to check the ignition system of a small engine. (See illustration below.)
8. If you do not have a compression gage, how can you check compression?
9. Describe a quick check to see if fuel is getting into the cylinder.

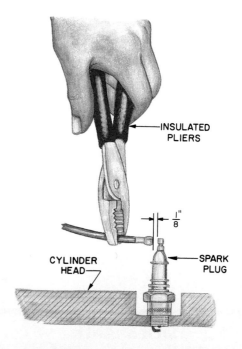

Applying Your Knowledge

Follow your teacher's instructions to complete these activities:

1. Change the oil on a small four-stroke engine. If you don't have an engine, list the steps you would follow in changing oil. Use the procedures described in this chapter.

2. Check and clean the air filter and fuel filter on a small engine. Identify the type of filters used on the engine. If you don't have an engine, list the steps you would follow. Identify the type of filters used on your "pencil and paper" engine.

3. Select a small engine at your home or at a friend's home. List the steps needed to prepare the engine for seasonal storage. (For example, a lawn mower is stored through the winter and a snow blower is stored through the summer.) If you don't have an engine available, visit a local store and prepare your report for one of the engines on display.

4. Prepare a list of tools needed to repair small engines. Divide your list into two parts:
   a. General tools
   b. Special tools
   You may obtain information from manufacturer's service manuals in your laboratory file. You might also obtain information from local tool supply companies.

Chapter 18

Equipment Powered by Small Engines

Devices powered by small engines have expanded the capability of individuals. They help us save time and effort.

Expanding Your Knowledge

As you study this chapter, you will learn to:

- Understand how small engines extend the strength of individuals and help them accomplish more work.
- Identify the characteristics of small engines which contribute to their extensive use.
- Recognize that small engines can provide power in any locations that can be reached by humans.
- Identify many safety procedures necessary to work safely with devices powered by small engines.
- Understand how to perform routine service and maintenance on some of the more common devices powered by small engines.

Building Your Word Power

The following terms are defined and explained in this chapter. Learning these will help you learn more about equipment powered by small engines.

blower
chain saw
edger/trimmer
lawn mower
snow blower
tiller/cultivator
trimmer, hedge

The small engine permits us to work faster and accomplish more. It also reduces the amount of individual effort and multiplies strength. Small engines power a variety of devices. Some may assist you in maintaining your home. Others may be used regularly on the job. A chain saw is a good example. It is used to cut firewood for homes and is also used in commercial logging. Professional gardeners use many of the same power devices used by homeowners.

This chapter identifies many uses of small engines. Some are familiar. You may have already used devices such as power lawn mowers and rotary cultivators. Others are quite unique, exemplifying the great potential for special uses.

Since use is very extensive, this chapter provides information on a selection of common and unique applications. Safety and equipment care are emphasized.

CHARACTERISTICS OF SMALL ENGINES

There are a number of characteristics of small engines which contribute to their extensive use. These include:
■ Portability.

Small engines are comparatively light and can be carried easily. As a result, they can be transported and used almost anywhere. The major requirement for location is *ventilation*. There must be a way for poisonous exhaust gases to escape from enclosed work areas and for fresh air to come in.
■ Operate in any position.

Depending on design, small engines can operate upside down or in any position desired.
■ Speed.

Small engines rotate at high speeds (high rpm). Through special gearing, the speed (rpm) can be varied from very fast to very slow.
■ Reliability.

While small engines were not always reliable in the past, they are now quite dependable and, with proper care, have a long life.

■ Cost.

High production and competition have kept small engine costs low. A few engine designs can be adapted to provide power for many different types of equipment.

COMMON USES OF SMALL ENGINES

Small engines number in the millions. The manufacture, sale, and repair of both the engines and equipment employ thousands of people throughout the nation. Some of the most common equipment powered by small engines are:
■ Lawn mowers
■ Chain saws
■ Garden and home maintenance equipment

Lawn Mowers

Small engines have eliminated much of the work of cutting lawns. **Lawn mowers** come in all sizes, varying from small mowers for home use to large mowing machines which carry the operator. See Fig. 18-1.

Fig. 18-1. Common sizes of lawn mowers.

The rotary mower shown in Fig. 18-1 is a simple design. The small engine is set on the mower with the crankshaft pointing towards the ground. A blade, as shown in Fig. 18-2, is attached to the crankshaft. The engine drives the blade at the same speed at which the engine rotates. This is fast enough to cut the grass. The outer edge of the blade does nearly all the cutting. It moves at a very rapid speed.

Rotary mowers can either be pushed by the operator or driven by the engine powering the blade. When the engine drives the wheels, a pulley attached to the crankshaft drives a belt which rotates the wheels. See Fig. 18-3. The engine speed needs to be geared down by pulley ratios and gears to normal walking speed, 2-3 mph. Riding mowers can operate at higher speeds.

Safety. The rotary mower can be dangerous. A blade having an edge speed of over 200 mph can pick up and throw rocks or other solid objects at deadly speeds. People have been injured—even killed—by thrown objects. All rotary mowers are designed to catch the grass and other debris. Some have special shields to protect the operator. Again, see Fig. 18-2. Even with these devices, accidents can happen. The operator must work carefully.

The following are a few safety procedures that should be observed when using a rotary mower:

■ Keep small children away from the mower. Never cut the lawn when other people are around or working in areas close by.

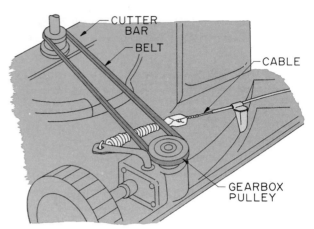

Fig. 18-3. The belt from the crankshaft drives the gearbox. The gearbox reduces the speed down to 2-3 miles per hour. The cable operates a clutch which engages and disengages the wheels from the engine.

■ Stop the engine before cleaning clogged grass from the blade and housing. Also, remove the spark plug high tension lead to prevent the engine from starting while rotating the blade during cleaning.
■ Wear heavy shoes but be sure to keep your feet clear of the mower. The blade can cut both your shoes and your feet.
■ Follow all safety rules for small engines listed in Chapter 16. These include proper use and storage of gasoline, the danger of exhaust fumes, and the high temperature of the engine.

Maintenance. All the small engine maintenance procedures described in Chapter 17 should be followed. The following are some special procedures for lawn mowers.

■ Rotary blades should be kept sharp. Dull blades break, rather than cut, the grass. Blades can be sharpened with a file. *Always* turn off the engine and remove the high tension lead before checking or touching the blade. Always remove a blade, following procedures outlined in the operators manual, before sharpening it.
■ Check belt tension on self-propelled mowers. Some mowers have automatic tension devices. Others require adjustment.
■ Keep mowers clean, and lubricate the wheels and other moving parts. Follow instructions given in the operator's manual.

Chain Saws

Chain saws were developed as a tool to assist loggers in cutting trees. But many people

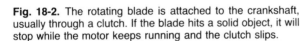

Fig. 18-2. The rotating blade is attached to the crankshaft, usually through a clutch. If the blade hits a solid object, it will stop while the motor keeps running and the clutch slips.

now use them to cut their own firewood or to trim or cut trees on the farm and around a home.

The chain saw is one of the *most dangerous* of the small engine applications. In order to do its job, the chain saw must have a long rotating chain operating without a protective shield. See Fig. 18-4. The small engine must drive the saw with considerable force. Even when used properly, a chain saw is a dangerous piece of equipment.

Figure 18-5 identifies the parts of a chain saw. Note the parts of the small engine driving the saw. Chain saw engines are almost always two-stroke-cycle engines with diaphragm carburetors. This design permits the engine to operate in any position.

Safety. A chain saw is a dangerous tool and should only be used by *adults* who understand how to use the saw and who are fully aware of the many hazards in using the saw.

Proper clothing is essential while using a chain saw. Each item has an important use. Eye protection protects the eyes from sawdust, dirt, and branches. Because a chain saw is noisy, ear protection is important, especially when the saw is used for long periods of time.

Each year, approximately 63,000 Americans are treated for chain saw injuries. A few of them die. Many of the problems are human errors. The operator might touch the moving chain while changing positions, lose balance, or trip over the saw. Some of the accidents can be prevented by saw design. About one-fifth of all accidents (the single largest cause) are from *kickback*. In a kickback, the saw is thrown up towards the operator when the upper part of the bar tip contacts an object. The contact transfers the energy moving the chain to the frame holding the chain. This throws the saw up. See Fig. 18-6.

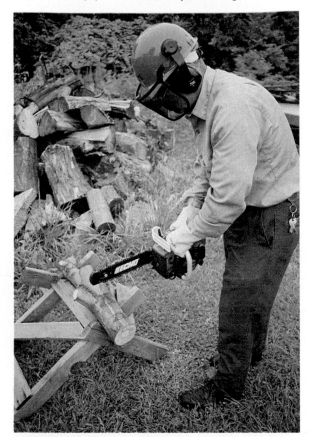

Fig. 18-4. A chain saw has many uses, but the operator must always use great care!

Chain saw manufacturers use a number of different safety devices. But a person operating a chain saw must use great care! An operator should keep the saw sharp, cut to one side rather than down or up towards the body, and *ALWAYS* turn off the saw blade between cuts. A person must *NEVER* move about carrying a running chain saw.

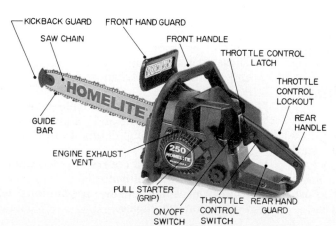

Fig. 18-5. The main parts of a chain saw.

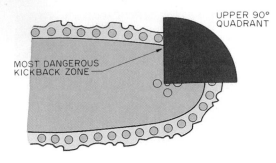

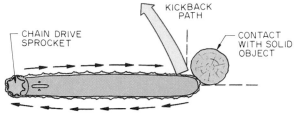

KICKBACK REACTION ZONE

Fig. 18-6. Kickback occurs when the upper curved surface of the blade strikes a solid object. The saw "kicks up" towards the operator. A chain saw should have a guard on the saw tip to prevent kickback.

Maintenance.
The most common form of maintenance is sharpening the chain saw. Operators can keep spare saw chains on hand. Dull chains can then be sharpened by a specialist. Or, the operator can obtain files and a special file holder and sharpen the chain as needed.

A routine operation is setting the tension of the chain. Tension is usually adjusted by a screw on the saw. The chain fits around the guide bar. It has tangs that fit into a groove on the outside of the bar. The chain must be tight enough to keep tangs inside the groove. This prevents the chain from slipping off. It must also be loose enough to prevent the chain from binding against the bar. During use, the saw should be turned off from time to time to check the tension and reset it if needed.

The operator may also need to adjust the safety brake and make general small engine adjustments. As with other small engine applications, all instructions given in the owner/operator manual should be followed carefully!

Garden and Home Maintenance Equipment

There is a variety of equipment powered by small engines which make gardening and yard maintenance quicker and easier. Devices include tiller/cultivators, edgers and trimmers, snow blowers, hedge trimmers, and blowers. The use of each of these devices has grown each year.

Fig. 18-7. A tiller being used to cultivate the area around garden plants.

Tiller/Cultivators. Tillers or cultivators operate under a variety of trade names many of which include the prefix "roto-" which is short for *rotary*. They vary in size, depending on the amount of land being gardened. Figure 18-7 shows a small tiller in operation. Some tillers operate without wheels, leaving movement and control to the operator.

Figure 18-8 shows a larger unit, powered by a choice of engines up to 8 horsepower in size. Each unit is designed to accomplish the same tasks—turning over soil, weeding, and maintaining small home gardens.

Many tiller/cultivators have detachable units which permit a variety of uses. Attachments can vary. See Fig. 18-9.

For *safety*, remember the most dangerous parts of tiller/cultivators are the cutters which break the soil. The belts and drive mechanism can also cause injury. Designs of tiller/cultivators vary. Always review the operating manual prior to use.

Special safety precautions to follow during operation include:
■ Always wear safety clothing. The tiller can throw dirt and rocks. Eye protection is especially important.
■ Watch for roots, rocks and other debris. These materials can jam the cutting blades, and throw you off balance; possibly into the equipment.
■ Avoid hills too steep to cultivate safely.
■ Always turn off engine and remove spark plug lead before clearing debris from blades or performing service.
■ Keep all guards and covers in place when operating the tiller/cultivator.
■ Follow all small engine precautions when working on the engine.

THROTTLE
CONTROL

DIRECTIONAL
CONTROL

SPEED LEVER

DEPTH GAUGE

TINES

ENGINE

PULL STARTER

CHOKE

Fig. 18-8. A typical tiller/cultivator.

Maintenance of tiller/cultivators center on keeping the digging units sharp so that they can break the soil quickly and effectively. Drive mechanisms from the small engine include gears, belts and pulleys, and chains and sprockets. On-off switching is provided for the engine and through clutches to disengage the engine from the cultivators and wheels.

Edgers and Trimmers. The knowledge that a string or line moving at high speed can cut grass, weeds, and even small shrubs introduced a whole new line of small engine applications. See Fig. 18-10. As shown, the line can be replaced by a metal or plastic blade. This makes it possible to cut down brush and larger bushes or very small trees.

Fig. 18-9. Attachments permit a tiller/cultivator to perform a variety of tasks.

Fig. 18-10. A trimmer can be used to cut weeds and grass in places that are difficult to reach with other equipment.

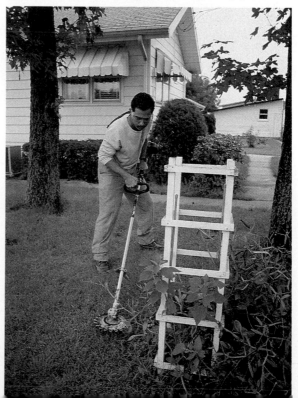

For *safety* always wear proper clothing when using trimmers. This includes shoes, preferably high tops, to protect the feet and ankles from the spinning string. Goggles or other eye protection should always be worn since trimmers can throw dirt, brush, and other debris which can cause severe eye injury. Metal and plastic blades are far more dangerous than the string. They can cause severe injuries if used improperly.

Maintenance of trimmers is relatively easy. The line, usually nylon, wears in use or breaks when cutting heavy objects or hitting rocks or curbs. Some trimmers have automatic feeds requiring only occasional line replacement. See Fig. 18-11. Others have easy systems for replacing single strings.

Snow Blowers. A very common use of small engines in colder climates is to power snow removal devices. Two basic cleaning principles are employed.

The first is using a high-speed reel which throws the snow forward. See Fig. 18-12. The second is using curved blades which pick up the snow and throw it to the side. See Fig. 18-13.

Fig. 18-11. Parts of a string trimmer. The string head assembly needs to be refilled occasionally.

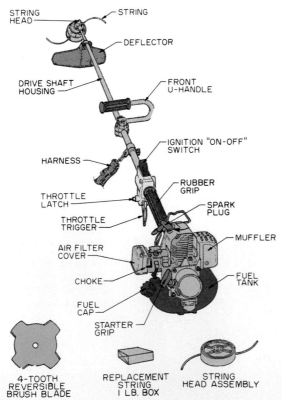

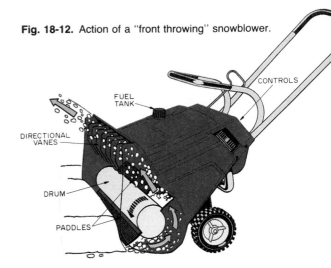

Fig. 18-12. Action of a "front throwing" snowblower.

For *safety*, remember the moving parts of snow blowers, especially the gears and/or belts, are dangerous and can cause injury. Never operate the unit without protective guards in place. Do *not* work on the blower while the engine is running.

Most *maintenance* problems of snow throwers involve either small engine maintenance or problems caused by working in heavy wet snow. These latter are more related to engine power and clogging rather than maintenance.

Hedge Trimmers. Hedge trimming is another small engine application. Figure 18-14 shows a trimmer in use.

Like the other cutting applications of small engines, *safety* precautions are necessary. Keep in mind that the running engine is hot and potentially dangerous. The blades of a trimmer are sharp and can cause serious injury. Trimmers should only be operated by adults who are familiar with the equipment and who are wearing eye protection and other heavy clothing.

Fig. 18-13. A snow blower can quickly clear snow from an area, saving much time and scooping effort for the user.

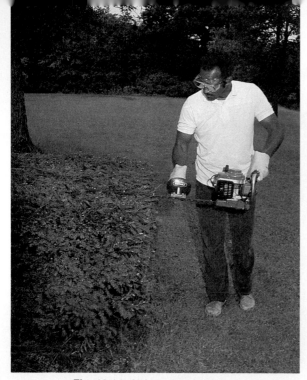

Fig. 18-14. Using a hedge trimmer.

Fig. 18-15. Power blowers are simple devices which can be used for keeping areas clear of debris and, sometimes, for spraying.

In addition to maintaining the small engine, there are two important areas of *maintenance*. First, the cutting blades must be kept adjusted and sharp. Worn blades should either be replaced or sharpened by a specialist. And secondly, the gear case requires periodic lubrication.

Blowers. Power blowers can be used to blow debris from driveways and other areas, as shown in Fig. 18-15. Special attachments permit the blowers to be used for spraying.

Operation of blowers is quite simple. The crankshaft drives a blower fan which moves large quantities of air.

For *safety*, wear eye, ear, and breathing protective devices. Never point the blower in the direction of people. Follow safe operating procedures for small engines, and always read and follow the manufacturer's operating instructions and safety precautions.

Maintenance consists primarily of care and routine service of the small engine.

ADDITIONAL USES OF SMALL ENGINES

Small engines have many additional uses. See Fig. 18-16. Many of these uses are for commercial applications, such as log splitters used for cutting firewood. Others are for home and small farm use.

Small engines are often used in transportation. These applications can sometimes be as complex as an automobile.

Care and maintenance of all of these devices should follow the procedures established by the manufacturer. Always obtain the manufacturer's operating manual. If you plan to do the servicing yourself, be sure to obtain the service manual pertaining to the equipment. It should provide detailed instructions.

SMALL ENGINE SAFETY

Safe use of equipment was stressed throughout this chapter. Many small engine applications involve cutting actions. These are especially dangerous since the force used to cut lawn, shrubs, or trees can cause severe injury and even death. Most of these devices are so dangerous, they should be operated by adults only.

Equipment should always be kept in good operating condition. Tools with dull cutting edges can often be more dangerous than sharp tools.

Technology Focus

A Whale of A Job

Time: October, 1988 **Place:** 312 miles north of the Arctic Circle, off the coast of Barrow, Alaska

They should have been migrating south, to the warm waters off the California coast. Instead, three young Gray whales were battling an ever-widening ice field that had them trapped. Their snouts were raw from breaking air holes in the ice. They were stressed and weakening rapidly.

A man on a snowmobile, *Roy Ahmaogak*, discovered the plight of the whales and told other residents of Barrow. Soon a handful of men mounted on snowmobiles and carrying hand tools and chain saws traveled to the site to help keep air holes open and to see if they could create a path for the whales to the open sea.

Government agencies became involved. The newspaper reported the situation and the word spread. Soon people around the world were following with interest the heroic efforts to free the whales.

In Minnesota, two brothers-in-law, *Rick Skluzacek* and *Greg Ferrian*, of Kasco® Marine, Inc., heard the news. They knew their de-icing equipment would maintain and enlarge the breathing holes and buy the most precious commodity of all—time. They packed up their De-icers and headed for Alaska.

At first, authorities feared the De-icers might startle the whales. But the situation was deteriorating, so why not try? As with the chain saws, the whales seemed to understand that the commotion created by the De-icers was occurring on their behalf. They followed the noise from breathing hole to breathing hole as rescuers slowly carved a trail to the sea.

Fig. 18-16. Other applications of small engines.

A. Electrical generator

B. Sprayer

C. Shredder

While small-scale efforts were in progress, large-scale efforts were also underway. National Guard helicopters were towing an icebreaking barge*. But it traveled only about three miles a day and was 190 miles away. Then word was received that Russian icebreakers (ships) were on their way. A large ridge of ice lay between them and the whales. Around-the-clock efforts continued.

The conditions of the whales had seemed to stabilize. But the smallest and the weakest of the three (shown here) disappeared beneath the ice and was lost forever. Would help arrive in time to save the two remaining whales?

The weather was amazingly good, odd for this area at this time of year. A turn for the worse would stop everything. But the weather held and a Russian icebreaker arrived. The whales were free at last and on their way to warmer waters.

The journey would not be without perils. Killer whales and Japanese whaling ships with powerful harpoons hunt in the Pacific. Will we ever know the fate of the two young whales? Probably not. But for a few days in October, humans used their technology not to kill whales, but to rescue them as fellow creatures on one earth.

Postscript: The rescue of the whales required phenomenal human effort, but equipment powered by small engines also played a critical role. Snowmobiles carried workers back and forth. And without chain saws, initial efforts would probably have failed.

The De-icers are powered by 1/2 or 3/4 hp motors. These do not heat the water; they continuously pump warmer, denser bottom water up to the surface to eliminate existing ice and prevent new ice from forming. Units weigh only 25 or 35 pounds and cost around $400 each. Behind the whale in the picture, you can see the flotation block that holds a De-icer suspended beneath the surface of the water.

Kasco® Marine, Inc. is a small company, employing only 10 people during its busiest time of year. As Rick Skluzacek said, "It [the rescue] just goes to prove that the 'little man' is not that far removed from world events." It also proves that small equipment in the right hands can perform big jobs.

*Belonging to VECO, Inc.

Protective equipment is especially important. Eye protection is necessary for nearly all small engine uses, especially cutting devices such as edgers and chain saws. Small engines are noisy and can cause hearing damage. This is especially true for long term use or for engines operating close to your ears (such as when carried on your back). Wear appropriate hearing protection.

The safety precautions presented in Chapter 16 apply to all small engine uses. *Follow them!* You should also read and follow the special instructions prepared by the manufacturers for each piece of equipment you use.

GASOLINE VS. ELECTRICAL POWER

Many of the applications shown in this chapter can also be powered by electric motors. Electric motors do not involve all of the hazards of gasoline engines but add the problem of electrical shock. In general, electric motors are less powerful and are confined to lighter applications. They usually require less maintenance than gasoline engines.

The electric cord needed to power the motor limits the range of use. The cord can also be a nuisance during use, especially with rotary lawn mowers. Cut cords occur, even to the careful user. Be sure the cord is properly grounded.

Testing Your Knowledge

Briefly answer each of the following questions. Write on a separate piece of paper.
1. Identify the five characteristics of small engines which contribute to their extensive use.
2. Name the two ways in which lawn mowers cut grass.
3. What two things must you do before cleaning clogged grass from the blade and housing of a lawn mower?
4. What is the single largest cause of accidents with chain saws?
5. Name five common garden and home maintenance devices powered by small engines.
6. Identify three ways in which small engines are used in transportation.

Expressing Your Knowledge

Using complete sentences, write your answers to the following on a separate sheet of paper:
1. Explain why a rotary mower should not be used when people are working or playing nearby.
2. Why is the chain saw often identified as one of the most dangerous pieces of equipment powered by a small engine?
3. Describe safety precautions to follow when operating a tiller/cultivator.
4. Briefly compare the use of electric motors and small gasoline engines.

Applying Your Knowledge

Follow your teacher's instructions to complete these activities:

1. Conduct a survey of the small engines used in your home, in the neighborhood, or around school. Write up your findings in a report that includes the condition of each engine and each piece of equipment.

2. Choose one of the engines you investigated in Activity 1. *With the approval and supervision of your teacher*, demonstrate how the engine powers the output device. Follow all safety rules when operating the engine and output device.

3. Prepare a report that shows as many different uses of small engines as you can find. Obtain photos and descriptive literature from magazines, newspapers, and promotional materials from sales and service dealers. Information can also be obtained by:

   ■ Visiting stores and asking for brochures on small engines and the equipment they operate.

   ■ Writing to small engine manufacturers.

   ■ Observing residential, commercial, agricultural, and recreational uses of small engines.

   Your report should emphasize unique applications not included or just briefly mentioned in this chapter. Your teacher may ask you to make an oral presentation on one of your applications.

Mechanical Power

SECTION

Chapter 19

Mechanical Power—Principles and Theory

Mechanical energy is the energy of motion. It can be harnessed, put to work, and measured. When timed, mechanical energy becomes *mechanical power*.

Expanding Your Knowledge

Learning about power and energy technology will help you understand more about the world around you. As you study this chapter, you will learn to:

- Describe what is meant by *mechanical advantage* and explain how it is determined by using force and distance in the *work* equation.
- Explain the difference between theoretical and actual mechanical advantage.
- Identify the six simple machines and explain how each is able to change the value for force and distance in the work equation.
- Identify two ways of determining the mechanical advantage of a simple machine.
- Solve problems involving simple machines, input and output forces, and mechanical advantage.

Building Your Word Power

Knowledge of the vocabulary used will help you develop greater understanding of power and energy. The following terms are defined and explained in this chapter. Learning these will help you learn more about mechanical power.

actual mechanical advantage	pulley
fulcrum	screw
inclined plane	theoretical mechanical advantage
lever	wedge
machine	wheel and axle
mechanical advantage	

Before mechanical power can be put to use, it usually must be changed. Many changes are possible. We can start it, stop it, change its direction, and make it stronger. We can slow it down, speed it up, and change it from one kind of motion to another. The work we want done determines the kind and number of changes.

Many different devices are used to modify mechanical power. We call these devices **machines**. A machine can be as simple as a wood-splitting wedge or as complex as a giant industrial press.

All machines work on the same basic principles. This chapter will introduce you to these principles. It will show you the simplest machines in which the principles are used.

The chapter first explains mechanical advantage. You will recognize the benefits of using machines and learn to calculate exactly what is gained and lost when using machines.

MECHANICAL ADVANTAGE

Unless you are very strong, you could not lift a 500-pound engine from a car by yourself. However, you could lift the engine with the help of a machine. The chain hoist in Fig. 19-1 is just such a machine. The hoist multiplies your strength, or force. This increase in force gained from using a machine is called a **mechanical advantage**. In Fig. 19-1, the worker is lifting a 500-pound engine with only 20 pounds of force. The hoist multiplies her strength by 25. We say that she has a mechanical advantage of 25. For every pound of force applied, she lifts 25 pounds of engine.

There are simple machines all around us. You have probably used many machines to gain a mechanical advantage. Doorknobs, for example, are simple machines. They make it easier to turn the latch. And screwdrivers, pliers, wheelbarrows, and countless other tools are all machines. They are devices that provide a mechanical advantage.

There are two ways to measure mechanical advantage: *theoretical* and *actual*. Actual mechanical advantage is always less than theoreti-

cal mechanical advantage. The difference between the two has to do with friction. Friction always causes a loss of power. **Theoretical mechanical advantage** does not take friction loss into account. **Actual mechanical advantage** refers to the theoretical advantage gained minus the friction loss.

How Machines Produce Mechanical Advantage

Chapter 6 presented material on the measurement of energy and power. This material is directly related to machines and mechanical advantage. Power, you recall, is work per unit of time. Work itself is useful motion. We calculate work by multiplying *force times distance*. This gives us an answer in *foot-pounds*. If metrics are used, the answer will be in *joules*.

A certain amount of power can do only a certain amount of work. Machines do not increase this amount. Machine output (work performed) is always the same as machine input (power applied).

Fig. 19-1. A chain hoist is a machine that gives mechanical advantage. With it a person can do work that would otherwise be impossible.

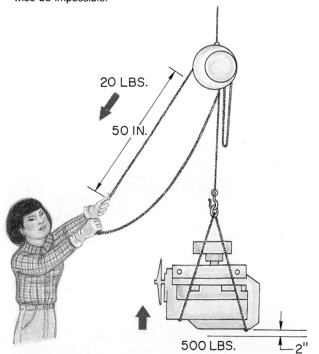

20 LBS.

50 IN.

500 LBS. 2"

Technology Focus

The Quest for Perpetual Motion

Throughout the ages, people have tried unsuccessfully to build a machine that would run forever—*perpetual motion*. People are still trying. The U.S. Patent Office often receives requests to patent perpetual motion machines.

One of the principles often tried is the "overbalanced wheel" shown here. It's true that a ball on the descending side of the wheel exerts more rotating force than an ascending ball. Unfortunately, there are more balls on the ascending side.

Perpetual motion machines are affected by *friction*[*]. Even the satellites circling the earth are not "in perpetual motion." The thin atmosphere through which they pass slows them by friction. All will eventually fall back to earth.

The concept of perpetual motion ignores the Law of Conservation of Energy which states that energy can be changed from one form to another, but can never be *created* or destroyed. Perpetual motion machines either must operate at 100% efficiency (which friction won't permit) or they must *create* energy.

So far perpetual motion remains an illusive, yet tantalizing, idea. Some people still believe it's possible to design and build such a machine. Do you have a design that you think will work?

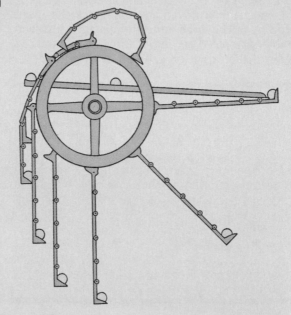

---

[*]Will superconductors enable us at last to create perpetual motion? See Chapter 27.

However, machines *can* change the amounts of force and distance in the work equation. Suppose we put 10 pounds of force into a machine at a distance of 5 feet. We will get 50 foot-pounds of work from the machine. We could put in 5 pounds of force at a distance of 10 feet. The work performed would be the same—50 foot-pounds. Only the amounts of force and distance have changed.

Input Work	Output Work
Force × Distance =	Force × Distance
10 lbs. × 5 ft. =	5 lbs. × 10 ft.
50 ft.-lbs. =	50 ft.-lbs.

Mechanical advantage usually refers to a gain in force and a loss of distance (MA_f). However, mechanical advantage can also refer to a gain in distance and a loss of force (MA_d).

Determining Mechanical Advantage

Every machine provides an exact amount of mechanical advantage. Engineers and technicians determine these amounts with several different formulas. All of the formulas produce ratios that compare *forces* or *distances*. The following paragraphs explain the most common formulas.

One way of calculating mechanical advantage is to compare output force to input force. See Fig. 19-2. A load (output force) of 30 pounds is being lifted by an input force of 6 pounds. The mechanical advantage is 30 to 6, or 30:6. This ratio is equal to 5:1, a mechanical advantage of 5. The mechanical advantage multiplies the input force by 5. However, note the distance involved in the example. The output force moves only ⅕ as far as the input force. Again, see Fig. 19-2.

Using Metrics

In the metric system, mechanical advantage is calculated the same way as in the customary system. The ratios remain the same no matter which system is used. For example, in the metric system, force is measured in *newtons (N)*. If 30 newtons is lifted by 6 newtons, the mechanical advantage is 30:6, or 5:1, or 5.

In the metric system, distance measurements are expressed in meters instead of feet. Again the ratios will stay the same no matter which system of measurement is used.

We can also determine mechanical advantage by comparing input distance to output distance. For example, if an input force moved a distance of 10 inches and the load moved 5 inches, the ratio would be 10 to 5, or 10:5. This is the same as 2:1, a mechanical advantage of 2.

Fig. 19-2. If 6 pounds of force moves a 30-pound load, the mechanical advantage is 30:6, or 5:1, or 5. However, the 6 pounds of force must move five times as far as the 30-pound load.

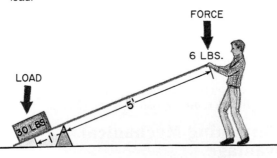

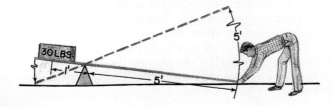

In any example, the theoretical distance and force ratios will be the same. Using the example of Fig. 19-2:

$$\frac{\text{Input Distance}}{\text{Output Distance}} = \frac{\text{Output Force}}{\text{Input Force}}$$

$$\frac{5 \text{ ft.}}{1 \text{ ft.}} = \frac{30 \text{ lbs.}}{6 \text{ lbs.}}$$

$$\frac{5}{1} = \frac{5}{1}$$

As you can see, we need to know only forces *or* distances to calculate mechanical advantage. The only difference is that when we figure mechanical advantage from distances, output distance is on the bottom. When we figure mechanical advantage from forces, input force is on the bottom.

PRINCIPLES OF MACHINES

There are basically six simple machines used to control and change mechanical power. All complex machines use the principles of one or more simple machines. The simple machines are:

- Lever
- Wheel and axle
- Pulley
- Inclined plane
- Wedge
- Screw

The six machines actually operate on just two basic principles. The lever, wheel and axle, and pulley operate on the principle of the *lever*. The inclined plane, wedge, and screw operate on the principle of the *inclined plane*. This section describes how basic machines produce mechanical advantage.

The Lever

A **lever** can be a long bar that rests on a pivot point. The pivot point is called a **fulcrum**. Somewhere along the bar a force is applied to move a load. The three types of levers are first-class, second-class, and third-class. See Figs. 19-3 and 19-4.

The levers differ in the placement of the fulcrum, force, and load along the bar. With different positioning, levers change mechanical advantage in different ways.

In *first-class levers*, the fulcrum is between the force and the load. The lever in Fig. 19-3A is a first-class lever. Note the distance from the force to the fulcrum. It is longer than the distance from the load to the fulcrum. This provides a mechanical advantage in force. First-class le-

Fig. 19-3. Types of levers: (A) first-class lever; (B) second-class lever; (C) third-class lever.

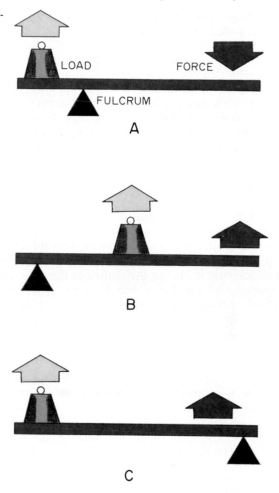

vers also change the direction of the force. A force applied downward exerts an upward push on the load.

A crowbar is an example of a first-class lever. A pair of scissors is a combination of two first-class levers. They use the same fulcrum.

In *second-class levers*, the load is between the force and the fulcrum. See Fig. 19-3B. Second-class levers provide mechanical advantage in force. However, they do not change the direction of the force. As with first-class levers, the force is farther away from the fulcrum than the load is. This determines the mechanical advantage. A wheelbarrow is an example of a second-class lever.

In *third-class levers*, the force is applied between the load and the fulcrum. See Fig. 19-3C. Third-class levers provide mechanical advantage in distance. Also, they do not change the direction of the force. The force is closer to the fulcrum than the load is. This results in a decrease in force and an increase in distance. In many cases a third-class lever is used because more distance means more speed. (Speed, you will recall, is distance per unit of time.) Brooms, hammers, and baseball bats are examples of third-class levers.

Fig. 19-4. Examples of the three classes of levers. Which type of lever is shown in each example?

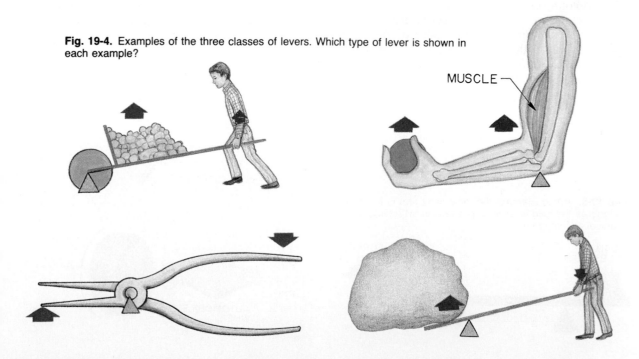

When you put a lever to work, it has two lever distances. The *force lever arm* is the distance from the fulcrum to the force. The *load lever arm* is the distance from the fulcrum to the load. We can calculate mechanical advantage by comparing these distances. In Fig. 19-5, the ratio is 5:1. This gives a mechanical advantage of 5. Two pounds of force will lift five times that amount (10 pounds). Note that the product of force times distance is the same for both sides of the lever.

The Wheel and Axle

The **wheel and axle** is another simple machine. It is a rod or shaft (axle) with a wheel attached to it. This machine works on the same principle as a *second-class lever*. See Fig. 19-6. The fulcrum is always the center of the axle. The positions of the force and load can vary. The wheel and axle can provide mechanical advantage in either force or distance. The gain in force or distance depends on the placement of the force and load.

With the input force applied to the *wheel*, the wheel and axle provides a gain in force with a loss in distance. The force travels a distance equal to the wheel's circumference. The load is attached to the axle. It travels a much shorter distance. The load travels a distance equal to the axle's circumference. See Fig. 19-7A.

When the input force is applied to the *axle*, the wheel and axle provides a gain in distance with a loss in force. The wheel makes one complete revolution for every revolution of the axle. The circumference of the wheel is greater than the axle's. Therefore, the outer edge of the wheel moves much farther than the outer edge of the axle. See Fig. 19-7B.

It is possible to calculate the mechanical advantage of a wheel and axle in one of three ways.

We can compare either the wheel's circumference, diameter, or radius to the corresponding (same) part of the axle. The most common method is to compare the radius of the wheel to the radius of the axle.

The Pulley

A **pulley** turns on an axis (center of rotation). Most pulleys are grooved to carry ropes or

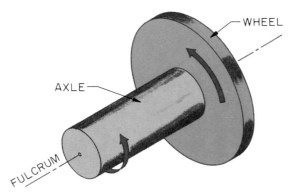

Fig. 19-6. The wheel and axle works on the same principle as the lever. The wheel acts as a lever and the center of the axle acts as the fulcrum.

Fig. 19-7. Depending on where the force and load are applied, a wheel and axle can provide a mechanical advantage in either force (A) or distance (B).

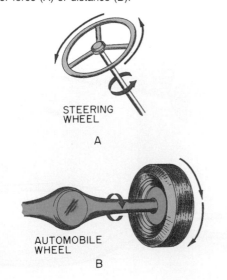

STEERING WHEEL

A

AUTOMOBILE WHEEL

B

Fig. 19-5. In this example, the force lever arm is five times as long as the load lever arm. The ratio is 5:1, giving a mechanical advantage of 5.

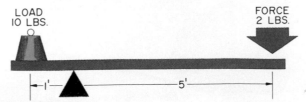

LOAD
10 LBS.

FORCE
2 LBS.

|← 1' →| |← 5' →|

belts. Pulleys are used with ropes and belts to do two things:

■ Change the direction of an applied force.
■ Increase the mechanical advantage of either force or distance.

Pulleys, like the wheel and axle, work on the principle of the lever. The center of the pulley—its axis—is the fulcrum. The pulley in Fig. 19-8 is an example of a simple fixed pulley. The center of the wheel is the fulcrum. This means that the lever distances are equal. (Each is a radius of the wheel.) The ratio is 1:1, which provides no mechanical advantage. To raise the load, you must apply a force equal to the load. This type of pulley is used only to change the direction of the force.

Pulley A in Fig. 19-9 is a movable pulley. It does not change the direction of the force. However, it does provide a mechanical advantage, using the principle of the *second-class lever*. The fulcrum is now at the edge of the pulley opposite the force. This makes the force lever arm equal to the diameter of the pulley. The load lever arm is still equal to the radius. The force arm is twice as long as the load arm. Therefore, the mechanical advantage is 2:1.

We can use many different pulley combinations to change force direction and provide mechanical advantage. In Fig. 19-9B, a fixed pulley has been added. This changes the direction of the force. However, it does not change the 2:1 mechanical advantage.

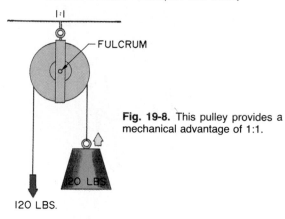

Fig. 19-8. This pulley provides a mechanical advantage of 1:1.

In Fig. 19-9C, a third pulley has been added. Three ropes now support the 120-pound weight. Each rope supports only 40 pounds. Therefore, the mechanical advantage is 3:1.

The Inclined Plane

The **inclined plane** is a machine that makes use of a sloping surface. You do not usually think of ramps, winding mountain roads, and staircases as machines. But they are all examples of inclined planes.

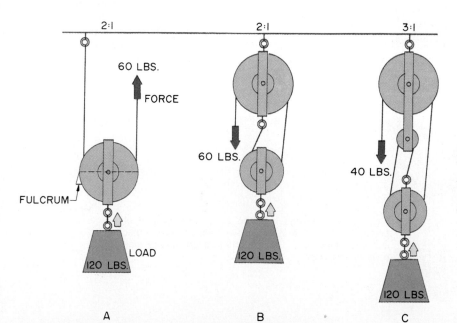

Fig. 19-9. Using additional pulleys can increase the mechanical advantage and provide directional changes. However, every increase in force is balanced by a loss in the distance moved.

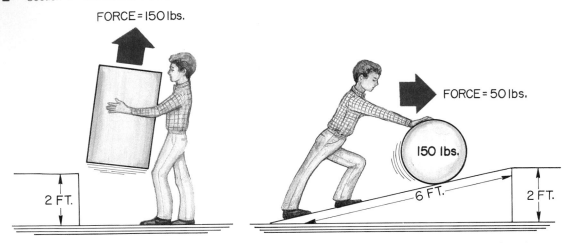

FORCE = 150 lbs.

2 FT.

FORCE = 50 lbs.

150 lbs.

6 FT.

2 FT.

Fig. 19-10. Using an inclined plane gives the person a 3:1 mechanical advantage in moving the barrel.

Figure 19-10 illustrates the mechanical advantage of the inclined plane. It is hard for the person to lift the 150-pound barrel and put it on the platform. It is much easier to roll the barrel up the inclined plane and onto the platform. We can calculate the mechanical advantage by comparing the length of the plane to the height of the platform. In this case the mechanical advantage is 6:2. This equals 3:1, or 3. A force of 50 pounds is enough to push the barrel up the inclined plane. Note, however, that this force is applied for 6 feet. This is three times the distance as in the lifting method.

The Wedge

A **wedge** is made up of two *inclined planes*. They are placed so that the sloping sides come together at a point. This arrangement makes a simple tool. It can be used to cut and pierce solid surfaces. Nails, axes, and wood-splitting wedges are simple examples of this principle.

The mechanical advantage of a wedge is the ratio of its length to its thickness. See Fig. 19-11. The splitting wedge multiplies the force of a hammer blow. It concentrates the force at the pointed end of the wedge. The mechanical advantage of this wedge is 6:2. This equals 3:1, or 3.

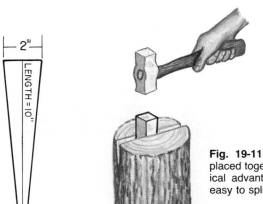

2"

LENGTH = 10"

Fig. 19-11. A wedge is made up of two inclined planes placed together. The wedge shown here provides a mechanical advantage of 5. This mechanical advantage makes it easy to split wood.

The Screw

The **screw** is an *inclined plane* cut in a spiral around a shaft. See Fig. 19-12. This provides a very long and gradual slope around the shaft. The slope gives a very high mechanical advantage. For example, a ½-inch bolt may have 20 threads per inch. This provides a mechanical advantage of more than 30:1. Figure 19-13 shows different applications of the screw.

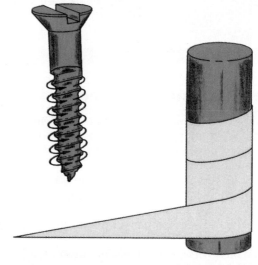

Fig. 19-12. A screw is basically an inclined plane wrapped around a shaft.

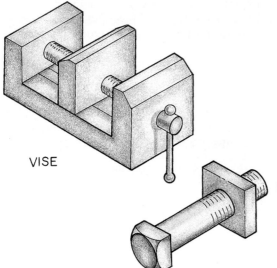

VISE

Fig. 19-13. Different applications of the screw.

NUT AND BOLT

Chapter 19—Review

Testing Your Knowledge

Briefly answer each of the following questions. Write on a separate piece of paper.

1. What do we call devices that modify mechanical power?
2. State two ways of determining the mechanical advantage of a simple machine.
3. Name the six simple machines.
4. Which three machines operate on the same principle as the lever?
5. Which three machines operate on the principle of the inclined plane?
6. Where is the fulcrum on a first-class lever?
7. Where is the force applied on a third-class lever?
8. What is the mechanical advantage of a single movable pulley?

Solve these problems:

9. A simple machine has an input force of 20 pounds, an input distance of 5 feet, and an output distance of 10 feet. What is the output force?
10. In the use of a series of pulleys, it is discovered that the rope must be pulled down 6 feet in order to move a weight up 1 foot. What is the mechanical advantage of the pulley system?
11. What is the force necessary to lift a 180-pound man when the mechanical advantage is 9:1?

Expressing Your Knowledge

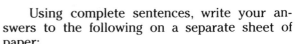

Using complete sentences, write your answers to the following on a separate sheet of paper:

1. Define mechanical advantage.
2. Explain the difference between theoretical and actual mechanical advantage.
3. How are force and distance affected by a wheel and axle when the input force is applied to the wheel?
4. Explain why a screw is an inclined plane.
5. Identify the types of levers shown in the illustration below. Explain your answers.

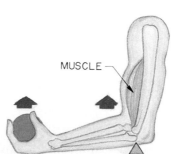

MUSCLE

Applying Your Knowledge

Follow your teacher's instructions to complete these activities:

1. Find devices in your home and in school that use the principle of simple machines. List each device and explain how it provides a mechanical advantage. There are many of these devices. They include saws, paper cutters, lawn mowers, bicycles, hand tools, can openers, knives, clothes driers, and washing machines. Your listing should look like this:

1. Screwdriver: The handle is larger in diameter than the blade. This provides the mechanical advantage of a second-class lever or a wheel and axle.

2. Knife: The knife blade provides the mechanical advantage of a wedge (inclined plane).

3. Nut and bolt: The threads provide the mechanical advantage of an inclined plane.

Now, continue and build your own list of at least 10 different items.

2. The chain hoist shown in Fig. 19-1 provides a very high mechanical advantage. Its operation is not explained in this chapter. Perform the necessary research needed to describe how a chain hoist provides mechanical advantage. Describe your findings in a brief report.

Chapter 20

Mechanical Power Systems

Mechanical power systems control and adapt power to practical uses. With them, we can do work that would otherwise be impossible.

Expanding Your Knowledge

As you study this chapter, you will learn to:
- Explain how mechanical devices are able to switch power on and off, change the direction of power, and change the power's force and speed.
- Describe the relationship of force and speed when either is changed by the advantage of a mechanical device.
- Describe how gears, pulleys and belts, sprockets and chains, clutches, and couplings (a) serve as on-and-off switches, (b) change power direction, and/or (c) change the force and speed of power.
- Identify the differences between spur gears, helical gears, bevel gears, miter gears, and worm gear sets.
- Explain the operation of an automotive friction clutch, a planetary gear system, and a universal joint.
- Describe the difference between friction and anti-friction bearings.
- Solve mathematical problems involving force and speed variations, mechanical advantage, and torque.

Building Your Word Power

The following terms are defined and explained in this chapter. Learning these will help you learn more about mechanical power systems.

aerodynamic drag
anti-friction bearings
clutch
couplings
gear ratio
gears
planetary gear system
sleeve bearings
sprocket

Sometimes mechanical power is put directly to work without changing it in any way. For example, the cutting blade of a lawn mower is connected directly to the power source, the engine's crankshaft.

For most uses, however, we need to change mechanical power in some way before putting it to use. We use control devices such as gears, pulleys, and clutches to make these changes. These devices control and transmit mechanical power. We connect them to power sources to create *mechanical power systems*. See Fig. 20-1.

In this chapter you will learn how we can change mechanical power in different ways. You will then learn about many of the control devices used in mechanical power systems. And you will begin to see the value of mechanical power systems.

TYPES OF CHANGES IN MECHANICAL POWER

In Chapter 1, you learned that the three basic parts of an energy control system are the source of energy, the conversion and transmission of energy, and the use of the energy. A mechanical power system basically has the same parts, except that we call the parts *input*, *control*,

and *output*. The input power comes from some type of power source. Special control devices can change the input power in three basic ways. They can:
■ Switch the power on and off.
■ Change the power's direction.
■ Change the power's force and speed.

The control devices can make one or all of these changes. They can also make one kind of change at several different times. The kinds and number of changes depend on the eventual use or power output of the system. The output may be the movement of a car, the spinning of a lawn mower blade, or the work of a complex piece of industrial machinery.

On-Off Switching

Sometimes we need to stop the power output in a system for just a short time. Then we turn it back on. We may need to do this quickly and frequently. We may not want to or be able to completely stop the input power. In these cases we need a *switching control device*. This device connects and disconnects the power output without stopping the input power.

A manual-shift car is an example of a mechanical power system that requires a switching control device. The engine provides the input power for driving the car. At stop signs we need to stop the car. This means we need to switch off the power output. It would be a lot of trouble to turn off the engine at every stop sign. This would also be hard on the car. Instead, we use a control device—a **clutch**. This device disconnects the input power from the power output. (Clutches are described later in this chapter.)

Fig. 20-1. The automobile engine converts fuel into mechanical power—the motion of the crankshaft. Various control devices then transmit and control this motion so that the car can start and stop, move forward, reverse direction, or accelerate. The movement of the car is the output or use of the entire power system.

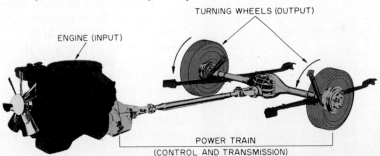

TURNING WHEELS (OUTPUT)

ENGINE (INPUT)

POWER TRAIN
(CONTROL AND TRANSMISSION)

On-off switching is needed in many types of mechanical power systems. Most transportation devices have controls for on-off switching. Many industrial machines need to be turned on and off again and again. This must be done without stopping the input power.

Changes in Direction

Input power usually takes the form of rotary motion. A shaft turning in a certain direction is one example. The direction of motion may need to be changed to do the needed work. Directional changes are usually one of three types:

■ Reversing.

We often need to make input motion turn in the opposite direction. Automobiles, for example, usually go forward but must occasionally go backwards.

■ Turning.

We sometimes need to *redirect* the power. The rear-end assembly of a rear-wheel-drive automobile, for example, redirects power 90° from the drive shaft to the rear wheels.

■ Converting one kind of motion to another.

We must often change linear motion to rotary motion or vice versa. Many machines change rotary motion to reciprocating motion or reciprocating to rotary. See Fig. 20-2. Changes of

this type are often needed in both home and industrial use. In most washing machines, the input motion is rotary. Control devices convert it into reciprocating motion. This motion moves an agitator back and forth. Another example is an industrial press that stamps forms from metal. This requires the conversion of rotary motion into reciprocating motion.

Speed and Force Changes

Mechanical power is often measured in terms of *force* and *speed*. These two parts of mechanical power are very closely related. If you increase one, you must decrease the other by the same amount. Chapter 19 explained this relationship in terms of force and distance. Speed is simply distance per unit of time. Therefore, we can substitute speed for distance when we speak of mechanical advantage.

For many mechanical power uses, we need to gain either force or speed. A gain in one of these always means a decrease in the other. For example, a stopped car needs a great deal of *torque* (turning force) to get moving. As the car starts moving, it needs less torque and more speed. We use control devices to regulate the engine's power. With them, we can produce the right amounts of force and speed at the right time.

CONTROL DEVICES

Mechanical power systems use several major control devices. These devices change the input power as needed for the work to be done. The most common types are:

■ Gears
■ Pulleys and belts
■ Sprockets and chains
■ Clutches
■ Couplings

Gears

Gears are basically wheels that have teeth cut around their outside surface, or circumference. There is also a hole in the center so that a shaft can be attached to the gear.

Gears work on the principle of the lever. See Fig. 20-3. The teeth of one gear mesh (fit in between) the teeth of another gear. When a power source turns one gear, the other gear also turns. The gear connected to the power source is called the *drive gear*. The other gear is called the *driven gear*.

Fig. 20-2. Motion can be converted from one form to another in a mechanical power system.

Technology Focus

The Racer's Edge

Progress is being made in bicycle technology. Designers study the interaction between the rider and the bicycle. For example, imagine that the rotation of your bicycle pedals follows the face of a clock. The greatest push from your legs on the pedals occurs between the one o-clock and the five o-clock positions. This two-thirds of the downstroke provides most of the power to move the bicycle. Recent bicycle designs take advantage of this fact.

One design, shown here, includes a device called ExO POWERCAM®. It uses the cam (center) to adjust the speed of the pedal crank. Two positions of the crank are shown:

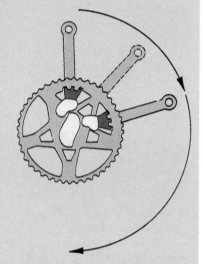

■ When the crank is up, note that the roller which rests on the cam is closer to the center of the cam. In this position, the crank driven by the roller moves comparatively slowly.

■ When the crank is moving down, the roller is extended. The crank driven by the roller is now moving faster.

Note the design of the cam. When the roller is down at the five o-clock position, it will "notch" around the cam just as it does at the top. The result is slower crank speed. This speed change permits the leg to surge (move faster) on the downstroke. The rider then relaxes when the crank slows through the "dead" zone. The result is more power and a more relaxed ride.

Since Powercam, other designs have been developed and still others are being tested. Many shapes and combination of parts are possible. In bicycle technology, even a small change may give you the "edge" you need, whether for racing or for pleasure riding.

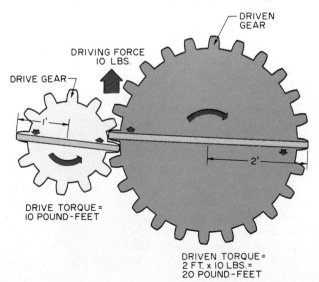

Fig. 20-3. Different size gears can be used to multiply torque. The green bars show the lever action of the gears.

DRIVEN GEAR

DRIVING FORCE 10 LBS.

DRIVE GEAR

DRIVE TORQUE = 10 POUND-FEET

DRIVEN TORQUE = 2 FT. x 10 LBS. = 20 POUND-FEET

We use gears to make all three basic power changes: on-off switching, directional changes, and changes in force and speed. The kind of change depends on the size, type, and position of the gears.

There are many kinds of gears. Five of the most common are:

■ Spur gears
■ Helical gears
■ Bevel gears
■ Miter gears
■ Worm gear sets

Spur Gears. The spur gear is the simplest and most common type of gear. It has teeth cut parallel to the shaft that runs through the gear. See Fig. 20-4. Spur gears can provide directional change. They can also change either force or speed.

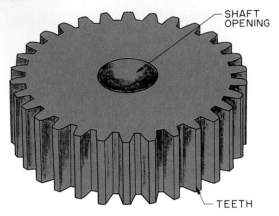

Fig. 20-4. In a spur gear, the teeth are parallel to the shaft.

Whenever two spur gears mesh, they reverse the direction of the power. If the power source turns one gear in a counterclockwise direction, the second gear turns clockwise. Three spur gears are needed to make the power output turn the same way as power input.

Refer again to Fig. 20-3. This illustration shows how two spur gears can multiply torque. Each tooth in the gears represents the end of a lever. The center of the gear acts as the fulcrum. The drive gear (on the left) has a 1-foot radius. It has a torque of 10 pound-feet. This force transfers to the larger gear. The larger gear has a radius of 2 feet. Therefore, it has a torque of 20 pound-feet at its shaft.

We calculate changes in speed and force with gears in terms of **gear ratio**. This is the ratio of the number of teeth on a driven gear to the number of teeth on the drive gear. For example, if the driven gear has 24 teeth and the drive gear has 12 teeth, the ratio for the gear set is 24:12, or 2:1. This means that the driven gear has twice as much torque as the drive gear.

A gain in force always means an equal loss in speed. In the previous example, the small gear makes two complete revolutions for every one of the larger gear. We measure speed in revolutions per unit of time. Therefore, the larger gear turns at half the speed of the smaller.

Spur gears can also be used to increase speed. In the same example, suppose the larger gear were driving the smaller. There would be an increase in speed. If the larger gear turned at 10 rpms, the smaller gear would turn at 20 rpms. Of course, the smaller gear would have only half the torque of the larger gear.

Helical Gears. The helical gear is similar to the spur gear. The difference is that helical gears have teeth cut at an angle. See Fig. 20-5. The angular cut of the teeth provides greater contact between gears. Usually more than one tooth from each gear is meshed. This increased contact allows more torque to be transferred. It also helps prevent excessive wear and breakage. However, the greater contact also produces more friction between the gears. This results in a greater power loss.

With their angular cut, helical gears can change power direction. Figure 20-5 shows helical gear sets being used in both parallel and right-angle positions. When used at right-angles, helical gears can be used instead of bevel or miter gears.

Bevel Gears and Miter Gears. We use both bevel gears and miter gears to change the direction of input power. See Fig. 20-6.

Bevel gears can also provide a mechanical advantage in either force or speed. When used to provide a mechanical advantage, the two halves of a bevel gear set have different sizes. We use gear ratio to determine the mechanical advantage.

The gear ratio in miter gear sets is always 1:1. Each gear has the same number of teeth. Therefore, miter gears provide only a directional change.

Bevel gears and miter gears may have straight-cut teeth, like spur gears. Or they may have spiral-shaped (helical) teeth. See Fig. 20-6B. The spiral teeth increase load capacity. They also reduce wear on the gear.

Fig. 20-5. Helical gears are designed to provide a change in power direction.

A. Parallel.   B. Right angles.

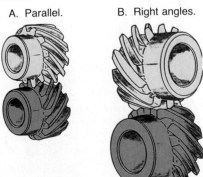

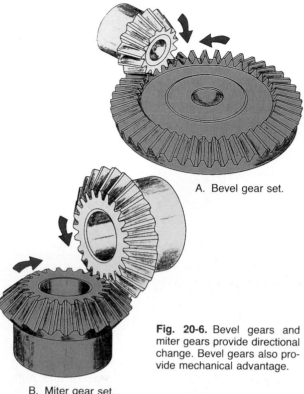

A. Bevel gear set.

Fig. 20-6. Bevel gears and miter gears provide directional change. Bevel gears also provide mechanical advantage.

B. Miter gear set.

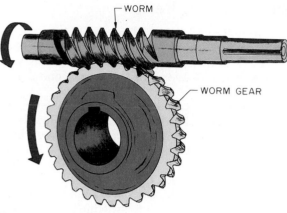

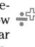

Fig. 20-7. In a worm gear set, the turning worm rotates the worm gear.

Worm Gear Sets. A worm gear set consists of a *worm* and a *worm gear*. See Fig. 20-7. Worm gear sets make major changes in torque and speed. They also change the direction of power.

The input power is usually applied to the worm. The worm acts like a screw to rotate the worm gear. The worm gear rotates only one tooth each time the worm makes one full revolution.

A very high mechanical advantage is possible with worm gear sets. For example, suppose a worm gear has 30 teeth. The worm must rotate 30 times to rotate the worm gear once. This is a mechanical advantage of 30:1. The output torque is 30 times greater than the input torque. This is an example of the main use of worm gear sets—to provide increased torque with reduced speed.

Worm gear sets are commonly used in automotive steering systems. Some steering systems use ratios as high as 28:1. These high ratios allow drivers to turn the front wheels easily with the steering wheel. It takes several turns of the steering wheel to turn the front wheels about 90°. The gear arrangement increases torque and decreases speed.

By connecting worm gear sets together, the ratios are multiplied and we get very high mechanical advantages. This produces very slow motion. For example, two connected worm gear sets, each with a ratio of 60:1, have a speed reduction of 3600:1.

Gear Uses. There are many home, industrial, and transportation uses for gears. The automobile transmission in Fig. 20-8 is one example. The gears in this transmission provide torque, speed, and directional changes.

Gears can also provide on-off switching. We can move them out of mesh. This cuts off the input power from the output gear. For example, automobile transmissions have a "neutral" position. Shifting into this position unmeshes two gears. When this happens, power cannot transfer from the engine to the drive wheels.

Fig. 20-8. This complex automotive transmission is a mechanical control device. It makes changes in the speed and force (torque) of a car's output power.

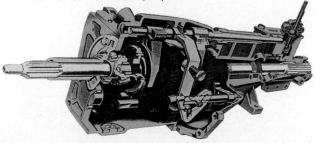

Pulleys and Belts

A pulley is basically a metal disk that is grooved around its circumference. It either drives or is driven by a flexible belt. In this way power transfers over a distance from one pulley to another.

The most common types of pulleys are called *V-pulleys*. See Fig. 20-9. These pulleys have a V-shaped groove that accepts a V-shaped belt. In an automotive engine, the V-belts on the crankshaft pulleys drive the water pump, alternator, and other equipment.

Pulleys and belts can provide all three major control functions: on-off switching, directional change, and speed and torque change. We can disconnect the power flow in a belt-and-pulley system by moving one of the pulleys toward the other. The belt slips and cannot transfer power through the system. We can connect the power flow by tightening the pulley.

We can change direction by twisting the belt or using idler pulleys. Idler pulleys act only as supports for the belt.

We do not often use pulleys and belts for on-off switching and directional change. We use them mainly to transmit power and to change force and speed. For example, we may connect a small-diameter driver pulley to a larger-diameter driven pulley. This increases torque but decreases speed. Reversing this setup has the opposite effect.

Sprockets and Chains

A **sprocket** is similar to a gear. The difference is that it drives or is driven by a chain instead of another gear. See Fig. 20-10. Sprockets provide mechanical advantage and speed changes in the same way as gears. However, chain and sprocket assemblies cannot change the direction of rotation as gears can. Sprockets

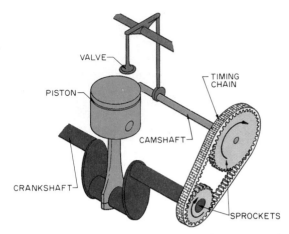

Fig. 20-10. Chain and sprocket assembly. Some automotive engines use sprockets and a chain to transfer crankshaft movement to the camshaft. Notice that the direction of rotation is the same in both sprockets.

and chains are a very strong way of transmitting power while changing force and speed. This high strength makes them suitable for many industrial uses.

Sprocket and chain assemblies are *positive-drive* units. The teeth of the sprockets mesh with the chain. This prevents any slippage as the sprockets move. The sprockets maintain a specific timing relationship to one another. This feature makes sprockets and chains very useful in situations in which timing is important.

Another type of positive drive unit uses a flexible *timing belt* instead of a chain. See Fig. 20-11. Timing belt assemblies have the same

Fig. 20-11. In this timing assembly, a belt takes the place of a chain.

Fig. 20-9. V-pulleys and belt.

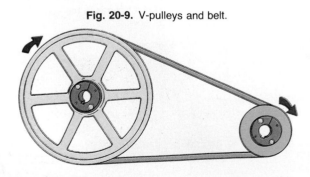

basic characteristics as chain assemblies. The difference is that timing belts are quieter-running and lighter. Timing belts also have some "give" during operation. This provides smoother operation than with chains. However, timing belts cannot transfer as much force as chains can.

We can use belt and chain drives to provide adjustable ratios of speed and torque. Figure 20-12 shows an *adjustable chain drive*. This assembly uses special cone pulleys instead of sprockets. We can change the working diameter of cone pulleys by opening or closing them. In **A**, the drive has one cone fully closed. The other is fully open. **B** shows a top view of the complete assembly. Note that a control screw is used to adjust the cone positions.

Variable-speed pulley drives operate in a way similar to the adjustable chain drive. They use V-belts and adjustable pulleys to produce variable ratios of speed and torque.

Clutches

We use *clutches* to perform on-off switching. There are many different kinds of clutches. Four of the most common are:
■ Friction clutch
■ Positive clutch
■ Centrifugal clutch
■ Cam (overrunning) clutch

Friction Clutch. The friction clutch is the type of clutch used on automobiles with manual transmissions. It consists of a *friction disk* (clutch plate) sandwiched between the engine's *flywheel* and a *pressure plate*. See Fig. 20-13. When the clutch is engaged, the pressure plate presses the friction disk against the flywheel. The friction disk grips the flywheel and turns with it. In this way, engine power transfers through the flywheel and friction disk to the transmission.

Fig. 20-13. The parts and operation of a friction clutch.

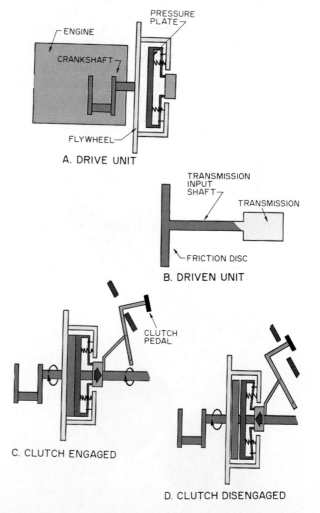

A. DRIVE UNIT

B. DRIVEN UNIT

C. CLUTCH ENGAGED

D. CLUTCH DISENGAGED

Fig. 20-12. When the cone pulleys of an adjustable chain drive are adjusted as in A, force is increased. A reversal of the pulleys' adjustments would cause an increase in speed. The method of adjusting the pulleys is shown in B.

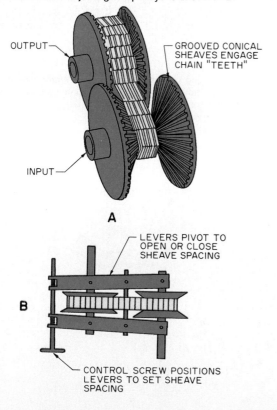

To disconnect the power flow, the driver pushes the clutch pedal down. This releases the pressure holding the friction disk to the flywheel. The disk disengages from the flywheel. The flywheel then turns freely without moving the disk. As a result, no engine power is transferred to the transmission.

Friction clutches have a very high capacity for transmitting power. However, they do have load limits. With too heavy a load, the friction disk will slip and generate heat. This heat will quickly destroy the clutch.

Note that we can apply or release friction clutches while the input power is on. This is one of their major advantages. We can engage or disengage the power source at any time. In this way, we have a high degree of control over the power system.

Positive Clutch.

A positive clutch will not slip. However, it must be engaged when it is either not rotating, rotating at a low speed, or both halves are rotating at the same speed.

Figure 20-14 shows two types of positive clutches. The clutch in **A** can transfer power in either direction. The clutch is shown disengaged. It is engaged by sliding one half into mesh with the other. The clutch in **B** can transfer power in only one direction—clockwise. This clutch is engaged in the same way as the clutch in **A**. Note

that each tooth is tapered (angled). The clutch will disengage whenever power is applied counterclockwise.

Centrifugal Clutch.

Centrifugal clutches work on the principle of centrifugal force. This is the force that causes an object to move away from the center of rotation. In Fig. 20-15, centrifugal force acts on the stone as the person spins it. To keep the stone going in a circular path, the person must apply a counter force. This force must be increased to increase the speed of rotation.

In the centrifugal clutch, a pair of weights attach to an input shaft. See Fig. 20-16. Centrifugal force moves the weights out as the shaft rotates. The output force of the weights increases as the rotation speed increases. A housing surrounds the weights. The housing is connected to an output shaft.

When the rotational speed is high enough, the weights are forced against the housing. Held by friction, the housing rotates at the same speed as the weights. Centrifugal force keeps the weights against the housing. Power transfers from the input shaft, through the weights, to the housing and output shaft.

Centrifugal clutches can rotate in either direction. As speed increases, the weights develop more centrifugal force. The higher the centrifugal force, the harder the weights press against the housing, and the higher the friction that is produced. This maintains a positive transfer of power.

Fig. 20-14. Once it is engaged, the positive clutch in A can transfer power in either direction. The clutch in B can transfer power in a clockwise direction only.

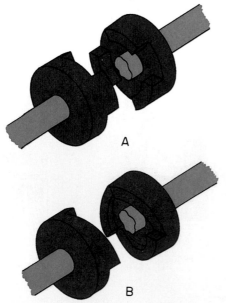

A

B

Fig. 20-15. Spinning a stone on a string illustrates centrifugal force. As the stone rotates, centrifugal force tries to move it away from the center of rotation.

CENTRIFUGAL FORCE

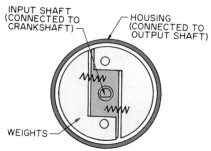

A. When the input shaft rotates slowly or not at all, the springs hold the weights in.

B. As the input shaft spins faster, centrifugal force throws the weights out. They contact the housing, and friction between the rotors and the housing causes the housing to rotate.

Fig. 20-16. The operation of a centrifugal clutch.

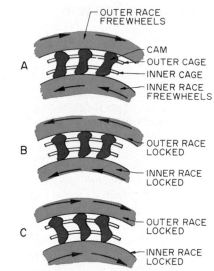

Fig. 20-17. Operation of a cam, or overrunning, clutch.

In small gas engines, the input power for a centrifugal clutch is supplied by the crankshaft. A gear or sprocket is attached to the clutch housing. As the housing rotates, the gear or sprocket transmits power to the power output. When the engine is starting or at an idle, the clutch does not engage. Therefore, the gear or sprocket does not turn. However, when engine speed is increased, the clutch engages. This turns the gear or sprocket.

Cam (Overrunning) Clutch.
Cam or overrunning clutches have a ring of cam-shaped parts that transfer power in only one direction. Figure 20-17 shows how overrunning clutches transmit input power to an output shaft. The *races* are metal shells that rotate with the input and output shafts.

In **A**, the low points of the cams touch the inner race. No power transfers. Each race turns free of the other. This is often called *freewheeling*.

In **B**, input power is applied to the outer race. Each cam turns slightly. This locks the races together. The outer race drives the inner race. If the inner race rotates faster than the outer race, the cams shift back to the position

shown in **A**. When the inner race runs faster, it *overruns* the outer race.

In **C**, input power is applied to the inner race in the reverse direction. The diagram shows the cams turned further. The inner race transmits a large amount of power to the outer race. In this case, the outer race could overrun the inner race. If the inner race is stopped, the outer race will freewheel.

Automotive automatic transmissions use an overrunning clutch. It is also used in special industrial applications. In these cases, the output shaft must rotate freely after the input shaft stops. See Fig. 20-18.

Fig. 20-18. Parts of a cam clutch.

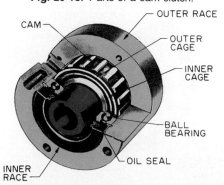

Planetary Gear System

A **planetary gear system** is a special combination of gears, brakes, and clutches. It provides a variety of directional, speed, and torque changes. Planetary gear systems have been used in cars almost from the beginning. The classic Model T Ford used a planetary gear system both in its steering mechanism and in the transmission. The latest model automatic transmissions also use planetary gears.

The planetary gear system has an *internal gear* and a *sun gear*. See Fig. 20-19. These two gears are separated by two or three *planet gears*. A *planet carrier* holds the planet gears. The planet gears mesh with both the sun gear and the internal gear. The three types of gears are always in mesh. They do not have to be shifted.

Figure 20-19 shows a shaft connected to the planet carrier. There is also a shaft connected to the sun gear. These shafts can be used for input or output. A shaft can also be attached to the internal gear. Planetary gear systems also have special brakes called *bands*. These are used to hold any of the three types of gears stationary during operation. Clutches are used to lock the input and output together. The brakes and clutches accomplish changes in speed, torque, and direction of movement. We will now see how the system operates.

Reverse. In Fig. 20-20, the planet carrier is held stationary. Input power is applied to the sun gear. As the sun gear rotates, the planet gears also rotate. As these gears rotate, they drive the internal gear. The internal gear rotates in a direction opposite that of the sun gear. The internal gear is larger than the sun gear. Therefore, it turns much slower. In the example shown, one revolution of the sun gear turns the internal gear only ⅓ of a revolution. The speed reduction is 3:1.

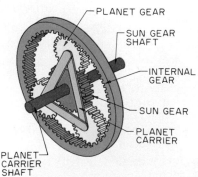

Fig. 20-19. In a planetary gear system, the planet gears are tied together by a carrier and shaft. The planet gears rotate as a unit.

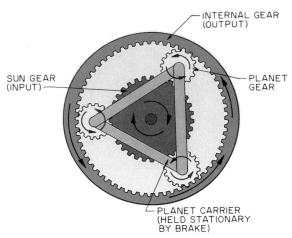

Fig. 20-20. A planetary gear system providing a speed reduction of 3 to 1.

An output shaft connected to the internal gear would revolve in reverse. It would also have three times the torque of the sun gear. We could increase speed instead of torque by applying the input power to the internal gear. This would cause a speed increase and torque reduction in the sun gear.

Speed Reduction—Forward. In Fig. 20-21, the sun gear is held stationary. Input power is applied to the internal gear. The output is at the planet carrier. As the internal gear ro-

Fig. 20-21. A planetary gear system providing a speed reduction and a force increase in a forward motion.

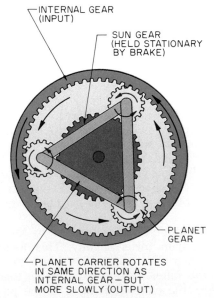

tates, it turns the planet gears. The planet gears "walk" around the sun gear in the same direction as the internal gear. This action turns the planet carrier in the same direction. However, the carrier turns at a slower speed than the internal gear.

Direct Drive. Planetary gear systems can also provide direct transfer of power. This is accomplished by locking any two units together with a clutch. In Fig. 20-22, the carrier and internal gear are locked together. The input power is applied to the sun gear. As the sun gear turns, it tries to turn the planet gears. Since the carrier and internal gear are locked together, the planet gears cannot turn. As a result, the entire system rotates together. In this situation, none of the gears rotate within or around another gear. In an automatic automobile transmission, this is the direct drive position. It is the position used most of the time. The gears touch only at certain points. Therefore, gear life is very long—with minimum failure.

Speed Increase—Forward. Planetary gear systems can also provide a forward speed increase. This is not a common use, but it is possible. Look back to Fig. 20-21. In that speed reduction arrangement, the input is to the internal gear. The output is from the planet carrier. A speed *increase* can be obtained by reversing the input and output. Applying the input power to the carrier will cause a speed increase of the internal gear.

A. Roller chain coupling

B. Disassembled coupling with protective housing.

Fig. 20-23. A roller chain coupling is a rigid coupling that uses two sprockets and a chain to transfer power.

Couplings

Couplings are permanent connections used to transmit power. We use them to produce directional changes or to connect lengths of shaft.

There are many types of industrial couplings in common use. Some are rigid. We use this type to connect separate shafts. Figure 20-23 shows a rigid coupling. This coupling consists of two toothed sprockets and a double roller chain. One sprocket fastens to the end of each shaft being connected. The chain is then wrapped around both sprockets. This locks them together. Power transfers from one shaft to the other through the chain.

The *universal joint* is a coupling that provides for alignment change. See Fig. 20-24. The universal joint permits the shafts connected to it to be out of alignment and still move. A rigid coupling would not allow this misalignment and motion.

One type of universal joint consists of two sets of bearings on a crosspiece. Each shaft connects to a set of bearings. The power transfers from one shaft to the other through the crosspiece. The bearings permit the shafts to move up-and-down during operation. This type of universal joint is used commonly on automotive drive shafts.

A simpler flexible coupling is a spring connection. This type of coupling is strong and needs no lubrication. It can withstand some shock and flexing.

Fig. 20-22. A planetary gear system in direct drive.

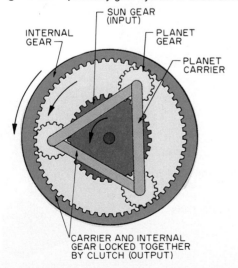

SUN GEAR (INPUT)

INTERNAL GEAR

PLANET GEAR

PLANET CARRIER

CARRIER AND INTERNAL GEAR LOCKED TOGETHER BY CLUTCH (OUTPUT)

A. Assembled "U-joint"

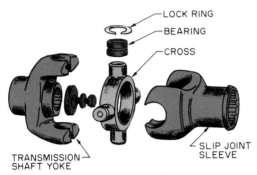

B. Disassembled joint

Fig. 20-24. A universal joint allows the connected shafts to be out of line with each other and still move.

POWER TRANSMISSION AND FRICTION

Moving power from place to place is called *power transmission*. The main power transmission devices are the control devices already described. These devices move the power to where it is needed. They also change or control the power to fit the needs of the system. For example, an automobile transmission contains control devices that modify the engine's power. The power must also be transmitted from the engine to the wheels. This is done with a driveshaft and a rear end assembly. The power can then be used to drive the car.

Not *all* the power can be controlled. There are power losses in every power system. Most power losses in a mechanical system are due to friction. The more complex the system, the greater the power loss.

Friction

As noted in Chapter 1, *friction* is an energy loss in the form of heat. In power systems, friction occurs in control devices. It also occurs along the line of transmission. This energy loss can seriously reduce the available power.

Friction occurs whenever surfaces moving at different speeds contact each other. It occurs between all materials in contact in varying degrees. Friction even occurs between air and a moving mechanical device. For example, air slows down a speeding automobile. This is called **aerodynamic drag**. The driver must accelerate (apply more power) to compensate for the friction.

Bearings

Bearings reduce friction between moving parts. They also provide support for rotating shafts. All mechanical power systems use bearings. For example, bearings are used in automobiles wherever moving parts make contact. This includes the engine, wheels, transmission, starting motor, and rear end assembly. There are many types of bearings. However, most of them can be classified into two groups:
■ Sleeve bearings
■ Anti-friction bearings

Sleeve Bearings. Figure 20-25A shows a sleeve bearing. Essentially, it is a sleeve held in a housing around a shaft. The part of the shaft

Fig. 20-25. Two common types of bearings.

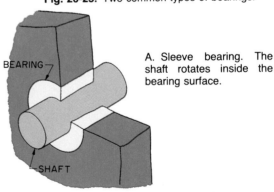

A. Sleeve bearing. The shaft rotates inside the bearing surface.

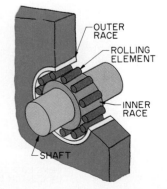

B. Anti-friction bearing. The rolling elements rotate between the inner and outer races.

that rotates inside the bearing is called the *journal*. The bearing is stationary. It supports the journal as the shaft rotates. One surface slides over the other surface, providing *sliding friction*.

Sleeve bearings are made of either metal or plastic. Metal bearings are normally lubricated by a film of oil. The oil provides a low-friction surface.

Metal sleeve bearings can carry heavy and variable loads. Bearings of this type are used throughout automotive engines to reduce friction and wear.

Some sleeve bearings need to be lubricated. Others are pre-lubricated. Pre-lubricated bearings are called *oil-impregnated bearings*. As the shaft rotates in the bearing, the heat generated by friction releases a small amount of oil. These bearings require no additional lubrication.

Plastics, especially nylon, are often used as a bearing surface for fairly light loads. Children's toys and many home devices use nylon bearings. They are trouble-free and never require lubrication. They also cost less than metal bearings.

Anti-Friction Bearings. Figure 20-25B shows a typical anti-friction bearing. This type of bearing provides *rolling friction* rather than sliding friction. The inner race holds tightly to the rotating shaft. The outer race is fixed in the housing. It supports the shaft. As the shaft rotates, the rollers turn. Anti-friction bearings must be lubricated for low-friction operation.

The most common types of anti-friction bearings are ball bearings, roller bearings, and tapered roller bearings. See Fig. 20-26. Ball bearings are commonly used in electric motors. They are designed for high-speed, moderate-load uses. Roller bearings are used when the loads are heavier. Rollers offer more support than balls. Tapered roller bearings provide excellent support and can also handle a heavy side thrust. Most automotive wheels use this type of bearing.

POWER OUTPUT

After we change input motion and transmit it to where we need it, we can put it to work. The *output* (final use) may be the motion of a car, the spinning of a lawn mower blade, or the work of a complex piece of industrial machinery.

SERVICE TOOLS AND EQUIPMENT

Small mechanical systems are serviced and maintained by general sets of tools as described for small engines in Chapter 17. However, many mechanical systems are very large, transmitting considerable power. For example, large conveyor systems can move ore a great distance. These require very large and heavy tools for servicing. The most prominent characteristic in the servicing of mechanical systems is the use of large heavy-duty tools.

A. Ball bearing

C. Tapered roller bearing

B. Cylindrical roller bearing

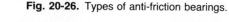

Fig. 20-26. Types of anti-friction bearings.

Chapter 20—Review

Testing Your Knowledge

Briefly answer each of the following questions. Write on a separate piece of paper.

1. List the three basic ways mechanical power systems can change input power.
2. Name the five most common mechanical control devices.
3. What is the main function of bevel gears and miter gears?
4. What is the main use of a worm gear set?
5. Gears can change input power in one way that sprocket and chain assemblies cannot. What is this advantage of using gears?
6. What special feature do adjustable chain drives have?
7. What are the three main types of gears in a planetary gear system?
8. What is the advantage of oil-impregnated bearings?
9. What are the three most common types of anti-friction bearings?

Solve these problems:

10. An automotive engine produces a torque of 120 pound-feet. This torque is transferred into the transmission, which is shifted into low gear. The gear provides a mechanical advantage in force of 3:1. What is the torque of the transmission output shaft?
11. If the input shaft of Item 10 is rotating at 1800 rpm, what is the speed of the transmission output shaft?
12. If the rear end assembly of an automobile has a fixed speed reduction of 4:1, and the input speed is 600 rpm, what is the output speed?
13. If the rear end assembly of Item 12 has an input torque of 400 pound-feet, what is its output torque?
14. If the rear wheels of the automobile of Item 12 have a diameter of 2 feet, what is the forward force being produced from the torque?

Expressing Your Knowledge

Using complete sentences, write your answers to the following on a separate sheet of paper:

1. Describe what happens to speed when force is increased by using the mechanical advantage of a machine.
2. What is a spur gear?
3. Identify the two major advantages of using helical gears instead of spur gears.
4. Give two advantages and one disadvantage of timing belts as compared to sprocket and chain assemblies.
5. Describe how an automotive friction clutch operates when it is engaged.
6. Describe the operation of a centrifugal clutch.
7. What is the function of a universal joint?

Applying Your Knowledge

Follow your teacher's instructions to complete these activities:

1. Clutches are important industrial devices. Identify as many applications of clutches that you can find. Use library and home resources to the extent available. Remember, clutches provide controlled on-and-off application of power. Two examples are:
   - ■ Automobile engine to transmission—The clutch permits the transmission to be shifted, and the engine runs while the car is standing still.
   - ■ Rotary lawn mower—A simple safety slipping clutch permits the blade to be stopped by an obstruction while the engine continues to run.

2. Prepare a written report that traces the transmission of power in a car from the pistons to the driven wheels. Describe the purpose of each part. Emphasize what happens during the following:
   - ■ Power stopping and starting
   - ■ Directional changes
   - ■ Changes in mechanical advantage

Fluid Power

Chapter 21
Fluid Power—Principles and Theory

Chapter 22
Fluid Power Systems

SECTION

Chapter 21

Fluid Power—Principles and Theory

Fluids work like machines in mechanical power systems. They also work like the electrons of electrical power systems. Fluid systems move and control power.

Expanding Your Knowledge

Learning about power and energy technology will help you understand more about the world around you. As you study this chapter, you will learn to:

- Explain what is meant by fluid power.
- Describe the differences between absolute and regular temperature and pressure scales.
- Explain how a Bourdon tube works as a pressure gage.
- Explain how the volume of a gas varies with changes in pressure and temperature.
- Describe how a fluid is able to transfer force as well as change the relationship between force and distance or speed.
- Solve mathematical problems involving changes in pressure, temperature, and volume in fluid power systems.

Building Your Word Power

Knowledge of the vocabulary used will help you develop greater understanding of power and energy. The following terms are defined and explained in this chapter. Learning these will help you learn more about fluid power systems.

absolute temperature scale
absolute zero
atmospheric pressure
Boyle's Law
Charles' Law
Fahrenheit temperature scale (°F)
fluid power
fluids
hydraulics
pneumatics
static head pressure
vacuum

Fluid power is the use of pressurized **fluids** (liquids and gases) to control and transmit power. The liquids and gases receive power from an outside source. The fluids then move through a system of transmission lines and control devices. They arrive at a location where the power is put to work.

We can use fluids in power systems because we know how they will react under certain conditions. Fluids react to changes in force, temperature, and volume. We can calculate the exact effect of any change.

Early experimenters developed an understanding of the basic principles of **pneumatics** (controlling gases) and **hydraulics** (controlling liquids). In this chapter, you will learn the most basic and important of the principles of fluid power.

FLUID PRESSURE

One of the most important measurements of fluid power is pressure. Chapter 6 explained pressure as a general unit of measurement. In this chapter, you will learn about atmospheric pressure, vacuums, and other factors that affect fluid pressure.

Atmospheric Pressure

Atmospheric pressure is the reference point, or standard, we use to measure fluid pressures. The air surrounding the earth applies a force of 14.7 pounds per square inch (psi) on the surface of the earth. We often round off this figure to 15 psi.

Most pressure gages are set so that atmospheric pressure registers as 0 psi. Some gages show pressures both above and below this point.

When we use gages in which 0 psi equals atmospheric pressure, we add the word *gage* to the reading. Therefore, **atmospheric pressure** is 0 pounds per square inch gage (psig). The *g* is often dropped from psig for convenience. Whenever you see a reading in psi, it means psig.

We usually measure pressure when we are using it to create motion. In most fluid power systems, no motion will occur until fluid pressure overcomes atmospheric pressure. Therefore, we are usually concerned with pressures above atmospheric pressure.

Vacuums

We refer to a pressure below atmospheric pressure as a **vacuum**. We base our measurements of vacuums on a method that shows that atmospheric pressure is about 15 psi. Mercury (symbolized as *Hg*) is a liquid metal. It weighs about ½-pound per cubic inch. A 1-square-inch column of mercury 30 inches high weighs about 15 pounds. This column of mercury equals atmospheric pressure. Therefore, we can use the column to measure fluid pressures.

Figure 21-1 shows several tubes standing in a dish of mercury. Unlike the other tubes, tube A

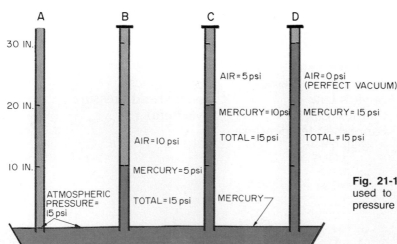

Fig. 21-1. The height of a column of mercury is used to measure a vacuum. A vacuum is any pressure less than atmospheric pressure.

A. REGULAR GAGE

B. COMPOUND GAGE

C. ABSOLUTE GAGE

Fig. 21-2. These commonly used gages all measure atmospheric pressure. A regular gage can be converted into an absolute gage by adjusting the dial to read 15 psi at atmospheric pressure.

is open at the top. Therefore, atmospheric pressure (15 psi) is equal inside and outside this tube.

Tube B is sealed at the top and ⅓ of the air in the tube has been pumped out. As a result, the pressure drops to 10 psi ⅓ of 15 is 5). Atmospheric pressure outside the tube then pushes mercury up the tube. It continues to do this until the pressure inside the tube equals the pressure outside the tube.

Using Metrics

In the metric system, pressure is measured in *pascals* instead of pounds per square inch. One pascal is the force of one newton acting on an area of one square meter. One kilopascal (kPa) equals 1000 pascals or 0.145 pound per square inch.

To achieve a balance of pressures, enough mercury to produce 5 psi must enter the tube. We know that mercury weighs ½ pound per cubic inch. At ½ psi for each inch, 10 inches produces 5 psi. Therefore, the mercury column must be 10 inches high. Added to the 10 psi of air pressure, the mercury balances atmospheric pressure.

Tube C of Fig. 21-1 shows a further removal of air (5 psi). The mercury now stands at 20 inches. This height is equal to 10 psi. Together, the mercury and the air balance atmospheric pressure. D in Fig. 21-1 shows all the air removed. No air pressure remains in the tube. This is an example of a *perfect vacuum*. It now takes a 30-inch column of mercury to balance the atmospheric pressure. This is the highest level to which atmospheric pressure can lift mercury.

You should now see that we can measure pressure by measuring the height of a column of mercury. Every inch of mercury equals ½ pound

of pressure below atmospheric pressure. Using this method, we can measure any vacuum.

Figure 21-2 compares some typical gage readings. Gage B measures pressures above atmospheric pressure in psi. It measures pressures below atmospheric pressure in inches of mercury. The zero point is atmospheric pressure. This gage is called a *compound gage*.

Gage A is the most common type of pressure gage. This gage is similar to gage B. It registers atmospheric pressure as 0. However, it does not show pressures below atmospheric pressure.

Gage C of Fig. 21-2 is an *absolute gage*. It registers atmospheric pressure at 15 psi. When we read this type of gage, we add the word "absolute" to the reading. Therefore, we read atmospheric pressure as 15 pounds per square inch absolute (psia). A perfect vacuum is 0 psia. Figure 21-3 shows a comparison of gage (psig) and absolute (psia) pressure readings.

Fig. 21-3. Compare the gage reading with the absolute reading. The bar shows that 0 psi gage is equal to 15 psi absolute. In the metric system, atmospheric pressure equals 0 kPa gage and 100 kPa absolute. (Use this chart for easy conversion when working with gas laws.)

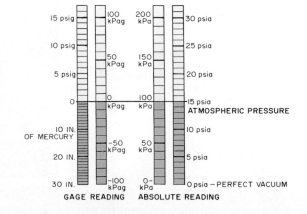

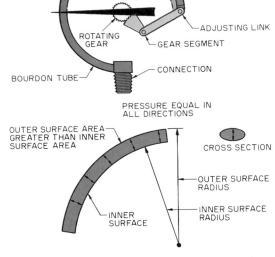

Fig. 21-4. The fluid pressure inside a Bourdon tube moves the tube. A gear-and-pointer arrangement connected to the tube indicates the pressure.

Pressures of Confined Fluids

In Chapter 6, you read that a force acting on a confined fluid exerts outward pressure equally in all directions. This property of fluids is the most basic principle of fluid power. We put it to use in many different fluid power applications. One example is the way in which we use it in pressure gages.

The most important part of most pressure gages is a *Bourdon tube.* This tube is circular in shape. In a gage, the tube connects with a source of pressurized gas or liquid. The Bourdon tube applies the principle of the even pressure of confined fluids.

Figure 21-4 shows the operation of a Bourdon tube. Notice how the shape of the tube affects the inner and outer surface areas. The outer surface area is greater than the inner. A fluid inside the tube applies the same pressure over any given area. However, since the outer surface has a greater area than the inner surface, the fluid pressure produces a greater force against the outer area. This difference in force tends to straighten the tube. The greater the pressure, the greater the difference in force. The tube straightens further as the pressure increases.

As the tube responds to added pressure, it rotates a gear segment. See Fig. 21-4 again. As the gear segment rotates, it moves a pointer. The pointer then shows the increase in pressure on the gage dial. A lessening of pressure has an opposite effect on the tube. This registers as a lower reading on the gage.

Static Head Pressure

A tank of liquid produces a varying amount of pressure from top to bottom. See Fig. 21-5.

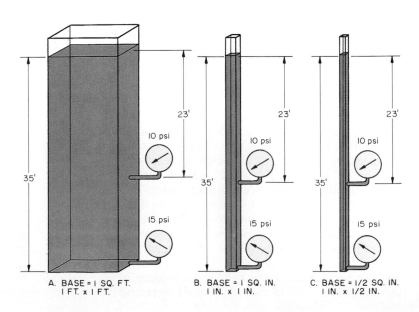

Fig. 21-5. The static head pressure in each of the three containers is 15 psi. As long as the height and the density of the liquid are the same, the psi measurement is not affected by changes in the total amount of liquid.

The weight of the liquid and the height of the tank determine this pressure. You can compare this pressure to the weight of the column of air in Fig. 21-1A. The pressure developed by the weight of a column of fluid is called **static head pressure**.

The pressure a column of liquid produces is the same regardless of the area it covers. We can apply this principle to the tubes of mercury in Fig. 21-1. The tubes may be smaller (or larger) than 1 square inch and still balance atmospheric pressure.

Note that in Fig. 21-5 the pressure in the middle of the column is less than that of the total column. This pressure is produced by the weight of the fluid above the point of the pressure reading.

PNEUMATICS—CONTROLLING GASES

Gases and liquids share many of the same properties. However, they are different in regard to volume. A fluid's *volume* is the amount of space it displaces. Liquids have a definite volume; gases do not. This means that pressure and temperature changes affect liquids differently than they affect gases. For example, as pressure increases, the volume of a gas decreases. The volume of a liquid does not change with pressure changes. See Fig. 21-6. This section describes what happens to gases when pressure and temperature changes occur.

Compression of Gases

Since a gas does not have a definite volume, it fills the volume of its container. A force applied to a gas confined in a container pushes the gas molecules closer together. We refer to this forcing together as *compression*.

Gas molecules resist compression. As force pushes the molecules closer together, they push back. They try to move further apart. The more the molecules are pushed together, the more they try to move apart.

This effort of the gas molecules to resist compression and move apart produces pressure. Scientists have found that the pressure of gas is *inversely proportional* to its volume. This means that any change in pressure produces an *equal but opposite* change in volume. For example, if we multiply the pressure by 2, the volume will be divided by 2.

This relationship between the pressure and volume of a gas is known as **Boyle's Law**. This law states, *"The volume of a gas varies inversely with the pressure applied to it, provided the temperature remains constant."* See Fig. 21-7. You can see by this statement that temperature also has an effect on the volume and pressure of a gas. You will learn more about this effect later in this chapter.

We can state Boyle's Law mathematically in several ways. One way is:

$$P_1V_1 = P_2V_2$$

Where:

P_1 = original pressure
V_1 = original volume
P_2 = new pressure
V_2 = new volume

Fig. 21-6. Both pressure and temperature affect the volume of gases, but not the volume of liquids. For example, when pressure is applied to a container of gas and liquid, only the gas is compressed.

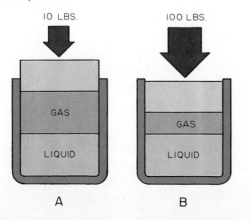

Fig. 21-7. Doubling the pressure on the gas from 15 psia to 30 psia reduces the volume by one-half. This is a demonstration of Boyle's law.

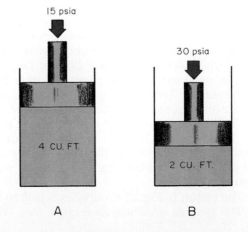

Technology Focus

It's In The Bag

A *pneumatic system* could soon provide millions of Americans with added protection during automobile accidents. In a collision, an air bag will inflate from under the dash or from within the steering column, cushion the front-seat passengers during impact, and then deflate. All of this will happen in 1/10th of a second! It happens so quickly that you'll simply feel the air bag, and then it will lay deflated in front of you—after the collision.

Air bags have been under development for years. Some cars already have them. By the early 1990s, many more new cars will be equipped with them, and someday air bags may be standard equipment. This type of pneumatic system could make driving safer and save thousands of lives.

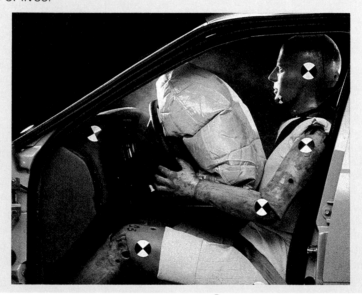

This formula assumes that the temperature stays the same. Notice how the formula works with the volumes and pressures in Fig. 21-7.

A: 15 psia (P_1) $\times$ 4 cu. ft. (V_1) = 60 (P_1V_1)
B: 30 psia (P_2) $\times$ 2 cu. ft. (V_2) = 60 (P_2V_2)

We can use the formula above to find the volume that will result from compressing a gas. (**Note**: Whenever we use the Boyle's Law formula, we must use *absolute* pressure rather than *gage* pressure. To change gage pressure (psig) into absolute pressure (psia), add 15. See Fig. 21-3. This is the correction for atmospheric pressure. If you use the formula to find an unknown pressure, you can convert the answer back into gage pressure by subtracting 15.)

Example problem:

The piston in Fig. 21-8A applies 5 psig to the gas. The gas has a volume of 8 cubic feet. What will be the volume of this gas if a piston compressed it to a pressure of 65 psig (Fig. 21-8B)?

1) Change gage pressure to absolute pressure:
$$psia = psig + 15; \text{ therefore,}$$
$$P_1 = 5 + 15$$
$$P_1 = 20 \text{ psia, and}$$
$$P_2 = 65 + 15$$
$$P_2 = 80 \text{ psia}$$

2) Solve for new volume:
$$P_1V_1 = P_2V_2$$
$$20 \text{ psia} \times 8 \text{ cu. ft.} = 80 \text{ psia} \times V_2$$
$$\frac{20 \text{ psia} \times 8 \text{ cu. ft.}}{80 \text{ psia}} = \frac{80 \text{ psia} \times V_2}{80 \text{ psia}}$$
$$V_2 = 2 \text{ cu. ft.}$$

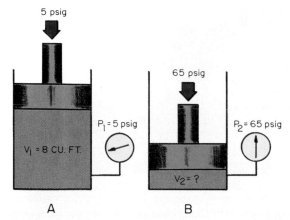

5 psig

65 psig

P₁ = 5 psig

P₂ = 65 psig

V₁ = 8 CU. FT.

V₂ = ?

A   B

Fig. 21-8. We can use a mathematical expression of Boyle's Law—$P_1 V_1 = P_2 V_2$—to find an unknown volume when we know the change in pressure.

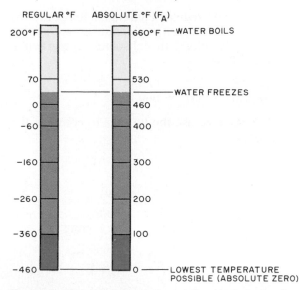

Fig. 21-9. This chart shows the relationship between the regular Fahrenheit temperature scale and the absolute Fahrenheit temperature scale. (Use this chart when converting temperatures for gas laws.)

You may have realized already that the volume-pressure relationship works in reverse. A change in volume creates an equal but opposite change in pressure. We can use the same formula to find the new pressure.

Effects of Heat on Gases

You have just read about how pressure affects the volume of a gas. The temperature of a gas also affects its volume. Whenever we talk about the volume of a gas, we must know the temperature at which the volume is measured.

Two scientists, *Jacques Charles* and *Joseph Gay-Lussac*, are given credit for explaining the relationship between the temperature and volume of a gas (**Charles' Law**). These scientists showed that the volume of a gas is *directly proportional* to the temperature. That is, any change in temperature produces an equal change in volume. However, this occurs only if the pressure stays the same. For example, if a gas's temperature doubles, its volume will also double as long as the pressure does not change. In equation form:

$$\frac{V_1}{T_1} = \frac{V_2}{T_2}$$

Where:

V_1 = original volume
T_1 = original temperature
V_2 = new volume
T_2 = new temperature

We can use this formula to calculate a change in volume due to heat. To do this, we must express the temperatures according to an

absolute temperature scale. On this type of scale, 0° is the temperature at which a material has no heat. This is the coldest possible condition. We call this temperature **absolute zero**. As you remember, heat is the motion of molecules. Absolute zero is the temperature at which molecular motion stops. Therefore, the material can get no colder. Figure 21-9 compares the absolute Fahrenheit scale with the regular **Fahrenheit temperature scale** (°F). Absolute Fahrenheit temperature is written °F_A (degrees Fahrenheit absolute).

The container in Fig. 21-10A holds 4 cubic feet of gas under a pressure of 15 psia at 68°F. In **B** the temperature has risen to 200°F. The pressure has stayed at 15 psia. After changing the regular temperatures to absolute temperatures, we can use our formula to determine the volume in **B**.

Fig. 21-10. As a gas is heated, its molecules move faster and faster. This increases the volume of the gas if the pressure stays the same.

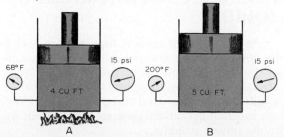

To change regular Fahrenheit temperatures to absolute Fahrenheit temperatures, we simply add 460°. Therefore, the absolute temperatures for **A** and **B** are:

A: $68° + 460° = 528°F_A$
B: $200° + 460° = 660°F_A$

We can now use the formula to compute the new volume:

$$\frac{V_1}{T_1} = \frac{V_2}{T_2}$$

$$\frac{4 \text{ cu. ft.}}{528° \text{ F}_A} = \frac{V_2}{660°F_A}$$

$$4 \text{ cu. ft.} \times \frac{660°F_A}{528°F_A} = \frac{V_2 \times 660°F_A}{660°F_A}$$

$$V_2 = 5 \text{ cu. ft.}$$

Temperature can affect the pressure of a gas in the same way that it affects volume. If the volume stays constant, the pressure increases or decreases in proportion to a temperature change. To express the temperature-pressure relationship, we can substitute pressure for volume in the formula used above. The result is:

$$\frac{P_1}{T_1} = \frac{P_2}{T_2}$$

This formula can be used only in situations in which the volume does not change. Also, the values for this formula must be in *absolute temperature and absolute pressure*.

In most cases, a temperature change affects both volume and pressure. Neither factor remains constant. When this happens, the combined change in volume and pressure is directly proportionate to the temperature change. We can express this relationship as:

$$\frac{P_1V_1}{T_1} = \frac{P_2V_2}{T_2}$$

HYDRAULICS—CONTROLLING LIQUIDS

As you learned earlier, liquids have a definite volume. Under normal conditions, they cannot be compressed. This property of liquids permits a direct and efficient transfer of force. Liquids can also be used to multiply force. Very high mechanical advantages are possible in hydraulic power systems.

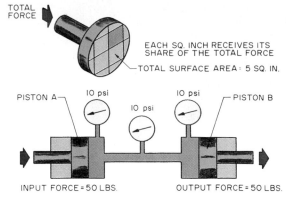

Fig. 21-11. In this fluid power system, the pressure is determined by two factors: the input force and the area of the piston.

Transferring Force Through Liquids

Figure 21-11 shows how liquids transfer force. The force applied to piston A produces a pressure on the fluid. The fluid then exerts the same amount of pressure equally in all directions. As a result, the pressure applied to piston A transfers to piston B.

Changes in the size or shape of the fluid's container do not affect its transmission of force. The diameter of the pipe between pistons A and B is much smaller than it is on either end. However, this does not affect the amount of force applied to piston B. As long as the pipe is large enough to permit fluid flow, the input and output forces will be equal.

This equal transmission of force occurs even if we change the direction of flow. In Fig. 21-12 fluid is flowing upward as it pushes on piston B. It still supplies the same input force (50 pounds) to piston B.

Fig. 21-12. Changes in direction do not change the transfer of force through a liquid.

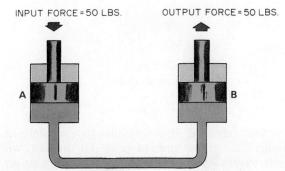

You should remember from Chapter 6 that pressure is force per unit of area. In equation form:

$$\text{Pressure} = \frac{\text{Force}}{\text{Area}}$$

Figure 21-11 shows how we determine pressure in a fluid power system. A force of 50 pounds is applied to the 5-square-inch piston. Each square inch of the piston receives ⅕ of the total force. Therefore, the mechanical force is equal to 10 psi. The amount of force has not changed, only the way in which the force is measured.

Multiplying Force with Liquids

We can use a fluid's ability to transmit forces to produce a gain in mechanical advantage. (For an explanation of mechanical advantage, see Chapter 19.) Figure 21-13 shows how this is done through the use of two pistons of different size. A force of 50 pounds is applied to piston A. Piston A has an area of 5 square inches. Therefore, the pressure throughout the fluid is 10 psi.

Piston B has an area of 20 square inches. The force of 10 psi pushes up on this piston. We can calculate output force with the following formula:

Force = Pressure × Area

Therefore, the output force is 10 × 20, or 200 pounds. The ratio of output force to input force is 200:50. This is a mechanical advantage of 4 to 1.

However, you will recall from Chapter 19 that gain in force always means an equal loss in distance or speed. In Fig. 21-13 the gain in force is offset by an equal loss in distance. The 50-pound input force must move 4 inches to move the 200-pound output force 1 inch.

The flow of fluid from one cylinder to the other makes piston movement possible. To move up 1 inch, the output piston needs 20 cubic inches of fluid. We determine this by multiplying the piston area (20 square inches) times the distance moved (1 inch). The input piston area is only ¼ that of the output piston. It displaces (moves) only 5 cubic inches of fluid for each inch of travel (5 square inches × 1 inch). As you can see, the input piston must travel 4 inches to displace the 20 cubic inches of fluid.

In the actual operation of a system such as the one in Fig. 21-13, motion occurs only after friction is overcome. The system is balanced with 10 psi. For motion to occur, the input force must be increased enough to overcome the friction within the system.

We usually refer to the movement of fluid as *flow*. With hydraulic systems, we measure flow in terms of *gallons per minute (gpm)*. With pneumatic systems, we measure the flow in *cubic feet per minute (cfm)*.

Fig. 21-13. We can multiply force by using different size cylinders and pistons. A four-inch downward movement of piston A produces only a one-inch upward movement of piston B. However, due to the relative piston sizes, there is a mechanical advantage in force of 4:1.

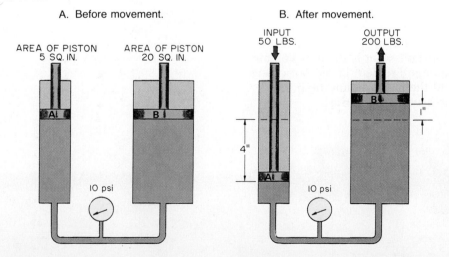

A. Before movement.

B. After movement.

Chapter 21—Review

Testing Your Knowledge

Briefly answer each of the following questions. Write on a separate piece of paper.
1. What amount of pressure does the atmosphere exert on the earth?
2. What is the pressure reading of a perfect vacuum on a compound gage?
3. On an absolute gage, what is the pressure reading of atmospheric pressure? of a perfect vacuum?
4. What design feature of the Bourdon tube makes it straighten as pressure increases?
5. What is static head pressure?
6. If the pressure on a gas remains constant and the temperature increases, what happens to the volume of the gas?
7. On the regular Fahrenheit scale, what is the temperature at which all molecules stop moving?
8. Show the mathematical relationship between temperature change and combined change in volume and pressure.

Solve these problems:

9. A gage reads *30 psig*. What would the reading be in absolute pressure (psia)?
10. The pressure at the top of Pike's Peak is 9 psia. What would the gage pressure (psig) be?
11. If 12 cubic feet of gas has a pressure increase from 10 psig to 45 psig without a temperature change, what is the new volume?
12. If a regular Fahrenheit thermometer reads 70°, what is the absolute Fahrenheit temperature?
13. A gas having a volume of 4 cubic feet is heated from 90°F to 640°F. If the pressure remains constant, what is the new volume?
14. If the volume in Problem 13 did not change, what would the new pressure be if the starting pressure was 35 psig?

Expressing Your Knowledge

Using complete sentences, write your answers to the following on a separate sheet of paper:
1. What is fluid power?
2. Describe the scale that uses psig (pounds per square inch gage) as a measure of pressure.
3. State Boyle's Law.
4. What is absolute zero?
5. Describe the relationship between the pressure and the temperature of a gas when the volume remains constant.
6. Describe how fluid transfers force.

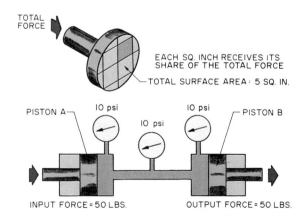

TOTAL FORCE

EACH SQ. INCH RECEIVES ITS SHARE OF THE TOTAL FORCE

TOTAL SURFACE AREA: 5 SQ. IN.

PISTON A — 10 psi · 10 psi · 10 psi — PISTON B

INPUT FORCE = 50 LBS. · OUTPUT FORCE = 50 LBS.

Knowledge Is Power

Applying Your Knowledge

Follow your teacher's instructions to complete these activities:

1. Measure the mechanical advantage of a hydraulic floor jack. Record and explain the results of your experiment on a separate sheet of paper.

   Pump up the jack, measuring the distance the jack moves up versus the distance the handle moves down. Determine theoretical mechanical advantage. The hydraulic jack gains mechanical advantage from both the hydraulic cylinder and lever action.

   The experiment provided theoretical mechanical advantage. How could you determine actual mechanical advantage?

2. A vacuum is a pressure below atmospheric pressure. It is measured in inches of mercury. Identify as many applications as you can for the use of a vacuum. Use the library to identify different uses. Select one use and describe how vacuum is used.

Chapter 22

Fluid Power Systems

Fluid power has served humanity throughout the ages. Wind and water were natural sources of fluid power. Today, fluid power systems are complex and highly developed. They are extremely important in our industrial society.

Expanding Your Knowledge

As you study this chapter, you will learn to:

- Identify and explain the function of each of the seven major parts of a fluid power system: fluid, reservoir or receiver, filter, pump or compressor, control valves, transmission lines, and actuators.
- Describe the function and operation of a filter, regulator, and lubricator (FRL) unit.
- Explain the operation of pumps and compressors, including the piston pump, lobe pump, gear pump, and continuous-flow air compressor.
- Describe the operation and use of valves, including globe valves, gate valves, plug valves, needle valves, two-way spool valves, three-way valves, four-way valves, check valves, pressure relief valves, and pressure control valves.
- Explain what is meant by *pressure drop* in a fluid power system.
- Identify the factors that determine the torque and speed of a fluid power motor.

Building Your Word Power

The following terms are defined and explained in this chapter. Learning these will help you learn more about fluid power systems.

actuator
compressor
connector
cylinder
filter
fluid power motor
fluid power system
pump
receiver
reservoir
valve

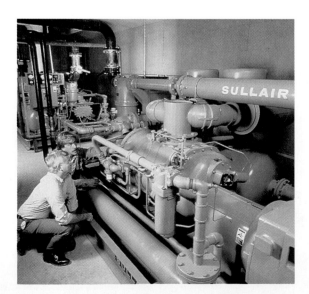

Fluid power systems convert mechanical power into fluid power. They transmit and control the fluid power. Then they change the power back into mechanical form. In this form, the power can do work. Fluid power systems are not sources of power. Outside sources must develop the original power. These sources are usually engines and electric motors.

Since it does not produce its own power, a fluid power system is most often one part of a larger power system. The larger system usually consists of mechanical systems, other fluid power systems, and electrical systems.

Fluid power systems have the ability to provide very high mechanical advantage. Because of this, they serve many valuable industrial functions. They produce huge gains in force in relatively small spaces. Fluid power systems are also very flexible. They can carry power to wherever a pipe, hose, or piece of tubing can be placed.

Fluid power systems provide much of the power for earth-moving equipment used in construction and mining. They provide the power to run production lines and pneumatic tools. They can power everything from dentist's drills to large industrial presses. Fluid systems are important means of transmitting and controlling power.

TYPES OF FLUID SYSTEMS

A **fluid power system** is an assembly of units that controls the flow of pressurized fluid. It transmits power from an energy source (input) to a power use (output).

There are two types of fluid power systems: hydraulic and pneumatic. *Hydraulic systems* use a liquid, usually oil, to transmit power. *Pneumatic systems* use a gas, usually air, to transmit power.

The basic operating principles of hydraulics and pneumatics are very similar. You read about these principles in Chapter 21. In this chapter, you will read about the actual parts of the two systems. All fluid power systems have the following parts:

- The *fluid* may be either a gas, a liquid, or both.
- A *reservoir or receiver* is a container that stores fluid.
- A *filter* is a device that cleans the fluid as it travels through the system.
- A *pump or compressor* is a device that converts mechanical power into fluid power. It supplies fluid under pressure to the system.
- *Control valves* are devices that regulate the fluid pressure, flow rate, and direction.
- *Transmission lines* consist of a system of pipes, hoses, and tubes. These parts contain the fluid so it can be transmitted under pressure.
- An *actuator* may be a cylinder, motor, or other converter that changes fluid pressure into the desired mechanical form.

Before learning about the parts of fluid power systems, we will compare the two types. We will follow the complete path of the fluid through both the hydraulic and the pheumatic systems, and then study the individual parts. You should be able to see how the parts work in an entire system.

Hydraulic Systems

Hydraulic systems are important parts of almost all transportation vehicles. Many braking devices, transmissions, power-assisting devices, and auxiliary power units are designed as fluid power systems.

Figure 22-1 shows the hydraulic system used to operate the landing gear of an airplane. The fluid in this system is oil. The same type of hydraulic system is used to operate automobile power steering and braking systems. Large industrial presses also use this type of system.

Figure 22-1 shows the path of the fluid as the pilot lowers the landing gear. The oil pump pumps the oil from the reservoir, through the filter, and into the transmission lines. The oil travels past the hand shutoff valve into a four-way valve. The pilot operates the four-way valve manually. With the valve in the position shown, the oil flows to the upper end of the double-acting cylinder. The oil is under pressure from the pump. Therefore, it pushes the piston inside the cylinder downward. This activates mechanical devices connected to the piston. These devices lower the landing gear.

The cylinder also contains oil below the piston. As the piston moves downward, it forces oil out the bottom of the cylinder. The oil travels

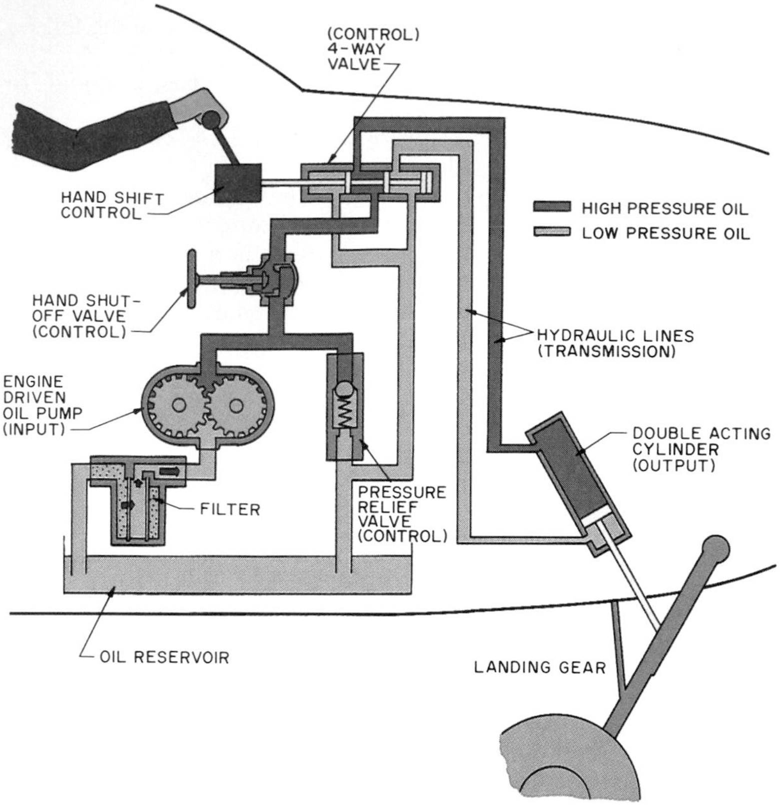

Fig. 22-1. A hydraulic system can be used to raise and lower an airplane landing gear. Here the system is in the gear *down* position.

through a transmission line under low pressure. It passes through the four-way valve. Then it returns to the reservoir. This completes the oil's circuit through the system. This kind of hydraulic system maintains a steady, constant flow of power.

Notice the pressure relief valve in Fig. 22-1. The oil did not pass through this valve on the path just described. However, this valve is a very important part of the system. The pressure relief valve protects the system. If the pressure gets too high, the pressure relief valve opens. This allows high-pressure oil to return to the reservoir, thus reducing system pressure.

To raise the landing gear, the pilot shifts the position of the four-way valve. See Fig. 22-2. The valve directs high-pressure oil to the other end of the double-acting cylinder. The oil pushes up on the piston. This raises the landing gear. At the same time, the oil in the top of the cylinder flows back through the four-way valve to the reservoir. This completes the circuit.

Pneumatic Systems

Industrial use of pneumatics has grown over the past century. In that short time, pneumatics has replaced vast amounts of manual labor. It

has also replaced many mechanical and electrical systems. In comparison with fluid systems, mechanical systems are slow and clumsy and electrical systems are costly and complex.

Figure 22-3 shows the parts of a typical pneumatic system. Garages use this system to lift automobiles and trucks for servicing and repairing. This is an *air-over-oil* system. It uses both air and oil.

The pneumatic circuit begins with air traveling from the compressor to a storage tank called a **receiver**. The receiver stores pressurized air until the system needs it. As the system uses air, more air flows from the receiver. It passes through a shutoff valve. Then it continues to an air-processing unit. This unit cleans the air. It also lubricates the air with a fine oil mist.

After processing, the high-pressure air travels through a three-way valve. From there it flows into a pressure cylinder. There is oil in the bottom of this cylinder. The incoming air forces the oil into the hydraulic cylinder. This raises the ram on which the car is mounted.

Like the hydraulic landing gear system, this pneumatic system has a pressure-relief valve. The valve protects the system from excessive pressure. This valve is at the left of the receiver in Fig. 22-3A.

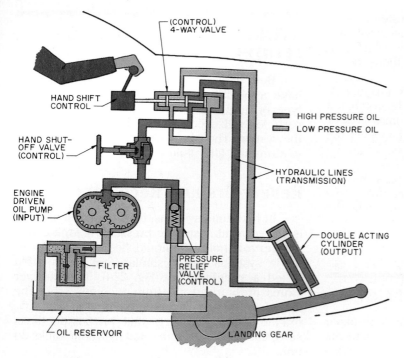

Fig. 22-2. A hydraulic landing gear system in the gear *up* position.

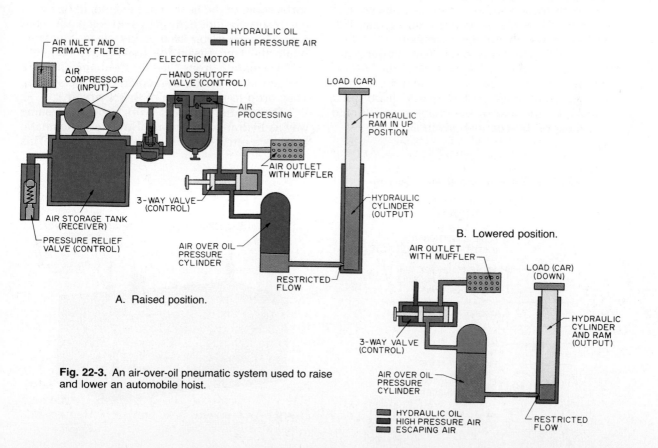

Fig. 22-3. An air-over-oil pneumatic system used to raise and lower an automobile hoist.

Figure 22-3B shows how the system lowers the ram. The operator shifts the three-way valve. This allows the air in the pressure cylinder to flow back through the valve. From there the air escapes into the atmosphere.

As the air escapes, the pressure pushing oil into the hydraulic cylinder drops. The combined weight of the car and the ram becomes greater than the air pressure. When this happens, the ram moves downward. It pushes oil back into the pressure cylinder.

On its way back, the oil must pass through a small opening. This restriction controls how fast the lift lowers. This safety feature keeps the hoist from coming down too fast.

FLUID SYSTEM DRAWINGS

Fluid power systems are designed on paper before they are produced. By first drawing the systems, engineers and technicians can quickly figure the materials and parts needed to do the job.

Engineers use symbols to show the different parts, positions, and fluids in fluid power systems. With these symbols, they can quickly and accurately illustrate an entire fluid system. Figure 22-4 shows several basic symbols.

You will see many other fluid power symbols in this chapter. They are near the discussions of the parts that they symbolize. As you study different fluid system parts, learn their symbols. By the end of the chapter, you should know most of the common symbols.

STORING AND FILTERING FLUIDS

Both hydraulic and pneumatic systems must have a plentiful supply of fluid. Whatever the type of fluid, it must be clean. Otherwise, dirt particles will decrease the efficiency and life of the system. The two systems use similar devices to store and filter fluids.

Reservoirs and Receivers

In hydraulic systems, the liquid (usually oil) is stored at atmospheric pressure. A tank called a **reservoir** holds the liquid. See Fig. 22-5. Pneumatic systems use a similar tank. It is often called a **receiver**. See Fig. 22-6. The receiver stores pressurized gas from a compressor. The major difference between pneumatic and hydraulic storage tanks is that pneumatic tanks store fluid under pressure and hydraulic tanks do not.

The typical hydraulic reservoir serves several important functions. Its main purpose, of course, is to store hydraulic liquid. Another purpose is cooling. The air around the reservoir absorbs some of the heat from the fluid. In this way, the reservoir indirectly helps to keep the fluid cool. The reservoir also helps clean the fluid. While the fluid sits in the tank, heavy contaminants separate from the oil. Contaminants are dirt and other matter that could clog the system. They drop to the bottom of the reservoir.

Pneumatic receivers work much the same way as hydraulic reservoirs. However, pneumatic tanks are often larger than hydraulic tanks. This

Fig. 22-4. Some basic fluid power symbols.

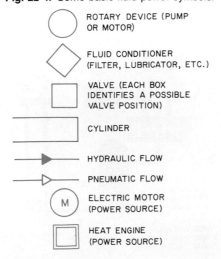

ROTARY DEVICE (PUMP OR MOTOR)

FLUID CONDITIONER (FILTER, LUBRICATOR, ETC.)

VALVE (EACH BOX IDENTIFIES A POSSIBLE VALVE POSITION)

CYLINDER

HYDRAULIC FLOW

PNEUMATIC FLOW

ELECTRIC MOTOR (POWER SOURCE)

HEAT ENGINE (POWER SOURCE)

Fig. 22-5. A typical oil reservoir.

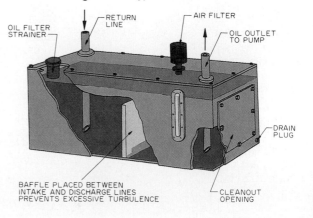

OIL FILTER STRAINER

RETURN LINE

AIR FILTER

OIL OUTLET TO PUMP

DRAIN PLUG

BAFFLE PLACED BETWEEN INTAKE AND DISCHARGE LINES PREVENTS EXCESSIVE TURBULENCE

CLEANOUT OPENING

Fig. 22-6. In pneumatic systems, the storage tank is often called a receiver. It receives pressurized air from the compressor.

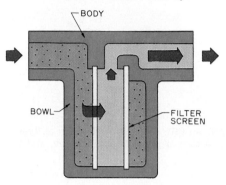

Fig. 22-7. Operation of a hydraulic oil filter.

is because gases require more space than liquids. Also, the tank itself needs more space in the system. Therefore, receivers are often farther from the output location than reservoirs are.

Filters

As fluids move through fluid systems, they pick up dirt and dust particles. The smallest bit of dirt or metal can damage a part. It can even cause a system to break down. Contamination will also cause parts to wear out faster. To function at peak efficiency, fluid systems must be kept clean. **Filters** help keep fluid systems clean by removing dirt and contaminants.

Hydraulic Filters. Hydraulic systems have at least one filter. Large systems and systems exposed to extremely dirty conditions may have many filters.

Hydraulic filters come in a wide variety of materials and designs. However, basic design and operation are the same for all filters. See Fig. 22-7. As liquid passes through the filter, it moves through a porous material. (*Porous* means having many small holes.) This material removes foreign matter from the liquid. Fluid power mechanics must periodically remove foreign matter from the filter. They do this by either cleaning or replacing the porous material.

Pneumatic Filters. The air used in pneumatic systems usually contains moisture and dirt. After compression, the air passes through a filter. See Fig. 22-8. The internal shape of the filter causes the air to swirl. Centrifugal force throws water and large particles of dirt out of the air. It deposits them on the inner surface of the filter bowl. The dirt and water eventually fall to the bottom.

The air then passes through the *filter element*. This element has a fine screen. The screen blocks any remaining dirt and moisture from entering the fluid lines.

Mechanics open the drain cock at the bottom of the filter periodically. They drain water that has condensed in the filter. They also remove dirt that has collected.

Fig. 22-8. As the air swirls in this pneumatic air filter, centrifugal force throws out dirt and water.

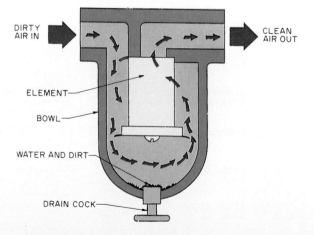

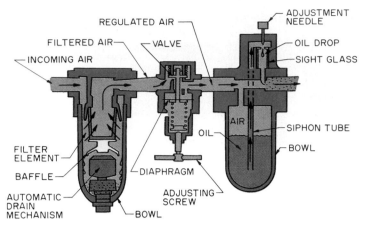

Fig. 22-9. An FRL unit is a combination of three devices: a filter, a pressure control valve, and a lubricator.

Many of the parts in a pneumatic system must be lubricated. Adding a small amount of oil to the air gives the system enough lubrication. A device called a *lubricator* adds oil to the air. In many pneumatic systems, the lubricator is combined with the filter. In other systems, the filter and lubricator are combined with a pressure control valve called a regulator. The entire assembly is called an *FRL unit*. FRL stands for filter, regulator, lubricator. See Figs. 22-9 and 22-10. You will learn about the pressure control valves later in this chapter.

PUMPS AND COMPRESSORS

As previously mentioned, fluid systems usually receive their power input from either an engine or an electric motor. The systems must have devices to convert mechanical input into fluid movement. *Pumps* have this function in hydraulic systems. *Compressors* serve the same purpose in pneumatic systems.

Pumps

The most important part of a hydraulic system is its pump. The **pump** converts incoming mechanical power into fluid power. It also moves the fluid under pressure throughout the system. The pump is the "heart" of the hydraulic system.

There are many different pump designs. In this section, we will consider three general types. The *piston pump* will show you the basic principles of pump operation. Then you will learn about *gear pumps* and *vane pumps*.

Most hydraulic pumps are *positive-displacement pumps*. These pumps take in a fixed amount of fluid. Then they push the fluid through the system under pressure. We measure the capacities, or outputs, of these pumps in terms of

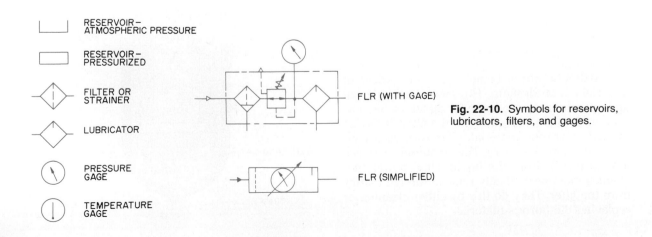

RESERVOIR–
ATMOSPHERIC PRESSURE

RESERVOIR–
PRESSURIZED

FILTER OR
STRAINER

LUBRICATOR

PRESSURE
GAGE

TEMPERATURE
GAGE

FLR (WITH GAGE)

FLR (SIMPLIFIED)

Fig. 22-10. Symbols for reservoirs, lubricators, filters, and gages.

total fluid displacement. We say that there are so many cubic inches of displacement per revolution of the mechanical power input shaft.

Manually Operated Piston Pump. Figure 22-11 shows a manually operated reciprocating piston pump. By pulling and pushing on the lever, a worker raises and lowers the input piston. This action raises the output piston. Pumps of this type are used in hydraulic jacks and some presses.

The upward movement of the input piston creates a low-pressure area in the piston chamber. See Fig. 22-11A. This allows atmospheric pressure to force open the intake check valve. Liquid then flows from the reservoir past the check valve. It flows through the charge line and into the input piston chamber.

Before the piston starts downward, the input piston chamber is filled with liquid. As the piston moves down, it increases the pressure of the liquid in the piston chamber. See Fig. 22-11B. First the liquid tries to go back into the reservoir. However, the reverse flow pushes the intake check valve shut. The pressurized liquid then pushes open the discharge check valve. At the same time, the load is pushing on liquid on the other side of the valve. The input side liquid must push harder than the load does. If this happens, the discharge check valve will open. The liquid will then flow into the discharge line. The pressure of the liquid on the output piston will raise the load. When the input piston starts back up, the whole series of actions repeats.

In-Line Multi-Piston Pump. Most piston pumps are powered by an engine or motor rather than by a manually operated lever. These power sources usually supply enough power to drive more than one piston. Pumps with several pistons are often called in-line multi-piston pumps. A rotating shaft provides the power input for this type of pump. The pistons operate with reciprocating (back-and-forth) motion. Therefore, the shaft's rotary motion must be changed to reciprocating motion. This is done by special devices. One such device is a wedge-shaped part called a *swashplate.*

A. Intake stroke. Piston moves up.

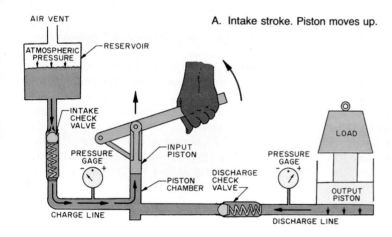

B. Discharge stroke. Piston moves down.

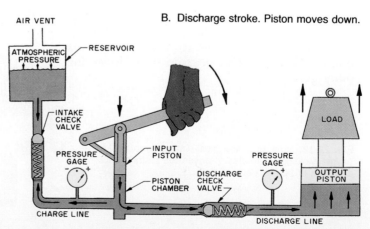

Fig. 22-11. Operation of a simple manually operated reciprocating piston pump.

Technology Focus

The Heart of The Matter

The world's most reliable fluid power pump is inside the human body. Yes, it's the heart! Think about it. Your heart runs itself, using energy from common food. It regulates itself, adjusting from heavy work loads to the light demands of sleep. Sometimes it even repairs itself, often recovering from a heart attack (partial failure) to provide many more years of good service.

In just one day, your heart will beat 100,000 times, pumping 2,000 gallons of blood. That's the same amount of work as is required to move 248 hundred-pound kegs of nails from the first floor to the second floor of a building.

Hearts work continuously, some for more than 100 years. While they require some care, proper food, and exercise, hearts are the most trouble-free pumps in the world.

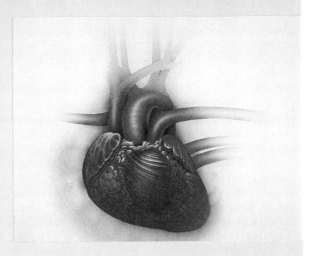

Figure 22-12 shows the operation of a typical in-line multi-piston pump. The swashplate attaches to the input shaft. The bottom of the pistons ride freely on top of the swashplate. As the swashplate turns, the pistons alternately raise and lower. They do this because of the angle of the swashplate. The moving pistons work like the input piston of a manually operated pump. The more pistons a pump has, the greater its output. More pistons also create a smoother flow of liquid through the system.

Gear Pumps. Gear pumps are fairly simple pumps. They consist of two gears inside a housing. See Fig. 22-13. The two gears mesh and rotate in opposite directions. An input shaft drives one of the gears. This gear, in turn, drives the other gear.

As the gear teeth turn past the inlet port, they pick up liquid. Each tooth pushes a certain amount of liquid along the inside of the pump housing. The teeth then force the liquid through the outlet (discharge) port.

Figure 22-14 shows a lobe pump. This is a variation of the gear pump. The lobe pump has the same pumping action as the gear pump. Its advantage is that its lobes can move more liquid faster than gear teeth can. The disadvantage is that one lobe cannot drive the other lobe. Both lobes must be driven.

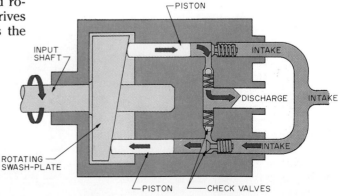

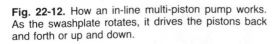
Fig. 22-12. How an in-line multi-piston pump works. As the swashplate rotates, it drives the pistons back and forth or up and down.

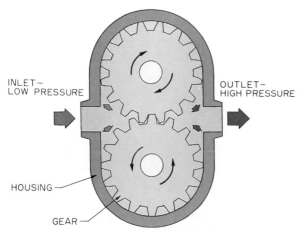

Fig. 22-13. The gears of a gear pump pick up fluid and carry it under pressure to the outlet side of the pump.

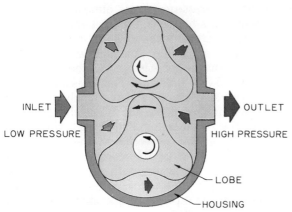

Fig. 22-14. In a lobe pump, the rotating lobes drive liquid through the pump.

low-pressure area in the chambers. The low pressure allows oil to flow into them. As the chambers approach the outlet side, they decrease in size. The smaller size creates higher pressure in the chambers. This forces the liquid into the discharge lines.

Compressors

The air **compressor** is the pump of a pneumatic system. It operates on the same basic principles as the hydraulic pump. Both convert mechanical power into fluid power. However, the air compressor pumps gases instead of liquids. Construction workers use this type of compressor to power pneumatic tools. See Fig. 22-16.

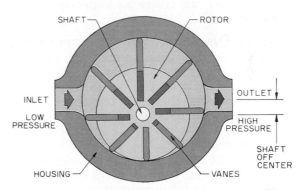

Fig. 22-15. As the rotor turns in a vane pump, two things happen: the vanes rotate and they slide out to the inner wall of the housing.

Vane Pumps. Vane pumps use sliding vanes to move liquid through the pump. This type of pump has four main parts. These are the rotor, sliding vanes, drive shaft, and housing. See Fig. 22-15. The rotor is not centered in the pump housing. It is offset to one side. This creates a large open space on the other side of the rotor.

In operation, the drive shaft turns the rotor clockwise. As the rotor turns, the vanes rotate. At the same time, centrifugal force or small springs push the vanes out against the housing.

As the rotor turns, liquid is trapped between the vanes on the inlet side of the pump. The vanes then carry the liquid to the discharge side of the pump. From there, the liquid passes into the discharge line.

The spaces between vanes are called *chambers*. Notice that the chambers increase in size as they approach the inlet. This action creates a

Fig. 22-16. This air compressor is powered by a gasoline engine. Because the compressor does not require electricity, it can be used almost anywhere.

There are many different designs of compressors used in pneumatic power systems. We can divide these designs into two different types:

■ Continuous-flow
■ Positive-displacement

Continuous-Flow Compressors.

Continuous-flow compressors are also called *variable (non-positive) displacement compressors*. This type of compressor uses high-speed rotating blades. See Fig. 22-17. These blades give the gas mechanical energy. In other words, the blades speed up a large volume of the gas. This type of gas flow is an example of kinetic energy. We cannot store this energy.

Continuous-flow compressors are used in industry to transport gases and added materials. Large volumes of compressed air also move grain, minerals, and chemicals from one location to another.

Positive-Displacement Compressors.

A positive-displacement compressor converts mechanical power into pneumatic power. It does this by both pumping and pressurizing air. To help you understand how a compressor works, we will look at a *single-piston reciprocating air compressor*. This is one of the most commonly used compressors.

Figure 22-18 shows how a reciprocating compressor works. The downward movement of the piston creates a low-pressure area above the piston. When the pressure is low enough, atmospheric pressure pushes the inlet valve open. See Fig. 22-18A. Air then flows into the cylinder until

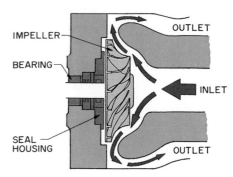

Fig. 22-17. Continuous-flow compressors use centrifugal force to move large volumes of air.

the cylinder pressure equals atmospheric pressure. When this happens, the inlet valve closes.

As the piston moves upward, it compresses the air into a smaller space. You learned in Chapter 21 that a decrease in volume causes an equal increase in pressure. This pressure forces the intake valve closed and the discharge valve open. The air then flows out the discharge valve and into the receiver. See Fig. 22-18B. This cycle continues to fill the receiver with pressurized air.

The operation of the compressor is controlled by the pressure in the receiver. If the power source is an electric motor, the receiver usually has a pressure-operated electrical switch. The switch is preset to a certain pressure for the system. When the receiver pressure falls

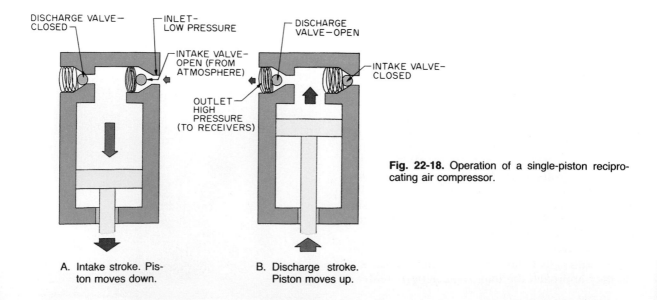

Fig. 22-18. Operation of a single-piston reciprocating air compressor.

below the set amount, the switch turns the compressor on. When the power source is an engine, a bypass valve usually controls the compressor.

There are several other kinds of positive-displacement compressors. But they all work on the same principles as the reciprocating compressor.

Figure 22-19 shows the symbols used to identify both oil pumps and air compressors.

CONTROL VALVES

Many types of **valves** are used in fluid power systems to control the flow of fluid. The operator uses the valves to start and stop the flow. The valves also change the fluid's force, speed, and direction. Some valves are preset to maintain safe pressures throughout the system.

On-Off Valves

Operators use many different kinds of valves to turn fluid flow on and off. They often refer to these valves as *two-way valves*. Two-way valves are mainly on-off valves. However, operators also use some two-way valves to meter (regulate) fluid flow. This section describes five common types of two-way valves.

Globe Valves.
Globe valves are simple and very reliable. They are used extensively in home and industry. Their main function is to provide on-off control of fluid flow.

Figure 22-20 shows how a globe valve works. Fluid passing through the valve must pass

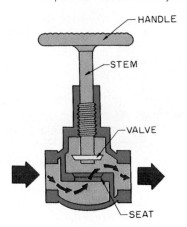

Fig. 22-20. A globe valve in the open position.

through the valve seat. When the operator turns the valve stem down, the valve rests tightly against the seat. This stops the flow of the fluid. Turning the stem up releases the flow.

Globe valves force fluid to change direction twice as it passes through. This creates some resistance. When the rate of flow is high, resistance can cause a loss of pressure. Usually this loss is small. In general, the globe valve is an inexpensive and reliable valve.

Gate Valves.
The gate valve is as reliable as the globe valve. In a gate valve, the fluid does not change direction as it passes through. This makes the gate valve more efficient than the globe valve. However, gate valves are more expensive. Gate valves are used on systems with high rates of flow.

Figure 22-21 shows how a gate valve works. Turning the stem up moves the tapered wedge (gate) up. This allows fluid to flow freely. Turning the stem down lowers the wedge and blocks the flow.

Fig. 22-21. A gate valve in the closed position.

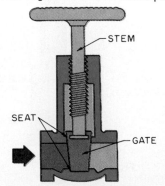

Fig. 22-19. Symbols for oil pumps and air compressors.

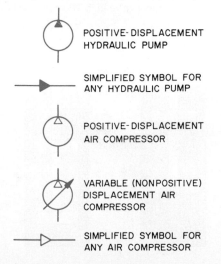

POSITIVE-DISPLACEMENT HYDRAULIC PUMP

SIMPLIFIED SYMBOL FOR ANY HYDRAULIC PUMP

POSITIVE-DISPLACEMENT AIR COMPRESSOR

VARIABLE (NONPOSITIVE) DISPLACEMENT AIR COMPRESSOR

SIMPLIFIED SYMBOL FOR ANY AIR COMPRESSOR

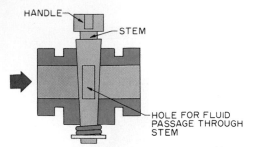

Fig. 22-22. A plug valve in the closed position.

Plug Valves. Figure 22-22 shows a plug valve. This is a simple variation of the gate valve. Plug valves are difficult to operate under high pressures. Therefore, they are used only in low-pressure systems.

Note the hole in the stem of the plug valve. The operator can turn the hole in line with the inlet and outlet. This allows fluid to flow freely. Turning the valve another one-quarter turn blocks the flow.

Needle Valves. Needle valves are used to control the amount of fluid flow. See Fig. 22-23. Needle valves have a tapered stem. As the operator opens the valve, the flow increases slowly. In this way, the flow may be adjusted gradually to the proper rate.

Spool Valves. The spool valve has many industrial uses. This valve consists of a plunger that moves up and down inside a housing. See Fig. 22-24. The plunger has spools attached to it. These spools fit tightly against the walls of the housing. This is similar to the way a piston fits inside a cylinder.

Spool valves may be two-way, three-way, or four-way valves. The two-way type is most commonly used as an on-off valve.

Figure 22-24 shows how a typical two-way spool valve works. In **A** the spring holds the plunger in an open position. This allows fluid to pass through the valve freely. In **B** the plunger has been pushed down. This compresses the spring. The top spool is now between the inlet and outlet ports. This blocks the fluid flow.

Only one of the two spools is needed to open and close the valve. The bottom spool prevents twisting and binding in the housing. It also provides a surface for the spring. Some spool valves use only one large spool.

Directional Control Valves

Many fluid power systems have several power sources, several outputs, or both. These systems often require a way of changing power sources and redirecting fluid flow to different parts of the system. Directional control valves provide a way to do this. There are three general types of directional control valves. They are three-way valves, four-way valves, and check valves.

Most directional control valves are spool valves. Their main function is to control the direction of fluid flow. However, they can sometimes be used as on-off valves.

Fig. 22-23. Needle valves are used to control the rate of fluid flow through the system.

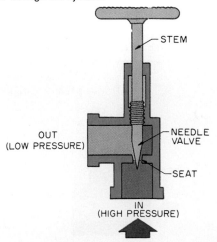

Fig. 22-24. A spool valve in its two common positions.

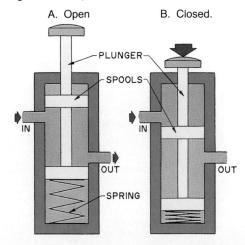

Three-Way Valves.

A three-way valve has three ports. One type of three-way valve has two input ports and one output port. With this valve, the operator can use two different sources of pressure. Another type of three-way valve has one input port and two output ports. The operator can direct pressurized fluid to either output port.

Figure 22-25 shows how a three-way valve works. The valve shown is a two-output type. In **A** the spring holds the plunger up. This is the valve's normal, or *nonactivated*, position. This position allows fluid to flow in port 1 and out port 2. The bottom spool blocks the flow from port 1 to port 3.

When the operator pushes the plunger down, the valve moves to the position shown in **B**. The fluid now flows out of port 3. It cannot flow through port 2.

Four-Way Valves.

Four-way valves can start, stop, or reverse the direction of fluid motion. They are most often used to control the reciprocating motion of a piston within a cylinder. Another common use is to reverse the rotation of a fluid motor. The landing gear system in Fig. 22-1 uses a four-way valve.

The four-way valve is a type of spool valve with four ports. See Fig. 22-26. The valve shown actually has five ports. However, the two exhaust ports are considered to be just one working port.

The four-way valve allows pressurized fluid to push on a piston in both directions. In Fig. 22-26A, pressurized fluid passes through port 1, then

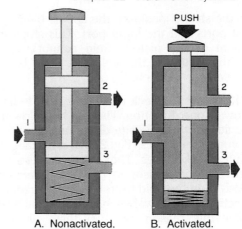

A. Nonactivated.　　B. Activated.

Fig. 22-25. This is a two-output type of three-way valve. Depending on the plunger position, fluid flows out of either port 2 or port 3.

port 3. The fluid enters the top end of the cylinder and forces the piston down. The downward piston movement forces the fluid in the bottom of the cylinder through port 2. It then passes out the lower exhaust port.

In Fig. 22-26B, the valve position is reversed. Pressurized fluid passes through port 1, then port 2. The fluid enters the rod end of the cylinder and forces the piston up. The upward piston movement forces the fluid in the top of the cylinder through port 3. It then passes out the upper exhaust port.

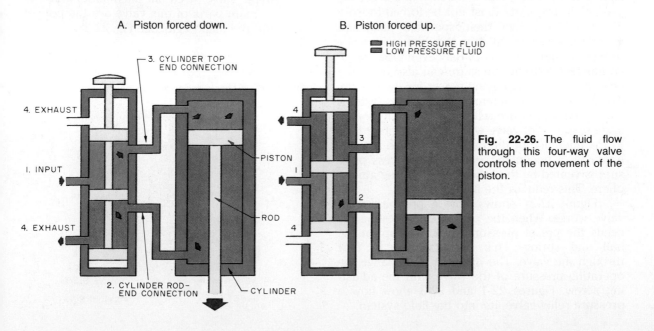

Fig. 22-26. The fluid flow through this four-way valve controls the movement of the piston.

In the shutoff position, the spools block the exhaust ports and the input port. This stops the movement of the piston. Fluid cannot escape from either side of the cylinder. This is the *closed-centered* position.

Check Valves. Check valves are used to limit fluid flow to one direction. They do not allow the fluid to flow in the opposite direction.

Compressor valves (Fig. 22-18) are examples of simple check valves. They allow fluid to flow through the compressor in only one direction. They also keep the fluid from reversing direction. All directional check valves have the same function. For this reason, we call them *one-way valves*.

Refer back to Fig. 22-18. The pressure of a lightweight spring forces a ball against a seat, sealing the opening. The valve opens when fluid pressure overcomes the spring pressure. The fluid pressure lifts the ball off the seat. This allows fluid to flow freely. If the fluid tries to reverse its flow, the valve closes. The reverse pressure exerts force on the back of the ball. This helps to keep the valve closed.

All check valves cause a small pressure loss in the fluid flow. The loss is about 5-10 psi. This is usually the amount of pressure needed to overcome the spring tension. In some cases, check valves are used deliberately to reduce pressure. Pressure reductions of 50 psi or more are possible.

Pressure Relief Valves

All parts of a fluid power system are designed to operate most efficiently under certain pressures. The parts must not be forced to work at pressures above their specified maximum pressure. Pressure that is too high will make them wear out faster. They may even break down completely. Extreme pressure can also harm the engine or motor supplying power for the system. To avoid these problems, fluid power systems usually have pressure relief valves. In a hydraulic system, the relief valve will open and direct fluid to the inlet side of the pump or back to the reservoir. In a pneumatic system, the excess pressure is vented by the relief valve into the atmosphere. This reduces the fluid pressure.

Figure 22-27 shows how a pressure relief valve works. When the pressure in the line exceeds the preset pressure, it pushes up on the ball and spring. This permits fluid to flow through the valve. The operator can change the operating pressure of the valve with the adjusting screw. Figures 22-1 and 22-3 show how a pressure relief valve fits into the fluid system.

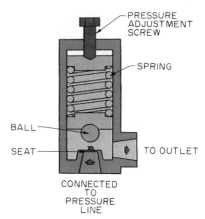

Fig. 22-27. In this pressure relief valve, fluid pressure has overcome the pressure of the spring.

Pressure Control Valves

Pressure control valves are an essential part of most fluid power systems. Many systems deliver pressurized fluid to several output units. The different units may require different pressures. However, the system must generate an overall pressure that will operate the unit needing the highest pressure. Pressure control valves are used to provide reduced pressures for lower-pressure units. These valves are placed in the system close to the lower-pressure output units. The valves maintain pressures below system pressure for these units.

There are many types of pressure control valves. One of the most widely used is the simple spring-type valve used in pneumatic systems. The two main parts of this valve are the poppet valve and the diaphragm. See Fig. 22-28.

Fig. 22-28. A simple spring-type pressure control valve.

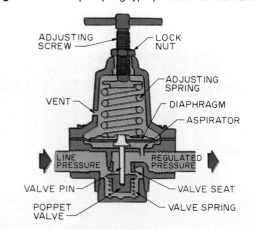

A spring-type pressure control valve regulates system pressure by balancing the following two forces:

■ The force trying to open the valve.

This force results from atmospheric pressure (through the vent) plus the adjustable spring force. Both forces push *down* on the diaphragm.

■ The force trying to close the valve.

This force results from the regulated system pressure plus the valve spring pressure. Both of these forces push *up* on the diaphragm.

When the adjusting spring is compressed, it pushes down on the valve pin. This opens the poppet valve. The regulated pressure increases until it is high enough to balance the added spring force. The result is a higher regulated pressure. If the adjusting spring tension is reduced, regulated pressure decreases by the same amount. In normal operation, the poppet valve stays open just enough to maintain the regulated pressure at a constant level.

Operation of Fluid Power Valves

Fluid power valves can be operated manually or automatically. In the simplest systems, the operator activates the valves with a hand lever, palm button, or foot pedal.

Valves used in more complex home and industrial systems usually require automatic control. The automatic transmission in an automobile is one example. In this fluid power system, the transmission fluid operates the valves automatically.

Fluid power valves can also be operated electrically. This is usually done with solenoids. (Solenoids are described in Chapter 24.)

Valve Symbols

Figure 22-29 shows the symbols for different fluid power valves. Each box represents a possible position of the valve. Connected lines and ar-

Fig. 22-29. Symbols for different types of fluid power activators, valves, and valve positions.

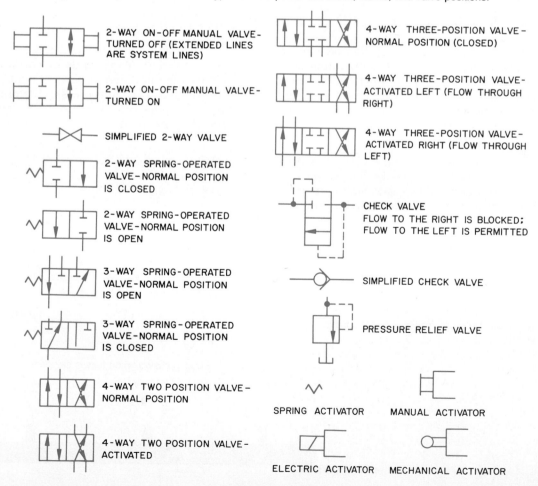

rows mean that fluid is flowing through the valve. A T-shaped ending on a line means the valve is blocking flow.

Note the end parts on the top two valves in the left-hand column. These parts indicate that the valves are operated manually. A wavy line on the end of a valve indicates a spring. The spring holds the valve in one position. Lines that cross inside a valve are not connected. An arrow aligned with an external line means that the valve connects into the system.

TRANSMISSION LINES AND CONNECTORS

Whether they are liquids or gases, fluids must have a container through which they can flow. In fluid systems, the containers are pipes, tubes, and hoses. These are called *transmission lines*. Transmission lines are rarely in one piece. Therefore, there must be a way of connecting them. This section explains transmission lines and their connectors.

Transmission Lines

Transmission lines may be either flexible or rigid. Flexible lines are used when an output unit must be movable or is subject to vibration. They are made from a variety of materials. The material used depends on the maximum working pressure of the system.

Plastic hoses are often used for small and moderately sized pressure systems. High pressures require stronger tubing. Some flexible lines are reinforced with steel wire.

Rigid lines are used whenever flexible lines are not required. Rigid lines are more economical. They also provide long, trouble-free service. They are usually made of copper or steel.

Pressure Drop

As fluids flow through transmission lines, friction develops. The resistance of friction causes a decrease in pressure. The farther the fluid flows, the greater the friction and the decrease in pressure. See Fig. 22-30. This pressure decrease is called a *pressure drop*.

Friction is not the only cause of pressure drops. *Turbulence* is any irregular or disrupted flow. It can also cause pressure drops. A quick change in direction causes turbulence. The smaller directional changes inside a valve can also cause turbulence. A third cause is any restriction in the system.

Connectors

The units and lines in a fluid power system must be connected. Many kinds of **connectors** are used to join the different parts of a fluid system. The amount of system pressure determines the kinds of connectors to be used. The type of line used also affects the choice of a connector.

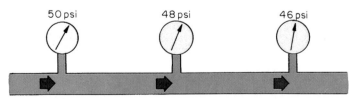

A. Pressure drop in free-flowing line.

Fig. 22-30. Pressure inside a fluid transmission line.

B. Equal pressure when flow is stopped.

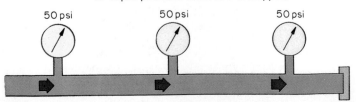

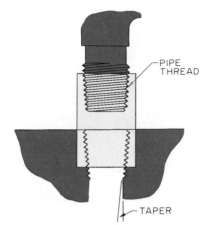

Fig. 22-31. Pipe threads are tapered (cut at an angle). When tightened, the threads come together to form a tight, leak-proof joint.

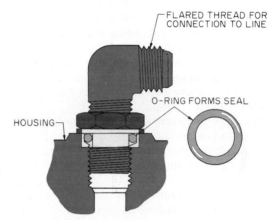

Fig. 22-32. An O-ring made of rubber or plastic is used to seal straight threads.

Rigid Connections.

Rigid Connections. One end of a connector must often fit into a unit, such as a valve. The input and output ports of the unit usually have threads. These threads may be either pipe (angled) threads or regular (straight) threads.

Figure 22-31 shows pipe threads on both a unit and a connector. Notice that the threads are tapered. As the connector is screwed into the unit, the connection becomes increasingly tighter.

However, there are always small gaps remaining in even the tightest connection. To fill these gaps, operators place pipe sealer on the threads before making connections. The sealer fills in the gaps as the threads are tightened together. If the threads are regular (not tapered), a rubber or synthetic ring is used. This *O-ring* presses tightly against the connector and the unit. This seals the joint. See Fig. 22-32. The other end of the connector attaches to the transmission line.

Rigid lines normally use either of two types of connections. These are the flared connection and the compression connection. In the *flared connection*, the tube is flared (spread outward) at one end. This flaring is done with a special tool. See Fig. 22-33. The connector end is machined to fit the angle of the flare. A special nut on the tubing threads onto the connector. It squeezes the flare onto the connector. The metal tubing must be soft enough to fill all gaps between the two parts. This ensures a good connection.

In a *compression connection*, the tubing end has a soft metal sleeve called a *ferrule*, slipped over it. Part of the sleeve fits into the connector. See Fig. 22-34. The compression nut screws onto the connector. Both the nut and the connector squeeze the sleeve. This distorts the sleeve so that it digs into the tubing for a tight seal.

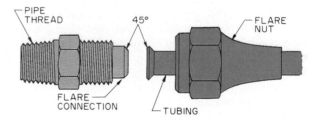

Fig. 22-33. A flared tubing connection.

Fig. 22-34. A compression connection.

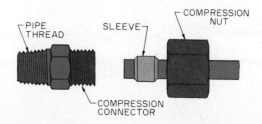

Flexible Connections. Flexible hoses also use flared and compression fittings for permanent connections. However, hoses that need to be connected and disconnected often use a different type of connector. The connector most commonly used is the *quick-disconnect coupling*. This connector has two parts. One end consists of a barbed stem and a socket. See Fig. 22-35. The barbed stem inserts into the hose. The stem is larger than the hose. Therefore, the hose tends to mold itself around the stem. This provides a seal. It also holds the hose on the stem.

The other end of the connector has a special plug designed to snap into the first end's socket. Again, see Fig. 22-35. An O-ring provides the seal between the plug and socket.

Quick-disconnect couplings may have threaded ends instead of barbed stems. This permits a wide variety of connections that can be quickly changed.

For high-pressure systems, a metal sleeve and threaded insert tightly grip the hose. This assures a leak-proof joint. Quick-disconnect couplings or other connectors can then be attached to the other end.

Figure 22-36 shows the different symbols used for fluid lines and couplings.

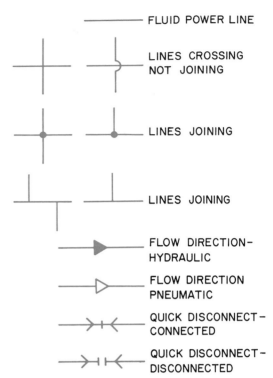

Fig. 22-36. Symbols for fluid lines and couplings.

ACTUATORS

Before we can put fluid power to work, we must change it into mechanical power. We make this change with an *actuator*. An **actuator** is a device that receives fluid power and changes it into mechanical motion. Actuators can produce either linear, reciprocating, or rotary motion. We use **cylinders** to produce linear and reciprocating motion. We use **fluid power motors** to produce rotary motion.

Pneumatic and hydraulic actuators have similar designs. They also operate in much the same way. This section describes both types together.

Cylinders

Figure 22-37 shows a typical cylinder and piston used as a linear actuator. When pressurized fluid enters the right port, the piston moves to the left. When pressurized fluid enters the left port, the piston moves to the right. In a pneumatic system, the gas can be released into the atmosphere after use. In hydraulic systems, the fluid is piped back to the reservoir and reused.

Many kinds of jobs can be done with the piston's reciprocating motion. Forming metals and plastics, moving objects, and operating power steering systems are just a few.

There are two basic types of cylinder actuators. These are single-acting and double-acting cylinders. Double-acting cylinders can be further divided into two types. These are differential and nondifferential cylinders.

Fig. 22-35. A quick-disconnect coupling is used to connect two pieces of flexible hose.

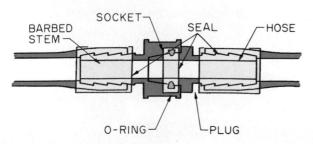

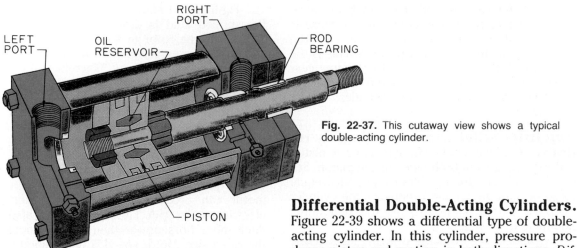

Fig. 22-37. This cutaway view shows a typical double-acting cylinder.

Single-Acting Cylinders. In single-acting cylinders, pressurized fluid exerts force on only one side of the piston or ram. Figure 22-38 shows a single-acting cylinder, called a ram that is used in hydraulic jacks and automobile lifts. A pump supplies fluid under pressure. This raises the ram and lifts the load (**A**). When the operator releases the pressure, the combined weight of the ram and load pushes the ram down (**B**).

Differential Double-Acting Cylinders. Figure 22-39 shows a differential type of double-acting cylinder. In this cylinder, pressure produces piston rod motion in both directions. *Differential* means that only one rod extends from the cylinder to do work. This rod can perform both a push (**A**) and a pull (**B**).

Differential also indicates a difference in force. The rod reduces the piston area on the rod side of the piston. Therefore, the total force in one direction is different from the force in the other direction. The piston has less force when moving *away* from the rod end of the cylinder. It produces more force when moving *toward* the rod end.

A three- or four-way valve is used to control the flow of fluid to the cylinder. In Fig. 22-39A, the valve provides pressurized fluid to the right side of the cylinder. This forces the piston to the

Fig. 22-38. A single-acting cylinder used as a hydraulic jack.

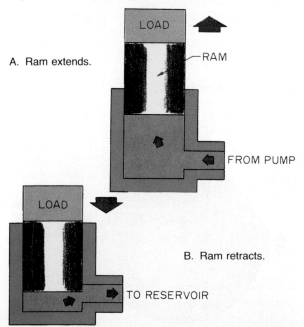

A. Ram extends.

B. Ram retracts.

Fig. 22-39. A differential-type double-acting cylinder.

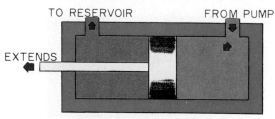

A. Piston rod moves to the left.

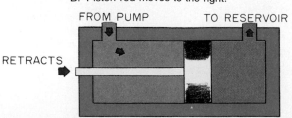

B. Piston rod moves to the right.

left. The rod extends out of the cylinder. After the motion to the left is complete, pressure is applied to the left side of the cylinder (**B**). The piston returns to its original position. This is the type of cylinder used for lifting the landing gear shown in Fig. 22-1. Figure 22-37 shows the inside construction of a double-acting cylinder.

Nondifferential Double-Acting Cylinders.

Nondifferential cylinders have a piston rod extending from both sides of the piston. See Fig. 22-40. This type of cylinder provides equal force in both directions. Otherwise, the cylinder operates in the same way as the differential double-acting cylinder.

Cylinders are available in many sizes. Their size depends on the force and distance needed for the output motion. Fluid pressure and piston area determine the force. The length of the cylinder determines the length of the stroke.

Fluid Motors

We use fluid motors to convert fluid power into rotary motion. Fluid motors are, in most cases, fluid pumps in reverse. In fact, some fluid pumps can be used either as pumps or motors.

A common type of fluid motor is the vane-type motor. This motor is similar to the vane pump shown in Fig. 22-15. As you recall, vane pumps hold the vanes against the housing with centrifugal force. Vane motors hold the vanes out with springs.

Figure 22-41 shows how a fluid motor works. Pressurized fluid is directed against the vanes. This turns the rotor to which the vanes are attached. The pressure exerts force against one or more vanes at all times. Therefore, the rotor turns at a steady rate. A shaft attached to the rotor can be used to do work.

Other types of hydraulic and pneumatic motors are available. In general, they have the same designs as the pumps with similar names.

Fluid pressure determines the torque of a fluid motor. As long as the pressure is constant, the torque is constant. This means that a fluid motor can produce high torque quicker than electric motors can. Fluid motors can also produce more horsepower than electric motors of the same size. Motor speed is determined by the flow of fluid. The greater the rate of flow (gallons or cubic feet per minute), the greater the motor speed.

Figure 22-42 shows the fluid power symbols used for cylinders and motors.

READING FLUID SYSTEM DRAWINGS

Drawings of fluid power systems are presented in Figs. 22-43 and 22-44. After reviewing Figs. 22-4, 22-10, 22-19, 22-29, 22-36, and 22-42, examine these drawings. By identifying the symbol for each part, you will be able to "read" the drawings to see how a fluid system operates.

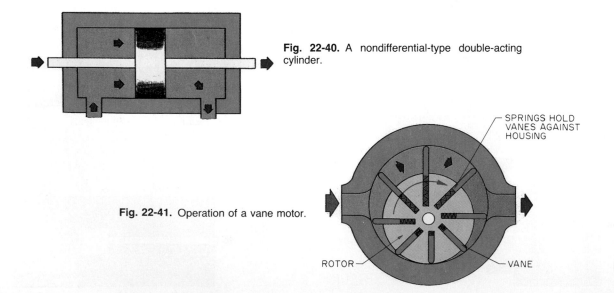

Fig. 22-40. A nondifferential-type double-acting cylinder.

Fig. 22-41. Operation of a vane motor.

SPRINGS HOLD VANES AGAINST HOUSING

ROTOR

VANE

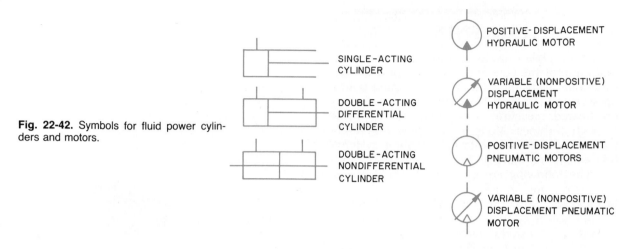

Fig. 22-42. Symbols for fluid power cylinders and motors.

SINGLE-ACTING CYLINDER

DOUBLE-ACTING DIFFERENTIAL CYLINDER

DOUBLE-ACTING NONDIFFERENTIAL CYLINDER

POSITIVE-DISPLACEMENT HYDRAULIC MOTOR

VARIABLE (NONPOSITIVE) DISPLACEMENT HYDRAULIC MOTOR

POSITIVE-DISPLACEMENT PNEUMATIC MOTORS

VARIABLE (NONPOSITIVE) DISPLACEMENT PNEUMATIC MOTOR

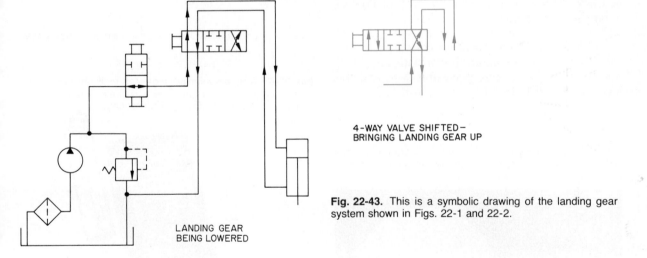

4-WAY VALVE SHIFTED— BRINGING LANDING GEAR UP

LANDING GEAR BEING LOWERED

Fig. 22-43. This is a symbolic drawing of the landing gear system shown in Figs. 22-1 and 22-2.

Fig. 22-44. This is a symbolic drawing of the air-over-oil hoist system shown in Fig. 22-3.

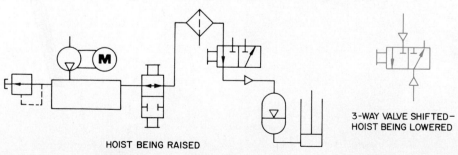

HOIST BEING RAISED

3-WAY VALVE SHIFTED— HOIST BEING LOWERED

TEST INSTRUMENTS

Fluid power systems require instruments that monitor the flow of fluids. Many of these are traditional instruments that measure fluid power pressure and rate of flow. Others are more sophisticated, measuring air velocity or flow rates through turbines. Modern fluid power systems pass these measurements to computer systems that adjust and manage the production process.

The following are some of the fluid power test instruments in use:

■ Pressure. Measuring the pressure within a fluid power system is basic to controlling the system. It can be measured by a pressure gage, as shown in Fig. 22-45. Pressure can also be converted to an electrical impulse by a transducer. The electrical measurement can be provided on a gage or sent to a computer.

■ Flow meter. Measuring the rate of fluid flow is important for many systems. See Fig. 22-46.

■ Gas velocity. It measures the rate of flow of air or other gases. See Fig. 22-47.

■ Level measurements. It measures the level of fluids in a reservoir or other container.

There are many additional measuring instruments that can measure pressure, flow, and the levels of fluids under different conditions.

Fig. 22-46. Flow meters measure flow in volume per unit/time. A typical measurement is in cubic centimeters per minute (cc/min). (Omega Engineering)

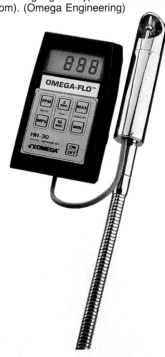

Fig. 22-47. This air velocity gage can measure the speed of air passing over the gauge. A typical measurement is in feet per minute (fpm). (Omega Engineering)

Fig. 22-45. Pressure gauges determine pressure in pounds per square inch (psi) or inches of mercury (in. of Hg) for a vacuum. (Omega Engineering)

Testing Your Knowledge

Briefly answer each of the following questions. Write on a separate piece of paper.
1. Identify the seven parts common to all fluid power systems.
2. In a pneumatic power system, what two contaminants does the filter remove from the air?
3. What is an FRL unit?
4. Name three basic types of hydraulic pumps.
5. Name the two classifications of air compressors.
6. What is the main use of needle valves?
7. Name the three types of spool valves.
8. What are the functions of a directional control valve?
9. What is the function of a check valve?
10. What causes a pressure drop in a fluid power system?
11. What are quick-disconnect couplings used with?
12. What is the function of a fluid power actuator?
13. Name two common fluid power actuators.
14. What determines the torque of a fluid power motor?
15. What determines the speed of a fluid power motor?

Expressing Your Knowledge

Using complete sentences, write your answers to the following on a separate sheet of paper:
1. Why are symbols used to represent fluid power parts on drawings?
2. What is the difference between a fluid reservoir and a fluid receiver?
3. What are positive displacement pumps?
4. Give one advantage and one disadvantage of the lobe pump as compared to the gear pump.

5. What advantage does the gate valve have over the globe valve?
6. Describe how pipe threads seal a connection when a unit and a connector are tightened.

Applying Your Knowledge

Follow your teacher's instructions to complete these activities:
1. Design and build a simple fluid power system. First, draw your system using the proper symbols. Then, with the help of your teacher, obtain a double-acting cylinder, a four-way valve, a pressure regulator, and lines. Put these together according to your design. Use an air compressor or compressed air from the school lab as the supply of fluid power.

Practicing Safety

Set the regulator to a low pressure.

2. Make a survey of your school, lab, home, or community for uses and applications of both pneumatic and hydraulic power systems.
    Select three of the uses and write a description of how pneumatics or hydraulics are used. How is the mechanical advantage of fluid power used in each of these three examples?
3. Name the different fluid power systems used on an automobile. Most automobiles have more than one. These systems include shock absorbers and heater controls, to name two. What other systems exist?
    Choose one of the systems and prepare a brief report describing how it operates. In the report, tell how the system provides mechanical advantage. Also try to figure out why fluid power was used instead of a mechanical or electrical system. Explain.

Electrical Power

Chapter 23
Electrical Power—Principles
and Theory

Chapter 24
Electrical Power Systems

SECTION

Chapter 23

Electrical Power—Principles and Theory

Electricity has made our modern way of life possible. We need power on a continuous basis. Electricity is the primary form in which power is transported to us.

Expanding Your Knowledge

Learning about power and energy technology will help you understand more about the world around you. As you study this chapter, you will learn to:

■ Identify the relationships and electrical charges of the neutron, proton, and electron in the structure of an atom.
■ Identify three characteristics that make some elements good conductors.
■ Explain how an electrical source can produce a flow of electrons in a conductor.
■ Describe magnetic polarity and the characteristics of a magnetic field.
■ Explain and use the mathematical relationship controlled by Ohm's Law.
■ Explain the difference between direct and alternating current.
■ Describe the flow of current through a series circuit and through a parallel circuit.

Building Your Word Power

Knowledge of the vocabulary used will help you develop greater understanding of power and energy. The following terms are defined and explained in this chapter. Learning these will help you learn more about electrical power.

alternating current (AC)	circuit, electrical
amperage	conductor
ampere	coulomb
atoms	current, electric

direct current (DC)
electricity
electromagnet
electron theory
hertz (Hz)
kilowatt-hour (kWh)
magnet
magnetic field
ohm
Ohm's Law
parallel circuit

polarity
protons
resistance, electrical
schematic drawings
series circuit
series-parallel circuit
volt
voltage
watt (W)
wattage

Electricity is now a part of nearly every American home. It provides us with light, heat, and useful motion. Electric motors, for example, convert electricity into motion. They operate household appliances and home workshop tools. We use heat produced by electricity to cook food, dry clothes, and heat our homes. Electricity also produces light whenever we need it. See Fig. 23-1.

Electricity also serves industry. Electric motors operate many tools and machines. Electric lighting allows workers to do their jobs at any time. Industry also uses heat from electricity to produce many materials.

Electricity powers radios, televisions, calculators and computers, digital watches, and telephones. These and many other communication devices make our lives easier and more enjoyable.

There are thousands of ways we can put electricity to work. This chapter will help you understand the principles and theory of electricity. Chapter 24 will explain how we control and use electricity.

ELECTRON THEORY

To understand electricity, you must first learn more about atoms. As you know from Section I, **atoms** are the smallest part of an element that retains the element's individual characteristics.

In simple terms, the **electron theory** states that atoms consist of three kinds of particles—protons, neutrons, and electrons. Together, the protons and neutrons form the nucleus. The electrons revolve around the nucleus. See Fig. 23-2.

Different atoms have different numbers of protons, neutrons, and electrons. Again, see Fig. 23-2. The nucleus usually has an equal number of protons and neutrons. The number of electrons circling the nucleus is always the same as the number of protons. When we study electricity, we are concerned only with protons and electrons. Neutrons do not affect electricity.

The Size of Atoms

An atom is only two billionths of an inch (.000000002″) in diameter. One million atoms can easily fit on the head of a pin.

The atom is a giant compared to its parts. For example, imagine that the proton of a hydrogen atom were the size of a golf ball. Its single

Fig. 23-1. Electrical power serves us by providing light, heat, and motion.

Fig. 23-2. Atoms are the building blocks of the universe. The difference between an oxygen atom and a helium atom is in the number of protons, neutrons, and electrons.

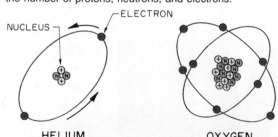

HELIUM
2 PROTONS, NEUTRONS, AND ELECTRONS

OXYGEN
8 PROTONS, NEUTRONS, AND ELECTRONS

electron would be circling in an orbit one mile away. Yet, this electron spins around the nucleus a hundred million billion times each second. That's almost like being everywhere at once! Also, a proton weighs 1836 times as much as an electron. Compared to protons, electrons are almost weightless.

Charged Particles

Electrons have a *negative* charge. **Protons** have a *positive* charge. A charged particle either attracts or repels other charged particles. See Fig. 23-3. Particles with the same charge have *like charges*. Like charges repel each other. *Unlike charges* attract each other. When a negative charge and a positive charge attract each other, they are in balance. Together, they neither attract nor repel other particles.

An atom is normally in a state of balance or *neutrality*. The nucleus is positively charged by the protons. This charge is balanced by an equal number of electrons rotating around the nucleus. The attraction between the protons and electrons keeps the orbiting electrons from being thrown off by centrifugal force.

The distance between protons and electrons determines the strength of attraction between them. The electrons orbit in orderly shells around the nucleus. Copper, for example, has four shells. See Fig. 23-4. The three inner shells contain 28 of the 29 electrons. The shell closest to the nucleus contains 2 electrons. The second shell contains 8 electrons. And the third shell contains 18 electrons. The outer shell has just one electron. This electron is farthest from the nucleus. Therefore, it has the weakest attraction

for the nucleus. As a result, it can easily be forced from its orbit to become a *free electron*. When this happens to an atom, it becomes positively charged. There are not enough electrons to balance the charge of the nucleus. A positively charged atom will try to attract a free electron from another atom. **Electricity** is the movement of electrons from one atom to another.

With its negative charge, an electron always moves toward a positively charged atom. Electricity always flows from negative to positive.

Conductors

Some elements, such as copper, hold their outer electrons with a weak force. We call these elements **conductors**. Conductors have only a few electrons in their outer shell. These electrons are easily pushed from their orbits. The atoms of good conductors are also close together. Their outer orbits overlap. This allows electrons to transfer easily from atom to atom. See Fig. 23-5.

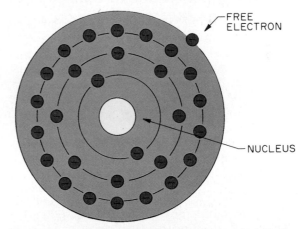

Fig. 23-4. The arrangement of electrons in a copper atom.

Fig. 23-3. A positive charge and a negative charge attract each other. Two positive charges or two negative charges repel each other.

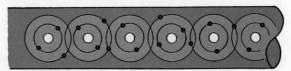

Fig. 23-5. In a conductor, the orbits of outer electrons overlap. This allows the electrons to transfer easily through the conductor.

To produce a flow of electricity, a conductor must be attached at one end to a source of free electrons. The other end must attach to a place for the electrons to go. The electron source may be either a generator or a battery. The source provides an imbalance of electrons. It develops a surplus of electrons at one terminal, and a shortage of electrons at the other terminal. See Fig. 23-6. Electrons flow through the conductor from the negative terminal to the positive terminal. We call this flow of electrons an **electric current**.

CURRENT FLOW

Let us look a little more closely at electric current. The battery in Fig. 23-6 moves electrons through a wire to light a bulb. Think of the battery terminals as two containers. One container (the negative terminal) holds many electrons.

The other container (the positive terminal) holds only a few. This creates an electrical pressure difference between the negative and positive terminals.

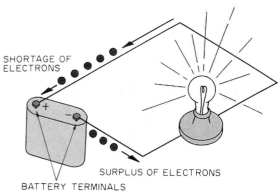

SHORTAGE OF ELECTRONS

SURPLUS OF ELECTRONS

BATTERY TERMINALS

Fig. 23-6. A battery develops a shortage of electrons at one terminal and a surplus at the other. When a wire is connected to the terminals, the electrons flow from the negative terminal to the positive terminal.

Technology Focus

Flying On Beam Power

The same microwaves that can cook dinner in a microwave oven and carry telephone messages across the country can be used to fly an airplane. Microwaves are electromagnetic beams of energy which can be used to produce heat (cooking), to transmit sound and television signals, and to transmit energy.

Recently, a small experimental plane[*], weighing just 10 pounds, flew at an altitude of 300 feet for 20 minutes powered by microwaves from earth. While a modest beginning, the flight proved the concept works— just like the first flight of 102 feet by Orville Wright proved that heavier-than-air flight was possible.

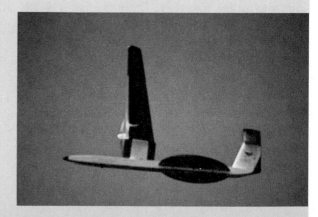

Planes powered by microwaves could stay in the air for months, rotating with others for service and repair. They could fly at various heights performing many tasks now performed by satellites, but at much less cost. In addition, they could be used for low-altitude operations such as watching for forest fires, inspecting farm crops, and tracking icebergs.

Transmitting electrical energy without wires—via microwaves—has been a long-sought goal. Proving that microwave-powered flight is possible is an important step toward achieving this goal.

[*]Designed and built by the University of Toronto Institute for Aerospace Studies.

Current begins to flow when the negative terminal pushes an electron into one end of the conductor. The conductor can hold only a set number of electrons. Therefore, an electron gets pushed off the other end. This keeps constant the number of electrons in the conductor. However, the addition and removal of single electrons produces a current through the entire wire.

Figure 23-7 shows another way of looking at electron flow. There is a line of 10 billiard balls. A single ball added to one end produces an almost immediate movement of the ball at the other end. The moment the first ball strikes, its force is transmitted through all the balls. This force drives the last ball from the other end.

This condition is also true with electrons producing an electric current. Actually, electrons move through a wire quite slowly. However, because the movement is transmitted through the entire wire, the resulting current flow is very rapid. Current travels at nearly the speed of light, which is 186,000 miles (300,000 km) per second.

MAGNETISM

We can best understand magnetism by observing its effects. **Magnets** can attract iron and steel. See Fig. 23-8. Each end of a magnet is different. One end of the magnet is called the *north pole* (abbreviated N). The other end is called the *south pole* (abbreviated S). The poles are named for the direction they will point if they are allowed to move freely. A north pole will always point toward the earth's north pole. It is often called a *north-seeking pole*. The poles are similar to electrical charges. Like poles repel and unlike poles attract. See Fig. 23-9.

A magnet can be shaped like a horseshoe, but most magnets are bar magnets, as in Fig. 23-9. Some magnets are shaped to fit the inside of an electric motor or another electric device.

A magnet develops a **magnetic field** around it. This field is the area in which magnetic attraction or repulsion takes place. We can "see" the magnetic field by placing a piece of paper over a magnet and sprinkling iron filings on the paper. See Fig. 23-10. More iron filings gather at the ends of the magnet than in the center. This shows that the attraction is strongest at the ends of the magnet. Repulsion between like poles will also be strongest at the ends.

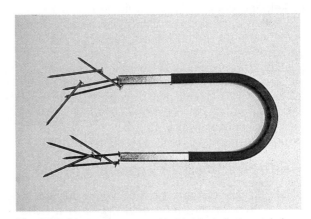

Fig. 23-8. Magnets attract and hold objects that contain iron.

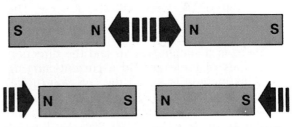

Fig. 23-9. Like poles of magnets repel each other. Unlike poles attract each other.

Fig. 23-10. When iron filings are sprinkled on a sheet of paper above a magnet, they form the pattern shown here. This pattern indicates the magnetic lines of force.

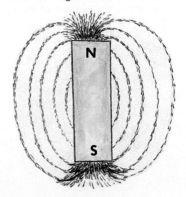

Fig. 23-7. A row of billiard balls demonstrates electric current. When the cue ball strikes the row of balls, it stops. The impact is transferred to the last ball, which rolls away. In the same way, electrons are added and released from a conductor.

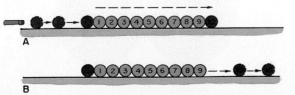

The magnetic field is often called the *magnetic flux*. It is made up of magnetic lines of force. These lines have both force and direction. See Fig. 23-11. Outside the magnet, the direction of the magnetic flux is from north to south. Inside the magnet, the direction is from south to north.

Types of Magnets

Magnets are made of iron, steel, alnico, and other materials. (Alnico is an alloy of aluminum, nickel, and cobalt.) Magnets made of hard steel are called *permanent magnets*. They retain their magnetism for a long time. Magnets made of pure iron or soft steels lose their magnetism very quickly. Pure iron may be used in either nonpermanent magnets or electromagnets. **Electromagnets** are magnets that receive their magnetism from an electric current. They lose most of their magnetism when the flow of current is stopped or reversed as in alternating current.

Magnetism and Current Flow

When an electric current flows through a wire, a circular magnetic field develops around the wire. The amount of current flowing through the wire determines the strength of the field.

If the current flow is reversed, the **polarity**, or direction, of the force will also reverse. The magnetic lines of force do not move or flow around the wire. They merely have direction.

There is a simple way to find the direction of the lines of force around a current-carrying wire. This method is called the *Left Hand Rule*. To apply the Left Hand Rule, grip the wire in your left hand with your thumb extended in the direction of electron flow. Your fingers will point in the same direction as the magnetic lines of force. See Fig. 23-12. These lines of force will always be at right angles to the conductor.

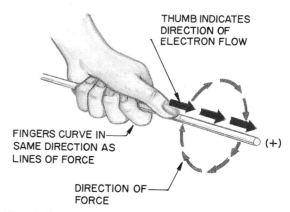

Fig. 23-12. You can use the Left Hand Rule to find the direction of the magnetic lines of force around a conductor.

You can also find the direction of electron flow if you know only the direction of the lines of force. Again with your left hand, grip the conductor with your fingers pointing with the magnetic lines of force. Your thumb will point in the direction of electron flow.

Strengthening Magnetic Fields

Figure 23-13 shows two wires placed close together. The wires are carrying electrons in opposite directions. In this situation, one conductor has clockwise lines of force. The other conductor has counterclockwise lines of force. However, the lines of force *between* the conductors are in the same direction. This creates a strong magnetic field between the wires. The strong field will tend to push the wires apart to weaken the field.

Fig. 23-13. Conductors carrying electrons in opposite directions will tend to move apart.

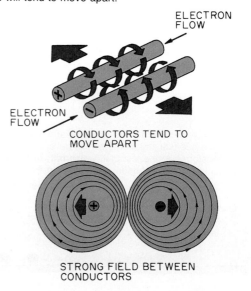

Fig. 23-11. The magnetic flux consists of magnetic lines of force. These lines form a continuous circular path as they travel inside and outside the magnet.

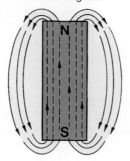

A different condition exists when two neighboring wires carry equal currents in the *same* direction. See Fig. 23-14. The lines of force around each conductor will be in the same direction. The lines of force between the conductors will be in opposite directions. These opposing lines of force will cancel each other out. No magnetic field will be left between the wires. One large magnetic field will surround both wires. This strong field will push the wires toward each other.

The field surrounding both conductors will be equal to that of one conductor carrying twice the electricity. Many wires can be placed side by side. This increases the magnetic effect even more. One large field will surround all the wires.

The magnetic field can be increased even more if the wire is coiled. A coiled wire will have the same effect as many wires carrying current in the same direction. See Fig. 23-15. This field is similar to that of the bar magnet in Fig. 23-11.

Placing a piece of soft iron inside a coil strengthens the magnetic field still more. The lines of force can pass more easily through the iron core than through the air. This concentrates the lines of force within the coil. The iron core increases the strength of the magnetic field over 300 times. It does this without requiring additional current.

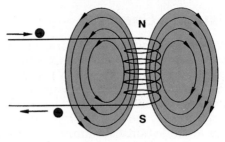

Fig. 23-15. A single coiled wire has the same magnetic effect as several conductors placed close together.

Electromagnets

A piece of soft iron with a current-carrying wire coiled around it forms an *electromagnet*. The current turns the iron core into a strong magnet. When the current is stopped, the core loses almost all its magnetism.

Different things happen when a piece of hard steel is used as the core. The magnetic field will be quite weak when the current is first turned on. However, the longer the current stays on, the stronger the field becomes. When the current is turned off, the core remains magnetized. It can be used as a permanent magnet.

You can find the polarity of an electromagnet by using the Left Hand Rule. Grip the coil with your fingers pointed in the direction of electron flow through the coil. Your thumb will point towards the north (N) pole of the magnet.

Magnetism is the link between mechanical and electrical energy. We produce motion with electric current by applying the principles of magnetism. The electric motor is one of many devices that use magnetism to produce motion.

Fig. 23-14. Conductors carrying electrons in the same direction will tend to move together, producing a single, stronger magnetic field surrounding both conductors.

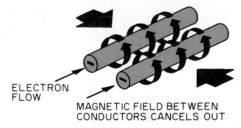

ELECTRON FLOW

MAGNETIC FIELD BETWEEN CONDUCTORS CANCELS OUT

CONDUCTORS TEND TO MOVE TOGETHER

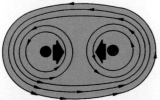

STRONGER MAGNETIC FIELD SURROUNDS BOTH

MEASURING ELECTRICITY

Electricity is the flow of electrons. We measure electrical energy by finding the number of electrons moved from one place to another. Since electrons are very small, an enormous number of electrons must move to generate a small amount of electricity.

The basic unit of measurement for electricity is the **coulomb**. One coulomb is 6.28×10^{18} (or 6,280,000,000,000,000,000) electrons. Although this is a very large number of electrons, it is still only a small amount of electricity. One coulomb is enough to light an average light bulb for one second.

Measuring Current

We cannot describe an electric current with coulombs alone. We must use three other basic units: the ampere (a), the volt (V), and the ohm (Ω). We use these units to measure an electric current flowing through a conductor.

Amperage is the rate at which current flows through a conductor. One **ampere** (or amp) is one coulomb of electricity passing a given point in one second. We can compare it to the rate at which water flows through a pipe. See Fig. 23-16. In calculations, the sign for amperage is I. We measure amperage with an *ammeter*.

Voltage is the pressure pushing the current through the conductor. One **volt** is the pressure exerted by one coulomb of electricity. We can compare voltage to the pressure in a water pipe. Again, see Fig. 23-16. Voltage is also known as *electromotive force*. In calculations, the sign for voltage is E. We measure voltage with a voltmeter.

Resistance (R) is the opposition to current flow through a conductor. Energy is lost as electrons move from atom to atom. The attraction of the nucleus for the outer electron produces resistance. This resistance produces heat.

We can compare resistance to the friction in fluid transmission lines. Resistance to the flow of fluid is measured as a pressure drop. Resistance in an electrical circuit has the same effect. It produces a drop in the voltage. We measure resistance in **ohms** with an *ohmeter*. In calculations, the sign for resistance is R.

Amps, volts, and ohms are all mathematically related. *It takes one volt to force one ampere of current through a resistance of one ohm.* This statement is known as **Ohm's Law**. Written as a mathematical formula, it becomes:

Voltage = Amperage × Resistance

or

$$E = I \times R$$

The formula can also be written with amperage or resistance as the first value:

$$I = \frac{E}{R} \quad \text{or} \quad R = \frac{E}{I}$$

An easy way to remember Ohm's Law is to use the Ohm's Law Circle. See Fig. 23-17. If you know any two values, you can find the third. For example, if a circuit has a voltage of 120 and an amperage of 10, what is the resistance?

$$R = \frac{E}{I}$$
$$R = \frac{120}{10}$$
$$R = 12 \text{ ohms}$$

If a circuit has a resistance of 20 ohms and a voltage of 120, what is the rate of current flow (amperage) through the circuit?

$$I = \frac{E}{R}$$
$$I = \frac{120}{20}$$
$$I = 6 \text{ amperes}$$

Fig. 23-16. The flow of electricity through a conductor can be compared with the flow of water through a water pipe.

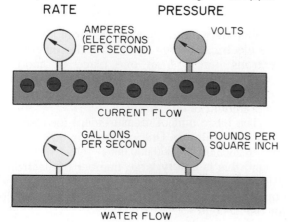

RATE   PRESSURE

AMPERES (ELECTRONS PER SECOND)   VOLTS

CURRENT FLOW

GALLONS PER SECOND   POUNDS PER SQUARE INCH

WATER FLOW

Fig. 23-17. You can use the Ohm's Law circle to find voltage, amperage, or resistance. Cover the value you want to find. This will identify the equation to use.

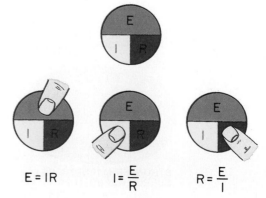

E = IR $I = \frac{E}{R}$ $R = \frac{E}{I}$

Measuring Electrical Power

Power is energy (work) per unit of time. We measure mechanical power in foot-pounds per second. We measure electrical power in **wattage**. Wattage is the measurement of power produced by the flow of current under pressure. We must know both the voltage (pressure) and the amperage (rate of flow) to measure wattage. One **watt (W)** of power is produced by a flow of one ampere at a pressure of one volt. In equation form:

$$\text{Wattage} = \text{Amperage} \times \text{Voltage}$$

or

$$W = I \times E$$

Using Metrics

The watt is used in both the customary system and the metric system to measure electrical power. In the metric system, the watt is also used to measure all other forms of power. In the customary system, however, the watt is used only to measure electrical power.

If you know two of the values, you can find the third. For example, if the current passing through a light bulb has a pressure of 120 volts and a rate of flow of 0.5 ampere, what is the wattage of the bulb?

$$W = I \times E$$
$$W = .5 \times 120$$
$$W = 60 \text{ watts}$$

One watt is a small amount of electrical power. It take 746 watts to equal one horsepower. The **kilowatt-hour (kWh)** is the basic measuring unit used by power companies. One kilowatt-hour is 1000 watts of electricity used in a period of one hour.

ELECTRICAL CIRCUITS

A **circuit** is a system of conductors and electric devices through which electric current moves. See Fig. 23-18. The word *circuit* means *a circle*. Electricity flows in a circle. It moves from and returns to its source. The source may be a battery or an electric generator.

An electrical circuit depends on an electron imbalance set up by the power source. In Fig. 23-18 the source is a battery. The battery's terminals are connected by a conductor and two lamps. Electrons move inside the battery by chemical action from the positive terminal to the negative terminal. This results in a surplus of electrons at the negative terminal. There is a shortage of electrons at the positive terminal. This is an unbalanced condition.

The conductor and lamps allow electrons to flow through the circuit from the negative terminal to the positive terminal. This current flow balances the electron distribution. The battery keeps the current flowing. It continues to move electrons internally from the positive terminal to the negative terminal. Therefore, the electrons move in a complete circle. The current will continue to flow as long as the battery maintains an internal unbalanced condition.

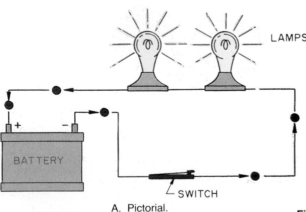

LAMPS

A. Pictorial.

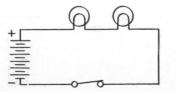

B. Schematic.

Fig. 23-18. A series circuit provides a single path for current flow.

Electrical Symbols

Since we cannot see electricity, we must rely on diagrams of circuits and electric devices. In very simple circuits, the circuit parts can be drawn pictorially (lifelike). But pictorial drawings can be confusing because different people draw circuit parts differently. To avoid this problem, symbols are used. Symbols are easy to draw. They also show exactly what is in the circuit. Drawings made with symbols are called **schematic drawings**. See Fig. 23-18.

Types of Circuits

There are three basic types of electrical circuits:
- Series
- Parallel
- Series-parallel

Series Circuit. The most basic circuit is the series circuit. Again, see Fig. 23-18. The series circuit provides only one path for current flow. Electrons flow through a single conductor. They flow from the negative side of the source to the positive side. If the circuit is interrupted or broken, no electricity will flow. For example, if one of the light bulbs in Fig. 23-18 burns out, current will stop flowing to the other light bulb.

An interruption of current flow is called an *open circuit*. An open circuit anywhere in a series circuit will cause the whole system to go dead.

For example, a switch connected *in series*, as in Fig. 23-18, allows you to control the whole circuit. When you close the switch, current flows through the circuit. When you open the switch, current flow stops.

Parallel Circuit. Parallel circuits have more than one path for current flow. In Fig. 23-19 the lamps are arranged *in parallel*. With this type of circuit, current can flow equally along different paths. A parallel circuit can be open at one point yet continue to conduct electricity. In Fig. 23-19, if one bulb burns out, the other bulb will keep burning. Current will flow as long as it has a complete path to follow.

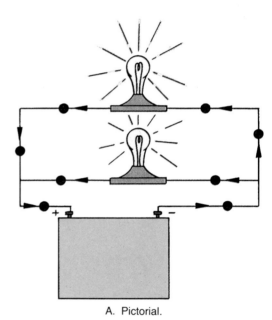

A. Pictorial.

Fig. 23-19. A parallel circuit provides at least two different paths for current flow.

B. Schematic.

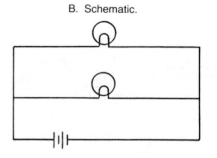

Series-Parallel Circuit. In a series-parallel circuit, both series and parallel circuits are used. See Fig. 23-20. In this circuit, the switch is in series with the lamps. If one bulb burns out, current flow will continue. However, if the switch is opened, all current flow will stop.

ALTERNATING AND DIRECT CURRENT

Current flow through a circuit may be one of two types. One type is **direct current (DC)**. This type has been used in all the circuits illustrated in this chapter. In direct current, the electrons flow in only one direction. The source must continue to supply electrons at the negative terminal by taking them away from the positive terminal. Figure 23-21 shows direct current on a graph in comparison with alternating current.

Alternating current (AC) is the most commonly used type of current. In alternating current, the polarity (direction) of the current changes rapidly. Again, see Fig. 23-21. Electrons flow first in one direction. They stop, then flow in the opposite direction. Again they stop, then flow in the first direction. This sequence makes up one *AC cycle.*

An AC cycle always takes place in a definite period of time. Usually, there are a number of cycles each second. In the United States, alternating current completes 60 cycles per second. This is fast enough to provide the appearance of a steady flow of current. The term "hertz" is often used instead of cycles per second. One **hertz (Hz)** is one cycle per second. Thus, alternating current in the U.S. is 60 hertz.

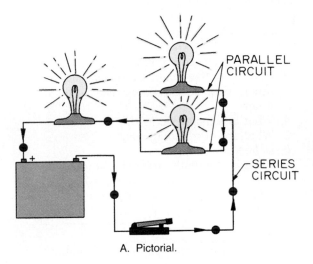

A. Pictorial.

B. Schematic.

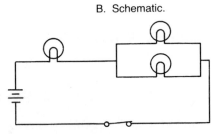

Fig. 23-20. A series-parallel circuit is a combination of series and parallel circuits.

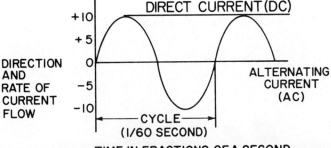

Fig. 23-21. A comparison of direct current (DC) and alternating current (AC).

Chapter 23—Review

Testing Your Knowledge

Briefly answer each of the following questions. Write on a separate piece of paper.

1. Name the three tiny particles that combine to make up atoms.
2. What is the electrical charge of an electron? a proton?
3. What is the main characteristic that makes an element a good conductor?
4. How fast does electricity travel through a conductor?
5. What is the Left Hand Rule used for?
6. How can the magnetic field of a coil of wire be strengthened?
7. What is a coulomb?
8. What basic unit is used to measure the rate at which current flows through a conductor?
9. How is electrical resistance measured?
10. What is electrical power measured in?
11. How many hertz is alternating current in the United States?

Solve these problems:

12. An automobile circuit has a voltage of 14. The ignition draws 7 amperes. What is the resistance of the circuit?
13. If the headlights of the automobile of Item 12 have a resistance of 1 ohm, what is the amperage? (The voltage is 14.)
14. The current flow in an automobile is 28 amperes and the resistance is 0.5 ohm. What is the voltage produced by the alternator?
15. During starting, an automotive starting motor draws a voltage of 9 and an amperage of 180. How many watts of power does the motor use?
16. Convert the wattage of Item 15 to horsepower.

Expressing Your Knowledge

Using complete sentences, write your answers to the following on a separate sheet of paper:

1. Define electricity and electric current.
2. Describe how an electrical source produces a flow of electricity in a conductor.
3. How do unlike magnetic poles react to each other? How do like poles react to each other?
4. What is a magnetic field?
5. What are electromagnets?
6. Define volt.
7. What is the mathematical relationship between volts, amps, and ohms?
8. What does it take to produce one watt of power?
9. What is the difference between a series circuit and a parallel circuit?
10. What is the difference between direct current and alternating current?

Applying Your Knowledge

Follow your teacher's directions to complete these activities:

1. Make a simple compass. Figure 23-22 shows the steps to follow.
   a. Obtain an old double-edge razor blade.

Practicing Safety

Handle the razor blade carefully to avoid getting cut.

   b. Using a honing stone, dull the edges of the blade.
   c. Rub one end of a horseshoe magnet (always in the same direction) against the blade as shown in **A**. Five or six times should magnetize the razor blade.

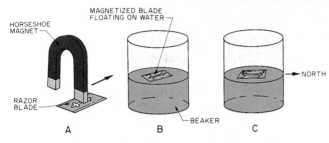

MAGNETIZED BLADE FLOATING ON WATER

RAZOR BLADE

A

B

C

BEAKER

NORTH

Fig. 23-22. Constructing a compass using a magnetized razor blade.

d. Place the magnetized blade carefully on top of water in a beaker. If placed gently, the blade will float. One end of the blade will point north. See **B**.
e. Determine which direction is north, and mark your blade as shown in **C**. As you turn the beaker, your blade will always point north.
f. Hold your horseshoe magnet so one end is near the blade. Watch the blade rotate. Reverse the magnet. Note what happens to the blade. Can you identify the north pole of your magnet? Be prepared to explain how you identified the north pole of your magnet.
g. Move your magnet slowly up and down near the glass. See if you can get the blade to rotate like a motor. This rotation is a simple demonstration of how a motor works.
2. Figure 23-23 shows a compass using two needles. Follow these steps to make this compass:
a. Slide a permanent magnet over two needles several times in the same direction to magnetize them.
b. Tape the needles to a folded paper. Mark the eye ends of the needles S and point ends N.
c. Insert a third needle in clay. Balance the center of the paper on top of the needle. Notice that the magnetized needles always point northward.

d. You can also fasten the paper to a pencil and thread. Insert it in a glass jar to protect it from wind. You can glue a card to the bottom of the jar with directions marked—north, south, east, and west. It can then be used as a regular compass.
3. Design and build a circuit demonstrator consisting of two "D" cells, a switch, and two #49 electric lamps. Prepare a series of demonstrations to be checked by your teacher. Include a switch in each circuit.
a. "D" cells in series with 2 lamps in series.
b. "D" cells in series with 2 lamps in parallel.
c. "D" cells in parallel with 2 lamps in series.
d. "D" cells in parallel with 2 lamps in parallel. Which circuit produces the brightest lamps?

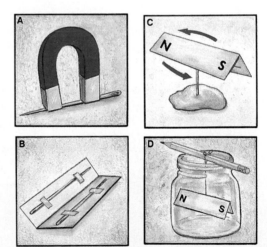

Fig. 23-23. Constructing a compass using magnetized needles.

Chapter 24

Electrical Power Systems

Electrical power systems are all around us. They may be simple or complex. Electricity is our major form of power.

Expanding Your Knowledge

As you study this chapter, you will learn to:

- Describe the operation of generators and alternators as they change motion into electricity.
- Explain how primary and secondary cells change chemical energy into electrical energy.
- Describe the function and operation of electrical control devices, including three- and four-way switches, relays, transistors, diodes, silicon-controlled rectifiers, fuses, circuit breakers, transformers, resistors, thermistors, and capacitors.
- Explain the difference between electron flow and hole flow in an electric current.
- Describe how electricity is used to provide motion, heat, light, and communications.
- Describe how a solenoid converts electricity into linear motion.
- Explain the operation of an electric motor and identify three types of motors.

Building Your Word Power

The following terms are defined and explained in this chapter. Learning these will help you learn more about electrical power systems.

alternator
battery
capacitor
cell
circuit breaker
diode
electrolyte
fuse
generator
induction
induction motor
primary cell
relay
resistor
secondary cell
semiconductor
short circuit
silicon-controlled rectifier (SCR)
solenoid
transformer
transistor
universal motor

We have all used both simple and complex electrical power systems. A flashlight, for example, is a simple power system. See Fig. 24-1. A battery serves as the source of power. A switch is used to control it, and the output is the light.

A home electrical system is more complex. This system gets its power input from a power company. The electrical power is then routed throughout the home. It is controlled with switches and other devices to operate lights and to provide heat. Electricity powers washing machines, refrigerators, and stoves. It is also the power source for electronic devices such as radios and televisions.

Electrical power systems also include electric tools such as power saws and drills. Industry uses electrical power systems to operate assembly lines and machinery. Automobiles and trucks have electrical power systems to operate the starting and ignition systems, lights, and accessories.

An electrical power system is basically the same as a mechanical or fluid power system. All three systems consist of:
■ Power input
■ Transmission and control
■ Power output

Electrical power has one great advantage. It can be transported over great distances with minimum power loss.

ELECTRICAL POWER INPUT

Electrical power input can come from two sources. The source can be self-contained. (A battery is a good example.) Or it can be the product of the conversion of mechanical energy into electrical energy. Most power sources are the second type. Devices such as generators and alternators convert rotary motion into electricity. This provides the input for an electrical power system.

Generators

A **generator** is a device used to convert rotary motion into electricity. It does this by using the principle of magnetism described in the last chapter. Magnetism is the link between mechanical and electrical power. It is also the link between electricity and motion. We can use magnetism to convert motion into electricity. We can also use it to convert electricity into motion.

In Chapter 23 you learned that passing a current through a conductor produces a magnetic field. In the generation of electricity, just the opposite occurs. A conductor is moved through a magnetic field. This produces a current in the conductor.

Figure 24-2 shows a simple method of producing current in a conductor. The conductor is moved through a magnetic field. (This magnetic field is produced by a permanent magnet. The N and S poles shown are from a single magnet. The rest of the magnet is not shown in order to keep the drawing simple.) As the conductor cuts through the lines of force, a current is developed, or *induced*, in it. The movement of the meter needle shows that current is flowing.

Notice that the conductor bends the lines of force as it passes through the field. As the conductor cuts through the lines of force, a current is generated in the conductor. The stronger the field, the stronger the current generated in the moving conductor.

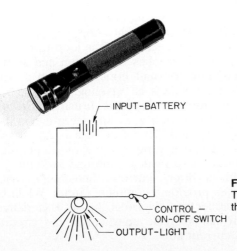

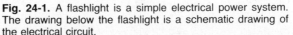

Fig. 24-1. A flashlight is a simple electrical power system. The drawing below the flashlight is a schematic drawing of the electrical circuit.

Figure 24-2 shows a conductor being moved both up and down through the field. Notice that when the direction is reversed, the current also reverses. Figure 24-3 shows a looped conductor being passed through a magnetic field. Rotating the loop produces an electric current. During rotation, the conductor cuts through the field from above and below. This direction change produces constant changes in the current's direction. This simple generator produces *alternating current (AC)*.

There must be a way of collecting the current from a generator. This is done with slip rings and brushes. A *slip ring* is attached to each end of the conductor. Again, see Fig. 24-3. The conductor and the slip rings rotate together. Special conductors called *brushes* rest on the slip rings. The brushes provide a path for the current flow. Note that there must be a complete circuit. The current leaving one slip ring must match the current entering the other slip ring. A break in the circuit will stop the current flow.

Alternating current is the most common form of electrical power. It is the power we use in our homes. It is also the form most often used by industry. However, some uses require *direct current (DC)*.

Fig. 24-2. An electric current can be produced by passing a conductor through a magnetic field.

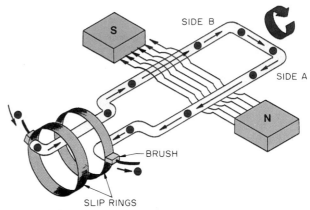

A. Side A on the right is moving down. Current flows in the direction shown.

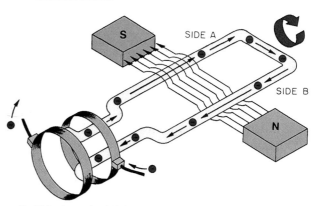

B. Side A on the left is moving up. Current flows in the reverse direction.

Fig. 24-3. A simple AC generator consists of a permanent magnet, a conductor, slip rings, and brushes. Follow side A and its current flow as the conductor rotates.

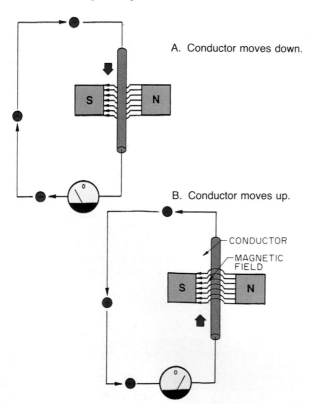

A. Conductor moves down.

B. Conductor moves up.

CONDUCTOR

MAGNETIC FIELD

Alternating current can easily be changed into direct current. Figure 24-4 shows one way of doing this. A DC generator uses a *commutator* instead of slip rings. The commutator shown consists of a slip ring cut in half. Each half connects to one side of the loop. Brush 2 collects electrons as the side B of the loop travels down. When side B reaches the bottom and starts up, its commutator half contacts brush 1. At the same time, side A is traveling down. Its half of the commutator contacts brush 2. Downward travel always produces an electron flow in the same direction. Therefore, brush 2 always collects current flowing in the same direction. The commutator provides continual switching. This produces direct current. Remember that the brushes provide a complete circuit. While brush 2 is collecting electrons, brush 1 is delivering electrons. A break anywhere in the circuit will stop current flow.

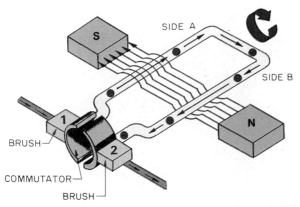

Fig. 24-4. A DC generator has a commutator instead of slip rings. The commutator allows direct current to flow from the generator.

Alternators

At one time, many DC generators were used to produce electrical current. One major use was to provide operating current for automobiles. Today few DC generators are used. Automobiles use an **alternator**. See Fig. 24-5.

Alternators are much simpler than DC generators. They also produce more electricity. Alternators generate alternating current. *Diodes* are then used to change the alternating current to direct current. (Diodes are explained later in this chapter.) This conversion is important in automobiles. All automobiles use direct current in their power systems.

Figure 24-3 showed you how a simple AC generator works. This generator developed only

Fig. 24-5. Parts of an alternator.

a small current. There are several ways to increase the electrical output of an AC generator. An electromagnet can be used instead of a simple permanent magnet. This increases the strength of the magnetic field. The number of wires cutting the lines of force can also be increased. A third way to increase output is to place more magnets along the wires. This way, the wires will continually cut through a strong magnetic field. A modern AC generator includes all of these improvements. The result is a generator that produces a substantial amount of alternating current.

Alternators and generators are constructed differently. Figure 24-5 shows an alternator. The positions of the magnetic field and the conductors are opposite those in a generator. See Fig. 24-6. Notice that the conductors do not move. An alternator has a circular assembly of conductors called a *stator*. It also has a *rotor* which produces the magnetic field. The rotor rotates inside the stator. Remember that in the generator the *field* was fixed and the *conductors* rotated.

Figure 24-7 shows the rotor by itself. The rotor is basically a rotating electromagnet. The battery supplies current to the rotor through the

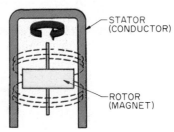

Fig. 24-6. In an alternator, a magnet rotates inside a conductor assembly called a stator.

Fig. 24-7. The rotor of an alternator is an electromagnet. The battery delivers current to the rotor through the brushes.

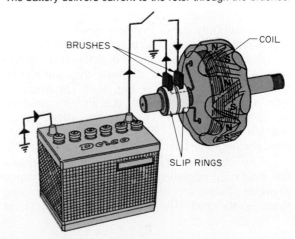

brushes and slip rings. The current magnetizes the poles of the rotor. The "fingers" of the rotor are interlaced. This provides alternating poles (N, S, N, S, etc.) around the rotor.

The stator consists of a frame and many loops of wire. As the rotor turns, each finger induces a magnetic field in each segment of the stator. The next finger collapses the field. This process induces a current in the stator. The amount of electricity going to the rotor controls the magnetic field's strength. The alternator output can be increased or decreased by controlling the electrical input. Typical automobile alternators can produce over 500 watts of power for long periods of time.

Cells and Batteries

Cells and batteries come in a variety of sizes. They store energy and deliver it on demand. Cells and batteries can also be easily moved. These features have made many industrial and consumer products possible. However, cells and batteries have the following disadvantages:

- The amount of electricity available from them is quite small.
- Electricity produced by cells and batteries is expensive.

Many people confuse the terms *cell* and *battery*. A **cell** converts chemical energy into electrical energy. Two or more cells grouped together form a **battery**. There are two basic types of cells:

- Primary
- Secondary

Primary Cells. A primary cell acts as a basic source of electricity. It produces power by direct chemical conversion. The power lasts as long as the chemicals in the cell react. The cell is then discarded. This type of cell is referred to as *primary* because it cannot be recharged.

The flashlight cell is one of many primary cells commonly used. Primary cells also power calculators, watches, and many other items.

A typical primary cell consists of a carbon rod, a zinc case, and a paste-like substance called the electrolyte. See Fig. 24-8. The **electrolyte** reacts chemically with the zinc to produce an electrical current. This occurs whenever an outside connection permits electrons to flow from the negative terminal to the positive terminal.

The chemical action within the cell makes the zinc case negative. The carbon rod becomes positive. There are more electrons in the case than in the rod. This represents an electrical

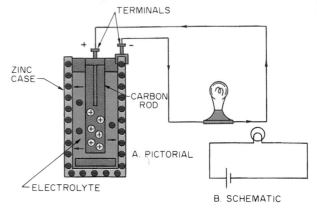

Fig. 24-8. The construction and operation of a primary cell.

pressure difference, or *potential*. This pressure (voltage) causes the current to flow in the circuit.

As you recall, electrons always flow from negative to positive in a circuit. The chemical reaction in the cell replaces the electrons at the negative terminal. The chemical reaction maintains voltage. It does this until reaction uses up the zinc.

Other primary cells include *alkaline* and *mercury* cells. These cells use different materials to produce electricity. Carbon-zinc cells lose their ability to produce electricity in a short period of time. In contrast, alkaline cells can last up to 10 times longer than carbon-zinc cells. Alkaline cells can also provide twice the electricity of carbon-zinc cells. Mercury cells last about twice as long as alkaline cells. Mercury cells are very small. However, they provide the greatest energy for weight and size. Mercury cells are most common where space is a problem. Both alkaline and mercury cells are more expensive than carbon-zinc cells.

One of the products of the chemical action in all types of cells is a watery liquid. This liquid is very corrosive and can seep out of a discharged cell. It can cause corrosion inside electrical equipment. Flashlights are easily ruined this way.

Primary cells come in many different sizes and shapes. See Fig. 24-9.

Secondary Cells. A secondary cell converts electricity into chemical energy. It also holds the energy in this form. When needed, the chemical energy is changed back into electricity. This type of cell is referred to as *secondary* because it can be recharged.

Automobile storage batteries are the most common secondary cells. These batteries usually consist of six cells connected together. The storage battery supplies electricity to start the engine. While the engine is running, an alternator recharges the battery. That is, the alternator supplies electricity to the battery. The battery then converts the electricity into chemical energy. It holds the electricity until the engine needs to be started again.

A more precise name for an automobile battery is *lead-acid battery*. See Fig. 24-10. Each cell of the battery consists of two groups of lead plates in an electrolyte. The electrolyte is a mixture of distilled water and sulfuric acid. Positive lead peroxide plates are alternately sandwiched between negative lead plates. The plates are insulated from each other by separators.

When the battery is used in a circuit, a chemical reaction takes place between the plates and the electrolyte. This reaction produces an electric current that is discharged into the circuit. During the reaction, the acid in the electrolyte combines with the lead plates. This releases electrons. During recharging, current passes back through the battery. Electrons are forced into the plates, thus reversing the original reaction. The sulfuric acid returns to the electrolyte. Figure 24-11 shows the chemical reactions involved in charging and discharging.

Fig. 24-9. Common primary cells.

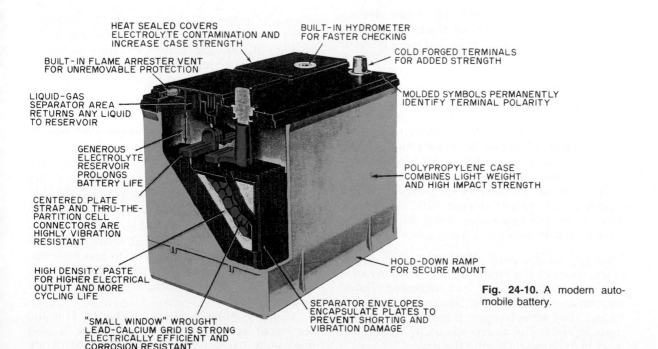

HEAT SEALED COVERS ELECTROLYTE CONTAMINATION AND INCREASE CASE STRENGTH

BUILT-IN HYDROMETER FOR FASTER CHECKING

COLD FORGED TERMINALS FOR ADDED STRENGTH

BUILT-IN FLAME ARRESTER VENT FOR UNREMOVABLE PROTECTION

MOLDED SYMBOLS PERMANENTLY IDENTIFY TERMINAL POLARITY

LIQUID-GAS SEPARATOR AREA RETURNS ANY LIQUID TO RESERVOIR

GENEROUS ELECTROLYTE RESERVOIR PROLONGS BATTERY LIFE

POLYPROPYLENE CASE COMBINES LIGHT WEIGHT AND HIGH IMPACT STRENGTH

CENTERED PLATE STRAP AND THRU-THE-PARTITION CELL CONNECTORS ARE HIGHLY VIBRATION RESISTANT

HIGH DENSITY PASTE FOR HIGHER ELECTRICAL OUTPUT AND MORE CYCLING LIFE

HOLD-DOWN RAMP FOR SECURE MOUNT

"SMALL WINDOW" WROUGHT LEAD-CALCIUM GRID IS STRONG ELECTRICALLY EFFICIENT AND CORROSION RESISTANT

SEPARATOR ENVELOPES ENCAPSULATE PLATES TO PREVENT SHORTING AND VIBRATION DAMAGE

Fig. 24-10. A modern automobile battery.

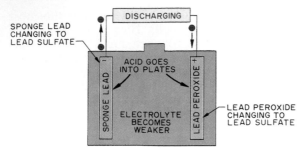

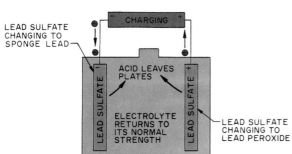

Fig. 24-11. Discharging and charging of a lead-acid battery.

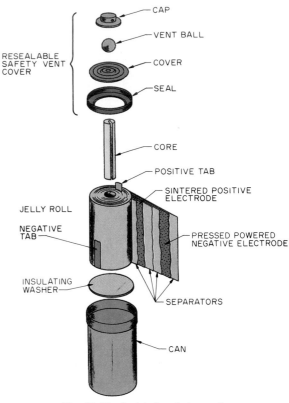

Fig. 24-12. A nickel-cadmium cell.

Both discharging and recharging produce hydrogen and oxygen. The battery has vent holes to permit these gases to escape. Batteries should never be turned over or placed on one side. This would allow the electrolyte to leak from the vents.

Lead-acid batteries have an advantage over some other secondary cells. The liquid electrolyte allows large numbers of electrons to move rapidly. Other secondary cells that use a paste or semisolid electrolyte cannot produce as much electricity.

The nickel-cadmium cell is another type of secondary cell. See Fig. 24-12. It can be used in place of carbon-zinc and alkaline cells for many uses. Nickel-cadmium cells use a paste of semi-solid electrolyte. A paste does not allow as much current to flow as a liquid does. However, the advantage is that nickel-cadmium cells do not leak. These cells can be used in any position. Nickel-cadmium cells power electric razors and many small tools and appliances. They can easily be recharged with small recharging units.

Future Cells and Batteries. In recent years, research in developing large-capacity storage cells and batteries has increased. Power companies are looking for ways of storing electricity. They want to store it during low-use periods at night. The stored electricity would help meet high demands during the day.

Electricity can be stored in many different ways. However, battery storage has one great advantage. It makes the electricity readily available.

Scientists are now trying to develop high-capacity lightweight batteries. These batteries could power automobiles. This would help reduce our dependency on fuels such as gasoline and diesel oil.

CONTROL OF ELECTRICAL ENERGY

We must control the electricity from power sources to put it to work. We do this with circuits and special control devices.

As earlier defined, a circuit is the path electric current follows as it travels to and from the power source. Electricity must readily pass through a circuit. Therefore, circuits are made of electrical conductors.

Copper is an excellent conductor. It is the one most commonly used. Aluminum is also used quite extensively. Wires made from it are larger than copper wires. However, aluminum wires weigh less than copper wires. By weight, aluminum is a better conductor than copper. This is an advantage in long-distance power transmission. The towers supporting aluminum wire can be farther apart. This makes the cost of an aluminum transmission system lower.

Symbols

Drawings of electrical circuits, like fluid power circuits, use symbols to represent actual parts. Knowing these symbols will help you read the drawings and gain a better understanding of electrical control. Figure 24-13 shows some of the basic symbols used for electrical control devices. You may wish to refer back to these as you study this chapter.

On-Off Control Devices

Circuits usually have electrical output units placed *in parallel*. This way, the units can work independently of each other. See Fig. 24-14. On-off control devices are placed *in series* with each unit. An open switch breaks the flow of electrons. This turns the light or heater off. A closed switch completes the circuit and turns the light or heater on.

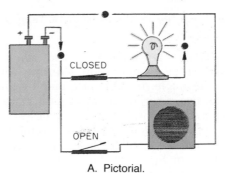

A. Pictorial.

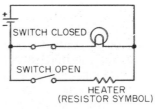

B. Schematic.

Fig. 24-14. In this circuit, the electric output units (the lamp and the heater) are placed in parallel. The switches in the circuit are placed in series with the output units.

Switches are the most common electrical control devices. Figure 24-15 shows the simplest type of on-off switch—the *knife switch*. All on-off switches operate basically like knife switches.

On-off switches come in many styles. In push-button types, current flows only when the button is pushed. Many switches operate with spring tension. The light switch used in most homes is a good example. This switch is called a *toggle switch*. Spring tension opens and closes the contact points quickly. This "snap action"

Fig. 24-15. A typical knife switch. This double-pole, double-throw switch is used to control the current on two different circuits.

Fig. 24-13. Basic symbols for electrical control devices.

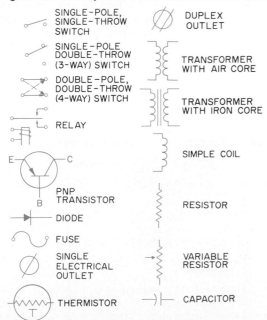

SINGLE-POLE, SINGLE-THROW SWITCH

SINGLE-POLE DOUBLE-THROW (3-WAY) SWITCH

DOUBLE-POLE, DOUBLE-THROW (4-WAY) SWITCH

RELAY

PNP TRANSISTOR

DIODE

FUSE

SINGLE ELECTRICAL OUTLET

THERMISTOR

DUPLEX OUTLET

TRANSFORMER WITH AIR CORE

TRANSFORMER WITH IRON CORE

SIMPLE COIL

RESISTOR

VARIABLE RESISTOR

CAPACITOR

helps to keep the contacts from burning during opening or closing.

Three-Way Switches. The three-way switch is a single-pole double-throw (SPDT) switch. The single movable arm may be thrown to one of two different contacts. Either "throw" completes the circuit. Figure 24-16 shows a common use of this switch—a lighting circuit. It may be turned on or off with either of the three-way switches (S_1 or S_3). Many homes have this type of circuit. Three-way switches may be placed at opposite ends of a room. The residents can control the lights from either end.

Four-Way Switches. Sometimes three switches are needed to control a circuit. A four-way switch is used as the third switch. Although a four-way switch looks like a regular toggle switch, it has four contacts for the wires in the circuit. A four-way switch always permits a current to flow through it.

Figure 24-17 shows a circuit with three switches controlling two lights. S_1 and S_3 are three-way switches. S_2 is a four-way switch. In **A**, the circuit is complete and the lights are on. Changing any of the three switches will turn the lights off. In **B**, S_2 has been turned to its second position. This opens the circuit and turns the lights off. Changing any of the three switches will turn the lights on.

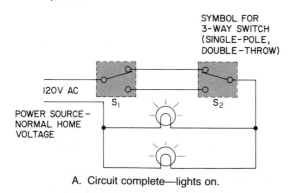

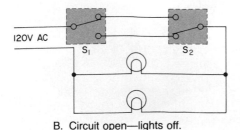

B. Circuit open—lights off.

Fig. 24-16. Three-way switches can control two lights connected in parallel.

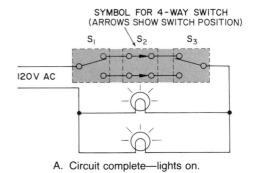

A. Circuit complete—lights on.

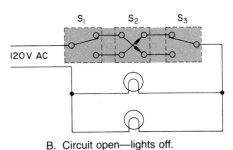

B. Circuit open—lights off.

Fig. 24-17. This light circuit uses two three-way switches and a four-way switch.

Sometimes more than three switches are needed to control a circuit. More four-way switches may be added. The switches are wired into the circuit between the two three-way switches. The operator can use any switch to turn the lights on or off.

Relays. A relay is an electrically operated switch used to control a circuit from a remote source. Relays can also serve as automatic control devices. A relay controls on-off switching with an electromagnet. See Fig. 24-18. In the relay, a coil surrounds a soft iron core. When the operator closes the switch, current flows through

Fig. 24-18. The operation of a relay in an electrical circuit.

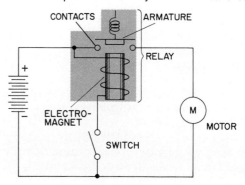

Technology Focus

Another Micro-Revolution?

The development of the microchip made possible the "computer revolution." Today we may be on the brink of a new technology revolution—one created by the development of *micromotors*.

The micromotor shown here is no larger than the width of a single human hair! It is less than three thousandths of an inch in diameter and about one ten-thousandth of an inch thick. The picture was taken through an electron microscope.

The same materials and techniques used to make microchips are used to make micromotors. Basically, layers of polysilicon and silicon dioxide are built up and then shaped into the mechanical elements by using lithographic and etching techniques.

The micromotor in the picture is powered by extremely small amounts of electricity. The structure in the middle of the motor is the *rotor*. *Stator poles* surround the rotor. The voltage difference between the poles of the rotor and the stator poles creates an *electrostatic force* that causes the rotor to turn. This electrostatic drive can *interface* with circuits on conventional microchips, a very promising feature for the future of micromotors!

At the time this book is being written, micromotors have not yet been developed for practical use. But much progress is being made. By the time you read this article, they may be in use in surgical and scientific instruments, manufacturing equipment, hearing aids, and many other products. As a matter of fact, you may be witnessing a "micromotor revolution." Researchers say it's possible!

the coil. The core becomes an electromagnet. An armature above the coil has switch contacts. The electromagnet pulls the armature down to make contact. This completes the circuit to the motor. When the operator opens the switch, the magnetic attraction stops. A strong spring then opens the contacts. This breaks the circuit and stops the motor.

Large relays are used to control circuits with large amounts of current. In these cases, the hand switch operating the relay can be located some distance from the motor. The relay itself needs very little current to operate.

Relays can be operated by switches controlled by clocks. Thermostats, light meters, and other sensing devices are also used to activate relays. These devices work by connecting two contacts to complete a circuit. This activates the relay. Many automatic circuits operate in this way. Relays operate burglar alarms, furnaces, refrigerators, and many other electric devices.

The strength of the electromagnet within the relay is based on ampere-turns. An *ampere-turn* is a current of 1 ampere (amp) passing through a wire making one complete turn around the core. For example, if an electromagnet has 1000 turns of wire and one amp passes through the wire, the strength of the electromagnet will be based on 1000 ampere-turns. The same strength can be achieved with only 100 turns of wire. However, 10 amps must pass through it. Therefore, a common method of determining magnetic effect is to multiply the current by the number of turns on the coil.

Figure 24-18 shows a relay wired in parallel with a motor. In such a system, the relay coil will have many thin turns carrying a low amperage. This will produce a strong magnet with a minimum use of electricity. We call this type of relay a *voltage-sensitive* or *voltage-operated relay*. It is the most common type of relay.

Relays can also be wired in series with the device being controlled. See Fig. 24-19. In this example, the coil is wired in series with an electric motor. In normal operation, a low current passes through both the motor and the relay coil. The amperage is enough to operate the motor. But it is not high enough to activate the relay.

If the load on the motor becomes too high, the motor will slow down. It will also draw more amperage from the power source. This increased amperage strengthens the coil's magnetic field. The relay closes and connects the warning light into the circuit. The light warns the operator that the motor may be overloaded and in danger of overheating. We call this type of relay a *current-sensitive* or *current-operated relay*. Its coil has fewer turns, but the wire is large. All the current for the circuit must pass through the coil. The large wires of the coil provide almost no resistance to current flow.

The two relays shown so far are both *normally-open (NO) relays*. When the relay is not operating, its points are open. *Normally-closed (NC) relays* are also available. In an NC relay, the points are closed when the relay is not operating. When the relay is activated, the points are open.

Transistors

Transistors are electric devices that can be used as on-off switches. They control circuits just as relays do. However, transistors have no moving parts. This is a great advantage. Moving parts can wear out or require servicing. Transistors operate entirely on electricity. They have an almost unlimited useful life. However, they must be protected from excessive heat. They must also be used for their designed purpose.

Transistors are one of several types of *solid-state devices*. This means they consist entirely of solid material. In transistors, insulators and semiconductors are solid materials.

Up to this point, we have considered only materials that are good electrical conductors. There are also many materials that are the opposite of conductors. These insulators resist the flow of electrons. Insulators have no free electrons. Therefore, they cannot transmit electric current.

There is a group of materials between conductors and insulators. This group has some of the properties of both conductors and insulators. These materials are called **semiconductors**.

Semiconductors are used in transistors and many other devices. The two semiconductors most commonly used are silicon and germanium. Both elements form crystals. Figure 24-20 shows a modern transistor. Figure 24-21 shows the construction of a silicon transistor. In its pure form, silicon is an insulator. However, the silicon used in transistors is not pure. Small quantities of an impurity, such as arsenic or aluminum, are needed. Arsenic causes the silicon to free some electrons. This makes the silicon a conductor. The free electrons are able to flow. Since this form of silicon has free electrons (negative charge), it is labeled *N* in Fig. 24-21.

Adding aluminum to silicon makes it react in an opposite way. This form of silicon can accept free electrons. It is labeled *P* (positive) in Fig. 24-21. Note that there are two pieces of P material and one piece of N material. These materials produce a *PNP* transistor. Transistors may also be made with two pieces of N material and one piece of P material (*NPN*). The three materials make up the *emitter (E), base (B),* and *collector (C)*. A wire is connected to each of the three parts.

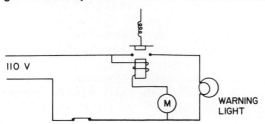

Fig. 24-19. A relay wired in series with an electric motor.

Fig. 24-20. A modern transistor.

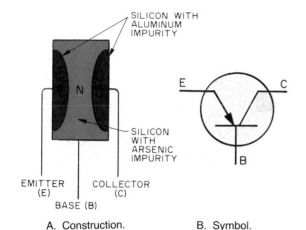

A. Construction.　　　　B. Symbol.

Fig. 24-21. The makeup of a PNP transistor.

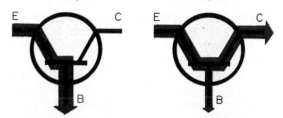

Fig. 24-23. A transistor operates when a small amount of current flows in the E-B circuit. The E-B circuit acts as a switch to activate the E-C circuit. The arrows show the direction of *hole* flow, not electron flow.

Transistors and Electron Flow.

Before you learn how transistors and other solid-state devices work, you must review the movement of electrons through a conductor. You will recall that electrons flow from negative to positive. As one electron enters the negative side of a conductor, one electron leaves the positive side.

Solid-state devices operate on the principle of *hole flow* rather than electron flow. Hole flow is in the opposite direction of electron flow. See Fig. 24-22.

Transistor Operation.

Figure 24-23 shows how a transistor works. The *emitter-collector (E-C) circuit* is the main path of the current flow. For current to flow through this path, a small amount of current must flow through the *emitter-base (E-B) circuit*. The E-B circuit acts as a switch. It activates the E-C circuit. If no current

flows through the E-B circuit, no current flows in the E-C circuit. Therefore, the E-B circuit acts as a switch. It turns the E-C circuit on or off.

Figure 24-24 shows a transistor in a circuit. Note that the flow of electrons (negative to positive) is from the base (B) to the emitter (E). This is opposite the direction of the arrow in the transistor symbol. The emitter (a positive material) has holes that can accept electrons from the base (a negative material). As current flows, the hole moves from the emitter to the base. As this happens, an electron from the negative side of the battery moves to the base to fill the hole. As this process continues, a small current flows through the E-B circuit.

Most of the holes provided by the emitter move to the collector. There, electrons from the battery can fill the holes. The resistor below the base permits only a limited flow of electrons. Therefore, most of the electrons pass from the collector to the emitter through the base. The base triggers this flow. However, the main flow of electrons is through the E-C circuit.

Note that the transistor in Fig. 24-24 takes the place of a relay. When the switch is closed, the availability of electrons at the base activates the E-B circuit. This, in turn, triggers the E-C circuit, which starts the motor. The motor will con-

Fig. 24-22. The direction of hole flow is opposite the direction of electron flow. This is shown by the row of billiard balls. When a ball (electron) is added on the left, a ball leaves on the right. This forms a hole. As more balls are added, the hole "moves" to the left.

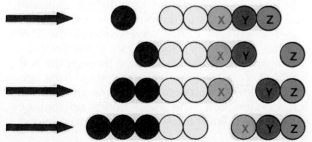

Fig. 24-24. Using a transistor as a switch in an electrical circuit.

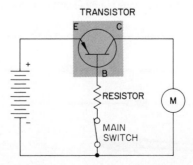

tinue running as long as a small amount of current flows through the E-B circuit. Carmakers have substituted transistors for some relays in modern automobile circuits.

Transistors have many uses in addition to functioning as on-off switches. They have replaced the vacuum tubes formerly used in radios, televisions, and early computers. Hundreds of transistors can fit on tiny chips. These chips are used in digital watches, calculators, computers, and microprocessors. Many products can be made almost completely with transistors and other solid-state parts.

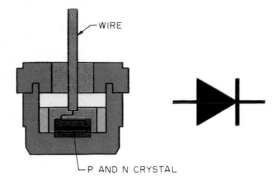

Fig. 24-26. Diode construction and symbol.

Directing Current Flow—Diodes

Another type of solid-state device is the diode. **Diodes** permit current to flow through them in only one direction. They act much like fluid power check valves. These valves, you will recall, allow liquid or gas to flow in only one direction.

Figure 24-25 shows several typical diodes. Figure 24-26 shows diode construction and the diode symbol. The arrow in the symbol points in the direction of *hole movement*, not electron flow.

Diodes are made by joining a small N-type semiconductor to a P-type semiconductor. In Fig. 24-26A, the P and N crystal is below the wire near the bottom. The case and surrounding parts protect the crystal from damage.

A diode has only two connections. The wire leading up from the diode acts as one connection. The case acts as the other. In many diodes, the crystal is insulated from the case. This type of diode has a second wire leading from the case.

Diodes can be used to change alternating current (AC) to direct current (DC). We call this

process *rectification*. The diode accomplishes rectification by passing current in only one direction. Rectified current can be used for charging batteries. This use for diodes has made rechargeable batteries practical for many devices. Computers, electric shavers, carving knives, and electric toothbrushes are examples. The most common use of rechargeable batteries is in our automobiles.

Controlling Current—SCRs

The characteristics of the transistor and diode can be combined. The result is a diode that can be turned on and off electrically. A diode that uses silicon is called a *silicon rectifier*. The control features of a transistor can be added to a silicon rectifier. It then becomes a **silicon-controlled rectifier (SCR)**. Another common name for the SCR is *thyristor*.

Figure 24-27 shows how an SCR has features of both the transistor and the diode. It consists of four semiconductor materials, two P-type and two N-type.

An SCR will not pass current in either direction until it is "triggered," or turned on. It will then pass current between the *anode* (positive side) and the *cathode* (negative side). Again, see Fig. 24-27. The SCR is triggered by a small current passing through the *gate* to the cathode. The gate connects to the power source.

The current easily travels across the P-N crystals as it moves from the gate to the cathode. The current flow causes leakage through the N-P junction (center line with arrows). This increased flow permits current to flow through the left P-N junction. The effect builds up rapidly. Current then flows freely between the anode and the cathode.

Fig. 24-25. Modern diodes are available in many shapes and sizes.

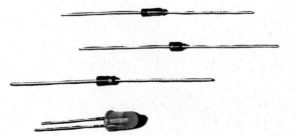

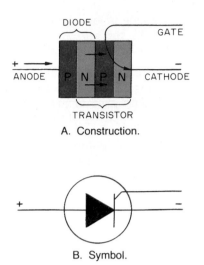

A. Construction.

B. Symbol.

Fig. 24-27. A silicon-controlled rectifier (SCR). The arrows indicate the direction of hole movement.

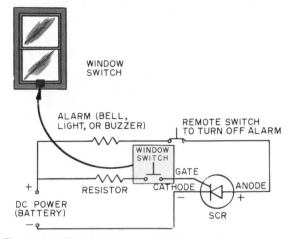

Fig. 24-28. This window-operated burglar alarm uses an SCR.

The current continues to flow through the SCR even when the current through the gate stops. The small current flow through the gate circuit is needed only to start the main flow from anode to cathode.

Breaking the system circuit with a switch stops the current flow through the SCR. The gate circuit must trigger the SCR again before current will flow again.

If the power input is alternating current, the SCR will rectify it into direct current. Each half-cycle of alternating current produces a stop as the current reverses. In this case, the gate circuit must remain in operation.

Remember, in SCR operation, current flow starts only when the gate circuit is triggered. This permits a flow of current across the anode-cathode circuit. The current stops *only* when the anode-cathode circuit is opened.

Figure 24-28 shows an SCR in a window-operated burglar alarm circuit. A battery provides the power. Under normal conditions, no current flows through the SCR in either direction. When someone opens the window, the window switch closes. This completes the gate circuit. The resistor in the system circuit keeps the current at a low level. The current in the gate-to-cathode circuit turns on the anode-cathode circuit. The alarm rings. Closing the window closes the window switch. However, the alarm will continue to ring. It will stop only when the remote switch is opened or the batteries wear out. This is only one example of many possible uses for an SCR.

Solar Cells

Solar (photovoltaic) cells are also semiconductors. As with other solid-state devices, solar cells contain no moving parts and are made mainly of silicon. The silicon is first mixed with a small amount of arsenic. This mixture is then formed into a large crystal. The crystal is cut into thin wafers, about $\frac{1}{25}$ of an inch (1 mm) thick. The wafer is then exposed to a vapor containing boron. The boron penetrates into the wafer about $\frac{1}{10,000}$ of an inch ($\frac{1}{400}$ mm). The wafer is cleaned and plated, and wires are attached. One wire attaches to the silicon center. The other wire attaches to the boron-penetrated surface. The wafer is now a solar cell.

The silicon/arsenic center of the wafer has a different electrical characteristic than the boron portion of the crystal. Figure 24-29 shows the construction of a solar cell. The boron layer is labeled N (negative). The silicon/arsenic layer is labeled P (positive). When light strikes the solar cell, it produces a voltage difference between

Fig. 24-29. The construction of a solar cell.

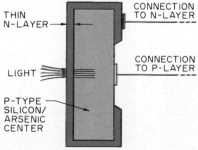

the P and N layers. About 0.45 volt is developed. While the electric current is small, when grouped together as described in Chapter 3, solar cells can develop large quantities of electrical energy.

Other Solid-State Devices

A great variety of solid-state devices has been developed since the transistor. These devices have changed the manner in which many industrial processes are controlled. The microprocessors and computers described in Chapter 7 use solid-state devices. These controls are now found throughout the home, as well as in business and industry.

Overload Control—Fuses and Circuit Breakers

Fuses and **circuit breakers** are switches that open quickly when too much current passes through a circuit. Excessive current can result from a short circuit or an overload.

A **short circuit** is produced whenever the electrons are allowed to return to the source without passing through the complete circuit. See Fig. 24-30. That is, the electrons bypass normal circuit resistance. In general terms, any electric device, such as a motor, lamp, heater, or radio, is referred to as a resistance. In Fig. 24-30, the light bulb is the resistance.

When resistances are bypassed, the electron flow (amperage) through the circuit is very high. Too much current flowing through a circuit is called an *overload*. This produces excessive heat. The heat, in turn, can burn the insulation from the wires. In a home or industrial plant, the heat developed by a short circuit or overload can ignite the insulation on the wires. Serious fires can result.

Excessive heat can also occur if the circuit has too many parallel resistances. Each added resistance reduces the total resistance of the cir-

cuit. If the resistance is low, the current may become greater than the wires can safely carry. This overload condition could result in a fire.

Fuses. A fuse protects a circuit from dangerous overloads. Figure 24-31 shows how a fuse works. In **B** the amperage of the shorted circuit is greater than the capacity of the fuse. The heat produced by the current melts the link within the fuse. This opens the circuit. All current flow stops. The short circuit must be corrected and the fuse must be replaced before normal current flow will begin again.

Figure 24-32 shows three different fuse designs. *Time-delay fuses* permit a momentary current flow above their designed capacity. They are used on motor circuits that require a high current for starting but a lower current for operation.

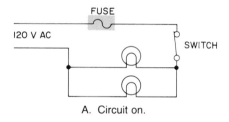
A. Circuit on.

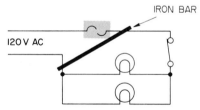
B. Circuit shorted. Fuse blows allowing no current flow.

Fig. 24-31. The connection within a fuse breaks whenever the circuit is overloaded.

Fig. 24-30. A short circuit permits current to bypass the resistors in a circuit.

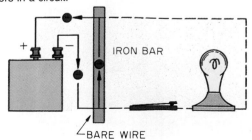

Fig. 24-32. Various fuse designs.

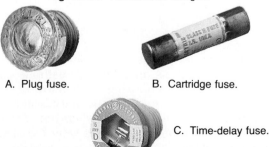

A. Plug fuse.

B. Cartridge fuse.

C. Time-delay fuse.

Circuit Breakers.

A circuit breaker serves the same purpose as a fuse. However, it can be reset by a switch after the circuit is opened.

A number of circuit breaker designs are commonly used. One operates on the same principle as the relay. Figure 24-33 shows a circuit protected by this type of circuit breaker. In **A** the current is flowing and the motor is running. The current flow may become too great. In this case the magnetic field of the circuit breaker coil will become strong enough to pivot the breaker arm. See Fig. 24-33B. When this happens, the circuit breaks and the motor stops. To start the motor, someone must reset the circuit breaker. This is done by moving a switch or pushing a button located on the circuit breaker.

All circuits are protected by either fuses or circuit breakers. If you replace either device, you must use a fuse or circuit breaker of the proper capacity. An over-capacity fuse provides little protection against fire or other types of circuit damage.

Ground Fault Circuit Interruption (GFCI).

In some special situations, fuses and circuit breakers do not provide protection against electrical shock. Your body offers some resistance to current flow. Therefore, touching a wire does not necessarily blow a fuse or open a circuit breaker.

Practicing Safety

Do not touch a "live" wire. Your body would provide an alternate path for the current flow. This danger is especially serious in any place where you might touch a live wire while in contact with water or some other good ground. Examples include bathrooms, damp basements, and anyplace outside.

In potentially dangerous situations, the circuit needs special protection. A ground fault circuit interrupter (GFCI) provides this protection. The GFCI can be a circuit breaker or a special type of electrical outlet. See Fig. 24-34.

The GFCI protects against shock by measuring the current flow in each of the two wires of an electrical circuit. Remember, every electrical circuit is a complete loop. It has a wire from the source to the use. It also has a wire that returns to the source. The current in one wire should be the same as the current in the other wire. A difference in the two currents indicates a circuit leak to ground. The leak to ground could be caused by a short circuit or someone touching a live wire. The GFCI immediately breaks the circuit whenever a leak to ground occurs. This prevents or reduces the chance of electrical shock. Many building codes now require electricians to use GFCI breakers in bathrooms, garages, and outside outlets.

Bimetallic Circuit Breaker.

Another type of overload protection is the bimetallic circuit breaker. (*Bimetallic* means made of two metals.) This type of circuit breaker protects motors from temporary overloads. Bimetallic circuit breakers are used in any situation where motors might be

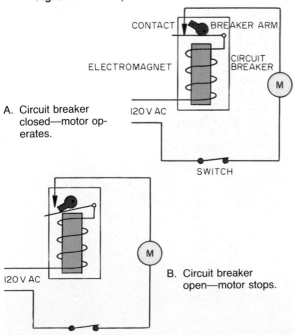

Fig. 24-33. The operation of a circuit breaker.

A. Circuit breaker closed—motor operates.

B. Circuit breaker open—motor stops.

Fig. 24-34. Ground Fault Circuit Interrupters are designed to protect humans and animals from serious electric shock.

overloaded. (An air conditioner running during a very hot day is a good example.) The main advantage of a bimetallic circuit breaker is that it can be self-setting. After the overload has been relieved, a self-setting circuit breaker cools and resets itself.

The bimetallic circuit breaker consists of a heating coil, a bimetal strip, and contacts. The heating coil generates heat that affects the bimetal strip. The metals in the strip expand at different rates when heated. This causes the strip to bend. The circuit breaker is wired in series in the circuit. Excessive heat causes the contacts to open, thus breaking the circuit. See Fig. 24-35.

When the circuit is open, the coil cools. This allows the bimetal strip to return to its original shape. The contacts then close again. This action turns the motor on. If the temporary overload has disappeared, the motor will run in a normal way. But if the circuit is still overloaded, the breaker cycle will repeat itself until the trouble is corrected.

Controlling the Amount of Current and Voltage

Besides starting and stopping current flow, we must often vary the amount of voltage and current. Several types of devices have been developed to provide this control. They include:

■ Transformers
■ Resistors
■ Thermistors

Transformers. A transformer changes the ratio of the voltage and amperage in a circuit.

For example, electrical power plants generate electricity at about 2200 volts. This voltage is too low for long-distance power transmission. Therefore, the power company uses transformers to boost the voltage to about 220,000 volts. At the same time, the transformers lower the current's amperage. High-voltage current loses less power over long distances than high-amperage current does. When the electricity reaches its area of use, other transformers reduce its voltage and raise its amperage. For home use, the voltage is reduced to 240 and 120 volts.

A change in voltage is *always* accompanied by a change in amperage. However, the amperage adjustment is in the opposite direction. As voltage increases, amperage decreases.

Transformers range in size from very large to very small. See Figs. 24-36 and 24-37.

Transformer Operation. Transformers operate on the principle of **induction**. They transmit energy from one circuit to another, modifying the energy in the process. This is similar to the way an automobile ignition coil works. Like automobile ignition coils, transformers have two sets of windings. These windings are called the *primary coil* and the *secondary coil*. Both coils of wire are usually wrapped around a soft iron core.

Fig. 24-36. A large transformer in an electrical substation. Electric fans cool the transformer during operation.

Fig. 24-35. These diagrams show how a bimetallic circuit breaker protects an electric motor. If the motor draws too much current, the bimetal strip gets hot and bends. This breaks the circuit until the bimetal strip cools.

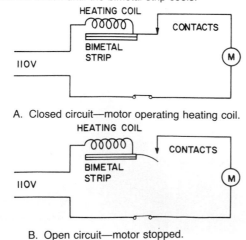

A. Closed circuit—motor operating heating coil.

B. Open circuit—motor stopped.

Fig. 24-37. This small transformer reduces voltage from 120 volts to 12.6 volts (AC).

Figure 24-38 shows the location of a transformer in a circuit. Note that the primary coil is not connected to the secondary coil. However, the two coils are very close to each other. When the switch is closed, a magnetic field builds up in the primary coil. This field is called the *primary field*. As it builds up, the primary field cuts through the secondary coil. This action generates current in the secondary coil. The current lights the lamp.

Induction takes place only when the electromagnetic field moves. Therefore, the lamp lights up only for a moment. Opening the switch will cause the primary field to collapse. As the field collapses, it will again cut through the secondary coil. This will cause the lamp to light for another instant.

To induce a current, the magnetic field must either build up or collapse. A circuit having a

transformer cannot use uninterrupted direct current. For example, in Fig. 24-38, the cell delivers a constant DC current. Induction takes place only when the switch is opened or closed. A constant flow of current from a DC source will overheat the transformer.

Induction is a continuous process in an alternating current circuit. See Fig. 24-39. Alternating current constantly changes direction. It produces an electromagnetic field that is either collapsing or building at all times. This happens so fast that the lamp appears to be lit constantly.

Step-up Transformers. The primary and secondary coils have different numbers of windings. See Fig. 24-40. The voltage induced in the secondary coil depends on the voltage in the primary coil. It also depends on the ratio between the number of windings in each coil. In Fig. 24-40A, the ratio of the primary windings to the secondary windings is 10:100 or 1:10. The voltage induced in the secondary coil will be 10 times that of the primary coil. The *amperage* of the

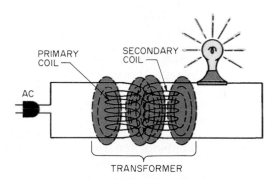

Fig. 24-39. Alternating current produces continuous induction of electric current from the primary coil to the secondary coil.

Fig. 24-38. Induction takes place when the primary circuit is connected or disconnected by a switch. Each buildup or collapse of the primary field lights the bulb for just an instant.

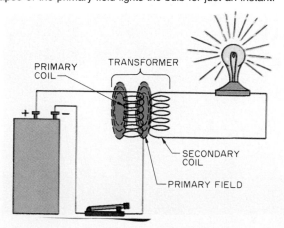

Fig. 24-40. A step-up transformer and transformer symbols.

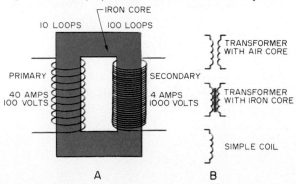

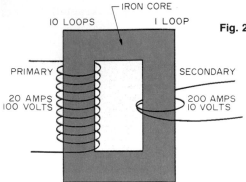

IRON CORE

10 LOOPS　　　　I LOOP

PRIMARY　　　　　SECONDARY

20 AMPS　　　　　200 AMPS
100 VOLTS　　　　10 VOLTS

Fig. 24-41. A step-down transformer.

secondary coil will be $\frac{1}{10}$ that of the primary coil. A transformer that changes current in this way is called a *step-up transformer*. It increases (steps up) voltage and decreases amperage. However, note that the *wattage* remains unchanged:

Input Wattage
Watts = Volts × Amps
Watts = 100 Volts × 40 Amps
Watts = 4000

Output Wattage
Watts = 1000 Volts × 4 Amps
Watts = 4000

Try to keep this point in mind. Control devices can change the *characteristics* of power, such as voltage and amperage. However, control devices cannot change the total *amount* of available power. The only way to increase power is to provide additional energy from another source.

In transformers some power in the form of heat is lost during induction. However, this loss is quite low. Transformers can change voltage and amperage with very little loss of energy.

Step-down Transformers. Figure 24-41 shows a step-down transformer. This type of transformer has fewer loops in the secondary coil. This arrangement decreases (steps down) the voltage from the primary coil to the secondary coil. At the same time, the transformer increases amperage. The wattage remains the same.

As stated earlier, electricity is transmitted through power lines in the form of high-voltage, low-amperage current. Step-down transformers are used at the end of the line to reduce voltage and increase amperage.

Resistors. In a circuit, resistance converts electrical energy into heat energy. All electric devices offer resistance to current flow. Resistance can also be deliberately added to a circuit to provide control. Special resistors are used for this purpose. These devices have one main function—to reduce current flow.

Figure 24-42 shows various types of commonly used resistors. Most resistors consist of an insulated and sealed coil of wire. The wire resists current flow. Resistors are rated in watts. The watt rating indicates the amount of heat the resistor can safely transfer to the surrounding air. The watt rating also determines the capacity of the circuit in which a resistor can be used. For example, a 10-ohm, 10-watt resistor provides 10 ohms of resistance. However, it can be safely used only in circuits carrying up to 10 watts.

Some resistors provide an adjustable resistance. This type of resistor is called a *variable resistor*. Other names for a variable resistor are *potentiometer* and *rheostat*.

A variable resistor is shown in the lower right of Fig. 24-42. The farther the current must travel through the coiled wire, the greater the resistance. Moving the sliding contact (center) toward the input (end) reduces the length of wire through which the current must pass. This in turn reduces the resistance.

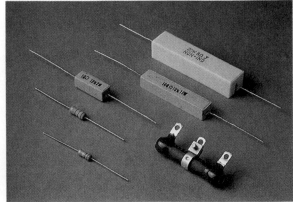

Fig. 24-42. Common resistors.

Fig. 24-43. The brightness of automobile dash lights is controlled by a variable resistor.

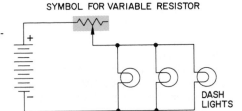

SYMBOL FOR VARIABLE RESISTOR

DASH LIGHTS

Resistors reduce voltage (electrical pressure). In this way, they limit the flow of current. See Fig. 24-43.

Thermistors. A thermistor is a temperature-sensitive resistor. See Fig. 24-44. The name comes from the words *thermal* and *resistor*. When it is cold, a thermistor has a high resistance to current flow. As the thermistor becomes warm, its resistance drops. This action is opposite to that of most electric heaters. Electric heaters have low beginning resistance. The resistance increases as they warm up.

Thermistors are commonly used in measuring temperature. See Fig. 24-45. They are also used in circuits where a low beginning resistance can be harmful. A transistor circuit is one example.

Capacitors. In many situations, we need to delay the flow of electric current. That is, we must temporarily restrict or remove current flow. In these cases, we use capacitors to control the current. A **capacitor** is a device that stores and holds an electrical charge. See Fig. 24-46.

A capacitor consists of two metallic plates (conductors) separated by an insulating material. The insulation is called a *dielectric*. The metal plates are good conductors. Therefore, they can store electrons. When current enters a capacitor, one plate collects a surplus of electrons. This plate is called the *negative plate*. The other plate loses electrons. This plate is the *positive plate*. An electrical charge can build up in a capacitor. Therefore, a charged capacitor can be a source of electrical power.

In a charged capacitor, there is a difference in the number of electrons on the negative and positive plates. This difference is the amount of the charge. We measure the charge contained by a capacitor in farads. One *farad (F)* is an electron difference of one coulomb (6.28×10^{18} electrons). A one-farad capacitor is quite large. Most capacitors are smaller. In fact, most capacitors are measured in *microfarads (μF)*. A microfarad is one-millionth of a farad.

Fig. 24-44. Thermistors are available in many shapes and sizes. Some are so small they can fit through the eye of a needle.

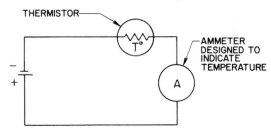

THERMISTOR

AMMETER DESIGNED TO INDICATE TEMPERATURE

Fig. 24-45. Thermistors can be used in measuring temperature. In this circuit, more current flows to the ammeter as the thermistor heats up.

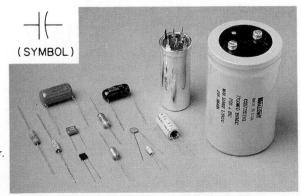

(SYMBOL)

Fig. 24-46. Typical capacitors and the symbol for capacitor.

Figure 24-47 shows how a battery charges a capacitor. In **A**, free electrons move from the negative terminal to the negative plate. The electrons build up on the plate. At the same time, electrons are being repelled from the positive plate. The dielectric insulates the two plates from each other. However, it adjusts to the surplus of electrons on the negative plate. It does this by forcing electrons from the positive plate to the positive battery terminal. Electron movement continues until the plate has the same level of surplus electrons as the battery. When this happens, the circuit is in balance. The electron flow stops. At this point, the capacitor is charged.

Figure 24-47B shows the circuit after the battery has been removed. The capacitor retains its charge. The charge can now be used. A common use is a camera flash unit. A switch connects the charge capacitor to the flash unit. The electrons rush through the unit. This causes the bright flash of light. See Fig. 24-47C.

Practicing Safety

If you touch the two leads of a charged high-voltage capacitor, you will get a severe shock. The larger the capacitor, the more severe the shock. Also, if you charge a capacitor at a voltage higher than its rating, it can explode. **Capacitors can be deadly.**

In a flash unit, the battery cannot provide the sudden surge of electrons needed for a bright flash. However, the battery *can* charge the capacitor in 10-15 seconds. The stored energy is then released quickly to produce a bright flash.

Note that the capacitor and flash unit are in a DC circuit. In an AC circuit, the capacitor will charge as current flows one way. When the current stops to reverse direction, the capacitor will discharge. This principle is used in capacitor-start motors. These motors are described later in this chapter.

Some electronic circuits use capacitors for units that need surges of current. Automobile ignition systems use capacitors to *contain* sudden surges. An automobile capacitor (or *condensor*) helps keep the breaker points from burning. Capacitors are also used to reduce radio interference.

TRANSMITTING CURRENT

Electricity is transmitted more efficiently than any other common form of power. As a result, power is carried as electricity to all parts of our nation.

Most current-carrying wires consist of a conductor surrounded by an insulating material. See Fig. 24-48. The insulation prevents current loss through short circuits. Insulators are *nonconductors*. They prevent the flow of electric current. Most plastics make good insulators. They are used to insulate the wiring in electric motors. Often "bare" copper wire is really wire insulated with a clear plastic. While most wires are insulated, some are not. Large power lines are not insulated. Rather, they are insulated from the towers supporting them.

A high-amperage flow produces heat in a conductor. This is due to the friction of the electrons traveling through the conductor. Power companies always transmit large amounts of electricity long distances at very high voltages and low amperages.

Fig. 24-47. A capacitor in three conditions.

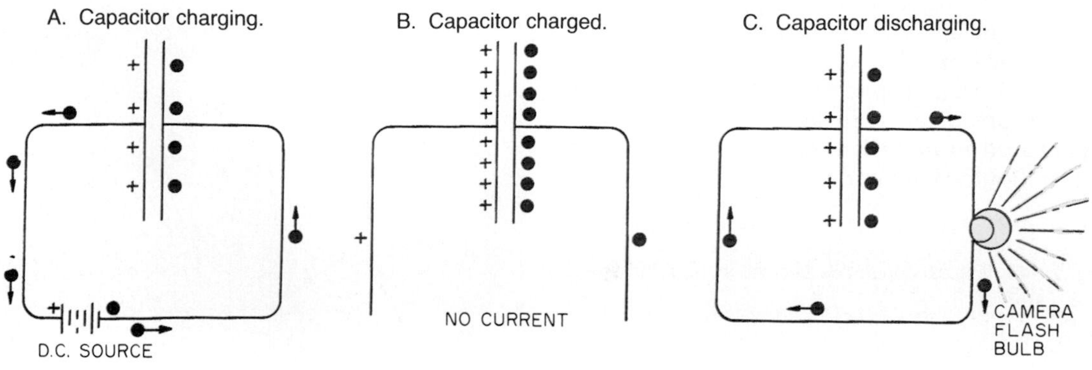

A. Capacitor charging. B. Capacitor charged. C. Capacitor discharging.

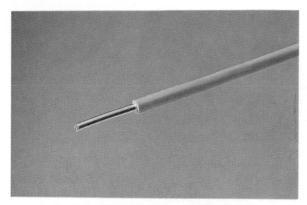

Fig. 24-48. An insulated electrical conductor.

ELECTRICAL POWER OUTPUT

The uses of electrical power may be grouped into four major categories:
- Motion
- Heat
- Light
- Communication

As you know, all devices using electricity act as resistors. In the process of producing light or motion, some of the electricity is changed to heat. This heat is produced by the friction of electrons moving through the conductor. The heat is released to the surrounding air. Output devices such as electric heaters use special conductors that offer higher resistance. The amount of heat produced by these devices can be controlled.

Conversion to Motion

Electricity can be changed into either linear or rotary motion. Solenoids produce linear motion. Electric motors produce rotary motion.

Solenoids

A **solenoid** is a simple variation of the relay. It is simply a relay with a movable core. A spring holds a plunger (the core) away from the center of a coil. Passing a current through the coil develops a magnetic field. The lines of force travel through the core as well as around it.

As described in Chapter 23, lines of force travel more easily through metal than through air. Lines of force also try to take the shortest path through the field. First the lines of force take the longer path through the iron core. Then the field develops enough force to pull the core

into the center of the coil. The two actions take place very quickly.

The core movement has considerable force. Therefore, we can use it to perform any linear work. Controlling fluid power valves and engaging gears are two examples.

Another common use is to bring heavy electrical contact points together. For example, the solenoid may act as a switch in an automobile starting system. See Fig. 24-49. The solenoid transmits 100 to 300 amps of current from the battery to the starter.

Motors

Electric motors work by converting electric current into rotary motion. They operate on the same principles used in generators. Figure 24-50 shows a magnetic field with a current-carrying wire within the field. The wire has its own lines of force. These lines react with the lines of force between the poles of the magnet.

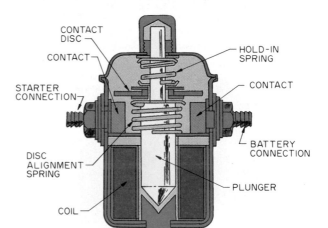

Fig. 24-49. This automobile solenoid is operated by the ignition key. When the key is turned, contact is made between the battery and the starter.

Fig. 24-50. Inside a motor, the lines of force surrounding a current-carrying conductor react with another magnetic field. The reaction produces a weaker field below the conductor. The conductor moves toward this weaker field.

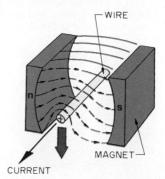

This reaction makes the wire move. Note that the wire's magnetic field moves in the same direction as the magnetic field above it. The two fields combine and become stronger. Below the conductor in Fig. 24-50, the wire's field opposes the other field. Therefore, the wire's field weakens the magnet's field. This causes a magnetic imbalance. The imbalance forces the conductor toward the weakened field.

If the same wire shown in Fig. 24-50 were shaped in a loop, the wire would start to rotate. See Fig. 24-51. The arrows on the wire show the direction of current flow. Figure 24-52 shows how current passing through the loop both strengthens and weakens the lines of force. This action produces a rotating force on the loop of wire. However, the loop cannot continue through a complete revolution unless the current direction changes.

Figure 24-52 will help you understand the need for current to reverse direction. When the loop on the left reaches the bottom and tries to start up on the right side, it will be pushed down rather than up. However, if the current flow

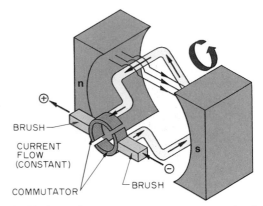

Fig. 24-53. In a DC motor, a commutator reverses the direction of current flow in the wire. This reversal occurs when the rotating wire is 90° vertical to the brushes.

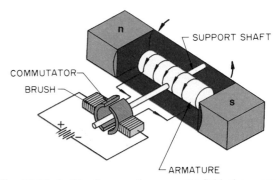

Fig. 24-54. In this diagram, the magnetic field of a current-carrying conductor has been strengthened by adding windings and adding an iron core. The result is a rotating electromagnet (armature).

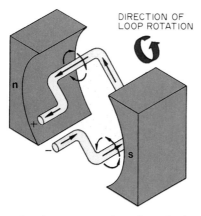

Fig. 24-51. Passing a current through a wire loop within a magnetic field causes the loop to rotate.

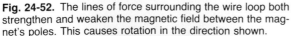

Fig. 24-52. The lines of force surrounding the wire loop both strengthen and weaken the magnetic field between the magnet's poles. This causes rotation in the direction shown.

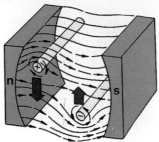

changes direction when the loop is at the bottom, the loop will be pushed up. Continual current reversal is needed to provide current flow in the same direction for the loop coming down and for the loop going up.

The method used to alternate current direction in the loop depends on the type of motor. Many motors use a *commutator*. See Fig. 24-53. A motor commutator works the same way as a generator commutator.

Motors can be strengthened by increasing the ampere-turns. This is done by increasing the number of windings and/or increasing the amperage. An iron core will also strengthen the conductor's magnetic field. This arrangement forms a rotating electromagnet. In motors, the rotating electromagnet is called the *armature*. See Fig. 24-54. The stationary magnet is called the *field*.

Figure 24-55 shows how an armature rotates within a field. Remember, like poles repel each

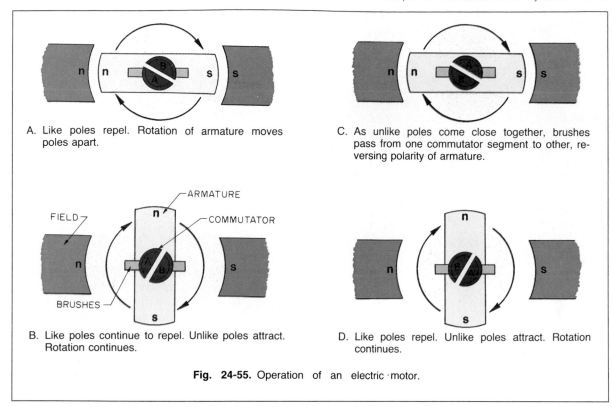

A. Like poles repel. Rotation of armature moves poles apart.

C. As unlike poles come close together, brushes pass from one commutator segment to other, reversing polarity of armature.

B. Like poles continue to repel. Unlike poles attract. Rotation continues.

D. Like poles repel. Unlike poles attract. Rotation continues.

Fig. 24-55. Operation of an electric motor.

other and unlike poles attract. In **A**, the like poles of the armature and field are aligned. This causes the armature to turn (**B**). Just as the unlike poles of the armature and field line up, the commutator reverses the current direction. This in turn reverses the armature's magnetic field (**C**). The like poles again repel each other and the armature continues to turn (**D**).

The armature always rotates in the same direction. Couplings, pulleys, or gears can be attached to the *armature shaft*. These devices put the armature's rotary motion into use.

A typical motor armature has many windings wrapped around a soft iron core. The commutator has many divisions. This allows it to reverse the current direction through each set of wire loops. Each loop has its own pair of commutator segments.

Universal Motors. The basic motor just described can operate on either DC or AC current. It is often referred to as a **universal motor**. Automobile starters are universal motors. The motor draws DC current from a battery. The current produces a magnetic field around the field windings and around the armature. This type of motor has a very high starting torque.

A universal motor can also run on alternating current. AC current reverses the current direction 120 times each second. However, the principle of operation stays the same. When current direction changes, both the field and the current direction in the armature reverse. The armature continues to rotate in the same direction.

Universal motors have many AC current uses. In and around the home, they power many portable and stationary devices. Vacuum cleaners, electric drills, food mixers, and electric lawn mowers are just a few examples. Universal motors are used in any appliance that has changing loads and requires high torque. See Fig. 24-56.

Induction Motors. Induction motors are simple motors that use AC current only. They run at a near-constant speed and do not use brushes. They are also more trouble-free than universal motors. However, both can provide years of service without failure.

In induction motors, the armature is called a *rotor*. There is no electrical connection to the rotor. The rotor gets its current through electromagnetic induction. We can view the induction motor as a transformer with a movable secondary coil.

Fig. 24-56. A universal motor used in a vacuum cleaner.

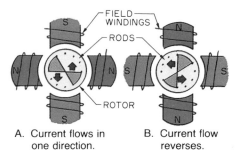

A. Current flows in one direction.　　B. Current flow reverses.

Fig. 24-58. In an induction motor, the polarity of the field windings changes as the current alternates. The rotor follows the changing polarity of the field windings.

Figure 24-57 shows a rotor. It has a series of copper rods. The metal surrounding the rods is nonmagnetic. The rotor looks like a cage. Therefore, it is often called a "squirrel-cage" rotor.

Most induction motors have a double field consisting of two sets of electromagnets. See Fig. 24-58. During operation, the magnetic field builds and collapses in the field windings each time the AC current reverses direction. This action induces a current in the rotor.

The current in the rotor produces its own magnetic field around the cage. The polarity of this field changes as the current reverses. This causes the cage to rotate. The cage rotates once every two cycles. Alternating current operates at 60 cycles per second. Therefore, the cage rotates about 30 times per second, or 1800 times per minute.

The rotor follows the changing polarity of its field. However, it is always slightly behind the magnetic field set up by the field coils. This time lag is called *slip*. Slip decreases the ideal rotation speed of the rotor. In reality, the motor rotates about 1725-1750 times per minute.

Unlike universal motors, induction motors are not self-starting. Also, they have very little low-speed torque. Therefore, a special starter winding is used to help start the motor. The current in this winding lags slightly behind that in the main windings. Therefore, the starter winding is said to be "out of phase" with the main winding. Together, the two windings achieve a gradual and stronger pull on the rotor. When the motor reaches about 75% of its full speed, a centrifugal switch disconnects the starter winding.

The lag in the starter winding is normally produced in one of two ways. The windings are in parallel in both. In one way, a resistor is in series with the starter winding. The resistor causes a slight delay in the buildup and collapse of the winding's field. This produces enough torque to start the motor. (The motor, however, must be under a minimum load.) This type of motor is called a *split-phase motor*. It is used on electrical appliances that do not need a high starting torque.

The second method of producing lag uses a capacitor instead of a resistor. When current flows in the main winding, the capacitor becomes charged. This cuts off the current to the starter winding. As the main winding field starts to collapse, the capacitor discharges. The starter winding then receives the current. Motors using this system are called *capacitor-start motors*. They have higher starting torque than split-phase motors. They are used whenever the starting load is similar to the running load. A furnace blower is a good example.

Fig. 24-57. An induction motor has a "squirrel-cage" rotor.

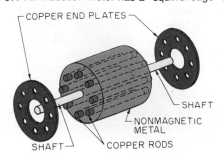

Fig. 24-59. Diagrams of single-phase and three-phase current are shown here. Homes use single-phase current. Three-phase current is used in industry, where more power is needed.

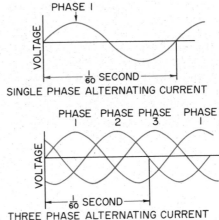

PHASE 1

$\frac{1}{60}$ SECOND

SINGLE PHASE ALTERNATING CURRENT

PHASE PHASE PHASE PHASE
1   2   3   1

$\frac{1}{60}$ SECOND

THREE PHASE ALTERNATING CURRENT

Three-Phase Motors. Some induction motors operate on a special three-phase AC current. The AC current described in Chapter 23 was *single-phase current.* Single-phase current completes 60 cycles per second. Three-phase current completes 180 cycles per second. See Fig. 24-59. Three-phase current provides a more constant source of power. Therefore, it is a better form of current for industry. Three-phase motors are more efficient and powerful than single-phase motors.

Conversion to Heat and Light

Electric current produces heat. In the home, we use electrical heat to prepare food, dry clothes, and heat air and water. Industry uses heat to liquify metals and plastics. Heat can also change the properties of many other materials. Therefore, it is essential in many manufacturing processes.

We use *high-resistance wire* to change electricity to heat. Passing current through this type of wire produces heat. Heaters and toasters use resistance wire to produce heat. Other items, such as electric stoves, use *resistance coils.*

Passing current through high-resistance wire can also produce light. A light bulb has a piece of high-resistance wire. Passing a current through the wire produces enough heat to make it white-hot. The white-hot wire produces light.

As you know, lighted bulbs become very hot. The resistance wire, or *filament*, is sealed in a vacuum. The vacuum keeps oxygen from coming into contact with the filament. Oxygen will oxidize and break the filament.

Use in Communication

Electricity plays an important part in helping us communicate. Many of our modern ways of transmitting information directly involve electricity. Telephones, radios, televisions, and computers all use electricity. This book does not have room for descriptions of how these relatively complex devices operate. But doorbells, buzzers, and door chimes are simple communication devices. They each use an electromagnetic coil.

Figure 24-60 shows a drawing of a simple doorbell circuit. In this circuit, current passes through a set of contacts connected to the clapper arm. From the contacts, the current flows through the coil, then back to the source.

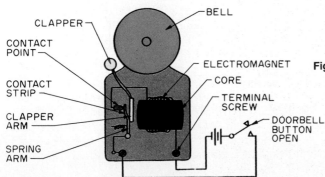

CLAPPER
CONTACT POINT
CONTACT STRIP
CLAPPER ARM
SPRING ARM
BELL
ELECTROMAGNET
CORE
TERMINAL SCREW
DOORBELL BUTTON OPEN

Fig. 24-60. Operation of an electric doorbell.

When the current flows, the coil pulls the clapper arm against the core. This causes the clapper to hit the bell. This movement also opens the contacts, which in turn disconnects the circuit. When the coil field weakens, a spring returns the arm to its original position. This brings the contacts together. Current restores the coil's magnetic field. This cycle repeats as long as electricity is available. The result is a continuous ringing of the bell.

A buzzer works in the same way. In a buzzer, the contact strip vibrates against the coil's core. This makes a buzzing sound.

A door chime uses a solenoid instead of a relay type of electromagnet. When current flows, the solenoid coil quickly pulls on the plunger. The plunger shoots into the center of the coil. This movement causes a hammer to strike a chime bar or tube.

Doorbells, buzzers, and chimes are all controlled by switches in other locations. The small coils and push-button switches operate on a low-voltage current. A small transformer reduces the 120-volt house current to 10-24 volts.

Common Electrical Circuits

We all use electricity every day. This section presents several electrical circuits to help you understand how electricity is controlled and used.

Source to Home. To produce electricity, we must begin with a power source. Heat engines, rushing water, and nuclear reactors are all power sources. At power plants they connect directly or indirectly to generators. The result is electricity.

Once generated, the electricity must be transmitted to homes and industry. Figure 24-61 shows how electricity is changed as it travels from the power plant to our homes. The power plant generates electricity at 2200 volts. A transformer (A) immediately steps up the current to 220,000 volts. High-voltage current can travel efficiently many miles to the area where it will be used (B). At this point, a step-down transformer reduces the voltage to 2200 volts. The current then travels to the city block where it will be used (C). Another transformer steps the voltage down to 120 volts.

House voltage circuits are a little different from simple two-wire circuits. Three wires leave the local step-down transformer. There are two 120-volt wires and a middle *neutral* wire. See Fig. 24-61 again. The neutral wire is a part of both 120-volt circuits. However, in some parts of the household system, the neutral wire is removed. This allows the two 120-volt wires to combine into a 240-volt wire. This arrangement provides two different voltages for home use without an additional transformer being used.

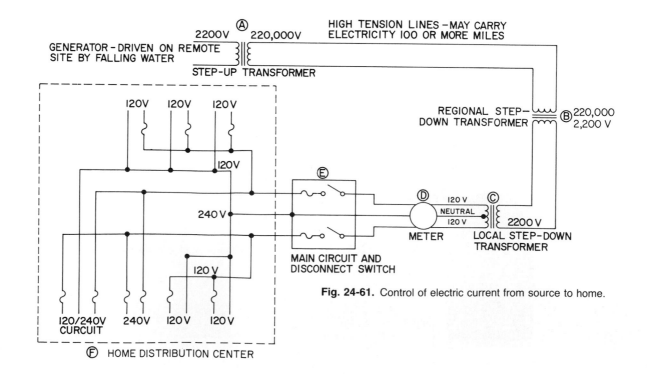

Fig. 24-61. Control of electric current from source to home.

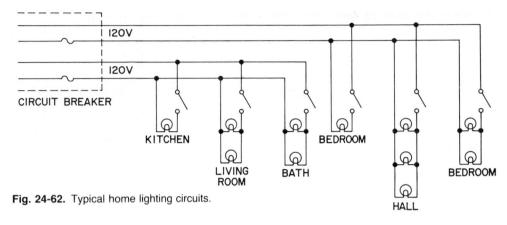

Fig. 24-62. Typical home lighting circuits.

The three-wire circuit passes through an electrical meter (D). This meter measures the amount of electricity being used in kilowatt-hours. A main switch and set of fuses or circuit breakers are located next. They are usually in a main disconnect box (E). From this point, the circuits are divided into 120-volt or 240-volt circuits. The division of the main 120- and 240-volt circuits into multiple circuits takes place in the distribution panel (F).

High-wattage electric devices use higher voltage (240 volts). Some examples are water heaters, stoves, and dryers. Other items use a lower voltage (120 volts). Lights, refrigerators, and televisions are a few examples.

Home Circuits. Individual circuits run from the distribution panel. A typical circuit might have 10-15 parallel lights and outlets. The circuit would be protected by a single fuse or circuit breaker. Each light or group of lights would have a switch to control the operation. Figure 24-62 shows how two typical circuits might appear on a wiring diagram.

Homes of the future may have special wiring systems and devices that control items and systems automatically. See Fig. 24-63.

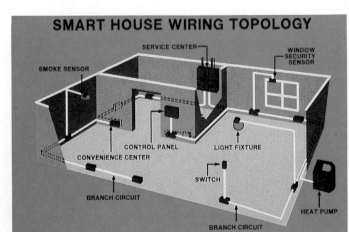

Fig. 24-63. Appliances, lights, and various other home operations can be controlled automatically. An experimental plan is shown here.

TEST INSTRUMENTS

Electrical test instruments are important in measuring the basic units of measurement in electricity. Measurement is accomplished by three meters: the voltmeter, ammeter, and ohmmeter. See Fig. 24-64. These meters can be combined into single meters. The readings can be combined to provide a measurement of power (watts).

While many electrical service procedures are provided indoors, electrical power companies often require outdoor repairs as shown in Fig. 24-65.

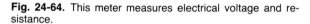

Fig. 24-64. This meter measures electrical voltage and resistance.

Fig. 24-65. Servicing electrical power line problems often involves the use of heavy equipment.

Chapter 24—Review

Testing Your Knowledge

Briefly answer each of the following questions. Write on a separate piece of paper.
1. What characteristic of electricity makes it our major form of power?
2. What is a generator?
3. What kind of device can change alternating current produced by an alternator into direct current?
4. Why is an on-off switch placed in series with a lamp or a motor?
5. What is the function of three-way and four-way electrical switches?
6. What is the main function of a relay?
7. What is the strength of the electromagnet within a relay based on?
8. Why is a transistor called a solid-state device?
9. What is meant by *rectification*?
10. What is the function of fuses and circuit breakers?
11. What is the function of a transformer?
12. According to what principle do transformers operate?
13. In transformer operation, what is the relationship between input and output wattage?
14. How do resistors reduce current flow in a circuit?
15. What is a solenoid?
16. What is a universal motor?
17. Name three types of induction motors.
18. What is used to change electricity to heat?
19. Name three home devices that use 240-volt current instead of 120-volt current.

Expressing Your Knowledge

Using complete sentences, write your answers to the following on a separate sheet of paper:
1. Describe how a generator changes rotary motion into electric current.
2. Give two advantages and two disadvantages of using cells and batteries as sources of electricity.
3. What is the difference between a primary cell and a secondary cell?
4. Why is aluminum used instead of copper for some long-distance power transmission?
5. What are semiconductors?
6. What is the difference between the electron flow and the hole flow of an electrical current?
7. Describe how a transistor can take the place of a relay.
8. How does current flow turn on and off in an SCR?
9. What is a capacitor? Give two common uses of capacitors.
10. Describe how a motor produces motion from electricity.
11. Explain how a door chime works.

Applying Your Knowledge

Follow your teacher's instructions to complete these activities:
1. Prepare a list of different home devices that operate on electricity. Categorize each device according to how the device uses electricity. The five categories are:
   - Motion (such as an electric mixer)
   - Heat (such as a toaster)
   - Light (such as a lamp)
   - Communication (such as a television set)
   - Combination uses (such as a dryer, which produces both motion and heat)
2. Find an electric motor in your home. Read the information plate. In a written report, explain what each item on the plate means.

Research and Development— Energy and Power Systems

SECTION

Chapter 25

Future Sources of Energy and Power

Want to "ride on a sunbeam"? It may become possible. Many new ideas are being explored in the search for future sources of energy and power.

Expanding Your Knowledge

Learning about power and energy technology will help you understand more about the world around you. As you study this chapter, you will learn to:

- Understand the role of research and development (R & D) in gaining new knowledge and solutions to existing problems.
- Explain the scientific method for seeking new knowledge and solving problems.
- Recognize that living plants and animals may be only one source of fossil fuels.
- Understand how solar energy can be captured in space for use there or on the earth.
- Explain how nuclear fusion may someday produce power using the same principles involved when the sun provides the earth with light and heat.

Building Your Word Power

Knowledge of the vocabulary used will help you develop greater understanding of power and energy. The following terms are defined and explained in this chapter. Learning these will help you learn more about sources of energy that may be used in the future.

development	plasma
hydrogen	research
hypothesis	scientific method
inertial confinement	solar sailing
law	theory
magnetic confinement	

This chapter introduces the concept of research and development (R & D). R & D has become an important part of industry. Various processes are used to investigate and find solutions to the power and energy problems we face.

R & D is being applied in the area of energy sources. Because fossil fuels will become increasingly scarce, engineers and scientists throughout the world are seeking alternative sources of energy. You have already learned about several possible sources: hydroelectric, nuclear fission, solar, geothermal, wind, biomass, and the oceans. But there are other possibilities. Some are still unproven theories. And some are very expensive to develop or need advanced technologies not yet available. But progress is based on exploring new ideas. "Maybe [these sources] will become a major source of power in the future, and maybe the concept will disappear and never be developed." Extensive R & D is underway to determine their potential for use in the future.

This chapter presents three possible sources. Each, if developed, could provide significant energy for the earth. They are:
- Petroleum from deep within the earth.
- Solar energy from collectors placed in orbit around the earth.
- Power from nuclear fusion, the source of the sun's energy.

RESEARCH AND DEVELOPMENT

Research is the process of obtaining new knowledge. **Development** is using this knowledge to solve problems and develop new products or processes. In industry, the two distinct processes have been combined into a single effort called *Research and Development (R & D)*.

At one time, research was mostly performed by colleges and universities. And many early discoveries resulted from individual efforts. The

electric light bulb, the telephone, the internal-combustion engine are inventions which led to the development of major industries.

Today, R & D is an important part of most major companies. The company which gains new knowledge leading to new or better products has a competitive edge over its rivals.

R & D is very important for our future energy needs. The ultimate use of alternative sources of energy depends on industries' ability to add to existing knowledge through research, and then using the knowledge to develop new cost-effective and efficient energy systems. R & D is also important in the continued improvement of our existing systems. Today, automobiles are safer, more fuel efficient, and more reliable due to effective R & D efforts by automotive companies. And similar improvements are occurring throughout industry.

The government also recognizes the importance of R & D. In 1977, the U.S. Congress established the *Department of Energy (DOE)*. DOE has been given the responsibilities of developing and implementing a national energy policy and promoting energy-related research and development.

The past chapters continually identified knowledge and areas needing further development. This section of the book, beginning with this chapter, will identify emerging ideas in energy sources, transmission, and utilization. The success of these ideas will depend on R & D.

THE SCIENTIFIC METHOD

The **scientific method** is a basic set of procedures used to obtain new knowledge and seek solutions to existing problems. It was first devised by scientists as a method of gaining new knowledge about science. Today it is a method used to solve almost any existing problem, whether it be scientific, industrial, or social.

The scientific method involves a series of steps. It starts with a problem and then proceeds in an organized fashion to solve the problem. The main steps in the scientific method are:
1. State the problem or question that needs to be solved.
2. Gather the information needed to understand the problem and seek a solution.
3. Identify a hypothesis or possible solution to the problem, based on the knowledge learned.
4. Plan a research procedure that will determine whether the hypothesis is correct.

This might involve an experiment, testing and analysis, or other procedures designed to gain the needed information.

5. Conduct the planned research, gathering evidence that supports the hypothesis or proposed solution or proves it incorrect.
6. Analyze the findings to determine whether the problem has been solved, or whether the process needs to be repeated.
7. If necessary, identify a new hypothesis or possible solution, and repeat the process.

There are some key elements in the procedure described. The **hypothesis**, or possible solution, is the researcher's analysis of the most likely solution to the problem. It is *not* the answer until proven. It merely establishes the direction for investigating the problem.

Planning and conducting the research is the most critical part of the scientific method. The information gained through careful investigation of the problem is critical for arriving at a solution. If the research proves the hypothesis correct, the problem is solved. If the problem is not solved, the process is repeated using a new hypothesis. This procedure continues until the problem is solved.

In science, a hypothesis that is proven through repeated experiments may become a theory. A **theory** is a concept or principle that has been verified by repeated testing. A theory is effective in predicting outcomes. Einstein's theory of relativity, which presents the relationship of matter and energy, is supported by considerable evidence. However, it has not yet become a law.

Eventually, if *all* evidence consistently supports a theory and no evidence contradicts its basic ideas, the theory becomes a **law** and is accepted as fact. The gas laws, law of gravity, and law of conservation of matter and energy have all emerged from hypotheses and theories.

The scientific method is an important procedure. Use it to solve problems you encounter as you work in school. You can also use it later in your job.

THE IMMEDIATE FUTURE

As countries become more highly industrialized, their need for controlled energy increases. As a result, the use of fossil fuels may increase rapidly in the years ahead. But continued development of alternative sources of energy could help offset this increase.

Nuclear power plants are being constructed in many countries. The United States has not started construction of a new nuclear power plant for many years. However, worldwide development continues.

Use of solar and wind energy and energy from the oceans should continue to increase. Research and development in these areas continues even during periods of decreasing fuel prices. If fuel prices rise as expected in the future, research and development in alternative sources of energy will increase rapidly. In the meantime, we will continue to see new ideas and inventions emerge. See Fig. 25-1.

Fig. 25-1. This vertical axis wind turbine stands 165 feet tall and is 110 feet in diameter. With a 28 mph wind, it can produce 500 kilowatts per hour of electricity.

The next sections will present some more venturesome concepts. Any of these concepts that can be developed could become a major source of energy. And energy could become more plentiful and inexpensive.

PETROLEUM FROM THE EARTH

"Petroleum and natural gas come from biomass (dead plants and animals) buried and compressed within the earth." This is the concept presented in Chapter 1, and the one generally accepted by scientists throughout the world as the source of *all* deep well petroleum and natural gas.

This concept is being challenged by *Thomas Gold*, a scientist from Cornell University. Gold believes that large quantities of the hydrocarbons (petroleum and natural gas) in the earth were formed by non-biological sources. His theory is that during the formation of the earth, large quantities of methane gas were trapped deep within the earth. The gas then bubbled up through the crust, sometimes becoming trapped in rock formations. He believes this produced some of the oil and gas fields now in use worldwide.

The theory is supported by many discoveries of hydrocarbons within the solar system. Hydrocarbons have been found in meteorites, where no plant or animal life was thought to have existed. Our space probes have found hydrocarbons to be common on other planets. The existence of hydrocarbons which did not originate from living plants and animals supports Gold's theory that the earth also has hydrocarbons which did not originate from plants and animals.

Many scientists dispute Gold's theory. They recognize that natural gas unrelated to fossil fuels exists. However, they believe the quantities are small and of no commercial value.

In the late 1980s, an effort to test Gold's theory was made in Sweden, but funds ran out before the test hole reached the planned depth of over 4 miles. The theory remains—unproven.

SOLAR ENERGY FROM SPACE

In outer space, solar energy is constant. There are no clouds to block the sun's rays and no night. If we could capture solar energy in space, then send it to the earth, we would have a constant supply of energy. Two systems have been proposed to accomplish this:

- Orbiting mirrors
- Orbiting photovoltaic cells

Both systems would collect solar energy for the production of electricity. And there are other possibilities for use of solar energy in space. See Fig. 25-2.

Orbiting Mirrors

Collecting solar energy on earth is an inconsistent process. Collection is most efficient when the sun is directly above the collectors, shining straight down. In the northern hemisphere, this only happens around noon each day, and then only in the summer. Placing mirrors in orbit around the earth could solve this problem.

The proposed system for putting mirrors in orbit is called the *Space-Orbiting Light-Augmentation Reflector Energy System (SOLARES)*. In this system, giant mirrors would be assembled in space and put into orbit. As the mirrors orbited, they would constantly be adjusted by computers to reflect sunlight onto a single location on earth. Since there is no night in outer space, the mirrors would reflect sunlight constantly. The sun's energy would then be used to produce electricity in one of the ways previously discussed.

Fig. 25-2. Devices in space could be a potential new source of nondepletable, clean, and continuously available energy.

Orbiting Photovoltaic Cells

Another proposed method of collecting solar energy in space is called the *Solar Power Satellite (SPS)*. This system is very similar to the solar energy collection system used in many of our space flights. Photovoltaic cells are used to gather solar energy and convert it into electricity.

In an orbiting solar collector, photovoltaic cells would collect and convert solar energy to electricity and transmit it to a collector site on earth. This would be done by microwaves.

Both SOLARES and SPS would capture solar energy on a constant basis. However, neither system has been developed to the testing stage.

Solar Sailing

A different use of solar energy is possible in space. Photons, the tiny particles of light energy, can be used to push a sail in a manner similar to the effects of wind on a sailboat. When used in space it is called **solar sailing**. In solar sailing, sunlight propels the space vehicle through space. Photons fall onto a vast sail and provide a push. This force is very small. However, in outer space the force would build up. It would become greater than that of today's most powerful rocket engine.

This "riding on a sunbeam" offers more than speed. Sunlight is always present in outer space. Therefore, photons can provide a push indefinitely. The result is a propulsion capability greater than that available from any other fuel. A solar-powered space probe could meet future comets or explore the outer reaches of our solar system and beyond.

Solar sailing has not been a major part of our space program. However, as space vehicles are sent greater distances, they may be equipped with sails. Sailing techniques in space are similar to those on water. But, unlike wind, the light from the sun is predictable. Thus solar sailing can be controlled by a computer.

Future Use

All three of these "space uses" of solar energy are possible. They are, however, expensive. Much of the technology needed to implement these concepts is available. Use, however, will require a large and long-range commitment of resources.

ENERGY FROM NUCLEAR FUSION

At the present time, nuclear fission is the source of all the electricity produced by nuclear power. As you learned in Chapter 5, *fission* is the splitting of a heavy nucleus of uranium. *Fusion* is just the opposite. In nuclear fusion, two light-weight nuclei *join* to form one heavier nucleus. See Fig. 25-3. When this happens, a tremendous amount of heat and light energy is released. Matter is converted into energy. The helium formed by fusion has less mass than the hydrogen fused to form the helium. This is the same reaction which produces the sun's energy.

Fusion is often called the *ultimate energy source*. Scientists understand the theory of fusion reactor operation. They have also successfully conducted fusion experiments. However, the construction of an experimental reactor is still far away. The research problem is to develop a *continuous* and *controlled* fusion reaction.

The Fusion Reaction

The fuel for a fusion reaction is **hydrogen**. Hydrogen is a very abundant element. It can be extracted from ordinary water. For hydrogen atoms to join, their nuclei must be forced together at extremely high temperatures and pressures. These temperatures and pressures are like those of the sun. The problem is to create sun-like conditions on earth. These conditions are extremely difficult to produce.

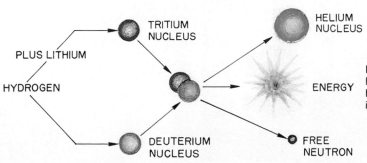

Fig. 25-3. In the fusion reaction, two isotopes of hydrogen-deuterium and tritium-combine to form helium. In the process, a small amount of matter is converted into a large amount of energy.

Scientists produce a fusion reaction by combining two isotopes of hydrogen: deuterium and tritium. The common hydrogen atom has a nucleus with one proton and no neutron. When a neutron is added to the proton, the hydrogen becomes *deuterium*. When a second neutron is added, *tritium* forms. The deuterium occurs naturally. It makes up a small part of the hydrogen in water. Tritium, however, is produced by bombarding the element *lithium* with high-energy neutrons. Again, see Fig. 25-3.

In the fusion process, deuterium and tritium are heated millions of degrees. They become a hot, gaseous mixture called **plasma**. At a high-enough temperature, the isotopes fuse (combine) to form helium nuclei. Each fusion reaction releases a fantastic amount of energy.

Containing the Fusion Reaction

The main problem in sustaining a fusion reaction is to *contain* the tremendously hot plasma. The plasma cannot be held in a solid container. All known solids would melt at such temperatures. Scientists are experimenting with two ways of containing the hot plasma:
- Magnetic confinement
- Inertial confinement

Magnetic Confinement. Russian scientists were the first to develop the magnetic method of confinement. Figure 25-4 shows a magnetic confinement test reactor. This type of reactor is also called a *tokamak*. "Tokamak" is the Russian acronym for this type of reactor.

A tokamak uses huge electromagnets to generate a powerful magnetic field. This field is needed to contain the plasma. The reactor also requires a large transformer. The transformer induces an electrical current in the plasma. This current does two things:
- It creates another magnetic field that helps hold the plasma in the reactor.
- It heats up the plasma to the temperature at which fusion can take place.

The tokamak machine at Princeton University is near a long-sought goal. Scientists have successfully operated the machine at 200 million ° Centigrade (360 million ° Fahrenheit). That temperature is 10 times hotter than the center of the sun. This development paves the way for the long-sought "*first goal*"—a fusion machine which generates as much energy as it consumes. It is hoped that this achievement will soon be accomplished. The "*second goal*," is to produce more energy than used. And the final goal will be the generation of a continuous flow of power from a nuclear fusion generating plant. See Fig. 25-5.

Magnetic confinement machines have generally been built bigger to produce greater temperatures. But a machine small enough to fit on a tabletop has been developed. If the small machine proves feasible, commercial reactors might someday be small enough to be hauled on a truck.

Inertial Confinement. The inertial confinement process involves using tiny glass spheres filled with deuterium and tritium. Each of the spheres is a small fuel pellet. The idea is to bom-

Fig. 25-4. Shown here is the tokamak test reactor at Princeton University. An electromagnet creates a magnetic field that squeezes and contains hot plasma within the donut shape.

Fig. 25-5. The interior of the tokamak vacuum vessel must be able to withstand extremely high temperatures.

REACTORS IN ORBIT

The need for large amounts of electrical power for space projects is growing. Most satellites now need only about one kilowatt of power. This amount is easily produced by solar cells.

The space shuttle now allows us to place more complex and larger satellites into orbit. These satellites may need 100 or more kilowatts of power. This much power is beyond the capability of existing space power stations.

Scientists are studying the possibility of placing small nuclear reactors into orbit around the earth. These reactors would be about the size of a small car. They would be put into orbit by astronauts from the space shuttle. The reactors would then be connected to satellites to provide power.

The possibility of nuclear reactors in space causes concern among many people. They fear that a faulty reactor might spread nuclear waste over part of the earth. In fact, this very thing happened in 1978 and 1983. The Soviet Union had nuclear-powered satellites in orbit. They accidentally reentered the earth's atmosphere and spread some contamination. Safety is a big concern. As with any new technology, there are both advantages and disadvantages to consider.

bard the fuel pellets with pulses of high-energy light. The light quickly raises the temperature of the fuel. The heat produces tiny fusion explosions as the two isotopes combine. Of course, energy is released during the explosions. Using many fuel pellets can provide a tremendous amount of energy.

The high-energy light used in inertial confinement is produced by a *laser*. (Lasers are described in detail in Chapter 27.)

Research efforts are directed toward the same goal as that for magnetic confinement. That is to obtain as much or more energy from the reaction as is used to produce it. See Fig. 25-6.

Laser fusion is not as close to break-even as magnetic confinement. Developers, however, believe that inertial confinement is simpler and will provide a less complex reactor.

The recent developments in superconductivity support both inertial and magnetic confinement research. Since electrical energy is critical in both processes, improvement in conductivity will help speed the development of a fusion reactor.

Scientists have not yet produced the kind of sustained and controlled reaction they are looking for. Most researchers believe that a successful fusion reactor will not be built until after the year 2000. And a commercial reactor may not exist until 2050.

Fig. 25-6. In this laser fusion device, a pulse of light is divided into 10 separate beams. Each beam is focused to about the width of three human hairs. Together the beams will deliver 100 trillion watts of power to cause the fusion of hydrogen isotopes.

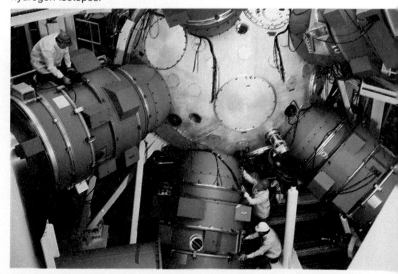

Technology Focus

A Solar Breeder?

The Solarex manufacturing facility in Frederick, Maryland, manufactures solar cells. Also, its main power system uses solar energy. The plant has 3000 solar modules capable of producing 800 kilowatt hours of electricity per day. It also has a 2.5-megawatt-hour battery storage capability.

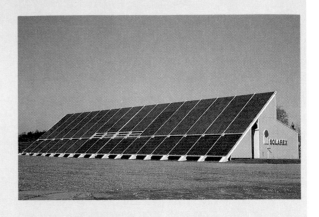

Plans were for the factory to be completely self-sustaining, relying completely on solar energy. Since solar cells were to be manufactured here, it was thought that the plant would be able to "reproduce itself." That is, it would become a *solar breeder*, producing more energy than it could use. This has not happened.

Actually, the plant comes close to being self-sustaining, but requires an outside source of electricity to maintain efficient operation. Still, such a goal is worth striving for. As new technology is developed, "solar breeders" may become possible, allowing us to make efficient use of our greatest source of energy, the sun.

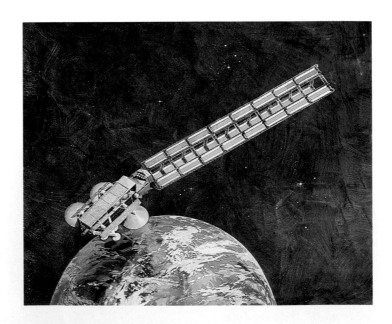

Testing Your Knowledge

Briefly answer each of the following questions. Write on a separate piece of paper.

1. Name the three major sources of energy presented in this chapter.
2. What evidence supports the theory that some hydrocarbons were formed by nonbiological sources?
3. Name the two systems that may someday be used to capture solar energy in space.
4. How can electricity generated in space be sent to earth?
5. Identify the long-sought first goal in the development of fusion power.
6. Name the two methods being used to produce the high temperatures needed to produce nuclear fusion.
7. What is the name of the basic set of procedures used to solve existing problems?
8. Name one theory.
9. Name one law.

Expressing Your Knowledge

Using complete sentences, write your answers to the following on a separate sheet of paper:

1. Explain the difference between research and development.
2. How can electricity generated in space be sent to earth?
3. What is solar sailing?
4. Explain a nuclear fusion reaction.
5. Why are nuclear reactors being considered as sources of power in space?
6. Explain how a theory becomes a law.
7. Explain how a hypothesis becomes a theory.

Applying Your Knowledge

Follow your teacher's instructions to complete these activities:

1. Prepare a chart or model showing how energy is obtained from nuclear fusion.
2. Research newspapers and journals regarding developments in petroleum from the earth, solar energy from space, and nuclear fusion. Also watch for new and unique sources of energy. Prepare a report on your findings. Share these with your class and add the information to your *Power Notebook*.
3. From the library or another source, identify a problem currently being worked on. An alternative would be to obtain a finished report describing a research project. Good sources are local companies with ongoing research. Look for a description of the methods being used to solve the problem. Prepare a report, briefly describing the following:
   a. State the problem or question being investigated.
   b. Describe the information known about the solution to the problem.
   c. Identify the proposed hypothesis, or possible solution.
   d. Briefly describe the research procedures being used.
   e. If the research has been completed, describe the findings.

Chapter 26

Storing and Using Energy

It is relatively easy to change large quantities of potential (stored) energy to kinetic energy (motion), but extremely difficult to do the opposite.

Expanding Your Knowledge

As you study this chapter, you will learn to:

- Understand the need for developing energy storage systems for both transportation and stationary needs.
- Recognize the difficulty in changing large quantities of kinetic energy into potential energy.
- Identify the use of batteries as power sources for transportation vehicles.
- Explain how hydrogen can be used to serve as a transportable fuel.
- Describe how hydrides may make hydrogen fuel systems safe and economical for automobile use.
- Explain how pumped-hydro and compressed-air systems can be used to increase utility company electrical outputs to meet peak demands.

Building Your Word Power

The following terms are defined and explained in this chapter. Learning these will help you learn more about storing and using energy.

compressed-air storage
electric vehicles (EV's)
electrolysis
pumped hydro storage

In order to take better advantage of alternative energy sources, methods of converting kinetic energy to potential energy need to be developed and used. This chapter will help you understand the extent of the problems we face in storing energy. It will review existing storage systems and look at potential developments in the future. These include batteries, pumped hydro, air storage, and hydrogen.

BATTERIES

In Chapter 24, you learned how batteries are able to store electricity. A storage battery converts electrical energy (kinetic) into chemical energy (potential). When needed, the process is reversed, and electricity is available for use.

Uses of Batteries

The amount of energy that can be stored in batteries is quite small. For example, it is not possible to have enough batteries to store the electricity needed by our cities at night. But batteries have extensive use in small and modest size applications. Home uses include portable radios and TV sets, electric razors, and the automobile storage battery used to start your car.

Batteries may also be used on a larger scale. See Fig. 26-1. During the day, solar cells collect energy and charge the batteries. Some of the solar electricity is used as generated, the rest is stored in these batteries for night use. The batteries also provide electricity for cloudy days. However, if the sun doesn't shine for a few days, a backup generator that operates on fossil fuels must be used. This type of storage for small communities without a regular source of electricity is becoming more common, especially in remote locations.

Fig. 26-1. In remote areas, solar cells produce electricity to charge storage batteries. The batteries provide nighttime electrical power.

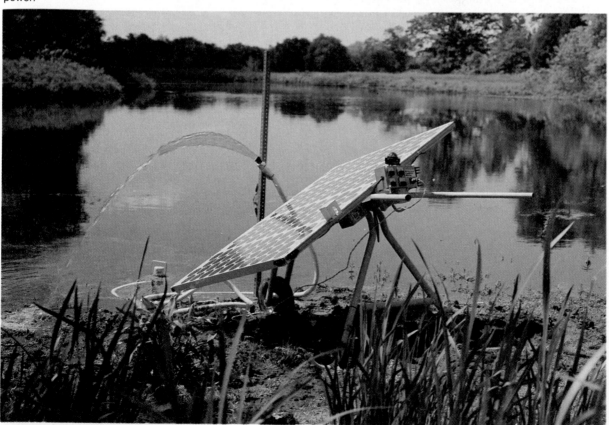

Batteries are transportable and can be used for transportation. **Electric vehicles (EV's)** include all types of home and industrial transportation vehicles. Today, there are many uses of EV's. Forklifts, golf carts, many vehicles driven in large industrial plants, and a variety of other vehicles used in business and industry operate on electricity. See Fig. 26-2.

Electric Automobiles

Interest in using electric automobiles remains. Today's electric motors are efficient and powerful, and electric motors at each wheel can provide multiple-wheel drive. However, the range of travel for battery-powered cars remains short.

In an electric car, as in all EV's, batteries store the energy required for operation. See Fig. 26-3. The range of the car is limited by battery capacity and by the number of batteries the car can carry. The car itself may also help charge the batteries to increase the driving range. For example, a car may be equipped with a *regenerative braking system*. In this system, when the brakes are applied, a generator connects with the wheels. The generator helps slow the car and recharge the batteries. Also, the energy released when going downhill could be used to charge the battery.

HYDROGEN

In Chapter 25, hydrogen was studied as a nuclear fuel, the fuel for a fusion reaction. Hydrogen can also be burned. It burns like natural gas and, as a result, can be used in place of gas for heating and cooking. Hydrogen is harmful if *inhaled* as a gas. But it is pollution-free when burned. When hydrogen burns it combines with oxygen from the air, producing water, which is released into the air as vapor.

Fig. 26-3. The batteries of electric vehicles must be recharged.

Fig. 26-2. Electrically powered vehicles, such as these golf carts, are quiet and nonpolluting.

Technology Focus

A "Current" Trend in Transportation

In the early 1900s, electric automobiles were common. They were the most reliable cars on the road. At the time, most travel was for 10 miles or less round trip. But as travel distances became greater, the distance limitations of electric cars lead to their disappearance.

Even after three-quarters of a century of battery development, electric cars can still only travel about 50 miles before the batteries need to be recharged. But electric vehicles are economical to operate and do not create air pollution. Companies are again considering producing them to offer as an alternative to vehicles that use gasoline or diesel fuel.

Use of electric cars may build slowly. New high-temperature, sodium-sulfur batteries will double travel range to 100 miles. These batteries are very expensive. But the combination of less cost for fuel (about half the cost of gasoline) coupled with low maintenance will help cover battery costs.

At first, the electric vehicles used most will probably be those that provide intracity transportation services, such as small delivery and service trucks. Shown here is a van with its battery pack beside it. For operation, the pack is mounted under the vehicle floor. A positive response to this type of vehicle would encourage the gradual return of electric cars.

Hydrogen could be used as the fuel for nearly all internal- or external-combustion engines. See Fig. 26-4. It is transportable. In Chapter 12, you learned that hydrogen is one of the fuels used to power rocket engines for space flights. It can also be used to power an automobile engine, but the carburetor and fuel system of the engine must be changed to accommodate hydrogen.

Transporting Hydrogen

Hydrogen is not an easy gas to store. It can be held as a liquid if kept at a very low temperature. Or, it can be kept as a highly compressed gas. Both systems are possible for industrial applications. But they become more complex and costly for transportation.

Fig. 26-4. Hydrogen can be used as a fuel in a modified internal-combustion engine. This experimental vehicle uses liquid hydrogen. The storage tank is shown here.

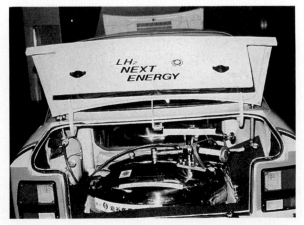

Fortunately, a new way to store and transport hydrogen has been found. Some *metallic compounds* (chemically combined metals) are able to absorb hydrogen. The process forms a new hydrogen-rich metallic compound called *hydride*.

One hydride, at a pressure of just 60 pounds per square inch gauge (psig), can safely store a quantity of hydrogen equal to that stored by a similar-sized container of *pure* hydrogen at a pressure of 15,000 psig. Further, if the hydride container develops a leak, the escaping hydrogen rapidly cools the hydride. This decreases the flow of hydrogen and the leak almost stops completely.

A group of experimental vehicles used by the U.S. Postal Service has proven that the system can work. But hydrogen has less power per unit volume than gasoline and requires larger fuel tanks. There is also a real concern for safety. Hydrogen is highly inflammable. And since hydrogen has small molecules, it is more difficult to provide leak-proof joints. Much additional research and development are needed to perfect the use of hydrogen for transportation.

Producing Hydrogen

For hydrogen to be used as a replacement for fossil fuels, the principle source will probably be water. A molecule of water (H_2O) consists of two atoms of hydrogen *bonded* (joined) to an atom of oxygen. The bond combining the oxygen and hydrogen is very strong. The process of breaking this bond requires large amounts of energy.

There are several ways in which hydrogen can be released from water. The most promising method is called *electrolysis*. In **electrolysis**, electricity is passed through water. This process separates the hydrogen from the oxygen atoms. The amount of electricity needed is high. Since electricity is costly, the process is expensive. If ways are developed to produce inexpensive electricity, hydrogen could become a cost-effective fuel.

PUMPED-HYDRO STORAGE

One practical and cost-effective method of storing energy is the use of **pumped-hydro storage**. In this process, water is pumped from a lower lake or reservoir to a higher lake or reservoir late at night when electrical usage is very low. When demand is high during the day, the water is released, producing hydroelectric power when needed the most. See Fig. 26-5.

Fig. 26-5. Operation of a pumped-hydro system presently in use.

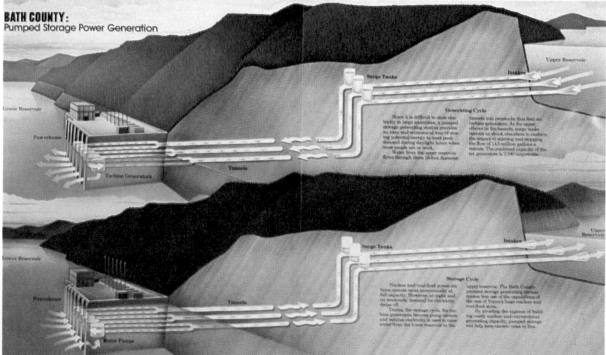

The advantage of this system is twofold:

■ All power plants are more efficient if operated at a steady high output. This system uses the extra electricity that is produced at night to keep the plant operating at high efficiency.

■ Additional plants to provide electricity at peak-use hours are unnecessary.

There are more than 30 pumped-hydro plants producing over 18,000 megawatts (MW) of electricity. Utility companies plan to expand the use of pumped-hydro storage. This system makes existing plants more efficient and increases electrical production capacity during daytime operation.

COMPRESSED-AIR STORAGE

Compressed-air storage can be used to accomplish the same goal as pumped-hydro storage. In **compressed-air storage**, air is pumped into a storage cavern at night. It is released during the day to help spin the plant's turbine-driven generators, providing additional electricity. See Fig. 26-6.

The plant would use large underground caves in salt deposits. Water would be pumped into the salt to dissolve it. The dissolved salt would be pumped out. The process would continue until the desired size cavern for air storage was obtained.

THE FUTURE

With the exception of batteries, the concept of storing energy has emerged as a major need only during the past 20 years. As a result, both the technology and the use are at beginning levels.

Because of its proven cost-effectiveness, the most advanced area is pumped-hydro storage. Compressed-air storage has potential, but will require more research and development.

The need for a plentiful and economical transportable fuel will probably emerge during the coming century. Hydrogen will be an important consideration. And new ways to store energy may be discovered as research and development continue.

SCHEMATIC OF COMPRESSED AIR ENERGY STORAGE POWER PLANT

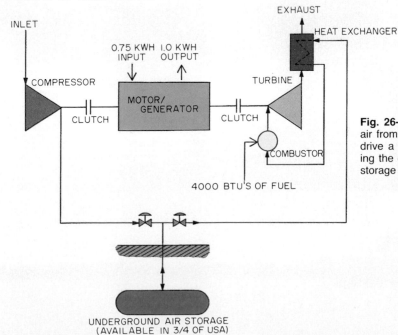

Fig. 26-6. In a compressed-air storage system, air from an underground cavern is used to help drive a turbine, producing added electricity during the day. The compressor pumps air into the storage cavern at night.

Chapter 26—Review

Testing Your Knowledge

Briefly answer each of the following questions. Write on a separate piece of paper.
1. Which is the most widely used form of potential energy?
2. Identify the major problem with electric powered automobiles.
3. What is a hydride?
4. What is the major problem solved by the use of hydrides, as related to transporting hydrogen?
5. In a compressed-air storage system, where do utilities plan to store the air?

Expressing Your Knowledge

Using complete sentences, write your answers to the following on a separate sheet of paper:
1. Why is there a need to develop a new transportable fuel?
2. Why is hydrogen considered a nonpolluting fuel?
3. What is electrolysis?
4. Give the advantages of developing and using a pumped-hydro storage system.

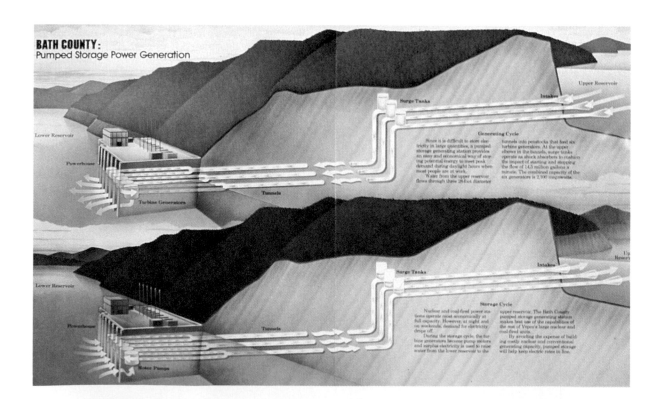

Applying Your Knowledge

Follow your teacher's instructions to complete these activities:

1. Conduct a survey to determine whether any of the concepts presented in this chapter are applied in your community or nearby areas. Include the use of electric vehicles used on golf courses and in business and industry. Do any groups use hydrogen-fueled vehicles? Does the utility company use any forms of *stored* energy? Prepare a written report on your findings.

2. Locate articles in newspapers and journals that tell about developments in:
   - ■ New battery designs for energy storage.
   - ■ Use of hydrogen for transportation.
   - ■ Pumped-hydro storage.
   - ■ Compressed-air and gas storage.
   - ■ New and unique methods of storing and using energy.

   Report your findings to the class and add the information to your *Power Notebook*.

Chapter 27

Emerging Power Applications

The field of power and energy technology is dynamic. New developments, wisely applied, promise an exciting future.

Expanding Your Knowledge

As you study this chapter, you will learn to:

- Describe how laser beams are produced in a ruby laser.
- Explain how lasers are used in communication, industry, and medicine.
- Define *cryogenics* and describe how cryogenic temperatures affect electrical conductivity.
- Identify three future uses of the superconductivity obtained with cryogenic temperatures.
- Describe how a fuel cell operates and is able to generate electricity in a public utility.

Building Your Word Power

The following terms are defined and explained in this chapter. Learning these will help you learn more about emerging power applications.

anode
cathode
coherence
cryogenics
fiber-optic system
fuel cell
laser beam
superconductor

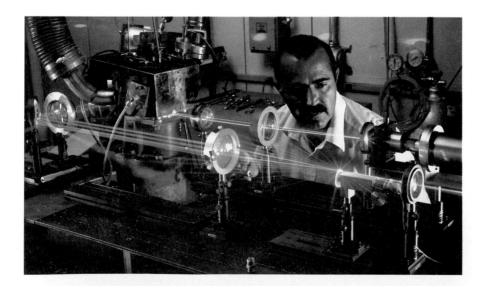

Many uses of energy have been discovered during the past few decades. Using light to transmit power and perform work is already a proven technology. *Laser beams* (coherent light beams) have many uses in industry, medicine, and research. And we can expect this list of uses to grow rapidly.

When materials become very cold, their properties change. The study of materials at very low temperatures is called *cryogenics*. As some conductors become very cold, they become *superconductors*. They conduct electricity with almost no power loss due to friction. This discovery has opened many possibilities in generating and transmitting electricity over long distances. The possibilities are almost endless, varying from superconducting generators to efficient transportation systems.

Fuel cells are a new source of electricity from public utility companies. They are nonpolluting and can be put into service quickly.

Each of these topics—lasers, cryogenics, and fuel cells, is covered in this chapter.

Fig. 27-1. Laser beams (concentrated beams of light) are being used in research.

Principles of Laser Operation

Laser beams consist of electromagnetic waves. These waves are at or near the wavelength of visible light. Normal light consists of waves of a variety of lengths. This produces mixed, or multiple-direction, light. The waves in a laser beam have almost identical lengths. Therefore, a laser beam can travel in a straight line for miles with very little spreading. This identical wavelength characteristic is called **coherence**.

Radio wavelengths are measured in yards (or meters). Television wavelengths are measured in feet (or tenths of a meter). The laser wavelength is very short. It is measured in millionths of an inch. With their short wavelength, lasers can carry more messages than radio or television signals can. This makes them excellent carriers of telephone conversations.

Laser beams can be produced by devices that use liquids, gases, and semiconductors. The result is the same. These lasers all produce an intense beam of light that travels in a straight line with almost no spread. The first laser beam was produced by a device that used synthetic rubies. The *ruby laser* is still in common use.

In operation, the laser's power supply provides an electric current. This current produces a flash in the lamp. The flash develops electromagnetic waves along the ruby rod. One end of the rod is coated with a reflecting film. The other end is partially coated. The light reflects back and forth between the reflecting surfaces. The light finally escapes past the partially coated end

LASERS

A **laser beam** is a concentrated beam of light that travels in a very narrow, straight path. See Fig. 27-1. The word "laser" comes from **L**ight **A**mplification by **S**timulated **E**mission of **R**adiation.

Until recently, power transmission has involved only mechanical devices, fluids, or electrical wire. Lasers are different. They can transmit power through the atmosphere without using any of these things. Also, the heat of laser beams can be controlled. It can range from very low temperatures to temperatures as hot as the sun. Lasers were first developed in 1960. They have become an important device in power transmission, in communication, and in industrial uses.

as a high-intensity, coherent beam of light. The beam can be focused with a lens and put to work.

Lasers in Communication

Until recently, laser beams were transmitted only through the atmosphere. The use of lasers in communication has introduced a new system of transmission—*fiber optics*. Lasers in **fiber-optic systems** use a semiconductor crystal. The laser is about the size of a pocket calculator. It produces one milliwatt (mW) of power. This is about 60,000 times less than the power used by a 60-watt light bulb.

In operation, a fiber-optic laser flashes bursts of light along hair-thin strands of flexible glass. New lasers are capable of handling the equivalent of 300,000 voice channels.

Fiber-optic systems have several important advantages over regular telephone systems. Cables made up of glass strands take up much less space than copper cables. Also, light signals need to be regenerated (strengthened) only about every six miles (10 km). This is much farther than the regeneration distance in regular systems. There are plans to join the United States and Europe with a fiber-optic system.

Fiber-optic systems can also work well alongside electrical conductors. Fiber-optic strands and electrical wires can share space without either system affecting the other. Therefore, fiber-optic lines can be run anywhere that electrical lines are run.

Fiber-optic telephone lines are now in use throughout the world. The great capacity of fiber-optic transmission will permit more economical two-way video and complex computer transmissions. The video telephone may become a reality instead of a novelty. Classes may be taught and conferences held using fiber-optic telephone lines. See Fig. 27-2.

Fig. 27-2. Communications using fiber optics can provide face-to-face conferences with people miles away. This photo shows a group holding a discussion by way of telecommunications.

Fig. 27-3. A laser beam cuts by vaporizing materials.

Lasers in Industry

Lasers are being used more and more in industry. They can *drill precision holes* without distorting surrounding materials. In drilling, the laser first melts the material. It then vaporizes the melted substance. This method is used to drill holes in materials that are too hard to be drilled with regular tools, such as diamonds. Lasers can also drill very soft materials. For example, holes in nipples for babies' bottles are drilled with lasers.

Lasers can also be used to *join metals* by brazing or welding. Very small, thin metal pieces can be joined without any distortion from heat.

Lasers can also be used to *cut materials*. A laser can cut extremely complex designs in very hard materials. See Fig. 27-3. In a production situation, the laser can be programmed to repeat the cuts.

Heat treating of metals is also possible with lasers. Wherever heat is needed, lasers can provide it with a precision impossible with other methods.

Lasers in Medicine

Lasers have been used in eye surgery since 1960. At that time they were used to treat one of the leading causes of blindness in the world—the rupturing of tiny blood vessels in the eye. A laser beam seals the vessels by cauterizing (eliminate by burning) the offending blood vessels. This prevents blood from flowing into the eye, causing blindness. The operation is nearly painless, since

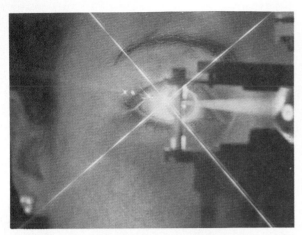

Fig. 27-4. A laser being used in eye surgery. (Phototake/R. Mansini)

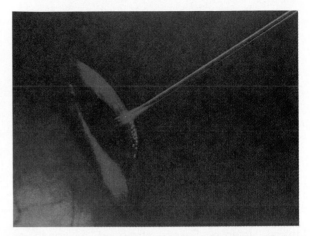

Fig. 27-5. A laser beam being used in eye surgery. (Phototake/R. Mansini)

the eye has few nerves to carry pain. See Fig. 27-4. Thousands of people have had their sight preserved by what has become simple outpatient surgery.

From this early beginning, laser surgery continues to gain new uses in medicine.

■ A carbon dioxide laser produces a light beam absorbed by water. Heat from the laser turns the water in the tissue into steam. The steam can vaporize cysts or other undesirable tissue in the body.

■ The argon laser reacts to the color red. It can penetrate the body until it reaches blood, where it can be used for treating skin disorders.

■ A new laser called the YAG laser can destroy tumors by "cooking" rather than cutting.

The initial eye surgery described has grown into a variety of surgery techniques. The future of lasers in medicine has almost no limits.

For example, the future may find a "smart laser" that can tell the difference between healthy and cancerous cells. It will then destroy the cancerous cells. A laser makes a cleaner cut with less pain and cell damage. It also seals blood vessels as it cuts, reducing loss of blood. See Fig. 27-5. Lasers may become the surgeon's knife in the years ahead.

Lasers in Everyday Life

Lasers are found in everyday use. Most people have already encountered lasers at the grocery store checkout counter. See Fig. 27-6. Such lasers are able to read the bar coding on the package identification tag, often reading around several bumps and towards the side of packages.

Fig. 27-6. The use of lasers speeds supermarket checkout. It also provides each customer with a complete list of products purchased, with their prices.

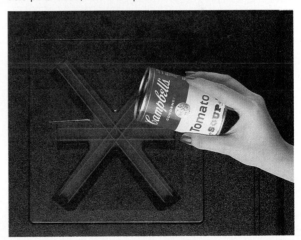

The result is a checkout slip that identifies the product purchased and the price of the product.

Lasers are also used for tasks varying from identifying fingerprints in a rapid and efficient manner, to cutting diamonds. Laser lighting is used in the entertainment industry. It is being used in discos and theater productions. New laser applications are being introduced with a growing frequency.

Future Uses of Lasers

In Chapter 25, you learned about the inertial confinement method of producing nuclear fusion. This method requires the use of the world's most powerful lasers. One laser used in research is called NOVA. When it is fully developed, NOVA will produce a beam of light with 150 *trillion* watts of power. The beam will last for just a fraction of a second. However, in this mini-second, it will duplicate the temperature of the sun. The result, if successful, will be a fusion reaction. Several different inertial confinement projects are now underway.

Lasers may also have a future role in national defense. Lasers stationed in space or mounted on mountaintops could be used to intercept enemy missiles.

The list of uses for lasers grows each year. Keep in mind that lasers harness *light*, a basic source of energy. At one time in history, people harnessed steam. The result of this was the Industrial Revolution. Someday, lasers may be seen as one of the greatest developments of the 20th century.

CRYOGENICS

Cryogenics, a science, is the study of the properties of materials at extremely low temperatures. Cryogenic temperatures range from −150°F (−101°C) to absolute zero (−460°F or −273°C). As the temperature drops into this range, air turns into a liquid and then freezes solid. Most metals become brittle enough to shatter like glass. Other metals, such as lead and mercury, react differently. At cryogenic temperatures, lead can be made into springs and clear-tone bells. Mercury can be made into a hammer.

There are many industrial and commercial uses for cryogenic refrigeration. Super-coldness is used to prepare freeze-dried foods and to freeze living cells. It is used in the manufacture of computer circuits and in space research. Cryogenic refrigeration also has an important future in the generation and transmission of power and even in transportation.

SUPERCONDUCTORS

In general, metal conducts electricity better as it becomes colder. This is because the electrons have less interference from molecular mo-

tion. In some metals, a strange thing happens as the temperature drops below −418°F (−250°C). All detectable electrical resistance suddenly vanishes. The metal becomes a **superconductor**. In one experiment, a superconductor conducted a current for two years without additional current input. The current flow was then stopped by warming the metal.

Scientists are mainly interested in two possible uses for superconductors:
- The production of super-efficient electrical generators and magnets.
- The super-efficient transmission of electricity.

In the past, the only superconductors were metals at cryogenic temperatures. But in recent years, research has turned to the use of other materials as superconductors.

In 1986, major breakthroughs began. Use of copper oxide "raised" the temperature at which a material would become a superconductor to −406°F (−243°C). This was the first major improvement since 1973 when −419°F (−250°C) was reached. Additional research with copper oxides have raised the temperature to −240°F (−151°C.) Research with other materials has not proven successful. While higher temperatures have been reported, they cannot be confirmed by repeated laboratory tests.

The new copper oxide materials tend to be brittle, making the forming of superconducting wires difficult. Wires or filaments are needed to manufacture magnets, motors, generators, and transformers. Progress is being made, as shown in Fig. 27-7. The process for manufacturing the flat wire involves combining the basic superconducting ceramic material with metals to form new alloys. The result is a more dense and stronger wire.

Fig. 27-7. The very thin superconductor ribbon (.010″) can carry the same current as the stranded copper cable (over an inch in diameter).

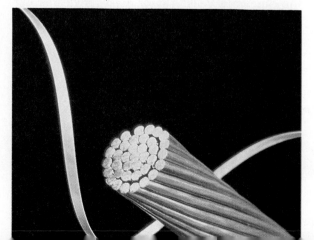

Research in superconducting materials continues in three major areas. The first is in developing the existing superconducting materials into useful products. The second area of research is in a continued search for new materials capable of conducting at higher temperatures. Perhaps the most important research is in the third area, the search to understand how a material "becomes a superconductor." While the results can be seen and used, the theoretical basis for superconductivity has yet to be established. Once understood, new materials and better fabrication techniques may be possible.

Many scientists believe that the development of superconductors may be among the greatest discoveries since the development of the semiconductor. Superconductors could revolutionize the way we move electricity from place to place, make magnetically propelled trains common, and create powerful and efficient motors. See Fig. 27-8.

Superconductor Generators and Magnets

A superconducting generator that can produce 18 million watts of alternating current could supply power for a community of 20,000 people. An experimental model that has been developed is only half the size and weight of a regular generator. It is also much more efficient. See Fig. 27-9.

Superconducting magnets can develop tremendously powerful magnetic fields using very small amounts of current. Later in this chapter, you will learn about the use of superconducting magnets in a new type of rail transportation.

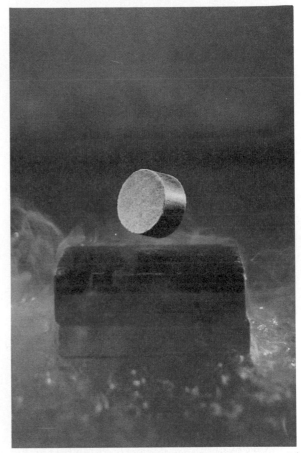

Fig. 27-8. A superconducting material suspends a metal sphere. Like magnetic poles repel, suspending the sphere.

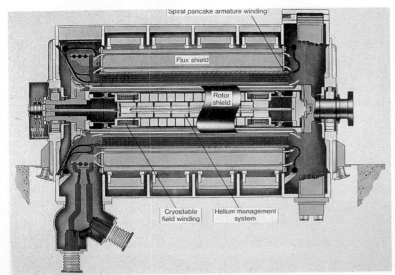

Fig. 27-9. Parts of a superconducting generator.

Superconductor Power Transmission

Savings in transmitting electricity with superconductors can be very great. Superconductors can transmit electricity for long distances without power loss. Superconducting wires are also much smaller than ordinary wires.

At the present time, power plants must be located fairly close to the area of use. Fuel must be transported to the plants, sometimes over great distances. With a superconducting transmission system, electricity could be generated at power plants near the fuel production site. Then the current could be transmitted through superconductors to the areas of use.

FUEL CELLS

Fuel cells are much like regular batteries. Both fuel cells and batteries convert chemical energy into electrical energy. Both types of devices also use an *electrolyte* (a solution or a polymer). However, the overall chemical reaction in a fuel cell is very simple. Hydrogen and oxygen combine to produce water and electricity.

Figure 27-10 shows the basic parts of the most common type of fuel cell. Hydrogen and oxygen are both fed into the cell from high-pressure containers. The hydrogen is the fuel of the fuel cell. The oxygen acts on the hydrogen and is called the *oxidizer*.

Technology Focus

When Is A Conductor Not A Conductor?

Progress continues in the development of a superconductor which will operate at room temperature. As you know, regular conductors must be insulated both for safety and to prevent short circuits. What form of insulation will be needed for superconductors? . . . None, except to prevent contact with other superconductors!

A superconductor provides no resistance to the flow of an electric current. As a result, the current will always stay with the superconductor. If you touch it, you won't receive a shock. If a regular piece of metal touches it, nothing will happen— no short circuit.

If, however, a superconducting wire is formed into a coil to generate a magnetic field, it must be insulated to keep the current spiraling around the many turns of the coil. If the wire were not insulated, the current would take a shortcut, traveling straight from one end of the superconducting coil to the other.

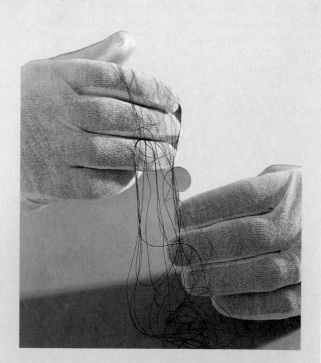

Almost any material that will seal the superconductor will serve as an insulator. Today, many scientists are using regular *conductors* as insulators! For example, silver is a very good—and very expensive—conductor. But to a superconductor, it's just another insulator.

The fuel cell has two electrodes: the **anode** (negative) and the **cathode** (positive). There is a polymer or an acid electrolyte between the electrodes.

In operation, hydrogen is fed constantly into the cell. At the anode, the hydrogen atoms release electrons. The positively charged particles which remains then travel through the electrolyte to the cathode. At the cathode, the hydrogen particles combine with the oxygen to produce water.

Meanwhile, the electrons released by the hydrogen atoms at the anode must be replaced. The replacement electrons come from the cathode. To maintain an electrical balance, the electrons released at the anode travel through the external circuit to the cathode. This produces a current to power the electric device.

Refer again to Fig. 27-10. Notice that the only by-product of fuel-cell operation is water. In addition, fuel cells are very efficient. Cells using pure hydrogen can reach efficiencies of nearly 70%.

Early research was done to develop fuel cells that could power electric automobiles. But most of today's research is directed toward developing fuel cells for the production of electricity by utility companies.

The heart of a commercial fuel-cell plant is the power section, made up of several stacks of fuel cells. See Fig. 27-11. (The fuel for commercial plants is a hydrogen-base fuel, such as natural gas, rather than pure hydrogen.) Such plants operate at about 40% efficiency and are expected to increase to 45-50%. This figure compares favorably to the 40% efficiency of conventional power plants.

The advantages of using fuel cells are numerous. They are clean, producing very little pollution. They can be quickly assembled in a variety of sizes and in various locations. Often waste heat can be used for cogeneration.

The major disadvantage of fuel cells is cost. It is hoped that mass production will lower cost to about $700 per kilowatt. This cost would be competitive with other generation options.

Fig. 27-11. A fuel cell stack. Each fuel cell produces a fraction of a kilowatt of DC power. When stacked together, the output is significant. In plants, several stacks are used.

Fig. 27-10. Parts of a fuel cell.

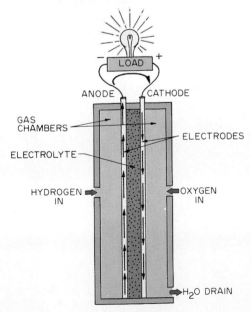

Chapter 27—Review

Testing Your Knowledge

Briefly answer each of the following questions. Write on a separate piece of paper.
1. What is a laser beam?
2. Identify four uses of lasers in industry.
3. Of what material are fiber-optic cables made?
4. When were lasers first used in medicine?
5. When used in medicine, the argon laser reacts to which color?
6. Name three possible uses for superconductors.
7. What are the waste products of fuel cells?
8. What is the principal problem holding back the expansion of fuel cells as sources of electricity for utility companies?

Expressing Your Knowledge

Using complete sentences, write your answers to the following on a separate sheet of paper:
1. What is meant by *coherence* in a laser beam?
2. Describe how a ruby laser produces a laser beam.
3. Describe how lasers are used in communications.
4. Describe one way a carbon dioxide laser is used in medicine.
5. Define cryogenics.
6. What is a superconductor?
7. What is a fuel cell?

Applying Your Knowledge

Follow your teacher's instructions to complete these activities:
1. Collect articles from newspapers and journals regarding developments in the use of laser, cryogenics, and fuel cells. Report your findings to your class and add the information to your *Power Notebook*.
2. Check with local industries in your area to see whether any companies are using lasers. Prepare a report describing the uses you find.
3. Repeat activity 2 for cryogenics.

Chapter 28

Future Transportation Systems

Transportation is the area of technology most sensitive to changes in the worldwide supply of fossil fuels. It is a dynamic area. Someday, perhaps in the near future, transportation will take us to other planets and beyond.

Expanding Your Knowledge

As you study this chapter you will learn to:

- Understand changes needed in transportation to lessen dependency on fossil fuels.
- Explain how hydrogen could become a primary transportation fuel in the future.
- Describe alternative methods of providing for transportation of people and goods.
- Identify problems in promoting changes in transportation.
- Describe a variety of possible changes which are being studied and considered for the transportation of people and goods.
- Explain existing plans and concepts for future space exploration.

Building Your Word Power

The following terms are defined and explained in this chapter. Learning these will help you learn more about future transportation systems.

air bags
anti-lock brakes
canard
ethanol
levitation magnets
maglev train system
propfan engine
propulsion magnets
Scotch yoke
space shuttle
space station
supersonic
tilt-rotor plane
unducted fan engine (UDF)

THE TEVan CONCEPT

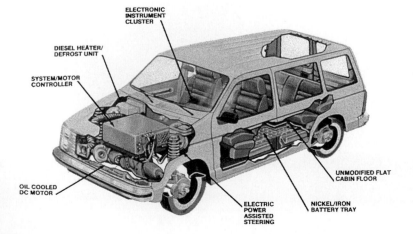

Transportation is important for everyone in the world. People in cities have food transported to them. Raw materials and goods are moved freely between nations. People travel between regions and between countries.

Transportation depends on a very large and steady supply of oil. Because of anticipated shortages of oil in the future, we must conserve the oil we have and begin to look at alternatives to oil as the primary fuel for transportation. Transportation is changing. Systems are being refined, and vehicle engines and designs are being improved.

Transportation is critical to space exploration. Exciting things are happening now, and plans for the future hold great promise.

TRANSPORTATION NEEDS

Transportation is essential for life. Over five billion (5,000,000,000) people on earth depend on transportation. Very few countries produce all the goods and food they need. Many countries import large quantities of food and export raw materials and/or manufactured products. Other countries reverse the process, selling or trading large quantities of food. Some countries import and export both. World commerce is essential to life as we know it on Earth.

All predictions for the future indicate a growing population. The need for food and manufactured products will increase. Therefore, the need for the transportation for both goods and people will continue to grow.

Since the supply of our main transportation fuel, oil, is limited, we must increase two efforts in the future:

- Increase conservation, thereby preserving fuel. Conservation can increase the number of years the world supply of oil will last.
- Seek alternative transportation fuels to oil, as well as other fossil fuels.

If successful, these efforts will move us away from our dependency on fossil fuels and towards the use of renewable and inexhaustible supplies of fuels. Our very existence depends on the success of these efforts. Our fossil fuels will not last for more than a century or two, considering the increased rate at which we are using them. We will, almost certainly, see shortages of natural gas and oil occur during the 21st century.

A very important by-product of this effort can be an improved environment. The burning of fossil fuels is the leading cause of air pollution. Smog in cities as well as parts of the countryside, the increase of carbon dioxide in the atmosphere and earth warming, acid rain, and other air pollution are the direct result of our high rate of burning fossil fuels. Shifting to other fuels, such as hydrogen, will provide cleaner air.

Conservation

Between 1960 and 1990, the number of miles driven in the United States increased from approximately .6 trillion to 1.5 trillion (600,000,000,000 to 1,500,000,000,000) miles. By the year 2000, the total will be approximately 2 trillion miles, if we maintain the expected 3-4% growth in miles traveled each year. See Fig. 28-1. Our automobile population is growing faster than our human population. The number of miles driven is expected to continue to increase at a rapid rate.

Fig. 28-1. Past and projected miles driven in the United States.

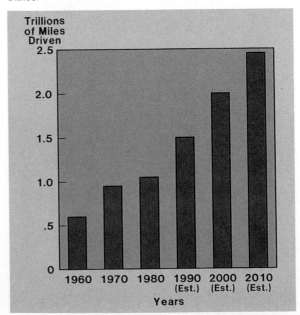

Between 1960 to 1990, fuel economy in U.S. automobiles went from an average of approximately 13 miles per gallon to 21 miles per gallon. Even with this increase of over 50% in fuel economy, gasoline consumption still increased by over 50% during the same period. The miles per gallon figures continue to improve each year.

The projection for the future is less promising. During the past few years, overall fuel economy has begun to stabilize as Americans are again driving larger cars. This has been encouraged by the low cost of fuel. Adjusted for inflation, early 1990 gasoline prices were the lowest they had been in 20 years.

Similar decreases in cost, though not as dramatic, have occurred in other forms of transportation. With less expensive fuel, people live farther from their place of employment.

Most efforts to reduce travel and fuel consumption are directed towards two factors:

- Our growing dependency on foreign oil contributes to our trade imbalance.
- Growing pollution and traffic congestion in cities decreases the quality of life.

These two concerns need to be combined with the greater need of conserving some of the remaining fossil fuels for future generations. For example, plastic products are made from fossil fuels. These may be far more important than burning the fossil fuels for heat and transportation.

The pressures for fuel economy will continue to grow. As the world demand for oil increases, prices will also increase. The oil price stability of the 1980s is not likely to continue through the 1990s. We should begin taking significant steps toward conservation, including:

- Increasing the fuel efficiency of automobiles, trucks, and recreational vehicles. In automobiles, efficiency can be increased to an average of 45 miles per gallon. Changes would include smaller engines, replacing heavy steel parts with plastics, and improving performance. See Fig. 28-2. Some of these changes will be presented later in this chapter.

The proposed increase in "average miles per gallon" will still leave the opportunity to build larger cars for special needs such as handicapped drivers. Miles per gallon can be increased to 51-78 by the year 2000 for production cars.

- Increasing the use of public transportation, especially in urban areas. See Fig. 28-3.
- Increasing the fuel efficiency of airplanes and other public transportation systems.

These changes will require a combination of government action and citizen support. Most require people to reduce comfort by riding in smaller cars or by giving up some freedom of movement by riding on public transportation systems. The benefits, however, can be substantial. These include:

- Cleaner air and a more healthy environment.
- More economical transportation. Efficient public transportation is less expensive than driving.
- Less stress. Driving conditions in heavy traffic congestion can produce considerable personal stress.

Fig. 28-2. A modern fuel-efficient automobile. This auto averages 53 miles per gallon, with 58 miles per gallon for highway driving.

Fig. 28-3. A light rail system can move people more economically than automobiles, and with less pollution.

A number of public actions can help accomplish these changes. Many are unpopular and will not be adopted without public support. Changes are taking place which will help promote conservation include:

- Implementing the proposed new federal fuel economy standards. These would increase average miles per gallon requirements for new cars from the current 27 to 40-45 miles per gallon by the year 2000.
- Increasing the gasoline tax. The increased tax will encourage the use of public transportation. The increased income from this tax can be used to finance and construct fuel-efficient public transportation systems.

There are many other ideas to encourage conservation. Some are even more controversial than the two suggested. We must, as a nation, put aside some personal interests and initiate and support plans which will conserve fuel.

In the meantime, each adult can develop his or her own conservation plan. Some things which should be included are:

- Use carpools or public transportation whenever possible.
- Minimize the use of car air conditioning. It consumes more than a gallon of gasoline for each tankful used.
- Avoid short trips. Instead, walk or ride a bicycle. A car burns more than twice as much gasoline during the first few minutes of operation than it does at other times.
- Inflate tires properly. Underinflated tires cause drag which can reduce fuel consumption by as much as 6%.
- Use radial tires. These improve fuel economy by about one mile per gallon.
- Always choose a fuel-efficient car when buying a new or used one.
- Keep automobiles properly tuned.
- Inspect and service emissions systems regularly.
- Replace the air filter at least every 15,000 miles.
- Drive at a steady speed.
- Drive more slowly. Less gasoline is burned at 45 mph than at 55 mph.
- Avoid idling. Thirty seconds of idling can consume more gasoline than the amount used to start a car.

Developing New Fuels

The second effort in transportation must be to seek alternative fuels. Potential alternatives were presented in Chapters 4 and 26. These are methanol, gasohol (mixture of ethanol and gasoline), electricity, and hydrogen. We can add compressed natural gas and solar power to this list.

Items on this list can be divided into two groups:

- Those easily developed and usable in the near future (or already in limited use)—methanol, gasohol, and compressed natural gas.
- Those which require extensive research and development prior to extensive use—electricity, hydrogen, and solar power.

Methanol, Gasohol, and Compressed Natural Gas. These fuels are presently in limited use with potential for expansion. All would decrease some of our reliance on world oil supplies, and will help provide cleaner air. However, none have the potential of replacing oil as the fuel of the future.

Methanol is an alcohol fuel made from coal, wood, natural gas, or garbage. If made from coal or natural gas, it is simply using a different fossil fuel. While coal is still abundant, natural gas will probably be in short supply during the next century.

The most effective use of methanol is a blend of 85% methanol with 15% gasoline. While producing less energy per gallon than gasoline, it is cleaner than gasoline and can be manufactured exclusively from U.S. products. Testing and use continues. See Fig. 28-4.

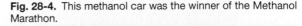

Fig. 28-4. This methanol car was the winner of the Methanol Marathon.

Gasohol, made of ethanol and gasoline, has had limited use in the past. **Ethanol** made from grain such as corn or from sugarcane can also be used as a fuel. However, the supply is limited. If 40% of the total U.S. grain harvest were used as ethanol, it would provide just 10% of the fuel consumed in the U.S. each year.

Compressed natural gas is already used for fleet vehicles, some school buses, and other limimted services. Compressed natural gas is currently less expensive than gasoline and less polluting. However, mileage is poorer, requiring refueling every 100 miles. Also, we are simply substituting one hydrocarbon which is in limited supply for another. The world supply of natural gas, while still plentiful, is less than the supply of oil.

Electricity.

Electricity is not a new fuel for transportation. It was one of the original automotive energy sources and is still in use in a variety of utility vehicles. Considerable research is underway on a number of different approaches to electric vehicles.

New advances in battery design, streamlining of vehicles, and use of lighter materials are making electric cars more practical. Figure 28-5 shows a prototype electric car planned for manufacturing and sales. Engineering reports indicate the car will operate for 120 miles between

Fig. 28-5. The aerodynamic design of this electric car contributes to its fuel efficiency.

battery charges, have a top speed of 110 mph, and will accelerate from 0 to 60 mph in eight seconds.

Another, more venturesome effort, is putting electric cables in roadbeds. See Fig. 28-6. Cars would receive electricity by way of electromagnetic induction. The induction plate must be 1½″ to 3″ above the roadbed, requiring a smooth and even roadway.

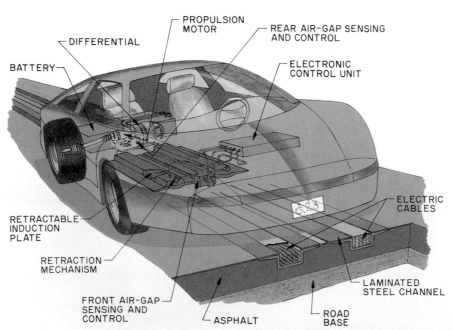

PROPULSION
MOTOR

REAR AIR-GAP SENSING
AND CONTROL

DIFFERENTIAL

BATTERY

ELECTRONIC
CONTROL UNIT

ELECTRIC
CABLES

RETRACTABLE
INDUCTION
PLATE

RETRACTION
MECHANISM

LAMINATED
STEEL CHANNEL

FRONT AIR-GAP
SENSING AND
CONTROL

ASPHALT

ROAD
BASE

Fig. 28-6. A roadway-powered electric car charges batteries and receives power to operate its motor—all through electromagnetic induction.

Fig. 28-7. A small electric fuel cell capable of generating electricity from many different fuels is shown on the left. Operation of the cell is shown below. The monolithic solid oxide fuel cell was invented by Argonne National Laboratory, Illinois.

MONOLITHIC FUEL CELL

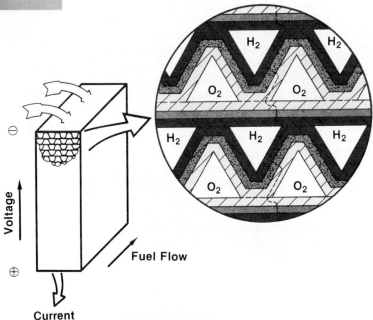

Induction would provide electricity to operate the car and to charge batteries. The batteries would operate the car when it was not over induction coils. Efforts are underway to construct a "demonstration roadway" in Los Angeles to study the possibility of widespread use of magnetic induction as an "electrical fuel" for automobiles.

Fuel cells, as described in Chapter 27, have been researched extensively as a potential source of power for automobiles. Past efforts to reduce weight and increase power were unsuccessful. At present, conventional fuel cells are too heavy for the power they produce and are not practical for automobiles, trucks, airplanes, and trains. However, recent research has developed a new fuel cell that is lightweight and compact. See Fig. 28-7.

When the new fuel cells are in operation, alternating streams of air and fuel flow by each other. The fuel and air react electrochemically across thin ceramic walls. The result is a flow of electric current which can be used to drive an automobile. It is projected that a 15-inch cube will produce 50 kilowatts of power, the equivalent of a 66-horsepower engine.

The operating temperature, 1500-1800°F (800-1000°C) will permit the use of practically any fuel including hydrogen, gasoline, methane, gassified coal, or ethanol. The concept is experimental. Considerable research is needed before being used in an automobile.

A final note on electricity as a fuel. As implied in the previous paragraph, electricity is a "secondary fuel." That is, electricity must be produced by some other fuel before it can be used for transportation or any other purpose. It is valuable as a transportation fuel only when the original fuel is readily available. To use gasoline to operate a fuel cell to drive an automobile might prove to be more efficient than using the gasoline in the internal-combustion engine. However, it does not solve the major problem of future shortages of fossil fuels.

Hydrogen. The use of hydrogen produced from solar energy to produce electricity uses an inexhaustible source of energy as the initial input.

Hydrogen was presented in Chapter 26 as a method of storing and using electricity. Its potential as a transportable fuel is significant, holding more promise as the "transportation fuel for future generations" than any other known fuel.

Considerable research and development is needed before hydrogen can become a major transportation fuel. Some predictions indicate that 20 years are needed, provided the pace of research and development is increased. Others feel that applications will soon be practical. Fortunately, all *theories* needed to utilize hydrogen as a fuel are already in place. Only the *technology to apply* the theories needs to be developed.

 An important area of Research and Development still needed is in the containment of hydrogen. Hydrogen is the lightest element, and atoms of hydrogen are the smallest atoms in existence. Hydrogen atoms can pass through small openings. Leaks can easily develop in transportation fuel tanks. Space shuttles have often been "grounded" due to hydrogen leaks. Efforts continue to develop leak-free systems.

In using hydrogen as a fuel, scientists can visualize a clear path from solar energy to transportation. See Fig. 28-8. Solar energy is a natural source since the production of hydrogen need not be continuous. Production can stop at night or whenever the sun does not shine.

Chapter 3 includes a description of how PV cells produce electricity. As efficiency increases, the cost of producing electricity decreases. When the cost per peak kilowatt-hour from PV cells drops to 50¢, the cost of hydrogen will become practical. At that time, the cost of the amount of hydrogen equivalent to a gallon of gasoline will fall below $2.00. On many world markets, hydrogen will then be competitive in cost to gasoline.

 While hydrogen has many uses, the first and most important use will be for transportation. Used in automobiles, hydrogen will create *no* pollution. The burning of hydrogen produces only water as a by-product. Thus the path from source to use begins when solar energy is used to produce hydrogen from water. Then, when burned as a fuel, hydrogen produces water and usable energy.

Hydrogen can be used with an internal-combustion engine as well as with fuel cells, as described earlier. See Fig. 28-9. Some experimental hydrogen-powered cars use a liquid hydrogen

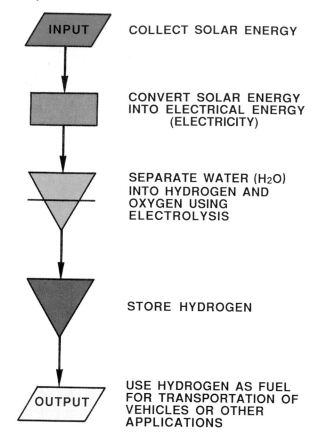

Fig. 28-8. The complete energy cycle from inexhaustible source of energy (solar), to fuel (hydrogen), to use (transportation and other applications).

system to provide added mileage. Other designs use metallic hydride, a very safe storage method. However, hydrides are heavy when storing large amounts of fuel.

Transportation systems using hydrogen are not limited to automobiles. Germany has a plane designed with a hump for hydrogen. Both the Soviet Union and the United States have converted planes to hydrogen use on an experimental basis.

Hydrogen uses can be extended beyond automobiles and airplanes to all transportation vehicles—trains, trucks, ships, etc. Hydrogen may indeed be the transportation fuel of the future.

Fig. 28-9. A hydrogen-powered experimental car has been developed. This shows the hydrogen tank behind the passenger compartment.

Benefits of Conservation and Alternative Fuels

The future can be very favorable if we adopt conservation efforts and successfully change to an inexhaustible supply of energy, such as the solar energy/hydrogen cycle. Some of the benefits have already been presented:

- Cleaner air. Burning of fossil fuels is one of the main sources of air pollution. Shifting to a non-polluting transportation fuel will make air much cleaner throughout the world.
- Balancing our national trade deficit. The United States has large deserts which can be used for solar energy collection and the production of hydrogen. Shifting to a domestic produced fuel will reduce or eliminate our importation of oil. This will be a major step towards balancing our national trade deficit.
- Preserving hydrocarbons. Hydrocarbons are used to produce plastics. The plastics industry produces strong, lightweight articles used throughout the world. Hydrocarbons are much more valuable as plastic products than when burned as fuel. Also, plastics can be recycled.
- Freedom from a limited fuel supply. At the present time, we are dependent on other countries for our fuel. Producing the fuel we need will protect our nation from the fear and concern of having our fuel supply limited, or stopped.
- Solving a critical problem. Someday we *must* find a substitute for oil as our transportation fuel. Developing a practical substitute will solve this problem and help assure future generations of enough fuel to maintain a desirable standard of living.

There are probably other benefits which can accrue in the future. These five, however, more than justify the need for research and the need to seek an inexhaustible substitute for oil as a transportation fuel.

POTENTIAL CHANGES IN TRANSPORTATION

Research and Development (R&D) is taking place in transportation modes and vehicles on a continuing basis. The previous section identified a need for conservation and a need for new transportation fuels. Research is underway and will lead us towards more energy-efficient vehicles and new and cleaner fuels.

This section will help you understand some of the R&D underway in major areas of the transportation industry: highway, rail, air, and water transportation.

Highway Transportation

The last section, "Transportation Needs," presented information on portions of the research directed toward making highway transportation more efficient in the future. Two areas of transportation receiving considerable R&D are fuel economy and safety, especially in the automotive area. The following developments will change highway transportation in the future.

Two-Stroke Automotive Engines. Two-stroke automotive engines are being developed which could replace many four-stroke automotive engines. A fuel-injection system injects fuel directly into the combustion chamber. Air intake can be provided in the manner described in Chapter 12, or a supercharger can be used to provide air through an intake valve. Most of the engines currently in development are using a supercharger which will provide greater power with less engine weight.

The use of fuel injection makes the engine more fuel-efficient. The amount of gasoline can be controlled to meet engine demands. The result is an engine lighter in weight which will significantly increase fuel economy.

Another design advance is being developed for two-stroke engines. A **Scotch yoke** replaces the traditional connecting rod/crankshaft design. See Fig. 28-10. It converts linear motion to rotary motion with less weight and internal friction. It also permits a design which will allow the placing of four cylinders at 90° intervals around the same crankshaft journal. Designs with two and three cylinders around a single crankshaft journal are also possible. One experimental three-cylinder two-stroke engine occupies about half the space required for a four-stroke four-cylinder engine. See Fig. 28-11.

The Scotch-yoke is not a new design. It has been used in other applications for many years. Its original use was in early stationary steam engines. Good ideas, even if old, often find use as design and needs change.

As with all ideas, there exists considerable controversy on the use of the two-stroke automobile engine. The four-stroke engine is well developed and designed. It will be difficult to replace.

Improved Vehicle Design. Wind tunnels and computer analysis have permitted auto and truck manufacturers to design vehicles with less wind resistance. These designs have helped produce greater fuel economy for both trucks and automobiles.

Designs still are not the most efficient. Trucks have made some progress through the use of wind deflectors and some streamlining. See Fig. 28-12.

The next big design step for automobiles will be a lower front hood. Refer back to Fig. 28-5. A lower hood design will also be possible with two-stroke engine using the Scotch-yoke design. As the need for fuel economy grows, streamlined design will continue to help reduce fuel consumption.

Fig. 28-11. A three-cylinder, two-stroke experimental engine is smaller than a four-cylinder four-stroke engine. It saves space in the engine compartment.

Fig. 28-10. A Scotch-yoke connecting-rod design with two opposed pistons.

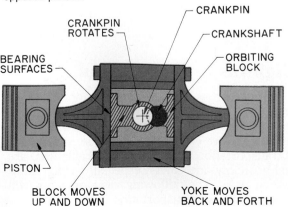

CRANKPIN

CRANKPIN ROTATES

CRANKSHAFT

BEARING SURFACES

ORBITING BLOCK

PISTON

BLOCK MOVES UP AND DOWN

YOKE MOVES BACK AND FORTH

Fig. 28-12. Wind deflectors help increase fuel economy. However, the massive size of trucks and the large engine have discouraged added streamlining. Also, economical fuel prices have discouraged placing funds into research and development on streamlining trucks.

Fig. 28-13. Large pickup truck, using a diesel engine.

Safety. A number of improved safety features have been developed and are gradually being introduced. In the future, many of these safety features will become standard equipment.

The two most important are **air bags** and **anti-lock brakes.** A pair of air bags, stored under the dash and/or in the steering wheel, will inflate instantly in an accident and protect the driver and front passenger. Inflation is so rapid that it occurs between the start of the collision and the action of persons being thrown forward and hitting the steering wheel or other portions of the dashboard. Refer back to "Technology Focus," p. 298.

Anti-lock braking is a significant safety improvement. In an emergency, an automobile with locked brakes skids farther than an automobile which does not have the wheels locked. The anti-locking device partially releases the brakes as the wheels begin to lock. In this way, they stop the automobile in the shortest possible distance.

Two other features also contribute to safety. These are four-wheel drive and four-wheel steering. Four-wheel drive has been common for trucks and off-road vehicles. It is now becoming popular in automobiles. Refer back to "Technology Focus," p. 175.

Four-wheel steering is a more recent development. It aids safety by providing better control of the car.

Diesel Improvements. Fuel economy has always been a strength of diesel engines. New diesel engines have overcome some of the past problems of diesel engines. Emissions, including particulates, have been decreased. New engines are also free of noxious exhaust emissions.

The growth of diesel usage in automobiles will probably continue, but at a slow rate. The diesel engine will permit larger cars to obtain good fuel mileage. The principal growth in the use of diesel engines will be in the larger pickup trucks, and recreational vehicles. See Fig. 28-13. Most large trucks already use diesel engines.

Diesel engines also provide an added fuel alternative to methanol and alcohol. A synthetic fuel can be made from vegetable oils. The key oil crops are soybeans, peanuts, sunflowers, linseed, corn, cotton, and palms. Initial uses will probably be blends of soybean and ethanol (alcohol). While not a total substitute, vegetable oils can reduce our need for imported oil.

Rail Transportation

You will recall from Chapter 14 that most of today's trains use diesel-electric engines. Compared to what rail transport could be, these trains are slow and noisy. They also produce a rough ride. These disadvantages could be overcome by using a relatively new transportation idea—levitation. (To *levitate* means to rise in the air.) Levitation can be accomplished by applying cryogenics to traditional rail transport.

In one **maglev** (magnetically levitated) **train system,** superconducting electromagnetic coils are mounted on the train. See Fig. 28-14A. Another set of magnets, called **levitation magnets,** are mounted on the surface. The superconducting magnets on the train induce magnetism of the same polarity in the levitation magnets. As a result, the two sets of magnets repel each other, pushing the train upward. The support wheels are used only when the superconducting magnets are not activated. That is when the train is picking up speed, rolling to a stop, or standing still. Otherwise, the train is raised above the surface and moves levitated on a magnetic field. The guide wheels keep the train centered over the levitation magnets.

Propulsion is provided by **propulsion magnets** mounted on the sides of the track. The propulsion magnets interact with the superconducting train magnets. Each train magnet is simultaneously pulled by a side magnet of opposite polarity and pushed by a side magnet of the same polarity. See Fig. 28-14B. The polarity of the side magnets is continually reversed. The speed of the train is determined by the speed at which the polarity is reversed.

Trains using a maglev system can reach speeds of over 300 miles per hour. They also provide a quiet, smooth ride.

Several countries are developing and testing maglev systems, including Japan, France, and Germany. The British have had a low speed maglev commuter in operation since 1987.

The first maglev system in the United States may be in Las Vegas, Nevada. A German firm has plans to build a maglev system from the airport to the downtown area. It hopes to introduce the maglev in the United States. See Fig. 28-15.

Trains are able to carry people and goods with more energy efficiency than automobiles and trucks. One way of reducing fuel consumption is to develop rail systems to transports people within and between cities. Also, existing rail lines could be used to carry more goods and passengers.

Fig. 28-15. Low-flying train. A scale model of a magnetically levitated train hovers above a special roadbed without touching the rails at Argonne National Laboratory's "Maglev" research center. A cutaway and a backdrop indicates how the train would look in open countryside.

Fig. 28-14. A maglev train uses magnetic force to lift the train above the surface and to provide forward propulsion.

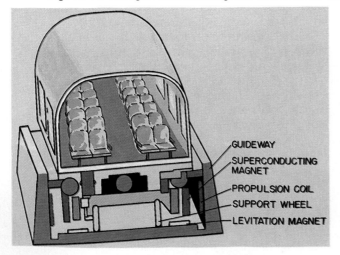

A. Levitation of train.

GUIDEWAY
SUPERCONDUCTING MAGNET
PROPULSION COIL
SUPPORT WHEEL
LEVITATION MAGNET

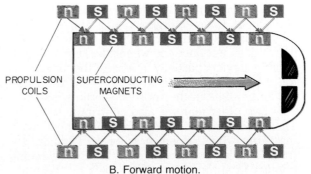

PROPULSION COILS

SUPERCONDUCTING MAGNETS

B. Forward motion.

Air Transportation

Airplane design interests continue in two directions:

■ Making airplanes more economical and safe. This emphasis recognizes that airplanes will continue to transport millions of people in a rapid manner for business and pleasure.

■ Making airplanes that fly faster to decrease travel time. Supersonic planes have the greatest potential for long distance transportation. Their greatest advantage would be transcontinental and transocean flights. See "Technology Focus," p. 166.

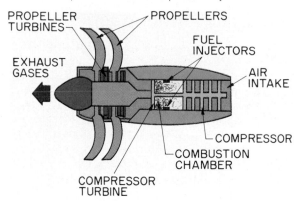

Fig. 28-16. A propfan (UDC) engine uses two swept blades on a single shaft. Each blade rotates in an opposite direction.

Profan Design. Most present-day jet planes are powered by turbofan engines. These engines propel the plane at 500-600 miles per hour. In contrast, regular propeller-driven (prop) planes have a top speed of about 450 miles per hour.

An engine with a propfan design combines the advantages of the prop plane with those of the turbofan design. A **propfan engine** is much the same as a turboprop engine, as described in Chapter 12. The difference is in propeller blade design. See Fig. 28-16.

The engine shown consists of two 11-foot diameter propellers, rotating in opposite directions (counter rotation). The engine is a turbofan jet engine. The more technical name for this turboprop is **unducted-fan engine** (UDF). The blades (eight on the engine shown) are curved and swept back. This curve delays the onset of blade drag. This permits higher air speed over the propellers and results in higher speed for the airplane. A second set of blades is attached and rotates in the opposite direction. This gives added power and smoothes the flow of air.

The UDF (propfan) uses 25 to 45% less fuel than jet aircraft now flying. The UDF powered plane will fly at the same speed, 500-600 miles per hour, just as existing jet aircraft do now.

Supersonic Flight. At the present time, only one supersonic commercial jet airplane is in operation, the *Concorde*. The military has many *supersonic* jets, but they are not readily adaptable to commercial use. **Supersonic** means flying faster than the speed of sound.

The failure to develop more supersonic commercial airplanes has been the result of high costs and low fuel economy. The cost of transporting a passenger across the Atlantic Ocean in the *Concorde* is considerably more than in subsonic jet aircraft.

Another concern is environmental. There is a growing fear that supersonic aircraft, flying at high altitudes, contribute to the destruction of the ozone layer protecting the earth. However, despite these limitations, a larger, more economical supersonic jet could still be a long distance jet plane in the future.

Research in supersonic jets continues in England, Germany, Japan, and the United States. See Fig. 28-17. England is considering a "second generation" *Concorde*. If developed, this plane would have a range of 5500 miles (50% farther than the existing *Concorde*) and carry 300 passengers. The current leader in supersonic planning is Germany where a commercial company has government backing to develop a newly designed supersonic jet. At present, private businesses in the U.S. made no commitment to develop a supersonic jet.

Fig. 28-17. An artist's conception of the second generation of the *Concorde* supersonic jet.

Fig. 28-18. This canard design airplane set a world's record for flying around the world nonstop. (Visions/Jeffrey Vock, 1986)

Fig. 28-20. Tilt-rotor plane able to take off and land vertically. It will be more economical, and faster, than helicopter service.

Future Designs. In the future we may use a host of new designs. Airplane designers have suggested a number of possibilities.

A **canard** design places the wing near the rear of the aircraft. See Fig. 28-18. The word canard is French for *duck.* Canard planes look somewhat like a duck in flight. They do not have a regular tail (rudder). The rear of the plane may have the vertical part of the tail. However, the horizontal part of the tail, the elevator, is placed in front of the wings. The carnard design results in planes that are light, fast, fuel-efficient, and very safe.

Early canard planes were designed for sports flying. Current designs are planned for business and small commercial carriers.

Another area of interest is the "flying wing." First planned as a military plane, it is also being considered for commercial flight. Fig. 28-19 shows a unique design for the future. This "wing" would fly through the air at an angle.

A **tilt-rotor plane** is shown in Fig. 28-20. This plane will make a vertical take-off, fly as a conventional plane flies, and land vertically. The plane could be used to commute between cities. It does not require an airport for take-offs and landings.

Water Transportation

One of the emphases in the future of water transportation will be increased safety, especially with oil tankers. Problems with oil spills from ruptured hulls have been a growing concern. One answer is the double-hulled tanker. This will reduce the growing danger of oil spills.

Another future development is the use of multi-hull ships. Multi-hull ships have potential for higher fuel efficiency and more comfortable rides. See Fig. 28-21.

Fig. 28-19. The flying wing moves through the air at an angle, powered by two engines.

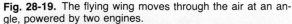

Fig. 28-21. Cruise liner of the future.

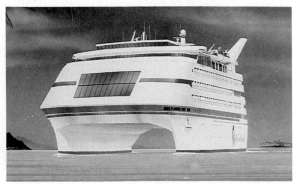

SPACE EXPLORATION

Exploration of space began in the 1950s and has continued at an ever-increasing rate to the present time. See Fig. 28-22. Today we are exploring space on ever-broadening frontiers. Immediate plans for the future include the establishment of a space station and the placement of a permanent base on the moon and eventually the planet Mars.

Part of space has already been explored and is being used. Many satellites have been launched from the surface of the Earth. These serve many purposes.

Some satellites help us predict the weather. They have given meteorologists (weather scientists) the opportunity to study weather patterns and learn how different weather conditions develop on Earth. Our weather predictions are far superior to those made just a decade ago. See Fig. 28-23.

Other satellites provide images and conduct scientific research. The Hubble Space Telescope, a 25,000-pound observatory, is now stationed in an orbit around the Earth. It is powered by photovoltaic cells and is providing data never before available to astronomers. Future launches will continue scientific research such as growing crystals in space, manufacturing perfectly round ball bearings, and studying geological features to better understand how the Earth continually changes.

One routine function of satellites is communication. Voice and television signals are relayed around the world by satellite. Telephone calls are possible, by direct dial, to most locations, and it is now routine to televise live news broadcasts from almost any place on earth.

Many of our uses of space have become routine. However, the frontier is great, and exciting activities are planned for the future.

Fig. 28-22. Milestones in space exploration.

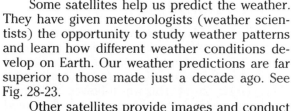

SPACE EXPLORATION TIME LINE

April, 1981   Columbia, John Young, Robert Crippen, U.S.A.
—First flight of space shuttle

May, 1973   Skylab 1, U.S.A.
—First American space station

April, 1971   Salyut, U.S.S.R.
—First space station tested

July, 1969   Apollo 11, Neil Armstrong, Edwin Aldrin, Michael Collins, U.S.A.
—First mission to successfully place people on the moon

December, 1968   Apollo 8, Frank Borman, James Lovell, William Anders, U.S.A.
—First people to orbit the moon

May, 1966   Surveyor 1, U.S.A.
—First controlled soft landing on the moon

August, 1962   Mariner 2, U.S.A.
—First successful interplanetary probe

February, 1962   John Glenn, U.S.A.
—First American to orbit Earth

August, 1961   Gherman Titov, U.S.S.R.
—First person to orbit Earth

May, 1961   Alan Shepard, U.S.A.
—First American in space

April, 1961   Yuri Gargarin, U.S.S.R.
—First person in space

August, 1960   Echo 1, U.S.A.
—First communications satellite

October, 1957   Sputnik I, U.S.S.R.
—World's first artificial satellite

Fig. 28-23. A weather satellite orbiting the earth.

Space Shuttle

A **space shuttle** is a plane which carries freight and passengers into space and returns to Earth. The space shuttle program began with the first successful flight of *Columbia* on April 12-14, 1981. See Fig. 28-24. This was followed by *twenty-three* successful flights. Then came the ill-fated flight of the *Challenger* on January 28, 1986.

Since the loss of the *Challenger* and the ships crew, the remaining shuttles have been checked out and redesigned with the hope of preventing future accidents. Space shuttles are again flying, but there exists added caution and great respect for the risks of space exploration.

One of our national goals is to develop a replacement for the space shuttle. A desired characteristic of a new shuttle is that it be able to take off like an airplane, accelerate into orbit around the Earth, and return for a runway landing. The "Technology Focus," p. 166, discusses the project presently underway by NASA. This project is now in its second phase—the development of concept and design characteristics.

Fig. 28-24. A space shuttle in flight. The shuttle shown has a telescope mounted for a series of special space experiments.

Fig. 28-25. Space Station Freedom—our first permanent manned venture in space.

Space Station

Our nation's next major venture in space will be the construction of a permanent **space station.** This facility is called Space Station Freedom. Assembly in orbit is planned to begin in 1994. Figure 28-25 shows an artist's drawing of the station in space.

The station will allow permanent presence of humans in space. The station will operate in orbit 220 miles above the surface of the earth. It should provide services for 20 to 30 years. Men and women will work in the station which is designed to operate 24 hours a day, 365 days a year.

Phase I will include the building of the basic station consisting of two polar-orbiting platforms and four pressurized modules. One module provides living quarters for the crew and research personnel. The other three laboratories are for research and development. Initial research will concentrate on material science and life science. Examples include growth of large protein crystals, metallurgy, and the understanding of fluid behavior. Life science research includes space physiology, gravitational biology, and controlled ecological life support systems.

The station will be designed to allow for expansion. More modules may be added in the future. Future phases will add support services for other spacecraft. Also it may be used as a base for sending humans on missions to the moon and to Mars. It could become a base support for transportation in the solar system.

The initial station will be a boom 508 feet (155 m) long, with four solar-cell "wings" on each end. The solar cells will supply 75,000 watts of electrical power. The station will be occupied by representatives of several nations, all contributing to this initial effort. The United States will supply the module containing living quarters plus one research module. Japan will supply a second research module, and the European Space Agency will supply the third. Canada will supply a mobile servicing center which will help assemble *Freedom* during construction.

This effort should be the first of many joint and cooperative space ventures. Hopefully, all peoples of the Earth will join in the exploration of our remaining frontier—space.

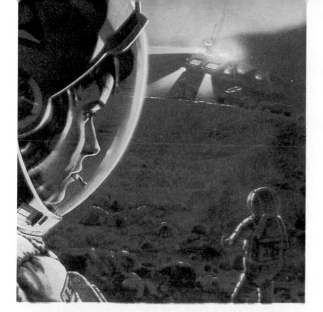

Fig. 28-26. Mars—Our next frontier.

The Space Exploration Initiative

"Why the moon? Why Mars?
Because it is humanity's destiny to strive, to see, to find. And because it is America's destiny to lead."

—The President of the
United States

The President was referring to an ambitious program, one which may bring humans to Mars by 2019. See Fig. 28-26. The exploration initiative is in the planning and development stage, and is a logical next step to the orbiting space station.

The principal reason for establishing the initial base on the moon is that it is the body closest to earth. On the moon, we can learn about living and working on another surface.

The next effort will be to launch robotic and human missions to Mars. Efforts will be made to search for signs of life, both past and present.

A long-range plan is to establish a permanent research base on Mars as a first step toward eventual colonization. The overall focus is to *be on* Mars, not just *go to* Mars.

Beginning with the first mission, Martian resources will be used to the fullest extent. A goal will be to maintain a presence on Mars.

Many of our nation's scientists believe Mars should be the focus of our efforts to establish a self-sustaining community, independent of Earth. The Boulder Center for Science and Policy conducted a conference on "The Case for Mars." The following reasons were developed which encourage a space station on Mars.[1]

[1]*The Case for Mars: Concept Development for a Mars Research Station,* Boulder Center for Science and Policy, April

■ Mars is the best possibility for settlement.

Of all the planets, Mars is the most hospitable and comparable to Earth. It is the only planet where a permanent settlement can be established with foreseeable technology.

■ Mars is abundantly endowed with all the resources necessary to sustain life.

Compared to the moon, Mars is a veritable "Garden of Eden." Using Mars resources will allow the settlement to become independent of Earth, virtually a requirement due to the long transit times and expense of transporting consumables.

■ Mars offers the potential for rapid achievement of self-sufficiency.

The Mars atmosphere is an accessible source of materials that allows a relatively low-technology approach to manufacturing. Water, breathable air, and rocket propellants can be obtained reliably from the Mars atmosphere beginning with the first mission carrying a crew.

■ A Mars base will have a high scientific payoff.

All aspects of Mars science will be well served by a Mars base program. In the near future, automated scientific missions will provide information required for a human landing crew to safely reach the surface.

■ A Mars program encompasses a wide spectrum of activities.

Activities range from short-term individual missions which are presently under development (for example, the Mars Observer Mission, MOM) through the establishment of the Mars base and the achievement of self-sufficiency of the base.

■ A Mars program will require contributions of knowledge, expertise, and effort from all branches of NASA, from universities, and from the private sector.

Science and its many applications and all types of support personnel have roles to play in a Mars program.

■ Mars has the potential for long-term economic payoff.

Mars and its satellites are likely to be a major source of commercial resources for transportation systems in the future. Mars may become the getaway to the outer solar system. It will become economically and strategically important when human interests extend to the outer solar system.

A Mars settlement may become a reality, or it may remain a dream and long-term goal. It is however, an excellent focus and one which will lead us to continue the exploration of today's frontier—space.

10, 1986. **Note:** Some of the materials have been edited for readability and presentation.

Chapter 28—Review

Testing Your Knowledge

Briefly answer each of the following questions. Write on a separate piece of paper.

1. What was the increase in miles driven in the United States since 1960?
2. During the same period (Item 1), what happened to fuel economy (miles per gallon)?
3. Using present technology, to what level could we increase miles per gallon by the year 2000?
4. What effect does the use of an automobile air conditioner have on fuel economy?
5. What effect does the use of radial tires have on fuel economy?
6. Name three alternative fuels presently in limited use, but capable of reducing our dependency on oil and gasoline.
7. Identify three ways electricity can be used to power cars in the future.
8. At present, what is the most promising fuel to replace gasoline as a transportable fuel?
9. Identify the potential advantage of two-stroke engines over four-stroke engines for automobile use.
10. About how fast will a maglev train be able to travel?
11. How fast can a propfan plane fly?
12. When did the first person set foot on the moon? What was the person's name?
13. When did the first space shuttle fly?

Expressing Your Knoweldge

Using complete sentences, write your answers to the following on a separate piece of paper.

1. Identify the two steps which must be taken to assure an adequate supply of transportation fuel in the future.
2. Describe how transportation is harmful to the environment.
3. Why is the future for fuel conservation in transportation less promising than it has been in the past decade?
4. Give two reasons why national efforts are being made to reduce travel and fuel consumption.
5. Explain why the use of ethanol will not replace the use of gasoline.
6. How will using hydrogen help eliminate pollution?
7. Briefly describe the operation of a maglev train.
8. What is a "canard designed" airplane?
9. Identify the contributions planned by different nations for the space station *Freedom*.
10. Identify seven reasons why Mars might become a location for a permanent self-sustaining base.

Applying Your Knowledge

Follow your teacher's instructions to complete these activities:

1. Conduct a class activity by writing a letter to the National Aeronautics and Space Administration (NASA), Washington, D.C. 20546. The letter should request information agreed upon by class discussion.

   NASA will provide information on projects under consideration, being developed, or already in operation. NASA also has lists of audiovisual materials available for school use, and often develops projects which can be used in school. NASA officials recognize the interest young people have in space exploration, and assists schools in providing current and accurate information.

   In your letter, be specific regarding areas of interest. You may wish information on the space station *Freedom* or research on manufacturing in space. Consider the different options and then, with the teacher's approval, write for information.

   Upon receipt of materials from NASA, prepare a report and present the report to the entire class.

2. Use your school and local library to identify new trends in automotive R & D. Libraries contain many magazines which present new and planned developments. Review these magazines and prepare a written report on future changes in automotive research and development. Be prepared to enter into a class discussion on your findings.

3. Repeat Activity 2 for the other areas of transportation: rail, air, and water. Also, you may wish to study existing R & D in the trucking industry and in the space program.

4. Conduct a survey of local public and private transportation groups to identify their current use of alternative fuels and/or their plans for the future. Conduct the survey with an understanding of the potential use of methanol, gasohol, ethanol, compressed natural gas, and hydrogen. Agencies to contact should include public transportation systems and local energy conservation offices or agencies. You may also wish to contact some rail, air, and trucking companies to determine whether they are considering alternative transportation fuels.

Chapter 29

Effects of Energy Use on Society

Energy controlled as power contributes to both the world's accomplishments and to its shortcomings. People must understand energy and use it wisely as they work towards making this a better world.

Expanding Your Knowledge

As you study this chapter you will learn to:

- Describe the ways controlled energy has contributed to the progress our world has enjoyed.
- Understand how the use of energy has permitted world population to grow.
- Explain the problems that energy use has caused, and how energy use has contributed to these problems.
- Describe how people can use their ability to control energy as we seek solutions to problems and improve our quality of life.

Building Your Word Power

The following terms are defined and explained in this chapter. Learning these will help you learn more about the effects of energy use on society.

energy conflicts
mechanization
quality of life
standard of living

Energy controlled as power has given people freedom to live in cities, to visit the far corners of the world, and to enjoy a comfortable way of life. Our understanding of electricity has permitted the development of computers, microprocessors, and robots. It has helped us land people on the moon, and will help us reach Mars and the universe beyond.

Unfortunately, use of controlled energy has come at a price. Our air, water, and land are becoming more and more polluted. The world population continues to grow and cities have become more crowded. Many people have jobs they find uninteresting, and many work in dangerous environments. Use of controlled energy is certainly *not the cause* of these and other problems of society. However, it is a major contributor.

When seeking ways to correct these problems, use of controlled energy becomes an important factor. Considerations such as pollution-free sources of energy, cost of fuel, and a sufficient supply of energy for all have become important. Energy is a significant factor in nearly all future world progress as well as in future problems the world faces.

people to live and work in cities and suburban communities. It also provides many labor-saving and recreational devices. However, the use of controlled energy is not "all for the good." Some uses also have some negative effects. Both positive and negative factors are presented here.

Where People Live

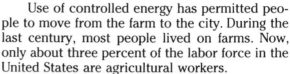

Use of controlled energy has permitted people to move from the farm to the city. During the last century, most people lived on farms. Now, only about three percent of the labor force in the United States are agricultural workers.

The move to cities occurred due to the development and use of mechanized farm equipment. See Fig 29-1. **Mechanization,** using mechanical power, permitted each farmer to produce more food by farming more land and farming it more intensely. Mechanization also led to specialization. Today's farms are businesses, usually producing just one or a limited number of crops.

While this condition exists in the United States and other developed countries, it does not exist in all countries. Countries such as China and Thailand still have the majority of their citizens living on small farms. See Fig. 29-2. However, many of these countries also are beginning to mechanize agriculture. In the future, we will continue to see fewer people growing the food used throughout the world.

BENEFITS FOR SOCIETY FROM CONTROLLED ENERGY

The *quality of life* is affected by the use of controlled energy. **Quality of life** is the sum of all elements and attributes which contribute to and detract from one's standard of living. These factors vary from person to person. Some people value a quiet life and the benefits of nature. Others value social relations and excitement. What might be a very good quality of life for some people may be a poor quality of life for others. As a result, quality of life is a personal value, one which has different elements for different people.

Use of controlled energy as power has made many positive contributions to the quality of life of many people. Controlled energy is used to provide convenient transportation, permitting

Fig. 29-1. Modern farm equipment has mechanized farming, permitting each farmer to till more land.

Fig. 29-2. Many countries still have many individual farmers working small plots of land.

Fig. 29-3A. The high cost of land in many cities makes apartments a popular housing choice.

Fig. 29-3B. Many Americans live in suburban neighborhoods in comfort.

In the United States and other developed countries, the majority of people live in or near cities. They may live right in the city, in suburbs, or in the country. They commute to work by public transportation or by private car. The combination of a selected career, living in the location desired, and having transportation and laborsaving devices available contributes to a good quality of life. See Fig. 29-3.

Unfortunately, not everyone has been able to profit from the mechanization of agriculture. Some people remain on small farms with poor soil. Their income is very low. Others with inadequate education or skills needed for employment have moved to the cities only to face unemployment or work at jobs with very low salaries. For many people, living conditions remain poor and the quality of life low.

Where people live continues to change. In the past, the large city or suburbs was considered desirable by most people. Today, there is a growing interest in returning to country living or living in smaller cities. Changes in job requirements coupled with a growing retired population is giving people more choices as to where they will live.

Transportation

Another major application of controlled energy is the vast array of transportation systems available for use. Varied transportation systems affect many aspects of society.

Transportation of Goods. Farm products, manufactured goods, and raw materials are transported by trains, trucks, ships, and airplanes.

During the past few years, improvements in air and sea transportation have permitted the development of a *world* economy. Some countries provide raw materials such as oil or metal ores. Others provide manufactured goods such as automobiles or computers. Still others supply food. The result is a growing world economy, with goods transported between nations. See Fig. 29-4.

Transportation to Work. Rapid transit systems and the freedom to drive highway vehicles to work permits people to work long distances from their homes. During past decades, travel to work has increased as people have sought better home locations. Low-cost energy and mass transportation by train, subway, or other modes have made these greater distances possible. See Fig. 29-5.

Commuting distances for many have grown due to housing costs. In many areas of the country, housing costs have risen around cities forcing workers to travel greater distances for affordable housing. Some workers travel two to four or more hours per day coming and going from work. This amount of travel each day reduces leisure and family time, and erodes the quality of life.

As this trend grows, serious problems are beginning to develop. The amount of driving done in cities is increasing at twice the national rate of traffic increase. Air pollution from transportation vehicles is increasing, and streets and highways are becoming more congested. As these problems are added to the growing problems of fuel consumption and the cost of this fuel, concern for the economic health of our country continues to grow. Solutions are not easy. Serious attention must be given to this growing problem, and soon.

Transportation for Leisure. Transportation for leisure activities continues to increase. It is possible to classify leisure transportation in two ways:

■ Transportation for pleasurable uses.
■ Transportation for traveling to desirable locations.

In the first group are a great variety of what might be described as "fun vehicles." These can provide both healthy exercise and/or enjoyment.

Fig. 29-4. Goods are shipped freely between countries.

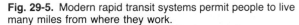

Fig. 29-5. Modern rapid transit systems permit people to live many miles from where they work.

Fig. 29-6. Many cycling enthusiasts wanted a bicycle that would combine some features of the English racer with the sturdiness of the traditional bicycle of the 1950s. The cross-country bicycle was the result.

These vehicles contribute to enjoyment and to one's quality of life. Examples are numerous and include the following:

- Bicycles—both for city and country roads and for cross-country trails and off-road use. See Fig. 29-6.
- Snowmobiles—for cross-country travel over snow. These can be used for both transportation and recreation.
- Sailboats and a variety of wind- and engine-powered vehicles for water sports. They can provide exercise and enjoyment on the water.

The second group of transportation vehicles carries people, in a pleasant setting, to distant locations. Cruise ships are once again growing in popularity and provide pleasant leisure travel with stops in interesting and educational locations. See Fig. 29-7.

People also use automobiles, buses, trains, and airplanes to travel to vacation locations throughout the country and the world. Transportation devices now permit people to travel to all parts of the world.

Changing Work Locations

The combination of developing technology and efficient transportation is changing our work locations. The development of computers and the growing use of computers and microprocessors is permitting some people to blend working

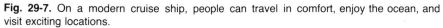

Fig. 29-7. On a modern cruise ship, people can travel in comfort, enjoy the ocean, and visit exciting locations.

at home and working at a central location. Some people are able to work at home, connecting their home computer to their business by telephone.

Efficient transportation of goods permits work to be performed anywhere people wish. The finished products can be transported to where they are needed. Entire countries or regions can specialize in a single product, shipping it to wherever it is needed. Automobiles built in the United States are sold worldwide, just as automobiles built in Europe and Japan are sold in all parts of the world including the United States.

Agriculture has also made use of transportation. Fruits and vegetables grown in the United States during the summer can be shipped to South America and Australia. When we have summer, they have winter. In our winter, we receive fruits and vegetables from South America and Australia.

Convenience Devices

The availability of economical and reliable power is permitting a gradual and steady change in devices which add to comfort and the quality of life. Numerous changes are gradually entering our lives, both at home and at work.

We have *not* reached the point at which robots will serve us as "human substitutes." However, most of the technology is available to build such robots.

Rather than an immediate change to robots, we are seeing a steady increase in the types and uses of automated devices. These can sense an increasing variety of conditions. We can now accurately sense and measure time, light, motion, heat, and odor. Although some of these conditions have become very subtle, we are still able to use these *senses* to control devices. Some examples include:

- A device can sense when someone enters a room (motion) and turn on the lights. The same device can also save energy by turning lights off when the room is empty. The same device can adjust thermostats up or down, thereby conserving energy.
- On a smaller level, a key chain can now be equipped with a beeper and sound sensor. When the owner loses keys and then claps his or her hands, the beeper sounds indicating the location of the lost keys.
- Devices can recognize sunlight and close blinds in the summer to keep heat out. The same device can open the blinds in winter to allow heat from the sun to enter.

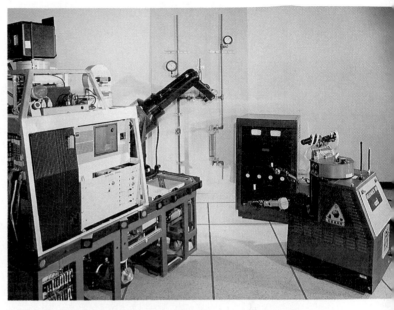

Fig. 29-8. These two robots are designed to cooperate in the performance of a task assignment.

These devices are steps towards automation. Many home appliances have microprocessors which can be programmed or which provide automated control. Ovens can be programmed to cook at different temperatures in order to complete the cooking process as people arrive home.

The combination of sensing devices and automated control permits the development of complex control systems. The only limitation is need and imagination. We can expect automatic convenience devices to gradually become more complex. It is expected that these devices will, in time, become more robotic in form and in service to humans. See Fig. 29-8.

Exploration of New Frontiers

Progress in transportation and the control of energy will permit businesses to explore new frontiers. The last chapter identified national goals of a permanent space station with live-in crews, as well as future settlements on the moon and on Mars. The future beyond those plans is almost limitless.

Another frontier, the depths of the ocean, has yet to be explored. Scientists are beginning to learn of life at great depths. However, the ocean is largely an unexplored frontier.

How Low Can We Go

Vast unexplored areas on Earth? In this time of high technology, of supersonic flight and instant communication, it's hard to believe. However, such areas do exist—far beneath the surface of the sea.

About 40% of the total volume of all oceans lies below 12,000 feet. Most deep-diving submersible vehicles in use today do not go much deeper than 20,000 feet. This leaves a total area about the size of the United States completely unexplored. Also these submersibles are slow and depend on surface ships for sustenance, which greatly limits the scope of their travels.

One company at work today may revolutionize undersea exploration. Headed by a husband and wife team, *Graham Hawkes* and *Sylvia Earle*, Deep Ocean Engineering, Inc. is designing what is described as the first underwater "aircraft." The vehicle, called *Deep Flight*, has wings and other features similar to those of airplanes, but is designed to operate underwater.

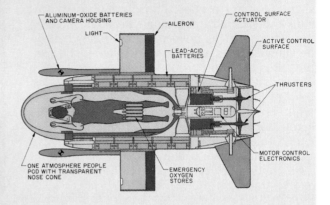

Utilizing the latest technological advances, the vehicle will be light (1½ tons), buoyant, strong, comparatively fast, and easy to manipulate underwater. It consists basically of a "people pod" within an exoskeleton.

The pod is a pressure-resistant chamber in which the pilot rides and operates the "flight controls" and other equipment such as cameras and research devices. If the exoskeleton should become ensnared underwater, the pod, which is also buoyant alone, can be released, and the pod and pilot will float to the surface. The exoskeleton protects the pod and holds the power and control equipment and research devices.

Deep Flight is powered by aluminum-oxide batteries similar to those used in buoy beacons but more powerful. These batteries cannot be recharged. They are simply aluminum plates that react chemically with sea water to create an electric current. Lead-acid gel batteries are included as backups but can also be used to supplement the aluminum batteries.

The batteries power twin thrusters at the rear of the craft. Speeds up to 15 knots* (approx. 17 mph) can be achieved, but cruise speed will be about 12 knots.

Perhaps the most exciting and revolutionary system in the craft is the ingenious control system. Wings near the center of the craft are actually upside-down airfoils which create a *downward* "lift." The control areas at the rear are designed to work like the tail of a dolphin to make the craft dive and ascend. Combinations of these controls allow the craft to perform "hydrobatics," pitching and rolling as do many animals of the sea.

How low can we go? Soon we may be "flying" to the greatest ocean depths, viewing exotic scenes and perhaps discovering animals with whom we share this Earth but could not imagine in our wildest dreams.

---

*A *knot* is one nautical mile per hour. One *nautical mile* is equal to 6076 feet (1852 m), and one *mile* is equal to 5280 feet (1584 m). Approximately how many mph is 12 knots? (Answer is given at the end of the chapter.)

POPULATION

The control of energy has been a major factor in permitting the world's population to grow. Not only has controlled energy in transportation allowed wide distribution of food, but it has also permitted the growing of more food per acre of land. Irrigation, made possible by pumped water or water from reservoirs, has turned deserts into farms. See Fig. 29-9.

In 1970, the world population was 3.6 billion (3,600,000,000) human beings. In 1990, the population was 5.3 billion. The projection for the year 2000 is 6.1 billion human beings. It is obvious that the world can support only a limited number of people. Some scientists believe that the population is already too large for the earth. They point to the physical problems of global warming, acid rain, and the growing problem with periodic holes in the ozone layer. Social problems include increasing crime rates, home-lessness, and viral epidemics. Millions (possibly billions) of people may live their lives in poverty with little hope of ever enjoying a reasonably good quality of life.

Other scientists believe the problems are not due to the increasing population. Instead they indicate that we have societies that encourage waste and pollution. We have governments which blunder into wars, and we have political systems which fail to address the needs of the people.

Perhaps there are no final answers. To make progress towards solutions to the problems, society must recognize the role of controlled energy in sustaining the population of the world. Controlled energy will continue to help provide for the growth in population. However, the present system can fail, and limits do exist. Society needs to plan and develop a world which helps all people attain a reasonably good quality of life. In that world, proper use of various forms of controlled energy can contribute in a positive way.

Fig. 29-9. Controlled energy was used when building the Aswan Dam on the Nile River in Egypt and now is used to control the flow of water to provide irrigation.

A. This part of the Aswan Dam has a power plant. Electric generators, driven by floodwater, are used to produce electrical power. The capacity is 2,100 megawatts.

B. The Aswan Dam is 364 feet (111 meters) high. It holds back an enormous volume of water. Some of the water is released as needed to irrigate farmland. Use of the water in this way has permitted year-round irrigation of farmland that was formerly irrigated only at the time of the annual Nile flood.

EMERGING PROBLEMS

Some of the problems resulting from energy use have already been described. These include poverty as people moved off of farms and into the cities, population growth, and increasingly longer commutes as cities have grown. There are other problems that need to be considered by our world leaders.

Pollution

Chapter 9 presented the problems of pollution from the use of controlled energy. As the world's population grows, and as nations consume more energy, problems such as global pollution will grow.

Oceans, seas, rivers, and lakes are being polluted by waste products from manufacturing and cities. As with air pollution, the amount of waste continues to increase, producing both land and water pollution. See Fig. 29-10.

The problems of pollution can be controlled. **Recycling**, recovering and reusing materials, can bring much of our waste under control. Biological products such as food and plant waste can be processed into fertilizer and used to restore soil. Plastics, paper products, and metals can be saved and recycled. Recycling will not only bring pollution of land and oceans under control, it will help preserve limited resources. However, we need to increase and expand recycling practices. Recycling must be promoted as a means of saving resources and preserving our environment. See Fig. 29-11.

Fig. 29-10. Manufacturing industries are heavy users of energy. Unless waste products from energy use are properly managed, the environment is damaged.

Energy Conflicts

Fossil fuels are now so important that the very existence of nations and social orders depends on a continuous supply of fuel. When supplies are threatened, nations react quickly and strongly. The oil embargos of the 1970s, and the invasion of Kuwait by Iraq in 1990 affected most nations. **Energy conflicts** are likely to increase and become more *severe* whenever the world supplies of fuel are threatened. See Fig. 29-12.

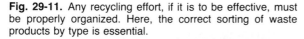

Fig. 29-11. Any recycling effort, if it is to be effective, must be properly organized. Here, the correct sorting of waste products by type is essential.

Fig. 29-12. Industrialized western nations are heavily dependent on foreign oil. Such dependence can lead to economic uncertainty. It also offers the potential for conflict.

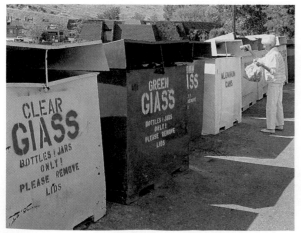

This condition does not need to continue. Efforts need to be expanded to utilize inexhaustible supplies of fuel. Solar energy, the use of hydrogen as a transportable fuel, fusion, and other alternatives need to be developed at a rapid rate.

Helping nations gain energy independence through an inexhaustible supply of energy may be a better way to build a peaceful world than armed defense. However, efforts must be increased far beyond the very limited efforts in the past decade. In terms of energy research and development, the 1980s may have been the "dark ages" of energy resource development compared to existing and future needs.

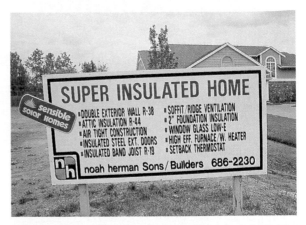

Fig. 29-13. More effective housing design can make homes more energy efficient. This sign details many of the features that make this house attractive to an energy-conscious consumer.

USING ENERGY TO IMPROVE THE WORLD OF THE FUTURE

The future of our world can be disasterous or it can be bright with each person having the opportunity for an enjoyable life on this Earth. The choice between possible disaster or opportunity rests with the people of the Earth.

World problems must be considered with intelligence. Plans must be made to consider and work towards solving each of the problems. Providing an adequate supply of controlled energy to each nation of the world is a critical step towards world peace. This can best be accomplished by developing major alternative sources and achieving independence from the fossil fuels. See Fig. 29-13.

An adequate supply of energy is not, of course, a solution to *all* the world's problems. However, energy plans a critical role. Solutions to present energy problems can be found, but it will take the best efforts of coming generations to find them. See Fig. 29-14.

Fig. 29-14. This house is being destroyed because it is in an area that has been polluted by industrial waste. Because this waste was not properly treated, it contaminated the soil.

Chapter 29—Review

Testing Your Knowledge

Briefly answer each of the following questions. Write on a separate piece of paper.

1. Agricultural workers make up what percentage of the labor force in the United States?
2. Today most people live in cities. What is an emerging future trend?
3. Improvements in which two forms of transportation have contributed most to the development of a world economy?
4. Name the two classifications of leisure transportation.
5. What are two sources of some of our fruits and vegetables during the winter?
6. What was the world population in 1990?
7. What is the projected world population for the year 2000?

Expressing Your Knowledge

Using complete sentences, write your answers to the following on a separate piece of paper:

1. What is meant by the phrase "quality of life"?
2. Explain why more and more people were able to move from the farm to the city.
3. Why have commute distances generally increased for city workers in some regions of the country?
4. Describe two examples of sensing devices in use today.
5. Why do some scientists believe world population is already too large?
6. Describe two emerging problems which are related to controlled energy.

Applying Your Knowledge

Follow your teacher's instructions to complete these activities:

1. Use your school library to seek some additional information on "quality of life." Based on these readings and a self-appraisal of your likes and dislikes, describe the elements and attributes which will give you the quality of life you desire. Also, identify major characteristics which would detract from that quality of life.

   Present your findings in the form of a written report. Be prepared to enter into a class discussion on the quality of life and how it is influenced by controlled energy.

2. The teacher will divide your class into two groups. One group is to be in favor of defending world population growth and the other is to be in favor of encouraging a stable or reduced world population. Identify a debate team for each group. The entire group should then research their position in the library and provide information to their debate team.

   Hold a class debate between the two teams.

3. Prepare a report on how controlled energy can be used to make the world a better place in which to live. Identify possible conditions which could prevent a better world for all.

Answer to problem p. 424: 12 knots is approximately 14 mph.

Choosing and Preparing for a Career

SECTION

Chapter 30

Career Exploration

There are hundreds of careers in the areas of energy sources, transportation, power transmission and control, and the use of power. These careers cover a wide range of interests and abilities. One of them may be right for you.

Expanding Your Knowledge

Learning about power and energy technology will help you understand more about the world around you. As you study this chapter, you will learn to:

■ Explain why knowledge about yourself should be matched with knowledge about careers during the process of selecting a career.
■ Understand how an individual's abilities, interests, and values relate to career choice and future career success.
■ Identify a variety of places where information about careers can be obtained.
■ Describe various career positions possible in such energy and power areas as the generation of electricity, energy exploration and research, transportation, conservation and the environment, automated control systems, and business.
■ Describe the five common career types, or job classifications, used in energy and power: production worker, mechanic, technician, technologist, and engineer.

Building Your Word Power

Knowledge of the vocabulary used will help you develop greater understanding of power and energy. The following terms are defined and explained in this chapter. Learning these will help you learn more about careers in the fields of power and energy.

career	technician
engineer	technologist
mechanic	values
production worker	

Your choice of a **career** (lifework) will be one of the most important decisions you will ever make. As an adult, you can expect to spend one-quarter or more of your time at work.

Your career also affects your personal life. Many friendships are made at work. Also the amount of money you earn will help determine your leisure-time activities. Make your career choice carefully!

Later in this chapter, you'll learn about various career possibilities. However, you should first learn about the work involved in *choosing* a career. To find the lifework that is right for you, you will want to spend some time and effort.

CHOOSING A CAREER

At some stage in life, everyone must make a career decision. A few people decide on a career very early. They work toward it without changing. But these people are the exceptions. Most people investigate many different careers before choosing one. Even then, they may enter a career, work in it for a while, and then decide to change careers.

It's true that you can't really know *all* the details about a career until you are involved in that career. However, planning ahead will help you avoid choosing or "drifting into" a career that you won't enjoy.

Choosing a career is one of the most important decisions you'll ever make. This chapter offers some general pointers on how to go about it. See Fig. 30-1.

Fig. 30-1. Choosing a fulfilling career requires careful career planning. Many different types of careers are available in the field of power and energy.

B. Research.

A. Production.

C. Technical.

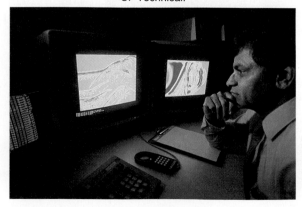

Knowing Yourself

You have interests, skills, and values that are unique (special). Your personal characteristics are the best guides you have in choosing the right career.

Knowing what you like and dislike is a matter of experience. To avoid choosing an unsatisfactory career, you must first *know yourself*. Take a good look at your abilities, interests, and values. This "soul-searching" can tell you a lot about the type of career you would be most happy and productive in.

Your Abilities. Think about your abilities in school, sports, and recreational activities. Also consider your abilities at doing household chores or handling the responsibilities of a part-time job. Think about the things you do well and the things you do poorly. (No one can do everything well.) See Fig. 30-2.

Compare your abilities with those of other students your age. As you make these comparisons, recognize that you can strengthen your abilities. You can improve your skills—if you are interested. *Don't* underrate yourself. *Do* develop an understanding of your own strengths and weaknesses.

Your Interests. Make a list of the things you like to do and the things you don't like to do. Try to relate these likes and dislikes to possible careers.

You may enjoy being outdoors and working by yourself. Or you may enjoy working as part of a group on school assignments. You may be interested in how things work. Or you may like to read and write stories.

Your interests are a major factor in choosing a career. For example, if you are interested in working by yourself, you may eventually eliminate careers that involve working with people, such as teaching. You may find being a mechanic, an engineer, or a technician more satisfying.

Interests, like abilities, can be developed. There are always activities you haven't tried. Keep an open mind as you list your likes and dislikes. As your abilities in an area improve, your interest in the area may also grow. Abilities and interests are often closely related.

Your Values. Values are the things that you feel are important in life. Values include family, religion, freedom, and many other things. Career values may include security, good working conditions, money, prestige, respect, the ability to set your own standards, the chance to help and serve others, or the opportunity to protect the environment. See Fig. 30-3.

Your values are an important guide in choosing a career. You should be aware that values can conflict. For example, you may be interested in protecting the environment and in making money. However, you may find that you can make money more easily in business than in environmental protection. As you consider different careers, think carefully about the things that are most important in your life.

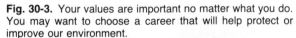
Fig. 30-3. Your values are important no matter what you do. You may want to choose a career that will help protect or improve our environment.

Fig. 30-2. A key factor in selecting the right career is recognizing your abilities. Try various types of work activities to help identify your aptitudes.

Finding Out About Careers

To make a wise career choice, you will want to compare your personal characteristics and needs with the requirements of the career. How do you find information about careers you're interested in? There are many answers to this question.

Start at School. School provides a great opportunity to explore various career areas. By taking different courses, you will have many experiences related to many different careers. For example, think about the things you learned while reading this book. Did you enjoy learning about electrical systems? If you did, you may enjoy a career in the electronics field.

School may also help you learn which career areas you *don't* like. You can learn even from bad experiences. These experiences will help you focus your attention on the things you enjoy most or do best. However, don't ignore the basics, such as reading, writing, math, science, and social studies. Knowledge in these areas is important no matter what career you go into.

Learn at Work. Summer and part-time jobs are excellent sources of career information. Each job you have will expose you in some way to a new career area. Of course, you'll be on the bottom, looking up. But you'll still get a firsthand look at the requirements for a career. Many part-time jobs also lead to full-time employment after graduation. See Fig. 30-4.

Do Research. Many careers are hard or impossible to experience through school or part-time work. Engineering and management are two examples. Research is a good way to learn about these careers. You can learn a great deal by sending for employment information, government publications, and career manuals. Your school resource center and the public library probably have reference areas for career information. Your school counselors are also good sources of career information. Using these different resources is a fast way to learn about many different careers.

Go on Field Trips. Your school may have a science club, a technology club, or a Junior Engineering Technical Society. Often these groups take field trips to local industries. You can learn a lot about careers by taking field trips. You can actually see where people work and what they do.

Talk with Workers. Most people are more than willing to talk about their careers to interested students. They will be especially helpful if you have questions to ask. Write your questions down beforehand so that you'll be prepared. You'll usually find that the more interested you are, the more information and help you'll receive. See Fig. 30-5.

CAREERS IN POWER AND ENERGY

Career opportunities in power and energy are many and varied. And as new technology is

Fig. 30-4. A part-time job is a good way to learn about a career. You can see first hand the responsibilities involved.

Fig. 30-5. Ask questions. You can learn a great deal from workers in the field.

developed, new opportunities become available. The future promises to be exciting. Perhaps there's a place for *you*!

The following divisions will give you an idea of some of the career possibilities. The careers mentioned are only a few of the hundreds possible.

Generation of Electricity

Electrical power is extremely important in our modern world. Thousands of plants across the country supply us with electricity. These plants need people in many different careers to operate them. *Engineers* plan and design more efficient power plants. They also direct the operation of existing plants. *Plant supervisors* oversee and direct plant operations and maintenance. *Technicians* and *tradespeople* construct, maintain, and repair electrical plants. They also work on the transmission lines that distribute power to homes and industry. See Fig. 30-6.

Fig. 30-6. Many careers are available in the area of power distribution.

Technology Focus

The Wizard of Research

Creativity and originality are two of the most important abilities a researcher can possess. *Thomas Edison* had these and more.

We all know that Edison invented the electric light bulb. But, did you know that he also invented the first electric-power station to provide electricity for his light bulb? The phonograph was his invention as well, and he improved motion pictures, telephone transmitters, typewriters, electric generators, and numerous other technical devices. Edison patented more than 1100 inventions in 60 years, most in the use of *electrical energy*. He became known as the "Wizard of Menlo Park" (New Jersey).

How did he do it? Thomas Edison is usually called a genius. But he defined "genius" as "1% inspiration and 99% perspiration." He worked days at a time, stopping only for short naps.

Failure never discouraged Edison. While trying to develop a storage battery, about 10,000 experiments failed. When friends tried to comfort him, Edison replied, "Why, I have not failed; I've just found 10,000 ways that won't work."

There are lessons in Thomas Edison's life for all of us. Hard work, persistence, and willingness to explore the unknown are proven paths to success in research and in life.

Fig. 30-7. People are needed to identify energy sources. This worker is checking the extraction of methane gas from a landfill.

Energy Exploration and Research

At the present time, energy exploration is a very active career field. Oil companies employ many people in this area. These people search much of the world for sources of oil, natural gas, and other fossil fuels. There are career opportunities in energy exploration for *geologists, chemists, surveyors, cartographers* (map-makers), and *engineers.*

Great efforts are being made to ease our dependency on fossil fuels. As a result, there are many new careers in the research and development of alternative energy sources. See Fig. 30-7.

Transportation

Our nationwide transportation system requires many people to put it into operation and to keep it going. Transportation workers are all trained to do specific jobs. Major types of careers in transportation include *managers, vehicle operators, vehicle maintenance personnel*, and *passenger service personnel*. What other examples can you name? See Fig. 30-8.

Conservation and the Environment

In the past 10 years, conservation and environmental control have become more important. People have recognized the growing shortage of fossil fuels. They have also seen the effects of pollution. There are now more jobs than ever before in conservation and environmental control. Workers in these areas look for ways to conserve energy and keep the air and water free from pollution.

Automated Control Systems

Automation and robotics are two of the fastest-growing career areas in the nation. The combination of instruments, computers, and automated manufacturing is changing how we build and assemble products.

Robotic systems are still quite new. Their future growth will depend on research and development. Many new and exciting careers will emerge. See Fig. 30-9.

Business

There are also many career opportunities for people interested in business. Careers include positions in sales, accounting, public relations, and management.

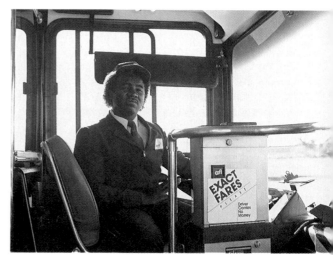

Fig. 30-8. Workers in transportation play an integral part in our daily lives.

Fig. 30-9. More and more workers will be needed to program, operate, and maintain automated systems.

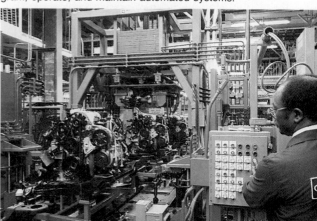

CAREER TYPES

Career types are broad categories of the type of work a person does. Career types also indicate the level and kind of education needed for a certain job. The following types are the most common ones.

Production Worker

Production workers usually operate machines which manufacture products in a factory. Some production jobs can be very repetitive, such as assembly line work. However, some people enjoy this kind of work.

Many production positions don't require prior training. You usually learn your duties on the job.

Mechanic

Mechanics are most commonly employed in vehicle repair areas. A mechanic is a *skilled* worker. He or she may learn the trade both in school and in an apprenticeship or a similar on-the-job training program. Many mechanics take *certification tests* after receiving their basic training. Being certified makes a mechanic more employable.

Technician

Technician is a career type that has much in common with the mechanic career type. Both involve the service and repair of power system equipment. Mechanics usually work on transportation equipment. Technicians work with other types of equipment.

Technologist

A **technologist** has more training than a technician. Techologists can get added training in one of two ways. They may complete a four-year college technology program. Or they may receive additional on-the-job training.

Technologist is a relatively new career type. The two main reasons for the development of this type are:
■ The continued growth of knowledge.
■ The need for engineers to become planners and designers.

Technologists work at a level midway between that of the technician and the engineer. They often serve as division supervisors or leaders of technician groups.

Engineer

Engineers are graduates of four-year colleges. Their education requires a great deal of math and science, plus specialized engineering courses. People interested in engineering should be strong in math. Mathematics is often called the "language of the engineer."

In the areas of power and energy, engineers plan, design, and develop power systems and system parts. An engineer's tasks may vary from planning manufacturing operations to researching and developing new products. As you can see, *engineer* is a very broad career classification. There are many different types of engineers. For example, you could become a mechanical engineer, an electrical engineer, or a production engineer.

YOUR CAREER DECISION

Choosing a career is not a "one-time" activity. It is an ongoing process. As you consider possible careers, try to learn as much as you can about each one. Find out the working conditions, entry requirements, and major duties. Match these with your own abilities, interests, and values. See Fig. 30-10.

Making a career decision is a process of elimination. You eliminate career areas and narrow your choices until only a few careers remain. Don't be impatient. Some people choose a career very early. Others don't choose a career until adulthood. Also, your choice doesn't have to be final. You can always reevaluate it and change it. In the end, choosing a career is an individual decision. Accept suggestions and information from parents and friends. But make the decision yourself.

Fig. 30-10. Career decisions are important. Read and think about the types of careers available. Find that which is right for you.

Chapter 30—Review

Testing Your Knowledge

Briefly answer each of the following questions. Write on a separate piece of paper.

1. What three personal areas can you examine to find out more about yourself to help you choose a career?
2. Name five ways to find information about careers.
3. List six general career areas involving energy and power.
4. List five career types.

Expressing Your Knowledge

Using complete sentences, write your answers to the following on a separate sheet of paper:

1. In what ways can you avoid choosing an unsatisfactory career?
2. Describe the two career types included in this chapter that you think you would find most interesting.

Applying Your Knowledge

Follow your teacher's instructions to complete these activities:

1. Plan a class discussion to identify efforts being made to eliminate discrimination in employment. Your list of research and discussion topics should include:
   - Employment of the handicapped.
   - Males in traditional female positions, and females in traditional male positions.
   - Employment of minorities.
   - Employment of young people; employment of seniors.

2. Prepare a list of questions you would like the school counselor to answer regarding job opportunities, searching for employment, work responsibilities in specific areas, and training for advancement.

   Your teacher may arrange for the counselor to speak to your class. Or you may visit the counselor yourself and obtain answers to your questions.

3. Plan a research activity to identify new jobs that have been created through recent technological advances. Your research should include reviewing library materials, questioning friends and industrial workers, and reviewing newspapers and journals. Prepare a report identifying the occupations, work activities, and entry requirements.

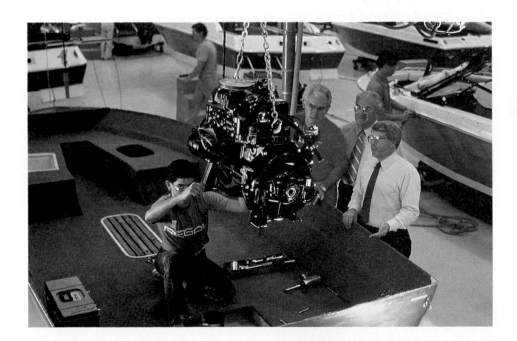

Chapter 31

Developing Special Career Skills

As you consider what career goal to choose, there are career-related skills and knowledge that you can acquire right now.

Expanding Your Knowledge

As you study this chapter, you will learn to:

- Understand the role of an entrepreneur in starting a business.
- Explain the difference between a proprietorship, a partnership, and a corporation.
- Identify the tasks and traits of an effective leader.
- Explain three styles of leadership.
- Find ways to develop personal leadership and participation skills in student associations.

Building Your Word Power

The following words and phrases are defined and explained in this chapter. Learning these will help you learn more about developing special career skills.

autocratic leadership style
corporation
democratic leadership style
entrepreneur
laissez-faire leadership style
leadership
partnership
proprietorship
shares
stock
venture capital

This chapter will introduce you to the basics of how businesses are started and operated. You will learn what characteristics leaders need to succeed in the business world. You will also find out about student organizations. As you participate in these, you can gain practical experience that will be useful in your career.

ENTREPRENEURSHIP

As you have learned, power and energy technology has been developed to serve the needs of people. Whether it is used to manufacture products, provide electricity to people's homes, or transport people or goods quickly and conveniently, this technology is vital to businesses today. You may someday want to develop expertise in this dynamic and challenging field. You could apply your expertise in a large company or at a smaller, more specialized company. You might even want to start your own company. What kind of a company would you like to work for? How do companies begin?

All businesses begin with an **entrepreneur** ("ahn-truh-pruh-noor"). The entrepreneur is the person who has an idea for a new product or service and goes into business to manufacture or provide it. See Fig. 31-1.

What do entrepreneurs have to do? First, they must have an idea for a product or service that they can sell. They have to find a need that isn't being met by businesses that are already in operation. Entrepreneurs must compete with all

Technology Focus

Play Is Child's Work

The concept of "play is child's work" is the secret behind the success of Discovery Toys, a company founded by *Lane Nemeth* in 1977. Nemeth started Discovery Toys when she couldn't find high-quality educational toys for her daughter, *Tara*.

Starting a new company was not easy. Nemeth began by borrowing $25,000 from family members and friends. Early years were a struggle. At one point, Nemeth was about to give up. But, instead, she applied determination, creativity, and intelligent problem-solving in an effort to save the company.

Lane Nemeth's abilities coupled with perseverance and confidence in the company won. Current sales are approaching $100 million per year. And she has an ad-

ministrative staff of 150, plus 12,000 independent salespeople who act as "educational consultants." These consultants give home demonstrations, showing parents how to use the toys for both the education and enjoyment of their children.

Discovery Toys is a company built on the addition of quality, safety, and education to a type of product (toys) which has been used by children for centuries. Opportunities are everywhere for those who are willing to accept the challenge.

Fig. 31-1. William R. Hewlett was a pioneer in the electronics industry. He and his partner, David Packard, first set up shop in a rented garage with little more than $500 capital. With hard work, creative thinking, and strong leadership, they built their company, Hewlett-Packard, into a multimillion-dollar business.

the other businesses to get people to buy their product or service. They go into business to make a *profit*.

Entrepreneurs may have ideas for things that are completely new or for improvements of some product or service that is already for sale. Besides good ideas, entrepreneurs must have money to finance the business venture. They may use their own funds, find people who are willing to invest money, or obtain a loan from a bank or other source.

Money invested so that a company can operate is called *capital*. The term used to refer to investments for starting a company is **venture capital**.

Once entrepreneurs have ideas and capital, they must plan how to produce what they want to sell, get the necessary materials, and see that the work is done. They also must inform consumers that the product or service is available. Then they distribute it so that people can find and buy it. Entrepreneurs have to be creative, skillful, and energetic.

Not all entrepreneurships are successful. Being an entrepreneur involves many risks and much hard work, but the rewards of starting a successful business can be worth the responsibility and effort.

TYPES OF COMPANY OWNERSHIP

There are three types of company ownership: proprietorship, partnership, and corporation.

A business often starts as a **proprietorship**. This kind of business is owned and operated by only one person. Proprietors contribute all the capital and take all the risks of starting a new business. If people don't buy the product or service, the proprietor will lose his or her investment. If the company makes money, however, proprietors receive all the profits.

If more than one person decides to start or operate a business, they can form a **partnership**. Each partner makes an investment in the business. Together, the partners operate the company and make planning and operating decisions. Under a partnership, the risk is divided; one person doesn't have all the responsibility. The profits of the business are also divided.

As a business grows, its owners usually decide to form a **corporation**. They file an application with the state, and after it is approved, they can divide the company's ownership, called **stock**, into **shares**. People who buy these shares of stock are investing in the company. The investors become part-owners.

After a corporation is formed, the shareholders elect a board of directors. This group then hires a manager, usually a president, to actually operate the business.

The profits are divided among many people, but so are the risks. A corporation has the same legal rights as an individual. Also, the business itself—not the individuals who share ownership—is responsible for any debts.

LEADERSHIP

No matter where you work in the business world, being a *leader* is important. **Leadership** involves deciding what direction to take and helping others reach a goal. In any field, people who can lead others and find solutions to problems are needed. What is a good leader like? How can you develop effective leadership skills?

Roles of a Leader

Good leaders need to play many roles. Often leaders of groups must be *initiators* (people who start a project). Leaders decide what the goals of a group should be and motivate the group members to achieve those goals.

Leaders must know about the job to be done so they can make plans and give directions to the group members on how to do it. They also act as guides. When the workers encounter a problem, leaders must have ideas on how to solve it or know where they can get the information the workers need. See Fig. 31-2.

Then, when a project is finished, the leaders evaluate the work and decide what improve-

Fig. 31-2. An important part of being a good leader is communicating with workers in the group.

ments could be made on the group's next project. Leaders are also needed to help maintain progress.

Traits of Good Leaders

What kind of people are needed as leaders? Leaders must be able to take the initiative. That is, they need to be able to start in new directions and begin new projects. They also need enthusiasm, resourcefulness, thoroughness, and good judgment.

Leaders must work well with other members in the group. They should make each member realize that his or her contributions are important. Leaders need to show an interest in others and listen well. They also should be tactful; that is, they should avoid embarrassing or offending others. Leaders need to treat all group members fairly and honestly.

Styles of Leadership

There are three different leadership styles. The first is called **autocratic leadership**. The leader decides what will be done and gives orders to the people in the group. The leader doesn't ask for any opinions or suggestions from the group members.

The next type of leadership is **democratic**. Group members are asked to contribute ideas and information before decisions are made. The leader directs activities and elicits cooperation from the group in meeting goals they have decided on together.

The last style of leadership is called **laissez-faire** ("lay-zay-fare"). This term comes from the French words for "Let the people do as they choose." In a group managed by this type of leadership, the group members reach decisions on their own. This leadership may sound appealing, but without a single person to make decisions, goals are usually hard to reach.

Different types of leadership can be used in different situations, and we all react in different

ways to the three styles. But in most cases democratic leadership uses people's skills most effectively.

PARTICIPATING IN STUDENT ASSOCIATIONS

All members of a group are important. To develop effectiveness both as a leader and a group member, you may decide to participate in student associations such as technology education or vocational associations. Any student enrolled in a course represented by the association can be a member of such a group.

Student associations usually resemble small businesses. They meet technology and business standards and give you the chance to learn more about the use, control, and effects of business and technology; learn about career opportunities; and focus attention on your school's educational programs.

Activities may include contests and achievement programs. You can meet and work with other students and with business and industrial leaders. You may even compete for scholarships. Student associations are usually part of state and national associations.

The activities of an association are planned and carried out by officers (leaders) and committees. As you work in groups, you can learn to think creatively, solve problems, and make decisions. You can take a turn at leading a group and be responsible for reaching a goal. And you will gain experience in communicating and cooperating with others. See Fig. 31-3.

Student groups also serve their communities through work projects, like helping to build a playground or raising funds for charity. In a student association, you can develop and apply special career skills that will benefit you all your life.

Fig. 31-3. Have fun while you learn. Participating in a technology assocation can be an interesting and enjoyable learning experience.

Testing Your Knowledge

Briefly answer each of the following questions. Write on a separate piece of paper.
1. Name two things entrepreneurs need to start a business.
2. Where can entrepreneurs obtain venture capital?
3. Name three types of company ownership.
4. Name two advantages of organizing a business as a corporation.
5. Identify three roles of a leader.
6. What five traits does an effective leader need?

Expressing Your Knowledge

Using complete sentences, write your answers to the following on a separate sheet of paper:
1. What is an entrepreneur?
2. Compare proprietorships and partnerships and give one advantage and one disadvantage of each.
3. How does a person acquire part of a corporation?
4. How can student associations help you develop leadership skills?

Applying Your Knowledge

Follow your teacher's instructions to complete these activities:

1. Find out about the history of a corporation in your area. Ask an adult who works for the company for information. Or go to the library; librarians often keep files of information on large local businesses. Or you could write to the corporation and request printed materials that contain the information. Try to discover what entrepreneurs started the business, what idea they used for a new or improved product or service, and when the company became a corporation. Also make notes on other interesting facts in the development of the business. Study and analyze annual reports of the company. Summarize the information, and give a short report to your class on the history of the company.

2. Interview an employee of a business. Find out about the leaders this person encounters on the job. What traits do leaders need in the employee's company? What leadership styles has he or she observed? How would the employee describe the ideal leader? If the employee leads a group, what problems has he or she experienced in leading? Write a report based on your findings.

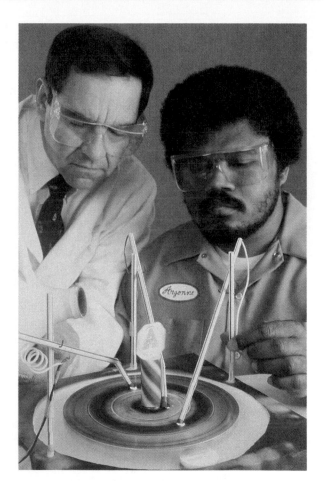

Projects and Activities

ACTIVITY 1: THE SOURCE OF ALL ENERGY

Chapters 1-5 describe the sources of all energy we have available. All of these sources have their origin within our solar system. They are either the direct result of the sun's effect on our earth, or they use materials provided during the formation of the earth and the solar system. The sun sustains the earth. As such, it acts as a control over all of the energy we have available.

In this activity, you will be presented with a series of diagrams. These diagrams show, in graphic form, all of the sources of energy discussed in Chapters 1-5. Your assignment is to prepare an essay describing how all energy can be traced to the sun, our solar system, or to the formation of the earth. Each figure will have questions and directions that will help you prepare your essay.

For this assignment, you should:
- Read and study Chapters 1-5 of this book.
- Study each diagram presented with this activity.
- Follow the directions and answer any questions presented as you write your essay on "The Source of All Energy."
- Look ahead to Step 6. It contains an outline of your finished essay. Use it as you develop and write your essay.

OBJECTIVES
- To gain an understanding of the source of all energy.
- To learn that sources are related, and can be traced back to the sun or solar system.
- To gain experience in writing an essay and presenting ideas about the sources of energy in an organized presentation.

PROCEDURE
1. Study Fig. A1-1. This figure shows all of the energy sources discussed in Chapters 1-5. *All* of these energy sources are connected to the sun.
   Write the introduction to your essay. We will come back to this chart as we complete the essay. For the introduction, include answers to the following:
   a. What is the source of all of our energy? Describe how the sun obtains its energy from a nuclear reaction.
   b. Describe the division provided by the power line. The power line is also the control line. In your introduction indicate that the sources above the line are all natural sources of power. Control is provided at the power line.

c. Identify the three final outputs and uses of all power at the bottom of the chart.

2. Study Fig. A1-2. This figure is an excerpt from Fig. A1-1. It shows all of the direct uses of the sun's energy. The title of this section is "Direct Uses of the Sun's Energy."

In this section you will trace and describe the different sources of energy presented on the chart. The following is an example of how your essay should appear for each tracing of energy source.

"Fossil Fuels"

Fossil fuels, from Fig. A1-2, trace their source to the sun. Plants, trees, and animals grew from the chemicals and minerals from the earth, and from the radiant energy of the sun. This combination of radiant energy and chemicals from the earth produced the hydrocarbons that make up the fossil fuels.

The plants, animals, and trees were compressed by earth forces, producing the fossil fuels.

The tracing of this process on Fig. A1-2 is from the sun, to radiant energy, to biological process. The second part is from the sun, to earth, to chemicals (minerals), to biological processes. Fossil fuels are produced from the biological process.

The use (or control) below the power line is by the chemical reaction of burning, to produce thermal energy. Thermal energy is most often used to produce mechanical power through both internal- and external-combustion engines. Thermal energy can also be converted directly to fluid power (heating gases, which expand) or electrical power.

Tracing the conversion and control of fossil fuels on Fig. A1-2 goes from fossil fuels, across the power line, to chemical reaction (burning), to thermal, and to the three applications of power—electrical, fluid, and mechanical.

a. Note that the above includes a description of how fossil fuels are formed, tracing on Fig. A1-2, and a description of how fossil fuels are controlled, tracing the control on the chart.

b. Repeat this process in your essay for each of the following areas:

   (1) Fossil fuels—you may use the presentation as shown. However, it would be better if you prepared your own presentation using your own words.

   (2) Other biological sources (wood, alcohol, ethanol, methanol, etc.).

   (3) Direct uses of radiant energy (Photovoltaic cells and direct use of radiant energy as heat). Note the direct line from radiant to thermal, via the short line from electrical power to thermal. This provides for the direct use of radiant energy as heat.

This section should also include OTEC and solar salt ponds.

   (4) Meteorological sources (wind and rain as hydroelectrical power).

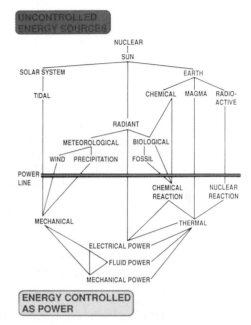

Fig. A1-1. The energy sources available to provide power for our use.

(5) Provide answers to the following questions, or provide the information as requested. Present your answers as part of the essay.

(i) Explain briefly how heat from the sun produces weather.

(ii) How is the power from the wind captured and used?

(iii) Explain how rain becomes a source of power.

3. Study Fig. A1-3. This figure is another excerpt from Fig. A1-1. It shows how the earth is used as a source of energy. The title of this section is "Using the Earth as a Source of Energy."

This section shows the existing resources on the earth used to produce controlled power. These sources were placed on the earth when it was formed. They include uranium and other radioactive materials, as well as hydrogen, the potential source of fusion energy.

a. Repeat the process of step 2, using the example of fossil fuels. Repeat for the following areas from Fig. A1-3.

(1) Magma—include all geothermal sources,

(2) Radioactive materials—includes both fusion and fission.

(3) Chemical—this section is very minor and may be omitted. It is included because other chemical sources can be used to produce electrical power, such as the power produced by a battery.

b. Provide answers to the following questions, or provide information as requested. Present your answers as part of the essay.

(1) What is the source of the heat used to keep the earth's core very hot and form magma?

(2) Explain the difference between fission and fusion.

4. Study Fig. A1-4. This figure is the final excerpt from Fig. A1-1. It shows the remaining energy source, which is from tides. This section should be titled "Using the Solar System as a Source of Energy—Tides".

For this section repeat the process of step 2 using the example of fossil fuels for the use of tides as a source of controlled power.

Provide answers to the following questions, or provide the information as requested. Present your answers as part of the essay.

a. What do we mean by *gravity?* How does gravity affect the solar system and cause tides?

b. Describe how a tidal power plant operates.

5. You should finish your essay with a Summary section. Refer back to Fig. A1-1. In this section discuss the complete interaction of the sun with all sources of energy within our solar system. If you wish, you could look ahead in this section to solar sailing, as described on page 377. You could also identify those sources that might be our most important sources of energy in the future.

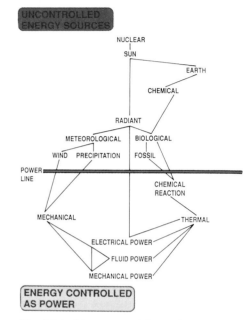

Fig. A1-2. Direct uses of the sun's energy.

6. The following is an outline for the finished essay.
   Title: The Source of All Energy
   Headings:
   I. Introduction
   (see Step 1 and Fig. A1-1)
   II. Direct Uses of the Sun's Energy
      A. Fossil Fuels
      B. Other Biological Sources
      C. Direct Uses of Radiant Energy
      D. Meteorological Sources
        (see Step 2 and Fig. A1-2)
   III. Using the Earth as a Source of Energy
      A. Magma
      B. Radioactive Materials
        (see Step 3 and Fig. A1-3)
   IV. Using the Solar System as a Source of Energy—Tides
      (see Step 4 and Fig. A1-4)
   V. Summary
      (see Step 5 and Fig. A1-1, again)
7. Your teacher may want you to prepare an appendix of articles and/or pictures of energy sources presented in your essay. They can be found in magazines and newspaper articles.

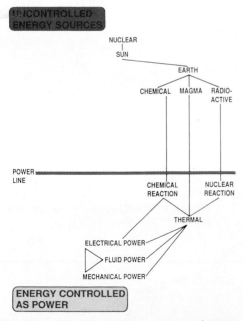

Fig. A1-3. Using the earth as a source of energy.

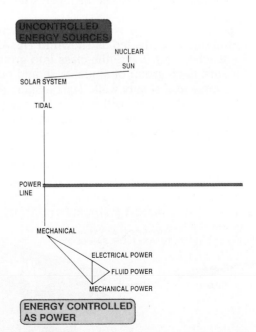

Fig. A1-4. Using the solar system as a source of energy.

ACTIVITY 2: EFFECTS OF TIRE INFLATION ON "OVER-THE-ROAD" RESISTANCE

Many factors influence the amount of resistance encountered by an automobile design. Manufacturers have made significant progress in reducing wind resistance. The use of wind tunnels and computer design has resulted in designs that decrease wind resistance.

One area which can be an important factor is tire pressure. This activity will provide an indication of the effects of tire pressure on resistance to automobile motion.

OBJECTIVES

■ To determine the effect of tire inflation on the resistance to automobile motion.
■ To determine the effect of varying automobile load on resistance to automobile motion.

EQUIPMENT AND SUPPLIES

Compact, mid-size, and full-size cars
1 Manila tow rope
1 Rugged spring scale
1 Portable (12V) tire inflator
1 Accurate tire gage
Masking tape or chalk

PROCEDURE

1. Following your teacher's instructions, mark out a level track on a parking lot. The distance should be 50-75 feet.
2. Prepare the tow rope with scale and attach it to the automobile to be tested as shown in Fig. A2-1.
3. The teacher may divide the class into groups of 8-10 students. Each group of students should pull a car over the course at a steady walk. Start a short distance behind the start line so the car is in steady motion as it crosses the line. Have one student read the scale. He or she should note the steady speed pull, not fluctuation. Use the average of three pulls over the course. (All pulls must be in the same direction over the course.)

PULL AREA

TOW ROPE ATTACHED TO AXLE OR CAR BODY

SCALE

Fig. A2-1. Attach tow rope to automobile. Note placement of scale.

Then prepare a graph as shown in Fig. A2-2. Show resistance at 5-pound variations in tire inflation.

4. Using the compact car, reduce tire pressure to 15 psi, and pull on the test course. One student should be inside the car. Note the force necessary to keep the car moving at a steady rate. Record the average of three pulls.
5. Complete the graph by repeating at 20 psi, 25 psi, 30 psi, 35 psi, and 40 psi.
6. Place four students in the car and repeat the experiment. Prepare a second graph.
7. Repeat steps 4, 5, and 6 with the mid-size car. Prepare two more graphs.
8. Repeat steps 4, 5, and 6 with the full-size car. Prepare two more graphs.
9. The experiment is now completed. Return tire pressure to the level recommended by the manufacturer.
10. Analyze the six graphs prepared during the activity. Include the following:
    ■ A description of the effects of tire inflation on rolling resistance.
    ■ A description of the effects of adding passengers to the car.
    ■ A comparison of the three cars, explaining the differences in needed force to keep the cars moving.
    ■ An explanation about which size car is more sensitive to changes in passengers.
11. Each group should prepare an analysis and submit a written report along with the six graphs.

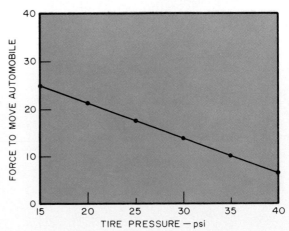

Fig. A2-2. Graph to record tire pressure and force. Use the average of three pulls. This graph is an example of what might occur.

ACTIVITY 3: COST OF OPERATING HOME APPLIANCES

Many home appliances operate continuously, like the refrigerator. Others operate when needed or desired. For example, the range is used when cooking, the TV for entertainment, and the electric iron whenever clothes are ironed. Use depends on need, the size of the family, and life style. Figure A3-1 shows the "typical" electrical consumption of most home appliances. Your actual use may vary from these figures.

Fig. A3-1. Estimated annual kWh consumption of electrical home appliances.

Electrical Appliances	Average Wattage	Annual kWh Consumption
range	12,200	1,175
oven (self-cleaning)	4,800	1,146
microwave oven	1,500	300
refrigerator/freezer, frostless (14 cu. ft.)	615	1,829
refrigerator/freezer (14 cu. ft.)	326	1,137
freezer, frostless (15 cu. ft.)	440	1,761
freezer (15 cu. ft.)	341	1,195
water heater (quick recovery)	4,474	4,811
water heater (standard)	2,475	4,219
air conditioner	1,566	1,389
clothes dryer	4,856	993
washing machine	350	90
dishwasher	1,301	363
waste disposal	445	30
trash compactor	400	50
vacuum cleaner	630	46
radio/record player	109	109
television	200	440
radio	71	86
coffee maker	894	106
toaster	1,146	39
blender	286	15
frying pan	1,196	186
broiler	1,436	100
deep fryer	1,448	83
mixer	127	13
carving knife	92	8
iron (hand)	1,008	144
sewing machine	75	11
fan (window)	200	170
fan (circulating)	88	43
heater (portable)	1,322	176
heater (infrared)	250	13
air cleaner	50	216
sunlamp	279	16
hair dryer	381	14
clock	2	17
shaver	14	1.8
toothbrush	7	0.5

OBJECTIVES

■ To determine the annual cost of operating home appliances within the home.
■ To identify ways of reducing operating costs through planned conservation.

PROCEDURE

1. Identify the appliances you have in your home which are shown on Fig. 3-1. Obtain the cost of electricity in your area. This information is often shown on your utility bill. If not, contact your local electrical utility company for the information. It's common to charge different rates for different amounts of electricity used. Use the rate which produced the largest portion of your most recent electrical bill if your company has variable rates.

2. From the information gathered for item 1, prepare a table showing the annual cost of each electric appliance. See Fig. A3-2. Arrange the table so that the highest cost item is listed first and each succeeding item progressively lower.

3. Use the top five items and prepare a report describing ways that you might be able to reduce the use of electricity. This will conserve energy and reduce costs. (If you have already taken conservation steps with these appliances, describe the results of your efforts.)

4. Some appliances will have wattage different from the average shown. In some cases, the wattage will change consumption. In others, it may not. For example, wattage on the water heater determines how fast the heater heats water. The actual amount of hot water used determines the kilowatt hour (kWh) consumption. A lower wattage on the television set or refrigerator will decrease the total kWh consumption.

   Some costs may vary significantly by climate or family use. For example, air-conditioning costs will be greater in Texas than in Maine. A large family will use more hot water than a small family. For the table shown, the family size is the national average, approximately four people per household.

   For this final step, check the wattage of the five top items. Discuss with your family whether you use more or less electricity than the average family. If you decide that you use 20% more hot water, raise your annual cost by 20%. Do this for each item and explain why you made the adjustment.

Appliances	Avg. Wattage	Annual kWh	Rate	Annual Cost
Water heater (standard)	2475	4219	.12032	$507.63
Range	12200	1175	.12032	$141.38
etc.				

Fig. A3-2. Table for determining annual electrical costs. Total at bottom to find costs for the year. Figures shown are typical figures and are an example only. Use your local per kWh costs.

ACTIVITY 4: TROUBLESHOOTING A SMALL ENGINE

A. LEARNING TO TROUBLESHOOT

Determining the cause of poor engine performance is the first step in returning an engine to normal service. It is also the most critical. Proper diagnosis will determine the corrective steps necessary.

This activity should be used to troubleshoot an engine which either isn't operating or has poor operating performance. As a result, all parts of this activity will not apply to each engine. Rather, start with an engine needing repair and use this activity to identify the difficulty and the procedures needed to repair the engine.

OBJECTIVES

■ To learn the steps necessary to determine the cause of poor engine performance.
■ To identify the procedures necessary to correct the identified problem.

PROCEDURE

This activity will proceed from the problem encountered to the probable cause of the problem. Keep in mind the content of Chapter 17, especially the troubleshooting section which describes many of the procedures used in this activity.

1. Identify the engine problem from the following list. Then refer to the troubleshooting chart indicated.
   ■ Engine fails to start or starts with difficulty. See Fig. A4-1.
   ■ Engine misses, lacks power, or surges (speeds up and slows down). See Fig. A4-2.
   ■ Engine stalls. See Fig. A4-3.
   ■ Engine vibrates, knocks, or is noisy. See Fig. A4-4.
   ■ Engine overheats. See Fig. A4-5.
   ■ Engine with electric starter fails to turn over or cranks slowly. See Fig. A4-6.
2. Review the possible causes for the problem. Use the knowledge you gained and check the engine for each cause to determine the problem. The more experience you have, the easier the process will be. In the beginning, you will spend considerable time checking each possible cause. As you gain experience, you will be able to quickly work through possible causes and determine the difficulty.
3. Identify the problem. If possible, repair the engine and return it to service.

Possible Cause	Remedy	Possible Cause	Remedy
■ Fuel not reaching carburetor	■ Fill tank; open vent hole in fuel tank cap; open shutoff valve; clean fuel filter and fuel line.	■ Too much oil in fuel (two-stroke cycle)	■ Drain fuel tank and fill with correct mixture.
■ Engine flooded	■ Close fuel shutoff valve, remove spark plug and crank engine. Dry and install plug. Open shutoff valve and crank engine until it starts.	■ Breaker points dirty, burned, or out of adjustment	■ Inspect breaker points. Clean or replace. Check spring tension. Adjust properly.
■ Engine over- or under-choked	■ Close choke all the way if the engine is cold when starting, halfway if engine is warm. Open choke when engine starts.	■ Flywheel-to-coil lamination air gap incorrect	■ Adjust air gap.
■ Carburetor adjustment incorrect	■ Adjust carburetor.	■ Loose or defective magneto system wiring or parts	■ Tighten connections, replace wires, repair or replace faulty parts.
■ Carburetor throttle plate not opening	■ Check throttle linkage. Be sure it is clean and free.	■ Spark plug fouled (clogged) or defective	■ Clean, inspect, and adjust or replace plug.
■ Fuel pump diaphragm leaks	■ Replace diaphragm or pump.	■ Fuel vapor lock	■ Allow engine to cool. Check engine cooling.
■ Carburetor fuel valves stick	■ Clean fuel screen and valves (in carburetor).	■ Ignition timing incorrect	■ Retime engine.
■ Governor faulty	■ Check parts. Repair or replace. Adjust linkage as necessary.	■ Gasket at carburetor or reed valve defective	■ Replace gasket.
■ Carburetor clogged	■ Overhaul and clean carburetor. Drain fuel and fill with clean fuel.	■ Poor compression	■ Take engine apart to find difficulty. Check pistons, rings, cylinders, valves, and gaskets. Repair and assemble.
■ Reed valve not working (two-stroke cycle)	■ Replace reed valve and gasket. Check reed stops.		

Fig. A4-1. Engine fails to start or starts with difficulty.

Possible Cause	Remedy	Possible Cause	Remedy
■ Spark plug fouled or defective	■ Clean and regap plug, or replace if defective.	■ Fuel foaming in tank (two-stroke cycle)	■ Keep fuel tank filled.
■ Dirt or water in fuel line or carburetor	■ Drain fuel system. Fill tank with clean fuel. If this does not correct the problem, clean fuel line and carburetor.	■ Governor faulty or linkage binding	■ Check and repair governor linkage.
■ Carburetor adjustment incorrect	■ Adjust carburetor.	■ Reed valve fouled or sluggish (two-stroke cycle)	■ Clean or replace reed valve, stops, and gasket.
■ Fuel filter clogged	■ Clean filter.	■ Breaker points dirty, burned, or out of adjustment	■ Inspect breaker points. Clean or replace. Check spring tension. Adjust properly.
■ Muffler or exhaust system clogged	■ Clean or replace muffler. Clean exhaust ports. Check fuel and air supply.	■ Faulty condenser or magneto system parts	■ Replace condenser or magneto system parts.
■ Fuel tank vent clogged	■ Clean tank vent.	■ Electrical wires worn or broken	■ Check wires and connections. Tighten loose connections. Replace worn or broken wires.
■ Fuel level low	■ Fill tank.	■ Ignition timing incorrect	■ Retime engine.
■ Fuel vapor lock	■ Allow engine to cool. Check engine cooling.	■ Flywheel-to-coil air gap incorrect	■ Adjust air gap.
■ Fuel-pump diaphragm leaks	■ Replace diaphragm or pump.	■ Crankcase seals or gasket leaking	■ Replace leaking seals and gasket.
■ Choke partially closed	■ Open choke.	■ Poor compression	■ Take engine apart to find difficulty. Check pistons, rings, cylinders, valves, and gaskets. Repair and assemble.
■ Carburetor throttle does not open	■ Check throttle linkage. Repair or replace broken or bent parts. Adjust so plate opens.	■ Worn or binding connecting rod	■ Overhaul engine. Replace worn parts.

Fig. A4-2. Engine misses, lacks power, or surges (speeds up and slows down).

Continued on next page.

Fig. A4-2. Continued.

Possible Cause	Remedy	Possible Cause	Remedy
■ Fuel valves stick	■ Clean and repair valves.	■ Valve clearance incorrect (four-stroke cycle)	■ Check and adjust valve clearance.
■ Fuel system dirty	■ Drain and clean fuel system. Replace with clean fuel.	■ Valves leaking or sticking (four-stroke cycle)	■ Clean and reseat valves. Check spring tension.
■ Air cleaner clogged	■ Clean air filter.	■ Cooling fins dirty	■ Clean cooling fins.
■ Carburetor clogged	■ Clean carburetor.	■ Exhaust fumes entering carburetor intake	■ Pipe exhaust away from air intake. Provide proper ventilation.

Fig. A4-4. Engine vibrates, knocks, or is noisy. ("Engine knock" is a dull thudding sound. It is the sound of fuel igniting at the wrong time—before the engine piston reaches the top of the stroke.)

Same possible causes as Fig. A4-2 plus the following:	
Possible Cause	**Remedy**
■ Engine overheated	■ Check for cause of overheating. Correct trouble.
■ Faulty shorting device (device to ground spark plug)	■ Replace shorting device.

Fig. A4-3. Engine stalls.

Possible Cause	Remedy
■ Loose flywheel	■ Check for loose nut and sheared or partially sheared key. Replace worn parts.
■ Carbon in combusion chamber	■ Remove cylinder head. Remove carbon from cylinder, head, and piston.
■ Worn engine parts: piston, rings, cylinder, connecting rod, bearings, crankshaft, or camshaft	■ Overhaul engine. Replace all worn parts.
■ Bent fan or blower housing	■ Remove housing. Straighten or replace fan and housing.
■ Incorrect ignition timing	■ Retime engine.
■ Wrong spark plug heat range	■ Install correct spark plug.
■ Parts loose or unbalanced	■ Tighten all parts. Balance as necessary.

Possible Cause	Remedy	Possible Cause	Remedy
■ Not enough oil in fuel mixture (two-stroke cycle)	■ Drain fuel system. Fill tank with proper mixture.	■ Condenser faulty	■ Replace condenser.
■ Crankcase oil level too low or too high, or oil grade incorrect (four-stroke cycle)	■ Fill crankcase with oil of proper grade. Check level.	■ Spark plug defective	■ Replace spark plug.
■ Cooling air flow blocked	■ Clean and straighten all shrouds, screens, fins, and blowers. Clean cooling fins.	■ Ignition timing incorrect	■ Retime engine.
■ Carburetor clogged	■ Clean carburetor.	■ Carburetor adjustment incorrect	■ Adjust carburetor.
■ Exhaust gas entering carburetor intake	■ Pipe exhaust away from air intake. Provide proper ventilation.	■ Fuel foaming in tank (two-stroke cycle)	■ Keep fuel tank filled.
■ Carbon in combustion chamber	■ Remove cylinder head. Remove carbon from cylinder, head, and piston.	■ Fuel tank vent clogged	■ Clean tank vent.
■ Excessive load on engine	■ Remove excessive load.	■ Fuel vapor lock	■ Allow engine to cool. Check engine cooling.
■ Breaker point adjustment incorrect	■ Adjust breaker points.		

Fig. A4-5. Engine overheats.

Fig. A4-6. Engine with electric starter fails to turn over or cranks slowly.

Possible Cause	Remedy	Possible Cause	Remedy
■ Run-down battery	■ Check battery. Recharge or replace. Engine may be started with different battery and jumper cables.	■ Defective solenoid in starter	■ Remove and inspect solenoid. Repair or replace.
■ Starting circuit open	■ Find and elmininate open point in circuit. Possibilities include loose or dirty battery cables, dirty or burnt starting switch contacts, faulty solenoid (switch) in starter.	■ Engine jammed	■ Take engine apart to find trouble. Repair.
■ Starter flywheel drive jammed	■ Remove and inspect starter motor. Unjam or repair drive mechanism.	■ Alternator or generator not charging battery	■ Condition same as run-down battery. Check alternator or generator. Repair or replace.
■ Defective starting motor	■ Remove and inspect starting motor. Repair or replace.	■ Voltage regulator defective	■ Repair or replace.

B. SMALL ENGINE TROUBLESHOOTING CONTEST

Troubleshooting of small engines is a skill developed by study and by actually working on engines. Preparation for this contest will help you develop greater knowledge of small engine theory, operation, and service.

OBJECTIVES

■ To gain experience in small engine troubleshooting under competitive conditions.
■ To develop additional knowledge and skills which will help you diagnose small engine problems.
■ To test your knowledge and abilities in competition with classmates.

EQUIPMENT AND SUPPLIES

■ Five or more small engines (one engine for every two students in the contest). All engines should be identical.
■ Appropriate engine stand for each engine.
■ Set of engine service tools for each team. Each set of tools should be identical and in good repair.
■ Scoring sheets (one for each team). See Fig. A4-7.

PROCEDURE

1. The teacher will divide the class into teams of two persons each.
2. Each team is assigned an engine and tools. You and your teammate should check your engine, operate it, and make certain it is in excellent working condition. Report any problems to your teacher.
3. Prior to the start of the contest, each engine will be "bugged." That is, each engine will have a series of problems, or "bugs," intentionally placed in the engine. All problems will be included in each engine, and all problems will be the same for each engine. The following are typical problems which may be introduced:
   ■ Parts which have been rendered inoperative or partially inoperative. (Example: Spark plug gap too small or too large.)
   ■ Blocks in fuel system. (Examples: Plugged fuel filter, fuel line, fittings, etc.)
   ■ Plugged fuel tank vent.
   ■ Incorrect carburetor adjustments. (Examples: Float level, mixture, etc.)
   ■ Open electrical conductors, or high-resistance wires, or disconnected or improperly connected electrical wiring.
4. The contest takes place within one class period. On the day of the contest, each team starts work on its engine at the same time. Your goal is to correct engine problems so the "engine operates properly at all speeds." When you and your teammate feel you've accomplished this goal, do the following:
   ■ Turn the engine off.
   ■ Advise judges you have finished. They will record your time.

■ The engine will either be judged at your work station or you will take it to the judges' stand, depending on procedures.

■ On order of the chief judge, you and your teammate will attempt to start your engine.

—If the engine starts, the judges will take over and do their measurements of performance, inspection of workmanship, etc.

— If your team cannot get the engine to start and run properly within 10 minutes, you will be disqualified.

—If the engine stalls during the judges' inspection, you will have 5 minutes to start the engine or be disqualified.

5. The judges will evaluate your work on two counts: visual inspection and performance. A *demerit system* will be used. That is, each fault found produces a demerit. Your goal is a minimum number of demerits. The checklist shown in Fig. A4-7 is typical, but your teacher may provide a different form or have the class or a student committee develop a checklist.

6. The team with the *fewest* demerits wins the contest.

FOLLOW-UP ACTIVITIES

7. Critique the contest. When the contest is over, discuss the following with your classmates:

■ Why the winning team came in first.

■ Weaknesses in "bugs" used, including their appropriateness.

■ Weaknesses of judging scale used.

■ Suggested changes and improvements for future contests.

8. If there is more than one class, winners can compete among classes. For example, if there are only two classes, the first three places in each class can compete. Other arrangements are possible, depending on the number of classes.

Each time the contest is repeated, new bugs will be identified and introduced. Also, each contest will be more difficult than the prior one. *Note:* These procedures are "typical." Your teacher may change or modify them to meet class needs, student abilities, and class goals.

9. With your teammate, prepare a written report critiquing the contest. Your report should include:

■ A list of the bugs you found.

■ Problems you encountered during the contest.

■ Aspects of the contest you felt were good.

■ Aspects of the contest you felt were poor or unfair.

■ Recommendations to improve contests in the future.

Team Members: _____   Time Finished: _____

_____

Score = Number of problems × Demerits

Criteria	Demerits	Score
■ **Visual inspection—engine not running:**		
1. Cooling ducts in place and secured	1	_____
2. Fuel and oil caps snug and in place	1	_____
3. Fuel leaks	3	_____
4. Oil leaks	2	_____
5. Loose fasteners	1	_____
6. Missing lock washers, stripped fasteners, etc.	2	_____
7. Misrouting of fuel or electrical lines	1	_____
8. General appearance of engine relative to grease, oil, and dirt	1	_____
9. Missing parts—fuel filter, air filter, etc.	1	_____
■ **Engine performance:**		
10. Does not idle properly	5	_____
11. Does not accelerate properly	5	_____
12. Does not operate at high speeds	5	_____
13. Does not operate at steady speed	5	_____
14. Misses	10	_____
■ **Time**		
15. Each additional minute after the first team (not disqualified) finishes	2	_____
TOTAL DEMERITS		_____

Fig. A4-7. Troubleshooting contest checklist.

Glossary*

absolute temperature scale—A temperature scale that registers absolute zero as 0°. (21)

absolute zero—The temperature at which all molecular motion stops (no heat remains). On the regular Fahrenheit scale, absolute zero is −460°F. (21)

acid rain—Rain containing an unusually high quantity of acid. Acid rain usually results from high concentrations of sulfur dioxide (SO_2) and nitrous oxides (NO_X) in the air. (9)

active solar heating system—A solar heating system that collects solar energy and moves it by mechanical means to where it is needed. (3)

actual mechanical advantage—Measured mechanical advantage which takes friction loss into account. (19)

actuator—A fluid power device that changes fluid power into rotary, linear, or reciprocating motion. (22)

aerodynamic drag—The friction that occurs between air and a moving vehicle. (20)

air bags—Automobile safety bags that inflate during an accident protecting passengers. (28)

alternating current—Current that alternately changes polarity (direction). The electrons flow in one direction, then reverse. (23)

alternative energy sources—New renewable and inexhaustible sources of energy. (4)

alternator—An electrical device that uses stationary conductors and a rotating magnet to generate alternating current. (24)

amperage—The rate at which current flows through a conductor. (23)

ampere—A unit of measurement for the rate of electric current flow. (23)

anode—The negative terminal of a battery. (27)

anti-friction bearings—Bearings which use balls or rollers to decrease friction. (20)

anti-lock brakes—Brakes that will not lock wheels during an emergency stop. (28)

atmospheric pressure—The pressure produced by the weight of the air surrounding the earth, about 14.7 pounds per square inch. (21)

atom—The smallest part of an element that retains the properties of the element and takes part in a chemical reaction. (23)

atomization—Changing a liquid into a fine mist. (15)

autocratic leadership style—A leadership style in which decisions are made by one person, without involving others. (31)

automated control—The continuous automatic operation done to perform a task such as operating industrial or home devices. (7)

automatic guided vehicles (AGVs)—Robotic trucks and carriers that move parts and products along pre-planned paths in manufacturing plants. (10)

automotive diagnostic service center—An automotive facility that provides a complete analysis of the condition of the automobile. (14)

barge—"Floating box" designed to carry products such as coal or grain on waterways. Often lashed together with other barges into groups called tows. (10)

battery—A group of two or more cells connected. (24)

bearings—Devices that reduce friction between moving surfaces. (15)

biofuels—Waste products of biological origin which can be used to produce energy. (4)

blower—A device powered by a small engine or electric motor that blows a large volume of air to remove debris, snow, etc. (18)

boiling-water reactor—A nuclear reactor which boils water in the containment vessel. (5)

Boyle's Law—The volume of a gas varies inversely with the pressure applied to it, provided the temperature remains constant. (21)

breeder reactor—A nuclear reactor that is fueled by uranium-238 and plutonium. The fissioning of the plutonium releases neutrons that strike the uranium and convert it into plutonium. (5)

British thermal unit (BTU)—The amount of heat needed to raise the temperature of one pound of water one degree Fahrenheit. (6)

calorie (c)—The metric unit of measurement for heat energy. It is the amount of heat needed to raise the temperature of one cubic centimeter of water one degree Celsius. (6)

Calorie (C)—A unit of measurement equal to 1000 calories. It is used to measure the amount of heat available in the food we eat. (6)

canard—Airplanes with the wing at the rear and the horizontal part of the tail at the front. (28)

capacitor—A device that stores an electrical charge. It can be discharged as needed. (24)

carbon monoxide (CO)—A poisonous gas emitted from internal-combustion engines. It is a compound of carbon and oxygen. (9)

carburetor—The part of a gasoline fuel system that provides the proper mixture of air and fuel. (17)

career—A job or position that is usually a person's main source of income. (30)

cargo—Goods or products being transported from one location to another. (10)

cathode—The positive terminal of a battery. (27)

celestial navigation—Using the stars and the sun to determine your location on earth. (10)

cell—Device that converts chemical energy into electrical energy. (24)

central processing unit (CPU)—The part of the computer which interprets and executes programs. (7)

centrifugal force—A force that causes a rotating object to move away from the center of rotation. (15)

chain reaction—A nuclear reaction. The splitting of an atom releases not only energy but neutrons which split other atoms, producing similar reactions. (5)

---

*All glossary terms are used in the textbook. The number in parentheses identifies the chapter in which the term was introduced.

chain saw—A device for cutting wood, usually powered by a small engine. (18)

charging system—System which provides electricity to keep the battery charged and to operate the electrical systems during engine operation. (13)

Charles' Law—The volume of a gas varies directly with the temperature applied to it, provided the pressure remains constant. (21)

chemical energy—Energy produced by chemical changes. Chemical energy is the source of energy for all living things. (1)

chronometer navigation—An accurate clock, used in celestial navigation. (14)

circuit breaker—A device that opens an electrical circuit when it is overloaded. (24)

circuit, electrical—A system of conductors and electric devices through which electric current moves. Electricity flows from and returns to its source in a complete "circle." (23)

clutch—A transmission device that controls the transfer of power from an input shaft to an output shaft. (20)

coal—See **fossil fuels**. (2)

cogeneration—Using a single energy source for two useful purposes. Example: Steam run through turbines for generating electricity can also be used for heating. (4)

coherence—A characteristic of laser beams; their light waves have almost identical wavelengths. (27)

compressed-air storage—The process of pumping compressed air into a large cavern during low demand hours, and using it to produce electricity during hours of heavy demand. (26)

compression—Increasing the pressure on the air-fuel mixture prior to ignition. (17)

compression ignition—System in which fuel is ignited by the intense heat of compression. (12)

compressor—A device which raises the pressure of a gas, converting mechanical power to fluid power. (22)

computer—An electronic device designed to store and manage information and solve problems. (7)

conduction—The movement of heat through a substance. (3)

conductor—Material that easily transmits (conducts) electricity. (23)

connector—A device used to join fluid power transmission lines or to join a transmission line to a component of the system. (22)

conservation of energy—Elimination of practices which waste energy. (8)

convection—The movement of heat through air, water, or other fluids. The heated fluid carries the heat from one place to another. (3)

cooling system—System which removes excess heat from the engine. (13)

corporation—A legal structure, licensed by a state or country. The corporation owns and operates the company or business. Many people share ownership. (31)

coulomb—The basic unit of measurement of electricity. It is 6.28×10^{18} electrons. (23)

coupling—A permanent connection between two shafts, used to transmit power. (20)

cryogenics—The science that deals with the properties and behavior of materials at very low temperatures. (27)

cultivator—A device for breaking up soil and destroying weeds around garden plants. (18)

current, electric—The movement of electrons through a conductor. (23)

customary system—The traditional measuring system used in the United States. Measurements include foot, quart, ounce, and degree Fahrenheit. (6)

cycle—A complete set of piston movements repeating in the same sequence. (12)

cylinder—In fluid power, an actuator to convert fluid pressure to a mechanical force through the use of a piston inside a closed container. (22)

dead reckoning—The laying down on a chart of the planned course line, including the distance and the time it will take to reach your destination. (10)

democratic leadership style—A leadership style in which people share in the decision-making. (31)

density—The number of molecules in a given volume of a material. (3)

development—Using new knowledge, gained through research, to develop new products or processes. (25)

diesel engine—An internal-combustion engine that burns diesel oil to produce heat. Pressure inside the combustion chamber causes the fuel to ignite. (12)

diode—A solid-state electrical device that permits electrons to flow in only one direction. (24)

direct current (DC)—Current that flows through a conductor in only one direction. (23)

dynamometer—A device used to measure the power produced by an engine or motor. (6)

earth warming—The long-range warming of the earth due to increased levels of carbon dioxide in the air. (9)

ecology—The relationship between living things and the environment in which they live, also known as environmental biology. (9)

edger—A device, sometimes powered by a small engine or electric motor, used to trim grass or cut weeds in tight and difficult places. (18)

electrical energy—The motion of electrons. Electrical energy is measured in joules. (1)

electricity—Movement of electrons from one atom to another. (23)

electric vehicles (EV's)—All types of home and industrial vehicles which use electricity as the source of power. (26)

electrolysis—Process of using electricity to separate water into oxygen and hydrogen. (26)

electrolyte—A substance that conducts electricity by transfer of ions, such as is used in storage batteries and fuel cells. (24)

electromagnet—A magnet consisting of an iron core wrapped with a current-carrying wire. (23)

electron—A negatively charged particle of an atom. (3)

electron theory—States that an atom consists of three major particles: protons, neutrons, and electrons. (23)

electronic navigation—Using an electronic system, such as radar or loran to determine location. (10)

emission control—A system of devices on automobile engines to reduce the amount of pollution produced by the engine. (13)

energy—The ability to do work or the capacity to produce motion, heat, or light. (1)

energy control system—A system for controlling energy that includes the original source of energy, all the conversions and transmissions the energy undergoes, and the eventual use of the energy. (1)

energy conflicts—Conflicts between nations that result from disagreements involving control and access to energy sources, particularly fossil fuels. (29)

energy conversion—The process of changing energy from one of its six forms to another. (1)

energy efficiency—The percentage of available energy converted into usable energy. (1)

energy efficiency rating (EER)—A rating attached to appliances which provides information on cost and energy consumption. (8)

engine—A device that converts any form of energy into mechanical energy. See **heat engine**. (11)

engineer—A person who plans and designs technical systems. (30)

engine thrust reverser—A device which takes the forward thrust of a jet engine and reverses the force to stop the airplane. (12)

entrepreneur—A person who starts a new business. (31)

ethanol—An alternative transportation fuel made from corn, sugarcane, and other grains. (28)

exhaustible energy sources (fuels)—Sources of energy that cannot be replaced after use. These sources include fossil fuels and uranium. (2)

exhaust system—System that removes burnt fuel from the engine. (13)

external-combustion engine—A heat engine that uses heat and pressure produced outside of the engine. (11)

Fahrenheit temperature scale (°F)—The customary temperature scale. On this scale, water freezes at 32° and boils at 212°. (21)

fiber-optic system—A communication system that uses semiconductor lasers and strands of flexible glass for transmission. (27)

filter—A device, usually containing a porous substance, used to remove solid particles and other contamination from a flowing fluid. (22)

fission—The splitting of atomic nuclei to release energy. (5)

fix—The exact location of a ship or airplane. The navigator uses known landmarks or aids to navigation to determine exact location. (10)

flight plan—The planned course and destination along each leg of an airplane's planned flight. (10)

fluid—Any liquid or gas. (21)

fluid power—The use of fluids under pressure to control and transmit power. Fluid power includes the use of both gases (pneumatics) and liquids (hydraulics). (21)

fluid power motor—Motor used to convert fluid power into rotary motion. (22)

fluid power system—An assembly of units that controls the flow of pressurized fluid. (22)

force—Any push or pull on an object. Force is measured in pounds or newtons. (6)

fossil fuels—Fuels that developed over millions of years from dead plants and animals, including coal, oil (petroleum), and natural gas. (2)

four-stroke cycle engine—An engine that requires four strokes of the piston to produce a single power stroke. The four strokes are intake, compression, power, and exhaust. (12)

freight—Another term for cargo. See **cargo**. (10)

friction—The resistance to motion produced when two objects rub against each other. Friction produces heat energy. (1)

fuel cell—A device that produces electricity from a chemical reaction between hydrogen and oxygen. (27)

fuel-injection system—System that supplies fuel to an engine's combustion chamber through an injection device rather than with a carburetor. (13)

fuel system—System that provides the correct mixture of air and fuel to the engine. (13)

fulcrum—Pivot point of a lever. (19)

fuse—An electrical device that protects a circuit from excessive current flow. (24)

fusion—The fusing (combining) of atoms to release energy. (5)

gas turbine engine—Engine that operates on the same principles as a turboprop engine, but without a propeller. It is used to power devices such as generators and ships. (12)

gasohol—A mixture of nine-tenths unleaded gasoline and one-tenth ethyl alcohol. (4)

gasoline piston engine—An internal-combustion engine that uses gasoline to produce heat. It is the most common type of automobile engine. (12)

gear ratio—The ratio of the number of teeth on a driven gear to the number of teeth on the drive gear. This ratio determines the relationship between force and speed (distance per unit of time). (20)

gears—Wheels with teeth cut around an outside or inside surface, used to transfer motion and change direction, speed, or force. (20)

generator—A device that converts rotary motion into electrical energy. (24)

geopressured energy—A solution of natural gas in hot water trapped at high pressure underground. (4)

geopressure reserves—Natural gas found dissolved under high pressure in brine (salt water) deep within the earth. (2)

geothermal energy—Heat energy generated within the earth. It is the result of the natural decay of radioactive materials. (4)

global pollution—Pollution that affects the entire world. (9)

glow plug—An electrically operated element used to heat fuel and sometimes air in a diesel engine during cold starting conditions. (14)

governor—A device that automatically regulates the speed of an engine. It is usually used on small engines. (15)

gravity—The attraction exerted by a large body (for example, the earth) for objects on or close to its surface. (6)

greenhouse effect—The effect that carbon dioxide has on the temperature of the earth. Carbon dioxide acts like greenhouse glass to trap solar heat in the atmosphere and warm the earth. (3)

grounding—An electrical connection that permits electricity to return to its source. (15)

heat—See **thermal energy**. (1)

heat engine—A device that converts heat energy into mechanical energy. (11)

heat exchanger—A device that transfers heat from one fluid to another. (5)

hertz (Hz)—Electrical cycles per second. In the United States, alternating current is 60 hertz. (23)

horsepower (hp)—A unit of measurement of power. One horsepower is the energy needed to lift 33,000 pounds 1 foot in 1 minute. (6)

hydraulics—The use of liquid under pressure to produce motion. (21)

hydrocarbons—Compounds consisting of combinations of carbon and hydrogen. Hydrocarbons include the fossil fuels and wood. (9)

hydroelectric energy—Electrical energy produced from falling water. Water is collected behind dams and used to rotate a turbine. (2)

hydrogen—The simplest element, consisting of a nucleus of one proton orbited by a single electron. (25)

hydrothermal energy—The thermal (heat) energy from natural steam and hot water from within the earth. (4)

hypothesis—A person or researcher's best solution to a problem being investigated. It is based on all knowledge available to the person. (25)

ignition—Setting the air-fuel mixture on fire in the combustion chamber of the engine. (17)

ignition system—System which delivers high voltage to the spark plug to start an engine. (13)

inclined plane—A sloping surface which provides mechanical advantage. (19)

inducted fan engine—The technical term for a prop-fan engine. (28)

induction—The process of transmitting electrical energy from one circuit to another through the building and collapsing of a magnetic field. (24)

induction motor—A type of electric motor in which the armature receives current through electromagnetic induction rather than through a direct electrical connection. (24)

inertial confinement—The use of lasers to bombard fuel pellets to produce a fusion reaction. (25)

inexhaustible energy sources—Energy sources that will always be available. These sources include solar energy, hydroelectric energy, tides, ocean thermal energy, solar salt ponds, and geothermal energy. (2)

input—The information provided to a computer, or the force provided to a power system. (7)

insulation—Material used to reduce heat flow. (8)

intermodal transportation—Use of more than one mode of transportation to move passengers and/or cargo from one location to another. (10)

internal-combustion engine—A heat engine in which the heat and pressure are produced inside the engine. (11)

International System of Units (SI)—An international system of measurement used throughout the world. Measurements include meter, liter, gram, and degree Celsius. (6)

inverter—An electrical device used to change direct current to alternating current. (4)

isotopes—Different atoms of the same element. The difference is in the number of neutrons in the nucleus. All isotopes of a single element have the same number of electrons. (5)

jet engine—An internal-combustion engine that produces linear motion through the principle of jet propulsion. (12)

jet propulsion—The principle of Newton's third law of motion: For every action there is an equal and opposite reaction. Escaping gases reduce pressure at one end of a cylinder, producing thrust (force) at the other end. (12)

kickback—A sharp, violent reversal of the starting direction of an engine. (16)

kilowatt (kW)—One thousand watts of electricity. (3)

kilowatt-hour (kWh)—One thousand watts of electricity used in a period of one hour. It is the basic measuring unit used by power companies. (23)

kinetic energy—Energy in motion. All energy performing work or producing power is kinetic energy. (1)

laissez-faire leadership style—A leadership style which permits members of the group to do as they wish. (31)

laser beam—A concentrated beam of light that travels in a very narrow straight path. (27)

lawn mower—A device used to cut lawns, usually powered by a small engine or electric motor. (18)

law—A proven and accepted fact, based on all evidence consistently supporting the concept or idea. (25)

Law of Conservation of Energy—Energy cannot be created or destroyed; the amount of energy in the universe is fixed. However, energy can be changed from one form to another. (1)

leadership—A personal responsibility for the performance and accomplishments of other people. (31)

lever—A simple machine which consists of a fixed bar resting on a pivot point called a fulcrum. (19)

levitation magnets—Magnets that raise a train off the rails. (28)

lift—The pressure difference above and below the wing which supports the weight of the plane, enabling it to fly. (10)

light energy—The visible part of radiant energy. Light consists of electromagnetic waves traveling through space. (1)

light-water reactor—A nuclear reactor which uses ordinary water to transfer heat. (5)

linear motion—Motion in a straight line, such as is produced by a jet engine or rocket. (11)
locomotive—A train's power source.
loran—A nagivation system that measures the time differences between two radio signals sent at the same time. (10)
lubrication system—System which provides for the lubrication of all moving engine parts. (13)

machine—A device that changes the relationship between force and speed (distance per unit of time). Simple machines include the lever, wheel and axle, pulley, inclined plane, wedge, and screw. (19)
maglev train system—A rail system involving *mag*netic *lev*itation. A train travels above the rail on a magnetic field created by electromagnetic coils. (27)
magnet—A body that can attract iron and steel. It creates a magnetic field around it. (23)
magnetic confinement—Use of powerful magnets to confine plasma for a fusion reaction. (25)
magnetic field—The area around a magnet or current-carrying wire in which magnetic attraction or repulsion takes place. (23)
mechanic—A person who services and repairs mechanical devices such as engines or other transportation devices. (30)
mechanical advantage—An increase in force or speed (distance per unit of time) gained through the use of a machine. (19)
mechanical energy—The energy of motion, the most common and visible form of energy. It is measured in foot-pounds or joules. (1)
mechanical system—The mechanical portion of an engine. It converts heat energy to mechanical motion, with the operation of the other engine systems. (13)
mechanization—using mechanical power to replace human or animal powered activities. (29)
megawatt (MW)—One million watts of electricity. (3)
memory—The computer unit which stores information. (7)
methanol—A clean-burning liquid fuel made from wood or plants. (4)
metric system—See **International System of Units.**
microprocessor—A single-purpose computer that has integrated memory and controller units which control a transportation, home, or industrial device. (7)
modes, transportation—The individual methods of transportation: highway, rail, air, water, and pipeline. (10)
momentum—The measured force of a moving body. The faster a body moves, or the greater its weight, the greater its momentum. (15)
motor—An electrical or fluid-operated device that produces rotary motion. (22 and 24)
multi-viscosity oil—Oil which fulfills both low- and high-viscosity oil requirements. (17)

natural gas—See **fossil fuels.** (2)
navigation—The total process of planning and maintaining knowledge of one's location. (10)
navigation fix—see **fix.**

neutron—A neutral particle that makes up part of the nucleus of an atom. (5)
Newton's Third Law of Motion—See **Third Law of Motion.**
nuclear battery—A type of battery that produces electrical energy from radioactive materials. (5)
nuclear energy—Energy produced by reactions in the nuclei of atoms. (1)
nuclear reactor—A device in which a fission or fusion reaction is started, continued, and controlled. (5)
nuclear wastes—The by-products of a nuclear reaction, usually very radioactive and dangerous. (5)
nucleus—The center of an atom, consisting of protons and neutrons. (The plural is nuclei.) (5)

Occupational Safety and Health Act (OSHA).—A federal law passed in 1970 requiring employers to provide worksites free of recognized hazards that are causing or likely to cause death or serious harm. The law also requests employees to comply with occupational safety and health standards. (16)
ocean thermal energy—Energy generated by the difference in water temperature between surface and deep ocean water. (4)
ohm (R)—The unit of measurement of electrical resistance. (23)
Ohm's Law—It takes one volt to force one ampere of current through a resistance of one ohm. (23)
oil (petroleum)—See **fossil fuels.** (2)
Omega—Uses the same principle as loran, but is applied to worldwide navigation. (10)
on-site transportation—Transportation over a short distance, occurring in one location. (10)
output—The product of a computer or a power system. (7)
overhaul—Disassembling, checking, and repairing all parts of a major unit, such as an engine. (17)
oxident—A chemical compound which can oxidize compounds not usually oxidized by oxygen. (9)
oxidize—The process in which a material combines with oxygen to form a new material. (9)
ozone—A harmful form of oxygen formed when sunlight strikes air containing hydrocarbons. Ozone is a major ingredient of smog. (9)

parallel circuit—An electrical circuit in which current flows in more than one path. (23)
particulates—Tiny particles of matter released into the air by burning fossil fuels. (9)
partnership—A business relationship in which two or more people share responsibility for starting and operating a business or company. (31)
passenger—A person being transported from one location to another. (10)
passive solar heating—A solar heating system that collects, stores, and transfers heat by natural means. Passive heating systems include both direct-gain and indirect-gain systems. (3)
peat—The first stage in the formation of coal. (2)
petroleum—See **fossil fuels.** (2)

petrothermal energy—The thermal (heat) energy from magma and hot rock within the earth. (4)

photon—A particle or "packet" of light energy. (3)

photosynthesis—The conversion by plants of sunlight, carbon dioxide, water, and nutrients into food and plant material. (1)

photovoltaic array—A group of PV cells; a battery. (3)

photovoltaic (PV) cell—A device that converts light into electrical energy. (3)

piloting—Determining the location of a ship or airplane from recognized landmarks or aids to navigation. (10)

planetary gear system—A gear assembly which uses internal and external gears to provide a variety of changes in force and direction. (20)

plasma—A gaseous mixture of active particles. In nuclear fusion, it is a very hot mixture of deuterium and tritium. (25)

plutonium—A radioactive element (239) found in small quantities naturally and produced from uranium-238 during nuclear fission. It can be used as a nuclear fuel. (5)

pneumatics—The use of air under pressure to produce motion and perform work. (21)

polarity, electric—The direction of current flow. Current always flows from negative (area of more electrons) to positive (area of less electrons). (23)

polarity, magnetic—The direction of magnetic lines of force. Around a magnet, the lines of force move from north to south. Inside a magnet, they move from south to north. (23)

pollution—Any undesirable change in the air, land, or water that harmfully affects living things. (9)

potential energy—Stored energy, or energy ready or available for use. When used, potential energy changes to kinetic energy. (1)

power—Energy (work) per unit of time, or work accomplished in a given period of time. In the customary system, power is measured in horsepower, BTUs per hour, and watts. In the metric system, power is measured in watts. (6)

power train—In automobiles, a way of delivering power to the wheels, usually including a clutch, transmission, drive shaft, and rear end assembly. (13)

pressure—A measurement of force determined by the area on which the force is applied. Pressure is force per unit of area. Pressure is measured in pounds per square inch, inches of mercury, and pascals. (6)

pressurized-water reactor—A nuclear reactor which heats pressurized water in the containment vessel. (5)

primary cell—A device that stores chemical energy. The chemical energy is converted to electricity as needed. Primary cells cannot be recharged. (24)

production worker—A person who builds products in a factory, usually on a production or assembly line. (30)

programming—Placing a planned set of instructions into the computer memory. The set of instructions is called a **program**. (7)

propfan—An airplane engine with propeller blades that are curved and swept back. (28)

proprietorship—A business owned and operated by one person. (31)

propulsion magnets—Magnets that move the train forward. (28)

proton—A positively charged particle located in the nucleus of an atom. (23)

pulley—A device which changes the direction of an applied force. (19)

pump—A device which raises the pressure on a liquid, converting mechanical power to fluid power. (22)

pumped-hydro storage—The process of pumping water into an upper reservoir during low-demand periods, and using it to produce electricity during hours of heavy demand. (26)

quality of life—The sum of all the elements and attributes that contribute to and distract from our standard of living. (29)

radar—Determining location by bouncing a radio signal off an object and measuring the length of time it took the signal to return. (10)

radiant energy—A form of energy produced by any warm or hot object, such as the sun. It is a combination of light and heat energy. Radiant energy changes to heat energy when it changes wavelengths from short to long. (2)

radiation, atomic—Energy released during changes in the nuclei of atoms. Atomic radiation includes alpha particles, beta particles, and gamma rays. (5)

radiation, thermal—The transfer of heat by electromagnetic waves through space and air. (3)

radioactivity—The release of atomic radiation during the disintegration of the nuclei of certain atoms. (5)

radio direction finder—A device that can determine the direction from which a radio signal is broadcast. (14)

ramjet engine—A jet engine that uses the forward motion of the engine to bring air into the combustion chamber and to compress the air. (12)

receiver—In a fluid power system, a storage tank for a gas. (22)

reciprocating motion—Back-and-forth movement, such as a piston moving inside a cylinder. (11)

recycling—The reprocessing of used materials into a usable product or products. (8)

refining—The process of separating a crude substance into purer, useful substances. In crude oil refining, this process is called **fractionating**. (2)

relay—A device which controls on-off switching of an electric circuit through the use of an electromagnet. (24)

renewable energy sources (fuels)—Sources of energy that, with proper management, will be available indefinitely. Renewable sources include wood, plants, and waste products. (2)

research—Process of gaining new knowledge. (25)

reservoir—In a fluid power system, a storage tank for a liquid. (22)

resistance, electrical—The opposition to current flow through a conductor. Resistance is measured in ohms. (23)

resistor—A device placed in a circuit to reduce current flow. (24)

robot—A computer-controlled device which performs operations usually done by humans. (7)

robotics—The field of study dealing with the construction, maintenance, and use of robots. (7)

rocket engine—An engine that operates on the principle of jet propulsion and which carries its own supply of fuel and oxygen. (12)

rotary engine—An internal-combustion engine in which a triangular rotor rotates within a housing. The motion of the rotor rotates an output shaft. (12)

rotary motion—Circular motion, such as the motion produced at the flywheel of an engine. (11)

R-value—The measurement of a material's resistance to heat flow. (8)

schematic drawings—Drawings that use symbols to represent parts of an electrical circuit. (23)

scientific method—A basic set of procedures used to obtain new knowledge and seek solutions to existing problems. (25)

Scotch yoke—A connecting rod/bearing connection that converts linear motion to rotary motion. (28)

screw—An inclined plane cut in a spiral around a shaft. (19)

secondary cell—A chemical storage cell that can be electrically discharged and recharged repeatedly. (24)

semiconductor—A material that has some of the properties of both insulators and conductors. Semiconductors are the basic materials for solid-state electrical devices. (24)

sensing devices—Units (instruments) which recognize and measure conditions such as distance, pressure, time, and temperature. (7)

series circuit—An electrical circuit that has only one path for current flow. (23)

series-parallel circuit—An electrical circuit that contains both a series circuit and a parallel circuit. (23)

sextant—A device to accurately measure angles. Used in celestial navigation—or in other places where accurate angle measurement is needed. (10)

shares—Parts into which the ownership of a company is divided. (31)

short circuit—An accidental bypassing of the normal resistance in an electrical circuit. (24)

silicon-controlled rectifier (SCR)—A semiconductor device with the characteristics of a transistor, except that once a current is established by the energization of the gate, it continues to flow even after the gate is de-energized. (24)

sleeve bearing—A stationary part held in a housing around a rotating shaft. (20)

slurry—A solution of a liquid and a ground-up solid material such as coal that can be transported through a pipeline. (2)

smog—A major form of air pollution produced from sunlight acting on hydrocarbons, sulfur oxides, and nitrogen oxides in the air. (9)

snow blower—A device to blow snow off sidewalks, driveways, and other areas, usually powered by a small engine or electric motor. (18)

solar cell—See **photovoltaic cell**.

solar energy—Energy from the sun. Solar energy is our most basic source of energy. (3)

solar panel (collector)—A device used in an active solar heating system to absorb solar energy. (3)

solar sailing—The use of photons of light energy to push a sail through space. (25)

solar salt pond—A pond of salt water. In energy development, a source of temperature difference between the surface and the bottom, used to generate electricity. (4)

solenoid—A device that converts electrical energy to linear motion. (24)

solvent—A petroleum-based fluid that dissolves dirt, oil, and grease. (16)

space navigation—Determining location in space, a three-dimensional position. (10)

space shuttle—A vehicle that carries people and goods between Earth and space. (28)

space station—A base in space with a permanent crew. (28)

speed—Distance per unit of time. (6)

sprocket—A toothed pulley, similar to a gear, driven by a chain and used to transmit mechanical energy and produce changes in force and speed. (20)

standard of living—The perceived level of attributes held that control one's quality of life. (29)

starting system—System in an automotive engine that starts the pistons moving to draw in the air-fuel mixture. (13)

static head pressure—The pressure developed by the weight of a column of fluid. (21)

steam engine—An external-combustion engine that converts the heat and pressure of steam into mechanical energy. (11)

steam turbine—An external-combustion engine used to produce rotary motion. Steam turbines are commonly used to produce electricity. (11)

Stirling Cycle engine—An external-combustion engine that operates on the heating and cooling of a gas within a cylinder. This causes a piston to move within the cylinder. (11)

stock—Ownership of a company, usually divided into shares. (31)

stroke—The movement of a piston from one end of a cylinder to the other. (12)

superconductor—An electrical conductor that has lost all detectable electrical resistance. (27)

supersonic—Faster than the speed of sound. (28)

synfuels (synthetic fuels)—Liquid or gaseous fuels made from existing solid fuels. Synfuels are produced from coal, tar sands, and oil shale. (2)

system—A group of parts that work together. (13)

tachometer—An instrument which measures engine speed in rpms. (6)

technician—Occupation performing repair and services to stationary devices. (30)

technologist—A person working in a position considered between a technician and engineer, performing such tasks as supervising production and operating divisions of power plants. (30)

temperature inversion—When warm air moves above cold air, creating a stable condition with minimum air movement. (9)

theoretical mechanical advantage—Mechanical advantage calculated from force/speed changes. It does not take friction into account. (19)

theory—A concept or principle that has been verified by repeated testing, but not to the extent of becoming a law. (25)

thermal energy (heat)—The motion of atoms or molecules. Heat is present wherever there is motion. (1)

thermal mass—A heat storage material, such as water, masonry, or concrete, used in passive solar heating systems. (3)

thermal pollution—The release of waste heat into air or water by power plants. This waste heat upsets the delicate balance of nature. (9)

thermoelectric coupling (thermocouple)—A device used to generate electricity from a heat source. The coupling uses two different materials joined together. Heat applied at one end produces electricity at the other. (5)

thermosiphoning—The circulation of water by natural convection. Thermosiphoning operates on the principle that as water is heated it changes density (expands and rises). (3)

thermostat—A device that senses and regulates temperature. (13)

Third Law of Motion—A law of nature discovered by Isaac Newton: For every action there is an equal and opposite reaction. (12)

thrust—A forward push or force produced by a jet or rocket engine. Thrust is measured, like force, in pounds or newtons. (12)

tidal energy (tides)—Energy generated by using the flow of ocean tides. (4)

tight sand reserves—Natural gas trapped in a type of hard, dense sandstone. (2)

tiller—Similar to a cultivator. It is used to turn soil for planting and weed removal. (18)

tilt-rotor plane—Airplanes that take off vertically like a helicopter. Then the rotor tilts, transforming the plane into a conventional propeller-powered plane. (28)

torque—A twisting or turning effort; also, a measurement of force applied to a radius. Torque is measured in pound-feet or newton-meters. (6)

tractor-trailer—Highway vehicle used to transport cargo. The tractor is the power unit and the trailer holds the cargo. (10)

transformer—A device that transmits electricity from one circuit to another by induction, changing amperage and voltage in the process. (24)

transistor—A solid-state electrical device that is used as an on-off switch. (24)

transportation—The movement of people and goods from one place to another. (10)

trimmer—A device used to trim bushes or hedges, powered by a small engine or electric motor. (18)

troubleshooting—Checking an engine to find out what part or condition is causing poor performance. (17)

turbine—A device which changes moving gases or liquids into rotating motion. (12)

turbocharger—A device using exhaust gases to drive a turbine which pumps air into the engine. (13)

turbofan engine—Similar to a turbojet engine, but includes a large fan powered by a turbine. (12)

turbojet engine—Jet engine which has air compressed by the forward motion of the engine and an air compressor driven by a turbine. (12)

turboprop engine—A jet engine which drives a propeller instead of using the reaction principle to propel the airplane. (12)

two-stroke cycle engine—A heat engine that requires two piston strokes to produce a single power stroke. The two strokes are compression and power. Intake and exhaust take place at the bottom of the power stroke. (12)

uducted fan engine (UDF)—A propeller airplane engine with curved blades. Operates as a turbofan jet engine. (28)

universal motor—An electric motor that can operate on either AC or DC current. (24)

uranium—A radioactive element used as fuel in nuclear reactors. (5)

vacuum—A pressure below atmospheric pressure. A *perfect vacuum* is Ø psia or 30 in of Hg. (21)

values—The things a person feels are important in life. (30)

valve—A device used to control the flow of fluids. (22)

vaporization—Changing from a liquid to a gas. (15)

vehicles—Devices used to move passengers and cargo. (10)

ventilation—System for admitting fresh air. (16)

venture capital—The funds used to start a new business. (31)

venturi—A narrow passage within a carburetor which produces an increase in air speed. The increased speed reduces the pressure of the air passing through.

viscosity—The rate at which a liquid flows. (17)

volt—A unit of measurement of electrical pressure. One coulomb of electricity exerts a pressure of one volt. (23)

voltage—The pressure pushing current through a conductor. (23)

waste disposal—The discarding or destroying of sewage, garbage, and unwanted items. (8)

watt (W)—The customary unit of measurement of electrical power, and the metric unit of measurement of electrical and mechanical power. One watt equals one joule of electrical energy per second. One watt is also equal to a flow of one ampere at a pressure of one volt. 746 watts equals one horsepower. (3)

wattage—Measurement of power produced by the flow of current under pressure. (23)

wedge—Basic tool that consists of two inclined planes placed so that the sloping sides come together at a point. (19)

weight—Force applied in a vertical direction. It is the result of the pull of gravity. (6)

wheel and axle—A rod or shaft and large wheel. Mechanical advantage is produced by the principles of the second-class lever. (19)

work—Motion that produces a desired outcome or accomplishment. Work is equal to force times distance and is measured in foot-pounds or joules. (6)

workman's compensation—State laws that provide benefits to workers injured on the job. Benefits include medical, death, rehabilitation, and disability. (16)

Illustration Credits

Art
Howard Davis
James Kasprzyk
Liz Purcell
Creative Slides & Advertising

Technical Consultant
Russell W. Meals, Sr.

Photos
ABB Process Automation, 112 (left)
Alaska Division of Tourism, 125, 130
Alcan Automotive Structures, 112 (right)
Ambassade de France, 66
American Nuclear Society, 84
American Petroleum Institute, 142 (top)
American Superconductor Corp., 394
Amtrak, 140 (top)
Archer Daniels Midland Co., 90-91
Arco Solar Inc., 16 (left), 21, 55, 57 (top right)
Argonne National Laboratory, 396 (bottom), 405, 410 (top)
Arizona Office of Tourism, 42
Arnold & Brown, 330 (top), 333 (top right), 349 (bottom right), 352 (bottom right), 354 (left column), 356 (bottom right), 357 (right), 359 (top left), 360 (bottom), 361, 363 (top left), 393 (bottom), 403 (left), 418, 420 (top right, middle right), 434 (left)
Arvin Industries, Inc., 129
Ashland Oil, Inc., 147
Atlantic Research Corp., 34 (bottom)

Roger B. Bean, 426, 427
Roger B. Bean, Woodruff High School, 437
BELLCORE, 392 (bottom left)
Berkeley Sensor & Actuator Center, University of California, 351
BMW of North America, Inc., 407
Ralph Bohn, 425
Briggs & Stratton Corp., 211 (top), 211 (bottom right), 218 (top right), 219, 227 (right), 240 (right), 243 (top), 243 (bottom)
British Aerospace, Inc., 411 (bottom)
British Airways, 137 (middle)

California Energy Commission, 73 (bottom right)
J.I. Case, a Tenneco Co., 14 (left)
Caterpillar Inc., 19 (right), 105
Celebration/Carnival Cruise Lines, 422 (bottom)
Certainteed Corp., 114, 116
Champion Spark Plugs, 222, 245 (right)
Champlin Petroleum Co., 32 (top)
Chevron Corp., 39
Chicago Police Department Bomb Squad, William Struke, 16 (right)
Chrysler Corp., 180, 400, 408 (top)
CILCO, 370
CILCO, Dick Etter, 30 358 (right), 371, 435 (top)
Cincinnati Milacron, 108, 111
Clayton Industries, 102
Clean Energy Research Institute, University of Miami, 385 (bottom)
Combustion Engineering, 73 (bottom left), 158
Paul Conklin/Photo Edit, 420

Conoco Inc., 135 (top)
Continental Oil Co., 32 (bottom)
©The Cousteau Society, a member-supported, non-profit environmental society, 111
Coventry Creative Graphics/Liz Purcell, 413
CSX Corporation, 10-11, 188
Cummins Engine Company Inc., Advertising & Sales Promotion Dept., 189

Dana Corp., 276
Datsun, 178
Deep Ocean Engineering/Howard T. Davis, 424
John Deere, 164 (bottom left), 196-197, 214 (bottom), 244 (top right), 292-293
Delco-Remy Div., General Motors, 345 (bottom left), 347 (top)
Delta Air Lines, 14 (top), 139
Department of Energy, 83, 375 (bottom), 378, 379, 381, 382, 383, 395 (top), 445
Detroit Diesel Corp., 191 (bottom)
Detroit Edison, 384 (top), 385 (top)
Detroit Transportation Corp., 402 (right)
The DeVilbiss Co., 308, 309 (top left), 313 (bottom)
Dexter Corp., 121
Discovery Toys, 411
Dresser Industries, Inc., 148, 264-265
Du Pont, 22

Electric Power Research Institute, 394 (top), 397 (right column)
Ethyl Corp., 432
The Eureka Company, 366 (top left)
Eveready Battery Co., 347 (bottom), 348 (right column)

Fafnir Bearing Div., of Textron Inc., 289
Randy Feuch Construction, Inc., 229
Figgie International, 303
Florida Solar Energy Center, 52 (left), 68, 76
Ford Motor Co., 174 (top), 175, 181, 281 (bottom), 297, 298, 436 (bottom)
Glenn Frank/Photo Edit, 421
David R. Frazier, 61, 122, 419, 426 (bottom left)

Garrett Auxiliary Power Division, Allied-Signal Aerospace Co., 168 (top right)
The Garrett Corp., Airesearch Industrial Division, 182 (top)
Ann Garvin, 18 (top), 20, 117 (bottom), 229, 241, 420
Gates Rubber Co., Denver, Colorado, 179
General Dynamics/Quincy Shipbuilding Division, 33
General Electric Power Generation, 392
General Motors Corp., 41, 42 (top), 390, 402 (left), 403, 404 (top), 409
General Motors Corp., Electro-Motor Division, 140 (bottom), 143
Gold's Gym, 96
Greater Los Angeles Visitor's Convention Bureau, 328-329
Greyhound Lines, Inc., 195
Grumman Corp., 139

Hewlett-Packard Company, 442
Highspeed Rail Association, 396
Homelite Textron, 255 (bottom), 256 (left), 258 (left), 260 (bottom)
Hunter Engineering Company, 185